Creation Regained: Disciplinary Perspectives

Creation Regained: Disciplinary Perspectives

Edited by Russell D. Kosits

Foreword by Albert M. Wolters

Dordt Press

Cover design by Benjy Weida
Layout by Carla Goslinga

ISBN: 978-0-932914-39-2

Printed in the United States of America.

Dordt Press
700 7th Street NE
Sioux Center, Iowa 51250

www.dordt.edu/DCPcatalog

The Library of Congress Cataloging-in-Publication Data is on file with the Library of Congress, Washington, D.C.

Library of Congress Control Number: 2025951594

To:

The Reformational Philosophy
Discussion Group

We had a good run.

Table of Contents

List of Contributors

Vahagn Asatryan, Ph.D., Associate Professor of Business, Redeemer University

Janet R. Danielson, Lecturer (retired) Simon Fraser University

Ben Faber, D. Phil., Associate Professor of English, Redeemer University

Kevin Flatt, Ph.D., Professor of History, Redeemer University

Calvin Jongsma, Ph.D., Emeritus Professor of Mathematics, Dordt University

Russell D. Kosits, Ph.D., Professor of Psychology, Grove City College

David T. Koyzis, Ph.D., Global Scholar, Politics & International Affairs, Global Scholars Canada

James J. Rusthoven, Ph.D., Professor Emeritus of Oncology, McMaster University

Derek C. Schuurman, Ph.D., Professor of Computer Science, Calvin University

Arnold E. Sikkema, Ph.D., Professor of Physics, Trinity Western University

Steven H. VanderLeest, Ph.D., Technical Fellow, Boeing Company

Kevin Vander Meulen, Ph.D., Professor of Mathematics, Redeemer University

James R. Vanderwoerd, Ph.D., Professor of Social Work, Redeemer University

Albert M. Wolters, Ph.D., Emeritus Professor of Religion, Redeemer University

Foreword

by Albert M. Wolters

I am greatly encouraged by the appearance of this collection of academic essays in the Reformed and Reformational tradition. Written by competent and seasoned scholars in a wide variety of disciplines, from mathematics to social work, and from engineering to music, these essays share a common commitment to the tradition of Reformed Christianity, especially as this has come to expression in the culturally engaged Neocalvinism associated with the name Abraham Kuyper.

Central to this tradition, and to the essays in this volume, is the emphasis on a good creation which is seriously marred by sin, but reclaimed in Christ, and ultimately to be restored in the new heavens and the new earth. Creation is understood in a comprehensive sense to include not only the subject matter of the academic disciplines, but also those disciplines themselves. The academic enterprise itself is part of the good creation, is subject to the distorting effects of sin, and is claimed by Christ as part of his wide-ranging kingdom.

This is an audacious, countercultural perspective which challenges fundamental assumptions both of the secular mainstream and of various two-kingdom versions of the Christian tradition. It requires tenacious dedication, fierce intelligence, and a measure of selflessness and fearlessness, to bring it creditably to bear on one's academic specialty. I salute the authors of this volume for their contributions to this ongoing endeavour.

Within the context of this broad Neocalvinist perspective, many of the authors also draw on the Reformational philosophy of Herman Dooyeweerd, especially his theory of fifteen irreducible modal aspects. Without necessarily adopting the whole of Dooyeweerd's complex systematic philosophy, these authors use his modal scale to guard against the ontological reductionism of so much contemporary scholarship, and to preserve an empirical openness to the multi-dimensional character of reality and human experience.

I am humbled by the fact that the title of this volume quite directly refers to the title of my own little book *Creation Regained: Biblical Basics for a Reformational Worldview* (1985; 2nd ed. with M. Goheen 2015). Of course, this shared title alludes to John Milton's great epic poem *Paradise Regained* (1671), which is one of the classics, not only of English literature but also of Reformed theology. In this way the title of the present volume signals at the outset that the essays which it contains are rooted in the same religious intellectual tradition as my book, namely that of Reformed Christianity.

It is my hope that these penetrating essays will serve as a model and an encouragement for others in the academy to forge a distinctively Christian academic path in their own disciplines, and in this way to make visible something of Christ's kingship in the world of scholarship.

Preface

Creation Regained: Disciplinary Perspectives attempts to put discipline-specific flesh on the bones of the Reformational vision epitomized by Al Wolters' classic book *Creation Regained: Biblical Basics for a Reformational Worldview*. While this Reformational vision goes far beyond Al's little book—and it wouldn't be accurate to say the chapters in this book are *based* on Al's book—the original *Creation Regained* nevertheless encapsulates the main contours of the neo-Calvinist vision that undergirds the present volume.

What are these contours? On the 30th anniversary of his book, Al described *Creation Regained* as "an introduction to a comprehensive Biblical worldview that stresses the breadth of Creation, the extent of the Fall, and most importantly, the fact that salvation in Jesus Christ really means a reclaiming, a regaining, of the entire length and breadth of Creation with all of its cultural domains." Whereas we tend to think of "creation" as being limited to, say, "nature," and of "sin" and "redemption" as applying solely to a narrow domain of life called "religion," the neo-Kuyperian tradition has a much broader and more satisfying vision. Wolters continues: "That tradition sees Creation as a very broad and differentiated thing, filled with distinctive structures which are made to move in certain directions. Structure refers to the way things are meant to be—the way God instituted family to be, the way God meant the state to be, the way God has a design for advertising. These are all developments of Creation which are corrupted by sin and all of which need to be redirected, need to be redeemed, reclaimed in order to conform more closely to the way God meant it to be from the beginning."[1]

Al's book has impacted an untold number of Christians, as they seek a more intellectually satisfying Christian vision of the world they inhabit. It has proved valuable to laypersons, undergraduate students, and—what is more relevant to this project—has been profitably used in mentoring programs at Christian colleges, to equip new faculty in the challenging task of carrying out their teaching and research in a distinctively Christian way.

One of our experiences at Redeemer University is that it is sometimes difficult to move from a theological or philosophical articulation of Reformational principles to their effective application in specific aca-

1 Al Wolters and Brian Dijkema, ""Creation Regained" at thirty," *Comment*, April 16, 2015, https://comment.org/creation-regained-at-thirty/.

demic disciplines. Mentoring of new faculty is often seriously hindered because young professors will read and appreciate books like *Creation Regained* but not have many good examples of how the ideas apply to their own work. Our hope for this book is that mentoring programs—and new faculty struggling to teach and research from an integrally Christian perspective—might be helped. But the chapters are written in such a way that non-specialists may also appreciate and learn from them. We hope this volume, the namesake of the original classic, may similarly have broad appeal.

Each chapter follows a general approach, though some latitude was granted to authors to implement the vision—articulated in the introduction—as they saw fit. In short, we hoped to provide chapters that engage a specific academic discipline but from the categories of God,[2] creation, fall, redemption, and consummation, as they have been understood in this broad, neo-Kuyperian sense. Authors were also asked to provide a list of discussion questions and resources that might be helpful to faculty as they attempt to apply these concepts on their own. They were also given the option to sketch out a Reformational research agenda. Each chapter underwent a non-blind peer review in which subject-matter experts generally sympathetic with the overall project of this book were asked to assess the accuracy and currency of each contribution. As this book attempts to provide examples of neo-Calvinist perspectives on the academic disciplines, we wanted to be assured that the authors were accurately representing those disciplines. It was the job of the editor[3] to assess the quality of application of Reformational perspective. One of the joys of editing this volume was to read the effusive praise heaped upon the chapter authors by these experts. They were: Andrew Goddard (Westminster Theological Centre), Jacob Ellens (Our Lady Seat of Wisdom Academy), Mark McCarthy (Dordt University), David Klanderman (Calvin University), Jill Risner (Calvin), Jason Stansbury (Calvin), Joh Zwart (Dordt), Daniel Chua (Hong Kong University), Lisa Hosack (Grove City College) Abram Steen (Crandall University), Gayle Elmer (Calvin), Bryan McGraw (Wheaton College), and Eric Johnson (Houston Christian University). We are profoundly grateful for their service.

I'd also like to acknowledge the incredibly helpful work of Richard Van Holst, who proofread every chapter, applied a uniform formatting, searched down missing references, incorporated revisions from chapter authors, and more. As he said, "I like to think of proofreading as polishing up the text and making it shine." His meticulous attention to detail

2 As it is unusual to include God in the typical creation, fall, redemption framework, not all authors have a section on God.

3 For several years, David Koyzis and I shared this responsibility. More on that later.

made my work much easier. The Research Office at Redeemer University provided multiple grants to support this work over the years. Calvin Jongsma suggested we change the title from *Academy Regained* (the former working title for the book) to *Creation Regained: Disciplinary Perspectives*. I'd also like to thank Kevin Vander Meulen, a longtime colleague at Redeemer who provided invaluable assistance and accountability to keep the project moving along. Finally, many thanks to all the chapter authors and the Redeemer administration for their great patience in seeing this book through until completion.

Now, let me give a bit more background to the long history of this book. In August 2022, pre-published chapters from this volume were used as part of a faculty development conference at Redeemer University. To introduce the project, I argued that the book might best be introduced through a story, a parable, a metaphor, a Psalm of David, and another parable. I'll discuss these below, and then conclude this preface with some final thoughts.

The Story of This Book

As the editor of this collection of essays, I thought I'd share a little bit about my own intellectual journey in neo-Calvinism, which overlaps quite a bit with the history of this book.

When I arrived at Redeemer University in 2006—it was called Redeemer University College then— I was very self-consciously in the Reformed tradition, particularly in the Presbyterian, Westminster Standards strain. I was very much influenced by Jonathan Edwards, and had been strongly shaped by one significant strain of Kuyperian thinking via Cornelius Van Til.

Now, I had heard that Redeemer was in another corner of the Reformed academic world, and the thing that distinguished Redeemer's heritage was its emphasis on the "Reformational philosophy" of Herman Dooyeweerd, Dirk Vollenhoven, Roy Clouser and others. I was curious. Not only had I heard about Dooyeweerd, but I had also heard about controversies back in the day, in which there were debates between "the Van Tillians" and "the Dooyeweerdians" that got so heated that the opposing parties were apparently anathematizing one another. One particularly vivid example of this I discovered in the late 1990s, when I was studying for my first master's degree at Geneva College in Pennsylvania. I had heard stories about an influential and controversial Dooyeweerdian named Peter Steen who had taught there. Though he taught at Geneva only four years, his impact was significant enough to make him one of the faculty members discussed in the institutional history of Geneva College published upon the sesquicentennial celebration in 1997.[4]

So, when I arrived in Ancaster, Ontario (where Redeemer is located), I wanted to learn more. In that first summer of 2006, we had a faculty retreat at what was then called the Canterbury Hills Conference Centre in Ancaster, Ontario. I approached Al Wolters—whom I had been told knew quite a bit about the topic—and told him that I'd love to find out more about Dooyeweerd and wondered if he would teach me. Much to my delight, he said he would, and that there were some other faculty members who had expressed a desire for something similar.

So we started a group, which eventually acquired the name of the Reformational Philosophy Discussion Group. We began meeting during my first semester, and continued to meet through the 2015-16 academic year, after which the Centre for Christian Scholarship took over that role of facilitating faculty reading. All in all, we had a pretty good ten-year run and a number of publications flowed from our conversations. This book is the final fruit of that group.

In those first meetings, those who attended included Theo Plantinga, Al Wolters, Harry Van Dyke, Keven Vander Meulen, Derek Schuurman, David Koyzis, and Robert MacLarkey. Tragically, Plantinga died soon after we began, in July 2008. But I'll never forget his enthusiastic participation and the joy he had seeing the Reformational tradition being passed along to the next generation. Very soon after the formation of the group, Vahagn Asatryan and Kevin Flatt became mainstays. Jim Vanderwoerd and Jim Rusthoven soon became essential members of the group as well. Other attendees included Jacob Ellens, Doug Needham, Robert Joustra, Deborah Bowen, Elaine Botha, Jitse van der Meer, Gene Haas, Dirk Windhorst and others. All made important contributions.

At first, we called the group the "Dooyeweerd discussion group" (except for Theo, who called it the "Dooyeweerd reading group"). Though our elders disagreed with some of his interpretations of Dooyeweerd, they nevertheless appreciated J. Glenn Friesen's online translation of Dooyeweerd's original 1935 Dutch-language work, the *Wijsbegeerte der Wetsidee*—luckily for me, a non-Dutch speaker, we simply referred to the work as "the *WdW*," which saved me the embarrassment of trying to pronounce the full title. We also read from Dooyeweerd's *New Critique of Theoretical Thought*, the first volume of which was originally published in 1953, which was a translation and revision of the *WdW*—but the edition we read was the one published by Paideia Press in 1984. 35/53 has always been a helpful mnemonic to me.

In 2008, we read selected chapters from Andrew Basden's *Philosoph-*

4 David M. Carson, *Pro Cristo et Patria: A History of Geneva College* (Virginia Beach, VA: The Donning Company Publishers, 1997), 119.

ical Frameworks for Understanding Information Systems which had been published the same year. In the fall of 2009, Sean Purcell led us through Vollenhoven's *Introduction to Philosophy*.

In 2010, we read chapter drafts from what would become David Koyzis's book *We Answer to Another: Authority, Office, and the Image of God.* We also read *Reason within the Bounds of Religion* by Nicholas Wolterstorff. We were treated, in May 2010, via Craig Bartholomew's Paideia Centre of Public Theology, to an intensive seminar on the *New Critique of Theoretical Thought* taught by Henk Geertsema.

In 2011-12 we read Jonathan Chaplin's *Herman Dooyeweerd: Christian Philosopher of State and Civil Society.*

And these are just a few of the titles we read.

But here's the key thing. As we read these books, we kept coming back to the same question. We wondered how the material we found in these outstanding works could be applied to our disciplines. The current volume is an attempt to do just that. Which brings me to the first parable.

The Parable of the Impressive Foundation

In 2014 we had a conference in which initial drafts of some of the chapters were presented, under the head of "Academy Regained," here at Redeemer and at McMaster University—it was a "satellite conference" overlapping with the annual meeting of the Canadian Scientific and Christian Affiliation. David Koyzis and I hosted, and Arnold Sikkema of Trinity Western University was instrumental in bringing this to pass.

To promote the conference, I sent the following email to the faculty and staff of Redeemer in June 2014:

> Hello colleagues!
>
> Here's a parable: There once was an architect who designed a beautiful building. The construction crew came in, dug a big hole, and laid a perfect foundation. Then, the crew left. A crowd gathered to admire the beautiful foundation. End of story.

Christian scholarship and teaching sometimes seem like this. We might have a wonderful mission or blueprint. Redeemer certainly does, i.e., to teach and do research "which is scripturally directed and explores the relation of faith, learning, and living from a Reformed Christian perspective." We might have wonderful foundations, like Al Wolters's book *Creation Regained.* And we rightly enjoy celebrating these foundations. But if that's as far as we get, we're like the crowd in the parable—justly impressed, yet lacking an appropriate sense of incompletion!

The point is that theological and philosophical foundations are not ends in themselves. And since faculty are typically untrained in "foundational" matters, building on these foundations can be difficult, time-consuming and lonely work. *Creation Regained: Disciplinary Perspectives*, thus, is an attempt to build on these solid foundations, and to move away from a model of mentoring in which the mere reading of foundational texts is thought to suffice.

The Toolbox Metaphor

When I arrived at Redeemer there was some negative feeling about the Reformational tradition. In the eyes of some, it had become something of a straitjacket or a test of orthodoxy. Providentially, around the time our discussion group began, Calvin University philosopher Jamie Smith published an article in *Comment* which I think helped set the tone for our reading group, in which he described Reformational concepts as conceptual *tools in a toolbox*.[5] It was the perfect approach, invitational but non-constraining, suggesting that we could engage the tradition as useful, without fear of being burdened again by a yoke of slavery, to borrow a Pauline phrase. I think that was the spirit of *Creation Regained: Disciplinary Perspectives*.

Indeed, this humbler approach opened up vistas to other Reformed approaches, such as my own, which was very Van Tillian at the time (and still is in many ways). I'll never forget when Al Wolters said that the difference between the Van Tillians and the Dooyeweerdians was a "family squabble." The intention was to say that we're all in the same family, that we all have a voice, and it's best for us to talk these things through. In 2001, Nicholas Wolterstorff argued that there were three major Kuyperian traditions in North America. The tradition of Herman Dooyeweerd, centered in Toronto at the Institute for Christian Studies (and Redeemer itself); the tradition of Cornelius Van Til, centered in Philadelphia—with its core apologetic conviction of the necessity of the Christian worldview to make sense of reality—at Westminster Theological Seminary; and the tradition of William Harry Jellema, centered at Calvin College in Grand Rapids, which gave rise to a tradition of deeper engagement with mainstream scholarship, featuring luminaries such as Alvin Plantinga, Richard Mouw, George Marsden, and Wolterstorff himself.[6] The openness of the toolbox metaphor has extended to all of these Kuyperian traditions—they all make an appearance in this book (though the Reformational voice is dominant). Indeed, some chapters

5 James K.A. Smith, "Neocalvinism…Maybe: A Peek into My Neocalvinist Toolbox," *Comment* (June 1, 2006), Neocalvinism . . . Maybe: A peek into my neocalvinist toolbox - Comment Magazine.

6 Nicholas Wolterstorff, "How Calvin Fathered a Renaissance in Christian Philosophy" (Calvin College 125th Anniversary Lecture, Grand Rapids, MI, Feb. 2 2001).

have borrowed freely from other Christian scholarly traditions as they saw fit. My chapter, for example, attempts to reconcile Dooyeweerd, Van Til (via John Frame) Edwards and Aquinas. Our open-hearted discussion group allowed for creative syntheses such as this.

A Psalm of David

Originally, I began this work as co-editor with David Koyzis, who served as political science professor at Redeemer for 30 years, and whose book *Political Visions and Illusions* was praised by the late Timothy Keller as "Definitely the best book I've read on the current state of political thinking happening among evangelicals in 2020." It has always struck me that David is aptly named because he is a great lover of the Psalms. He reads the Psalms daily, and, in 2021, he completed a 35-year project of versifying the entire Psalter. For those versifications, he has also written his own harmonizations for the original Genevan Psalter tunes.

Not only has David been a dear friend and a trusted brother to me all these years. One of his favorite Psalms is the darkest of all the laments, Psalm 88 which contains the haunting phrase "*darkness has become my only companion*" (verse 18b). I mention this because the history of this volume has overlapped with some of the darkest and most difficult times, for David and for myself. One outworking of these challenges is that David pulled back from his role as co-editor, thinking he had not contributed enough to be given editorial credit. I disagreed with this assessment, but after it became clear that I could not persuade him otherwise, I honored his wish. The reader should know that David was involved behind the scenes in innumerable ways, and whatever virtues the book possesses are due, in part, to his presence and participation.

The Parable of the Tulips

Let me close with one last parable. Imagine there was a certain species of flower; let's say a tulip. Imagine further that as these flowers reproduced, they created a rich ecosystem in which even more tulips could flourish. Finally, imagine that this ecosystem, so nourishing to tulips, simultaneously created an environment toxic to other flowers. It would essentially be an environment in which some species thrived, while others languished.

I am a psychologist by training, not a biologist. Google tells me that there is actually a process that operates like this[7]. Regardless, as far as par-

7 The process is called *allelopathy*. See James J. Ferguson, Bala Rathinasabapathi and Carlene A. Chase, "Allelopathy: How Plants Suppress Other Plants," *UF/IFAS Extension* (March 2013), ferg-and-rath-ifas-ext.pdf (mssoy.org). The good news is that tulips, as far as I know, do not have allelopathic properties!

ables go, it works. It illustrates a concern about the intellectual tradition with which we wrestle in this volume, and the broader ecclesial tradition from which it flows. Can the Dutch neo-Calvinist Kuyperian intellectual tradition provide a context in which a thousand flowers bloom?

I want to suggest from my own non-Dutch experience that the answer to this question is yes.

Raphael's "School of Athens" is a famous 16th century fresco found in the Vatican. It depicts an older Plato, who points upward, indicating the importance of the eternal forms, while a young Aristotle points downward to the earth, signaling attentiveness to earthy realities.

The differentiation between the Puritan tradition of my Reformed Presbyterianism and the Reformational tradition I encountered at Redeemer might be understood as the difference between those two impulses.

When I arrived at Redeemer, I had a thoroughly Reformed and Augustinian sort of understanding—and of course Augustine had achieved a great synthesis of Christian and Platonic thought. According to this view, human nature is perfected by the well-ordering of its loves. Human beings flourish as they value that which has supreme value. Human goodness is a result of that beatific vision; in seeing God, we become transfixed by the beauty of God, and we are ourselves beautified. This was a major theme in the psychology of Jonathan Edwards.

But a potential problem with the emphases of this tradition is a de-emphasis on the richness and goodness of created reality. Taken to an extreme, my own tradition may struggle to differentiate between human beings and angels. Just as the angels find their *telos* in the "holy, holy, holy" of Isaiah 6, so too do we, of course. But without some deep grounding in creation, we might mistakenly conclude that's all we need to know about human beings.

This is the great value I found in the Reformational philosophical tradition. By paying careful attention to creation structure, the laws and norms that constrain and shape our human lives, we find a different but complementary vision of human flourishing. Perhaps it reflects less the Pauline and the Johannine vison and more the earthy vision of Proverbs: that as we conform our lives to the laws of creation, things tend to go well for us. Both visions are true.

In the Reformed and Reformational personality theory I developed over the last 17 years here at Redeemer (and which I finally get to share more broadly in my chapter in this book), I try to marry these two impulses. On the one hand, there is the vertical, worshipping side, the part of us that places its happiness *somewhere*, that trusts and loves *something* supremely. (And this isn't only Edwards and the Puritans who emphasized this—as my chapter details this is an important though sometimes neglected aspect of Reformational philosophy as well).

Second, there is the horizontal aspect, whether that be the biotic, the sensory, the fiduciary, the ethical, the logical, the lingual, the social, the cultural, the economic, the justicial, or the aesthetic. These are the laws and norms that govern our lives, and in fact, these are the laws and norms that shaped even the God-man Jesus Christ. By taking true human form, he himself was influenced by those laws and norms. And he himself, by taking true human form, declared those laws and norms good. In Christ, we are blessed to experience our creatureliness as the wonderful gift that it is.

So may a thousand flowers bloom? In my experience, yes! I feel that my Christianity has been expanded and completed in some way, through the wedding of these two traditions. Our hope is that readers of this volume would likewise something of value in this tradition, regardless of their position within the body of Christ.

Conclusion

During the faculty development conference at Redeemer in August 2022, as we discussed many of the chapters in this book, a moment of anxiety quickly changed into joy and gratitude. I had been anxious that none of that first generation of scholars, such as Al Wolters or Harry Van Dyke, whom we had relied upon for so long, were there to help us wrestle through tricky matters of interpretation. But at one moment I realized that *there we were*, the children and grandchildren of that preceding generation, taking the good things they had taught us, and passing them along to the next, in our own way and as best as we could. I was filled with a sense of God's blessing and grace.

Just as my first action as a Redeemer professor was to approach Al Wolters and help launch the Reformational Philosophy Discussion Group, my last action as a Redeemer professor is to submit the manuscript of this book for publication. As I take my family back to my wife's native Western Pennsylvania, and take a position at another wonderful Christian institution, it is with deep gratitude and the earnest hope that I may build upon what I learned at Redeemer, just as all the authors hope their contributions will prove useful.

Russ Kosits—Ancaster, Ontario
June 30, 2023

A Note of Gratitude

In God's kind providence, this volume—the namesake of Al Wolter's *Creation Regained: Biblical Basics for a Reformational Worldview*—has reached its final stages of preparation during the 40th anniversary year of that consequential little book. And as this anniversary year draws to a close, the subsequent appearance of this volume will, by God's grace, represent a continuation and constructive extension of the vision that *Creation Regained* helped illumine. In view of this, and since it's been more than two years since the preface to this volume was written, it seems appropriate to include this brief note of gratitude. Many of the authors in this book were personally mentored by Al during their time at Redeemer University; all of us were shaped by his book. We thus feel a further debt of gratitude. On a personal note, after seventeen years at Redeemer, and now in my third year at Grove City College, my appreciation for the usefulness and impact of *Creation Regained* has only grown. In a recent conversation with Al, I was able, with joy and thanksgiving, to share with him that we are using his book in both a pilot mentoring program for new faculty and also a new course on worldview and psychological science here at GCC. But this is certainly not the first time the work has been used here. Al told me that back in the 1970s, while still working for the Institute for Christian Studies in Toronto, he gave lectures at GCC on the material that would become *Creation Regained*. Along these lines, I recently learned from Paul McNulty (Grove City College's ninth president) that Kuyperian presuppositionalism had vivified the intellectual climate here while he was an undergraduate. Certainly, Al's lectures would have been part of that vivification.

I'm also grateful to John Kok, a champion of Reformational thought and longtime editor at Dordt University Press, who agreed to publish this volume. His untimely passing—along with the recent announcement of the closing of Trinity Christian College in Illinois—is a reminder of the impermanence of our earthly sojourn. And yet, the continued existence and flourishing of institutions like Redeemer and Grove City, and of the Christian intellectual tradition that this volume represents, reminds us that God graciously allows our imperfect labors to bear fruit. I'd also like to thank Carla Goslinga at Dordt Press who, after Dr. Kok's passing, in the midst of multiple other responsibilities, soldiered on, formatting the manuscript and handling many subsequent corrections. The cover design was inspired by the promotional images for the 40th anniversary celebration of *Creation Regained* held at Redeemer University on November 14. It alludes to the original 1985 cover design for *Creation Regained*, which featured a single leaf. The multiplicity of leaves on our cover captures our aspiration to multiply and build on Al's book and the Christian intellectual tradition it represents. Thanks to Benjy Weida for his excellent rendering of this vision. Finally, I'd like to thank again the authors of the various chapters whose patience in seeing this volume to fruition can only be described as Christ-like. For that, I am grateful beyond what I can express in words.

Perhaps God allows denominations and different Christian intellectual traditions to exist so that no one group can claim ownership of his manifold wisdom. We certainly don't claim a corner on Christian truth. Rather, it's our hope that the essays in this humble volume—which attempt to show how the Scriptural vision represented by *Creation Regained* and the wisdom of the Reformed and Reformational tradition may be applied to various academic disciplines and professions—will shape future generations and thus play a role—alongside other intellectual traditions flowing from historic Christian faith—in the continued advancement of the Kingdom of God in the realm of teaching and scholarship, as aspects of discipleship to Jesus Christ.

Maranatha!

Russ Kosits—Grove City, Pennsylvania
Thanksgiving Day, 2025

Introduction:
Scholarship for the Kingdom

David T. Koyzis and Russell D. Kosits

The Scriptures tell us that "The fear of the LORD is the beginning of knowledge" (Prov. 1:7). Human beings are his image-bearing creatures and are part of an orderly creation, which they are called, among other things, to study and explore. Over the centuries we have set up educational institutions at all levels to engage in this important task, including post-secondary schools known as colleges and universities. In North America there are over one hundred Christian colleges and universities established on the conviction that faith in the God who has revealed himself in Jesus Christ is foundational to the larger effort to understand his world. The Council for Christian Colleges and Universities (CCCU) has more than 180 member institutions, and at most of these there is a concerted effort to integrate faith and learning, as it is usually expressed.

However, efforts at integration are not necessarily easy, especially within those disciplines whose foundational roots have not yet been adequately explored from the vantage point of a Christian worldview. Junior faculty at such institutions are often given the mandate to integrate faith and learning but are left to feel their way to this elusive destination. They may know intuitively that it cannot be merely a matter of praying before class or being professionally ethical or seeking excellence in their teaching and research. There has got to be more. But what?

God

We believe that the tradition associated with Abraham Kuyper offers a way forward that will help our colleagues, along with graduate students, as they set about this task of integrating faith and scholarship. The place to begin here is with the biblical redemptive narrative, which properly starts with a consideration of God himself. The Christian worldview is theocentric. The very first verse of the Bible runs: "In the beginning God. . . ." Before anything else existed there was God, who is creator of heaven and earth. God is self-revealing. The main point of God's revelation—expressed in the Book of his Words (the Bible) and the Book of his Works (creation)—is God himself. He is independent of all else and is eternal, with no beginning and no end. God wishes to know us and for us to know him. He has revealed himself as Father, Son, and Holy Spirit, corresponding to the three persons of the Trinity. Followers of the two other major monotheistic faiths, namely, Judaism and Islam, erroneously think that Christians are tritheists – that we believe in three gods. Certainly the Trinity defies an easy explanation that will satisfy such objections. But if we remember that number is a created category and that God transcends his creation, then we can perhaps more easily accept that unity and plurality come together in God because they are his creatures. This is perhaps already evident in the Hebrew word for God, *Elohim* (אלוהים), which is, grammatically speaking, a plural noun, but applied to the one God (Deuteronomy 6:4).

God is a personal being, not merely an impersonal force. Since the release of the first of the *Star Wars* films back in 1977, the greeting, "May the Force be with you," has entered the English language. But God is not "the Force," for his is a conscious presence superintending the entire cosmos and directing it to its ultimate fulfilment. Nor is he the Supreme Being of Enlightenment Deism. He is not reducible to the Highest Cause or Pure Actuality, as some might have it, because causation and actuality are, once again, created phenomena. God is not an abstract principle of any sort. He is, quite simply, God, the Father Almighty, creator of heaven and earth, who deigned to become incarnate in Jesus Christ, and upholds and empowers us by his Spirit. He is who he is. More to the point for our purposes, he is who he has revealed himself to be.

This God demands our worship, which is the *telos* of human life. St. Augustine famously wrote: "You have made us for yourself, and our hearts are restless until they rest in you."[1] He further defined virtue as the right ordering of things loved. To worship God means to love him above all that he has created and to pay him due homage. To love inordinately—to love the creature rather than the Creator—amounts to what the Bible calls idolatry, which is prohibited in the first two commandments of the Decalogue. But if we are to love ordinately, then this love of God must be closely followed by the love of neighbour, which Jesus calls the second great commandment in his summary of the law (Matt. 22:37-40).

Because we are creatures, of course, it is difficult to talk about God without immediately discussing his creation. After all, God has chosen to relate to us in concrete creational ways. It could scarcely be otherwise. If God transcends his creation, then he must accommodate himself to us in ways we can understand. Even God's miracles, which we tend to think of as "supernatural," presuppose the regularities of creation and the ordinary laws of physics, astronomy, biology, and so forth. A miraculous healing involves the created phenomena associated with corporeal life, such as

1. Augustine, *Confessions* ed. Carolyn J.-B. Hammond, trans. William Watts, Loeb Classical Library 26 (Cambridge, MA: Harvard University Press, 2014), 1.1.

heart, lungs, blood circulation, antibodies, skin cells, and muscles. To this creation we then turn.

Creation

"In the beginning God created the heaven and earth." Another way to put this is that God created everything that is not God. It cannot be emphasized strongly enough that creation is cosmic in scope. If you can see it, feel it, hear it, smell it, taste it, or even just imagine it in your mind's eye, it is one of God's creatures. Creation is not just the fields and forests, lakes and rivers, oceans and glaciers, mountains and valleys. "Creation care" is often seen to consist of stewardship of our physical environment, but it might just as well include human society too. Families, marriages, political communities, business enterprises, labour unions, dance troupes, and agricultural co-operatives are part of God's creation and thus proper objects of concern for anyone interested in creation care. Not just the natural world, but the whole world of human culture, with its rich array of activities, communities, relationships, and artefacts, is part of creation in this total sense.

Creation exists entirely by God's grace. God did not have to create, after all, but he did so anyway. Grace is something freely given which cannot be merited by the recipient. Some Christian traditions make much of the distinction between nature and grace, but this distinction does not adequately recognize that even the natural world exists by God's grace. According to Russian Orthodox theologian Alexander Schmemann, "All that exists is God's gift to man, and it all exists to make God known to man, to make man's life communion with God "[2] The fact that we are alive, that we are here on earth, looking up into the skies, enjoying the mountains, oceans, rivers, and lakes, comes as the free gift of God. That we can marry, have children, organize business enterprises, and establish schools is entirely due to God's grace. Nothing that we might claim for ourselves comes *from* ourselves, but from God alone, whether or not we acknowledge it. Even our own gifts to God, e.g., of time, effort, or money, are merely returned to their source from the store of riches over which he has appointed us stewards. As William Howe's famous hymn lyric puts it,

We give thee but thine own,
Whate'er the gift may be,
For all we have is thine alone,
A trust, O Lord, from thee.

Creation thus finds its meaning outside itself, a recognition of which

2. Alexander Schmemann, *For the Life of the World: Sacraments and Orthodoxy* (Crestwood, NY: St. Vladimir's Seminary Press, 1973), 15.

already puts the Christian scholar on a very different footing from that of her unbelieving counterpart in the academy. Jonathan Edwards observes that God created the world for the manifestation of his glory, and it is only in seeing and delighting in this glory that human beings can find their greatest happiness.[3] David Kelsey further labels all human existence "eccentric" in that it derives its meaning outside of itself.[4] Meaning and joy are found in God who approaches us from the very outset as creator. Once again, this acknowledgement that we ourselves are God's gift using his gifts for his glory makes for a distinctive approach, not only to the academic enterprise, but to the whole of life.

For close to a century and a half, Christians hearing the word *creation* have often seen this as standing in opposition to *biological evolution.* We do not propose to address this controversy here, but we believe it is necessary to emphasize that the true opposite of the conviction that God created everything *ex nihilo* (out of nothing) is not evolution as such, but the belief that everything that exists is self-existent and self-sustaining, i.e., independent of God. Exactly how God brought everything, including human beings, into existence is a highly contentious and emotional issue in the church today and we hope this volume will prove useful to orthodox Christians of all stripes. But *that* God brought everything into existence is a nonnegotiable for the Christian. In this respect we are all *creationists,* even if we may object to how that label has been used in some circles. We do not believe, as did Aristotle, that matter and energy are eternal. We believe that they were created by a gracious God.

Still, God did not create everything in its final or complete form, and creation includes the further development and unfolding of its richness. In particular, God has given human beings a special place in his creation as caretakers responsible for "tending the garden" in answer to his call. We engage in this cultural activity not only as individuals but as communities. In engaging in these activities we are unique among his creatures. We are created to commune with God and to commune with each other as those created in his image. That we worship in community finds its significance in that we are members of the church of Jesus Christ, which gathers for the explicit purpose of liturgical worship but which is also manifest in every sphere of activity, whether formal or informal, organized or spontaneous, communal or associational. In the Reformed tradition this is generally known as the Cultural Mandate and is found

3. Jonathan Edwards, *A Dissertation on the End for Which God Created the World* in *The Works of Jonathan Edwards*, ed. Edward Hickman (Edinburgh: Banner of Truth Trust, 1974), vol 1: 94—121. page number needed].

4. David Kelsey, *Eccentric Existence* (Louisville, KY: Westminster John Knox Press, 2009).

in Genesis 1:26-30:

> Then God said, "Let us make man in our image, after our likeness. And let them have dominion over the fish of the sea and over the birds of the heavens and over the livestock and over all the earth and over every creeping thing that creeps on the earth." . . . And God said to them, "Be fruitful and multiply and fill the earth and subdue it, and have dominion over the fish of the sea and over the birds of the heavens and over every living thing that moves on the earth."

Although God as such is perfect, he pronounces his creation merely "good" and "very good," its goodness deriving from his own goodness. Nevertheless, it is incomplete and, as was evidently God's purpose from the outset, it requires human tending to attain that completeness. Consider the difference between a meadow and a formal garden. The meadow is filled with tall grasses and wild flowers and carries a certain pristine beauty of its own. But we marvel at, say, the *Jardin des Tuileries*, the formal gardens of the French kings in Paris, or the Royal Botanical Gardens in Hamilton, Ontario, Canada. Visitors from all over the world come to see these gardens and to enjoy these pleasing products of man's relationship with nature. Similarly, while we enjoy hiking in the forests or mountains, we love to visit our cities, such as New York, Paris, and London, where we can experience the best fruits of our diverse cultures, including classical or gothic architecture, stage plays, concerts, museums, zoos, and, once again, parks, and gardens.

The creation we undertake to explore is thus a dynamic and unfolding creation. More than one of the chapters in this collection will touch on technology, which we believe is in principle good, even as it is capable of distortion in practice. The world of Abraham and the patriarchs consisted of human beings employing fairly simple techniques appropriate to nomadic and tribal peoples. The Old Testament itself makes us aware of the technological gap between the Bronze-Age Israelites and their predatory neighbours, the Philistines, whose Iron-Age technologies gave them military superiority over the people of God. Our forebears born in the early years of the last century would have written on typewriters and communicated by telegraph across great distances, while a century later the words our own minds generated in digital form have an ethereal quality that makes them easy to edit or erase and to send across the globe instantaneously using highly sophisticated computer technology. It is important to recall that the potentialities making possible these developments were latent in the creation from the beginning, and it has been God's good pleasure that these should be discovered and developed. The physical properties making the microchip possible were already present at the time of Abraham or even of the much earlier Neanderthals.

This creation is a *lawful* creation. Even the randomness of certain processes, as studied by physicists, biologists, and other natural and social scientists, conforms to certain laws capable of exploration by those created in God's image.[5] In these early decades of the twenty-first century we may tend to view law as an external imposition on our wills, as something to which we are compelled to conform whether or not we like it. It cannot be denied that there is a coercive side to the law, but this is not the whole story. Law is, in reality, the very condition of our existence. The fact that we can express our desires at all is due to the lawful character of our created nature. Even when we depart from the law in specific ways, we do so in a manner that inevitably follows orderly patterns beyond our wills. We are bound, in the first place, to laws of nature which we cannot but obey for fear of suffering consequences for failing to do so. The law of gravity enforces itself with merciless immediacy, especially if we attempt to defy it by walking off the edge of, say, the Niagara Escarpment or jumping from the Empire State Building. But we ourselves bear responsibility for following *norms,* which can be disobeyed, at least in the short term. The proscriptions against theft and adultery are norms which God's human image-bearers are called to practise and to implement in specific ways in specific contexts. This form of lawfulness, which we might label *normativity,* is unique to God's image-bearers. Some traditions call this the moral law in that it governs the contingent choices human beings make on a day-to-day basis. These norms are embodied in general fashion in the Decalogue and in the biblical command to love God and neighbour. We bear responsibility for translating these norms into the various patterns, rules and regulations that govern our lives in a huge variety of communal contexts.

Some people think that any emphasis on law runs the risk of legalism. Perhaps, they think, we should emphasize human flourishing and seeking shalom in our communities instead of obedience to law. Nicholas Wolterstorff has argued that, rather than focussing on the "inner nature of the State" and similar institutions, we should be asking how empirical states serve humanity.[6] We believe that this is a false dichotomy. Indeed, as Jonathan Chaplin has recently argued, as we struggle to understand and submit to the laws and norms pervading and upholding creation, we will flourish. These require that we seek to understand the normative tasks of the huge diversity of institutions, associations, and relationships

5. The long-run relative frequency interpretation of probability so prevalent in the social sciences, for example, presupposes orderly probability distributions which make prediction and probabilistic knowledge possible.

6. Nicholas Wolterstorff, *Until Justice and Peace Embrace* (Grand Rapids, MI: Eerdmans, 1983), 63.

that make up a normal society. If we do not ask the proper structural questions, we could be faced, e.g., with a state claiming to serve humanity while grossly overextending its own competence in totalitarian fashion, with an economy in which the validity of the free market is extended into areas primarily and properly governed by other, noneconomic norms, or with social sciences that fail to address and remedy patterns of behaviour that undermine human flourishing.

The Reformational philosophical tradition associated with Herman Dooyeweerd and Dirk Vollenhoven is best known for its effort to elaborate upon the deep modal structure of the creation. Based on empirical observation, they assert that the whole of creation is subject to several irreducible laws and norms governing all of creaturely life. Many of our authors will employ this modal analysis in their chapters as a way of understanding the relationship between their particular fields and a complex creation. This approach can be helpful in several ways: it can help us to identify individual academic disciplines and the deep structure of academic inquiry. It can also help us to get a full-orbed, holistic sense of creational reality which can be useful in the design of products and machines, and in approaches to human well-being. Here are the modal aspects in descending order as set forth by Dooyeweerd in his mature philosophy:[7]

- pistical—faith, certainty
- ethical—love in temporal relations
- jural—retribution, justice
- aesthetic—harmony, beautiful proportion
- economic—thrift, frugality
- social—social intercourse
- lingual—language, symbolic signification
- historical—cultural formation, power
- analytical—logic, cognition, theory
- psychical—sensation, feeling
- biotic—organic life
- physical—energy, physico-chemical
- kinematic—motion, extensive movement
- spatial—continuous extension
- numerical—discrete quantity

For all these different ways in which the things of reality function, the creation itself has a coherence, complexity, and integrity that deserves

7. Herman Dooyeweerd, *A New Critique of Theoretical Thought*, trans. David H. Freeman and H. De Jongste (Jordan Station, ON: Paideia, 1984), We should note that the number and order of modalities is rightly contested in Reformational circles.

careful attention. This is why each discipline is divided into many subfields. Each particular part of the creation is worth careful study and is capable of rewarding sustained attention.

Fall into Sin

The Bible takes the first two chapters of Genesis to tell the story of creation, its initial unfolding, and the special place of human beings within it. However, the second act of the drama comes already in the third chapter, and this is the fall into sin by our first parents in the Garden. The entire rest of the Bible is preoccupied with the tragic after-effects of sin as experienced by subsequent generations over the course of millennia. But what is sin? Some parts of our popular culture tend to view it as harmlessly transgressive, as in the familiar advertising campaigns referring to a particular brand of chocolate or baked goods as "sinfully delicious." Some tend to associate sinfulness with *the other*, i.e., those outside of our own political or moral tribe. But sin is no trifle, and it affects us all. There are many facets to sin, of course, but it basically amounts to a disobedience to God's will incurring divine judgement. In the short term, we may tend to think that sin makes us happy, but as social scientific research increasingly demonstrates, our violation of God's law—whether it be through overeating, sexual infidelity, lack of gratitude, selfishness, nursing grudges and unforgiveness, laziness and lack of exercise, worry, and lack of sincere spiritual engagement—undermine well-being and flourishing. We all, sadly, know at least some of these things from personal experience: our collective failure to live in accordance with God's good law is misery-producing.

Sin, then, simply means that the world is not as it should be. One line of evidence that nearly everyone understands this is the fact that the world's religions have long attempted to account for this reality in some fashion. Even Platonic philosophy carries an implicit conception of sin, which, in Plato's eyes, amounts to a failure of the human person to think abstractly about the good, the true, and the beautiful. More recently, Marxism has been aptly labelled a Christian heresy. Not surprisingly, the Marxist believes that the original division of labour during a presumed ancient stage of primitive communism is the source of the world's many ills. As Reinhold Niebuhr famously observed, "The doctrine of original sin is the only empirically verifiable doctrine of the Christian faith."[8] We see the effects of sin within us and all around us; only with the greatest of difficulties can we deny it.

8. Reinhold Niebuhr, *Man's Nature and His Communities: Essays on the Dynamics and Enigmas of Man's Personal and Social Existence* (New York: Charles Scribner's Sons, 1965), 24.

That God has allowed lawlessness into our world and experience there can be no experiential or theological doubt. There is no "problem of evil" in that sense—sin and misery are precisely what the Christian worldview predicts. But *why* did God allow sin to come into the world? This we cannot know, because he has chosen not to reveal it to us. Presumably he could have created a world in which no one would be subject to temptation and in which it would be impossible for anyone to sin. We may be tempted to think that such a world would have been better than the real world of which we are a part. But, of course, we cannot presume to be wiser than the God who has created us. For reasons unknown to us God deliberately created human beings with the capacity to obey or to disobey the norms he has given them in creation. There is good biblical reason to conclude that this human responsibility is a crucial element of what it means to be created in God's image. God willed to relate to someone capable of consciously responding to his call. The capacity to respond presupposes the possibility of failing to respond accordingly, which is exactly what Genesis 3 records.

We must immediately warn against a defective view of sin and its effects that is found in many Christian and non-Christian circles. This view amounts to the belief that a structural component of creation is *a*, if not *the*, source of evil in the world. Libertarians tend to think that we would be much better off with as little external authority as possible, assuming that government is at best a necessary evil, but an evil all the same. Socialists generally assume that individual ownership of property is an evil to be combated. Prohibitionists think that alcoholic beverages are a source of evil, ignoring the reality that their abuse issues, not from their existence as such, but from the human heart that wills such abuse. Similarly, some Christians may be persuaded that psychology or politics are off-limits to the believer, thinking them to be intrinsically corrupt or corrupting. In so concluding, they risk falling into the ancient Gnostic heresy. Gnosticism locates evil, not in the human heart, but in some structural element of creation. But sin cannot be so easily identified and avoided. Certain types of pietists would have us eschew a lengthy laundry list of items, such as drinking, smoking, dancing, card-playing, and perhaps even the cinema. We will not weigh in on the respective merits or dangers of these activities except to note that the rejection of these does not by any means lessen the power of sin in our lives. In fact, it may encourage in us an unhealthy pride in our own righteousness, as illustrated in Jesus' parable of the Pharisee and the tax collector (Luke 18:9-14).

Sin, in other words, is cosmic in scope, but it has not destroyed or cancelled out the goodness of creation, which remains even after the fall. We continue to enjoy the sunshine, the flowers in our gardens, the beasts of the fields and forests, a performance of *Swan Lake*, prompt mail delivery, and fulfilling marriages – which taken together Kuyper refers to as common grace, which is distinct from the special grace that works salvation in Jesus Christ. The relationship between creation and sin is a complex one, and it is no simple matter to tease the two apart. As St. Augustine understood already sixteen centuries ago, sin has no substance of its own but is parasitical on God's good creation.[9] Or, as Cornelius Plantinga expresses it, sin vandalizes shalom.[10] The path of disobedience, as of obedience, is utterly dependent on the creation as its natural setting.

How then do we go about differentiating between the good creation and its sinful distortion? It is not difficult to discern that prostitution is a misuse of our created sexuality. But what of the internal combustion engine? Is that a structural component of creation? Is it a legitimate technological development drawing on the created potentialities of the natural world? Or is it an abuse of these natural resources that intrinsically pollutes, defaces our urban centres, and dangerously warms the world's climate? The answer to these questions is not immediately forthcoming, and well-meaning people, including Christians, are likely to disagree. But the ongoing task of distinguishing between creation and its distortion is one we cannot avoid, whether in ordinary day-to-day living or in our academic inquiry.

Vollenhoven expresses this distinction in terms of *structure* and *direction*, which Wolters picks up on and develops in *Creation Regained*.[11] Structure might be called the "stuff" of creation, for example, beasts, birds, reptiles, fish, plants, rocks, people, churches, states, labour unions, business enterprises, museums, and so forth. It includes animate and inanimate objects, emotions and thoughts, abstract concepts and ideas, institutions and associations, friendships and market exchanges. Each of these is governed by its own law and finds its place within an orderly creation upheld by God. Direction has to do with the visions and worldviews we bring to the stuff of creation. Here the chasm between unbelief and belief—between sin and redemption—finds its home. Here we find the diversity of basic orientations that grip the human heart – among the various loves that determine the nature of the communities of which we are part. Or, as Augustine puts it, between the City of God and the City of this world. Here we would include such phenomena as Christianity,

9. Augustine, *Concerning the City of God against the Pagans,* trans. Henry Bettenson, introduction G.R. Evans (London: Penguin, 2003), 12.3.

10. Cornelius Plantinga, *Not the Way It's Supposed to Be: A Breviary of Sin* (Grand Rapids, MI: Wm. B. Eerdmans, 1996), 197.

11. Albert M. Wolters, *Creation Regained: Biblical Basics for a Reformational Worldview*, 2nd ed. (Grand Rapids: Eerdmans, 2005), 87-114.

Judaism, Buddhism, Islam, socialism, liberalism, anarchism, nationalism, Darwinism, Freudianism, Marxism, and Hegelianism. These are not to be reified as if they were part of the structure of God's creation order. They presuppose that order, to be sure, but they are worldviews that *direct* our affections and actions as we live within that order.

How does sin affect the scholarly enterprise? In general sin *estranges us from God*. We no longer love God above everything he has created but love the creature more. This is nothing less than what the Bible terms *idolatry*, which is arguably the root of all other sins. Our loves are disordered, which leads to disordered lives lived for ourselves rather than for God. Estrangement from God further *estranges us from God's creation* in many ways. It alienates us from the true character of what we study. Even if we may have intimate familiarity with the details of the things we explore, we lose sight of that most fundamental characteristic of all things, namely, that they are upheld by a gracious God. In other words, we no longer see what we study as coming from God, as distinct from God, as revealing God, as inherently good, and as controlled by God. Instead, although we may admit on one level that creation is ultimately from God, we come up with narratives that either exclude God or push him so far into the background as to render him irrelevant.

A typical—but certainly not the only—way in which idolatry is manifested in academic pursuits is effectively to absolutize some aspect of the creation while at the same time identifying another aspect as the source of what's wrong with the world. The Freudian focuses on sexual and aggressive motives as definitive of the human person, assuming that a failure to successfully negotiate and sublimate this libido is the source of society's ills. Similarly, the Marxist assumes that productive forces determine the human person and that any supposed diversity of human motivations can ultimately be traced to these. This leads to a defective anthropology in which it is assumed, especially in its Leninist variant, that manipulation of these forces so as to eliminate economic classes will resolve all human conflicts, thereby ushering in the liberating classless society. When this society stubbornly refuses to arrive through their efforts, proponents turn to coercive means to accomplish their goals, generally at the expense of flesh and blood persons with their real-life aspirations. Within physics we also observe the decades-old quest to locate the smallest subatomic particle, an endeavor which in itself is legitimate. But the motivation for the quest is often unduly reductive. If we can find the most basic component of material reality, many assume, we can perhaps rule out any essential differences amongst the diverse phenomena we experience. If granite, quartz, water, frogs, and human beings are all composed of the same subatomic particle, we can correct our experience of diversity in a monistic direction. This, we believe, is tantamount to idolatry: failing to acknowledge the full diversity of God's creation and assuming that something within it is the linchpin for everything else.

What are the practical effects of this sin within the academy? These can be summarized as follows:

1. The most obvious effect can be seen when someone deliberately fabricates data in support of a shaky hypothesis. Here *wilful deception* is at issue. Everyone can presumably agree that such activities are wrong and that perpetrators should be penalized accordingly.
2. A second effect sees *sin compounding our created limitations.* As creatures, our knowledge is necessarily limited, and by itself this is unrelated to sin. Regardless of sin, we all need to learn that correlation does not imply causation, or that behaviour is multiply determined, for example. But sin can increase the likelihood that we make such mistakes, particularly when these mistakes are in our own selfish interests.
3. A related manifestation might be seen in *failing to accept the legitimate conclusions of the scientific method* when they conflict with our prejudices, although it must immediately be admitted that questioning of such conclusions is properly a part of the scholarly enterprise when good reasons can be adduced for doing so.
4. Another effect of sin occurs when an academic *claims too much for his or her methods,* such as the positivist error that we cannot know that which we cannot empirically verify. A related error is that of *interpretation of data.* An evolutionary psychologist claims that Darwin's mechanism of natural selection can—indeed, must—explain the origin of virtually any phenomenon from colour vision and the hardness of a tortoise shell to the French Revolution and Picasso's Cubist-era paintings.
5. Closely related to this is the *failure to admit one's own worldview assumptions* undergirding one's academic pursuit. This is a problem, not just for individuals, but for entire communities, including academic communities, which are inevitably—but typically unconsciously—in the grip of some religious worldview. For example, the larger academy tends to accept the assumptions of naturalism, "the orthodoxy of the academy," which deliberately excludes God from its purview. Even Christian scientists have been known to claim that a methodological atheism must be the basis of any sound scientific inquiry. But in so claiming, they risk overlooking the extent to which their own—or their discipline's—unstated, unacknowledged worldview assumptions affect their research. This too is due to the outworking of sin.

6. Attending all of these manifestations of sin within the academy, we have experienced a *fragmentation of knowledge* accompanying its steady growth. As our knowledge of God's creation expands, we are tempted to focus on smaller and smaller facets of creation, ignoring the larger context that would make sense of the whole. This has given rise to what George Parkin Grant aptly calls the "multiversity," where inquiry is so focused on fairly narrow sub-subfields that we lose a sense of what—or rather Who—holds it all together.[12]

Redemption in Jesus Christ

The church universal has taught that at the birth of Jesus Christ the second Person of the triune God became flesh and dwelt among us. It has also taught that he lived a perfect life, was crucified for our transgressions, and raised again for our salvation. If Genesis 3 begins the second act of the biblical drama, Matthew 1, which starts the New Testament, ushers in the third act, which sees our redemption accomplished. God in his grace did not give up on his fallen creation, leaving it to its own resources. Rather he intervened in history, taking our sins upon himself in the person of Jesus Christ, thus ensuring our redemption from the power and eternal consequences of sin. The implications of this are huge. For one, creation was reaffirmed in the incarnation of the Son, as is particularly emphasized in the Orthodox tradition. As truly and fully human, Jesus came to reclaim the fallen creation and to save fallen human nature from sin. The remarkable thing about Jesus Christ is that he lived a righteous life before the face of God, as a child obeying with all of his heart the wisdom of his parents and elders, and, throughout his entire life, the commandments of God. In his ministry he relentlessly sought justice and the restoration of shalom. In his obedience to God's law he was a man of joy (John 15:11), a tree planted by streams of water, yielding its fruit in season (Psalm 1:3). But he was also a man of sorrows: his obedience to God carried him to death on the cross, where he "became sin for us" (2 Corinthians 5:21), taking upon himself the condemnation due those who disobey God's commands. Jesus was then raised to a new and undying life, a life that he offers now to the world.

Some Christians seem to believe that Jesus came to rescue us *from* creation—to remove us from a doomed world, much as passengers on a sinking ocean liner might be saved in lifeboats from a watery death. Many popular revival hymns reinforce this notion: "When the roll is called up yonder, I'll be there," "This world is not my home; I'm just a-passing through." Some of us have attended funerals in which the deceased's

12. George P. Grant, *Techonology and Justice* (Toronto: Anansi, 1986), 35-77.

body is dismissed as an insignificant shell, as if the intermediate state is the final state, with little attention being given to the general resurrection of the body and the renewal of creation. Or we may have heard sermons about a "great tribulation" to be preceded by "the rapture," an apparently miraculous removal of the righteous from earth.[13] But these popular forms of eschatology, more widespread in North America than elsewhere, miss the true richness of God's grace to his creation. The familiar verse, John 3:16, which virtually every Christian memorizes as a child, tells us that "God so loved the world." St. Paul tells us that "the creation itself will be set free from its bondage to corruption and obtain the freedom of the glory of the children of God" (Romans 8:21).

Nevertheless, while it is true that Christ's redemption is cosmic in scope and has implications for the whole creation, it is above all centred in the human heart. Calvin once said that "as long as Christ remains outside of us . . . all that he has suffered and done for the salvation of the human race remains useless and of no value for us."[14] So how does Jesus Christ come to live within a sinner? The Scriptures say that those whom God foreknew he also predestined to be conformed to the image of his son (Romans 8:29). How does this transformation take place? The Reformed tradition teaches that the good news about Jesus is preached outwardly to all and that some are inwardly changed by the Spirit of God to hear and take it to heart. In coming to faith in Christ, the human heart is released in principle from its bondage and captivity to sin. This release is called regeneration, in which sinners are made new in union with Christ, so that they live the new life to his glory.

Kuyper made much of this idea of regeneration or "*palingenesis*" (Titus 3:5), as he called it. It is the reality of this *palingenesis* that forms the foundation of a renewed scholarship within the academy. Regeneration begins to reverse the effects of sin in human lives. Just as sin disordered our loves and our lives, regeneration begins the process of redirecting and reordering love, so that we may love God supremely, and our neighbours as ourselves. Just as sin vandalizes shalom, regenerated Christians can now seek to restore shalom. And just as sin pervades cultural developments, regeneration can begin to restore obedience in every square inch of culture, including scholarship. Above all, regeneration turns sinners and scholars into witnesses to the coming kingdom of God, which is already present in this world in the body of Christ and its many

---

13. This belief is associated with dispensationalism, invented by John Nelson Darby in the first half of the nineteenth century and popularized in the twentieth century by the runaway success of the Scofield Study Bible (1909).

14. John Calvin, *Institutes of the Christian Religion*, ed. John T. McNeill, trans. Ford Lewis Battles (Philadelphia: Westminster Press, 1960), 3.I.1.

activities in his behalf.

Regeneration introduces in principle a division within humanity between those who are in Christ and those who are not – between those who seek God's glory and those who follow their own devices. Inevitably, those wishing to conform their lives to God's intentions for creation will meet resistance. Building on Augustine's distinction between the two cities, Kuyper refers to this as an *antithesis* between belief and unbelief. This antithesis is not just limited to an apparent "spiritual" realm set apart from the rest of life; it has profound implications for the whole of life, including the theoretical life of the mind. Nevertheless, we must not underestimate the effect of God's common grace on non-Christians, which makes collaboration and tolerance at least possible. And we must not underestimate the effect of sin on Christians—the antithesis does not merely separate communities from each other; it runs straight through the heart of every single believer, as St. Paul affirms (Romans 7:13-25). Or as Aleksandr Solzhenitsyn famously puts it, "the line dividing good and evil cuts through the heart of every human being."[15] Not surprisingly, then, many Christian scholars have confessed their sins, accepted God's forgiveness, and strive to live the new life. They attend church on Sundays, pray with their families and try to be hard-working, decent and honest persons. Yet their scholarship is virtually indistinguishable from that of their unbelieving colleagues. To be sure, as Christian scholars have long observed, it is not necessary that everything the Christian scholar does will differ from that of their unbelieving counterparts. Nevertheless, if they accept the same paradigms and find no difficulty building their own research on them, they risk ignoring the extent to which their outlook may be reductionistic and thus incompatible with a biblical worldview. Hence the academy is filled with Christians who are effectively Hegelians, Kantians, Marxists, Positivists, and so forth, seemingly unaware of the spiritual underpinnings of the Hegelian, Kantian, Marxian, and Positivist projects.

Yet we also know that these same thinkers have had valuable insights from which we have learnt much. Although much of the Freudian corpus has been subject to criticism in the years since Freud's death (including his notion of the unconscious), the existence and centrality of the unconscious is now nevertheless widely embraced by those attentive to the findings of recent science. Marx similarly understood the power of economic factors in history, and one need hardly be a Marxist to see the validity of any approach that takes these seriously. This once again points to Kuyper's notion of common grace. In fact, when it comes to

15. Aleksandr I. Solzhenitsyn, *Gulag Archipelago 1918-1956: An Experiment in Literary Investigation, I-II* (London: Collins, 1974), 1: 168.

detailed scientific observation, it may not be immediately obvious that heart-level worldview commitments make a difference. Kuyper argued that Christians and non-Christians alike can agree on a huge proportion of the scientific enterprise, especially on those matters which are easily quantifiable. "Two plus two equals four" is an equation valid for believers and unbelievers, and many of the results of academic research fall into this category. All can agree through observation that a shot glass of ouzo will immediately turn cloudy when even a small drop of water comes into contact with it. Some people will call these "facts," or, perhaps better, "replicable observations," while Dooyeweerd describes them, somewhat inelegantly, as "undeniable states of affairs."

Kuyper likened scholarship to a tree. The trunk encompasses "a very broad realm of investigation"[16] and is the place where diverse groups with differing ultimate commitments can most easily work side-by-side. Because of the givenness of God's world, we readily recognize that even those who do not acknowledge him can achieve significant scientific discoveries, technological innovations, and aesthetic works. We do not question whether Alexander Graham Bell was a Christian before we pick up the telephone, nor do we ask whether Maurice Ravel was a believer before listening to his *Pavane pour une infante défunte* in concert or on an mp3 player. This is the trunk of the tree. But at some point differences in starting point will cause the tree to divide into branches, leading to two different sciences, two different "houses" or "structures . . . each of which purposes to be a complete building of science."[17] This is the case even as "formally . . . both are at work at a common task."[18] While there are definitely grounds for co-operation, there are also differences that will inevitably produce conflict and disagreement, and each community needs to give the others an account of its own starting point and how it leads to this divergence.

Kuyper thought it would take time for *palingenesis* to work itself out in the scholarly domain. "It is the slow process which must ensue before any activity can develop itself from what potentially is given in palingenesis."[19] He thought the progress of Christian scholarship would be slow for a variety of reasons, including the recent ascendancy of naturalism as a dominant paradigm and the tendency for overtly Christian scholars to be denied university posts. Kuyper also believed that nine out of ten scientists were likely to be concerned with the sort of theoretical work

16. Abraham Kuyper, *Encyclopedia of Sacred Theology* (New York: Charles Scribner`s Sons, 1898), 157.

17. Kuyper, *Encyclopedia*, 156.

18. Kuyper, *Encyclopedia*, 159.

19. Kuyper, *Encyclopedia*, 162.

constituting the "trunk" rather than with the perspectival work more characteristic of the "branches." "There is a broad field of detail-study in which laurels can be won, without penetrating to the deep antithesis of the two world-views. . . . In this class of studies success is won with less talent, with less power of thought, with less sacrifice of time and toil; one also works with greater certainty; more immediate results are obtained . . . [which] accounts for the fact that of ten scientists, nine will prefer this class of studies."[20] As a result, we might expect that overtly integrative scholarship would suffer from neglect.

It is not enough simply to do the best we can with the talents and resources at our disposal. The quest for guild-approved excellence is sometimes thought to cover adequately the task of the Christian in the academy. But this in itself can become an idol if it is seen to substitute for nurturing and maintaining an awareness of the worldviews undergirding our own efforts. Moreover, even within that range of activities where the follower of Christ ostensibly shares so much with the unbeliever, worldview matters. Are the principles of quantum mechanics *created* principles to which we are all subject? Or are they independent of any divine will, standing alone in godlike fashion? Might God himself be subject to these principles? No matter how objective the field of inquiry, worldview enters in *somewhere*. A Christian scholar needs to become expert in detecting—and correcting—this influence.

What then does redemption mean for our academic work? Although there is much to be said here, we must content ourselves to list the most significant implications, upon which our colleagues and students should feel free to expand:

1. Above all *we seek the glory of God*, who delights in the work of his (metaphorical) hands and in what we make of this work with our own (literal) hands, particularly when our work clearly expresses rather than suppresses the way his creation displays his eternal power and divine nature (Romans1:19-20). Living out the cultural mandate is not a sideline to the Christian life; it is central to it. Obedience to God's law is not uselessly contemplative in the manner of the ancient Greek philosophers; it results in concrete actions, including academic pursuits which glorify the One who has made us for his own purposes.

2. *Redeemed scholarship attempts to produce nonreductive, doxological, and non-idolatrous works*, based on a recognition of the deep-level diversity of God's creation. It will, accordingly, reject any theory

20. Kuyper, *Encyclopedia*, 166. Kuyper's comment does not do justice to the genius of much scientific accomplishment, but it does highlight a real phenomenon.

that will make a single created principle, e.g., psycho-sexual motives, natural selection, historical dynamism, or productive forces, paramount. It will seek to take into account—and even marvel at—the rich variegated character of created reality.

3. *Redeemed scholarship engages with the larger scholarly enterprise* by enabling us to identify our own presuppositions, to identify those of others, and to call the academy to a genuine pluralism in which the diversity of worldviews can be freely worked out. A redeemed scholarship will have an apologetic edge, will seek truth above all, and will communicate it in winsome fashion.

4. *Redeemed scholarship is humble scholarship*, recognizing that our efforts to grasp theoretically God's creation will always be partial and incomplete. Although it will rigorously seek out proximate explanations for the most puzzling phenomena, it will not deny mystery and that there will continue to exist much that we do not and may never fully understand. This humility should keep us from the sort of hubris characteristic of so much of the academy today, and it is implied by our recognition of creation's diversity.

5. *Redeemed scholarship is communal scholarship.* As scholars we are members of a variety of overlapping communities, some of which are academic in nature. Many of us teach at Christian universities where the task of Christian scholarship is carried on explicitly in the context of a larger collegial effort. For those of us who teach at nonconfessional institutions, we may not share the same ultimate commitments as our most immediate colleagues. We are, nevertheless, part of a larger communal enterprise, and we should try as much as possible to reach out to our Christian—and whenever we can, non-Christian—colleagues elsewhere.

6. *Redeemed scholarship is attentive to methods and to what might be called liturgies of inquiry.* Patterns of worship are reinforced and engrained in cultural practices or, as Jamie Smith, calls them, "cultural liturgies." We believe that research methods are an important example of such cultural practice. As we identify idolatrous practices in our own disciplines, we must seek to correct, rather than to reject or replace, those practices. Redemption frees us to consider alternative ways of looking at scholarship and the practices of scholarly communities. Conversely, if we uncritically adopt the liturgies of inquiry that are taught in mainstream academic disciplines, we are likely to perpetuate their idolatries, including the reductionisms mentioned above.

7. *Redeemed scholarship must be connected to and encourage human flourishing and shalom.* Our scholarly efforts should be conducive to shalom – to transforming our relationships with God, the self, other image-bearing creatures, and the rest of the created world. We should always be considering the practical implications of our research. This is not to say that there is no place for basic research or seeking knowledge for the pure joy of it. Nevertheless, redemption frees us to recognize the potential for idolatry in an autonomous attitude of "inquiry for inquiry's sake." Redemption, in short, should bridge the gap between theory and application.

Consummation

In this introductory chapter we have attempted to articulate what is admittedly an ambitious agenda for Christian scholarship – an agenda reflective of the abundant salvation that God has lavished on his people. This is ample reason for us to aim high. However, we must also recognize that the unfathomable complexity of created reality would require an eternity for us to unfold and develop by our own efforts. In the present age we can truthfully hope only to contribute a few bricks to what in centuries past used to be called the temple that is human knowledge.

The Bible tells us that God is uniting, gathering together, and summing up all things under Christ (Ephesians 1:10). We look forward to the day when Christ has the supremacy in all things (Colossians 1:18). For the moment, however, we live in between the times – between the already and the not yet. The kingdom is present among us, but it awaits its ultimate consummation at Christ's return. We engage in our scholarly activities in hope of this coming kingdom, when all things will be made new and God's glory will finally be vindicated. As Syd Hielema reminded us years ago during a faculty workshop, we work with this end in view, seeking to build on the foundation of Christ with gold, silver, and precious stones rather than with wood, hay, and straw, knowing that on that final day each person's work will be tested by fire (I Cor 3:12-13). Of course, we know that sin will continue to corrupt our work, however pure our motives and despite all our efforts to transcend the idolatries dominating our disciplines. This is more than enough reason for us to remain humble, recognizing that we will never get it perfectly right. So we look forward to the day when sin will finally be conquered and the opposition between Augustine's two cities will finally be over. Then we will at last be freed to explore God's good creation without hindrance, and our scholarship will perfectly praise the God of glory.

Jonathan Edwards has speculated that the new creation will see the eternal unfolding of God's perfections so that his people will never tire of praising him.[21] Perhaps there is an analogy in terms of exploring and understanding God's creation. There is a seemingly infinite complexity in what God has made, as reflected in the differentiation of the sciences and the explosion of scientific knowledge in recent centuries. If so, it may be that we really will require an eternity to see our projects through to completion. And, unhindered by time or sin, we may, together with our brothers and sisters, pursue our exploration of the new heavens and new earth in such a way that each new discovery increases our joy – in the complexity and beauty of the creation and, especially, in the wisdom and love of the One who fashioned it.

Bibliography

Augustine. *Confessions*. Edited by Carolyn J.-B. Hammond. Translated by William Watts. Loeb Classical Library, 26-27. Cambridge, MA: Harvard University Press, 2014.

Augustine. *Concerning the City of God against the Pagans*. Translated by Henry Bettenson. Introduction by G.R. Evans. London: Penguin, 2003.

Calvin, John. *Institutes of the Christian Religion.* Edited by John T. McNeill. Translated by Ford Lewis Battles. Philadelphia: Westminster Press, 1960.

Dooyeweerd, Herman. *A New Critique of Theoretical Thought.* Trans. David H. Freeman and H. De Jongste. Jordan Station, ON: Paideia, 1984.

Edwards, Jonathan. *A Dissertation on the End for Which God Created the World* in *The Works of Jonathan Edwards.* Edited by Edward Hickman. Edinburgh: Banner of Truth Trust, 1974. vol 1. 94—121.

Grant, George P. *Techonology and Justice.* Toronto: Anansi, 1986.

Kelsey, David. *Eccentric Existence.* Louisville, KY: Westminster John Knox Press, 2009.

Kuyper, Abraham. *Encyclopedia of Sacred Theology.* New York: Charles Scribner`s Sons, 1898.

Niebuhr, Reinhold. *Man's Nature and His Communities: Essays on the Dynamics and Enigmas of Man's Personal and Social Existence.* New York: Charles Scribner's Sons, 1965.

Plantinga, Cornelius. *Not the Way It's Supposed to Be: A Breviary of Sin.* Grand Rapids, MI: Wm. B. Eerdmans, 1996.

Schmemann, Alexander. *For the Life of the World: Sacraments and Orthodoxy.* Crestwood, NY: St. Vladimir's Seminary Press, 1973.

21. Edwards, *End for Which God Created the World.*

Solzhenitsyn, Aleksandr I. *The Gulag Archipelago, 1918-1956: An Experiment in Literary Investigation, I-II.* London: Collins, 1974.

Wolters, Albert M. *Creation Regained: Biblical Basics for a Reformational Worldview.* 2nd ed. Grand Rapids: Eerdmans, 2005.

Wolterstorff, Nicholas. *Until Justice and Peace Embrace.* Grand Rapids, MI: Eerdmans, 1983.

A Neo-Kuyperian Approach to Mathematics

Calvin Jongsma and Kevin Vander Meulen

Introduction

Few, if any, academic disciplines today claim to be absolutely certain or objectively true. If exceptions are granted, pure mathematics and logic rise to the top, though most postmodern intellectuals judge their traditional standing to be a vestige of a now-discredited, typically-Western, rationalist point of view.[1] What is deemed true in our era gets constructed by social convention, political rhetoric, or cultural context, by people who have attained the position and power to persuade others of the correctness of their ideas as a basis for thought and action. What's important for mathematics according to this view is not whether it is true but whether it is useful.

Christians of all stripes have a difficult time reconciling such sentiments with their understanding of God and the Bible. Doesn't Scripture provide us with unfailing truths about God and our world, and hasn't God established timeless norms for ethical behavior and holy living? Isn't it possible to know that some things are true beyond the shadow of a doubt? At the very least, shouldn't we accept mathematical truths as absolute certainties, as either self-evident truths or deduced from such via rigorous argumentation? Don't mathematical theories provide the firm foundation required by science to uncover the deep structure of the universe? In fact, wouldn't mathematical results remain true even if the nature of the cosmos was appreciably different? Aren't the truths of mathematics independent of human experience, and thus necessarily true of any world we could imagine? And aren't these results and theories in principle knowable by all capable students, regardless of religious orientation, social status, or cultural conditioning?

It would seem reasonable, therefore, for Christians to be predisposed toward a traditional modernist take on mathematics: as the Greek origin of the word itself indicates, mathematics seems to present us with absolutely true knowledge, as opposed to opinion, which is merely sub-

1. For an earlier discussion and critique of both modern and postmodern views of mathematics, see *Mathematics in a Postmodern Age: A Christian Perspective*, ed. Russell Howell and W. James Bradley (Grand Rapids, MI: W.B. Eerdmans, 2001).

jective. A Christian perspective on mathematics would then amount to affirming this exalted standing for mathematics, which entails that personal beliefs have no distinctive bearing on the technical details of the field itself. Mathematics proper would be religiously neutral, and hence no different for Christians than for anyone else.

Is Mathematics Religiously Neutral? Kuyper's Perspective

The Dutch cultural reformer Abraham Kuyper seems to have held a position somewhat along these lines, though, to our knowledge, he never explicitly discussed topics in the philosophy of mathematics.[2] As he saw it, in the pursuit of natural science,[3] both believers and unbelievers begin with a shared set of empirical data uncovered by observation, measurement, and experimentation, and everyone further calculates and reasons with this raw material according to the same set of procedural rules, regardless of religious or philosophical affiliation. This commonality is due to God's common grace, whereby he upholds his whole creation, including human culture, and restrains evil. Mathematical activities and theories would thus seem, for Kuyper, to fall within the scope of a belief-independent arena of shared ideas and methods.

On the other hand, Kuyper strongly rejected the dualistic medieval idea that all humans share a natural realm in common while Christians receive the added gift of supernatural grace enabling them to believe revealed truths about God and spiritual realities. For Kuyper, in contrast, God's saving grace restores or renews a fallen creation and extends to all aspects of life. Common grace should therefore not be identified with certain structural components of thought and life where all responsible human beings innately reason and behave in the same way. In accord with Kuyper's thinking, then, it would seem that mathematics cannot be taken as belonging to such a neutral realm, either. If this is the case, how should it be taken instead?

The key to resolving this dilemma may lie in Kuyper's view of world-

2. Kuyper's seminal chapter, "Calvinism and Science" is contained in his 1898 Stone Lectures given at Princeton Theological Seminary, *Lectures on Calvinism* (Grand Rapids, MI: W.B. Eerdmans, 1998). His book opens with the chapter titled "Calvinism: A Life-System," in which he introduces his ideas on worldview.

3. Kuyper's notion of *science* is that of a systematic discipline; it is not restricted to natural science. For a detailed analysis of "Abraham Kuyper's Philosophy of Science," see Del Ratzsch's lead chapter in *Facets of Faith and Science,* vol. 2, *The Role of Beliefs in Mathematics and the Natural Sciences,* ed. J.M. van der Meer (Ancaster, ON and Lanham, MD: Pascal Centre and University Press of America, 1996), 1-32. James Bratt's definitive biography *Abraham Kuyper: Modern Calvinist, Christian Democrat* (Grand Rapids, MI: W.B. Eerdmans, 2013) provides the broader cultural context for Kuyper's thought.

view and antithesis. Science, according to Kuyper, is incomplete at its lowest level of shared information and methodology. No discipline is worthy of being called a science until it has been incorporated into a unified system of thought and life, into a worldview or philosophy. In this broader context, of course, one's religious orientation and philosophical outlook can produce major differences. Some common elements may be shared by opposing viewpoints, but these can function very differently within a full system of thought. Kuyper's notion of antithesis also comes into play here, providing a counterweight to his notion of common grace. Different religious starting points about the nature of God, man, and the world will, he says, inevitably lead to divergent sciences, taken in their fullest sense. Knowledge is shaped by faith, by our most basic beliefs about the universe and about the role humans are meant to play within it. And, since one always interprets the basic building blocks of any science in the light of its encompassing context and supposed meaning, religious presuppositions and dispositions will color mathematics as well as any other academic discipline. This should lead to distinct attitudes, interpretations, and undertakings among mathematicians embracing different worldviews. It is in this sense that we can talk about a distinctly Christian approach to mathematics, counterintuitive as this notion may seem at first. In this chapter we sketch out the contours of what a full-orbed Christian approach to mathematics might entail.

While Kuyper specifies little about all this with respect to mathematics or other technical fields, some of his intellectual heirs do. We will first explore in a more general way how a number of prominent North American Kuyperian scholars suggest integrating religion and science/mathematics, and then we will briefly describe a neo-Kuyperian view that derives from the position proposed and developed by the Reformational Dutch philosopher Herman Dooyeweerd, the Canadian worldview thinker Albert Wolters, and the American philosopher Roy Clouser. As we discuss a number of biblical themes central to this neo-Kuyperian approach, we will consider their implications for a Christian approach to mathematics and mathematics education. We will conclude this chapter by raising a few issues for further reflection.

Kuyperian Affirmation of a Christian Approach to Mathematics

Protestant Christian scholars have found many of Kuyper's ideas on worldview and science quite attractive. In the past, evangelical thinkers have been accused, even by some of their own leaders,[4] of lacking an adequate intellectual framework for genuinely integrating faith and learning. But by following Kuyper in affirming at the outset a broader and more

4. Cf. Mark Noll, *The Scandal of the Evangelical Mind* (Grand Rapids, MI: W. B. Eerdmans, 1994).

robust notion of creation rather than focusing prematurely on Christ's salvific life and death, scholars have developed a deep biblical foundation for conceptualizing their field's connection to God and religion. And by conceiving the impact of Christianity on academic work as mediated through worldview and philosophy, scholars have exposed linkages that, despite being indirect, are nevertheless integral to the field—not superficially tacked on or aimed at producing analogy-based apologetics for the reasonableness of the Christian faith or the existence of God. Certain Reformed Kuyperian thinkers,[5] such as Nicholas Wolterstorff,[6] George Marsden,[7] and others,[8] though few mathematicians or philosophers of mathematics, have argued for the importance of the religious and philosophical contexts in which technical work takes place.

According to this way of thinking, one's religious beliefs don't dictate axioms from which to deduce mathematical theorems, but they can give motivation and a broad basis for doing mathematics and they can inform research programs' priorities and concerns in certain ways. By assuming that a sovereign being has created a multifaceted ordered and cohesive cosmos, Christians view the meaning and import of mathematics very differently than if they were to assume, like philosophical naturalists, that the world is a randomly evolved self-organized or unstructured material reality having no transcendent origin or connections. Religious commitment and worldview orientation form the background and meaning ma-

5. Not all Reformed philosophers agree with all aspects of the position we're outlining here. Del Ratzsch, for instance, believes that there is very little room for any genuine differences between scientists who disagree on religious matters; cf. his "Tightening Some (Loose) Screws: Prospects for a Christian Natural Science" in *Facets of Faith and Science*, vol. 2, *The Role of Beliefs in Mathematics and the Natural Sciences*, ed. J.M. van der Meer (Ancaster, ON and Lanham, MD: Pascal Centre and University Press of America, 1996), 173-190. And Alvin Plantinga, while a strong proponent of Christian scholars setting their own research agendas, sees scant disagreement among practitioners of mathematics and logic; cf. his "Methodological Naturalism?" in *Facets of Faith and Science*, vol. 1, *Historiography and Modes of Interaction*, ed. J.M. van der Meer (Ancaster, ON and Lanham, MD: Pascal Centre and University Press of America 1996), 177-221.

6. Cf. Nicholas Wolterstorff, *Reason within the Bounds of Religion*, 2nd ed. (Grand Rapids, MI: W.B. Eerdmans, 1984). This book has been a significant encouragement to others to think more seriously about the influence of religious commitment and beliefs on scholarship of all types.

7. Cf. George Marsden, *The Outrageous Idea of Christian Scholarship* (New York: Oxford University Press, 1997). This book seeks to convince secular thinkers that they should set a place at the table of scholarship for people with faith-informed approaches.

8. Cf. Joel Carpenter's thoughtful response to Michael Hamilton's reflection on "The Elusive Idea of Christian Scholarship" in "Response to Hamilton," *Christian Scholar's Review* 31, no. 1 (2001), 21-24.

trix undergirding scholarly work in mathematics as in other disciplines, providing Christians and others with certain control beliefs that shape professional expectations and give programmatic meaning to their work. Moreover, religious outlooks and philosophical frameworks centrally impact what foundational questions are raised and how they're answered, the ways mathematics gets related to other fields of thought, and how one actively pursues mathematics as a calling, whether or not religion directly affects the technical details of particular mathematical models and abstract theories.

As Christians, therefore, committed to the Lordship of Jesus Christ over all of life, we should not rest content with an approach that admits no real impact on or lacks a good fit with what we do in mathematics. Mathematics, too, to use an Augustinian image, is engaged in the ongoing struggle between the City of God and the City of Man. Mathematics, too, lies under Christ's rule, as Kuyper's clarion call, delivered during his opening address at the founding of the Free University in 1880, makes abundantly clear: "There is not a square inch in the whole domain of our human existence over which Christ, who is Sovereign over *all*, does not cry: '*Mine*!'"

Development of a Neo-Kuyperian Christian Approach to Mathematics

Kuyper's appeal for scholars to develop a consistent Christ-centered approach to science has found enthusiastic but qualified support in various places at different times. In his home country and at the Christian university he had helped to establish, twentieth-century scholars worked diligently to deepen his vision by developing the overarching Christian philosophy he had called for earlier. In the 1920s, the 1930s, and beyond, Herman Dooyeweerd, Dirk Vollenhoven, and others set forth what is now often referred to as Reformational Christian philosophy. Dooyeweerd challenged the "pretended autonomy of theoretical thought" by delineating a structural connection between religious stands on the origin, coherence, and unity of the cosmos and the ways in which philosophical and scientific theories are constructed.[9] He then outlined his own approach to philosophy, discussing the biblical ground motive of Creation, Fall, and Redemption that motivated his approach, and spelling out some ontological and epistemological fundamentals in dialogue with mainstream Western philosophers and by drawing upon the history, content, and methods of the various academic disciplines.

9. Cf. Herman Dooyeweerd, *De Wijsbegeerte der wetsidee*, (Amsterdam: H.J. Paris, 1935-1936). Translated as *The New Critique of Theoretical Thought*, (Philadelphia: Presbyterian and Reformed Pub. Co., 1953-1958).

During the second half of the last century, Dooyeweerd's insights were further expounded by a number of Reformed Christian academics. Popular academic books in the mid-1980s by Brian Walsh and Richard Middleton and by Albert Wolters made Reformational philosophy accessible on a worldview level.[10] Shortly thereafter, Roy Clouser gave fresh expression to Dooyeweerd's argument about the religious character of scientific theories and about how Christianity impacts our scholarly work.[11] Two key ideas in Clouser's presentations focus on how the notion of divinity relates to theorizing. First of all, something is (taken as) divine when it exists absolutely independently and is the supreme source or cause of the existence and meaning of all other things. Second, philosophical theories about how the world is structured exhibit some divinity commitment by what they presuppose to be unconditionally primary and nondependent, either some being that transcends the world or something that is a privileged part of reality. A basic religious orientation to what is supposed as divine gives guidance to human thinking about what is ultimately real and what sort of overall purpose and meaning it has. Scientific theorizing fits within this broader philosophical context. The way in which a field's central entities, properties, and relations are conceived also depends upon notions of basic meaning and how these things are believed to be properly positioned relative to the subject matter of other disciplines.

Christians affirm the God revealed in the Bible as the transcendent divine being, all other realities being completely dependent upon him as their sovereign Creator. This thesis has as a corollary that nothing in created reality should be singled out as absolute or autonomous nor as giving ultimate meaning or existence to anything else. A reductionist view of science or mathematics, which denies the richness of creation, can thus be seen as the theoretical expression of idolatry, putting something creaturely in the place reserved for God. A non-reductionist religious outlook gives Christians a certain pre-theoretical disposition that regulates their concept-formation in an indirect but pervasive way. Negatively, this outlook rejects explanations that attempt to explain all of reality in terms of

10. Cf. Brian J. Walsh and J. Richard Middleton, *The Transforming Vision: Shaping a Christian World View* (Downers Grove, IL: InterVarsity Press, 1984) and Albert M. Wolters, *Creation Regained: Biblical Basics for a Reformational Worldview*, 2nd ed. (Grand Rapids, MI: Wm. B. Eerdmans, 2005).

11. Cf. Roy A. Clouser, *The Myth of Religious Neutrality: An Essay on the Hidden Role of Religious Belief in Theories*, 2nd ed. (Notre Dame, IN: Notre Dame Press, 2005). For a condensed version of his argument, see his "A Blueprint for a Non-Reductionist Theory of Reality," September 2007, http://www.allofliferedeemed.co.uk/Clouser/RCBluePrint.pdf. and especially his "Is There a Christian View of Everything from Soup to Nuts?" in *Pro Rege* 31, no. 4 (June, 2003): 1-10, which ends with a few pages that discuss how a divinity belief impacts mathematics.

one or two aspects; positively, it is committed to developing a theory of reality that recognizes a diverse multifaceted creation with many coherent interconnections, all under God's sovereign control and care. These commitments will impact mathematics much as any other scientific undertaking. In this way, it makes eminent sense to talk about a Christian approach to mathematics even though specific beliefs don't function as theoretical hypotheses for drawing any particular conclusions in, say, geometry or calculus or linear algebra. Mathematics is not hermetically sealed off from other fields, nor is it impervious to one's religious stand on what is absolute.

This does not mean, however, to reiterate a point made above, that religious beliefs determine the contents of a scholarly discipline. The Bible is not a textbook for mathematics. No specific biblical statements about numbers or shapes or change provide us with a Christian foundation for number theory or geometry or calculus; one must investigate patterns of connections between numerical and spatial realities in creation in order to develop mathematical theories about such things.[12] The influence of religion on mathematics is more indirect and more global. Various biblical themes will inform our ideas about God and humans and the world overall, and these things will give guidance and a particular slant to various aspects of the way in which we pursue the study of mathematics as Christians.

The Theme of Creation: the Structure and Nature of Mathematics

Many definitions have been proposed for mathematics over the centuries. The earliest civilizations that consciously studied mathematics in a systematic way thought of it largely in quantitative algorithmic terms: mathematics calculates concrete quantities according to certain standard procedures. Even geometry fit into this mold for them, being a sort of applied arithmetic; determining length and area and volume were their main spatial concerns because these related to work projects, economic transactions, and bureaucratic record-keeping. This conception of mathematics also corresponds with the practice of much early astronomy. Computational procedures needed for predicting the future locations of heavenly bodies were often presented as a prerequisite component of textbooks on astronomy.

The ancient Greeks, who transformed mathematics into a theoretical discipline, recognized mathematical sciences for two distinct types of

12. For a general discussion of the underlying neo-Kuyperian distinction upon which we are drawing here—the one between structure and direction—see Albert M. Wolters, *Creation Regained.*

quantity—discrete and continuous. The former field (number theory) treated properties of and relations between positive whole numbers; the art of calculating with these numbers (arithmetic) was relegated to the marketplace, being too mundane to include in pure mathematics. The latter field (geometry) dealt with the continuous magnitudes of space. Here, too, the Greeks were mainly interested in the universal properties of and relations between line segments, two-dimensional regions, and solid figures rather than in how to calculate specific numeric measures for them, which was the focus for other ancient cultures.

Mathematical theories later went far beyond the traditional notions of mathematics as the art of calculation and even as the science of number and space, treating ideas such as that of motion and change with new forms of reasoning and becoming much more abstract in the process; but this beginning characterization is still a good way to ground our thinking about mathematics. It helps to remind us that mathematics is the science that investigates patterns in certain features of the world around us, and that it often provides quantitative information and tools useful for our daily lives. Following Dooyeweerd, we can generalize these early definitions without losing the focal points they identify: *mathematics is the systematic study of the numerical and spatial aspects of creation.* Let's parse this definition in more detail.

First, note that the ultimate focus and context of this study is the universe God created. Mathematicians do not invent their subject matter from whole cloth or determine what laws mathematical entities should obey. They attempt to uncover and account for the created order inherent in what they encounter. Creation in all its multi-faceted character, even in its abstract features, is God-given and divinely structured. Mathematics is rooted in our everyday experience. It does not study eternally existing objects in some suprasensory realm but characteristics abstracted from the created world. This is a significant part of our neo-Kuyperian definition of mathematics; it differs from popular Platonic accounts, which would have mathematics study ideal numbers and shapes located in some ethereal region behind the world we experience, possibly in the mind of God. Mathematics involves a focused process of abstraction from the created order. Exploring fairly abstract mathematical ideas can create the illusion that one's focus is otherworldly, but mathematical concepts, even broad generalizations and abstractions of abstractions, can always be grounded in the creation by investigating what they are abstracted *from,* possibly via a chain of abstractions. For example, a group in abstract algebra is any collection of elements having a binary operation that satisfies certain algebraic laws, such as the Associative Law. Many important structures, including familiar number systems like the integers under addition, form groups, but this concept was originally abstracted in the late nineteenth century from the earlier notions of permuting roots of polynomials, modular arithmetic, and geometric transformations, notions which themselves can be traced farther back to more concrete problem solving, computation, and movement of shapes.

All created things have numerical and spatial properties, so mathematical analysis is foundational for a wide range of disciplines. Focusing on the quantitative features of a situation is always worthwhile and may be important, even when these features are not the principal ones. They may reveal unexpected connections and open up areas for consideration that would have been less well known otherwise. Focusing on the dynamic interaction of predators and their prey, for instance, can lead to an understanding of whether and how these populations might be kept in equilibrium over time. Also, throughout mathematics, one finds that concepts abstracted from one situation often turn out to have applications elsewhere as well. Conic sections, which were first explored by the Greeks, quite possibly in connection with ancient sundial construction, were used much later by Galileo and Kepler to analyze the paths of projectiles and planets. The occurrence of shared numerical and spatial patterns in very different contexts manifests the wonderful coherence and unity built into the universe by its Creator, at times prompting our amazement and awe.

Lifting numbers and spatial configurations out of their natural embedded habitats, one can explore properties and relations that might be difficult to recognize within the complexity of a concrete situation. This simplifying tactic is extremely helpful in doing mathematics. Mathematics gains its power from abstraction and generalization; working with abstractions gives mathematics a certain economy of thought. Some people are concerned that this insulates mathematics from reality, making it seem self-contained. But mathematics is never completely severed from its original object, even when that object is no longer immediately in view; concepts retain a residue or a connection that links them back to the creation. At times conceptual entities, properties, or relations may be postulated (asked to be granted) without fully understanding their meaning (the nature and arithmetic of complex numbers is a good example of this; the notion of parallel lines in non-Euclidean geometry is another), but they are tentatively accepted and explored because of their usefulness to a given theory. Only later may meaningful connections be discovered that tether them to other areas of thought or concrete reality.

Second, the study of mathematics has a limited (though extensive) two-fold focus: it explores the *numerical* and *spatial* aspects of reality.[13]

13. A case might be made for including the kinematic aspect, but this would not affect our overall perspective here.

This part of the definition is meant to emphasize that mathematics constitutes only part of the full study of creation: it explores two main aspects. Recognizing this, however, does not mean mathematics can ignore other matters. When working on a modeling problem, other aspects of the situation need to be well understood and taken into consideration or the mathematics developed may miss what is significant. The created world has a wonderful complexity that involves many different aspects. On the basis of his study of a wide range of academic disciplines, Dooyeweerd recognizes fifteen distinct aspects, in order, as: numerical, spatial, kinematic, physical, biotic, psychic, analytical, formative, lingual, social, economic, aesthetic, juridical, ethical, and pistic.[14] This list, while not asserted dogmatically, is meant to encapsulate the essential order and complexity of the created world in the many ways/modes in which it functions. Each of these aspects captures some irreducible dimension of the world. Note that those studied by mathematics are foundational, appearing first in the list, since they are presupposed by the rest. But Dooyeweerd's structure also emphasized the interconnectedness of the modal aspects, noting that each of the earlier aspects anticipate the later aspects, thus countering a one-way relationship that might be assumed by using the word "foundational."

Given the rich variety of modes in which creation functions, it is not accurate to think of the world merely as a physical universe; reality has many more aspects than those treated by, say, mathematics and physics. The rich variety of things and aspects that we see in creation evidently reveals God's love of abundant diversity. Attempts to limit our understanding of how things work to one or two aspects often signal a reductionist viewpoint that can lead to paradoxical results. In fact, as Dooyeweerd taught, encountering "antinomies" or paradoxes is one of the ways we can recognize attempts to over-simplify the irreducible complexity of creation. For example, the Pythagorean discovery that the side and diagonal of a square are incommensurable[15] indicates that continuous magnitudes cannot be fully explained in terms of discrete quantity. This led the Greeks to develop a geometry instead that is almost completely number-free. Mathematics focuses on more than one aspect, each of which is very rich, and this creational diversity must be respected. Danie Strauss has analyzed various episodes in the history of mathematics in which, when attempts were made to reduce all of mathematics to just one aspect, paradoxes arose, emphasizing "the uniqueness and the

14. See the introductory chapter for additional information on Dooyeweerd's philosophical position.

15. In other words, these magnitudes cannot both be measured by whole numbers of any common measure—or, in modern terms, the square root of two is irrational.

mutual coherence of number and space as aspects of the richly varied creational order-diversity."[16]

While it is necessary to distinguish fundamental aspects of reality, these nevertheless remain dimensions of a creation that form a coherent whole, a unified cosmos. So, we also expect to see vital connections between different aspects.[17] We are not surprised, therefore, as some are,[18] to discover that mathematics can provide significant insights for other fields. In fact, we can see the fruitful interplay between numerical and spatial aspects within the field of mathematics itself. Recognizing this opens us up to a fuller experience of mathematics. Certain concepts in algebra, for example, have their origins in or have close connections to geometry, though algebra is often thought of as a generalization of arithmetic. Incorporating these relationships into our study of mathematics gives us a richer understanding of the meaning and complexity of a topic.

Geometric representation can sometimes illuminate concepts in algebra, making them easier to learn. For instance, the square of a number, such as $3^2 = 9$, can be thought of purely numerically as $3 \times 3 = 9$, but recognizing its relation to geometry allows us to picture a square with sides of length 3 and an area of 9. Similarly, the algebraic process of completing the square has geometric roots; in fact, it was this linkage that first enabled ancient Babylonian scribes to construct a systematic approach to solving complex quadratic problems, inaugurating algebra as a problem-solving discipline. Later, medieval Arabic mathematicians used geometry both to illustrate and demonstrate the validity of their problem-solving procedures, making algebra a systematic science of sorts.

In linear algebra, to give another example, the most basic notion of a vector arises in physics and geometry from attempts to capture displacement by means of directed line segments; yet vectors can also be formulated numerically using Cartesian coordinates. A vector operation such as addition can be described algebraically, but it also has geometric

16. D.F.M. Strauss, *Paradigms in Mathematics, Physics and Biology* (Bloemfontein: Tekskor, 2004), 18. See also his *Philosophy: Discipline of the Disciplines* (Grand Rapids, MI: Paideia Press, 2009) for a systematic presentation of Reformational philosophy.

17. In Dooyeweerd's philosophy these linkages are explored both by his theory of *enkapsis*, which looks at how aspects of situations are colored by what they are aspects of, and his theory of *anticipations* and *retrocipations*, which looks at how certain types of properties and relations find their counterparts in other aspects. We will not delve into these theories in any detail here.

18. The classic expression of this surprise is given by physicist Eugene Wigner in his 1959 Courant lecture, "The Unreasonable Effectiveness of Mathematics in the Natural Sciences," *Communications in Pure and Applied Mathematics* 13, no. 1 (February 1960): 1-14.

and physical interpretations via the Parallelogram Rule.

Depending on context, one viewpoint may be more helpful than another in understanding or using an idea. The recent calculus-reform movement in North American education recognizes this fact with its Rule of Four, which says that, whenever possible, functions should be considered numerically (tabulated calculations or observed data), algebraically or analytically (explicit formulas), geometrically (graphs), and verbally (described in words).

Or, in real analysis, while the rigorous algebraic description of the continuity of a function can be difficult for students to comprehend, its geometric meaning is intuitively clear. Nevertheless, there are complicated functions for which we cannot provide a picture, while the algebraic description still allows us to determine whether they are continuous.

To consider one last example, Boolean algebra illustrates this point in a more abstract algebraic setting. Some of its results are easier to grasp if the operations are conceived as meets and joins for a partial order, while others can be understood as legitimate generalizations of laws from ordinary arithmetic.

Finally, our definition recognizes that mathematics is a creative human endeavour. Mathematical terms and symbols identify and denote conceptual entities, properties, and relations: the words used in mathematics name ways in which we perceive the world to work, subject to God's ordering. Mathematical concepts, terms, and notation are neither independent of the world nor independent of human participation. Mathematics remains a human activity, as we will discuss next. This involves naming, exploring properties and relationships, deducing consequences, and modeling, as well as pattern recognition, conceptualization, representation, and verification.

The Theme of Creation: Human Development and Application of Mathematics

Developing the field of mathematics gets its warrant from God in the cultural mandate given in Genesis 1:28: we are appointed as stewards to responsibly manage and cultivate the creation. This includes maintaining what God has created, but it also involves unfolding the potential found within creation.[19] Culture-making is thus rooted in our character as God's image bearers, as his representatives within creation. We are commissioned to care for the world around us in a way that promotes its flourishing. Doing this well requires a deep understanding of the nature of what we are to rule over and steward. Mathematical activity mines the

19. Andy Crouch describes this task as "culture making" in his book *Culture Making: Recovering Our Creative Calling* (Downers Grove, IL: IVP Books, 2008).

numerical and spatial sides of creation and uncovers their connections to everyday life and other ways of knowing. Specialized mathematical knowledge contributes to this cultural undertaking as a whole, but developing mathematical concepts and theories to explicate numerical and spatial features of creation is already a type of culture-making and can be seen as a legitimate calling from God. Moreover, as we explore the order in creation via mathematics, we have an excellent opportunity to reflect on the source of all order and consistency, prompting us to acknowledge God's divinity, wisdom, and faithfulness. Comprehending the interconnected intricacies and wide applicability of mathematics can elicit expressions of awe and praise toward the Creator; seeing very different approaches to solving a problem yield the same answer teaches us that the world God has made and upholds is wonderfully reliable.

While mathematics has an important role to play in uncovering creational order, it also helps us to care for and develop the creation. Mathematical models can be used to analyze the spread of pathogens, ascertain the health of an ecosystem, observe the rise or decline of populations, and monitor the effects of pollution on the environment.[20] Mathematics is also an instrument for developing human culture: linear algebra plays a significant role in the ability of search engines to find data, game theory provides insights on the nature of economic transactions, Boolean algebra underlies the development of computer systems, fractal geometry allows for the small antennae that are needed for cell phones, and calculus provides the analysis of planetary motion due to gravitational attraction. Mathematics helps make modern science and technological artifacts possible and affects the way we gather, communicate, and validate information. These are but a few of the many mathematical contributions that have shaped culture into what it is today.

One significant part of mathematics is developing concepts and names. This task is deeply rooted in the original cultural mandate. The Bible says that God brought all the animals to Adam "to see what he would name them." This may seem a mere curiosity, except that naming had a particular significance in Near Eastern cultures. Naming something indicated having authority and power over what was named.[21] In the biblical creation story, God himself named parts of the creation, signifying that he was sovereign over the whole universe, even those creaturely beings worshiped by neighbouring cultures, such as the Sun, which the

20. These examples mostly reflect our role as stewards after the Fall. The Bible refers to the fact that the creation groans as a result of the Fall and awaits its restoration most fully in the second coming. See Romans 8:19-21.

21. Craig G. Bartholomew and Michael W. Goheen, *The Drama of Scripture: Finding Our Place in the Biblical Story*, (Grand Rapids, MI: Baker Academic, 2004), 34.

Egyptians revered as their god Ra. That God asked Adam to name the animals reinforces the creation mandate that Adam was to rule over and look after what he was naming.

This naming task continues today, especially in academic disciplines. Characterizing and categorizing things is a form of naming. Identifying important distinctions grounded in reality and singling them out by an appropriate name and notation gives one entry into the knowledge of things that would otherwise remain obscure or hidden. Mathematics is significantly about naming things found in the numerical and spatial dimensions of creation. This has multiple benefits: we have the opportunity to understand the order which God has sovereignly created; we are able to use mathematical concepts to develop other parts of culture; and we have resources for being better stewards of the creation overall. It is important to note that while naming is a human activity, it is not arbitrary or a mere formalism. It is meant to capture important distinctions found within creation. Concepts in mathematics, no matter how abstract, are derived from the way things function within the created order. The notion of divisibility, for instance, is rooted in a simple multiplicative relation among whole numbers. But it took genuine mathematical insight on the part of Pythagoras, Euler, Gauss, and others to recognize this as an important concept that would help us better understand the structure of number systems and provide a basis for modular arithmetic and various contemporary applications such as the use of UPC codes.

Naming is definitely a creative activity. While it is not creating *ex nihilo*, it does require isolating and comprehending what is being named. That God brought the animals to Adam "to see what he would name them" shows that God wanted Adam to exercise his capacities and suggests that he would take joy in this creative human activity, much as he took joy in the creation of the parts of the universe. In mathematics, we have some flexibility in making definitions for the concepts we are creating, and a degree of flexibility is likewise present in choosing axioms to govern these concepts within our deductive theories. Once these choices are made, there are limits to what can be deduced about the concepts formed. The way we understand the notion of *number*, for example, affects the ways we can use the concept. At an early point in history, number simply meant plurality. But the concept of number was later extended to take on other meanings in different cultural contexts (including commercial and scientific). For example, number now includes both quantity and direction, such as when we refer to positive and negative numbers. In all such contexts, numbers continue to satisfy a variety of algebraic rules, but these may vary as the concept is expanded. Enlarging the real number system to include complex numbers (where now any two-dimensional direction is permitted), a development that took mathematicians centuries to fully understand and accept, is a type of renaming in which the number concept has fewer restrictions on permissible algebraic operations. With complex numbers one can take the square root of any number, but when working within the real number system, square roots of negative numbers are not permitted. Thus, the development of concepts is a form of renaming, done for the purpose of more fully uncovering truths about the created order.

Naming things is part of our cultural responsibility in mathematics, but it is also culturally embedded. How we make distinctions and what we call the concepts we are naming are influenced by personal and social circumstances and also by historical context, and they in turn impact how these ideas are received and further developed. Calling a negative solution to an equation a false or fictitious root, as was initially done, for instance, indicates and perpetuates a belief that negative numbers aren't truly real in the way that positive numbers are. Mathematicians also seem stuck with the unhelpful practice begun by Descartes of calling square roots of negative numbers imaginary; this, too, arose out of a belief that these impossible numbers exist only in our imagination and have no connection to the world of sensory experience. When complex numbers first weaseled their way into mathematics in connection with solving cubic equations in the sixteenth century (Cardano, Bombelli), they weren't much understood, so disparaging them as imaginary seemed reasonable. Centuries later, however, when they were finally given a geometric representation and a connection with electricity was understood, the terminology was too deeply entrenched to change.

Naming things is also meant to keep us in relationship to God. We name what God has first made. This is part of being God's representatives in the midst of creation. We are also to take delight in this mathematical ability, in being able to discover new patterns and connections. The more we capture of the order of creation, the more we stand in awe of what God has made and how it is structured. Of course, given our sinful tendencies, we can all too easily think that we are masters of what we are creating, creating mathematics *ex nihilo*, and we can be tempted to take all the credit for our mathematics. Instead, we should adopt a humble attitude that recognizes that a better model might exist or that we may still not have uncovered some important connections in our theory.

Once mathematicians have identified key conceptual realities needed for a model or within a theory—various types of entities, properties, and relations—they then investigate logical linkages among these things. This is done in a number of ways. Some are more exploratory, part of the discovery process: studying the features of particular cases in depth, looking for similarities and analogies among things, conjecturing intuited or observed connections and testing them out with typical or boundary examples, exploring the deductive consequences of what-if scenarios, modifying the conditions of conjectures to fit what we discover or to strengthen our results, etc. But once a connection seems well established, a proof for its correctness is sought. In mathematics, justification of a result requires a conclusive proof from what is already known. As a theoretical area like geometry or linear algebra or group theory matures, conceptual pieces are put on an axiomatic basis and systematically developed into a deductive structure from first principles, each result being argued from what has already been established up to that point. In this way complex mathematical results are organized and given a relatively firm foundation, and their truth can be communicated to and evaluated by others. Proofs are ordinarily given informally, with certain background connections assumed and left unargued, but it is tacitly understood that, if pressed, someone familiar with the material and the process of deduction would be able to provide a rigorous argument for the result, based on what is commonly accepted as already known.

Mathematics is the field of thought that has been most closely allied with valid deductive reasoning. It was a major catalyst for the development of logic by Aristotle in Athens around 325 B.C., and it remains closely linked to logic today. Since the middle of the nineteenth century, in fact, this connection has become ever stronger with the development of mathematical logic by Boole, Frege, Peano, Russell, Hilbert, Gödel, Tarski, and others. By the early to mid-1900s, foundations of mathematics had become almost synonymous with mathematical logic. Logic advanced to the point where formal arguments could be made fully rigorous, leading even to the development of automated theorem-proving systems in certain areas of mathematics. Along the way, mathematicians discovered methods for treating the meta-mathematical issues of the completeness and consistency of formalized theories and the logical independence of various axioms from other axioms. In this context, notable results by Gödel and others definitively indicated some of the limits of using axiomatic deductive reasoning for developing mathematical theories.

Humans have been created with the wonderful capacity for rational thought, which allows us to trace and predict consequences of whatever principles we accept. Deductive reasoning is used throughout mathematics, but given how extensively mathematics has been used in the natural sciences and modern technology since the early modern era, its influence is felt throughout Western culture. The striking successes of mathematical physics in the early modern period led many thinkers over subsequent centuries to idolize Reason and seek to reorganize life on a fully rational basis. Mathematicians may be particularly susceptible to the allure of this outlook because deductive reasoning is so pervasively a part of their professional life and because they have seen how powerful the deductive axiomatic method has been for acquiring knowledge of the world, but twentieth-century developments in logic and foundations of mathematics also point out the limitations of such an approach, even within the discipline of mathematics itself. As noted above, mathematics involves mental activities besides proving. Moreover, human theorizing, also in mathematics, always takes place within the broader arena of worldviews and socio-cultural contexts. The sorts of theories that are pursued and the ways in which these are developed is largely constrained by past work in the field, but discontinuities have arisen within the history of mathematics, and these are at times due to tendencies within the broader culture that have important if subtle effects on its practitioners. The rise of commercial arithmetic in late medieval and Renaissance times encouraged the attendant development of symbolic algebra, which by the mid-seventeenth century provided resources for both analytic geometry and calculus.

While mathematics is a powerful conceptual tool for helping us steward the creation and develop its potential, it should never simply be about exercising power and control over our world. We need to go beyond abstract and utilitarian views of mathematics to play with and enjoy mathematical ideas. Algebra as originally developed by Babylonian scribes may well owe its existence to recreational mathematics, to a tradition among surveyors of solving riddles after-hours to hone their skills. We can see beauty in proofs and be surprised by the elegant ways in which ideas can be logically interconnected and provide insight into multiple situations in the world around us. The derivative in calculus, for example, provides us with a way to capture the elusive notion of instantaneous change (though nothing actually changes at each instant), and this can be used to calculate the velocity and acceleration of moving bodies in physics, the slope and curvature of graphs in coordinate geometry, and marginal profit in economics, among other things. Surprisingly enough, this concept also provides a theoretical bridge to an entirely different set of phenomena handled by integration via the two-part Fundamental Theorem of Calculus. Contemplating what is being done in and by mathematics helps us cultivate a sense of awe and wonder, seeing the scope and richness of what God has created in the mathematical dimensions of reality.

Distortions to the Structure and Nature of Mathematics

God created the cosmos and found what he had made to be very good. This includes its numerical and spatial aspects. When humans fell into sin, God continued to maintain the world according to his creation ordinances; this is a significant part of his common grace, according to Kuyperian thinking. For mathematics, this means that quantities and spatial configurations continue to be ordered by God's laws as they were before the Fall. Perhaps, as the Bible seems to suggest, the Fall affected plant and animal functioning in addition to the human condition, but so far as we can tell, it did not affect mathematical structures or states of affairs.

God's common grace also extends to many of the ways in which humans think about and make use of mathematics—people throughout a given culture calculate in roughly the same way and come up with the same correct answers; we all recognize the central importance of functions across mathematics today; and every calculus teacher uses the Fundamental Theorem of Calculus to connect integral calculus with the ideas and procedures of differential calculus. While a neo-Kuyperian approach rightly recognizes the antithesis between Christian and non-Christian approaches, the concept of common grace keeps us from becoming triumphalist or isolationist. In particular, since everyone is created in God's image, we all have the ability to develop creation and to theorize about the world. Christians do not have a peculiar advantage in doing mathematical research or learning mathematics, except insofar as these may be assisted by keeping mathematics in balanced perspective and recognizing the value of different approaches to a topic.

The Fall does affect in significant ways how humans think about the world and act within it, however. Our views of the nature of mathematics and of our reasoning processes are tainted by sin, altering as well some of our theorizing within mathematics and the ways in which we attempt to apply it. Naturally, as we have just noted, this does not mean that the minute details of mathematics will differ substantially on account of religious and worldview orientations, but our relationship to God does in principle[22] impact how we relate mathematics to other things, how we conceive of its overall goals and meaning, and how we practice it as a full-fledged activity.

To talk about this in a way that minimizes confusion, it may help to consciously distinguish two senses of mathematics that are sometimes

22. Of course, humans are notoriously inconsistent, often without realizing it. Our viewpoints on one subject may conflict with our ideas on another one or even with deeply held commitments whose implications we do not fully realize. This is as true of Kuyperian thinkers as of everyone else, though it is usually hardest to recognize faults and shortcomings in ourselves.

conflated,[23] especially in an era when some believe mathematicians invent their subject matter. "Mathematics" is sometimes taken in the sense of the ordered numerical and spatial realities being studied, but according to the way we defined "mathematics" above, we are using the term in the sense of our human theorizing about that order.[24] Taken in the first sense, there is no distortion in mathematics, so we have nothing new to add here. Taken in the second sense, however, human worldviews have introduced a number of distortions of various sorts. This notion of mathematics (as theory) is the older and more primitive sense, and this is what we intend with the term in our discussion here.

The neo-Kuyperian view that we are proposing sees mathematics as based in our human experience of reality with all its many dimensions. It is creation-bound and limited in scope, not divine or transcendent or all-important. We see two different but often related types of distortions, therefore, in thinking about the structure and nature of mathematics: distortions that misconstrue the creational character of mathematics by absolutizing its importance within creation, and distortions that locate mathematics outside creation itself within the divine being of God.

Looking to find something permanent and absolute within the world itself, some Greek philosophers elevated mathematical knowledge to divine levels. The Pythagoreans, for example, claimed that number was the sure foundation of all true and certain knowledge. Their thinking had a mystical element involving numerological speculation and veneration of number, but it also contained a scientific component in which phenomena like musical harmonies were explained via genuine quantitative relationships. And, of course, it strongly encouraged a deep investigation of number theory and geometry. A century or so later, Plato conceptualized mathematical truths as being about a realm of immutable ideal forms, not about the corruptible world that we inhabit. The study of mathematics thus liberates the soul, he thought, from the transient world of material things in order to contemplate the permanent world of unsullied intelligible and timeless truths. Plato also claimed that God used the five regular polyhedra (now called Platonic solids) as the geometric forms for the four basic elements of the world (fire, air, water, and earth) and for the shape of the universe as a whole.

23. See Calvin Jongsma, "Mathematics: Always Important, Never Enough. A Christian Perspective on Mathematics and Mathematics Education," *Journal of the Association of Christians in the Mathematical Sciences* (Oct. 2006), http://www.acmsonline.org/journal/2006/Jongsma.htm.

24. This dual meaning given to a discipline's name is not unique to mathematics; other fields, such as history, experience a similar ambiguity: *history* can mean that part of the past which is being studied, or it can mean the study of that past. The confusion here is roughly that of conflating a field's ontology with its epistemology.

These Greek views of mathematics thus make it essentially divine. As such, this promotes a dualism that was present in broader Greek culture: the truths of mathematics were treated as more absolute and real than those of other subjects, which downgraded the empirical certainty experienced in daily life and in other fields. It is true, of course, that our senses occasionally "trick" us, but we can likewise be fooled by logical argumentation, and, as all mathematicians know from experience, one may occasionally be misled into accepting incorrect proofs. But for the most part, both are accurate and give a reliable grasp of reality. In contrast to Greek thinking, a neo-Kuyperian approach recognizes the validity of multiple lines of inquiry without idolizing one particular way of knowing.

Nevertheless, some early Christians were profoundly attracted to Plato's dualistic separation of body and soul and to his emphasis on non-material spiritual reality as what is enduring. They also incorporated some of his ideas about the role of mathematics into their thinking, placing the ideas of numbers and perfect geometric shapes as well as truths about these things in the Mind of God. St. Augustine, for instance, was influenced by Platonic notions of wisdom. Mathematical knowledge, he thought, helped God to plan for and construct the universe.[25] Augustine claims that while he does not know just how wisdom and mathematics (number) are linked, "it is clear that both are true and immutably true."[26] Augustine quotes from Ecclesiastes 7:25 to support his position: "Not without reason was number joined to wisdom in the Holy Scriptures where it is said, 'I and my heart have gone round to know and to consider and to search out wisdom and number.'"[27] While Augustine sees the word *number* in this passage, this is not an apt translation of the Hebrew *heshbon*, which the New International Version renders instead as "the scheme of things." The formulation used by Augustine shows the influence of Platonic thinking.[28]

25. Augustine is sometimes oppositely portrayed as being highly suspicious of mathematics. Morris Kline in his popular *Mathematics in Western Culture* (London: Oxford University Press, 1953), 3, misleadingly quotes Augustine as saying, "The good Christian should beware the mathematician and all those who make empty prophecies. The danger already exists that the mathematicians have made a covenant with the devil to darken the spirit and to confine man in the bonds of hell." (original: *De Genesi ad Litteram*, 2.18.37) This quote, however, warns Christians against accepting the practices and predictions of astrologers, not those of mathematicians, as we now understand the term.

26. St. Augustine, *On Free Choice of the Will*, trans. Anna S. Benjamin and L.H. Hackstaff (Indianapolis: Bobbs-Merrill, 1964), 2.11.

27. St. Augustine, *On Free Choice of the Will*, 2.7.

28. Albert Wolters, private communication: Augustine is quoting from a Latin translation of the Septuagint, the Greek translation of the Hebrew Scriptures.

Plato's outlook has had a major impact on thinking about mathematics throughout its history, both for good and for bad. As a form of realism, it rightly acknowledges that mathematics is about an existing reality and that mathematics is about discovering numerical and spatial regularities rather than inventing them. However, it also posits mathematical results as necessary knowledge dependent neither on human experience nor on the created order. Mathematics is thought to study abstract objects existing in some separate uncreated mathematical world, objects that comprise the pre-existing archetypes of their faint imitations in the world of human experience. In the Christian version of Platonism, these are located in God's Mind, which makes them part of God's nature and being, coeternal with God Himself.[29] Mathematics as we know it, then, becomes thinking God's thoughts after him. For many, mathematics is also the primary medium for understanding the deep structure of the universe, which has been largely reduced to its mathematical and physical dimensions. This neo-Pythagorean way of thinking had a powerful resurgence during the early modern period in the work of scientists such as Kepler, Galileo, and Descartes. Mathematics, for them, takes on something of an imperial role, providing the only solid basis for whatever can be counted as genuine knowledge.[30] Mathematical realities are deemed more real than other aspects of the world, which are then denigrated to a secondary status, and the rich variety of creation is denied or fades into the background.

In contrast, a neo-Kuyperian stance with respect to the divine source of mathematics harks back to the work of John Calvin. Calvin emphasized the importance of knowing God as a prerequisite for human knowledge, but he says it is futile "to attempt with bold curiosity to penetrate to the investigation of his essence."[31] With respect to creation, we know God primarily by his actions, not his attributes. Speculation about the true being or essential nature of God is empty, because such knowledge is inaccessible to the human mind. One problem with plac-

29. For additional information, see the discussion of Christian Platonism in Chapter 10 of Russell W. Howell and W. James Bradley, *Mathematics through the Eyes of Faith* (New York: HarperOne, 2011).

30. A more detailed historical analysis of this mathematization trend for both the premodern and the modern periods is provided by Calvin Jongsma in chapters 5 and 6 of W.J. Bradley and R.W. Howell (eds.), *Mathematics in a Postmodern Age: A Christian Perspective* (Grand Rapids, MI: W.B. Eerdmans, 2001). For a critique of contemporary efforts to quantify the world of human experience, see Philip J. Davis and Reuben Hersh, *Descartes' Dream: The World According to Mathematics* (San Diego, CA: Harcourt Brace Jovanovich, 1986).

31. John Calvin, *Institutes of the Christian Religion,* ed. John T. McNeill, trans. Ford Lewis Battles (Philadelphia: Westminster Press, 1960), 1.5.9.

ing mathematics in the Mind of God, therefore, is that it presumes that humans can grasp how God thinks. Such attribution does not sufficiently recognize the transcendence of the Creator over his creation, even if one distinguishes God's features as having maximal degree or as having them in some analogical sense. In Isaiah 55:8-9, God declares that his way of thinking does not match up with our limited human ways:

> "For my thoughts are not your thoughts, neither are your ways my ways," declares the LORD. "As the heavens are higher than the earth, so are my ways higher than your ways and my thoughts than your thoughts."

In this passage God is saying that, unlike us, with our overwhelming desire for revenge, he is a God of compassion and mercy and wishes to be generous to those he created. But as an added layer of meaning, especially given the second half of the passage, we can take it to say that we should be careful not to attribute to God explicitly creaturely (human) ways of thinking.

According to scriptural revelation, God does accommodate himself to his creatures by taking on certain creaturely properties and relations,[32] acting as he has promised in his covenant with creation[33] as its sovereign architect and not because he is ruled by independently existing laws. Acknowledging this, however, is quite another thing from asserting that these creaturely features derive from some similar eternally existing features characteristic of the essential nature of God. Thus, while logic and mathematics are instrumental for our human understanding of the world, it seems presumptuous to say that God is subject to the laws of these fields in creating and upholding his creation. God institutes and faithfully upholds the structure we experience in creation, including mathematical and logical order. We can understand who God is in a limited way by how he has revealed himself to us, but this revelation includes the key fact that God transcends creation and will brook no rival taking credit for what he has made—no imagined deity, but also no god-like creaturely assistant, no mathematical or logical wisdom.

The concept of the Trinity is an example where our ordinary number concept doesn't quite fit. In the context of justifying a Platonist ontology of mathematics, the concept of the Trinity is used by some to suggest that mathematics or logic is fundamentally a part of the nature of God.[34]

---

32. See Chapter 4 in Gordon Spykman's *Reformational Theology: A New Paradigm for Doing Dogmatics* (Grand Rapids, MI: W.B. Eerdmans, 1992). These ideas are developed further by Roy Clouser as he analyzes different views of the nature of God in Chapter 10 of *The Myth of Religious Neutrality*.

33. Cf. Jeremiah 33:25.

34. See R. W. Howell and W.J. Bradley (eds.), *Mathematics through the Eyes of Faith*,

Supposedly, this can then be used as a partial foundation for a Christian approach to these fields.[35] Curiously, however, the concept of the Trinity does not do as good a job of grounding number as it does of demonstrating God's *accommodation* to his creation and to our understanding of it. Ultimately the Trinity is a mystery: God is one, but in three persons. Treating the Trinity as a foundation for our concept of number would seem to be analogous to taking God being our Father as a basis for our biological ideas about fatherhood, which has obvious limitations. Our neo-Kuyperian approach comes at this from the opposite direction and recognizes a healthy degree of mystery in our conception of God. We cannot penetrate beyond the boundary of creation to analyze or identify a divine analogue or repository for the truths about logic, number, and space; our concepts and understandings of number, spatial configuration, and logic are instead derived via abstraction from what God has created and can function in a limited fashion for helping us understand God.

In improperly elevating mathematics to divine heights, Platonism of whatever sort fails to recognize the embeddedness of mathematics in creation and the active role humans play in its development. Mathematical features of our world are only some among many that we experience in a holistic everyday way. These features must be recognized and abstracted by humans from full reality; they do not exist separately on their own, unrelated to other aspects. There are no pure numbers or shapes existing in their own world, even though quantities and configurations are real. The age-old debate over whether mathematics is discovered or invented is thus too black and white; mathematics is in a qualified sense both discovered (it is grounded in reality, broadly conceived) and invented (humans abstract mathematical traits, postulate conceptual entities, explore their properties and connections using imagination and ingenuity, symbolize their ideas with specialized notation and terminology, and adopt axioms to capture their fundamental features).

Some mathematicians and especially mathematics educators today take the opposite position from Platonists on these issues. Denying that mathematics is about some Platonic realm of abstract entities, they emphasize instead that humans socially construct the concepts they use. Since the time of Kant, this option has seemed more reasonable to many: we use

p. 227. See also J. Bradley, A. Busch, D. Klanderman, E. Ricketts, and G. Talsma, *Mathematics: a Christian Perspective* (Grand Rapids, MI: Kuyers Institute, 2008).

35. The notion of the Trinity is also taken as the basis for a Christian approach to mathematics and logic, respectively, by James Nickel in *Mathematics: Is God Silent?* (Vallecito, CA: Ross House Books, 2001) and by Vern Poythress in *Logic: A God-Centered Approach to the Foundation of Western Thought* (Wheaton, IL: Crossway, 2013). Their treatments derive from the philosophical views of Rousas J. Rushdoony, Cornelius Van Til, and John Frame.

our mental categories to structure our experience and make sense out of a chaotic world. For example, some conceive of mathematical modeling not as a way of approximating the quantitative and spatial facets of a given situation but as superimposing an independently created theory of concepts and results onto that reality. Reality, it is thought, may suggest some of this to us as a fuzzy prompt, but reality itself doesn't have a lawful structure that we are trying to capture with our theorizing. If a model generates good results, we will pragmatically accept it, but that doesn't mean the modeled situation really has the structure we've developed. There is a commendable degree of humility attached to this approach, but when this is combined with a view that rejects any God-given order for the creation itself, we believe it leads to a distorted notion of mathematical modeling.

A subjectivist approach to mathematical knowledge is also stressed by radical constructivists in mathematics education.[36] This is due in part to the legitimate recognition that mathematical ideas have a history, developing over time and in various ways in different cultures. It is true that mathematics does not consist of eternal truths and predetermined techniques dictated from on high. Egyptian fraction arithmetic, for instance, is very different from Chinese fraction arithmetic, and both of these differ in important ways from the way we think about and operate with fractions today. Subjective factors should indeed be taken into account in learning mathematics, but when this is overemphasized, one loses the sense that mathematics at all times and places arises from attempts to understand a given reality that is already divinely structured. Our neo-Kuyperian approach to mathematics refuses to go down this path, even if, like postmodern thinkers, we are critical of Platonism. The patterned structure of reality is what makes our experience of it possible. By using inquiry-based procedures to learn key ideas and techniques in mathematics, students gain a robust understanding of mathematics and make it their own, but we should not conclude from this that they are constructing mathematical meaning in any absolute sense. The mathematical features we experience really are part of the reality we live in, and their behavior is governed by God, not us. Moreover, it is impractical—impossible, really—for students to learn the entire discipline through personal discovery; that would discount the huge amount of time and the difficult struggles it took to develop refined mathematical ideas in the first place. Mathematics education should seek a balance that recognizes both the need for discovery learning and for directed teaching, both of which can be done in an interactive manner.

36. See Dave Klanderman's "Teaching and Learning Mathematics: the Influence of Constructivism," in *Mathematics in a Postmodern Age*, ed. R. Howell and W.J. Bradley, 333-359.

Distortions in the Development and Application of Mathematics

Since humans are finite creatures, our understanding of how the world works and how we should apply what we learn has its limits. Theory and practice always undergo historical development and, we believe, would have done so even had the Fall not occurred. However, with the advent of the Fall, we must now also contend with further complications, with theories and applications that can be distorted and that may even be harmful to us and the world that we inhabit. We discussed some distorted notions of the nature of mathematics above and will mention more below, so here we will focus on problematic uses of mathematics.

There is, of course, the more flagrant, evil uses to which mathematics can be put: using mathematics to help design weapons of indiscriminate mass destruction; using mathematics to maximize short-term profits in a business without concern for conserving resources or for avoiding any potentially destructive impact on the environment; using mathematics to justify acceptance of highly risky investments based on financial derivatives; using statistical analyses on biased samples to promote a product or practice or to deny their harmful effects; using inappropriate measures in politics (e.g., citing the percent increase of educational funding instead of noting the decreased funding per pupil) to make a situation look rosier than it is; and so on. In such cases, one can argue that the mathematics, strictly speaking, is not what's at fault: it's how mathematical knowledge is applied; the same technical mathematics may be put to very beneficial use. True enough; but the sorts of mathematical theories that get developed are influenced by the intended use that prompted their development, so mathematics as a whole may develop in a somewhat lopsided way. Moreover, mathematical practice cannot be so neatly compartmentalized—practitioners pursue mathematics with goals and perspectives that color the work they do overall, even if others are unaware of those things or emphasize other goals as they make use of the same ideas and procedures for their own purposes. Furthermore, the reputation of mathematics for uncovering absolutely certain truths may blind one to its genuine limitations in analyzing a particular situation.

In addition to exploring specific applications of mathematics, then, we should look at the unquestioned role of mathematics in science and culture more broadly. Our modern world assumes the validity of a secular perspective, that there are realms of life that are public, such as science and mathematics and business and politics, and realms that are private, such as personal morality and religion. Of course, things are not always so sharply delineated in everyday life, but the intention of the modernist distinction is clear. In the public arena, it is thought, we should act on the basis of a shared rationality and put our private views and individual concerns aside. Ever since the early modern era, mathematical sciences have been taken as the touchstone for what is truly objective and objectively true.

This perspective brings us back to the purported nature and value of mathematics. It may be difficult for us contemporary Westerners to fathom, but mathematics has not always had as central a role in culture as it has in ours. We tend to believe that something has been established beyond the shadow of a doubt only if quantitative measurements and calculations are significantly and prominently involved. Mathematics is thought to generate objective knowledge, while qualitative subjective experience generates only biased opinions—mathematics is believed to reveal truth like nothing else in our world. Other sources of revelation are limited to the social group or the culture that holds them dear; hence, the Bible, the Qur'an, and astrology have no authority to challenge the claims of modern science and mathematics. Science and mathematics, on the other hand, are considered to be impartially justified, providing a common basis for public decision-making and action.

This attitude has grown stronger as modern Western culture progressed, to the point where during Enlightenment[37] times and later attempts were even made to establish morality on a rational quantitative basis, to develop a utilitarian calculus that would determine the greatest good for the greatest number. Such an approach made sense to many, as we indicated above, because of the amazing success of mathematical physics in the work of Galileo and Kepler and Newton, which was extended in the eighteenth century to areas of physical science such as hydrodynamics, acoustics, magnetism, and electricity. It was this tendency to restrict one's attention to what could be measured and quantified that seemed to make scientific progress possible. Mathematics was held up as the language of science, alone able to explain the intricate structure of the universe in all empirical aspects.[38] This trend toward mathematization revived emphases that were strongly present in earlier Pythagorean and Platonic perspectives, but in the modern era they were combined with the goal of using mathematics to exploit, control, and even restructure the world to make it more suitable for human purposes. A secularized view of the cultural mandate was joined to an imperial view of mathematics, making mathematical modeling essential to ongoing human progress everywhere, even if the fit was initially less than perfect. In this

37 This term itself—coined later in the nineteenth century—indicates a bias in favor of scientific rationality.

38 For further discussion of this trend, see chapters 5 - 7 in *Mathematics in a Postmodern Age: A Christian Perspective* (Eerdmans, 2001).

way mathematics is pushed to become more than it can or should be.

We should again note, to avoid misunderstanding, that we believe mathematics has critical, necessary, and important insights to provide, alongside those of other fields of thought, in all sorts of ventures. But that does not mean, as many leading Western thinkers believe, that mathematics is the supreme arbiter of truth. Quantifying phenomena in order to understand them became for many the holy grail of science and of objective knowledge generally. Naturally, since not everything is quantifiable, this tendency was rejected by its opponents, both during the Romantic era of the nineteenth century and also in our postmodern era. Other parts of life were deemed more important—nothing of significance can be converted to numbers, they thought; mathematical science is unable to provide support for making truly important decisions in life. A neo-Kuyperian approach rejects this dichotomy, holding that mathematics has an important part to play in human knowledge of the world, but that it must be tempered and complemented by other ways of knowing that may be more important in certain respects.

Restoration: Implications of a Neo-Kuyperian Approach for Mathematics

The third component of the biblical motif of Creation-Fall-Redemption/Restoration has to do with God rescuing his creation from the evil effects of the Fall through the life and death and resurrection of his son, Jesus Christ. We who have been saved and given new life are tasked, as God's children empowered by the Holy Spirit, to live as grateful members of God's kingdom, serving God in all that we do. While we do not and cannot bring in the kingdom in an absolute sense, we are to act here and now in obedient ways that seek to realize how God always intended us to live in his world. We strive to fulfill the cultural mandate in ways that bring shalom to various parts of creation and that bring awe-filled praise to our Creator and Redeemer for how he cares for his world. For mathematics, this means that we must use it in appropriate and beneficial ways, that we should put mathematics into proper perspective, combating the distorted views that have been put forward over the years, and that we should recognize God as the ultimate source behind mathematical truths. Without repeating what we have already said in earlier sections, we will look at some further implications of a neo-Kuyperian view of mathematics with respect to a world being restored to its original created purpose.

In focusing on the lawful order and diverse modal complexity of created reality, the Dooyeweerdian conceptual model provides a fruitful framework for doing work in mathematics. When applying mathematics, it can be helpful to think of the various modal aspects as a checklist of sorts to ensure a full-orbed approach,[39] to avoid overlooking crucial aspects of the phenomena involved. This gives us a tool for resisting mathematization, the assumption that certainty is guaranteed by the mathematics being applied. We've already noted the importance of taking into account that mathematics does not merely deal with one aspect, that its primary focus is on the two aspects of number and space. Paying attention to other modal aspects can create an even richer experience, both for the further development of mathematics and for the application of mathematics.

All modal aspects play a role in the human development of mathematics and mathematics education. Most obviously, the logical (analytical) aspect has played an important role in the historical advance of mathematical theories, ever since the time of the ancient Greeks. Mathematicians prove their results on the basis of already accepted axioms and theorems, using valid forms of reasoning. This differs somewhat from the practice of other sciences. Reflecting on the distinction between inductive and deductive reasoning fits nicely into a lesson on mathematical induction. Similarly, as students explore the Four-Color Theorem in graph theory, there is an opportunity to discuss computer-aided proofs and to think about the nature of proof in our day.[40]

The social aspect is crucially important for doing mathematics. It has played a significant role in the professionalization of mathematics, which occurred in the nineteenth and twentieth centuries as various specialized mathematical societies sprang up to support mathematical research and education. Mathematical researchers often team up to work on a particular problem (think of the prolific twentieth-century mathematics collaborator Paul Erdös), but even when this is not the case (take, for example, Andrew Wiles' solitary work on Fermat's Last Theorem), the cumulative nature of mathematics means that nobody is working alone: one always builds on what was done by others, and there is always

---

39. A similar approach is taken by the authors of *Responsible Technology: A Christian Perspective* (Grand Rapids, MI: Eerdmans, 1986) in their discussion of various norms that engineering applications should attend to. This approach has been carefully delineated for computer technology in Derek Schuurman's *Shaping a Digital World: Faith, Culture and Computer Technology* (Downers Grove, IL: IVP Academic, 2013) and in *A Christian Field Guide to Technology for Engineers and Designers* by Ethan Brue, Derek Schuurman, and Steven Vanderleest (Downers Grove, IL: IVP Academic, 2022). See also the chapter on engineering and technology in this volume.

40. For a discussion of this issue, see Thomas Tymoczko, "The Four-Color Problem and Its Philosophical Significance," in *New Directions in the Philosophy of Mathematics: An Anthology*, ed. Thomas Tymoczko (Boston: Birkhäuser, 1986), 243-266.

a community of peer experts in each field who judge the validity of what is being produced and who help out when problems are discovered. In education, the social nature of mathematics is evident, for example, in the calculus-reform movement, which has promoted written and oral communication as an effective means of learning mathematical ideas and algorithms.

The economic and political conditions of a culture also have an effect on mathematics; they can either encourage or discourage its development, nudging it in one direction or another. Patronage from rulers or from industry may push mathematicians to develop a field in certain ways over other ways because of vested interests. The concerns of Mesopotamian bureaucrats around 2150 B.C. regarding the confusing variety of metrological systems then in existence, for instance, were instrumental in leading them to develop a more efficient system of calculation, the well-known sexagesimal (base-sixty, place-value) numeration system.

Mathematical concepts develop over time from rudimentary beginnings, exhibiting their historical embeddedness. Reflecting on this while teaching mathematics can provide particular pedagogical or curricular insights. Learning about the role played by calculus and subsequent probability theory in Enlightenment thought shows students that mathematics has not been culturally neutral or inert. Attending to the history of algebra in an abstract algebra course can help students recognize that mathematical concepts originate and are shaped in particular theoretical contexts. Discussing these helps students understand how the abstract notions of group and field, so different from what is studied in elementary algebra, evolved from earlier work with solving polynomials and an expanding number concept. Teaching Euclidean and non-Euclidean geometry in rough chronological order—seeing mathematicians hone the axiomatic method used by Euclid in order to shore up the foundations of geometry—provides some cognitive dissonance in the classroom that mimics the historical record regarding the discovery of non-Euclidean geometry. Such an approach can open up students' desire to explore the philosophical ramifications of those developments, if only for their own peace of mind, but ultimately it helps them recognize the important role mathematics has played in our culture's philosophical understanding of the nature of mathematics and its relation to the world. Students can learn about the role Euclidean geometry and the axiomatic method had in shaping modernity, and the subsequent role non-Euclidean geometry played in shaping postmodernity.[41]

41. For varied treatments of this, see Morris Kline's *Mathematics: The Loss of Certainty* (New York: Oxford University Press, 1980), Joan Richards' *Mathematical Visions: The Pursuit of Geometry in Victorian England* (Boston: Academic Press, 1988),

The Dooyeweerdian modal-aspects scheme thus provides a redemptive non-reductive framework for acknowledging cultural influences on the development of mathematics and of mathematics' reciprocal impact on culture. Introducing relevant topics connected with a variety of modal aspects in the mathematics classroom fits the neo-Kuyperian definition of mathematics we have adopted and is meant to honor and illustrate this fuller (and truer) context of mathematics.

A neo-Kuyperian outlook also helps raise our awareness of the worldview context of mathematical developments. The intellectual pursuit of mathematics, as we have defined it, certainly assumes God's common grace both in structuring reality and in making this accessible to mathematical theorizing. There is a non-arbitrary order given in reality waiting to be discovered, and we are equipped as image bearers to understand and develop all aspects of creation. How we do this, however, depends to some extent on religious worldview, philosophical perspective, intellectual heritage, cultural circumstances, etc. The neo-Kuyperian emphasis on worldview and antithesis points out the religious non-neutrality of mathematical practice. For example, it has been conjectured that probability theory did not develop in Greek culture in part due to a worldview that said *chance* could not be studied because events happened at the whim of the gods. Similarly, the Platonic view that mathematics studies immutable eternal truths may have led classical mathematicians to shy away from trying to develop a mathematical theory of change. The openness of ancient Chinese mathematics to an arithmetic of negative numbers in addition to that of positive numbers may be attributed in part to their emphasis on balancing contradictory opposites, yin and yang. Cultural outlooks may suppress or fail to recognize legitimate mathematical theories that develop at other times and in other places due to different conditions and perspectives.

The religious nexus of mathematics is apparent not only in the broad multi-dimensional context in which it is practiced and applied. One can see traces of religious and philosophical perspectives in the field itself. This is something someone with a neo-Kuyperian viewpoint on mathematics is predisposed to recognize. Such connections are most obvious in the area of foundations of mathematics. We'll illustrate this by briefly sketching some late nineteenth- and early twentieth-century developments that attempted to establish once and for all the self-contained absolute certainty of mathematics—a goal with a very long history, as we have noted, and one that illustrates the worldview motivations behind

---

Vladimir Tasić's *Mathematics and the Roots of Postmodern Thought* (New York: Oxford University Press, 2001), and Jeremy Gray's *Plato's Ghost: The Modernist Transformation of Mathematics* (Princeton, NJ: Princeton University Press, 2008).

certain developments in mathematics.

The school of philosophy known as *logicism* was inaugurated by Gottlob Frege during the last two decades of the nineteenth century. Like Dedekind and Peano, he found it scandalous that some of the most basic notions of mathematics, such as positive integer, hadn't been rigorously analyzed and defined. His aim was to remedy this, to establish the absolute certainty and truth of mathematics by reducing it completely to logic. To accomplish this, he first had to further develop the field of logic itself, introducing key ideas such as quantifiers that are part of what we now call *predicate logic*. He then identified certain laws of logic as axiomatic and showed how rigorous deductions from them could be constructed by logical rules of inference. With these things in hand, he could define the concept of number and deduce the rules of ordinary arithmetic, putting this elementary part of mathematics on a fully rational basis.

The logicist program was proceeding according to plan until 1902, when Bertrand Russell discovered that Frege's Basic Law V could be used to produce a logical contradiction—the death knell for a deductive theory. After some attempts to repair his foundation, Frege decided that the obstacles were insurmountable and gave up. Russell, on the other hand, was so strongly committed to Frege's vision of mathematics that he vowed to continue the program. As he admitted late in life, Russell pursued this goal religiously, because he felt mathematics was the one field of human thought where absolute certainty might be achieved. Enlisting his colleague Alfred North Whitehead, they spent the next couple of decades in what turned out to be a monumental project, trying to develop an unassailable logical foundation for mathematics. Although Russell concluded in the end that their three-volume work *Principia Mathematica* also failed to reduce mathematics to logic, the work done by them, following up on what Frege had begun, changed the face of mathematical logic and converted foundations of mathematics from a specialized philosophical topic into a technical prolegomena within mathematics itself.[42]

While Russell and Whitehead were busy working out their research program, the intuitionist L. E. J. Brouwer was challenging various aspects of classical mathematics that he thought had gone beyond what one could accept as absolutely certain—parts of Cantor's set theory, some results in real analysis, some proof strategies that led to questionable results. He wanted to ground all of mathematics on the basic human intuition of a temporal sequence, drawing upon some ideas that had first been put for-

42. Neo-logicist philosophy of mathematics arising in the last quarter of the twentieth century has revived a version of Frege's original proposal. See Paolo Mancosu's *Abstraction and Infinity* (Oxford: Oxford University Press, 2017) for an analysis of this development.

ward by Kant. Mathematics for Brouwer is created by the human mind; it is not about an external reality, nor is it dependent upon language or logic. Its certainty is thus guaranteed by how humans conceptually construct mathematics. These ideas led him and his followers to develop parts of mathematics in an alternative constructivist fashion that some found attractive but that repelled many mainstream mathematicians.

One mathematician who sought to answer Brouwer's critiques in an irrefutable way and so save classical mathematics was David Hilbert. Hilbert thought Brouwer's methods were too stringent and his rejection of parts of mathematics and logic unwarranted. However, he did not think that one needed to adopt a strictly logical basis, as did Frege and Russell, in order to show that mathematics was absolutely certain. He advocated the formal axiomatic method, which he helped to redefine around 1900 in his work on geometry, as the correct approach to take in mathematics overall. Every mathematical theory would be based upon an appropriate system of axioms, treated as formal/uninterpreted statements (hence his program is often called *Formalism*). From these statements mathematicians would rigorously derive the theorems of the field in question, using any valid form of reasoning. The axiomatic method, however, would do more than help to organize mathematical theories. He believed it would also help him establish the absolute certainty of mathematics. Hilbert treated the axiomatic statements themselves as formal mathematical objects about which he could deduce results—his so-called proof theory or meta-mathematics. Here he would use more restrictive methods of reasoning and some simple ideas from mathematics that even intuitionists would recognize as legitimate. In this way, he hoped to prove incontrovertibly that the axiom systems for various mathematical theories were logically consistent, that they would never lead to contradictory results like $0 = 1$, and so were completely safe to use as a deductive basis in mathematics.

Hilbert and his colleagues were still busy developing the analytical tools needed to pursue proof theory when Gödel proved his famous Incompleteness Theorems in 1931, demonstrating decisively that consistent systems rich enough to include a sub-theory of arithmetic are intrinsically incomplete; in particular, they are unable to establish their own consistency. These results were taken by many as the demise of the logicist and formalist programs. More generally, this was seen as a blow against any effort to rigorously prove what had long been an article of faith for mathematicians and others—that mathematics was a science of absolutely certain truths. For later postmodern thinkers, Gödel's results seemed to confirm their view that such an article of faith was misguided. For modernist thinkers, these results meant that the outcome they had hoped for couldn't be demonstrated by elementary reasoning within a closed system, even though it could still be true. Of course, there were also mathematicians—perhaps the large majority—who took these developments as indications that concerns with foundational matters weren't very fruitful, that they could continue to pursue their own mathematical interests in blissful ignorance of what the appropriate foundations of mathematics might be.

Whatever conclusions one might draw from these developments, the foundational ferment of the early twentieth century had several long-lasting impacts on mathematics. For one thing, mathematicians began to lose faith and interest in grand foundational schemes designed to establish the certainty of mathematics. Some came to believe that mathematics might just be a collection of theories developed from conventionally accepted formal postulates, providing a palette of results available to those working in applied mathematics whenever they found them useful for modeling real-life phenomena. But while foundations of mathematics lost its earlier reason for existence (to prove the absolute certainty of mathematics), it didn't wither away and die. It became an active sub-field of mathematics exploring the logical basis and structure of axiomatic theories—their consistency and completeness, and the independence of various results from the rest of the theory. The field was grounded in modern logic, but it was also based upon set theory, which had been axiomatized in the early decades of the twentieth century by Zermelo, Fraenkel, von Neumann, and others. To some, such as the Bourbaki group mid-century and certain New Math proponents in the '60s, set theory seemed able to sustain all of mathematics, given appropriate definitions and clever ways of modeling things with set-theoretic constructs. One might not be able to demonstrate the consistency or the certainty of set theory in a rigorously absolute way, but its role as a theoretical foundation and universal language for mathematics seemed to give mathematics a unity or coherence of sorts.

Philosophy of mathematics was also greatly changed by these developments. In many circles, it became nearly synonymous with foundations of mathematics, considered as dealing with the deductive basis and structure of mathematics. To be a philosopher of mathematics one had to be well versed in technical logic and foundational mathematics in addition to philosophical matters. But because demonstrating the certainty of mathematics turned out to be an illusory goal, mathematicians and philosophers also began to entertain other aims and concerns connected with mathematical practice, a focus that has become more popular in recent years. In recent years this has come to be challenged on a number of fronts, many now emphasizing the need to account for how mathematicians practice mathematics, not just provide a theoretical foundation for its results.

A neo-Kuyperian outlook on mathematics helps us to recognize the humanistic religious motivation behind the various foundational approaches attempting to demonstrate that absolute certainty can be achieved within the field of mathematics, and it sees the subsequent developments in foundations of mathematics as a verdict against such a view. This does not mean that Christians should steer clear of foundations of mathematics or ignore philosophical developments. Rather, we should be involved in it with our own agenda, actively choosing appropriate foundations for mathematical theories and gearing them to more modest aims. Pursuing meta-mathematical goals remains a legitimate concern as well, for it helps to reveal the logical connections and limitations to the foundations chosen for a theory. And we should be engaged in the broader discussion and evaluation of genuine mathematical practice.

A neo-Kuyperian approach to mathematics thus rejects the pretensions and deep-seated yearning for the security of grandiose one-sided foundational programs, advocating instead a more-humble acceptance of mathematics as a field of study of certain aspects of reality, intertwined with many others. We can recognize the significance of mathematics and the contributions it makes to our understanding and reshaping of the world around us without treating mathematics as divine or as the key that will unlock all the secrets of the universe. We can also acknowledge that mathematics has a part to play in restoring creation, in working to make things right, without taking it to be the field that, joined to information sciences and technology, will ultimately save us from the world's problems and usher in a recreated world. God is both the Creator and Redeemer of the cosmos; mathematics is an activity that assumes and functions within this overarching reality.

Some Brief Reflections for Further Work

We live today in an era where both modernist and postmodernist viewpoints are prominent. Most practicing mathematicians probably still feel more at home with a modernist outlook, but those familiar with the history and philosophy of mathematics understand that such an outlook has run into difficulties and can no longer be held as robustly as in the past. So what possibilities does this fluid state of affairs open up for those interested in a more holistic view of mathematics?

One topic that can be explored by scholars interested in the history and philosophy of mathematics is the secularization of mathematics. The religious context and significance of mathematics was certainly apparent to ancient mathematicians; not only were mathematics and religion not separate, they were closely allied in Greek culture. The same thing was true for medieval Arabic mathematics and Latin medieval mathematics. Certain mathematical topics were important to these cultures because of what they had to offer the practice of religion (calculating the direction of Mecca for prayers, determining the exact date of Easter). Medieval mathematics and natural philosophy in general were considered handmaidens to theology and religion, helping to clarify difficult topics that might arise in interpreting Scripture or in comprehending the nature of God, considered as an eternal being everywhere present with infinite power and knowledge.

In the Renaissance and the early modern period, though mathematicians didn't often reflect in public about how their faith impacted their mathematics, such connections would not be denied. Prominent mathematicians such as Kepler, Galileo, and Newton sought to use mathematics to better understand how God worked in nature. A more secular view of the purpose and nature of mathematics developed gradually, along with secular thinking in general, as deism gave rise to agnosticism and atheism. Such an anti-religious perspective came to typify Enlightenment thinkers in the later eighteenth and nineteenth centuries, but even that did not lead to the complete demise of religious viewpoints. For example, Leonhard Euler, the most prolific mathematician who ever lived, remained a devout Calvinist in the middle of the eighteenth century as the Enlightenment was making strong inroads throughout Europe and defended conservative Christianity against the freethinkers of his day. And as Daniel Cohen argues in *Equations from God: Pure Mathematics and Victorian Faith*, the Platonic view of mathematics as a way to the divine was still intellectually acceptable around 1850 and later in Great Britain and the United States, though this eventually gave way to more secular philosophies. It is rather striking, therefore, to realize that the widely held conception of mathematics as a purely secular discipline is a historical anomaly of relatively recent vintage. Much further scholarly work could be done to explore the significant transition to a secular view of mathematics. A book review of Cohen's work by James Bradley[43] suggests that this book is a call for Christians to produce a "change in the professional culture of the mathematics community—in which the notion that mathematics consists of transcendent ideas in the mind of God is seen as a legitimate interpretation." We would suggest to the contrary that drawing sustenance from such a neo-Platonic view of mathematics is neither necessary nor salutary. As one of us notes in reviewing Cohen's book elsewhere: "taking mathematical ideas to be divine may have

43. Bradley's review appears in the 2007 issue of the ACMS Journal. See https://pillars.taylor.edu/acmsjournal-2007/2/.

a pious motivation, but such a viewpoint has within it the seeds of a full-fledged anti-Christian religion stemming from its pagan pedigree."[44] We would recommend instead that the neo-Kuyperian view described in these pages is a more faithful position for Christians to endorse in combating secularism. Such a neo-Kuyperian approach to the trend of secularism would also treat this issue as being more about how worldviews influence mathematical developments than about looking for direct or analogical connections between religious beliefs or theological doctrines and mathematics.

Other areas that seem ripe for Christian mathematical engagement are history and philosophy of mathematics. While contemporary scholars may not always welcome the intrusion of religious and worldview concerns, these fields now deal with a much wider range of topics and approaches than they did several generations ago, when history was restricted mostly to technical mathematics and philosophy was equated with the technical foundations of mathematics.[45] Both fields are now more open to paying attention to aspects of human participation, to motivating factors, and to surrounding cultural contexts than earlier. There could be a role to play here for those espousing a neo-Kuyperian view of mathematics, where these sorts of concerns are almost second nature.

But beyond contributing to areas of mathematical practice where perspective is a direct concern, we believe that a neo-Kuyperian outlook on mathematics provides a healthy viewpoint for doing mathematics. As mathematicians, it is our calling to explore the many aspects of the cosmos God made, to serve others and the world around us, and to bring glory to God, our Creator and Redeemer. Without pretending that what we have to offer provides the key to unlocking all the secrets of the universe, we can do our work with humility and joy, realizing that we have something important to offer in the ongoing task of unfolding culture. By disclosing the marvelous structure, deep interconnectedness, and import of mathematical reality, we reveal the greatness, wisdom, and dependability of God, giving a voice to this part of creation, too, to declare his glory and manifest handiwork.

---

44. See the review by Calvin Jongsma in *Perspectives on Science and Christian Faith* 60, no. 2 (2008), 133-4.

45. We have already mentioned works by Jeremy Gray and Vladimir Tasić on the broader cultural context of mathematics. A work devoted to the varied connections between mathematics and religion is *Mathematics and the Divine: A Historical Study*, ed. T Koetsier and L. Bergmans (Boston: Elsevier, 2005).

Questions for Reflection and Further Exploration

1. This chapter organizes ideas about a Christian perspective on mathematics around the main biblical themes of Creation, Fall, and Redemption and adopts a neo-Kuyperian worldview and Reformational philosophical framework for elaborating them. Other Christian approaches focus primarily on how mathematics is related to God or how analogues of theological ideas like the Trinity or the nature of faith are reflected in mathematical concepts and practice. Which approach do you find most helpful for understanding an integral relationship between Christianity and mathematics? Are these approaches compatible, or do they exhibit different understandings of God and the roles of theology and philosophy relative to mathematics?
2. This chapter points out that a neo-Kuyperian approach to mathematics is at odds with a Christian Platonist approach. Compare and contrast these two perspectives in their overall aims and in their views of how God should be related to mathematical realities and truths. What mathematicians throughout history have promoted a Christian Platonist viewpoint in their writings about mathematics? Why did Plato develop his idealistic view of mathematics in the first place, and how did later philosophers, such as Aristotle, evaluate his ideas? What has been the reception of mid-twentieth-century philosophers of mathematics to his ideas about mathematical knowledge?
3. Number and space often appear as the first or most basic aspects in lists of modal aspects given by Reformational philosophers. Does this make them more foundational than other aspects? Might this legitimately account for why mathematics has been so highly valued by modernists for developing science? Shouldn't a robust philosophy of mathematics not only present a faithful account of the field's subject matter and how it is developed but also account for why people find alternative approaches attractive? In what ways, if any, is mathematics genuinely foundational for other fields of inquiry? Does such a view downplay or fail to recognize the interdependence and complementarity of all the aspects?
4. Should our definition of mathematics be expanded to include other modal aspects of reality? For instance, should it include kinematic functioning, given that the nature of motion and change is an important focus of differential calculus? Or is this merely an applica-

tion of mathematics applied to a different modal sphere? In what ways would expanding the focus of mathematics change our basic understanding of the nature of mathematics? Would this bring new insights or perspectives to mathematics?

5. Logic undergirds any field of thought that makes extensive use of argumentation, but mathematics may be the most prototypical field of inquiry with respect to this facet of its methodology. Over the last two centuries logic has been developed by mathematicians as a foundation for some of its basic ideas and for developments in computer science. Does this indicate that mathematics has wrongly overextended its focus or that logic has assumed too great a foundational role for mathematics? What legitimate fruitful connections are there between logic and mathematics? Given that the analytic modal aspect (with logic as a focal point) is not contiguous with the modal aspects of number and space, what are the implications for thinking about the relationship of logic and mathematics? To what extent is our understanding of logic and proof expanded by developments in computer science (theorem proving, artificial intelligence, etc.)? How should these be incorporated into our understanding of mathematical methodology? How should these developments be embraced or resisted?

Resources

The ACMS (Association for Christians in the Mathematical Sciences) has a biennial conference and publishes proceedings from those conferences, available at https://pillars.taylor.edu/acms/. The journal *Perspectives on Science and Christian Faith*, a journal of the ASA (American Scientific Affiliation), also often has essays and book reviews on faith and mathematics.

The following list of resources is a good starting point and provides helpful contextual reading. Some of the sources emphasize Christian approaches different from the one presented here, including a Christian Platonist approach by Bradley and Howell and an analogical approach by Poythress. The chapter on ontology in *Mathematics through the Eyes of Faith* includes both a Christian Platonist approach and a summary of the approach presented here, labeled therein as Christian Empiricism. The first author of this chapter maintains an online annotated bibliographic database on *Religious Faith and the Mathematical Sciences*, which should be publicly available early in 2026.

Bradley, W. James. "Theology and Mathematics–Key Themes and Central Historical Figures." *Theology and Science* 9 no. 1 (2011): 5-26.

Bradley, W. James, and Russell W. Howell, eds. *Mathematics through the Eyes of Faith*. New York: HarperOne, 2011.

Clouser, Roy. *The Myth of Religious Neutrality: An Essay on the Hidden Role of Religious Belief in Theories*. 2nd ed. Notre Dame, IN: Notre Dame Press, 2005.

Cohen, Daniel J. *Equations from God: Pure Mathematics and Victorian Faith*. Baltimore: Johns Hopkins, 2007.

Diedrichs, D.R. "Mathematics Reveals Patterns that Reflect the Orderly Character of God." *Perspectives on Science and Christian Faith* 71, no. 2 (2019): 107-118.

Howell, Russell W. "The Matter of Mathematics." *Perspectives on Science and Christian Faith* 67, no. 2 (June, 2015): 74-88.

Howell, Russell W, and W. James Bradley, eds. *Mathematics in a Postmodern Age: A Christian Perspective*. Grand Rapids, MI: Eerdmans, 2001.

Jongsma, Calvin. "Mathematics: Always Important, Never Enough. A Christian Perspective on Mathematics and Mathematics Education," *Journal of the Association of Christians in the Mathematical Sciences* (Oct. 2006). https://pillars.taylor.edu/acmsjournal-2006/3/.

Jongsma, Calvin. "Poythress's Trinitarian Logic: A Review Essay." *Pro Rege* 42, no.4 (2014): 6-15.

Jongsma, Calvin. "Reuben Hersh's What Is Mathematics, Really?" (Book Review). ACMS Journal and *Proceedings* 24: 272-282. May, 2025. https://pillars.taylor.edu/acms-2024/24/.

Koetsier, T., and L. Bergmans, eds. *Mathematics and the Divine: A Historical Study* Oxford: Elsevier, 2004.

Lawrence, Snezana, and Mark McCartney, eds. *Mathematicians and their Gods: Interactions between Mathematics and Religious Beliefs*. New York: Oxford University Press, 2015.

Poythress, Vern. *Redeeming Mathematics: A God-Centered Approach*. Wheaton, IL: Crossway, 2015.

Schuurman, Derek. *Shaping a Digital World: Faith, Culture and Computer Technology*. Downers Grove, IL: IVP Academic, 2013.

Strauss, D.F.M. *Paradigms in Mathematics, Physics and Biology*. Bloemfontein: Tekskor, 2004.

Su, Francis. Mathematics for Human Flourishing. New Haven: Yale University Press. 2020.

Van der Meer, J.M., ed. *Facets of Faith and Science.* Vol. 2, *The Role of Beliefs in Mathematics and the Natural Sciences,* Ancaster, ON and Lanham, MD: Pascal Centre and University Press of America, 1996.

Vander Meulen, Kevin. "'*Redeeming Mathematics: A God-Centered Approach*' by Vern Poythress," [book review]. *Perspectives on Science and Christian Faith* 69, no. 1 (2017): 52-54.

Bibliography

Augustine. *On Free Choice of the Will.* Trans. Anna S. Benjamin and L.H. Hackstaff. Indianapolis: Bobbs-Merrill, 1964.

Bartholomew, Craig G., and Michael W. Goheen, *The Drama of Scripture: Finding Our Place in the Biblical Story*. Grand Rapids, MI: Baker Academic, 2004.

Bradley, W. James. "Theology and Mathematics - Key Themes and Central Historical Figures." *Theology and Science* 9 no. 1 (2011): 5-26.

Bradley, W. James, and Russell W. Howell, eds. *Mathematics through the Eyes of Faith*. New York: HarperOne, 2011.

Bradley, W.J., A. Busch, D. Klanderman, E. Ricketts, and G. Talsma. *Mathematics: a Christian Perspective*. Grand Rapids, MI: Kuyers Institute, 2008.

Bratt, James. *Abraham Kuyper: Modern Calvinist, Christian Democrat.* Grand Rapids, MI: W.B. Eerdmans, 2013.

Calvin, John. *Institutes of the Christian Religion.* Edited by John T. McNeill. Translated by Ford Lewis Battles. Philadelphia: Westminster Press, 1960.

Carpenter, Joel. "Response to Hamilton." *Christian Scholar's Review* 31, no. 1 (2001): 21-24.

Clouser, Roy A. "A Blueprint for a Non-Reductionist Theory of Reality, "September 1, 2011, Metanexus Essay, https://metanexus.net/blueprint-non-reductionist-theory-reality/

Clouser, Roy A. "Is There a Christian View of Everything from Soup to Nuts?" *Pro Rege* 31, no. 4 (June, 2003): 1-10.

Clouser, Roy A. *The Myth of Religious Neutrality: An Essay on the Hidden Role of Religious Belief in Theories*. 2nd ed. Notre Dame, IN: Notre Dame Press, 2005.

Crouch, Andy. *Culture Making: Recovering Our Creative Calling.* Downers Grove, IL: IVP Books, 2008.

Davis, Philip J., and Reuben Hersh, *Descartes' Dream: The World According to Mathematics*. San Diego, CA: Harcourt Brace Jovanovich, 1986.

Dooyeweerd, Herman. *De Wijsbegeerte der wetsidee*. Amsterdam: H.J. Paris, 1935-1936. Translated as *The New Critique of Theoretical Thought*. Philadelphia: Presbyterian and Reformed Pub. Co., 1953-1958.

Gray, Jeremy. *Plato's Ghost: The Modernist Transformation of Mathematics*. Princeton, NJ: Princeton University Press, 2008.

Howell, Russell W, and W. James Bradley, eds. *Mathematics in a Postmodern Age: A Christian Perspective*. Grand Rapids, MI: Eerdmans, 2001.

Howell, Russell W. "The Matter of Mathematics." *Perspectives on Science and Christian Faith* 67, no. 2 (June, 2015): 74-88.

Jongsma, Calvin. "Mathematics: Always Important, Never Enough. A Christian Perspective on Mathematics and Mathematics Education." Pro Rege 35, no. 4 (June, 2007): 21-38. https://digitalcollections.dordt.edu/pro_rege/vol35/iss4/3/.

Jongsma, Calvin. Review of *Equations from God: Pure Mathematics and Victorian Faith*, by Daniel J. Cohen. *Perspectives on Science and Christian Faith* 60, no. 2 (2008): 133-4. https://digitalcollections.dordt.edu/faculty_work/307/.

Jongsma, Calvin. *Poythress's Trinitarian Logic: A Review Essay*. Pro Rege 42 no. 4 (June, 2014): 6-15. https://digitalcollections.dordt.edu/pro_rege/vol42/iss4/2/.

Kline, Morris. *Mathematics in Western Culture*. London: Oxford University Press, 1953.

Kline, Morris *Mathematics: The Loss of Certainty*. New York: Oxford University Press, 1980.

Koetsier, T., and L. Bergmans, eds. *Mathematics and the Divine: A Historical Study*. Boston: Elsevier, 2005.

Kuyper, Abraham. *Lectures on Calvinism*. Grand Rapids, MI: W.B. Eerdmans, 1998.

Mancosu, Paolo. *Abstraction and Infinity*. Oxford: Oxford University Press, 2017.

Mancosu, Paolo, ed. *The Philosophy of Mathematical Practice*. New York: Oxford University Press, 2008.

Marsden, George. *The Outrageous Idea of Christian Scholarship*. New York: Oxford University Press, 1997.

Monsma, Stephen, Clifford Christians, Eugene R. Dykema, Arie Leegwater, Egbert Schuurman, and Lambert Van Poolen. *Responsible Technology: A Christian Perspective*. Grand Rapids, MI: Eerdmans, 1986.

Nickel, James. *Mathematics: Is God Silent?* Vallecito, CA: Ross House Books, 2001.

Noll, Mark. *The Scandal of the Evangelical Mind.* Grand Rapids, MI: W. B. Eerdmans, 1994.

Poythress, Vern. *Logic: A God-Centered Approach to the Foundation of Western Thought.* Wheaton, IL: Crossway, 2013.

Richards, Joan. *Mathematical Visions: The Pursuit of Geometry in Victorian England.* Boston: Academic Press, 1988.

Schuurman, Derek. *Shaping a Digital World: Faith, Culture and Computer Technology.* Downers Grove, IL: IVP Academic, 2013.

Spykman, Gordon. *Reformational Theology: A New Paradigm for Doing Dogmatics.* Grand Rapids, MI: W.B. Eerdmans, 1992.

Strauss, D.F.M. *Paradigms in Mathematics, Physics and Biology.* Bloemfontein: Tekskor, 2004.

Strauss, D.F.M. *Philosophy: Discipline of the Disciplines.* Grand Rapids, MI: Paideia Press, 2009.

Tasić, Vladimir. *Mathematics and the Roots of Postmodern Thought.* New York: Oxford University Press, 2001.

Tymoczko, Thomas. "The Four-Color Problem and Its Philosophical Significance." In *New Directions in the Philosophy of Mathematics: An Anthology,* edited by Thomas Tymoczko, 243-266. Boston: Birkhäuser, 1986.

Van der Meer, J.M., ed. *Facets of Faith and Science.* Vol. 1, *Historiography and Modes of Interaction.* Ancaster, ON and Lanham, MD: Pascal Centre and University Press of America, 1996.

Van der Meer, J.M., ed. *Facets of Faith and Science.* Vol. 2, *The Role of Beliefs in Mathematics and the Natural Sciences.* Ancaster, ON and Lanham, MD: Pascal Centre and University Press of America, 1996.

Walsh, Brian J., and J. Richard Middleton. *The Transforming Vision: Shaping a Christian World View.* Downers Grove, IL: InterVarsity Press, 1984.

Wigner, Eugene. "The Unreasonable Effectiveness of Mathematics in the Natural Sciences." *Communications in Pure and Applied Mathematics* 13, no. I (February 1960): 1-14.

Wolters, Albert M. *Creation Regained: Biblical Basics for a Reformational Worldview.* 2nd ed. Grand Rapids, MI: Wm. B. Eerdmans, 2005.

Wolterstorff, Nicholas. *Reason within the Bounds of Religion.* 2nd ed. Grand Rapids, MI: W.B. Eerdmans, 1984.

The Physicality of the World in Context: A Reformational Perspective on the Disciplines of Physical Science[1]

Arnold E. Sikkema

What Is Physics?

Imagine a universe being created in a sequence of steps. First, a number of single individual structureless point particles (three of them, say) are brought into being. Second, these individual point particles are placed into spatial relationships with one another. (Prior to that, "space" had not existed.) Third, something about the particles and/or their spatial relationships is given the capacity to undergo change; perhaps the particles move about. (Prior to that, "change", including "motion", did not exist.) Fourth, these particles are equipped with the ability to interact with one another.

This is a little "parable of creation" I sometimes use to explain certain aspects of Reformational philosophy, particularly as it concerns the subject matter of the disciplines of mathematics and physics. It certainly misses deep features of Dooyeweerd's thought, but I believe it communicates some of its themes.

The parable has nothing at all to do with the order of events in the actual creation of this world. Instead, it simply demonstrates among other things our intrinsic unifying recognition of reality, and some of the difficulties of theorizing and abstracting. When we start by introducing three individual particles, we automatically want them to be at different places and have difficulty conceiving of them at one place, let alone conceiving of them without space yet existing. When we see three billiard balls moving about on a table, we readily think of the whole show; yet it requires effort to abstract out number, space, change, and interaction. We also see that different disciplines address different aspects: mathematics studies the first three aspects, and physics the fourth.[2] The interdepen-

1. While most of this chapter engages physics, and often the physical sciences more generally, much applies to the natural sciences more broadly.

2. While the kinematical aspect is sometimes included within what physics studies, I have framed it here as referring to change broadly construed, not just motion,

dencies of the disciplines, too, are exemplified: mathematics is indispensable in doing physics which (among other things) explains kinematics (motion and change of motion) by way of mechanics (force is key in Newton's theory of interacting bodies).

Physics is sometimes defined brashly in the opening pages of first-year university textbooks as the study of the universe. However, it quickly becomes apparent that physics does not involve the study of the Canadian legal system, or of the history of marriage traditions, or of the challenges of urbanization, even though those are certainly all found within the universe. A better, narrower, definition often offered is: the empirical study of matter, energy, and their interactions. Here "empirical" refers to a reliance upon observation and experiment, which includes its in-principle accessibility to all persons. Key in the definition is "interaction" as suggested in the parable of creation at the opening of this chapter.

Physics as a discipline makes heavy use of mathematics in both theoretical and experimental work. In fact, many areas of mathematics were developed specifically because of the need for them in the solutions of particular problems in physics. Even though physics employs mathematics as much as it does, it cannot rightly be called applied mathematics. Mathematics may *describe* and help *analyze* things in physics, but it cannot *explain* them.[3] Furthermore, mathematics can be applied to many additional areas of study besides physics (e.g. chemistry, biology, engineering, psychology, sociology, and politics).

Chemistry is very closely related to physics, being a physical science as well, though it is distinguished by its focus on interatomic bonds: reactions between substances that result in the formation, breakage, and/or alteration of molecular bonds in which energy is required or released, as well as the synthesis, purification, and characterization of substances. Much of this chapter applies in general to what are called the "natural sciences," which include astronomy, physics, chemistry, geology, meteorology, physical cosmology, biology, and parts of environmental science. The focus, however, will be on the physical sciences.

I find it important to use the words "physical" and "physically" in their technical sense, as it relates to physics and the physical aspect of interaction. Every created thing which exists within our universe exhibits every one of the modal aspects. Thus it is not correct, for example, for a student to ask, "May I email my paper to you, or would you like a physical copy?" The student has set up a false dichotomy. An emailed paper is

without regard for its cause. Furthermore, mathematics includes studies of rates of change, for example in calculus.

3. Taking mathematical description as explanation is an example of reductionism, which Reformational thought strongly rejects as described later in this chapter.

also a physical copy, as it is stored and sent electronically using the physical interactions of electricity and magnetism. The "paper" is the report or essay that can find its physical instantiation in the neuronal firing patterns of the student who has memorized it, in the air-pressure variations of the spoken word in its oral delivery, in the digital format of a word processor (or audio and/or video) file stored on a USB drive or a remote server in "the cloud," in the grooves of a vinyl record, or, yes, possibly in the ink patterns on paper. No version of any paper is non-physical.

Physics has come a long way since Aristotle's table of 4+1 elements (the terrestrial elements of earth, water, air, and fire, in addition to the quintessence of the heavenly bodies) and the associated concept of natural place. He analyzed all motion from his non-experimental observation post as being either natural (moving without force toward natural place), violent (being forced away from natural place), or circular (the orbits of the heavenly bodies about the earth). Though Aristotelian physics was adopted by Thomas Aquinas, along with Ptolemaic astronomy, as being of a piece with Christian doctrine, this was dismissed from the emerging natural philosophy, later called *physics*, of Kepler, Galileo, and Newton. There is of course more to the story, but modern science was born when meticulous quantification of astronomical observations was coupled with systematic experimental measurements and abstract idealization in theoretical thought, and the unifying recognition that "heavenly" bodies, having "terrestrial" features, are subject to the same interactions. Newton's physics also introduced the mechanical perspective as a replacement of the medieval view of world as organism, in which the various parts of reality function within the larger whole, all undergoing their natural activity like so many organs.

Physics is well-known for "laws of physics"—Kepler's three laws of planetary orbits, Newton's law of gravity and his three laws of motion, the zeroth through third laws of thermodynamics, conservation laws, etc. By the year 1900, many thought physics was at its end, with the only expectation being an increase in accuracy in the numerical values of the constants appearing in these mathematical relationships. But the twentieth century opened entirely new vistas, as laboratory curiosities and *gedanken* experiments led to special and general relativity as well as quantum physics. A good number of physical constants are now known to twelve significant figures (such as the mass of the electron which is $548.579909070 \pm 0.000000016 \times 10^{-6}$ u, where the atomic mass unit u is defined as 1/12 of the mass of the carbon atom ^{12}C).[4] At laboratories such as CERN's Large Hadron Collider, special relativity and quantum

4. P.A. Zyla et al., "Review of Particle Physics," *Progress of Theoretical and Experimental Physics* 2020, no. 8 (August 2020): 083C01.

physics are subjected to comprehensive rigorous testing during every one of its approximately one billion collisions per second; any slight deviation from basic relativistic relationships between energy E, mass m, and speed v (such as $E^2 = m^2c^4/[1 - v^2/c^2]$, where c is the speed of light) and conservation of energy and momentum would immediately show up in a multitude of ways in the many types and levels of detectors. Advances in observational and theoretical astrophysics in the past century, and especially in the past few decades, have provided a vast spatiotemporal perspective on the observable cosmos, with its hundreds of billions of galaxies each with hundreds of billions of stars and copious mysterious "dark matter," whose expansion from a big bang is accelerating due to some unexplained "dark energy."

The cosmos within our empirical observational scope is a universe exhibiting unity in diversity. A most fruitful approach in physics has been unification: the assumption that widely different behaviours or properties might very well be aspects of one deeper and broader type of physical interaction. For example, electric force, magnetism, and light, though superficially exceptionally different from one another, have in fact all been very well described and explained as *electromagnetic* phenomena, first in the mid-nineteenth century through Maxwell's equations and since the mid-twentieth century via quantum electrodynamics.

Much of the physics of today is characterized by global collaborations examining details of the very small and the very large. Many physicists also consider mesoscopic physics to be a frontier, probing novel phenomena at scales between the microscopic and the telescopic. In this range are found nonlinearity, chaos, complex systems, collective behaviour, and emergence, features that are considered important in the application of physics to biological systems as well. In the biophysics community, there is a wide range of perspectives on whether and how fruitfully the methods of physics can be applied to biological systems; these views differ on matters such as the role of historical contingency, function, and teleology in biology.

Some physicists who become public intellectuals, such as Stephen Hawking, Lawrence Krauss, and Neil deGrasse Tyson, exhibit rampant reductionism and epistemological arrogance. They think of physics as so utterly foundational for everything else that it is competent in principle to address problems in every other discipline (which are thus not truly disciplines in their own right). Thankfully, there are also both Christian and unbelieving physicists of high stature who are holding them to account.[5]

5. See (e.g.) John Horgan, "Physicist George Ellis Knocks Physicists for Knocking Philosophy, Falsification, Free Will," *Cross-Check (Scientific American)*, 22 July 2014, https://www.scientificamerican.com/blog/cross-check/physicist-george-el-

While the discipline of physics *per se* attempts to understand the nature of the world in its physical aspect, a number of interdisciplinary fields explore broader connections. The now well-established field of physics education research examines how students perceive the physical world, explores pedagogical techniques, and sets out to establish best practices in the teaching and learning of physics, focusing mostly on high-school through second-year university physics. A number of university departments of physics (and sometimes of education) have active collaborations in physics education research and offer graduate degrees in the field. The American Physical Society, with over 55,000 members, publishes (along with the American Association of Physics Teachers) the journal *Physical Review Physics Education Research*, first called *Physical Review Special Topics – Physics Education Research* from 2005 to 2015.[6] A strong knowledge of physics is also required for valuable contributions to the fields of history of physics and philosophy of physics, which are being published in journals such as *Physics in Perspective*, founded in 1999.

Taking God Seriously in Physics

Trinitarian and Covenantal

A Reformational perspective recognizes the God revealed in Scripture as trinitarian and covenantal.

It is quite insufficient for a Christian to develop a merely "theistic" approach to science, even if that affords some commonality between Christianity and other faiths that acknowledge some kind of ultimate divine personal being. One very common placement of the word "theistic" is in the significantly problematic label "theistic evolution," which is used to describe any number of views relating God to biological change. No Christian working in or writing about the physical sciences advocates for "theistic meteorology" to account for God's activity in weather or "theistic gravitation" to express how God holds the solar system together. Isaac Newton, as much a theologian as a natural philosopher, felt no need to seek a physical explanation of the force of gravity, saying only that God, being omnipresent, provides action at a distance. The Christian physicist today, though, seeks physical explanations while recognizing God

lis-knocks-physicists-for-knocking-philosophy-falsification-free-will/ and Sean Carroll, "Physicists Should Stop Saying Silly Things about Philosophy," 23 June 2014, preposterousuniverse.com/blog/2014/06/23/physicists-should-stop-saying-silly-things-about-philosophy.

6. Charles Henderson, "Editorial: Renaming Physical Review Special Topics—Physics Education Research," *Physical Review Physics Education Research* 12, no. 1 (25 January 2016): 010001.

as foundational, properly joining with the unbelieving physicist in fully agreeing on and exploring the limitations of the physical laws and principles involved, while not being on the same (metaphysical) page with respect to the origin and utterly universal application of those laws and principles.

Psalm 33:6 is often poetically interpreted as depicting the Trinity creating the cosmos: "By the word of the Lord the heavens were made, their starry host by the breath of his mouth" (NIV). This is because "word" is interpreted via John 1:1 as being Jesus Christ; "Lord" refers to Yahweh, the Covenant God, the Father; and "breath" refers to the Holy Spirit (the Hebrew *ruach* meaning breath, wind, and spirit). God as Trinity is the foundation for the unity and diversity of the cosmos, in which the "laws of physics" are apparently generally applicable to the astonishing diversity of structures of all scales observed throughout the universe. God's word for creation gives it existence, meaning, and regularity. Science cannot provide a rationale for the cosmos continuing to function, but all scientific activity fully depends upon (and effectively expresses) God's faithfulness to his covenant with creation. This dependability of natural cycles is articulated, though of course not initiated, in God's post-Flood promise in Genesis 8:22 (NIV):

> As long as the earth endures,
> seedtime and harvest,
> cold and heat,
> summer and winter,
> day and night
> will never cease.

God refers to his "covenant with day and night" and his having "established the laws of heaven and earth" in Jeremiah 33:20, 25 (NIV). The aim of physical science is the discovery of the lawfulness of the physical reality, and as James Jordan describes it, "a study of the terms of the Noahic covenant."[7] In our quest to do this, we cannot simply conclude, as Kepler did, that we "think God's thoughts after Him," in part because distinctions ought to be drawn between what I call "laws for the physical aspect of creation" and "laws of physics."[8] Stafleu distinguishes between these as well, calling them "laws" and "law statements" respectively.[9] Pri-

7. James Jordan, *Through New Eyes: Developing a Biblical View of the World* (Eugene, OR: Wipf & Stock, 1999), 109.

8. Arnold E. Sikkema, "Laws of Nature and God's Word for Creation," *Fideles* 2 (2007): 27–43.

9. M.D. Stafleu, *Theories at Work: On the Structure and Functioning of Theories in Science, in Particular During the Copernican Revolution* (Lanham, MD: University Press of America, 1987), 25.

mary among these is that God's laws govern, while our laws describe and explain. Our laws of physics are limited human expressions in mathematical form meant to describe and explain the patterns of regularity by which the Creator has chosen to govern the creation in its physical aspect.

Taking God and his covenant with creation seriously must also go hand in hand with accepting our God-given stewardly task in which we bear responsibility for creation care. God's promise of regular patterns does not negate the fact that we have been given the capability of significant disruption of our world's proper functioning. God's promise to "never again destroy every living thing" (Genesis 8:21, NIV) does not absolve us of our responsibility for a changing climate, warming atmosphere and oceans, melting glaciers, and rising sea levels, or for the disproportionate effects these are having on our most vulnerable global neighbours.[10] In the past, we learned of the damage done by certain gases used in refrigeration and aerosol sprays (the now strictly regulated chlorofluorocarbons, CFCs) to the earth's ozone layer which God in his providence established for our protection. In the same way, we should be thankful for scientific advances which have found that, while fossil fuels have been very beneficial to cultural development, their use has come with its own problems requiring international collaborative efforts for mitigation and adaptation.

Divine Revelation and Physics

What can be said regarding the role of divine revelation in physics? Does God provide helpful data in Scripture to supplement or guide our empirical studies? The key role of Christianity in the rise of modern science, acknowledged by Christian and non-Christian historians alike, was not the mining of specific biblical facts to be scientifically confirmed, but general worldview principles such as the non-divinity of the natural world and the idea of nature being governed by divinely ordained laws.[11] Biblical hermeneutics, especially in the Reformed tradition, emphasizes the redemptive-historical approach in which Christ is seen as the centre of Scripture, along with the use of Scripture to interpret Scripture, the

10. Katharine Hayhoe, "Christians, Climate Science, & Our Culture," presented at "From Sea to Sea … *to Sky!* Science and Christianity in Canada," a conference of the Canadian Scientific & Christian Affiliation, Trinity Western University, 12 May 2018.

11. H. Floris Cohen, *The Scientific Revolution: A Historiographical Inquiry* (Chicago, IL: University of Chicago Press, 1994); Peter Harrison, *The Cambridge Companion to Science and Religion* (Cambridge: Cambridge University Press, 2010); Nancy R. Pearcey, and Charles B. Thaxton, *The Soul of Science: Christian Faith and Natural Philosophy* (Wheaton, IL: Crossway, 1994).

importance of linguistic, literary, cultural, and historical contexts, the duality of divine and human authorship, and the revelation of the salvation message. With the Belgic Confession, for example, I "believe that this Holy Scripture fully contains the will of God and that all that man must believe in order to be saved is sufficiently taught therein" (Article 7). This, besides the fact that science, as it is now understood as a cultural enterprise, did not exist in biblical times, should suffice to dismiss the idea that Scripture provides scientists with helpful scientific data or tools to aid Christians today in our judgment of scientific theories. This has in the past been learned the hard way: Copernicus's heliocentric theory and Galileo's observations in its support were once considered antagonistic to the "clear biblical teaching" of geocentrism. Instead of seeing specific biblical passages as teaching the structures and processes of the cosmos, one can recognize the legitimate use of contemporary cultural expressions or knowledge of the human context to communicate divine truth.

General revelation, however, is the broad sense of God's divinity, power, and glory with which the created reality confronts everyone. The cosmos is described as a book in the Belgic Confession: "We know [God] by two means. First, by the creation, preservation, and government of the universe; which is before our eyes as a most beautiful book, wherein all creatures, great and small, are as so many letters leading us to perceive clearly the invisible things of God, namely, His eternal power and deity, as the apostle Paul says (Romans 1:20)" (Article 2). This self-revelation of God is general in that it does not provide the kind of detailed specific information God provides in Scripture (and in Jesus Christ) and in that it is directed to everyone regardless of time, place, culture, age, intellect, etc. Acknowledging the God revealed in creation can be followed by recognizing other aspects of God's character, some of which could be enhanced by natural-scientific study. God's wisdom is seen in the coherence of different levels of explanation and in the wondrous intricacies found in created forms as well as in our explanations thereof. God's love and goodness are seen in the consistency and stability of the world and its parts so that people and other creatures can depend upon their regularity. The Christian astronomer Jennifer Wiseman articulates God's power, creativity, beauty, patience, and faithfulness, showing that "this all points to a God who *loves*."[12] The more we study the world in all its aspects, including the physical, the more we deepen in our appreciation of these details.

Calvin speaks of creation as a mirror. McNutt points out that, unlike the unclear and distorting mirrors of the sixteenth century, creation

12. Jennifer Wiseman, "Science as an Instrument of Worship," *BioLogos* (7 March 2019), biologos.org/articles/science-as-an-instrument-of-worship; emphasis in the original.

is a clear, trustworthy, and unfailing reflection of God to us. In creation, God demonstrates his sovereignly transcendent qualities of glory, wisdom, justice, and power. Calvin's emphasis, though, with the mirror metaphor, is how creation reflects to us God's immanent qualities: his kindness, goodness, and fatherly benevolence toward us in its orderliness and aesthetic beauty. Any failure to perceive God properly is our faltering weakness, and God graciously gives us the additional glasses of Scripture to see the world (and him) properly.[13] The physical sciences especially afford us opportunities to gaze deeply into the pattern and process of created reality and to perceive with increasing clarity these qualities of the Creator.

God's attributes can be divided into communicable and incommunicable categories in terms of whether and to what degree humans as image bearers share them. Created reality also bears the stamp of God in ways that are worth exploring in detail. How God as an intrinsically interrelational Trinity is reflected in the world is discussed by Hastings.[14] He emphasizes the concepts of mutual indwelling of the persons of the Trinity, and perceives echoes of this coinherence in the world as explored through the sciences. Under the heading "Physics and Relational Ontology" below, I explain how the deepest levels of physical reality as studied in quantum field theory reveal an intrinsic relationality even of electrons and photons, demonstrating that the breadth of ontological relationality reaches beyond what we might expect.

Limits of Physical Science

Not infrequently, scientists addressing a popular audience are known to make claims about the origin of the universe. More will be said about this later, but it is important to note that claims of origin, meaning, and purpose of the universe are not within the domain of the natural sciences. Instead, these are within the realms of metaphysics, philosophy, and/or theology, and for the Christian are taught in Scripture, God as Creator being the Origin of all things. Such questions are not subject to empirical studies. The Big Bang Theory, for example, is not a theory of the *origin* of the universe, but only of its *history*, back to 10^{-43} seconds.[15] This history

13. Jennifer Powell McNutt, "The Mirror of Creation: An Unfailing Witness in Scripture and in the Theology of John Calvin," presented at "Exploring Creation," a conference of the American Scientific Affiliation, Wheaton College, 22 July 2019.

14. W. Ross Hastings, *Echoes of Coinherence: Trinitarian Theology and Science Together* (Eugene, OR: Cascade Books, 2017).

15. It is worthwhile pointing out that in the actual history of cosmology, the Christian priest Georges Lemaître was the first to propose the Big Bang Theory, and atheist physicist Fred Hoyle initially rejected it, not on scientific grounds, but due to it

is very well understood through multiple independent converging lines of evidence, but cannot be traced back to an extrapolated "time zero." Even less can the theory be used to obtain information to address the ultimate question of the origin or source of the universe. Science can only interrogate the universe from within the universe; it cannot address the coming-to-be of the universe itself. It is also important to remember that God created the universe neither at some moment in time nor at some location within space. Instead, as part of his creation of the universe, time was one of God's creations, along with space itself; in fact, God created both space and time. The deep connection between space and time is hinted at in the ways modern physics works with "spacetime" as an integral whole.

That the limits of science ought to be respected was also pointed out by Abraham Kuyper. In a volume translated only recently, he correctly notes that "it was only special revelation that shed such indispensable light upon the weightiest issues, especially those involving the origin, government, and destiny of all things."[16] Kuyper writes,

> To the extent that results are governed by factual observation, obtained by weighing and measuring and counting, all scientific researchers are equal. As soon as people move above this lower kind of science, however, to higher forms of science, at that point the personal subject makes a contribution, in terms of which the difference between the "natural" man and the "spiritual" man comes into play. This phenomenon is definitely not restricted to the science of theology, but is present in every spiritual science, including the philosophical framework for the natural sciences.[17]

Further, "all investigators can work together in those studies done outside subjective differences, but [believers and nonbelievers] must separate and go their own ways as soon as their study focuses on the spiritual sciences and on the higher scientific summary of the totality."[18] And finally,

> science fails as soon as it attempts to penetrate from the observable to the spiritual background of reality, and from the acquired data proceeds to attempt to build an entire construct. It puts forth with great fanfare what appears in God's light to be foolishness, that is, in conflict with essentiality and reality.... [R]esistance [must be] mounted

sounding too much like Genesis.

16. Abraham Kuyper, *Wisdom & Wonder: Common Grace in Science & Art* (Grand Rapids, MI: Christian's Library Press, 2011), 82.
17. Kuyper, *Wisdom & Wonder*, 79.
18. Kuyper, *Wisdom & Wonder*, 92.

> against the inclination to subject the spiritual sciences to the methods of the natural sciences.[19]

In short, one of the ways we take God seriously in physics is to properly recognize the limits of the discipline. For Kuyper, physical science is a "lower kind of science," in which "all investigators" can work together. More will be said about this in the discussion on methodological naturalism below. Physics cannot study the "origin, government, and destiny of all things," and physics methods are unsuited for studying the "higher" sciences, because in those the "personal subject" and the "spiritual background of reality" are involved. The movement of metaphysics out of the natural sciences proper is thus an appropriate advance.

One misconception worth addressing in terms of the limits of physical science is the idea that certain developments in science can be minimized as being only theoretical. One might say, for example, "The Big Bang is just a theory, and is not proven!" Indeed, in everyday human speech, "theory" usually refers to any individual's guess, idea, whim, or notion. But quite unlike that popular usage, in the language of the natural sciences, a "theory" is a particularly rigorous claim that has been extremely well supported by converging lines of evidence coming from multiple independent lines of inquiry and a wide range of research teams. Furthermore, theories in science are never proven. Proof is done in mathematics and logic, but in science one cannot get beyond significant evidential support. However entrenched a theory is, it remains a main goal of all science to find (and solve) problems within existing theories.[20] Disproving the Big Bang Theory, for example, would (after being subjected to rigorous peer evaluation) represent a significant advance in cosmology and be worthy of great acclamation.

Taking Creation Seriously in Physics

The Apostles' Creed begins: "I believe in God the Father, Creator of heaven and earth." Due to the creative activity of the Creator, created reality is real; it really exists. We acknowledge the legitimacy of sense experience. God has created a world, including us humans, and has intentionally endowed us with the capacity to have legitimate sensory experience of the world. This counters the pagan idea of brains-in-a-vat being fed false sensory impressions, and is connected with the concepts of realism, *imago Dei*, and God's goodness and common grace. All scientists, especially Christians, should be deeply concerned with faithfully

19. Kuyper, *Wisdom & Wonder*, 91.
20. Thomas Kuhn, *The Structure of Scientific Revolutions*, 3rd ed. (Chicago, IL: The University of Chicago Press, 1996).

investigating reality, through diligent discovery and honest and accurate descriptions and explanations of what is actually there.

Senses: Indirect Experience

The Christian who is a scientist has in the doctrine of creation further support than just the evidence of her senses that the things being studied are not mere mental constructs or sense impressions. Jesus Christ and the Apostle John clearly affirm and endorse the value of our senses. In John 20:27 (NIV) we read: "[Jesus] said to Thomas, 'Put your *finger* here; *see* my hands. Reach out your *hand* and put it into my side. Stop doubting and believe.'" I John 1:1–3a (NIV) tells us: "That which was from the beginning, which we have *heard*, which we have *seen with our eyes*, which we have *looked at* and *our hands have touched*—this we proclaim concerning the Word of life. The life *appeared*; we have *seen* it and testify to it, and we proclaim to you the eternal life, which was with the Father and has *appeared* to us. We proclaim to you what we have *seen* and *heard*, so that you also may have fellowship with us." The sacraments, with their water, wine, and bread, are Biblical endorsements of the physical as well as affirmations of the senses of touch, sight, taste, and smell, as they complement the hearing of God's word as means of grace in and through the church. Our world is not a world of mere ideas and appearances, as Gnosticism and Docetism would have it.

In everyday thought and speech, we often express our connection to reality as though it were direct perception: "That is obviously a tree in the yard." But we most certainly do *not* have direct access to the world. Our senses are the indispensable portals through which the world is known to us. Our experience of the physical world and our place in it is mediated through physical interaction, picked up by our senses of sight, touch, hearing, smell, taste, and proprioception. Neuroscience and psychology include descriptions and explanations of how our senses result in our mental perceptions.

The sense of *sight* is primary in the physical sciences. Tycho Brahe made two decades of meticulous naked-eye observations of stars and planets, recording angles and times, allowing Johannes Kepler to quantitatively develop and confirm his models of elliptical planetary motion. Significant advances have occurred in recent centuries as we extended our visual senses using telescopes and microscopes, first remaining in the human-visible portion of the electromagnetic spectrum and then expanding that to wavelengths and frequencies many orders of magnitude (powers of 10) beyond the visible, spanning the range from gamma rays to radio waves. Using microscopes we can see "Brownian motion" in which particles from long dead pollen (apparently) randomly move about in water, explained 78 years after Brown's 1827 observations (and 120 years after Ingenhousz's 1785 report on the motion of coal particles on the surface of alcohol) by Einstein as being due to their getting jostled about by invisible water molecules, thus giving significant (and of course indirect) confirmation of the kinetic-molecular theory of matter.[21] In 1986, the Hubble Space Telescope showed from its orbit around the earth that what was until then thought of as empty space actually contains hundreds of billions of galaxies. And the ongoing Kepler Mission, by examining periodic shifts in wavelengths and brightnesses of stars, has found that most stars in our Milky Way Galaxy have at least one planet. These observations significantly deepen the senses of wonder, insignificance, and gratitude for God's care for us expressed millennia ago in David's Psalm 8. Truly "The heavens declare the glory of God" (Ps. 19:1a, NIV).

Our sense of *touch* is extended by probing deep within materials, and then progressing deeper yet into atoms, nuclei, and even protons and neutrons using high-energy beams of electrons, protons, neutrons, muons, and other particles. We examine the way these beams transmit, reflect, and scatter to learn details about small-scale structures. In 1989, IBM used a scanning tunneling microscope to precisely position individual atoms to spell out its name. Atomic force microscopes "touch" atoms and their electron density waves to produce a visual map, and the same is done for chemical bonds in individual molecules. Our sense of touch is further extended into probing the vibration patterns resulting from earthquakes to develop working models of earth's crust, mantle, core, etc. We detect neutrinos coming from the sun and from elsewhere in space including especially supernovae (exploding stars). And starting in 2015, the relative vibrations of sets of perpendicular 4-km long laser pathways (the Laser Interferometer Gravitational-Wave Observatory, LIGO) have been able to "feel" extremely tiny wiggles rippling out into the fabric of spacetime itself from remote collisions of black holes with one another (dozens of times the mass of our sun),[22] of neutron stars, and more as this new astrophysical window into the universe opens up.

Einstein's 1915 general theory of relativity describes gravity as a consequence of the bending of spacetime by the presence of mass and energy. A black hole is a region of space with gravity so strong that even light cannot escape from within its event horizon (the point of no return). For a number of decades we have had several types of ob-

21. American Physical Society, "August 1827: Robert Brown and Molecular Motion in a Pollen-filled Puddle," *APS News* 25, no. 8 (Aug./Sept. 2016): 2–3.

22. B.P. Abbott et al., "Observation of Gravitational Waves from a Binary Black Hole Merger," *Physical Review Letters* 116 (11 February 2016): 061102.

servational evidence for their existence, including the motions of stars near the centre of our galaxy around an invisible source of gravitational attraction and occasional flashes as infalling objects were rapidly heated and swallowed up. Then on 10 April 2019, the Event Horizon Telescope Collaboration published images of a black hole,[23] as the team leader remarked at the press conference, "We have seen, and taken pictures of, a black hole." Many are under the impression that these are direct telescopic visual photographs of the event horizon. Of course, as noted above, every observation is indirect and mediated, including those via our senses and even more those using instruments to extend our senses. Furthermore, in this case, the iconic "pictures" presented were radio-wave intensity images of the event horizon "shadow," that began as four days of observations by eight radio-telescopes across the world, and were ultimately produced by aircraft bringing together the resulting huge quantities of data and supercomputers processing them intensively for almost two years using innovative custom techniques. Still, these images can be regarded as faithful representations of reality, far more so than artistic impressions of extra-solar planets that are occasionally presented in the news media.

Nothing is directly observed, but there is a sense in which observations can be more or less direct. Our senses—extended, quantified, and processed—are what give us access to the physical features of our world. We can be thankful for our curiosity, implanted uniquely into humans as a gift of God who created us with the senses, and for the earth's astonishing suitability as a platform for observation,[24] needed to develop and satisfy our curiosity as we explore our cosmos in its physical aspect. God's good gift of curiosity is in harmony with humankind's royal commission to explore: "It is the glory of God to conceal a matter; to search out a matter is the glory of kings" (Prov. 25:2, NIV).

Natural science is not simply an instrument to allow us to cope with the world and make predictions. It addresses the real state of affairs within our world. Our senses truly engage a created reality with at least some reliability, and God's good gift of human communal knowledge is worth acknowledging within physical science.

Critical Realism

But rather than simply asserting that our observations exactly cor-

23. Shep Doeleman, "Focus on the First Event Horizon Telescope Results," *The Astrophysical Journal Letters* 875, no. 1 (April 2019).

24. Guillermo Gonzalez and Jay Wesley Richards, *The Privileged Planet: How Our Place in the Cosmos Is Designed for Discovery* (Washington, DC: Regnery Publishing, 2004).

respond to, or perfectly describe, the world, we take the stance of *critical* realism. Critical realism in science is superbly introduced by physicist and priest John Polkinghorne in his book, *Belief in God in an Age of Science*.[25] An important aspect of many presentations of critical realism is the recognition of the multi-leveled character of reality, somewhat related to Dooyeweerd's philosophy. Polkinghorne's characterization of critical realism is well-known for the epithet "Epistemology models Ontology"[26]—"what we can know … is a reliable guide to what is the case."[27] Our knowledge is real, but never complete or perfect. Scientific models are increasingly verisimilitudinous, bearing an ever closer resemblance to the truth of the matter in a tightening grasp of reality. In physics, the special and general theories of relativity show that space and time are not as simple as we think from everyday experience. Quantum physics unveils a microscopic world that violates our cherished ideas of certainty and straightforward epistemology, showing that uncertainty and probability are real, as are collapsing wave functions, superposition, and entanglement. Polkinghorne notes that critical realism mediates postmodernism and modernism, "the adjective [critical] acknowledging the need to recognize that something is involved that is more subtle than encounter with unproblematic objectivity, while the noun [realism] signifies the nature of the understanding that it actually proves possible to attain."[28]

Diversity and Methodological Naturalism

The diversity in research teams reflects the diversity of creation, for God equips different people differently. David Chettle, a professor of medical physics at McMaster University, uses 1 Corinthians 12 as a manual for leading a research team: "A research group should work together as a team, although it comprises disparate individuals, each with her/his own needs, desires, talents and sources of motivation."[29] In addition to the benefit of improving the functioning of a team of scientists, diversity (in religion, ethnicity, age, language, disciplinary background, skills, in-

25. John Polkinghorne, *Belief in God in an Age of Science* (New Haven, CT: Yale University Press, 1998).
26. John Polkinghorne, *Science and the Trinity: The Christian Encounter with Reality* (New Haven, CT: Yale University Press, 2004), 79.
27. John Polkinghorne, *The Faith of a Physicist: Reflections of a Bottom-up Thinker* (Princeton, NJ: Princeton University Press, 1994), 156.
28. John Polkinghorne, *Quantum Physics and Theology: An Unexpected Kinship* (New Haven, CT: Yale University Press, 2007), 5ff.
29. David Chettle, "A Manual for Leading a Research Group," *CSCA* (2 January 2013), csca.ca/2013/01/02/chettle-research-group-manual.

terests, etc.) helps mitigate the possible ideological influence of a uniform background.[30] Stafleu notes, "Science is in need of many types of people, careful besides adventurous, conservative besides progressive, normal scientists besides paradigm builders."[31] Furthermore, Stafleu suggests that a diversity of worldview perspectives is actually essential in scientific work, arguing that because "certain world views are more successfully working in one direction [of research] than in another [...,] different points of view are necessary to obtain a fully developed insight into nature."[32]

Diversity of scientific research teams fits well with methodological naturalism. M.L. Peterson defines methodological naturalism as

> the idea that we should view science as a certain epistemological portal that we have refined over time and through which people of different religions, philosophies, and moral theories can make progress explaining natural phenomena by reference to natural causes.[33]

Thus methodological naturalism is used to define what (natural) science is. Taking creation seriously affirms some form of methodological naturalism (not to be confused with philosophical, ontological, or metaphysical naturalism, that purport that nature is all that exists, or that God is not involved in the world). That is, recognizing causality as real affirms the creation as real: creation is the creation not just of *things* but also of *processes*. These are the processes and interactions studied in the disciplines of the natural sciences in the search for and appeal to empirically accessible descriptions and explanations, without having to explicitly invoke the Creator in their *scientific* explanations.[34] Methodological naturalism was part and parcel of the theistic origins of modern science.[35] Hans Halvorson robustly argues that "theism provides a good motivation for methodological naturalism," pointing out that a number of objections to methodological naturalism do not properly take into account

30. Jitse M. van der Meer, "Background Beliefs, Ideology, and Science," *Perspectives on Science and Christian Faith* 65, no. 2 (June 2013): 87–103.

31. Stafleu, *Theories at Work*, 116.

32. Stafleu, *Theories at Work*, 157. The "four directions of research" Stafleu delineates are searches for objectivity, application, universality, and structure.

33. As quoted in Kathryn Applegate, "A Defense of Methodological Naturalism," *Perspectives on Science and Christian Faith* 65, no. 1 (March 2013): 37–45 (p. 42).

34. Applegate, "Defense."

35. Robert C. Bishop, "God and Methodological Naturalism in the Scientific Revolution and Beyond," *Perspectives on Science and Christian Faith* 65, no. 1 (March 2013): 10–23; see also Robert C. Bishop, "Recovering the Doctrine of Creation: A Theological View of Science," *BioLogos* (31 January 2011), biologos.org/articles/recovering-the-doctrine-of-creation-a-theological-view-of-science.

the character and limits of science.[36] It should be noted that, as discussed by Geertsema, methodological naturalism is consonant with a Christian approach to epistemology only if we properly acknowledge the limited scope and domain of the natural sciences, which is the position a Reformational perspective takes.[37] After all, I have already pointed out that science cannot be viewed as a total explanation of reality. Stafleu defines methodological naturalism as the claim "that supernatural intervention ... cannot be a principle of explanation *in [natural] science*."[38] Affirming methodological naturalism, far from implying that human knowledge is captured in its entirety by science, is simply a delineation of what science is. We know more than we can legitimately claim as empirical scientific knowledge. Each form of human knowledge takes its particular place within the epistemological enterprise.

Science, Scripture, and Epistemological Humility

When we take creation seriously, we note that physical science, and natural science in general, has a valuable role in helping us in understanding divine revelation in Scripture. This is because the Word is given within the world. In the context of realism, we cannot dismiss what we find in creation; in some cases we may come to realize that we had invested Scripture with a meaning that depended upon an earlier (now obsolete) cosmology. An example mentioned above was the shift from geocentrism. Given what we now know about the structure of the earth and the solar system, the passage "the world is established; it shall never be moved" (Psalm 93:1, ESV)[39] and the kenotic hymn's reference to "in heaven and on earth and under the earth" (Phil. 2:10, NIV) cannot be regarded as passages providing divine instruction that created reality is structured as a cosmos having a motionless earth as the middle of three tiers. Given our modern observation that the atmosphere materially consists of gases (mostly nitrogen and oxygen, along with a recently rapid increase of carbon dioxide) whose density decreases exponentially with height, it cannot be possible that Genesis 1:6–8 teaches that the earth

36. Hans Halvorson, "Why Methodological Naturalism?" in *The Blackwell Companion to Naturalism*, ed. Kelly James Clark (Hoboken, NJ: Wiley-Blackwell, 2016), 136–149.

37. Henk G. Geertsema, "Cyborg: Myth or reality?" *Zygon* 41/2 (June 2006): 289–328 (pp. 322–4).

38. M.D. Stafleu, *A World Full of Relations: Character and Meaning of Natural Things and Events* (2001), 262, scribd.com/doc/29057727/M-D-Stafleu-A-World-Full-of-Relations. Emphasis added.

39. Note that the NIV (2011) translation alleviates the tension: "the world is established, firm and secure."

is surrounded by a thin hammered metal shell (*raqia*),[40] though that is what most Biblical scholars agree the word means. This passage simply teaches that what the original audience thought of as *raqia*—whatever its true physical nature—was made by the Creator God. And so, advancing our physical knowledge turns the question of biblical interpretation back upon biblical scholars, who ought to take into account with appreciation our growing knowledge of what is found in creation in order to avoid misinterpreting Scripture.

A helpful stance for any academic is one of epistemological humility. Each discipline—including physics—has its limits, and the Christian academic must reject positivistic scientism which claims that every question worth asking can in principle be answered via the scientific method. Within this volume other forms of human knowledge besides the empirical are prominent. This affirms the breadth and depth of created reality. Beyond the scope of science are specific personal human knowledge (e.g. that my wife loves me) and most events in the remote past (e.g. miracles recorded in Scripture). Furthermore, scientism is easily shown to be self-contradictory: if it is true, its truth must be demonstrable by scientific inquiry, but as it is a statement *about* science, and not a statement *of* science, its veracity cannot be adjudicated by any method of science. Alvin Plantinga offers a sustained demonstration of the intrinsic contradiction between ontological naturalism and natural science while also showing a rich relationship between science and Christian faith.[41]

Science and Miracles

The most widespread idea regarding miracles is that they are violations of laws of nature, and those who believe that science has proven that scientific laws cannot be or have not been broken dismiss religion or religious miracle claims. However, this depends on the false assumption that human law statements have some form of autonomy and governing power over creation, thus conflating "laws *of* nature" and "laws *for* nature" that I have distinguished above. It also incorrectly assumes that "nature" itself is autonomous. Considering miracles "interventions into the natural order" ignores the Christian theological idea that God is intimately and personally sustaining the world by his word, and so it is incoherent to suggest that God intervenes in what he is doing. Ard Louis notes, "It is important to remember that [miracles] are not just 'wonders' (*teras*) for us to marvel at, but signs (*semion*) or works of power (*duna-*

40. *Raqia* is sometimes translated to avoid confusion as "expanse" or "sky."

41. Alvin Plantinga, *Where the Conflict Really Lies: Science, Religion, and Naturalism* (Oxford, UK: Oxford University Press, 2011).

mis). They occur when, to achieve his divine purposes, God chooses to sustain the world in a manner that is different from the way he normally does."[42] Chief among the purposes of miracles is their communication of divine revelation to humans within a specific redemptive-historical context. And Morris and Petcher engage the subject in a chapter with the chiasmic title "Supernatural Laws and Natural Miracles."[43]

Our analysis of God's "normal" working with the world in sustaining it allows us to discern patterns of regularity in its physical aspect that we articulate as our laws of physics. When, in history and in people's lives, certain events don't seem to fit these patterns, this may be a sign of God's special involvement, worthy of being deemed a miracle. However, physics (along with the other natural sciences) is incompetent to investigate miracle claims, since they belong to one of the many categories of human experience not subject to empirical tests of the nature demanded by physics. The best we could say from within physics is that perhaps a recalled or documented event might not have a physical explanation. The Christian physicist, knowing that the universe is subject to God and not to autonomous laws, will be more open to such a possibility, and the unbelieving physicist may be more doubtful but would still not be able to subject the event to testing. Along with Thomas Torrance[44] and critical realism, Reformational philosophy insists that the nature of an investigation must conform to the nature of that which is being investigated. Since miracles bear theological meaning and extrabiblical claims of miracles are likely highly personal, disciplines like theology and psychology—as well as the Church—ought to be consulted in assessing such claims.

Aspects of Science

In the media and in science textbooks, historical and contemporary scientists (including physicists) are often portrayed as being solitary figures hunched over a lab bench; instead, science is an irreducibly *human* activity. It exhibits and is subject to the full range of aspects as does any other thing in created reality. Natural science, especially physics, is a human cultural activity that aims to discover the laws by which creation functions. The subject matter of physics is the causal interactions

---

42. Ard Louis, "The Flawed Theology and Philosophy Behind Christian Resistance to Evolution," *BioLogos* (11 January 2011), biologos.org/articles/common-concerns-about-the-implication-of-biologos-science.

43. Tim Morris and Don Petcher, *Science and Grace: God's Reign in the Natural Sciences* (Wheaton, IL: Crossway Books, 2006).

44. Thomas F. Torrance, *The Ground and Grammar of Theology* (Charlottesville, VA: University Press of Virginia, 1980), 8.

(forces) between bodies. Physics as a discipline exhibits the whole range of aspects. While focusing on the Copernican revolution in astronomy, Stafleu's theory of theory (or meta-theory) applies generally to much of theory, especially in physics.[45] He details how physics is described by various aspects and norms (either directly or by analogy[46]). Consider the following summary points, in which many of Dooyeweerd's aspects are underlined:

- kinematic: "Because *theories* are characterized by deduction, their structure has a typical kinematic aspect, deduction being the logical movement from one statement to another,"[47] and "Prediction [is] the 'kinematic' function of a theory, to be distinguished from its 'physical' function, which is to explain [causally]."[48]
- physical: "A discussion (in a logical sense) has a *physical* foundation, because it is based on a logical *interaction* between arguments."[49]
- biotic: While *growth* and *development* are biological phenomena, we can speak of scientific theories as growing and developing by using these terms analogously. In this analogous sense, theories in physics exhibit a biotic aspect.

Work in physics is subject to:

- "the lingual norm of clarity and
- the social norm of evading offence…
- the economic norm of parsimony, and
- the aesthetic norm of harmony."[50]

Additionally, speaking of scientific theories in general, there are also:

- "juridical aspects of the use of theories: criticism and decision making"[51] and
- "the ethical principle of commitment."[52]

45. Stafleu, *Theories at Work.*
46. The technical sense of intermodal analogy is explained in Jonathan Chaplin, *Herman Dooyeweerd: Christian Philosopher of State and Civil Society* (Notre Dame, IN: University of Notre Dame Press, 2016), 59ff.
47. Stafleu, *Theories at Work*, 29.
48. Stafleu, *Theories at Work.*, 31.
49. Stafleu, *Theories at Work*, 29; emphasis added to manifest the connection between "physical" and "interaction."
50. Stafleu, *Theories at Work*, 186.
51. Stafleu, *Theories at Work*, 200.
52. Stafleu, *Theories at Work*, 216.

Respecting these and related aspects of science and seeking to follow the norms of human cultural activity within scientific practice are integral to taking creation seriously.

Taking the Fall Seriously in Physics

In the optimistic days at the beginning of the twentieth century, physicists openly proclaimed their confidence in the completion of the discipline's work. All that remained was to pin down various physical quantities, like the gravitational and electric constants, with more accuracy; a few more significant digits would wrap things up for good. This optimism, however, was abandoned in a few short years, as the early twentieth century gave rise to the revolutionary theories of quantum physics and relativity. Townes, writing in 1966, presents an accessible and relevant summary of these developments, concluding, "Scientists have now become a good deal more cautious and modest about extending scientific ideas into realms where they have not yet been thoroughly tested."[53] Physics, like every human enterprise, is a work in progress. We have neither universal nor perfect knowledge of the physical aspect of the universe.

There are some who believe that before the fall into sin, human knowledge knew no bounds. Kuyper's overly optimistic view of pre-fall human scientific knowledge can be seen in his *Wisdom & Wonder*, where he writes:

> In our current situation we can arrive at the knowledge of things only by observation and analysis. But that is not how it was in paradise. For we read that God brought the animals to Adam and that when he first saw them, Adam immediately perceived the nature of these animals in such a way that he immediately gave them names (Gen. 2:18–20).[54] .... Adam ... enjoyed a similar position with respect to the plant world, indeed, the entire natural world. We no longer possess that characteristic, that capacity immediately to perceive and understand the essence of plants and animals.[55] .... Adam would have arrived almost immediately at a knowledge of the entire creation if sin had not intervened. This knowledge would have led to a direct understanding of the entire creation in the context of its origin and its destiny.[56] .... Adam possessed a clarity, insight, and unity that we

53. Charles H. Townes, "The Convergence of Science and Religion," *Think* 32, no. 3 (March–April 1966): 2–7.

54. Kuyper, *Wisdom & Wonder*, 57.

55. Kuyper, *Wisdom & Wonder*, 57.

56. Kuyper, *Wisdom & Wonder*, 58.

> have lost.[57] .... Science was an immediate possession for Adam, but for us science is bread we can taste in no other way than in the sweat of our spirits, by means of difficult and strenuous labor. ... in that manner science has acquired an entirely different character as a consequence of sin.[58]

More recently, John Byl writes,[59] "The first man, Adam, no doubt knew quite well how God had created the universe." Even if we concede an intuitive superiority due to sinlessness, I cannot support such views regarding Adam's scientific prowess for several reasons. First, pre-fall humanity was already commanded to work, with verbs translated as "subdue," "guard," "serve," and "protect" that indicate challenging, strenuous, and diligent work. Second, there is no "science" without a *community* of scientists, with its methodological and technological advance required to supersede an inherently limited intuitive approach. Third, the God-given joy in discovery is missed with instant knowledge. Fourth, there are physical and biological limits to human knowledge (given its neurological foundation in the brain), which are not likely of the type to have been produced by the fall. Fifth, even if Adam received the revelation now recorded as the first chapter of Genesis, knowing *that* God's creation of all things is described by a sequence of divine fiats of the form "Let there be ..." neither exhausts knowledge of *how* God created nor settles modern scientific questions on the early developments of the cosmos.

Effect of the Curse

Traditionally, two passages in Scripture have led many to expect the fall, or at least God's curse thereafter, to have an effect on the physical aspect of creation.

The first of these is Genesis 3:17b–19 (NIV):

> Cursed is the ground because of you;
>   through painful toil you will eat food from it
>   all the days of your life.
>
> It will produce thorns and thistles for you,
>   and you will eat the plants of the field.
> By the sweat of your brow
>   you will eat your food
> until you return to the ground,

---

57. Kuyper, *Wisdom & Wonder*, 58.
58. Kuyper, *Wisdom & Wonder*, 59.
59. John Byl, *God and Cosmos: A Christian View of Time, Space, and the Universe* (Glasgow: Banner of Truth, 2001), 15.

since from it you were taken;
for dust you are
and to dust you will return.

Here we read, "Cursed is the ground because of you" (NIV). It is worth noting that the ground's curse is not so much a curse upon the ground itself (the physical material of our planet) but in what the ground will produce and result in for humanity, namely the famous "thorns and thistles" and the "painful toil" and "sweat of your brow."

The second relevant passage is Romans 8:19–22 (NIV):

> For the creation waits in eager expectation for the children of God to be revealed. For the creation was subjected to frustration, not by its own choice, but by the will of the one who subjected it, in hope that the creation itself will be liberated from its bondage to decay and brought into the freedom and glory of the children of God. We know that the whole creation has been groaning as in the pains of childbirth right up to the present time.

Here Paul speaks of "the creation" (and "the whole creation") experiencing "eager expectation," being "subjected to frustration" and in "bondage to decay" while "groaning as in the pains of childbirth."

The Curse and Entropy

It is not uncommon to encounter the idea that part of the curse on the ground and the whole creation's bondage to decay is the increase of entropy or disorder as described by the second law of thermodynamics.

For example, Bradnick argues that "entropy provides a feasible scientific explanation for the degeneration of nature in Genesis 1–3,"[60] providing as one supporting argument the universality of both the curse and the law of entropy. He affirmatively quotes R.J. Russell as noting, "if evil is real in nature, entropy is what one would expect to find at the level of physical processes,"[61] and presses further to claim a more than metaphorical connection between evil and entropy.

Making such connections between evil and entropy reveals a serious misunderstanding of entropy, in which one supposes, as Bradnick does, that "Systems are predisposed to proceed towards increased chaos and disorder."[62] Apart from the subtle but important differences between entropy (a precisely defined and measurable quantity) and disorder (an

60. David Bradnick, "Entropy, the Fall, and Tillich: A Multidisciplinary Approach to Original Sin," *Theology and Science* 7, no. 1 (2009): 67–83 (p. 73).

61. Bradnick, "Entropy, the Fall, and Tillich," p. 75.

62. Bradnick, "Entropy, the Fall, and Tillich," p. 77.

equivocal subjective quality), it is the failure to include the word "closed" or "isolated" as a qualifying descriptor of the system that removes all wind from the sails of the idea that entropy is evil. In fact, not all systems increase in disorder; it is only closed or isolated systems that have an overall increase in entropy. The transfer of heat from a higher-temperature body to a lower-temperature one is a classic thermodynamics example. The overall system including the two bodies increases in entropy, but, considered separately, while the cooler body increases in entropy (becomes more disordered), the warmer body decreases in entropy (becomes more ordered). If the increase of entropy is a result of the fall, then no heat transfer—such as the earth being warmed by the sun—could have occurred prior to the fall! In fact, since every physical process is subject to the second law of thermodynamics, overall entropy increase (along with local sub-system entropy decreases) has certainly always been occurring as a part of the good creation order. The only way to sustain the idea that the fall resulted in the second law of thermodynamics is to insist upon a notion, without any biblical or scientific support, of an unfathomable chasm of utter discontinuity from pre- to post-fall worlds, so that the objects (such as stars) in the pre-fall world are thoroughly unrelated to those of the post-fall world.

The Curse and Natural Evil

A second candidate for evidence of the fall on creation itself is what is sometimes called "natural evil." In the physical world, this includes events such as volcanoes, earthquakes, meteorites, floods, storms, asteroid impacts, tsunamis, solar flares, and nuclear radiation. As this chapter is on physical science, which does not include biology, I will restrict discussion of natural evil to "physical evil" only. There is no doubt that many of these types of events have caused and continue to cause death, destruction, disease, and disruption in humans and human communities. Such suffering is rightly acknowledged as part of our general sense that things in this fallen world are not as they ought to be. And the Christian hope includes a restored world where all things are set to rights. But it is difficult to justify an assumption that the physical events in and of themselves are a consequence of the fall and the curse, for two basic reasons: events like these predate the fall, and they have been used positively by God in the formation of our wondrous planet and cosmos.

According to the scientific picture of earth history, the geological (and biological) diversity we experience is due in large part to its seismic activity. This diversity is readily considered to be a signpost of God's good creation. The beautiful islands of Hawaii have a detailed chronological formation history, being built up of lava through the forty million years of the Pacific Plate's movement to the northwest over a volcanic "hot spot." The Nile River's annual flooding has since ancient times produced an agriculturally fertile valley and delta. Many genetic mutations are caused by nuclear radiation, and they can result in cancer or produce minor variations resulting in adaptation and diversification.[63] In terms of timing, we have fossil evidence of cancer predating modern humans and our fall. In addition, the same nuclear processes occur within the sun and stars throughout the universe, and the light we see from most of those stars has been travelling toward us for millions and billions of years. In fact, God speaks to Job out of the whirlwind, identifying his creative power shown in hail, thunder, lightning, snow, ice, and floods (Job 38; see also Psalm 29).

Thus, the curse does not mean that physical events are in themselves evil. This is perhaps a variation upon Al Wolters's idea of structure and direction.[64] The events, processes, and patterns of the natural world can be directed toward positive or negative results in terms of their human impact. In Wolters's analysis, the direction is usually the result of some form of human agency, usually by way of a sinful choice; in cases of physical evil, however, this is not often the case. A volcano can produce spectacular new landforms and thriving habitats, and it can result in terror and loss for humans.

A particularly valuable way of understanding creation, fall, and redemption is offered by Nicholas Wolterstorff in terms of human flourishing and *shalom*.[65] Each person has four basic relationships: with God, with self, with other humans, and with the non-human creation. Those relationships were created good and for our flourishing as humans. The fall and the curse result in the brokenness of each of these relationships, and our hope for redemption is in the restoration of full thriving in each. In connection with the concept of "natural evil," perhaps one could say that apart from the fall and curse, relations between humans and volcanoes, for example, were and would have remained harmonious in some sense. A possible picture of this is offered in C.S. Lewis's space trilogy. In a pre-fall scenario depicted in *Out of the Silent Planet*, the sentient *hrossa* even experience mortality without being "bent." And in *That Hideous*

63. The randomness occurring in quantum physics simply means that outcomes are intrinsically not predictable by us even if we were given complete knowledge of the present state of the universe, and it is not counter to the Christian confession of God's sovereign providence over all things.

64. Albert M. Wolters, *Creation Regained: Biblical Basics for a Reformational Worldview* (Grand Rapids, MI: Eerdmans, 1985), 72f.

65. Nicholas Wolterstorff, *Until Justice and Peace Embrace* (Grand Rapids, MI: Eerdmans, 1983), 69–72.

Strength, the manor at St. Anne's is a picture of our future hope of *shalom* (c.f. "the wolf will dwell with the lamb," Isaiah 11:6 NASB) as unexpected harmony exists between humans and mice: "Humans want crumbs removed; mice are anxious to remove them. It ought never to have been a cause of war."

Clearly humans do not at present live in harmony with the physical (and biotic) creation. We build homes on floodplains and mountain slopes without regard for the ecological impact of our action, and experience the natural consequences of floods and mudslides. In terms of the "thorns and thistles" of Genesis 3, we have fossil evidence for these biological realities long preceding humanity. So it may be not so much that these structures are now, as a result of the fall and curse, given the ability to physically puncture human skin and cause the experience of pain, but that our fallen disharmonious human response to such interactions tends to be sinful, including cursing, anger, disruption, lashing out, despair, etc.

There are other alternative approaches to the source of natural evil. C.S. Lewis was among those who suggested that Satan and the other fallen angels brought about natural evil: Satan "had already been at work for ill on the material universe, or the solar system, or, at least, the planet Earth, before ever man came on the scene."[66] And William Dembski writes, "an omnipotent God unbound by time can make natural evil predate the fall and yet make the fall the reason for natural evil."[67] Both of these approaches risk removing credit from God for the diversity and wonder of creation that "natural evil" gave rise to. Bethany Sollereder helpfully distinguishes the satanic fall, the human fall, and the cosmic fall, arguing that there was no cosmic fall, and provides historical resources on the views of Augustine and Athanasius as support for the idea that "looking for natural evil in a cosmic fall due to human sin was *not* the default position of the early church."[68]

Sin in Physical Science

Sin affects the practice of physics itself, as when unchecked we have a tendency to overlook, ignore, and suppress data or ideas we don't like. Sin is seen in the nature of some of the conflicts between scientists and other scientists, the general public, government, industry, and non-sci-

66. C.S. Lewis, *The Problem of Pain* (New York, NY: Macmillan, 1953), pp. 122—3.

67. William Dembski, *The End of Christianity: Finding a Good God in an Evil World* (Nashville, TN: B&H Publishing Group, 2009), 50.

68. Bethany Sollereder, *God, Evolution, and Animal Suffering: Theodicy without a Fall* (London, UK: Routledge, 2018), 14 (emphasis in original).

entist Christians. As in other areas of human activity, scientists are prone to pride and arrogance; we ridicule, spread rumours about and otherwise attack competitors or opponents, or we misconstrue the claims of science. We demonstrate unwillingness to listen, selfishness, and greed. For physicists in particular, arrogance is quite common. Physics is regarded by many physicists as the only valuable discipline of science, the only worthwhile human quest, the only way to certain knowledge. Ernest Rutherford, the father of nuclear physics, said, "All science is either physics or stamp collecting."[69] Ironically, he won a Nobel Prize in *Chemistry* in 1908 "for his investigations into the disintegration of the elements, and the chemistry of radioactive substances."[70]

Physicists are particularly prone to reductionism. At one level, this shows itself in the assumption that the search for ever smaller and more fundamental particles will be able in principle to explain everything in created reality. Rutherford, whom I have just mentioned above, correctly showed the gold atom to have a very dense and heavy positively-charged nucleus and a widely distributed collection of lightweight negatively-charged electrons. The nucleus was later shown to consist of protons and neutrons, and these in turn were shown to be composed of quarks. Determining the number and types of particles and the interactions between these and the other subatomic constituents of matter is an excellent endeavour and remains a valuable contribution to physics. But assuming that knowing the fundamentals means knowing everything is where this form of reductionism goes wrong.

Another manifestation of reductionism is the idea that materiality *is* reality, that all of reality is or depends upon the physical; this, however, is a form of idolatry. Clouser explains: "The teaching that nothing in the universe is self-existent forbids us from theories that reduce everything to X on the ground that everything is either X or is generated by X. Moreover, since Colossians 1 says that only Christ mediates God's sustaining power to creation, neither is anything in creation what all the rest of creation depends on."[71]

There have also been among public spokespersons of science a number of physicists who join with the so-called "new atheists" in ridiculing religion, including Stephen Hawking, Lawrence Krauss, P.W. Atkins, and

69. Quoted in J.B. Birks, ed., *Rutherford at Manchester* (London: Heywood, 1962), 108.

70. Nobel Prize Outreach, "The Nobel Prize in Chemistry 1908." nobelprize.org/prizes/chemistry/1908/summary.

71. Roy Clouser, personal communication via *ThinkNet*, 23 May 2014 (used with permission).

Neil deGrasse Tyson. Hawking, writing with Mlodinow, claims that science shows that laws can produce universes apart from a Creator:

> Because there is a law like gravity, the universe can and will create itself from nothing... Spontaneous creation is the reason there is something rather than nothing, why the universe exists, why we exist.[72]
>
> M-theory predicts that a great many universes were created out of nothing. Their creation does not require the intervention of some supernatural being or god. Rather, these multiple universes arise naturally from physical law.[73]
>
> [T]he beginning of the universe was governed by the laws of science and doesn't need to be set in motion by some god.[74]

As I wrote in my review of their book, it is clear that for Hawking and Mlodinow "these laws and theories function ... as an unarticulated divine self-existence and omnipotence, rather than human formulations of divine providential faithfulness."[75] They completely miss the simple fact that laws of nature can only work within the universe; these laws are plainly not beyond or outside of our universe somehow prescribing what must occur within the universe.

When individual physicists such as these make their raucous claims, they do so not *qua* physicists, but *qua* fallen human persons. To its credit, physics as a discipline has succeeded in defining itself more clearly, and metaphysical questions have moved to their rightful place in other disciplines.[76] To whatever degree they may have originated within the physics community or found a home in it or may be considered consistent with or founded upon physics, physical reductionism, ontological naturalism, epistemological arrogance, and the like are alive and well in the academy at large including physicists. But one does not find metaphysical questions addressed in the physics literature proper, as they are rightly not considered physics. This does not imply that unless they are empirically verifiable, events did not occur or entities do not exist, but simply that they are not within the domain of the particular discipline.

The more a discipline encounters the human dimension, the less

72. Stephen Hawking and Leonard Mlodinow, *The Grand Design* (New York: Bantam, 2010), 180.

73. Hawking and Mlodinow, *The Grand Design*, 8-9.

74. Hawking and Mlodinow, *The Grand Design*, 135.

75. Arnold E. Sikkema, "Review of Stephen Hawking and Leonard Mlodinow, *The Grand Design*," *Perspectives on Science and Christian Faith* 63, no. 2 (June 2011): 132–3.

76. For example, consider the journal *Perspectives in Physics*.

empirical and universal it becomes, and the more inescapable the human factors become. Theories of gravity differ vastly from theories of pedagogy and of interpretation. The best theory of gravity will be agreed upon by physicists regardless of their politics, economics, religion, gender, and ethnicity. But approaches to physics education will vary significantly depending on the socioeconomic standing of the school, the general philosophy of education in the region, the background and motivations of the teacher, etc. The fact that physics *per se* is universal can engender the false assumption that physics education is also universal. Pride and prejudice can blind our recognition that approaches which prove effective in one context will not simply translate to another. The consideration of philosophical, historical, and theological perspectives in physics is even more personal and subject to one's worldview.

The exaltation, and even the idolization, of natural science, as if it can be our saviour, is an idea sometimes promoted by members of the scientific community, but it is ultimately an illegitimate human attempt to displace the one true God. Everyone knows the world is not as it should be, and the gospel is the message that God as Trinity is restoring and renewing all things.[77] But many look to science and technology to provide the full solution to the world's most significant problems, not only disease, hunger, and climate change where science (along with technology and political leadership) can rightly be part of the solution, but also poverty, homelessness, religious persecution, war, and injustice. This is in part because of our failure to recognize the interconnections between the four types of relationships (with God, self, others, creation) that are all broken and need the gospel. Our broken relationship with our natural environment cannot be fully restored while we ignore our broken relationship with God. Related to the ultimate hope that many falsely place in science is a widespread idea that science is the only way to achieve knowledge, certainty, and confidence about any topic. Science indeed has its place, but it is only one part of our epistemological framework. Dealing with and preparing for global climate change or earthquake risks, for example, require not just cold reasoning via mathematical and physical-scientific models and blunt communication regarding them, but also knowledge and wisdom regarding psychology, society, politics, economics, and religion, as well as the passionate and committed transmission of knowledge and wisdom through creative communication.

77. Michael F. Bird, *Evangelical Theology: A Biblical and Systematic Introduction* (Grand Rapids, MI: Zondervan, 2013), 47–54.

Taking Redemption Seriously in Physics

Acknowledging Jesus Christ as not only creator and sustainer, but also redeemer, of all things (Colossians 1:15–20) can give the Christian in science great delight, confidence, and motivation. We can see our work in physics (and in natural science generally) as participating in the redemptive work of Jesus Christ. When the disillusioned John the Baptist sent his followers to find out if Jesus was indeed the Messiah, Jesus replied, "Go and report to John what you hear and see: the blind receive sight and the lame walk, the lepers are cleansed and the deaf hear, the dead are raised up, and the poor have the gospel preached to them" (Matthew 11:4–5, NASB). Jesus did not come to whisk people's disembodied souls off to a state of eternal bliss, but addressed both their present and eternal needs. God's good creation had been disrupted by the fall, and one day a new earth will be the place where God dwells with his people.

Consider a few illustrative examples of how physical science can be used to participate in the restoration of all things, keeping in mind Jesus's reply to John the Baptist and the fact that "God … gave us the ministry of reconciliation" (2 Cor. 5:18, NIV). We can be thankful that in his common grace God uses even the non-Christian to bring restoration to brokenness, and believers can take this as a deep motivation and calling. The development of the laser, originally a scientific curiosity based on obscure principles of quantum physics, is being used to restore sight to the blind. The lame are able to walk through the appearance of advanced materials and nerve-interfaced control systems, and there is significant new hope for paraplegic spinal cord repair based on biocompatible graphene nanoribbons.[78] Horrendous skin diseases are being studied and combated by artificial materials and molecular biochemistry. Piezoelectric crystal cochlear implants deliver auditory signals to the deaf. People whose hearts have stopped (which was for a long time the definition of death) are restored to life by the recombination of a significant quantity of opposite charges stored separately on the electrodes of a capacitor. Through the use of electromagnetic and gravitational theory, the monitoring of oceans by satellite systems allows the poor to receive advance warning of the possible arrival of an earthquake-triggered tsunami and its disastrous effects. In these and multitudes of other ways, the gospel is being preached through the use of science and technology. In this way, the redemptive work of Jesus Christ

78. I am humbled and grateful for the restoration-motivated work of my son; for example, see C.-Y. Kim, W.K.A. Sikkema, et al., "Effect of Graphene Nanoribbons (TexasPEG) on locomotor function recovery in a rat model of lumbar spinal cord transection," *Neural Regeneration Research* 13, no. 8 (2018): 1440–1446.

is continued by our participation in these advances, bringing shalom, wholeness, and human flourishing by addressing areas of brokenness. The structure of technologies based on physical science can certainly be directed toward evil instead of good, so discernment is called for. Also, receiving positive medical restoration is only part of the full reconciliation to God which acknowledges and trusts God as the great physician and healer of the whole person both now and in the new creation, not just of the body in this world.

Creation points everyone to its creator, as already discussed above in reference to Psalm 19 and Romans 1. This is true in all of its aspects, including the physical. Physics reveals deep, intricate, harmonious, and beautiful relationships, structures, and processes at all levels from quarks to quasars. Discovering, learning about, and teaching general principles (e.g. conservation laws, symmetry principles, interconnections between space and time, and unification of phenomena) as well as particular structures (e.g. atomic orbitals, face-centred cubic lattices, ferromagnetic domains, planetary magnetic fields, solar convection patterns, spiral galaxies, and superclusters) and processes (e.g. nuclear fusion, superconductivity, quantum tunneling, droplet formation, earthquakes, supernovae, black hole collisions) can certainly foster awe and wonder. While the Scriptures do not suggest that human recognition of the Creator is possible only through advances of science, the witness that our growing knowledge of the physical aspect of creation gives to the Creator reaches ever-increasing heights and is ever more difficult to suppress. And with the eyes of faith, redeemed by Christ, we are able to more clearly acknowledge, experience, and give voice to the praise that all creation offers to its creator. The physical creation responds to God's redemptive work in his people:

> "For you will go out with joy
>   And be led forth with peace;
> The mountains and the hills will break forth into shouts of
>   joy before you,
> And all the trees of the field will clap their hands."
>
> (Isaiah 55:11, NASB).[79]

God created and declared the world "good." For this and many other Scriptural reasons, Christians' future hope includes what we in the Apostles' Creed confess as "the resurrection of the body and the life everlasting." Christ was resurrected as "the firstfruits of those who have fallen asleep" (1 Cor. 15:20, NIV). His resurrected body evidently had physical

79. This is artfully explored in Virginia Stem Owens, *And the Trees Clap Their Hands: Faith, Perception, and the New Physics* (Grand Rapids, MI: Eerdmans, 1983).

features both similar to and different from those of his body prior to his death, and he was clearly not a ghost or spirit. So too in our bodily resurrection, there will be some mysterious combination of continuity and discontinuity, accomplished by the power of God (Matt. 22:29, Mark 12:24). Christ's bodily ascension into heaven, in which he brought into heaven our atoms and molecules of earth, signals a deeper connection than ever before between heaven and earth. The connection is ultimately established and consummated in what the Apostle John experienced in his eschatological vision: "the new Jerusalem, coming down out of heaven from God… God's dwelling place is now among the people, and he will dwell with them. They will be his people, and God himself will be with them and be their God" (Rev. 21:2,3, NIV).

An important place where we can see the implications of redemption for physical science is in a renewed research agenda for physics.

A Reformational Research Agenda in Physics

Research in physics proper, being subject as it is to the standards of the discipline (rightly including methodological naturalism) cannot have a particularly Reformational slant. Choices of topics and worldview assumptions can play a role in the researcher's motivation, but when a manuscript is submitted for publication and subjected to peer review, it is now one of the standard expectations of the discipline that work in physics *per se* be empirically accessible to the entire diversity of perspectives. It is valuable to recognize the distinction between the context of discovery and the context of justification. A Christian can agree that evidence supports a theory even if some of the people who proposed the theory or found the evidence did so out of an unbelieving motivation.

However, research on the connections between physics and other disciplines—such as mathematics, biology, chemistry, engineering, education, history, sociology, theology, and philosophy—can and should be more strongly influenced by Reformational perspectives. This is exactly as noted by Kuyper in the passages I have quoted above.

One of the key ideas of Reformational thought is its singular opposition to reductionism. In the physical sciences, much more work can and ought to be done in the exploration and articulation of the ways in which physics is not reducible to mathematics or biology to physics. Even the distinctions between chemistry and physics ought to be further examined.

Responding to Reductionism

Levels of Explanation

One of the ways reductionism can be critiqued is by pointing out the validity of science among the various legitimate levels of explanation.

In 1965, Frank H.T. Rhodes aptly demonstrated the existence of levels of explanation with reference to the question, "Why, I may ask, is that kettle boiling?"[80] There is a physical-science answer in terms of the thermodynamics of energy transformations, heat transfer, and phase transitions. There is also a personal answer in terms of someone kind enough to serve a cup of tea. The two explanations are sometimes described as scientific and "bottom-up" (the physics explanation of thermodynamics) and non-scientific and "top-down" (the desire for tea). These two causes neither contradict nor compete; instead they complement one another.

There is of course more that can be said scientifically, both by giving more detail about the physics, and by noting that other sciences are at play. These include the antibacterial effect of heating water for human health reasons, the efficiency of steeping tea improving at higher temperature, the way humans can tolerate hot beverages and benefit nutritionally from tea, etc. And it might be inaccurate to say that the desire for a cup of tea is truly complementary in not being scientific, given that desires are in fact amenable to scientific inquiry in fields like neuroscience.

Interestingly, many examples of so-called multiple levels of explanation actually refer to only two levels. It is insufficient to consider just top-down and bottom-up causes. There are many more things occurring that can be explored through a systematic philosophical lens, such as the social dimension of tea drinking and hospitality, the cultural positioning of the tea drinker, the economic and logistical factors of energy and water distribution and metal manufacturing. This brings the analysis of the one event of the kettle boiling more toward a fully-orbed and nuanced account, and we are thus less susceptible to a dualist top-down or bottom-up simplification. Instead we are driven to a *coherent* explanation: all the aspects of the event are interconnected and in fact cohere with one another because of the way our good and wise Creator establishes the world with its multiplicity of aspects: the numerical, spatial, kinematic, biological, psychological, linguistic, social, economic, aesthetic, and faith aspects, etc.

80. Frank H.T. Rhodes, "Christianity in a Mechanistic Universe," in *Christianity in a Mechanistic Universe and Other Essays*, ed. D.M. MacKay (London: InterVarsity Fellowship, 1965), 11–48 (p. 42). Rhodes attributes this example without citation to Douglas Spanner, though Spanner in his online book *Creation and Evolution* (2004; creationandevolution.co.uk/intro.htm) refers to this 39 years later.

On this perspective, for an event such as the raising of my hand, it is not just that the electrons and atoms and molecules are doing their physical thing making it so, and it is not just that my mind is instructing my body to act to make it so, but *I* am doing this, coherently, across the full range of aspects.

Emergence

Another criticism can be leveled against reductionism by acknowledging the reality of emergence. Emergence refers to a situation in which either a collective whole has properties not possessed by its parts, or a system undergoes a gradual development or a sharp transition that results in properties emerging that had not been present earlier. An example of the first kind, synchronic emergence, is the wetness of water: liquid water is wet, though no individual water molecule is wet. An example of the second kind, diachronic emergence, is a phase transition: ice has distinct crystal planes in particular directions, but the liquid water from which the ice emerged had a higher symmetry in which all directions were equivalent. Prediction is generally impossible: nothing about a complete study of a water molecule, prior to our observation of and familiarity with wetness, could have led anyone to predict wetness. Comprehensive knowledge of liquid water, apart from our prior experience with crystallization, is insufficient to predict the structure, much less the orientation, of the ice crystal. Reductionism, which claims that universal knowledge is in principle accessible by knowing everything about the fundamental constituents of matter, fails spectacularly. Further explication of such failures is possible by continued research on emergence.

The examples provided above are all within physics. Emergence in general is conceived much more broadly, including the emergence of life from non-life (relating physics and biology) and the emergence of the mind and consciousness from the brain (relating biology and psychology). It is important to remember the distinctions between synchronic and diachronic emergence. Thus we can plainly recognize the (synchronic) reality that living things are composed of non-living things; after all, the parts of a cell are not alive. It is a different matter altogether to assume that in the history of the earth non-living things naturally and autonomously (diachronically) transformed into living things, or to expect that an overarching theory in biophysics will explain abiogenesis. The problematic nature of emergence within physics is a caution against expecting too much in terms of explanation or prediction from such studies. A Reformational perspective acknowledges the distinction between laws for the physical aspect and laws for the biotic aspect, God's sovereign trinitarian activity in the world (both in history and in the present) to bring about biotic realities from physical realities, and the irreducibility of biotic laws to physical laws. On the other hand, many who espouse ontological naturalism expect that physical laws are supremely overarching and capable of bringing about biotic realities on their own.

The study of emergence in general has the potential to benefit from Reformational ideas such as idionomy, order of succession, anticipation, and encapsis.[81] Idionomy is the Kuyperian idea of "sphere sovereignty" applied to academics, in which each discipline has its own unique subjects and methods. Dooyeweerd's idea of the "order of succession" refers to the way in which something at one level has the necessary properties for the next level to exist and function. Anticipation refers to the way earlier aspects contain analogies to later aspects. And encapsis addresses whole-part relations at a philosophical level. Each of these are worthy of further study, and I will give a few remarks on anticipation and idionomy in the context of biophysics below.

Mathematics, Physics, and Biology

As I have already mentioned, one of the key contributions of Reformational philosophy is its opposition to reduction. Let me outline a few ideas on how this can be valuable in connecting physics with mathematics and with biology.

Mathematics is astonishingly useful in physics.[82] But physics is not simply applied mathematics. Mathematics can *describe* motion, but using mathematics to *explain* motion is fruitless. The cause of motion (or, more precisely, the cause of changes in motion) is in the irreducible *interaction* between bodies. Mathematics says nothing about observation, which is an *interaction* between a system and an observer. The quantum reality of the wave function, of wave-particle duality, and of uncertainty indicates that the microscopic world involves more than specifically quantifiable position and momentum: *interaction*.

Often the hope is expressed that if only biology would adopt the methods of physics, it would see significant advances, such as the development of mathematical laws. It is true that biological creatures have physical composition, but they are *more than* physical. This indicates that there will be biological structures and processes for which methods of physics are inadequate. Biological *function* is not something that physics

81. Arnold E. Sikkema, "Nuancing Emergentist Claims: Lessons from Physics," in *The Future of Creation Order*, vol. 1 of Philosophical, Scientific, and Religious Perspectives on Order and Emergence, ed. G. Glas and J. de Ridder (Cham, Switzerland: Springer, 2017), pp. 135–149.

82. Eugene Wigner, "The Unreasonable Effectiveness of Mathematics in the Natural Sciences," *Communications on Pure and Applied Mathematics* 13 (1960): 1–14.

can assess; Kauffman, for example, has pointed out that while the heart has many physical effects, deciding which one is its function is a biological assessment.[83] Function simply does not play a role in physics.

It is also true that biological systems follow thermodynamic and other physical laws. However, unlike most purely physical systems, biological creatures do not tend toward equilibrium. Their being subject to physical laws while going beyond them is analogous to the agential way in which the players of a game of chess obey its rules with strategy, prediction, and creativity. Biological creatures are subject to physical laws, but they are also subject to biotic laws.[84] Biotic and physical laws are interconnected to varying degrees. A striking example is the detailed way in which many of the genetic mutations that occur in evolutionary variation (e.g. the rapid changes in viruses, such as in the COVID-19 pandemic) are triggered by quantum events; early evidence of this was given in terms of the spatial and numerical features of genes and the temperature-dependence of the stability of genetic information as described by Erwin Schrödinger, one of the developers of quantum theory in the 1920s.[85]

Many biological creatures exhibit agency, in which one action among a set of possibilities is taken in response to environmental conditions. Clearly, physical reality is of such a nature that biological agency is possible. In Dooyeweerd's schema, this is related to "order of succession." The physical reality is the "substratum" of the biotic.

Still, we need to say more than that the physical world has the properties necessary for the biotic world to exist and have its properties. It is as though a world that has the physical properties of our world but not yet its biotic properties is incomplete without the biotic world. To that end, teleologically, it brims with possibilities for further development by God in bringing the biotic realities into being, not unlike the creation fiat of Genesis 1:20, "Let the waters teem with swarms of living creatures" (NASB). All of this seems to be implied in Dooyeweerd's notions of anticipation and the "opening process." Since "*anticipations* are expressions of a particular aspect within a later one,"[86] one might say that the physical aspect in some sense contains, or looks ahead to, the biotic aspect.

Klapwijk writes, "a believer has good reason to confess that the id-

83. Stuart A. Kauffman, *Reinventing the Sacred: A New View of Science, Reason, and Religion* (New York: Basic Books, 2008), 34f.

84. Uko Zylstra, "Intelligent-Design Theory: An Argument for Biotic Laws," *Zygon* 39 no.1 (March 2004): 175–191.

85. Erwin Schrödinger, *What is Life? The Physical Aspect of the Living Cell* (Cambridge: Cambridge University Press, 1944); see also Krishna R. Dronamraju, "Erwin Schrödinger and the Origins of Molecular Biology," *Genetics* 153 no. 3 (1 November 1999): 1071–1076.

86. Chaplin, *Herman Dooyeweerd*, 60; emphasis in the original.

ionomy that we encounter in distinct levels of being … is, in the final analysis, grounded in … laws of the creator God. … [W]e see a world that is open to its Creator, [that] shows a fundamental receptivity to laws of a higher order …. The world of becoming … is responding to divine orderings."[87] That is, the fact that different disciplines have different laws (e.g. there are laws of physics and laws of biology) is possible only because the world depends on its Creator who establishes the lawfulness of the creation. God has made the world in such a way that through his word and Spirit he worked with the world to bring into being new kinds of created things in history. Created reality is not static, but developing. God works with geological processes on earth as he grows the Hawaiian Islands. God works with gravitational and nuclear processes as he brings new stars into being, forms and disperses the chemical elements through supernovae, and constructs new planets through their subsequent accretion. Sometimes this unfolding of the potentialities embedded within creation happens via the involvement of humankind; this Wolters calls *creatio tertia* in distinction from the natural processes of *creatio secunda*.[88]

A crucial feature of the world needed for biological reality to exist may well be its physical indeterminism, in which the direction taken by processes is not fixed, or determined, by anything in physical reality. Certainly within the quantum world, though starting with exactly the same initial conditions, any number of options are available, and the more we study such situations the more it appears that there is neither any way we could predict which option becomes reality nor anything in the physical reality itself that makes the selection. It appears that physical indeterminism is fruitful for biology because it is a feature of the quantum world, and the scale of biochemical processes (e.g. in neurons) is both small enough for quantum events to be important and large enough that macroscopic consequences can occur. It is currently an open question as to whether, how, and to what degree biological agency and other biological processes depend upon or even harness quantum indeterminism. But this possible connection between biology and physics is another example showing how the biotic is founded upon the physical but not reducible to it.

Physics and Relational Ontology

The physical aspect is all about interaction. Change occurs as a result of mutual interaction. Interaction is inherently relational. How things relate to one another affects, or even determines, how the interaction

87. Jacob Klapwijk, "Creation Belief and the Paradigm of Emergent Evolution," *Philosophia Reformata* 76 (2011): 11–31.

88. Wolters, *Creation Regained*, 36.

effects change. Many things are commonly thought to be intrinsically isolatable, with change occurring when they are brought into potential or actual relations of interaction with other things. This common conception, which we might call atomic individuality, is, however, a serious error. For relationality is absolutely integral to ontology.

We already know that relationships are indispensable when we think of human nature. One cannot begin to describe oneself if one is required to avoid all mention of any other person. Our very identity is fully integrated with our relationships with other people and social structures, our parents, siblings, friends, home countries, educational background, colleagues, clients, and employers, not to mention our activities within community, the establishments we frequent, the institutions we respect, and the entertainment and news we consume. In a very real sense, we *are* the full set of our relationships with others.

In his development of electromagnetic field theory in the nineteenth century, Maxwell had already recognized this about charged particles. Neidhardt writes, "The relationships between particles as represented by the continuous, space-filling electromagnetic field were an *intrinsic part of what the particles really are*."[89] Neidhardt provides evidence that Maxwell's intuition of such a connection between particles and fields was motivated by his thinking about human relationships. Torrance noted that Maxwell saw that, for his predecessor Faraday, "lines of force belonging to bodies were in some sense part of them."[90] Thus, in Torrance's analysis, Maxwell "claimed, 'in a scientific point of view the relation is the most important thing to know' .... Relations ... belong to reality as much as things do, for the inter-relations of things are, in part at least, constitutive of what they are."[91] This brings Neidhardt to conclude that, for Maxwell,[92]

> Central to the biblical understanding of the person is the *reality of human relationships as an integral part of what persons really are*. You as a person are not an isolated individual, like the Newtonian particle separated from other autonomous particles [but] are interrelated with others, your parents, your friends, even people with whom you disagree. These *interrelationships constitute the very stuff of personal* being.... [T]his deep appreciation led to Clerk Maxwell's development

89. W. Jim Neidhardt, "Biblical Humanism: The Tacit Grounding of James Clerk Maxwell's Creativity," *Perspectives on Science and Christian Faith* 41, no. 3 (September 1989): 137–142 (p. 140, emphasis in original).

90. Thomas F. Torrance, *Transformation and Convergence in the Frame of Knowledge* (Grand Rapids, MI: Eerdmans, 1984), 228.

91. Torrance, *Transformation and Convergence*, 230.

92. Neidhardt, "Biblical Humanism," p. 140 (emphasis in original).

of the electromagnetic field in order to describe particles as never separable from their interactions.

Thus in classical electromagnetism, we have an example of the integrality of relatedness within identity, echoing what is the case for human persons.

Quantum field theory, developed from the unification of Einstein's 1905 special theory of relativity and the 1920s formulations of quantum mechanics, demonstrates even more intensely the relationality of ontology. In this theory, interactions between particles are understood as being due to mediating particles. Electrons feel each other not directly but by the mutual back-and-forth emission and absorption of photons. For the simplest aspect of the interaction between two electrons, we have one electron emitting one photon that gets absorbed by the other electron. But this process could be repeated, or switched around in terms of which electron emits and which receives. Or, the emitted photon could terminate in the spontaneous creation of a short-lived electron-positron pair (a positron is an anti-electron, that is, the antiparticle of the electron) that upon their mutual annihilation could form a new photon. Or, one of the electrons could emit a photon only to absorb it again before or after emitting the photon that was absorbed by the other electron. It goes on and on, like a fractal, but more complex. Especially helpful in showing such possibilities are the famous Feynman diagrams, which feature interaction vertices and simple combinatorial rules.

There are clear implications of quantum field theory for particles themselves as well, not just their interactions. For example, for an electron to get from point A to point B (or even to remain at a point in space, given that as explained in relativity theory, there is no essential difference between uniformly moving and being at rest), it could do so without any interactions. But it could also emit and reabsorb a photon, or two, or three, or any number in any sequence of emission and reabsorption. And any of these photons could spontaneously result in the creation and annihilation of electron-positron pairs, and any of the electrons or positrons could be themselves emitting and reabsorbing photons, etc. But it is not the case that one of these scenarios occurs in a particular motion under consideration. In fact, every single possibility occurs, in what is called a sum over histories. This can be seen from the fact that leaving some out produces a different (and incorrect) result of the mathematical calculation (an integral, using calculus) that the Feynman diagrams represent. In its calculations, quantum field theory profitably employs the mantra, "Anything that can happen does happen."

This means that an electron is not simply a passive particle with which another particle may interact, since every kind of interaction is always happening even if there are no other particles to interact with. The relationality of the electron is built into the very ontology of the electron. The same is true for every particle. Ontology is irreducibly relational, at the quantum mechanical level, at the level of electric charges and fields, in biology with its highly relationally integrated ecosystems, in anthropology, and even in theology (in the perichoretic Trinity).[93]

These and further insights from quantum field theory are and will be instructive for our reflection upon the nature of relations between God, law, and creation, namely that lawfulness should be seen as being built into thingness. There is no inert "thing" upon which "law" acts, for the nature of a thing's relationships with other things is inextricably wrapped up in its very essence.[94]

Summary and Conclusion

The unification of disparate physical phenomena under the ever-widening banner of broadly applicable theoretical frameworks has been an effective goal of physics. Classical electromagnetism and quantum field theory were mentioned above as examples of this. A significant push in much of theoretical physics remains the development of what is sometimes called a theory of everything (TOE), understood most narrowly as one that describes and explains both quantum field theory and general relativity, the two fundamental theories remaining elusively incompatible. Understood far too broadly, as by Nobel laureate Stephen Weinberg[95] (for example), a TOE would in principle explain literally everything about the universe. The "standard model" of particle physics seems to have no more holes, though it is widely considered to feature an embarrassingly large number of physical constants that cannot be theoretically calculated but only experimentally measured. A significant reason for considering the standard model complete is the 2012 discovery of the Higgs boson predicted 50 years earlier, hailed in popular media as the "God particle" because it is responsible for the mass of every other particle. And there are suggestions that some versions of string theory could simultaneously contribute to a "grand unified theory" and require the reality of a multiverse, from which our universe is but one of an

93. Hastings, *Echoes of Coinherence.*

94. I first wrote about this in Arnold E. Sikkema, "Death of the Watchmaker: Modern Science and the Providence of God," in *Living in the LambLight: Christianity and Contemporary Challenges to the Gospel*, ed. Hans Boersma (Vancouver: Regent College Publishing, 2001), 97–108 (pp. 101f.).

95. Steven Weinberg, *Facing Up: Science and Its Cultural Adversaries* (Cambridge, MA: Harvard University Press, 2001).

infinitude of many that bubble up via quantum fluctuations. The multiverse is considered by some as a way to get around the implications that a divine being is responsible for the exceptional "fine tuning" needed to have just the right parameters for our Big Bang to have produced a universe fruitful enough to include humans. Even if the motivation of some for advancing the multiverse idea was to avoid acknowledging the Creator, Christians can work together on fleshing out the idea into a theory, identifying its predictions, and considering the degree to which observations provide evidence for or against the theory. In fact, a good number of Christians who work in cosmology see the multiverse as God's creation and therefore worthy of investigation.[96] Our human ability to make so much sense of the cosmos and the beautifully harmonious patterns evidenced in the physical universe are a testimony to the goodness and faithfulness of the Triune God.

In Dooyeweerd's modal scale, the physical aspect is flanked by the kinematic and biotic. While physics and mathematics have mutually benefited one another for hundreds of years, connections between biology and physics are only now beginning to emerge. Understanding the defining characteristics of these three disciplines helps detail their mutual irreducibility as well as their possibilities for constructive engagement, especially when considering the developments of modern physics. Furthermore, a critical-realist and model-oriented approach to the laws of physics can encourage humble epistemology and limited ontology, much needed correctives to rampant reductionist and atheist claims. Casting all this within a trinitarian, covenantal, and creation-fall-redemption narrative, in which Scripture as well as creation are taken seriously, provides a nuanced perspective that, among other benefits, offers hope for resolving conflicts the scientific community experiences with many laypersons.

QUESTIONS FOR REFLECTION AND DISCUSSION

1. What is it about physics that leads many, including Christians, to consider physics as the most fundamental discipline?
2. What reasons might you give against thinking of physics as particularly fundamental in and foundational for reality?
3. Why is it not appropriate to consider physics as applied mathematics?
4. How do you react when you hear public spokespersons for science

96. For example, Robert B. Mann "Physics at the Theological Frontiers," *Perspectives on Science and Christian Faith* 66, no. 1 (March 2014): 2–12 and Don N. Page, "Does God So Love the Multiverse?" in *Science and Religion in Dialogue*, ed. M.Y. Stewart (Oxford: Wiley-Blackwell, 2010), 380–395.

address religious and philosophical claims?

5. What motivates your interest in physical science?
6. How do you picture the effects of the fall on the physical creation?
7. How do you see the work of physical scientists in helping restore relationships of the four types (with God, self, others, creation)?
8. What role does the physical play in your eschatology?

HELPFUL RESOURCES ON FAITH AND PHYSICAL SCIENCE

There is a significant amount of academic and popular literature on science and faith, especially on science and *Christian* faith in particular. Many works address the natural sciences in general, and often interweave historical, philosophical, and theological perspectives. An excellent starting point for such topics is this accessible and scholarly volume:

Harrison, Peter. *The Cambridge Companion to Science and Religion*. Cambridge: Cambridge University Press, 2010.

The physicist with the longest and deepest engagement with the Association for Reformational Philosophy is M.D. "Dick" Stafleu, who has been a prolific author in its academic journal *Philosophia Reformata* since 1966. He provides an in-depth explanation of the foundations of physics from a Reformational perspective, as well as an explanation of Dooyeweerdian philosophy in general, with a focus on the first few modal aspects, in his 1980 volume *Time and Again*. Stafleu also provides a thorough analysis of the actual "on-the-ground" use and development of scientific theories by a detailed case study of the Copernican revolution in his 1987 book *Theories at Work*. He has also advanced his own approach to Reformational philosophy by highlighting the relational character of reality in his 2001 book *A World Full of Relations*.

Stafleu, M.D. *Time and Again: A Systematic Analysis of the Foundations of Physics*. Toronto: Wedge, 1980.

Stafleu, M.D. *Theories at Work: On the Structure and Functioning of Theories in Science, in Particular During the Copernican Revolution*. Lanham, MD: University Press of America, 1987.

Stafleu, M.D. *A World Full of Relations: Character and meaning of natural things and events*. 2001. Translation by the author of Stafleu, M.D. *Een wereld vol relaties, Karakter en zin van natuurlijke dingen en processen*. Amsterdam:

Buijten & Schipperheijn, 2002. Online: scribd.com/doc/29057727/M-D-Stafleu-A-World-Full-of-Relations via *All of Life Redeemed* allofliferedeemed.co.uk (accessed 10 May 2021).

John Polkinghorne became an Anglican priest and theologian after an accomplished career in theoretical particle physics, culminating in work on quark theory. The single most important book on physics and Christianity is his *Faith of a Physicist.* Tim Morris and Don Petcher, biology and physics professors (respectively) at Covenant College, provide a covenantal approach to science. Stephen Barr, a frequent contributor to *First Things*, is a thoughtful Catholic and provides a careful analysis of worldview shifts accompanying the rise of modern (twentieth-century) physics. And George Ellis, a Quaker working in cosmology, published a seminal article explaining the importance of emergence vis-à-vis reductionism.

Polkinghorne, John. *The Faith of a Physicist: Reflections of a Bottom-up Thinker.* Princeton, NJ: Princeton University Press, 1994.

Morris, Tim, and Don Petcher. *Science and Grace: God's Reign in the Natural Sciences*. Wheaton, IL: Crossway Books, 2006.

Barr, Stephen. *Modern Physics and Ancient Faith*. Notre Dame, IN: University of Notre Dame Press, 2003.

Ellis, George F.R. "Physics and the Real World," *Physics Today* 58/7 (July 2005) 49–54.

Networking and mentorship are very important to science students and early career scientists, and Christian fellowship and academic rigour go hand in hand with the work of the American Scientific Affiliation asa3.org and its Canadian expression, the Canadian Scientific & Christian Affiliation csca.ca , which publish a peer-reviewed journal and a membership newsletter, and hold local and online events and annual international conferences. Similar organizations exist in other countries, mostly functioning in the English language, including Christians in Science (www.cis.org.uk in the United Kingdom) and Christians in Science and Technology (www.iscast.org in Australia).

Bibliography

Abbott, B.P., R. Abbott, T.D. Abbott, M.R. Abernathy, F. Acernese, K. Ackley, C. Adams, et al. "Observation of Gravitational Waves from a Binary Black Hole Merger." *Physical Review Letters* 116 (11 February 2016): 061102.

American Physical Society. "August 1827: Robert Brown and Molecular Motion in a Pollen-filled Puddle." *APS News* 25 no. 8 (Aug./Sept. 2016): 2–3.

Applegate, Kathryn. "A Defense of Methodological Naturalism." *Perspectives on Science and Christian Faith* 65 no. 1 (March 2013): 37–45. Accessed 10 May 2021. asa3.org/ASA/PSCF/2013/PSCF3-13Applegate.pdf.

Bird, Michael F. *Evangelical Theology: A Biblical and Systematic Introduction*. Grand Rapids, MI: Zondervan, 2013.

Birks, J.B., ed. *Rutherford at Manchester*. London: Heywood, 1962.

Bishop, Robert C. "Recovering the Doctrine of Creation: A Theological View of Science." *BioLogos* (31 January 2011). Accessed 10 May 2021. biologos.org/articles/recovering-the-doctrine-of-creation-a-theological-view-of-science.

Bishop, Robert C. "God and Methodological Naturalism in the Scientific Revolution and Beyond." *Perspectives on Science and Christian Faith* 65/1 (March 2013): 10–23. Accessed 10 May 2021. asa3.org/ASA/PSCF/2013/PSCF3-13Bishop.pdf.

Bradnick, David. "Entropy, the Fall, and Tillich: A Multidisciplinary Approach to Original Sin." *Theology and Science* 7 no. 1 (2009): 67–83.

Byl, John. *God and Cosmos: A Christian View of Time, Space, and the Universe*. Glasgow: Banner of Truth, 2001.

Carroll, Sean. "Physicists Should Stop Saying Silly Things about Philosophy." 23 June 2014. Accessed 10 May 2021. preposterousuniverse.com/blog/2014/06/23/physicists-should-stop-saying-silly-things-about-philosophy.

Chaplin, Jonathan. *Herman Dooyeweerd: Christian Philosopher of State and Civil Society*. Notre Dame, IN: University of Notre Dame Press, 2016.

Chettle, David. "A Manual for Leading a Research Group." *CSCA* (2 January 2013). Accessed 10 May 2021. csca.ca/2013/01/02/chettle-research-group-manual.

Clouser, Roy A. *The Myth of Religious Neutrality: An Essay on the Hidden Role of Religious Belief in Theories*. Notre Dame, IN: University of Notre Dame Press, 1991.

Cohen, H. Floris. *The Scientific Revolution: A Historiographical Inquiry*. Chicago, IL: University of Chicago Press, 1994.

Dembski, William. *The End of Christianity: Finding a Good God in an Evil World*. Nashville, TN: B&H Publishing Group, 2009.

Doeleman, Shep. "Focus on the First Event Horizon Telescope Results." *The Astrophysical Journal Letters* 875 no. 1 (April 2019). Accessed 24 May 2019. iopscience.iop.org/journal/2041-8205/page/Focus_on_EHT.

Dronamraju, Krishna R. "Erwin Schrödinger and the Origins of Molecular Biology." *Genetics* 153 no. 3 (1 November 1999): 1071–1076.

Geertsema, Henk G. "Cyborg: Myth or reality?" *Zygon* 41 no. 2 (June 2006): 289–328.

Gonzalez, Guillermo, and Jay Wesley Richards. *The Privileged Planet: How Our Place in the Cosmos Is Designed for Discovery.* Washington, DC: Regnery Publishing, 2004.

Halvorson, Hans. "Why Methodological Naturalism?" In *The Blackwell Companion to Naturalism,* edited by Kelly James Clark, 136–149. Hoboken, NJ: Wiley-Blackwell, 2016.

Harrison, Peter. *The Cambridge Companion to Science and Religion.* Cambridge: Cambridge University Press, 2010.

Hastings, W. Ross. *Echoes of Coinherence: Trinitarian Theology and Science Together.* Eugene, OR: Cascade Books, 2017.

Hawking, Stephen, and Leonard Mlodinow. *The Grand Design.* New York: Bantam, 2010.

Hayhoe, Katharine. "Christians, Climate Science, & Our Culture." Paper presented at "From Sea to Sea … *to Sky!* Science and Christianity in Canada," a conference of the Canadian Scientific & Christian Affiliation, Trinity Western University, 12 May 2018. Accessed 10 May 2021. youtu.be/1GgcxlOegrI.

Henderson, Charles. "Editorial: Renaming Physical Review Special Topics—Physics Education Research." *Physical Review Physics Education Research* 12 no. 1 (25 January 2016): 010001.

Henderson, Roger D., and Arnold E. Sikkema. "Review of Alister E. McGrath, *A Scientific Theology, Vol. I: Nature.*" *Pro Rege* 30 no. 4 (June 2002): 33–35.

Horgan, John. "Physicist George Ellis Knocks Physicists for Knocking Philosophy, Falsification, Free Will." *Cross-Check (Scientific American),* 22 July 2014. Accessed 10 May 2021. https://www.scientificamerican.com/blog/cross-check/physicist-george-ellis-knocks-physicists-for-knocking-philosophy-falsification-free-will/

Jordan, James. *Through New Eyes: Developing a Biblical View of the World.* Eugene, OR: Wipf & Stock, 1999.

Kauffman, Stuart A. *Reinventing the Sacred: A New View of Science, Reason, and Religion.* New York: Basic Books, 2008.

Kim, C.-Y., W.K.A. Sikkema, et al. "Effect of Graphene Nanoribbons (TexasPEG) on locomotor function recovery in a rat model of lumbar spinal cord transection." *Neural Regeneration Research* 13 no. 8 (2018): 1440–1446.

Klapwijk, Jacob. "Creation Belief and the Paradigm of Emergent Evolution." *Philosophia Reformata* 76 (2011): 11–31.

Kuhn, Thomas. *The Structure of Scientific Revolutions.* 3rd ed. Chicago, IL: The University of Chicago Press, 1996.

Kuyper, Abraham. *Wisdom & Wonder: Common Grace in Science & Art.* Translated by Nelson Kloosterman. Grand Rapids, MI: Christian's Library Press, 2011.

Lewis, C.S. *The Problem of Pain.* New York, NY: Macmillan, 1953.

Louis, Ard. "The Flawed Theology and Philosophy Behind Christian Resistance to Evolution." *BioLogos* (11 January 2011). Accessed 10 May 2021. biologos.org/articles/common-concerns-about-the-implication-of-biologos-science.

Mann, Robert B. "Physics at the Theological Frontiers," *Perspectives on Science and Christian Faith* 66 no. 1 (March 2014): 2–12. Accessed 10 May 2021. asa3.org/ASA/PSCF/2014/PSCF3-14Mann.pdf

McNutt, Jennifer Powell. "The Mirror of Creation: An Unfailing Witness in Scripture and in the Theology of John Calvin." Paper presented at "Exploring Creation," a conference of the American Scientific Affiliation, Wheaton College, 22 July 2019. Accessed 10 May 2021. youtu.be/2nLf69ZVAR4.

Morris, Tim, and Don Petcher. *Science and Grace: God's Reign in the Natural Sciences.* Wheaton, IL: Crossway Books, 2006.

Neidhardt, W. Jim. "Biblical Humanism: The Tacit Grounding of James Clerk Maxwell's Creativity." *Perspectives on Science and Christian Faith* 41/3 (September 1989): 137–142. Accessed 10 May 2021. asa3.org/ASA/PSCF/1989/PSCF9-89Neidhardt.html .

Nobel Prize Outreach, "The Nobel Prize in Chemistry 1908." nobelprize.org/prizes/chemistry/1908/summary.

Owens, Virginia Stem. *And the Trees Clap Their Hands: Faith, Perception, and the New Physics.* Grand Rapids, MI: Eerdmans, 1983.

Page, Don N. "Does God So Love the Multiverse?" In *Science and Religion in Dialogue*, edited by M.Y. Stewart, 380–395. Oxford: Wiley-Blackwell, 2010.

Pearcey, Nancy R., and Charles B. Thaxton. *The Soul of Science: Christian Faith and Natural Philosophy.* Wheaton, IL: Crossway, 1994.

Plantinga, Alvin. *Where the Conflict Really Lies: Science, Religion, and Naturalism.* Oxford, UK: Oxford University Press, 2011.

Polkinghorne, John. *The Faith of a Physicist: Reflections of a Bottom-up Thinker.* Princeton, NJ: Princeton University Press, 1994.

Polkinghorne, John. *Belief in God in an Age of Science.* New Haven, CT: Yale University Press, 1998.

Polkinghorne, John. *Science and the Trinity: The Christian Encounter with Reality.* New Haven, CT: Yale University Press, 2004.

Polkinghorne, John. *Quantum Physics and Theology: An Unexpected Kinship*. New Haven, CT: Yale University Press, 2007.

Rhodes, Frank H.T. "Christianity in a Mechanistic Universe." In *Christianity in a Mechanistic Universe and other essays*, edited by D.M. MacKay, 11–48. London: InterVarsity Fellowship, 1965.

Schrödinger, Erwin. *What is Life? The Physical Aspect of the Living Cell.* Cambridge: Cambridge University Press, 1944.

Sikkema, Arnold E. "Death of the Watchmaker: Modern Science and the Providence of God." In *Living in the LambLight: Christianity and Contemporary Challenges to the Gospel*, edited by Hans Boersma, 97–108. Vancouver: Regent College Publishing, 2001.

Sikkema, Arnold E. "Laws of Nature and God's Word for Creation." *Fideles* 2 (2007): 27–43.

Sikkema, Arnold E. "Review of Stephen Hawking and Leonard Mlodinow, *The Grand Design*." *Perspectives on Science and Christian Faith* 63 no. 2 (June 2011): 132–3. Accessed 10 May 2021. asa3.org/ASA/PSCF/2011/PSCF6-11BookReviews.pdf.

Sikkema, Arnold E. "Nuancing Emergentist Claims: Lessons from Physics." In *The Future of Creation Order*. Vol. 1 of Philosophical, Scientific, and Religious Perspectives on Order and Emergence, edited by G. Glas and J. de Ridder, 135–149. Cham, Switzerland: Springer, 2017.

Sollereder, Bethany. *God, Evolution, and Animal Suffering: Theodicy without a Fall.* London, UK: Routledge, 2018.

Spanner, Douglas C. *Creation and Evolution*. 2004. Accessed 10 May 2021. creationandevolution.co.uk/intro.htm.

Stafleu, M.D. *Time and Again: A Systematic Analysis of the Foundations of Physics.* Toronto: Wedge, 1980.

Stafleu, M.D. *Theories at Work: On the Structure and Functioning of Theories in Science, in Particular During the Copernican Revolution*. Lanham, MD: University Press of America, 1987.

Stafleu, M.D. *A World Full of Relations: Character and Meaning of Natural Things and Events*. 2001. Translation by the author of Stafleu, M.D. *Een wereld vol relaties, Karakter en zin van natuurlijke dingen en processen*. Amsterdam: Buijten & Schipperheijn, 2002. Accessed 10 May 2021. scribd.com/doc/29057727/M-D-Stafleu-A-World-Full-of-Relations via *All of Life Redeemed* allofliferedeemed.co.uk .

Torrance, Thomas F. *The Ground and Grammar of Theology*, Charlottesville, VA: University Press of Virginia, 1980.

Torrance, Thomas F. *Transformation and Convergence in the Frame of Knowledge*. Grand Rapids, MI: Eerdmans, 1984.

Townes, Charles H. "The Convergence of Science and Religion." *Think* 32 no. 3 (March–April 1966): 2–7.

Van der Meer, Jitse M. "Background Beliefs, Ideology, and Science." *Perspectives on Science and Christian Faith* 65/2 (June 2013): 87–103. Accessed 10 May 2021. asa3.org/ASA/PSCF/2013/PSCF6-13vanderMeer.pdf.

Weinberg, Steven. *Facing Up: Science and Its Cultural Adversaries*. Cambridge, MA: Harvard University Press, 2001.

Wigner, Eugene. "The Unreasonable Effectiveness of Mathematics in the Natural Sciences." *Communications on Pure and Applied Mathematics* 13 (1960): 1–14.

Wiseman, Jennifer. "Science as an Instrument of Worship." *BioLogos* (7 March 2019). Accessed 10 May 2021. biologos.org/articles/science-as-an-instrument-of-worship.

Wolters, Albert M. *Creation Regained: Biblical Basics for a Reformational Worldview*. Grand Rapids, MI: Eerdmans, 1985.

Wolterstorff, Nicholas. *Until Justice and Peace Embrace*. Grand Rapids, MI: Eerdmans, 1983.

Zyla, P.A., R.M. Barnett, J. Beringer, O. Dahl, D.A. Dwyer, D.E. Groom, C.-J. Lin, et al. "Review of Particle Physics." *Progress of Theoretical and Experimental Physics* 2020 no. 8 (August 2020): 083C01. Accessed 10 May 2021. pdg.lbl.gov.

Zylstra, Uko. "Intelligent-Design Theory: An Argument for Biotic Laws." *Zygon* 39 no. 1 (March 2004): 175–191.

A Reformed Christian Perspective of Engineering and Technology

Derek C. Schuurman and Steven H. VanderLeest[1]

Introduction

This chapter examines the discipline of engineering from a Christian perspective, more specifically, from within the Reformed tradition. Abraham Kuyper famously declared, "There is not a square inch in the whole domain of our human existence over which Christ, who is sovereign over all, does not cry: 'Mine!'."[2] The whole world is being redeemed in Christ—this includes the academy and disciplines such as engineering which are part of every "square inch" over which Christ is Lord. Engineering as an activity is part of the cultural bounty of creation, marred by sin, but reclaimed by Christ's redemptive power. We start this chapter by defining the discipline of engineering and outlining where it stands today. We then explore several important ways that the biblical narrative of Creation, Fall, Redemption, and Restoration frames our approach to engineering. Finally, we suggest some areas that merit further analysis and thought by Christian engineers.

Distinguishing Engineering and Technology

Engineering is the design of technology. Technology includes all the tools that you see around you: instruments, devices, gadgets, buildings, processes, software, and more. The president of the National Academy of Engineering defines engineering as "design under constraint."[3] Accomplished engineer and historian of technology Walter Vincenti defines engineering as "the practice of organizing the design, production, and

1. The authors would like to thank the Calvin College *Communitas* visiting scholar program for the opportunities it provided for the initial collaboration on this chapter. We are also grateful for feedback from a variety of reviewers who provided helpful comments and feedback.

2. Richard J. Mouw, *Abraham Kuyper: A Short and Personal Introduction*, (Grand Rapids, MI: Eerdmans, 2011), 4.

3. William Wulf, "The Urgency of Engineering Education Reform," *The Bridge* 28, no. 1 (Spring 1998). http://www.nae.edu/Publications/Bridge/EngineeringCrossroads/TheUrgencyofEngineeringEducationReform.aspx.

operation of an artifact or process that transforms the physical world to some recognized human end."[4] The respected engineering educator Billy Koen characterizes engineers as those who use a common method, which he defines as "the strategy for causing the best change in a poorly understood or uncertain situation within the available resources."[5] The technological products that engineers design are tools that serve practical means, including smartphones, nanotechnology, and space shuttles. They also include less obvious technologies such as wrinkle-resistant clothing, hammers, bicycles, highways, refrigerators, and espresso machines. We define a Christian approach to engineering as the human cultural activity of technology design with an eye on holistic considerations, transforming natural resources into useful tools, for the love of God and neighbor.

Some view engineering as a branch of science or merely "applied" science. Nevertheless, there are important differences between engineering and science. Frederick Brooks describes the difference this way: "the scientist builds in order to study; the engineer studies in order to build."[6] Charlie Adams, a Christian engineering academic, suggests that technology is distinct from science in that "Instead of seeking to understand what is already there, technology seeks to bring into being what exists only in potential."[7] The Christian philosopher of technology, Egbert Schuurman, suggests that the scientific method is one of "analysis and abstraction" whereas technology seeks a solution to a real-world problem that is not abstract.[8] Sometimes it is the case that scientific progress is stimulated by technological progress: the science of thermodynamics was preceded by the technology of the steam engine, the science of astronomy blossomed with the technology of the telescope. It has been suggested that science was granted cultural primacy in the era of modernism, and that pendulum has since swung with postmodernity towards favoring technology. "Certainly the view ... that science discovers and technol-

4. Walter G. Vincenti, "Engineering Knowledge, Type of Design, and Level of Hierarchy: Further Thoughts about What Engineers Know," in *Technological Development and Science in the Industrial Age: New Perspectives on the Science–Technology Relationship*, ed. Peter Kroes and Martijn Bakker (Dordrecht: Kluwer Academic Publishers, 1992), 18-19.

5. Billy Vaughn Koen, *Definition of the Engineering Method*, (Washington D.C: American Society for Engineering Education, 1985), 5.

6. Frederick P. Brooks, "The Computer Scientist as Toolsmith II", *Communications of the ACM* 39, no. 3 (March 1996): 62.

7. Charles Adams, "Galileo, Biotechnology, and Epistemological Humility: Moving Stewardship beyond the Development-Conservation Debate," *Pro Rege* 35, no. 3 (March 2007): 14.

8. Egbert Schuurman, *Technology and the Future: A Philosophical Challenge* (Toronto, ON: Wedge Publishing Foundation, 1980), 25.

ogy applies will no longer suffice."[9] Paul Forman, a historian of science, claims that beginning around 1980, with the global transformation from modernity to postmodernity, technology has replaced science in cultural primacy.[10] This shift is nowhere more evident than in the scientist's pursuit of usefulness in order to attract funding.[11] A more nuanced understanding recognizes that science and engineering are related -- not positioned one over the other, but more like "dancing partners" that interact in complex, dynamic ways.[12] Engineering uses the results of science, as well as other disciplines (mathematics and psychology to name a few) but its use does not limit engineering to mere application. Engineering has its own body of knowledge which includes concepts such as technology processes, design processes, heuristics, project management techniques, requirements definition, verification and validation techniques, and simulation tools. Engineering also has its own set of professional standards, its own accreditation bodies, and its own distinct goals.

The discipline of engineering has undergone tremendous specialization, branching into various subfields distinguished by the type of technology and tools. This reflects the normal process of *differentiation* which accompanies the unfolding of creation. Engineering subdisciplines include a wide variety of technical areas:

- Electrical engineers design devices that use electricity or magnetism, such as integrated circuits, communication gear, consumer electronics, manufacturing control systems, antennas, electrical propulsion systems and electrical power distribution networks.
- Computer engineers design computers and other digital devices, such as smartphones.
- Mechanical engineers design machines, thermodynamic systems for heating and cooling, automobiles, airplanes, engines, and robots.
- Chemical engineers design chemical processing plants, stain-resistant clothing, and pharmaceuticals.

9. Trevor Pinch and Wiebe Bijker, "The Social Construction of Facts and Artefacts: Or, How the Sociology of Science and the Sociology of Technology Might Benefit Each Other," *Social Studies of Science* 14, no. 3 (1984): 403.
10. Paul Forman, "The Primacy of Science in Modernity, of Technology in Postmodernity, and of Ideology in the History of Technology," *History and Technology* 23, no. 1-2 (2007): 2.
11. Forman, "The Primacy of Science," 11.
12. Steven VanderLeest, "Engineering is Not Science," *Perspectives on Science and Christian Faith* 64, no. 1 (March 2012): 26.

- Industrial engineers design complex organizational processes, such as a manufacturing line.
- Nuclear engineers design nuclear power plants and nuclear-powered ships.
- Software engineers design and develop computer software.
- Biomedical engineers design devices that measure or augment the human body, such as pacemakers, hip replacements, and prosthetics.
- Civil engineers design infrastructure such as buildings, highways, and bridges.
- Environmental engineers design systems to clean up the environment and analyze the impact of proposed developments.

In many universities, these differentiated branches of engineering often form their own distinct departments within the larger school of engineering. This specialization is further driven in academia by the need to publish novel results, thus pushing researchers into narrower niches of knowledge that have not yet been mined. Novelty can also drive specialization in a free market economy. Specialization is a natural and necessary consequence of finite humans trying to understand a vast and complex creation, or even a single, yet complex technological design. However, the cost of specialization is a fracturing of an overall understanding. When no one has a global view, not only does the design team miss opportunities for creative combination, integration and harmonization, it also makes it more difficult to identify (and thus avoid) dangerous interactions. As the discipline continues to differentiate, engineering teams should strive to maintain a coherent and holistic approach to design. The authors of this chapter recognize that we are also products of this specialization and humbly acknowledge that we cannot presume to completely describe the entirety of the discipline.

What is the state of engineering today? We can get one snapshot by using Google *ngrams* to compare the number of occurrences of disciplinary keywords in published books that Google indexes[13], shown in Figure 1.

13. Google ngram. Accessed August 3, 2021. http://goo.gl/4hwK5o/.

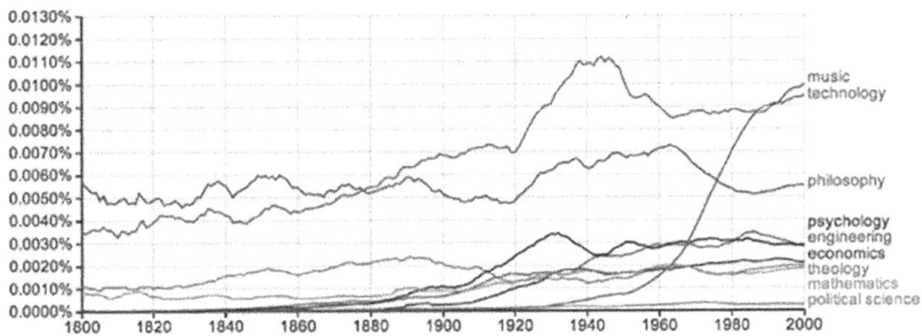

Figure 1: Frequency of select keywords in publications indexed over time

The graph readily shows that "engineering" is a relatively young term that has grown recently. The term "technology" is even younger, but has grown even more quickly. Although engineers may often think that technology falls within their discipline alone, others claim a share in this cultural artifact and activity, including scientists, artists, philosophers, politicians, historians, and media experts. Perhaps technology is like the other broad term in the graph, music: "Never forget that music is much too important to be left entirely in the hands of professionals."[14] Indeed, technology is a creational gift from God and thus a cultural good that all humans should steward and unfold.

Throughout this chapter, a practical engineering example—the electric vehicle—will illustrate the concepts. The design and manufacture of an electric vehicle requires a team representing multiple engineering disciplines: mechanical, electrical, chemical, computer, etc. It also relies on other disciplines such as business, psychology, public policy, law, environmental science and others. The electric vehicle cannot be simply discovered, as if it were a basic science; it must be invented by leveraging various sciences but also with creativity and innovation. As a technology embedded in our society, it must also be designed to operate safely in a wide variety of complex circumstances and environments. Through this running example we will demonstrate how a Christian perspective can inform our approach to engineering.

Technology and Values

The discipline of engineering has long recognized an ethical responsibility: the major engineering professional societies have all published "codes of ethics." However, these codes often speak only to the personal

14. Robert Fulghum, *Maybe (Maybe Not): Second Thoughts from a Secret Life* (New York: Ivy Books, 1993), 188.

behavior of the individual engineer, rather than examining the broader moral implications of the ends to which we focus our means. In the United States, the Accreditation Board for Engineering and Technology (ABET) evaluates engineering curricula for scientific and mathematical competence, but it also recognizes the social, cultural, and ethical implications of engineering. Despite this expectation, the authors of the book *Engineering and Society* point out that "as the technical content of engineering programs has increased, treatment of broader social issues has tended to be squeezed out. An underlying assumption has been that technology is value-free and that therefore any consideration of human emotions, needs, and aspirations is extraneous, if not irrational. Many engineering courses have been structured so that they avoid explicit value judgments."[15] This notion that technical artifacts are simply neutral tools is sometimes referred to as *instrumentalism*.[16] This problem is compounded by working in narrow disciplinary silos where it is easy to lose sight of broader cultural issues. The most challenging problems we face as a society are frequently multifaceted, cross-disciplinary conundrums. As more people become specialized, no one person, institution, or discipline seems to take complete responsibility or ownership for the wider issues.

Engineers always develop technology with one or more goals in mind, and these goals bias their design choices and are embedded in the final product. Furthermore, most modern technology is the product of a team of designers and developed in the context of a corporation. Multiple stakeholders all build in further bias to the end product. In his book *Technopoly*, Neil Postman writes, "Embedded in every tool is an ideological bias, a predisposition to construct the world as one thing rather than another, to value one thing over another, to amplify one sense or skill or attitude more loudly than another."[17] Let us consider two examples. The first is the microwave oven, which is not just a neutral kitchen appliance. It emphasizes efficiency in cooking and has subsequently affected how and what people eat. The second is the clock, which is not just a neutral device that tells time. It "is a piece of power machinery whose 'product' is seconds and minutes: by its essential nature it dissociates time from human events."[18] The clock has a bias towards the quantification of time,

15. Stephen F. Johnston, J. P. Gostelow, and W. Joseph King, *Engineering and Society: Challenges of Professional Practice* (Upper Saddle River, NJ: Prentice Hall, 2000), 544.

16. Nicholas Carr, *The Shallows: What the Internet Is Doing to Our Brains* (New York: W.W. Norton, 2010), 46.

17. Neil Postman, *Technopoly: The Surrender of Culture to Technology* (New York: Vintage, 1993), 13.

18. Lewis Mumford, *Technics and Civilization* (Chicago: University of Chicago Press, 1934), 15.

and it has fundamentally changed the pattern of our lives as we synchronize our activities according to the time it keeps.

A seminal book about technology through a Reformed lens is *Responsible Technology,* which notes that "each technological object, given its properties and capabilities, opens up some possibilities for interaction with both its cultural and natural environment, and correspondingly closes down other possibilities."[19] Author Andy Crouch echoes this idea when he suggests questioning not only what a new cultural artifact makes easier, but also what it makes more difficult.[20]

Furthermore, the bias embedded in technological devices impacts the surrounding culture. This impact, as the field of media ecology suggests, is akin to introducing new species into the environment. Postman describes this ecological effect of technology: "after the printing press was invented, you did not have old Europe plus the printing press. You had a different Europe. After television, America was not America plus television. Television gave a new coloration to every political campaign, to every home, to every school, to every church, to every industry, and so on."[21] Digital technology has brought about similar ecological changes: after the Internet and smartphones we do not just have the same world with these technologies added, we have a changed world. It is these changes to our lives and our world that demonstrate technology is value-laden.

Likewise, the electric vehicle is also value-laden. Like all automobiles, the electric vehicle is not simply a neutral tool for getting from point A to point B. Cars embody the values of individual freedom and choice in transportation (in contradistinction to public transportation). Cars have fundamentally reshaped our cities and neighbourhoods. They have separated where we live from where we work, worship, and shop. Cars also include a number of unintended consequences: pollution and traffic accidents, to name two. The electric vehicle may seem like a clean slate for a new design, but it must contend with the historical-cultural biases already set in motion by earlier automotive technologies. The engineering team and the automotive corporation make choices about the vehicle that embed a number of biases. Those embedded values include environmental aspects. With zero-emissions power generation, the electric vehicle can avoid atmospheric pollution. Even so, the electric vehicle transfers ecological impact from atmospheric pollution due

19. Stephen V. Monsma, ed., *Responsible Technology: A Christian Perspective* (Grand Rapids, MI: Eerdmans, 1986), 32-33.

20. Andy Crouch, *Culture Making: Recovering Our Creative Calling* (Downers Grove, IL: InterVarsity Press, 2008), 29-30.

21. Neil Postman, "Five Things We Need to Know About Technological Change," (speech, Denver, Colorado, March 28, 1998).

to fossil fuels, shifting it to the challenge of recycling a large lithium ion battery and other exotic materials. The infrastructure required to support electric vehicles (charging stations and grid capacity) is different from the infrastructure required to support gasoline-fueled vehicles (gasoline stations, oil refineries, and pipelines). The design of electric vehicles may be approached with different goals, for instance with an eye to improve range, safety, charging time, image or cost. Each of these design directions involves values, which impact drivers and the communities where they are used. These value choices also impact communities far from the point of use, such as locations where scarce minerals are mined or the environment surrounding a landfill where car parts are discarded.

Engineering and Technology: A Biblical Perspective

Christians developing technology have an important responsibility as they create the tools that shape our world, especially when their technological products may impact thousands or even millions of people. If it is true that "we shape our tools and thereafter our tools shape us"[22], how do we engineer tools that shape us in ways that are obedient to God? If technology is, in fact, value-laden, then how should Christian values influence the world of engineering?

Our Response to God

The book *Responsible Technology* defines technology as "a distinct cultural activity in which human beings exercise freedom and responsibility in response to God by forming and transforming the natural creation, with the aid of tools and procedures, for practical ends or purposes."[23] Developing technology in response to God is at the heart of the discipline of engineering. By God's grace, fallen humans are still responding to God as they create culture in the form of technological gadgets—even those who do not acknowledge their creator or do so unwittingly. We live *coram Deo*, before the face of God. Everything we do is a response to God, and our response can be one of obedience or disobedience.

We have suggested that technology embeds the values of the designer, but these values are shaped by a worldview. In essence, a worldview

22. John M. Culkin, "A Schoolman's Guide to Marshall McLuhan," *Saturday Review*, March 18, 1967, 70.

23. Monsma, ed., *Responsible Technology*, 19.

is a "comprehensive framework of one's basic beliefs about things."[24] A Christian worldview is one that is "shaped and tested by Scripture."[25] Since worldviews provide an orientation to the world, they give shape to our cultural activities, including technological development. The Bible is a guide for our lives, but how do we approach the Scriptures to inform us how to live obediently in the area of engineering? In the following sections, we will structure our examination of engineering around our response to God and the biblical themes of creation, fall, redemption, and restoration. Each of these themes has important implications for our work in engineering, as they do for other academic disciplines. However, we will not limit our analysis to this scriptural narrative—other biblical precepts will also be important.

Creation

The idea of an original, good creatin may not seem applicable to technology, until we enlarge our notion of creation. It is not limited to rocks, trees, plants, and planets. Creation includes everything that God has ordained to exist; "there is nothing in human life that does not belong to the created order."[26] This includes culture and the latent potential in creation for cultural unfolding, including technology. Furthermore, God continues to sustain his creation with providential care. The biblical creation story has significant implications for how we view and practice engineering, including the concepts of *imago Dei*, stewardship, and the cultural mandate.

Imago Dei

The Latin term *imago Dei* translates literally as "image of God." The creation of humankind is distinct from other aspects of creation because we are made in God's image (Gen. 1:27). What does this mean? We image God in a variety of ways including our ability to love, to relate, and to think rationally and creatively, to name a few. This has important implications for what it means to be human in a technological age. We need to reject materialistic reductions of what it means to be human; we are not simply machines, whose determinism would deny us both freedom and responsibility. Another important way that we image God is by creating new things. We are *homo faber* (man the maker), culture makers who unfold the possibilities in creation. In his book, *The Mythical Man-*

24. Albert M. Wolters, *Creation Regained: Biblical Basics for a Reformational Worldview* (Grand Rapids, MI: Eerdmans, 1985), 2.
25. Wolters, *Creation Regained*, 6.
26. Wolters, *Creation Regained*, 25.

Month, the computer scientist Frederick Brooks describes the delight we can have in making things: "Why is programming fun? What delights may its practitioner expect as his reward? First is the sheer joy of making things. As the child delights in his mud pie, so the adult enjoys building things, especially things of his own design. I think this delight must be an image of God's delight in making things, a delight shown in the distinctness and newness of each leaf and each snowflake."[27] Engineers often experience this delight that accompanies the design and building of new technologies.

Although made in God's image, human beings are still finite creatures. We are not God who is the all-powerful creator who can create from nothing. Furthermore, unlike God, human engineers cannot foresee all the implications of a design choice. Thus engineers must design with humble modesty, knowing they may make mistakes and they cannot predict all the impacts of their technology. Our technological work ought to be accompanied by *epistemological humility*, which can be defined as "a posture of appropriate servanthood and creatureliness with respect to our relationship with God and the non-human creation."[28] The engineer thus needs wisdom to discern the effects, good and bad, of her technological design choices, but also wisdom to realize that her knowledge is limited, leading to a posture of humility.

Our best picture of the true image of God is found in Jesus (Col. 1:15). To the extent that we become more Christ-like, we become better images of God who made us. It is difficult to imagine what Jesus would do with technology design and use. His first miracle, turning water into wine at a wedding, shows a caring for the physical needs of those around him, but also a participation in the joys of creation and the culture humans have unfolded in the creation, including the institution of marriage and the joy of fine wine. Jesus' ministry was both teaching and serving. He not only communicated the good news of the kingdom of God, but also healed the sick. Thus we might emulate Christ in our technological development through tools that help heal and serve our neighbors as well as bringing glory to God. To discern what it means to be Christ-like in engineering requires prayer and a knowledge of scriptural themes and principles, as well as a measure of "sanctified common sense" when determining how to practically live out our faith.[29] Finally, we can follow Christ by celebrating the creation while unwrapping the gift of technological development, which leads us to the next biblical concept with

27. Frederick Brooks, *The Mythical Man-Month: Essays on Software Engineering* (Reading, MA: Addison-Wesley Professional, 1995), 7.

28. Charles Adams, "Galileo, Biotechnology, and Epistemological Humility," 12.

29. Wolters, *Creation Regained*, 36.

relevance for engineering, the *cultural mandate.*

Stewardship and the Cultural Mandate

After God created humankind, he placed them in the Garden of Eden and gave them a mandate to "be fruitful and increase in number; fill the earth and subdue it" (Gen. 1:28). This is sometimes referred to as the *cultural mandate.* While this mandate has been misused as a license to plunder and exploit the world's resources, God's intention is for us to be stewards and caretakers of the earth (Gen. 2:15) while unfolding and developing its many possibilities.

Engineering is part of this cultural mandate. God granted us the basic materials and resources in his creation so that we could build technological products. Genesis 2:12 notes the presence of certain raw materials in the creation: "The gold of that land is good; aromatic resin and onyx are also there." Furthermore, God created humans with creativity and abilities that enable us to invent and develop technology to serve God and neighbor. Engineers must keep in mind the two goals of both tending as well as developing creation. A Reformational worldview calls us neither to pillage creation, nor to leave it untouched and untended; instead, it emphasizes that those working in technology are called to cultivate, bringing out the many possibilities in God's creation while still allowing it to flourish. This implies that sustainability will be an important consideration as we unfold the technical possibilities in creation. God created us able to respond to his call, and hence we have both freedom and responsibility in how we carry out this cultural mandate.

Dooyeweerd's Modalities

Dooyeweerd's modal aspects provide an ontological framework that can be a helpful tool for engineers. Creation is both complex and diverse, and these modal aspects can help people working in specialized disciplines to avoid the pitfall of reductionism. We can't treat everything like a machine or a technical optimization problem to be solved. Rather, we must see creation in a multi-aspectual and holistic way.

Furthermore, Dooyeweerd's modal aspects include both *laws* and *norms.* Certain physical laws are familiar to engineers: the law of gravity, Hooke's law, Ohm's law, and so on. These are based on the "earlier" aspects that we have no choice but to obey: the physical, kinematic, spatial, and numeric aspects. But creation also includes norms, areas in which humans beings exercise both freedom and responsibility. These are represented by the "later" modal aspects. We cannot choose whether or not to follow the law of gravity, but we can choose whether to follow the norm of justice. Prior work in the Christian philosophy of technology has focused on the seven highest Dooyeweerdian aspects of reality, deriving from them a set of "design norms."[30] These design norms are cultural appropriateness (historical norm), open communication (social and lingual norms), stewardship (economic norm), delightful harmony (aesthetic norm), justice (juridical norm), caring (ethical norm) and trust (pistic norm).

Dooyeweerd's modalities are a useful tool to help us remember the diversity and interconnectedness of creation. Engineers need to avoid focusing only on the earlier physical and kinematic laws of creation—they must be aware that technology is value-laden, and has cultural, social, economic, aesthetic, juridical, ethical and faith implications as well. Recognizing these aspects and identifying design norms can help engineers to avoid developing tunnel vision. The totality and holistic nature of creative design requires that we consider all the norms. They help us to contemplate the consequences of our choices in designing technology. These design norms will be discussed in more detail and expanded in the section dealing with redemption.

What do electric vehicles have to do with creation? First, creation embeds the latent possibility of vehicles, travel, and conversion of energy that allows stored energy in a battery to be converted into a rotating magnetic flux in an electric motor which, in turn, can be converted into mechanical energy. Creation includes the possibility of batteries, electric motors, semiconductors, and computers—all the components that are integrated into a vehicle. The cultural mandate calls us to develop technology, and that may include vehicles. Design of an electric vehicle requires working with sophisticated technologies, necessitating creativity and teamwork (two aspects of the *imago Dei*). The electric vehicle is not limited to its electrical and mechanical aspects, it has substantial social, aesthetic, legal, ethical, and trust aspects as well. The electric vehicle is also a provocative example of balancing two aspects of stewardship: that of conserving and protecting the environment versus that of developing new technology. Finally, the electric vehicle can also open up new possibilities, enabling us to travel with lower environmental impact so that we can carry out other kingdom service.

30. The introduction of design norms for technology development (based on Dooyeweerd's modalities) can be found in Monsma, ed., *Responsible Technology*. The design norms are explored in more detail in chapter 4 of Ethan J. Brue, Derek C. Schuurman, and Steven H. VanderLeest, *A Christian Field Guide to Technology for Engineers and Designers,* Intervarsity Academic Press, 2022.

The Fall and Engineering

Somewhere near the beginning, the human family fell into sin. The effects of sin are comprehensive and catastrophic, touching all areas of creation. Paul tells us that "the whole creation has been groaning" (Romans 8:22). Sin manifests itself in many ways: disease, death, conflict, theft and so on. But sin has also affected cultural activities and institutions producing corrupt governments, dysfunctional families, distasteful art (sometimes referred to as *kitsch*), and poor scholarship. It also has had an effect on engineering, such as technology that promotes injustice, disorders love, misdirects worship, or that is used for harm. Furthermore, there is the temptation towards *technicism*: putting our trust in technology to solve humanity's problems. Egbert Schuurman defines technicism as "the pretension of humans, as self-declared lords and masters using the scientific-technical method of control, to bend all of reality to their will in order to solve all problems, old and new, and to guarantee increasing material prosperity and progress."[31] To put our trust in technology is to replace the living God with some aspect of creation and to make it into an idol.

When thinking about the fall, it is also important to note that sin cannot create anything. Rather, it attaches itself to God's good creation like a parasite and distorts it. To better appreciate this concept, it is helpful to distinguish between *structure* and *direction*. Wolters describes *structure* as "the order of creation, to the constant creational constitution of any thing" and the concept of *direction* as one of two ways that structure is oriented: either toward God or away from God, i.e., "the distortion or perversion of creation through the fall."[32] Using the concepts of structure and direction further illuminates the value-ladenness of technology: technology is possible because of the possibilities latent in creation, but it can be directed in obedience to God or in ways that go against God's intents for his creation.

Although sin is pervasive, it is difficult to discern precisely how sin affects the physical world. When certain materials crack under stress, is this due to sin or is it part of how the good creation functions? Is the noise present in semiconductors or signal cables a result of sin, or is it part of the way things are meant to be? Just because material failures and noise complicate engineering designs does not mean they are necessarily the result of sin. This is yet another area where we ought to exercise humility; we don't really know exactly what the pristine creation was like,

31. Egbert Schuurman, *Faith and Hope in Technology*, trans. John Vriend (Toronto, ON: Clements Publishing, 2003), 69.

32. Wolters, *Creation Regained,* 49.

nor precisely how sin has distorted it.

The impact of sin also impacts our relationships with God and neighbor. Among other things, common grace reduces the impact of sin, holding back its full effects from completely damaging the fabric of our society. We see common grace in the codes of ethics used by engineers, which are largely aligned with Christian principles. The international agreements on standards of weights and measures are an example of common grace in action.[33] Cooperation around standard weights and measures helps engineers in their work and provides standards for the honest trading of goods. Proverbs 16:11 reminds us that "Honest scales and balances belong to the Lord; all the weights in the bag are of his making."

The normative aspects help us identify the effects of sin more clearly in engineering such as when we exercise poor stewardship, contribute to injustice, neglect to show due care for others, or when we pursue inappropriate technology. Technologies that ignore norms may nudge users to adopt practices that can subtly redirect hearts and distort worship. Anti-normative technology reduces flourishing and leads to negative consequences. If we consider each of the design norms listed earlier, we can identify corresponding "anti-norms" that arise when these aspects are ignored or misdirected. For example, disregarding open communication leads to confusion and obfuscation, ignoring stewardship leads to wastefulness, forgetting justice leads to injustice, neglecting delightful harmony leads to unintuitive designs that frustrate the user, and disregarding trust leads to unreliability and suspicion.

We must also recognize an important distinction between the sinful state of humankind and our finiteness. As noted in the section on creation, we are limited because we are intrinsically finite creatures. Aside from our fallenness, our finite nature means we are not all-knowing and cannot predict all of the consequences of our designs decisions. For example, the electric vehicle emits little pollution while running, but to build an electric vehicle we use batteries and other technologies that may be difficult to obtain or difficult to recycle.[34] Furthermore, the electric vehicle avoids using fossil fuels to run, but charging it might still rely on electricity that was generated using fossil fuels. Design trade-offs arise and are often difficult to balance. For example, choosing a light-weight material for the body of the vehicle improves fuel efficiency, but reduces safety in a crash. Furthermore, will people choose to drive more if their cars are more fuel efficient? Will recycling batteries lead to other environmental challenges? Will increased need for electricity lead to other issues in power distribution? Because of human finiteness, we cannot know all

33. We are grateful to Douglas De Boer for suggesting this example.

34. Ozzie Zehner, "Unclean at Any Speed," *IEEE Spectrum* 50, no. 7 (July 2013): 40-45.

the consequences of our design decisions.

When thinking of sin and engineering, we might consider technological failures such as the Challenger space shuttle exploding due to the failure of an O-ring seal in a solid rocket booster. Another example is the Therac-25 incident in which a radiation machine malfunctioned, delivering fatally high doses of radiation to some patients.[35] How do we discern the differences between our finiteness and our fallenness? For example, it is interesting to ponder if a software bug is due to fallenness or finiteness. In a perfect world, could humans write bug-free code? Certainly the harmful effects that may result from computer bugs are due to the fall, but it might be that debugging is part of the natural process of writing complex code.[36]

It is important to recognize fallenness and finiteness as distinct because we are called to fight the former but accept the latter. In fact, if we do not accept our limitations as creatures then we have fallen into the sin of pride, thinking more of ourselves than we ought. Moreover, not accepting our limitations as creatures can result in negligence, omitting appropriate care and understanding to work within one's competence. As engineers, we need to recognize our shortcomings and employ good design practices to minimize the impact and severity of flaws. This can be achieved in part by employing safety factors in designs as well as performing rigorous testing. We need to recognize both our finiteness and fallenness, avoiding hubris and cultivating a posture of appropriate humility. Humility can help us design with more caution, taking steps to build in redundant design features that help limit damage when unexpected things happen.

Another useful distinction is to divide design flaws into categories of *intentional* and *unintentional*. An example of an intentional flaw in software engineering would be the inclusion of a so-called "back-door" in a computer system, allowing illicit access later. A flaw that is willfully introduced in a system is clearly due to our fallen nature. One example of this is the "clever and sneaky algorithm" used to manipulate the emissions-control module in certain Volkswagen cars.[37] An example of an unintentional flaw might be a design that neglects to provide accessibility features or a software design that inadvertently opens up security

35. N.G. Leveson, and C.S.Turner, "An Investigation of the Therac-25 Accidents," *Computer* 26, no. 7 (1993): 18-41.

36. Derek C. Schuurman, *Shaping a Digital World: Faith, Culture and Computer Technology* (Downers Grove, IL: InterVarsity Academic Press, 2013), 67-69.

37. Prachi Patel, "Engineers, Ethics, and the VW Scandal," *IEEE Spectrum* (September 25, 2015), https://spectrum.ieee.org/vw-scandal-shocking-but-not-surprising-ethicists-say.

vulnerabilities. Here we see a more complex interplay between our finite nature that simply cannot comprehend all impacts and our fallen nature that seeps into our designs in different ways, leading to unintended consequences.

How does sin affect an electric vehicle? It may lead to distortions in each of the stages of design, manufacturing, purchasing, and disposal. For example, when acquiring the rare earth materials required for permanent magnets in the electric motors, greed may lead to environmentally destructive mining practices. During construction of the electric vehicle, injustice may occur if we do not pay manufacturing workers fair wages. Injustice can also creep into the supply chainthrough purchasing materials from areas where they are used to finance ongoing conflict and war.[38] For consumers purchasing an electric vehicle, the sin of pride may motivate the purchase of the car for conspicuous consumption or to promote an image of environmental superiority. Some may choose to drive an electric vehicle as a "virtue signal," taking pride in the sense that they are more "green" than their neighbors. Moreover, the freedom associated with vehicles and the open road may foster a false sense of autonomy which reduces our sense of dependence on God. Habitual practices like these may work on us unawares, redirecting our love and worship away from God and towards ourselves (sin of pride) or toward things which we associate with our freedom (sin of idolatry). When driving an electric vehicle, a lack of care may result in injury to innocent pedestrians. At the end of the vehicle life-cycle, improper disposal of certain electric vehicle components can lead to environmental consequences. Even with apparently responsible technologies such as electric vehicles, the effects of sin are present.

Redemption and Engineering

In the fullness of time God sent his son, Jesus Christ, to redeem the world. Through Christ, God is reconciling all things to himself (Col. 1:20). The previous section highlighted the pervasiveness of the fall, but "the scope of redemption is as great as that of the fall."[39] Jesus' ministry announced the arrival of the kingdom of God, a kingdom established with his first coming but which will not be complete until his second coming. In between, we are called to be agents of shalom, to "promote renewal in every department of creation."[40] Renewal must be directed to-

38. Eliza Strickland, "Cracking Down on Conflict Minerals," *IEEE Spectrum* 48, no. 12 (December 2011): 11-12.

39. Wolters, *Creation Regained*, 72.

40. Wolters, *Creation Regained*, 73.

ward restoration of our relationship with God, worshiping and glorifying him, as well as a restoration of our relationship with others and the rest of creation.

Being an agent of shalom and renewal requires that we start with allowing the gospel of Jesus Christ to change our own hearts and lives. Out of gratitude to God, we are then called to bring the gospel to bear in all areas of life, including technology. Aspects of technology that are misdirected and distorted need to be re-aligned in obedience with God's intents. We ought to employ technology in loving service of our neighbor and in service to God. We are not called to return to a pristine garden; rather we are called via the cultural mandate to cultivate appropriate technology.

One often hears philosophers, cultural pundits, and even Christians calling for us to resist the allure of technology. Indeed, technology has the potential to become an idol. However, this temptation is not solely a problem with the technological forms of culture. One can become addicted to any of the good things in creation such as music, leisure, or food. Once again, it is helpful to distinguish between structure and direction. The possibility for sinful distortions in technology should not lead us to reject technology. Just as we would not call for the rejection of music or literature, so we should not call for rejection of technology, *per se*. We should reject the sinful *directions* of technology while still embracing all of the creational possibilities. As Christians we are called to develop the creation through developing culture, including music, sculpture, literature, legislation, science, and technology in ways that honor God.

As a first step towards redeeming the profession of engineering, one can review the codes of ethics that are published by a number of engineering professional societies. These codes outline the ways engineers should act in their professional roles and also identifies behaviors considered unethical. As an example of encouraged behavior, the National Society of Professional Engineers (NSPE) calls for engineers to "hold paramount the safety, health, and welfare of the public."[41] The Institute for Electrical and Electronic Engineers (IEEE) provides an example of discouraged behavior, calling for engineers "to reject bribery in all its forms."[42] The codes rarely suggest guidelines for design itself, implicitly considering technology neutral, leaving only engineers' personal behavior within their jurisdiction. Thus, while these codes are helpful, they are not sufficient. We suggest that the Reformational perspective highlights

41. National Society for Professional Engineers, "NSPE Code of Ethics for Engineers," accessed August 11, 2014, http://www.nspe.org/resources/ethics/code-ethics.

42. Institute of Electrical and Electronics Engineers, "IEEE Code of Ethics," accessed August 3, 2021, http://www.ieee.org/about/corporate/governance/p7-8.html.

the fact that norms are embedded in technology and thus are essential in thinking faithfully about engineering.

Design Norms

As stated earlier, technology embeds a bias and is value-laden. Thus, engineers must not be myopic (the "narrowness tendency in design"[43]), but ought to look beyond narrow technical specifications to consider the wider implications of new technologies. A helpful framework to avoid this tendency is to apply the design norms introduced earlier. The design norms do not provide easy answers, but rather point a way forward and "are meant only as guides to more focused thinking by corporations and individuals as to the telos [purpose] of design."[44]

<table>
<tr><th>Dooyeweerd</th><th>Monsma, et. al</th><th>Ermer, VanderLeest</th></tr>
<tr><td>Historical (culture formation)</td><td>Cultural Appropriateness</td><td>Cultural Appropriateness</td></tr>
<tr><td>Lingual (symbolic)</td><td rowspan="2">Open Communication</td><td rowspan="2">Transparency</td></tr>
<tr><td>Social</td></tr>
<tr><td>Economic</td><td>Stewardship</td><td>Stewardship</td></tr>
<tr><td>Aesthetic</td><td>Delightful Harmony</td><td>Integrity</td></tr>
<tr><td>Juridical</td><td>Justice</td><td>Justice</td></tr>
<tr><td>Moral</td><td>Caring</td><td>Caring</td></tr>
<tr><td>Pistic</td><td>Trust</td><td>Trust</td></tr>
<tr><td></td><td></td><td>Humility</td></tr>
</table>

Table 1: Adapting the norms to categories helpful in engineering

The list of modal aspects originally proposed by Dooyeweerd is shown in the first column in Table 1. The corresponding design norms as translated and mapped by the authors of *Responsible Technology* are shown in the second column. Note that in this list the lingual and social norms are retained, but combined into a single norm called "open communication."[45] Furthermore, several norms are focused to provide more precise guidelines in the context of engineering.[46] We expect these normative

43. Lambert J. Van Poolen, "Technological Design: A Philosophical Perspective," *ASEE Annual Conference Proceedings* (1987): 785.

44. Lambert J. Van Poolen, "A Philosophical Perspective on Technological Design," *International Journal of Engineering Education* 5 no. 3 (1989): 325.

45. Monsma, ed. *Responsible Technology*, 72-73.

46. Note that the design norms do not capture the whole idea of each modal aspect.

aspects might have a somewhat different emphasis when applied in other disciplines. This focusing of the aspects into norms for technology can be seen in the mapping of the aesthetic aspect into engineering, honing in on the delightful integration of form and function that produces a particular beauty or elegance that engineers recognize.[47] Likewise, the economic norm becomes stewardship, the moral norm becomes caring, and so on. In the third column, these norms are slightly modified again by Ermer and VanderLeest so that "open communication" becomes labelled as "transparency" and "delightful harmony" becomes "integrity."[48] A full list of design norms helpful for engineering and technology is summarized in Table 2.

VanderLeest has also suggested an additional norm that does not easily fit into any of the existing categories: humility.[49] Unlike the builders of Babel who sought to make a name for themselves (Gen 11:4), engineers need to maintain a posture of humility. Because reality is complex, inserting new technological objects into the so-called "real world" comes with certain risks. A lack of humility can lead to overconfidence and recklessness in our designs. For example, an electric vehicle that includes diagnostics and warning lights for situations the designer did not anticipate exhibits greater humility because it acknowledges the driver may behave differently than the designer can envision. Designing with safety factors and testing in mind is a humble acknowledgement that we anticipate mistakes in the design. Providing redundancy, such as multiple computers to control the flight of an aircraft, each checking the other, is a recognition that physical flaws may cause incorrect operation on one of them. Whether humility is considered a design norm or simply a virtue that informs all the norms, it is an important attribute for the Christian as well as the Christian engineer.

Another important consideration for the pistic norm is how technology nudges us to adopt certain "liturgies," rituals, and practices. These rituals and practices have a way of shaping our hearts over time.[50] The

These norms have been derived to highlight concepts relevant to the specific area of technology.

47. For example, see the designs described in Don Norman, *The Design of Everyday Things* (New York: Basic Books, 2002).

48. Gayle E. Ermer and Steven H. VanderLeest, "Using Design Norms to Teach Engineering Ethics," *Proceedings of the 2002 American Society for Engineering Education (ASEE) Conference*, Montreal, Quebec, Canada, June, 2002: 9,025-9,034.

49. Steven H. VanderLeest, "Wider and Deeper Design Norms," *Proceedings of the 2008 Christian Engineering Education Conference (CEEC)*, (Beaver Falls, PA, June, 2008): 36-48.

50. Derek C. Schuurman, "Modern Devices and Ancient Disciplines", *Faith Today*, (November/December 2017): 39-41.

philosopher James K. A. Smith writes that "technologies come pre-loaded with ways of seeing and construing and 'making' the world" and that "the way we use them unconsciously trains us to inhabit the world with a certain posture."[51] Smith goes on to suggest a number of questions that might be helpful with evaluating certain types of technology:[52]

- What do such technologies make more difficult?
- How might some technologies shut down capacities for relating to God, our neighbor, and God's creation?
- Do some technologies actually make it harder to be open to God's call to love God and neighbor?
- Might some technologies functionally encourage disordered, sinful ways of being?
- Might other technologies actually make us more responsive to the gospel?

An engineer who appreciates the role practices play in faith formation will be sensitive to the pistic norm.

Design Norm	**Application to Engineering**	**Sample Questions**
Cultural Appropriate-ness	Technology products should take into account the culture into which they are embedded, cultivating improvement without disrespectful or unnecessary disruption	Does the technology relieve burdens while preserving what is good in a culture?
Transparency	Technology ought to be sufficiently understandable by users, so that they recognize potential dangers and can diagnose failures. For example, car brake pads include a liner that "squeaks" when it is time for them to be replaced.	Is the documentation clear? Are potential dan-gers clearly indicated to users? How will the user know when a part fails?
Stewardship	Use of creational resources should be respectful, frugal, and caring.	Does the design take into account the entire life cycle of the product?

51. James K.A. Smith, "In the Beginning Was . . . Technology," *The Banner*, 3 February 2016. https://www.thebanner.org/features/2016/02/in-the-beginning-was-technology

52. Smith, "In the Beginning Was . . . Technology."

Integrity	The form of the technological device should align with, and even suggest the function. For example, a hammer's form implies its function (of pounding).	Can new users easily intuit the function of this design?
Justice	Technology should correct (not cause) injustice and should encourage justice, i.e., equity and fairness.	Does this device promote fairness? Could this design be used for unjust purposes?
Caring	Our tools should help us to serve one another, to heal the sick, to love our neighbor, to enable our fellow creatures to flourish.	In what ways does this design show care for others? Who may be harmed if this device is used?
Trust	Technological devices ought to be reliable, but we must be wary of the temptation to rely solely or primarily on them, rather than God. Does the device contribute to practices that might distract us from God?	Does "shake and bake" testing indicate the design is robust? What "liturgical practices" are associated with the device?

Table 2: Description of norms focused for use in engineering

One example of a product that incorporates many of the proposed design norms is the fairphone, a smartphone designed and produced with considerations to minimize harm to people (justice) and planet (stewardship).[53] The fairphone project uses conflict-free minerals (justice), uses an open design (transparency) that users can easily configure (integrity), is manufactured in safe conditions with fair wages for workers (justice), and is designed with reuse and safe recycling in mind (stewardship). To our knowledge, fairphone is not a Christian organization but they have wisely recognized several creational norms. Sometimes the difference between distinctively Christian engineering and secular efforts are barely distinguishable, but Christians will be motivated to pursue normative designs out of service to God and love for neighbor. We should not be dismayed with instances where there is little apparent difference between secular and Christian approaches. Christian philosopher Nicholas Wolterstorff suggests that "difference must be a consequence, not an aim... difference is not a condition of fidelity—though, to say it once more, it will often be a *consequence*."[54]

53. Fairphone website, accessed August 3, 2021, https://www.fairphone.com.

54. Nicholas Wolterstorff, "On Christian Learning," in *Stained Glass: Worldviews and Social Sciences,* ed. Paul A. Marshall, Sander Griffioen and Richard J. Mouw (Lanham, MD: University Press of America, 1989), 70.

In addition to norms, there are a variety of other scriptural principles that ought to inform the practice of engineering. These include cultivating the fruits of the Spirit such as love, faithfulness, and self-control. The call to show mercy is an important motivation for developing caring products that help less fortunate people to flourish. The Ten Commandments also have many implications for how we show love to God and our neighbor. The Great Commission (Matt. 28:18-20) provides a strong motivation to develop technologies for spreading the gospel throughout the world.

Another scriptural principle is the importance of guarding our hearts (Prov. 4:23). Our hearts are shaped by our daily habits and "liturgies." Smith encourages his readers to take a "liturgical audit" to discern how our liturgies have the "power to calibrate our hearts" and "acknowledge that our domestic rituals might need to be recalibrated as a result of our auditing work."[55] Recognizing that technology scripts much of the daily liturgies in people's lives suggests that Christian engineers and users might benefit from performing a "liturgical audit" of designs being proposed.

How might this look if these normative and scriptural principles were applied to an electric vehicle? Does the electric vehicle honor God and does it enable human flourishing (shalom)? An electric vehicle enables us to do all the tasks a regular automobile does, but with a smaller environmental footprint. Even so, the complete lifecycle for the electric vehicle may not be as friendly as we first thought.[56] We need to continue to strive to build vehicles in ways that promote flourishing. By working with organizations such as the Responsible Materials Initiative, we can avoid conflict materials in supply chains.[57] Furthermore, we can ensure that an electric vehicle is manufactured in safe and fair working conditions. The electric vehicle is one solution to a problem, but perhaps we should also look for ways to reduce our reliance on automobiles through innovative city planning, effective mass transit and bike lanes, and living nearer to the communities where we work and worship.

In his book, the *Design of Design*, Fred Brooks observes that "an articulated guess beats an unspoken assumption."[58] For this reason, it is helpful to review all the normative aspects during the design process. In the words of Brad Kallenberg, "ethical reasoning is already inside of, and

55. James K.A. Smith, *You Are What You Love* (Grand Rapids, MI: Brazos Press, 2016), 114.

56. Ozzie Zehner, "Unclean at Any Speed."

57. Responsible Materials Initiative. Accessed August 3, 2021. https://www.responsiblemineralsinitiative.org/.

58. Frederick P. Brooks, *The Design of Design: Essays from a Computer Scientist* (Reading, MA: Addison-Wesley Professional, 2010), 116.

everywhere within, the entire design process."[59] One tool that can aid in this process is the decision matrix, something familiar to most engineering students. The rows in the matrix specify different design criteria while the columns show the weighted ranking of these criteria for different solutions. Typically a decision matrix only includes technical considerations, but Ermer and VanderLeest have suggested that design norms could also be included.[60] The inclusion of norms ensures that design trade-offs take into account more than technical and economic considerations. One of the potential pitfalls of this approach is the need to quantify things that are difficult to quantify: costs and energy consumption are more readily quantified, whereas assigning a weight to criteria such as justice and caring require experience and discernment. Furthermore, a quantitative chart does not capture the many nuances that are often involved. Thus the design matrix is only an aid, not a precise solution.

Design Trade-offs

As we seek to meet the various design constraints and norms we often encounter trade-offs. A trade-off involves "a compromise between two conflicting desirable features or goals."[61] Ideally we wish to maximize all our design goals and norms simultaneously, but frequently we are not able to meet all design criteria. As we improve one desirable feature, we often need to make compromises to another desirable feature. Trade-offs are implicit in any real-world design. For example, time, cost, and quality are three competing constraints that frequently arise in project management, leading to the maxim "better, cheaper, faster—choose any two." Another balance that often arises is one between safety and cost.[62] Although we should strive to maximize all the design norms, certain aspects may compete for finite resources. For example, an electric vehicle might be made safer for its occupants by using heavier steel in the body design, but this would directly decrease the energy efficiency and increase the cost of manufacture. Efforts to protect occupants of vehicles by using heavier materials might also compromise the safety of pedestrians in the case of a collision. An improved battery may provide better travel range and shorter charge times, but it may come at an environmental cost if the

59. Brad J. Kallenberg, *By Design: Ethics, Theology, and the Practice of Engineering* (Eugene, OR: Cascade Books, 2013), 49.

60. Ermer and VanderLeest, "Using Design Norms. A related approach of assigning numerical scores to various norms was also described in Andrew Basden, *Philosophical Frameworks for Understanding Information Systems* (Hershey, PA: IGI Publishing, 2008), 156-158.

61. Monsma, ed., *Responsible Technology*, 187.

62. Kallenberg, *By Design*, 39.

battery is comprised of more toxic materials. A particular electric drive motor may be more efficient, but it may require rare-earth materials that are costly, difficult to recycle, and mined in conflict zones. These design decisions all require skilled value judgments. Nevertheless, as far as possible, we should strive for the simultaneous realization of norms, making responsible design decisions and trade-offs from a balanced and holistic perspective.[63] Van Poolen refers to this as *sufficient design*, which he describes as follows: "Designs are deemed sufficient when they not only meet the criteria of financial and engineering efficiency, but also meet in a real way the criteria set down by proper design norms applied as much as possible in a simultaneous, holistic manner."[64]

Restoration

The Bible begins with the story of a garden, but ends with a marvelous garden city: the new heavens and the new earth. It is not humans who will usher in the new heavens and earth, but rather Jesus who will make all things new. This is a city not built with human hands, but one whose "architect and builder is God" (Heb. 11:10). Until Jesus comes again, we are called to be signposts of the kingdom and agents of shalom. We need to avoid the pitfall of technological triumphalism, realizing that our technology will never be able to usher in a perfect world. At the same time, we should also avoid an attitude of technological defeatism and pessimism. Technology is one of the "talents" God has given us, and we must put it to work, not bury it.

Let us look once more at our example of the electric vehicle. The electric vehicle represents our desire to live sustainable lives: we wish to flourish without compromising the ability of other creatures to flourish. The underlying premise of this desire is respect for other creatures (a form of justice), caring for other creatures (a form of love), a desire for fellowship and community (a form of peace), and the glory and praise of God. Thus, the electric vehicle is a small step towards shalom. Taken a step further, one may ask: will there be electric vehicles in the new heavens and new earth? The new heavens and earth are not simply a return to the "pristine" Garden of Eden. Rather, some technological artifacts such as the city appear in Revelation. In the end, "they will beat their swords into plowshares and their spears into pruning hooks" (Micah 4:3). Technology will be present, but that which was misdirected for harm will be redirected for the purposes of cultivation and flourishing. It may not be such a stretch to imagine some kind of vehicles on the streets of the new

63. Kallenberg, *By Design*, 188.

64. Van Poolen, "A Philosophical Perspective on Technological Design," 327.

Jerusalem -- purged of any sin and misdirections, but perhaps still recognizable as vehicles. Humility is important since we cannot know exactly what a world without sin will look like. However, the authors of this chapter will not be surprised if we find vehicles and many other familiar cultural and technological artifacts in the new heavens and earth, purified from sin, restored to their original goodness. In the words of Lewis Smedes: "In the end, God will come to fix his world and make it altogether good again. In between, his children are to go into the world and create some imperfect models of the good world to come."[65]

Articulating a Research Agenda

The discipline of engineering has many specialized subfields, each of which has its own unique technical research agendas. The authors of this chapter will not presume to articulate what these technical agendas ought to be. To get a thumbnail sketch of where the technical work is heading, the National Academy of Engineering solicited input from an international group of leading technological thinkers and identified a list of "grand challenge" engineering problems for the 21st century. These grand challenges are summarized in Table 3.

Make solar energy economical Provide energy from fusion Develop carbon sequestration methods Manage the nitrogen cycle Provide access to clean water Restore and improve urban infrastructure Advance health informatics	Engineer better medicines Reverse-engineer the brain Prevent nuclear terror Secure cyberspace Enhance virtual reality Advance personalized learning Engineer the tools of scientific discovery

Table 3: Engineering Grand Challenges[66]

At this broad level of perspective, values start becoming more obvious when choosing which agendas to pursue. On the one hand, many of these "grand challenge" engineering problems are ones that Christians can enthusiastically support. Some obviously address stewardship, such as securing sustainable energy and reducing pollution. Other challenges

65. Lewis Smedes, *My God and I* (Grand Rapids, MI: Eerdmans, 2003), 59.

66. National Academy of Engineering, "NAE Grand Challenges for Engineering," accessed July 11, 2014, accessed August 4, 2021, http://www.engineeringchallenges.org/challenges.aspx

provide concrete ways of showing love and care for our neighbors and promoting justice, such as supplying clean water, advancing medicine, and preventing nuclear terror. Still other challenges can assist in the cultural mandate, such as providing tools to enable further discoveries and better understand creation. On the other hand, we must be mindful of our presuppositions, particularly in any expansive research agendas. Reverse-engineering the brain should not presuppose that we are like a machine; we must be careful to avoid reductionism. Questions of structure and direction in these challenges are also important. Will the enhancement of virtual reality be directed in ways that increase flourishing, or will it be used to de-emphasize the importance of the physical world, perhaps encouraging a new type of Gnosticism?

Alongside ongoing technical research, Christian engineers should also be reflecting on what it means to be faithful engineers. Even in small design choices there is an opportunity for "proximate justice," incremental improvements toward more appropriate and responsible technology. Some engineers rise to significant positions of responsibility in governments or corporations and, like Daniel in Babylon, have opportunities to use their influence for the common good. All of us can pray for our companies and workplaces. Needless to say, there is much more work that needs to be done. In the rest of this section we suggest a few areas that deserve further investigation.

Deeper Design Norms

Christian engineering scholars could do more work to evaluate design norms as guidelines to faithful development of technology. What solutions can we offer here that will work in practice, beyond academics in the ivory tower? Are the modalities enough? How should humility shape our approach? Are there other ways to structure our guidelines for normative design of technology? For example, we could use Micah 6:8 to focus on three key requirements: justice, humility, and mercy. Alternatively, we could explore how Christian virtues might inform our work with technology. Each of these approaches may provide helpful insights for guiding Christian engineers in their work.

In addition, scholars could develop better curriculum and pedagogy to incorporate normative thinking into engineering education. Consideration of norms, using tools like the decision matrix suggested earlier in this chapter, can be useful to begin taking a more holistic approach to engineering. How can we help train engineers to handle the value judgments necessary when faced with design trade-offs? How do our technology liturgies shape human life and worship? Nesting an engineering education within a breadth of liberal arts courses can also train young engineers to think more holistically and appreciate the diversity in creation.

Reverse Engineering the Bias

Christian engineering scholars could do more work to understand the biases that are built into technology. Many technologies are designed by non-Christians or by Christians who are not thoughtfully applying their Christian faith to their designs. Can we analyze existing technology and reverse engineer it to find the biases built in, perhaps unintentionally? Could some of the tools from fields such as media ecology be adapted to help us better understand the strengths and weaknesses of our technological products by explicitly evaluating them against the norms? The results of this work may provide helpful methods for predicting the consequences of our technologies before it is too late and those consequences become painfully obvious in practice.

The Complexity of Integration

Finally, Christian engineering scholars could do more work to provide tools for understanding the consequences of very complex technologies. When we integrate individually engineered components into a more complex system, how do we evaluate the attributes that appear at the system-level that were not necessarily present in the individual components? As the number of components increases, the number of possible interactions increases exponentially, making the whole much harder to understand than the sum of the parts. Evaluating safety, predicting consequences, honoring norms—these all become much more challenging with increasing complexity. What methods, tools, or processes can we employ to help us design and use complex systems responsibly?

Conclusion

The biblical themes of Creation, Fall, Redemption, and Restoration have application to engineering and technology. Design norms adapted from Dooyeweerd's modal aspects can help guide our development of technology. However, more work could be done to understand how design norms can be used in practice with exemplars of how they can be incorporated into engineering design processes. In our engineering work we should cultivate humility since our fallen nature clouds our vision and insight at the same time that our finite nature hinders us from thinking through all the consequences of our technological activities. Engineers need to keep a holistic perspective as they make design decisions and trade-offs, because technology design is part of the work we are called to do in the kingdom of God. In the end, it will not be our technology that solves all our problems but rather the return of Jesus Christ who will restore all things. In his book, *Visions of Vocation*, Steven Garber encourages the reader to ask herself: "Knowing what I know, what am I going to do?"[67] The question could be posed for the engineer as well: "Knowing what I know, what am I going to design?" When Christ returns, will we be found faithful in the technologies we have developed?

Discussion Questions

1. Have you experienced a "call" to engineering? What influences attracted you to the discipline?
2. What technologies can you see around you right now? How do they impact how you live? What norms might be evident in these devices?
3. During the next worship service you attend, note the technology around you. How does it contribute to the liturgy, supporting the worship and glory of God? How could you design it differently to better contribute to worship?
4. Perform a "liturgical audit" of the devices in your life. How do they shape your daily habits and rituals?
5. How might a Christian engineer advocate for various design norms in a secular setting?
6. Consider the smartphone. How do the design norms apply to this technology?
7. Which of the "grand challenge" engineering problems seem most compelling to you? How does this interest relate to your faith?

Helpful Resources on Faith and Engineering

In addition to the books and articles referenced in the bibliography, here is a further list of resources that the interested reader may wish to use for further exploration of a Christian perspective on engineering:

Adams, Charles C. "Automobiles, Computers and Assault Rifles: The Value-ladenness of Technology and the Engineering Curriculum." *Pro Rege* 19, no. 3 (1991):1-7.

Borgmann, Albert. *Power Failure: Christianity in the Culture of Technology*. Grand Rapids, MI: Brazos Press, 2003.

67. Steven Garber, *Visions of Vocation: Common Grace for the Common Good* (Downers Grove, IL: InterVarsity Press, 2014), 222.

Brue, Ethan J., Derek C. Schuurman, and Steven H. VanderLeest. *A Christian Field Guide to Technology for Engineers and Designers*. IVP Academic, 2022.

Dyer, John. *From the Garden to the City: The Redeeming and Corrupting Power of Technology.* Grand Rapids, MI: Kregel Publications, 2011.

Goudzwaard, Bob. *Aid for the Overdeveloped West.* Toronto, ON: Wedge Publishing Foundation, 1975.

Mitcham, Carl. *Thinking through Technology: The Path Between Engineering and Philosophy*. Chicago, IL: University of Chicago Press, 1994.

Newberry, Byron. "The Challenge of Vocation in Engineering Education." *Christian Scholar's Review* 35, no. 1 (Fall 2005): 49-62.

Schultze, Quentin J. *Habits of the High-Tech Heart: Living Virtuously in the Information Age*. Grand Rapids, MI: Baker Academic, 2002.

Schuurman, Derek C. "Responsible Automation: Faith and Work in an Age of Intelligent Machines." In *The Wonder and Fear of Technology: Commissioned Essays on Faith and Technology*, edited by David H. Kim, 42-56. [New York]: Center for Faith & Work, 2016.

Schuurman, Derek C. "Technology and the Biblical Story," *Pro Rege* 46, no. 1 (September, 2017): 4-11.

Swearengen, Jack Clayton. *Beyond Paradise: Technology and the Kingdom of God*, Eugene, OR: Wipf & Stock, 2007.

Van Poolen, Lambert J. "Towards a Christian Theory of Technological Things." *Christian Scholar's Review* 33, no. 3 (Spring 2004): 367-378.

VanderLeest, Steven H. "Justice and Humility in Technology Design." *Proceedings of the 2006 American Society for Engineering Education (ASEE) Conference*, Chicago, IL, June, 2006: 11.851.1-12.

VanderLeest, Steven H., and Derek C. Schuurman. "A Christian Perspective on Artificial Intelligence: How Should Christians Think about Thinking Machines?" *Proceedings of the 2015 Christian Engineering Conference (CEC)*, (Seattle Pacific University, Seattle, WA, June 2015): 91-107.

Organizations, Web sites

The following websites may also be helpful:

- American Scientific Affiliation: http://network.asa3.org/
- Association of Christians in the Mathematical Sciences: http://www.acmsonline.org/
- Christian Engineering Society: http://www.christianengineering.org/

Bibliography

Adams, Charles. "Galileo, Biotechnology, and Epistemological Humility: Moving Stewardship beyond the Development-Conservation Debate." *Pro Rege* 35, no. 3 (March 2007): 1-19.

Basden, Andrew. *Philosophical Frameworks for Understanding Information Systems.* Hershey, PA: IGI Publishing, 2008.

Brooks, Frederick P. "The Computer Scientist as Toolsmith II." *Communications of the ACM* 39, no. 3 (March 1996): 61-68.

Brooks, Frederick P. *The Design of Design: Essays from a Computer Scientist.* Reading, MA: Addison-Wesley Professional, 2010.

Brooks, Frederick P. *The Mythical Man-Month: Essays on Software Engineering.* Reading, MA: Addison-Wesley Professional, 1995.

Brue, Ethan J., Derek C. Schuurman, and Steven H. VanderLeest. *A Christian Field Guide to Technology for Engineers and Designers,* InterVarsity Academic Press, 2022.

Carr, Nicholas. *The Shallows: What the Internet Is Doing to Our Brains.* New York: W.W. Norton, 2010.

Crouch, Andy. *Culture Making: Recovering Our Creative Calling.* Downers Grove, IL: InterVarsity Press, 2008.

Crouch, Andy. *Playing God: Redeeming the Gift of Power.* Downers Grove, IL: InterVarsity Press, 2013.

Ermer, Gayle E., and Steven H. VanderLeest. "Using Design Norms to Teach Engineering Ethics." *Proceedings of the 2002 American Society for Engineering Education (ASEE) Conference.* Montreal, Quebec, Canada, June, 2002: 9,025-9,034.

Forman, Paul. "The Primacy of Science in Modernity, of Technology in Postmodernity, and of Ideology in the History of Technology." *History and Technology* 23, no. 1-2 (2007): 1-152.

Fulghum, Robert. *Maybe (Maybe Not): Second Thoughts from a Secret Life.* New York: Ivy Books, 1993.

Garber, Steven. *Visions of Vocation: Common Grace for the Common Good.* Downers Grove, IL: InterVarsity Press, 2014.

Institute of Electrical and Electronics Engineers. "IEEE Code of Ethics." Accessed August 4, 2021. http://www.ieee.org/about/corporate/governance/p7-8.html.

Johnston, Stephen F., J. P. Gostelow, and W. Joseph King. *Engineering and Society: Challenges of Professional Practice.* Upper Saddle River, NJ: Prentice Hall, 2000.

Kallenberg, Brad J. *By Design: Ethics, Theology, and the Practice of Engineering.* Eugene, OR: Cascade Books, 2013.

Koen, Billy Vaughn. *Definition of the Engineering Method.* Washington D.C: American Society for Engineering Education, 1985.

Leveson, N.G., and C.S.Turner. "An Investigation of the Therac-25 Accidents." *Computer* 26, no, 7 (1993): 18-41.

Monsma, Stephen V., ed. *Responsible Technology: A Christian Perspective.* Grand Rapids, MI: Eerdmans, 1986.

Mouw, Richard J. *Abraham Kuyper: A Short and Personal Introduction.* Grand Rapids, MI: Eerdmans, 2011.

Mumford, Lewis. *Technics and Civilization.* Chicago: University of Chicago Press, 1934.

National Academy of Engineering. "NAE Grand Challenges for Engineering." Accessed August 4, 2021. http://www.engineeringchallenges.org/challenges.

National Society for Professional Engineers. "NSPE Code of Ethics for Engineers." Accessed August 11, 2014. https://www.nspe.org/resources/ethics/code-ethics.

Norman, Don. *The Design of Everyday Things.* New York: Basic Books, 2002.

Patel, Prachi. "Engineers, Ethics, and the VW Scandal." *IEEE Spectrum* (September 25, 2015). https://spectrum.ieee.org/vw-scandal-shocking-but-not-surprising-ethicists-say.

Pinch, Trevor, and Wiebe Bijker. "The Social Construction of Facts and Artefacts: Or, How the Sociology of Science and the Sociology of Technology Might Benefit Each Other." *Social Studies of Science* 14, no. 3 (1984): 399-441.

Postman, Neil. "Five Things We Need to Know About Technological Change." Speech, Denver, Colorado, March 28, 1998.

Postman, Neil. *Technopoly: The Surrender of Culture to Technology.* New York: Vintage, 1993.

Schuurman, Derek C. "Modern Devices and Ancient Disciplines." *Faith Today*, (November/December 2017): 39-41.

Schuurman, Derek C. *Shaping a Digital World: Faith, Culture and Computer Technology.* Downers Grove, IL: InterVarsity Academic Press, 2013.

Schuurman, Egbert. *Technology and the Future: A Philosophical Challenge.* Toronto, ON: Wedge Publishing Foundation, 1980.

Schuurman, Egbert. *Faith and Hope in Technology.* Translated by John Vriend. Toronto, ON: Clements Publishing, 2003.

Smedes, Lewis. *My God and I.* Grand Rapids, MI: Eerdmans, 2003.

Smith, James K.A. "In the Beginning Was . . . Technology." *The Banner* (3 February 2016).

Smith, James K.A. *You Are What You Love.* Grand Rapids, MI: Brazos Press, 2016.

Strickland, Eliza. "Cracking Down on Conflict Minerals." *IEEE Spectrum* 48, no. 12 (December 2011): 11-12.

Van Poolen, Lambert J. "A Philosophical Perspective on Technological Design." *International Journal of Engineering Education* 5 no. 3 (1989): 319-329.

Van Poolen, Lambert J. "Technological Design: A Philosophical Perspective." *ASEE Annual Conference Proceedings* (1987): 767-789.

VanderLeest, Steven H. "Engineering is Not Science." *Perspectives on Science and Christian Faith* 64, no. 1 (March 2012): 20-30.

VanderLeest, Steven H. "Wider and Deeper Design Norms." *Proceedings of the 2008 Christian Engineering Education Conference (CEEC).* (Beaver Falls, PA, June, 2008): 36-48.

Vincenti, Walter G. "Engineering Knowledge, Type of Design, and Level of Hierarchy: Further Thoughts about What Engineers Know." In *Technological Development and Science in the Industrial Age: New Perspectives on the Science–Technology Relationship*, edited by Peter Kroes and Martijn Bakker, 17-34. Dordrecht: Kluwer Academic Publishers, 1992.

Wolters, Albert M. *Creation Regained: Biblical Basics for a Reformational Worldview.* Grand Rapids, MI: Eerdmans, 1985.

Wolterstorff, Nicholas. "On Christian Learning." In *Stained Glass: Worldviews and Social Sciences,* edited by Paul A. Marshall, Sander Griffioen, and Richard J. Mouw, 56-80. Lanham, MD: University Press of America, 1989.

Wulf, William. "The Urgency of Engineering Education Reform." *The Bridge* 28, no. 1 (Spring 1998). http://www.nae.edu/Publications/Bridge/Engineering-Crossroads/TheUrgencyofEngineeringEducationReform.aspx.

Zehner, Ozzie. "Unclean at Any Speed." *IEEE Spectrum* 50, no. 7 (July 2013):40-45.

A Christian Theory of Personality: Toward a Comprehensive Framework for Psychology, Counseling, and Human Flourishing

Russell D. Kosits

The State of the Discipline: Psychology as Science and Worldview

Perhaps the best place to discover the state of the discipline of psychology is by looking at introductory psychology textbooks. Here we see that psychology is understood as the science of mental life and behavior– most definitions closely approximate that. You'll see that psychology covers a vast terrain, from a discussion of research methods, through the biological underpinnings of psychological experience, to sensation and perception, motivation and emotion, cognition and language, social psychology, personality, abnormal psychology, psychotherapy, and more. Those last two domains belong mostly to practitioners, i.e., those who offer psychological services, whereas the former topics belong to the scientists. But even that is imprecise because the latter chapters are also rooted in science. Still, a battle between the scientists and the practitioners has been the very core of psychology's last century.[1]

One of the most encouraging developments, ironically perhaps, is the result of the so-called "replication crisis" of the last decade in which many high-profile findings which had been taken as sacrosanct have failed to replicate. Although this has been an embarrassment—especially to areas like social psychology—it has also caused the field to redouble its efforts to improve the quality of its scientific work, especially through preregistered open science. Many leaders of the field painstakingly now try to sift wheat from chaff.

That's the first half of the story—psychology is a science. But here is the other half of the story, almost inevitably neglected in mainstream accounts—modern psychology is also a (non-Christian) worldview. In other words, it is powerfully shaped by and clings to certain contested assumptions about the nature of reality.

1. A major theme in Ludy T. Benjamin, *A Brief History of Modern Psychology* (Malden, MA: Blackwell, 2007).

The Historical Origins of Psychology's Worldview Commitments

While psychology readily claims the mantle of science (as it should), it almost never recognizes the fact that it is under the control of contestable worldview assumptions (as it also should). One of the main ways this worldview blindness is perpetuated is—surprisingly, perhaps—through historical narrative. Most introduction to psychology textbooks begin with a history of the field, as do the textbooks in many of psychology's subfields (such as cognitive psychology, for example). When students and professors alike read these narratives, they assume essentially an understanding of history like that of Leopold von Ranke, i.e., that history is simply a presentation of "the facts" of what happened in the past (see Kevin Flatt's chapter in this volume).

It's not widely recognized that history of psychology is an area of scholarship within our field. Specialists understand that Ranke's account is severely misleading, as any historian's biases will always shape their historical work. It's never merely the gathering of facts (though worthwhile historical accounts will always be rooted in facts). Specialists also recognize that "textbook history" often engages in "presentism" (sometimes called "Whig history"). As Butterfield explained, presentist narratives look to the past to justify the present, they emphasize "likenesses" and "anticipations" of currently accepted ideas, while ignoring as irrelevant any dissimilarities.[2]

North American academic psychology emerged in universities that once were Christian. Newsflash: That's different from today. In other words, all of the Christianity in psychology's past is typically ignored as uninteresting, irrelevant, or incomprehensible. In short, presentism amounts to a secular filter—it's almost axiomatic: if there are any Christian components to psychology's past they are reliably filtered out or de-emphasized. For those of us teaching and learning in a Christian context, this is deeply problematic. It essentially teaches would-be psychologists that the Christian faith has little to do with psychological science and that psychology advances as we move *away* from Christian faith. Such narratives essentially baptize us into the modern myth of worldview neutrality and the dogmatic separation of facts and values, science and religion, observation and interpretation. Rankean narratives justify Rankean disciplines which are convinced of their own neutrality, a conviction deeply opposed not only to reality, but also to the most basic convictions of Kuyperian presuppositionalism.

2. Herbert Butterfield, *The Whig Interpretation of History* (London: G. Bell & Sons, 1931).

In 2020, I served as president of Division 26 of the American Psychological Association, the Society for the History of Psychology. My presidential address[3]—which drew heavily from the history of psychology course I've been developing for the last few decades—takes this worldview neutrality head-on. Still, lest one think that my ambition is a Christian takeover of the field, my "presidential theme" was "viewpoint diversity in the history of psychology: the quest for worldview pluralism," which reflects my ongoing concern about the lack of ideological diversity and the growing illiberalism within the field and the contemporary academy more broadly. Building on the work of Jonathan Haidt and other scientists who—in view of a seemingly intolerant progressivism emerging within the field—have been promoting viewpoint diversity through organizations like Heterodox Academy, I put psychology's current worldview struggles into historical context.

The historiographical innovation of my course—and my presidential address—is to periodize North American psychology's institutional past across crucial *worldview* changes. In brief, the periodization is:

1636-1758: Confessional Era. Psychology rooted in Christian theology and philosophy. Christianity routinely asserted as true.

1758-1890: Non-sectarian Era: Psychology's commitment to empiricism/naïve scientific realism emerges as Christians embrace the Enlightenment. Christianity thought to be supported by the science.

1890-1913: Transitional Era. Historic Christianity replaced by what we might call Protestant Liberalism—the "first cancellation" of historic Christianity in psychology. Epistemological commitment expands to include the natural science methods of Wundt and others though introspection retained as main method.

1913-present: Secular era. Psychology's commitment to naturalism emerges; John Watson declares "no dividing line" between man and animals. The "second cancellation" of Christianity in psychology.

1968-present: Ambiguous era. Psychology's commitment to progressivism emerges. The "third cancellation" of historic Christianity. Progressives have for 50 years been in tension with the naturalists, but both worldviews are freely asserted as true within psychology today.

3. Russell D. Kosits, "Sacredness and Heresy in the History of North American Psychology" (Presidential Address, Society for the History of Psychology, Division 26 of the American Psychological Association, 2020).

There is a major potential benefit of such a narrative for mainstream psychology, i.e., embracing the fact that psychology always has been, and I believe always will be, shaped profoundly by worldview commitments, we're given the opportunity to move from psychology's current worldview "control" (in which naturalism and progressivism dominate) to that of peaceful "co-existence" as John Inazu[4] would put it. In short, the take-home message I had for my secular audience as president of Division 26 was to promote worldview pluralism,[5] the open-minded acknowledgement that psychology inevitably contains worldview assumptions and that the discipline therefore ought to create a space in which psychologists feel free to discuss and defend these assumptions without fear of persecution or "cancellation," as they maintain the highest standards of empirical inquiry and evidence.

Conceptualizing the Relation between Worldview and Science: A Christian Critical Realist Approach[6]

All of this means we need some way to conceptualize psychology that embraces our shared commitments to science, while being honest about the role of worldview, making discussion across worldview differences possible. To do this we need to think very briefly about the nature of psychological theory.

Psychological theory occurs at multiple levels, ranging from the most proximate, observation-based level, to the most ultimate, worldviewish level. Mainstream psychological science, however, imagines that worldviews and "bias" occur at the level of the individual, and are weeded out through method. As I've argued in the brief historical account of our field, however, worldview concerns have primarily been conveyed through a *sociological* commitment to shared narratives. So while psychologists might imagine that the demarcation line between worldview and science is carefully guarded, in reality, psychological science today looks something like this:

4. John Inazu, *Confident Pluralism: Surviving and Thriving Through Deep Difference* (Chicago: University of Chicago Press, 2016).

5. Russell D. Kosits, "Toward Worldview Pluralism in Psychology," in *The Hidden Worldviews of Psychology's Theory, Research, and Practice*, ed. Brent D. Slife, Kari A. O'Grady, and Russell D. Kosits (New York: Routledge, 2017).

6. For an elaboration of a Christian critical realism, please see Eric L. Johnson and Russell D. Kosits, "Teaching and Learning in the Social Sciences," in *Christian Higher Education: Faith, Teaching, and Learning in the Evangelical Tradition*, ed. David S. Dockery and Christopher W. Morgan (Wheaton: Crossway, 2018).

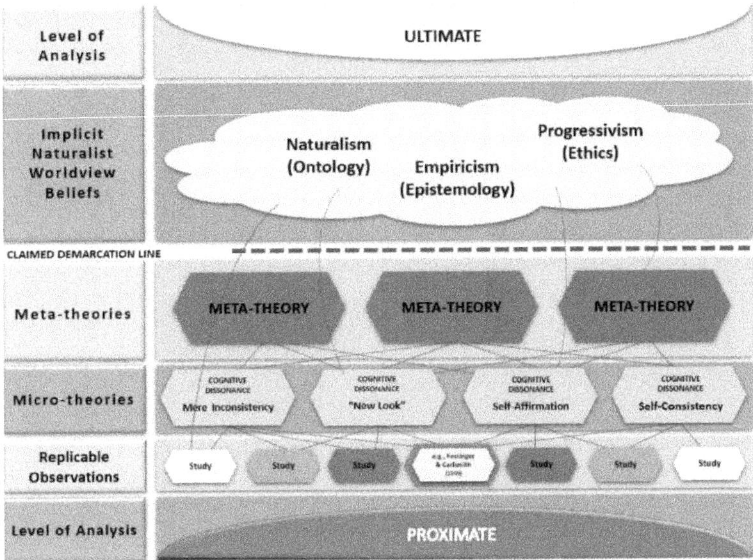

Figure 1: A model of theoretical activity in contemporary psychological science.

At the most proximate level, psychological science does indeed specialize in replicable observations, which are organized and interpreted through *micro-theories* which attempt to explain a narrow range of observations in strictly limited fields of inquiry. I've used cognitive dissonance research here as an example. The next level up we have what we might call *meta-theories*, in which hundreds of studies are synthesized to make broader points, such as the idea that human beings have a need to belong.[7] The claimed demarcation line is the classic modern mythology of worldview neutrality. But within the cloud of often inarticulate worldview assumptions, psychology's three main worldview commitments of ontological naturalism, ethical progressivism, and epistemological empiricism or naïve scientific realism, exert a tremendous amount of control over the discipline.

A better way of conceiving psychology, both descriptively and prescriptively, would be something like this:

7 Roy F. Baumeister and Mark R. Leary, "The Need to Belong: Desire for Interpersonal Attachments as a Fundamental Human Motivation," *Psychological Bulletin* 10, no. 3 (1995).

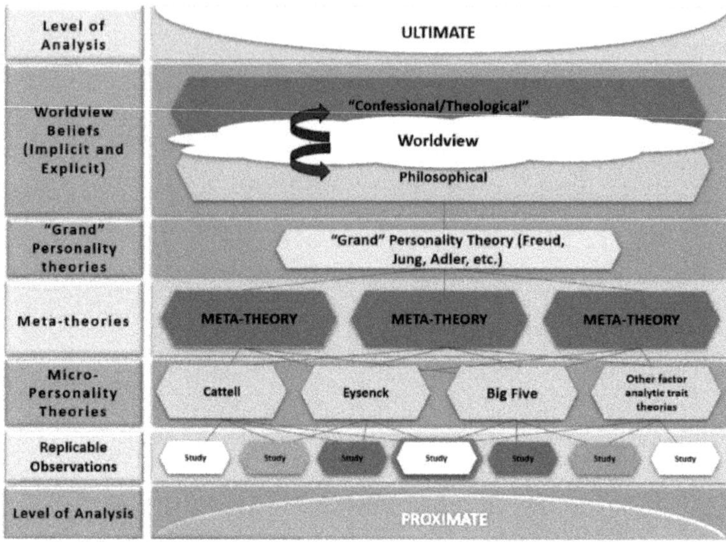

Figure 2: An expanded model of theoretical activity in contemporary psychological science.

Here, psychology's commitment to replicable observations, micro-theories and meta-theories remains intact. But instead of pretending to be worldview neutral, an overt articulation of worldview beliefs is called for. This diagram also includes *personality theory* – that is to say, theories such as those by Freud, Jung, and Horney, which are more worldview-ish than the micro-theories—such as Big 5—that tend to dominate psychological science. Still, the discipline allows these *grand theories* to be taught, via the personality theories course.[8] While some psychologists are skeptical of such grand theories because they all fall short of their lofty aspirations, I'm convinced that the failure of these grand theories has less to do with their audacity and more to do with their faulty worldview assumptions. I believe that Christians are uniquely equipped to develop personality theories in the grand old style, and this chapter will focus on one such theory that I have been developing over the course of my career.

One final diagram. If psychology were to embrace worldview pluralism, the discipline would then look something like this:

8. There are roughly two types of personality psychology textbooks. One of these focuses on explication of the classic theories of Freud, Jung, Adler, Horney, Allport, Maslow, Rogers, and others; the other focuses on personality science. Both are valuable and necessary, but personality theory in the more ultimate sense is the focus here.

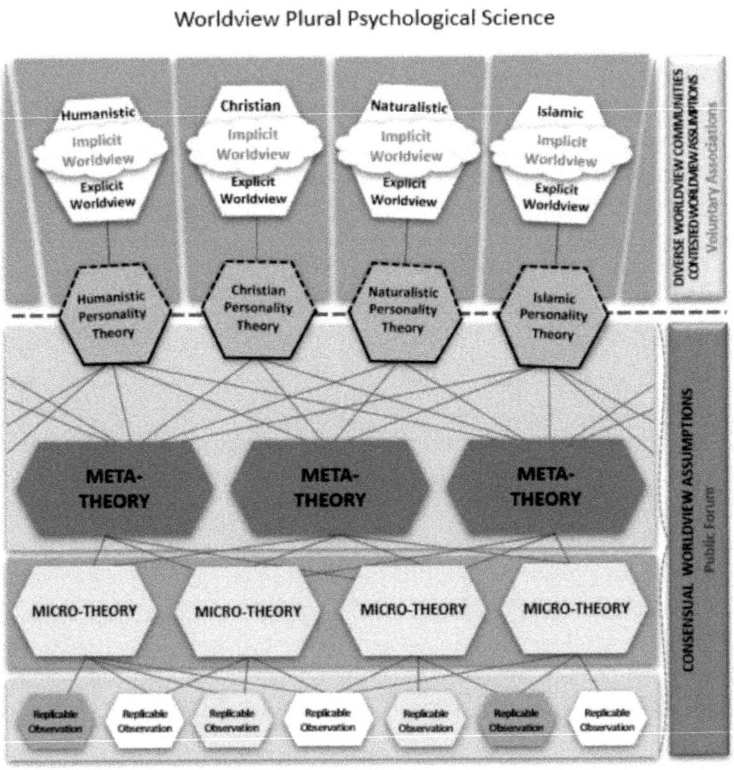

Worldview Plural Psychological Science

Figure 3: A model of worldview plural psychological science.

In this conceptualization, the level of replicable observations, micro-theories and meta-theories might be understood as the *empirical core* of psychology, shared by psychologists of all worldviews. Then, at a more ultimate level, different worldview communities within psychology would make the case that the contents of the empirical core fit the predictions and expectations of their worldview and personality theories. Kuyper's metaphor for science as a tree comes to mind. The empirical core is like the trunk of Kuyper's tree, the various personality theories and worldview assumptions the branches.

The remainder of this chapter summarizes such a personality theory.[9] Consistent with the grand theories of the past, this theory will attempt to articulate a comprehensive, multi-dimensional, multi-aspectual vision of the person. Unlike those theories, however, which are shaped by the dom-

9. In my chapter with Joshua Knabb, we envision Christian engagement with psychology as a five-step process. Step three is the articulation of grand theories. See section on helpful resources for more on that. See Kosits and Knabb, "A Christian Psychology View."

inant worldview assumptions of modern psychology, this theory attempts to be formed by the Christian worldview, primarily as understood by the Reformed and Reformational intellectual tradition. It thus aims to articulate an integrative framework for situating the various subfields of psychology, with multitudinous possible implications for research, counseling, and the pursuit of human flourishing. It's a theory whose basic principles can be articulated in secular terms, but whose Christian foundations will be emphasized below.

Taking God Seriously in Psychology

Dooyeweerd taught that all theoretical thought is related to some transcendental ground idea, which, in turn, is rooted in a ground motive, and that the *Christian* ground motive is "creation, fall, and redemption in Christ."[10] As the words "in Christ" suggest, the deepest motive of the Christian heart is God himself, and thus, the Christian ground motive might be more fully understood as *God*, creation, fall, and redemption. We cannot properly understand the creation if we don't understand the Creator, i.e., the One who created all things.

It is a marvel to realize that before the universe was created, indeed, before space and time itself, there was God. One God, the Scriptures reveal, existing in three persons,[11] perfect in love, happiness, and contentment in the enjoyment of his own glory and splendor.

One may legitimately ask—as the tradition has done—why would a Triune God of perfect happiness create anything at all? Certainly not out of lack. But then why? The "Sunday school answer" to the question comes from the Children's Catechism which says that God made all things "for his own glory." But this says too little. What does it mean that God made things for his own glory? Perhaps no one has answered this question more splendidly than Jonathan Edwards, who argued that God made the world to reflect his own beauty, i.e., that the moral beauty that he has *ad intra* (in himself) may be externally displayed, or manifested *ad extra* (outside of himself). It's in *this sense* that psychology is not primarily about the soul or mind. Nothing within creation is primarily about itself. The heavens declare the glory of God—and we've not understood anything unless and until we have understood it in relation to

10. Friesen, J. Glenn, "Motive," 2010, https://jgfriesen.wordpress.com/glossary/motive/.

11. As the Niceno-Constantinopolitan Creed puts it, this Triune God consists of the Father almighty, maker of heaven and earth, of all things visible and invisible, the Son, begotten from the Father before all ages, and the Holy Spirit, proceeding from the Father and the Son, a formulation that will become important later on as we consider the structure of the soul.

God. In Kuhnian terms, this theocentrism is the necessary "paradigm" to understand anything in the world. As we will see, this truth applies more strongly when we talk about the (human) creation, because it is only human beings that are made expressly to image forth God. Humanity, and the human psyche in particular, is the unique manifestation of the glory of God *ad extra*. When we discuss the creation we must keep this in mind if we're not to lose our step.

If it is true that humans are like God, we must ask: What is God like? There is a strange reticence in the Reformational tradition to answer this question, as if we were violating the creature/creator distinction or "putting God under a microscope" in doing so, but, whatever the merits of this concern, too strong a hesitation to describe God contradicts both the Scriptures (which readily describe God), the history of Christian thought, and faith itself (how can I trust a God I do not know?). It may even cause us to be *overly* concerned about the creation itself, to the neglect of the One who made it.[12] How strange it would be if Christians of all people could not name their own "divinity belief."[13] And we have. For example, the Westminster Shorter Catechism describes God as "a spirit, infinite, unchangeable, and eternal, in his being, wisdom, power, holiness, justice, goodness, and truth." Embedded within this necessarily imperfect but still helpful description are what theologians call the "in-

12. One of the complaints about the neo-Kuyperian tradition is it is so focused on "redeeming creation" that we forget the one whose creation it is. Michael Allen's book *Grounded in Heaven* is a helpful in-house exposition of this concern, which challenges the "eschatological naturalism" of some Kuyperian thought, by which he means "a theological approach that speaks of God instrumentally as a means or instigator of an end but fails to confess substantively that God's identity is our one true end.... In the hands of eschatological naturalism, the secondary is elevated to the primary position in terms of Christian hope, and that which is in fact primary is relegated (at best) to the fringes, if not outright dismissed." In the Reformational tradition, this eschatological naturalism might manifest itself in an intimation that God's primary purpose was the revelation and unfurling of his creational law, rather than the revelation of his own glory. There is no "false dichotomy" here: does our analysis lead us back to God, to see God, to praise God, or do we remain fixated on the creation itself? It was precisely this concern that led me to propose that the chapters in this volume begin with God, before we dive into the traditional creation, fall, redemption scheme. After all, our understanding of the creation will be immeasurably helped if we understand the purposes and character of the one who created it. While not all chapters took up this challenge, a chapter on psychology *must,* I believe, begin with God. See Michael Allen, *Grounded in Heaven: Recentering Christian Hope and Life on God* (Grand Rapids: Eerdmans), 39-40.

13. The reference here is to Roy Clouser's notion of divinity belief, which he correctly argues, are inevitable in all systems of thought. Roy A. Clouser, *The Myth of Religious Neutrality: An Essay on the Hidden Role of Religious Belief in Theories*, Revised ed. (Notre Dame, IN: University of Notre Dame Press, 2005).

communicable attributes of God," i.e., those characteristics which God alone possesses, i.e., his infinity, unchangeability, and eternality, and his "communicable attributes," i.e., those of his attributes that he gives, in a limited and creaturely way, to human beings, e.g., being, wisdom, power, holiness, justice, goodness, and truth. Precisely how he bestows and restores the gift of likeness to himself is discussed under creation and redemption but suffice it to say that our origin is beauty; our origin is goodness; our origin is truth. And as we will see, the historical Christian psychological tradition has always found its starting point in the God revealed in Holy Scripture.

Here are a few other relevant points about God. First, as John Frame repeatedly taught, it is enormously significant that the universe begins with a personal God, with personhood. Secular systems are hard-pressed to account for personhood if the universe has non-personal origins.

Second, the sovereignty of God is an aspect of God's nature that is crucial to psychology. The fact that God directs "whatsoever comes to pass," and "governs all his creatures and all their actions," underlies the idea of the lawfulness which is the presupposition of science itself,[14] and the reality that undergirds the human soul. And it is this notion of creation law that of course is expounded so brilliantly by Dooyeweerd, Vollenhoven, Clouser and others, to which we shall return as we turn to discuss the creation as it pertains to human psychology.

In short, the belief that we can study human beings without knowing the God in whose image they are made is deeply wrong, an error of the first order. It is out of accord with Calvin who said that of all kinds of knowledge, the knowledge of God and the knowledge of ourselves are the most important, and they are mutually interrelated. Further, as we shall see, this belief is historically novel in the psychological tradition of the North American academy. It is a tremendous grace of God that a field may still learn much about mind and behavior without reference to himself, but any field that leaves out God is at a severe disadvantage and more prone to error than it otherwise would be.

Taking Creation Seriously in Psychology

Because of the modern tendency to compartmentalize "religion" from other areas of life, we don't tend to think of human beings first and foremost as creatures, made by God, for God. The challenge is to

14. Paul Davies argued that when scientists assume the lawfulness of their subject matter, they are adopting "an essentially theological worldview." Paul Davies, "God and design: The teleological argument and modern science," ed. Neil A. Manson (London: Routledge, 2003), 148.

bring our faith with us into the lab or the counselling room. We've been trained to do the opposite. To take creation seriously in psychology is to ask questions such as: What would psychology look like if we didn't compartmentalize our faith into a separate sphere called "religion"? What would it look like if we conceived of the subject matter of psychology as *creational*?[15]

The Subject Matter of Psychology as Creational

Psychology is often defined as the scientific study of mind and behavior. This is fine as far as it goes, but tils us in a secular direction. Perhaps a more adequate definition is "Psychology is the 'logos of the psyche,' or the science of the soul, it's embeddedness within biology and culture, and its relation to human acts."[16]

Regardless of our definition, the subject matter we examine in psychology is the height of creation. Humans are special as they bear the image of God. Indeed, the soul has long been understood to be at the very least an important part—if not the entirety—of the image of God. Since psychology is the logos of the psyche, the millennia of reflection on the nature of the soul is highly relevant. Indeed, the retrieval of the Christian psychology of the past is "step one" of a Kuyperian Christian psychology.[17]

There was something ennobling about the historic Christian view of the soul. The *rational soul,* as it was taught for more than a millennium, was comprised of intellect and will, a capacity for truth and goodness, by which human beings image forth the God of truth and goodness. This captured, in part, how human beings are the glory of God *ad extra*. Though the Reformational tradition has historically been severely critical of the scholastic view of the soul, raising important points to consider, a deep dive into the psychological system of Aquinas is desperately needed today and it would surely reveal deep compatibilities with the Reformational tradition. Without concluding that debate, it is important to note that the Reformational tradition has put forward an alternative anthropology to that of the rational soul which has not always been conducive to engaging psychology.[18] After

15. Originally, I had also hoped to address an additional question in this chapter: what would it look like if we conceived of the *study* of psychology as creational? Space prohibits this discussion. Part of my answer to this question is contained in Kosits and Knabb, "A Christian Psychology View."

16. In an earlier draft of this chapter, I had a 400-word elaboration on this definition, which I am happy to share with any interested reader. Throughout this chapter, several very long footnotes have been removed to ensure it stays within reasonable limits.

17. Kosits and Knabb, "A Christian Psychology View."

18. One line of evidence for this assertion is that Basden's exploration of applications

all, how can a philosophy so critical of traditional views of the psyche be helpful in describing the "logos of the psyche"? Still, a closer look will show it bears much fruit.

In what is to follow, an attempt will be made to describe the *structure* of the human person, i.e., the ineradicable created nature of human beings, and its relation to the psychological.

Augustine taught that the human mind or soul images God's triune nature. In this vein, then, let us begin by asserting what I can only begin in this chapter to argue, i.e., that the human self—and the psyche *per se*—may be understood as a reflection of the three persons of the Trinity, and, consequentially, may also be understood tri-Perspectivally (Frame) and from the perspective of the three transcendental ground ideas (Dooyeweerd). The Father is reflected in the *ideal self*, the internal witness of the perfection from which we came and the source of Calvin's *sensus divinitatus*. We may also call this the normative self (Frame), which is the ineradicable testimony of our Origin (Dooyeweerd). The Son is imaged in the *horizontal self* which has to do with our modal functioning, arguably the best-known aspect of Reformational philosophy. The horizontal self may also be called the situational self (Frame) or understood as the modal diversity of our personhood (Dooyeweerd). Finally, the human heart, the core religious direction and center of the human person, or the *vertical self*, is the image of the Holy Spirit, the Love and Worship proceeding from the Father and Son in the Godhead. We may refer to the vertical self as the existential self (Frame) or the principle of unity, which Dooyeweerd believed to be the religious center of the human being or the human heart. As Frame's model suggests, each of these "dimensional" selves represents a *perspective* (not a different "part") on the person. Let's begin our discussion with the emphasis of modern psychology, i.e., the horizontal.

Horizontal (Modal) Functioning and the Subject Matter of Psychology (The "What")

The Reformational philosophical tradition is best known for what I'll call *horizontal* or modal functioning, so this is a good place to begin our discussion. Created things are shaped by God's law, which is revealed to us through everyday experience and empirical observation. Dooyeweerd argued there are fifteen irreducible ways of functioning, each of which has a meaning nucleus.[19]

---

of Dooyeweerd's philosophy in the academic disciplines has very little at all to say about psychology. Andrew Basden, *Foundations and Practice of Research: Adventures in Dooyeweerd's Philosophy* (United Kingdom: Taylor & Francis, 2019).

19. According to Basden, the order and meaning nuclei may be arranged as follows: quantitative (discrete amount) , spatial (continuous extension), kinematic (move-

Several Reformational thinkers (e.g., Van Belle, Ouweneel) have argued that Dooyeweerd and Vollenhoven's reduction of psychology to the *sensitive* aspect, which included both sensation and feeling, is inadequate and have proposed various solutions. I join those voices, though in a novel way.

The problem of reducing the "special science" of psychology to the sensory/psychical modality is obvious to anyone familiar with the field of psychology. They will know that sensation and perception is only one chapter in an intro psych textbook, and emotion is another. If the Reformational tradition is going to be serviceable for modern psychology (rather than criticize it from above based upon a pre-conceived definition[20]), it will need to help us understand the typical table of contents for an introduction to psychology book, which usually looks something like this:

History of psychology
Research methods
Personality
Biological bases
Sleep/drugs
Stress & health
Sensation & Perception
Motivation & Emotion
Learning
Memory
Cognitive psychology
Intelligence
Language
Social Psychology
Development
Psychological disorders and treatments

---

ment), physical (energy), biotic (life functions + organisms), sensitive/psychic (sense, feeling, emotion), analytical (distinction, conceptualization), formative (deliberate shaping, history, culture, technology, goals, achievement), lingual (meaning carried by symbols), social ("we': sociality, relationships, roles, respect), economic (frugal management of resources), aesthetic (harmony, surprise, fun, play, enjoyment), juridical (due: responsibilities + rights), ethical (self-giving love, generosity), pistic (vision, aspiration, commitment, belief). See Basden, *Foundations and Practice of Research:*, chapter 9. His website is also a treasure trove on this and all things Dooyeweerd: http://dooy.info/aspects.to1005.html.

20. Vollenhoven said, "By the psychic, we are to understand exclusively that which is studied by a scientific psychology that is mindful of its limits." His understanding sounds similar to the Aristotelian and Thomistic idea of the sensitive soul, i.e., "the mode of behavior (in animals and humans) that is of a primary sensitive kind..." Dirk H. T. Vollenhoven, *Introduction to philosophy* (Sioux Center, IA: Dordt College Press, 1930/2005), 26.

Such an array of topics does not fit the idea that the special science of psychology is the study of sensitive functioning only. Thankfully, there are tools within a Reformational ontology to engage psychology as it exists, but it will require us to think flexibly and creatively about the modal scale. As George Miller argued, psychology has always been a bit of an "intellectual zoo," (and within the field we see a wide variety of professional sub-divisions) but if we adopt "consciousness" or "immediate experience" as the subject matter of psychology, "we need reject little of what passes for psychology today."[21] Though we must not discount the importance of the unconscious, or the embeddedness of the soul within biology and culture, this emphasis on subjectivity or consciousness gets at the heart of what we mean by mind *per se* and may thus be helpful in developing a Reformational understanding of contemporary psychology: are there modalities or types of functioning that are inherently subjective, i.e., aspects of human consciousness *per se*?

A careful inspection of the modal scale reveals that five of the modalities are aspects of subjective experience *per se*, the sensitive, the fiduciary, the ethical, the analytic, and the lingual (with the first and the last being liminal modalities). Whether we are sensing,[22] believing/trusting,[23] feeling/desiring,[24]

21. George A. Miller, "The constitutive problem of psychology," in *A century of psychology as science*, ed. Sigmund Koch and David E. Leary (Washington, DC: American Psychological Association, 1992), 42.

22. The sensitive aspect is thought to have "feeling, emotion" as its kernel but also to include "sense" and "perception" and "smell, hear, see" as contained within its constellation (Basden, *Foundations and Practice of Research* 190). In psychology, however, there's a clear demarcation between sensation/perception, and feeling. So I am separating the sensory/perceptual from the aspect of feeling, as does Ouweneel.

23. My original footnote for the pistic or fiduciary modality began to get quite long. I think the full justification for this assertion will have to be made at a later time, but this quote from Basden's earlier thinking, with its combination of believing and trusting, gets at my meaning, "Activities like dignifying, aspiring, trusting, worshipping, praying, religious ritual and celebration are primarily pistic. Dooyeweerd's main explicit discussion of the pistic/faith aspect itself is in [1955,II:291-334], but his entire *New Critique of Theoretical Thought* [1955] can be seen as an argument that faith underlies all else." Why then, given the "order of succession" in which later modalities presuppose earlier ones, would belief/trust be placed as the last modality? Trust is psychologically basic, not something that emerges, say, post economic or justicial. "The Pistic Aspect," 1998, https://dooy.info/pistic.html; Basden, *Foundations and Practice of Research:*, 208.

24. After trust, is love, or what Reformational thought has called *ethical functioning*—undergirding the entire psychology of emotion. Ouweneel rightly argued that the sensory and the emotional are not reducible to one modality. But instead of dividing the sensitive into perceptive and sensitive (as in Ouweneel) I simply move the ethical into its proper location following the fiduciary. As Aquinas (and Edwards) argued, all emotions are rooted in love, and Edwards referred to the realm of affect

thinking,[25] or using language (which is deeply connected to thinking),[26] these are subjective kinds of functioning. It may thus be better to think of psychology not as a special science, but as a grouping of special sciences.[27] Underlying these fields are the biotic and earlier modalities, i.e., those aspects we share in common with animals and, below the biotic, with all physical entities.[28] After the psychological modalities, we have social/normative modalities, in which humans uniquely function as subjects[29] but are not aspects of subjectivity *per se.*

Let's first try to conceptualize this proposal. John Frame, who hails from the Van Tillian tradition has long argued that all of reality may be understood tri-perspectivally, i.e., things may be seen from what he called a "situational" (objective) perspective, an "existential" (subjective) perspective, and a "normative" perspective. Basden observes that some have found it helpful to arrange the aspects into groups, though he warns we must not erroneously con-

and desire as the realm of *moral* causation hence the designation "ethical" seems apt. (It is better to refer to human emotions as moral rather than merely sensibilities as Aristotle, Aquinas, and even Dooyeweerd do, as this fails to distinguish the key difference between human and animal emotion). Willem Ouweneel, *Heart and Soul: A Christian View of Psychology* (Grand Rapids: Paideia Press, 2009), 15; Harry Van Belle, The Meaning of the Psychical, 1985.

25. Next we have thought, the *analytic modality*, which includes the capacity to detect contradiction (something infants are capable of), estimate probabilities, use reason. Basden includes cognitive psychology as one of the sciences that pertain to this aspect.

26. Next is the *lingual modality*. Evidence of the close relation between the cognitive and lingual is that these two are often included in one chapter in introductory psychology textbooks.

27. For Reformationals, claiming more than one modality for an academic discipline feels imperialistic, but other scholars have similarly argued (implicitly or explicitly) that psychology involves more than one modality (e.g., Van Belle, Basden, Ouweneel), though this certainly is the first attempt to claim five, although it should immediately be noted that the broad field of psychology is divided into a range of subdisciplines which focus on one modality at a time. Likewise, psychology's emphasis is on subjectivity *per se*. Other academic disciplines may focus on certain modalities but from other vantage points—so this isn't to claim that psychology "owns" the modalities which are inherently subjective functioning. Dooyeweerd desired to define psychology "univocally" (as dealing with one modality) and thus demanded we give up the notion of a soul which is "a collective idea of modal functions." Whether we want to use the term "soul" or not, psychology as it exists today, the study of conscious experience *per se*, seems to me to be precisely what Dooyeweerd tried to deny, i.e., a grouping of modal functions. See Herman Dooyeweerd, *A New Critique of Theoretical Thought*, vol. 2: The General Theory of the Modal Spheres (Philadelphia: Presbyterian & Reformed, 1955), 111.

28. Ouweneel, *Heart and Soul: A Christian View of Psychology*, 14.

29. Dooyeweerd argued persuasively that only human beings function in the normative modalities as subjects. We can engage in social, cultural, economic functioning, for example, in a way that non-humans cannot.

clude that some aspects are more important than others.[30] Interestingly, one of the "common groupings" sounds much like Frame's tri-perspectivalism (and like the bio-psycho-social distinction that is so prevalent in psychology), i.e., the distinction between the physical, the mental, and the social.[31] Thus, the modal scale has been understood by some to have a tri-partite structure, which might be taken to imply that Frame's three perspectives are grounded in the nature of reality.[32] Of course, Reformational philosophy typically divides the modal scale into "laws" and "norms," a bipartite grouping. This tri-partite approach is not far removed from this, distinguishing between "situational" modalities (we may call *these* "laws"), "existential" or subjective modalities, and the social or "normative modalities." But to do this requires that we re-order the modal scale, by bringing fiduciary functioning (which has to do with the subjective functioning of belief/certainty and trust[33]) and ethical functioning (which has to do with subjective functioning of love), earlier on the scale. See Figure 4 for a summary.

This arrangement of the modal scale also clearly illustrates the embeddedness of the psyche within the biotic and the social/normative modalities. Further, it shows that sensation and language are both *liminal* modalities. The sensory is the bridge between the physical and the psychological (indeed, the neural apparatus is designed to transduce stimulus energies into biological signals which occasion our perceptions), and the lingual is the bridge between the private, inner, subjective world of the soul or mind and the social world.[34] We may "talk to ourselves," using

30. Basden also notes that though "Dooyeweerd is adamant that there are no *genus proxima* [*sic*] (NC, II, 14), no 'super-aspects' that group the aspects together," (p. 209), he himself did occasionally group aspects together. Basden, *Foundations and Practice of Research:*, 209.

31. Basden, *Foundations and Practice of Research:*, 209.

32. Having three different categories of functioning isn't the same as having three perspectives that may be taken on all things, but the former may underlie the latter. As all things are structured by God's law, and function (objectively at least) in all fifteen modalities, what Frame calls "normative" perspective may simply be highlighting the normative modalities pertinent to the thing being analyzed. Likewise the "existential" perspective may simply be focusing on the "existential" modalities that pertain to whatever is being considered. Situational perspective focuses on the objective characteristics of the topic in question, i.e., things that can be measured, seen, or empirically observed.

33. Basden at times places trust in the ethical (in his book) and at times in the fiduciary (on the Dooy pages). He also argues very helpfully that each modality exists as a continuum, with some types of functioning adjacent to the earlier modality, and some adjacent to the latter modality. Perhaps trust might be included in the fiduciary, but adjacent to the ethical. We don't need the pistic to capture religion because the vertical does that.

34. Van Belle criticizes Ouweneel for paying too close attention to inner-outer dynamics,but these are precisely what we should pay attention to as we attempt toproperly order the modal scale. Van Belle, The Meaning of the Psychical, 3.

Categorical distinctions						As continuous:	Modality	Faculties of soul	Images/witnesses to the God who:	Subfield within psychology
Norms	Normative	Normative	Social	Social		More normative	Aesthetic (pure norm)		is in the sum of his perfections, holy and beautiful	Positive psychology; Psy of aesthetics
							Justicial		acts justly/righteously; gives all their due	Moral psychology; Forensic psychology
							Economic		provides for his people and stewards resources	Behavioral economics
							Formative		is creator	Cultural psychology
							Social		exists in social harmony/perichoresis	Social psychology
Normed Laws	Existential	Subjective	Psycho	Mental	Soul/Mind/Psyche		Lingual (liminal)	The intellect, our structural orientation toward the true	speaks	Psycholinguistics
							Analytical		is truth	Cognitive psychology
							Ethical/love	The will, our structural orientation toward the good	is lovely/worthy of love	Affective science
							Fiduciary/trust		is trustworthy	Psychology of trust
							Sensory (liminal)	The senses	sees things as they are	Sensation & Perception
Laws	Situational	Objective	Bio	Physical	Body		Biotic		is life	Behavioral neuroscience
							Physical		holds all things together	
							Kinematic		is said to move	
							Spatial		is omnipresent	
						More lawful	Quantitative (pure law)		is One and Three	

Figure 4: A Modal Conceptualization of Psychology.

language internally on a purely subjective level, but we may also talk or write to others. The lingual is thus liminal between the subjective/existential and the social/normative modalities.[35]

Additionally, this arrangement of the subjective/existential modalities helps us to connect to the Christian psychology of the past, with the fiduciary and the ethical together constituting what has historically been called "will,"[36] and the analytical and lingual the "intellect." This is more

35. Indeed, this arrangement opens us to another interesting possibility, that the distinction between laws and norms is continuous in addition to categorical, i.e.., that it isn't only the psychological modalities that possess the characteristic of normed lawfulness. For example, cancer would suggest a violation of the normative side of the biotic, and the inevitability of social relatedness is the lawfulness of the social, etc. Perhaps we may posit only two "pure" modalities, with the quantitative being pure law, and the aesthetic pure norm. All of these ideas would need to be developed elsewhere, but complement the proposed tripartite division of the modal scale and shed further light on perennial mysteries of psychology, such as the deep connection of mind and body.

36. William Ames placed fiducia or trust in the will (but assensus in the intellect), so including certainty/trust along with love in the will seems appropriate. William Ames, *The Marrow of Theology*, trans. John Dykstra Eusden (Grand Rapids, MI: Baker Books, 1643/1968), 80.

than a curious historical comment—again, as the tradition taught, these faculties imply norms and connect to the image of God (a far more ennobling view of the mind than the prevailing Psychologies[37] today provide). As Aquinas said, the will acts under the aspect of the good, i.e., we trust, choose and desire that which appears good to us. The implicit norm is that we ought to trust and desire that which is *truly* good. Neurologically and developmentally, our conception of the good begins merely with bodily needs but is designed to expand to eventually include the good of God himself.[38] Likewise, Aquinas argued the intellect is adapted to the true. The implicit norm behind thinking and of languages is truth. Even "secular" research in cognitive psychology, which talks about cognitive "distortions" implicitly assume the norm of truth; everyday use of language assumes the truthfulness of the words we use. Cynicism, humor, and deception are all interesting because they depart from the norm pertaining to the intellect.

Something more needs to be said in order to complete this modal conceptualization of the field of psychology. The discipline is vast and goes beyond the study of the soul or mind *per se* as defined above. There are a host of what we might call analogical psychologies[39] in which the pre-sensory, (i.e., biotic) and post-lingual social/normative modalities qualify psychological functioning *per se*. In the former category, we have behavioral neuroscience or physiological psychology. In the latter category, each of the post-lingual modalities might be understood as implying a subfield of psychology, a certain psychological need, and norms and corresponding virtues, each of which entails a unique aspect of the image of God (see table above). This would of course, make the *social modality* next by order of succession, giving rise to the field of social psychology, the study of how real or imagined interaction shapes psychological functioning *per se*. The need for affiliation or belonging is one of the best-established psychological needs. A host of virtues, such as friendship, would seem relevant to this modality.

---

37. I here invoke the distinction between capital P Psychology, and lowercase p psychology. The former has to do with the basic assumptions we make about the mind, the latter the data we use to support these assumptions. All psychological systems include both. It's best, of course, if the Psychology that undergirds our work is Christian. See Kosits and Knabb, "A Christian Psychology View."

38. That this is the case developmentally is uncontroversial. The behavioral neuroscience is very interesting in that the basic "primitive" centers of the brain associated with desire, pleasure and pain, undergird human pleasure in charity, virtue, and in God. We have Augustinian brains.

39. This application of Dooyeweerd's concept of analogy to the subfields of psychology is based on D.F.M. Strauss, *The Philosophy of Herman Dooyeweerd* (Jordan Station, ON: Paideia Press, 2021), 46-47.

From there, we come to the *cultural/formative modality*, the "making" aspect of human functioning, a topic sometimes considered in vocational psychology and various areas of empirical research (such as achievement motivation, flow, and goal-setting). A virtue of excellence or craftsmanship in one's calling would seem to pertain. And of course we image forth God as creator in this modality.

Then comes the economic (based on the value of the things we make), having to do with stewardship and the creation of value; fields like behavioral economics would consider the relation between human psychology *per se* and economic functioning.[40] The need for competence likely also applies here as well, though we may also talk about economic needs on both the individual and societal level. The virtue of frugality and stewardship pertain to this modality, and herein we image forth the good stewardship and provision of God.

Next we have the justicial, or the modality corresponding to justice. The modal kernel of justice remains "giving each their due" and includes not only the legal system *per se* (and hence the field of forensic psychology) but also the entire natural and moral law and is related—among other things—to the field of moral psychology. Further, in keeping with Scripture's broad conceptualization of justice, it contains the key norms pertaining to all the psychological modalities, including trust and love. Thus, the psychological modalities are "normed laws," occupying a space between laws and norms. All of the virtues pertaining to the Ten Commandments would be relevant here. Of course we image forth the God of tzadeqah and mishpat as we act justly.[41]

Finally, whereas Dooyeweerd placed the fiduciary last on the modal scale, as the "means by which humans immediately relate to the origin of temporal existence."[42] I believe that role more properly applies to *the aesthetic*. While aesthetic functioning might connect to a field like the psychology of aesthetics, I see beauty as an emergent property, i.e., as a human being functions according to design in each of the modal aspects, they manifest *arete*, i.e., excellence and virtue, and are beautified, reflecting more and more the God who made them. Socrates argued that virtue

40. For example, the psychologist Daniel Kahneman would win the Nobel prize in Economics.

41. Keller argues there are three key "justice" terms in scripture, "tzadeqah," which is social conformity to a just norm, "mishpat" which is the corrective action by which we right wrongs, and "chesedh" which is the heart disposed toward justice, normative, situational, and existential See Timothy Keller, *Generous Justice: How God's Grace Makes Us Just* (New York: Dutton, 2010), chapter 1. I don't think Keller makes the tri-perspectivalism explicit.

42. James H. Olthuis, "Dooyeweerd on Religion and Faith," in *The Legacy of Herman Dooyeweerd*, ed. C.T. McIntire (New York: University Press of America, 1985), 26.

is the beauty of the soul; what he perhaps didn't understand is the full array of virtues, and how they manifest the glory of God *ad extra*.

This formulation expands—but does not exhaust—the notion of the image of God—we do not image God merely in intellect and will, as the tradition had emphasized, but also in our social, cultural, economic, and justice-related functioning. I will say more on the divine image below. But human nature properly ordered is glorious like the God who made us, the manifestation of the glory of God *ad extra*. Contrary to the dominant worldview of naturalism, our nature points clearly to transcendent beauties/realities beyond themselves and is inherently an elevating and non-cynical psychology. And contrary to the infinite malleability and self-defining autonomy of secular progressivism, a Christian psychology argues that conformity to these norms clearly implies human flourishing. Indeed, as the section on common grace will argue, there is ample empirical evidence that proper functioning within each modality is associated with human happiness. A proper understanding of human psychology is thus aspirational. It ought to create within us a longing to live into the glorious telos for which we were made.

Vertical Functioning—The Religious Direction of Human Life (The "Why")

So we are arguing (and there is strong evidence[43]) that there is a law for our being, that this law (structurally) underlies the field of psychology as it currently exists, and, Reformational ontology predicts, (directional) conformity to this will be associated with shalom. So far we've thought of human beings functioning *horizontally*, i.e., in all modalities, with some of these modalities being the subject matter of psychology *per se* (the sensory, fiduciary, ethical, analytical, and lingual), and other modalities functioning analogically within the field (e.g., in behavioral neuroscience, social psychology, or behavioral economics). Given the multi-modal nature of the field, psychology is probably best understood as a collection of special sciences or as Dooyeweerd put it, "a collective… of modal functions."[44] However, horizontal functioning contains only one of three dimensions of the subjective functioning of human beings made in the image of the triune God. Subjective functioning, i.e., the subject matter of psychology, may be considered three ways: modally (horizontally), religiously (vertically) and ideally. At this point, we'll focus on the vertical, i.e., an aspect of functioning that is even more important than the horizontal, the functioning, Dooyeweerd said, of "the

43. To be discussed in section on common grace and horizontal functioning.

44. As discussed above, Dooyeweerd of course tried to limit psychology to a single modality: Dooyeweerd, *A New Critique of Theoretical Thought*, 2: The General Theory of the Modal Spheres, 111.

heart," which is the religious direction of the human person, toward or away from the living God. Using Framean language, we might call this dimension "existential."

Calvin Seerveld, reflecting Dooyeweerd's work on the heart, famously portrayed this dynamic in his "tin-can theory" of human nature,

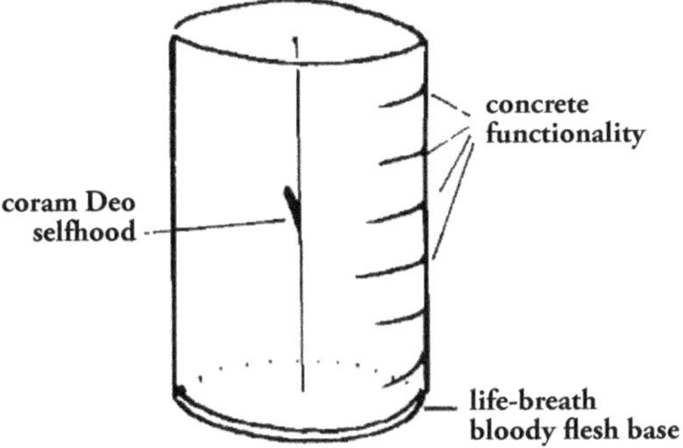

Figure 5: The vertical-horizontal distinction in Seerveld's tin-can theory.

where what I call the vertical functioning of the human being is like the axis that runs through the center of the can, which runs through each of the horizontal or modal aspects of functioning.[45]

The tin can helps us to understand that our horizontal functioning is always shaped by the direction of the heart, and when the heart is fully directed toward God, our horizontal functioning will be affected.

It's important to avoid the conflation of the horizontal and vertical, both structurally and directionally. Structurally, the difference is captured in the tin can theory, and in Dooyeweerd's own work.[46] Directionally, however, these two are sometimes conflated. So it is very important to distinguish proper horizontal direction from proper vertical direction.[47]

45. Figure originally published in Calvin Seerveld, "A Christian Tin-Can Theory of Man," *Journal of the American Scientific Affiliation* 33, no. 2 (1981): 76, https://www.asa3.org/ASA/PSCF/1981/JASA6-81Complete.pdf. Used by permission.

46. Structurally, people will function in the biotic, sensory, economic, etc. That is horizontal or modal functioning. It is also structural that people's hearts will be directed either toward or away from God, that is vertical or existential functioning, the worshipping aspect of human nature..

47. Proper *horizontal* direction occurs when human beings conform to the laws for any particular modality. For example, if we get enough sleep we are properly horizontally directed in that aspect of the biotic; if we don't violate the law of contradiction we are properly horizontally directed in that aspect of the analytic; if we maintain frugal business practices, we are properly horizontally directed in that aspect of the economic modality. Proper *vertical* direction, on the other hand, has to do with the *why* behind any particular modal *what*. Here as Dooyeweerd said, there are two options, toward or away from the God of Scripture. Proper vertical functioning takes

Ideal Functioning—The Sense of "Ought" (The "Where")

So if our modal functioning is the situational or *horizontal* self, and our existential/religious functioning is our *vertical* self, what about the normative self? Just as we can discern a difference between the horizontal and vertical, we can also discern a difference between those and our sense of how we *ought* to be functioning in each of these dimensions. For example, we may assess our lingual functioning and be pleased or displeased with it. We may assess our vertical functioning and be pleased or displeased. The normative or *ideal* self, in short, is our sense of how we ought to be and is related to conscience.[48]

Psychology has a large literature on the ideal self. In addition to the term *ideal self*, other similar terms, such as the real self, the intrinsic self, the essential self and the deep self have been used.[49] Carver and Shier emphasize that we tend to compare our actions (what we have called the horizontal) with some sort of "standard" (what is here called the ideal).[50] While a more extensive synthesis of this literature would be in order, there is little reason to doubt of the structural status of the ideal self.

Despite these firm empirical grounds, secular approaches to personality have had a very hard time making sense of this aspect of human experience, recognizing its centrality and yet not knowing precisely what to make of it because of the relativistic leanings of the field. Instead of treating the ideal self as a witness to the law of God within, it has treated

---

place when, whether we eat or drink or whatever we do, we do it all for the glory of God (1 Cor 10:31). It is the scriptural promise that we may no longer live for ourselves, but for Christ (2 Cor 5:15). Sometimes Reformational thinking conflates the two, imagining that proper horizontal functioning implies God-directedness, i.e., proper vertical functioning. But this is clearly not the case. It is possible, for example, to regulate sleep, and be rigorously logical, and impressively frugal, and yet do it for selfish reasons—that seems clear enough. On the other hand, proper vertical direction will tend toward non-idolatrous (i.e., better) horizontal functioning, and so there should be some correlation between the two. But there are far too many examples of non-Christians excelling—and of we Christians faltering— in the various horizontal modalities that the correlation is probably modest. There is empirical evidence of this claim as well, though it is crude. If we take religiosity as a very rough proxy for proper vertical functioning, i.e., of looking at individuals who are at least trying to direct their lives toward God, we expect performance to be better across modalities, and this is what we generally see, though the effect sizes are modest—a point to which we shall return in the section on common grace.

48. Technically speaking, conscience is what we might call an interaction between the ideal and the other dimensional selves. See the section on interactive selves.

49. Nina Strohminger, Joshua Knobe, and George Neman, "The True Self: A Psychological Concept Distinct from the Self," *Perspectives on Psychological Science* 12 (2017): 552.

50. Charles S. Carver and Michael F. Scheier, "Origins and Functions of Positive and Negative Affect: A Control-Process View," *Psychological Review* 97 (1990).

it as an introject (Freud), or a defense mechanism (Horney), or social construct.

A Christian worldview, on the other hand, provides a way of understanding the ideal self, which completes the triune image of God in human beings. Just as the vertical images the Spirit, and the horizontal the Son, the ideal self is the ineradicable internal witness to the perfection of God the Father and to our obligation to "be perfect, as your heavenly-Father is perfect" (Matt 5:48).

Our ideal self is deeply connected to questions of identity—of what we are called to be. Here we may distinguish between structure and direction as it pertains to the ideal self. Structurally, human beings will have some sense of what they ought to be, holding themselves against some ideal or standard, consciously or unconsciously, thereby taking upon themselves some identity. Directionally, human beings may hold themselves to actual or false ideals, and have accurate or false identities. At creation, these ideals or standards were God-given and true, i.e., they were properly directed.

The ideal self may further be divided into the universal and particular. The universal ideal is that which pertains to all human beings universally, i.e., all human beings ought to be properly vertically aligned, function appropriately in all the horizontal modalities as they unfold slowly over time, and evaluating themselves accurately—against an accurate ideal—as they develop. In a *particular* sense, however, the ideal self refers to the giftings and callings bestowed upon any given individual, which God expects each particular person to actualize for his glory and for the good of the world. The universal is the deeper, truer self, whereas the particular is qualified by the universal. Still, the particular is essential to proper human functioning.

Man as Trinity; Pyramidal Functioning

We may therefore think of the human soul as a trinity, as did Augustine. But instead of locating this trinity in memory, intellect, and will (which Calvin found untenable), we may perhaps more plausibly locate it in our horizontal, vertical, and ideal functioning. In the horizontal self, we manifest the modal diversity of the creation, as an image of the Son of God through whom God made all things and who entered himself into the fullness of our creaturely experience. In the vertical self, the unifying center and heart of our nature, we experience what Dooyeweerd called "the innate impulse of human selfhood to direct itself toward the *true* or toward a *pretended* absolute Origin..."[51], an image of the Spirit who proceeds from

51. Herman Dooyeweerd, *A New Critique of Theoretical Thought*, vol. 1: The Necessary Presuppositions of Philosophy (Philadelphia: Presbyterian & Reformed, 1953), 57.

the first and second persons of the Godhead. And finally, in the ideal self, we retain the whispers of that true Origin, God the Father almighty, the God of perfection and beauty, which subserves both the internal sense of what we ought to be (a prerequisite of conscience), and also the subception of the Perfection which is our true Origin, the *sensus divinitatus*.

Figure 6: Classroom demonstration of the pyramidal theory.

To illustrate this functioning, I have found the image of a pyramid to be useful, particularly one derived from a Sierpinski triangle, a well-known fractal. Just as fractals have been used to model various aspects of the material world, this "Sierpinski pyramid" provides a useful model of the human person. Each of the three sides of this pyramid represents one of the dimensional selves. In the paper model I have students create in my personality class, I have them draw in a vertical line to denote the vertical self, a horizontal line to signify the horizontal self and, for the ideal self which proceeds from the vertical and horizontal, an intersection of a vertical and a horizontal line. The photograph here depicts the horizontal and vertical, with the ideal self invisible.

Holding the physical pyramid raises other theoretical questions. The horizontal, vertical, and ideal are the three "dimensional" selves of this theory. When looking at the physical model, these are represented by focusing on one side of the pyramid at a time. But it is interesting that several other views of the pyramid are possible (which is obvious when one holds the model in one's hands). To wrap up our discussion of our created nature, we'll briefly address these in turn.

Interactive Selves

For example, it is possible to look at two sides at once. This view signifies what might be called interactive selves, conveying the idea that functioning in one dimension may influence—or be influenced by—functioning in another dimension. These influences may go either way (e.g., the horizontal might affect the ideal and the ideal the horizontal). With this in mind, there are 3! = 3 x 2 x 1 = 6 interactive selves. When we begin to consider interactive selves our appreciation of the created complexity of functioning begins to settle in.[52]

The Frame, Foundation and Fount of Life (The "How")

Another view of the pyramid is from the base or foundation. Is there anything foundational to horizontal, vertical, and ideal functioning? The Christian tradition says there is, and this is a crucial—perhaps *the* crucial—piece in any theory of human nature. It is the question of the *how*. Yes, we may—via the ideal self—have a sense of our goals and calling, of *where* we want to go both vertically and horizontally. But *how* precisely are we going to get there?

God did not make human beings to be Pelagians, endowing them with an autonomous power to image forth God—as if a sort of psychological deism applies to human functioning. Yes, humans are designed to stand upright before God, worshipping him only, in their vertical selves. They are, horizontally, designed to function properly in their multi-aspectual uniqueness. And they are—in their ideal selves—designed to have a accurate sense of what they ought to be, in both a universal and particular sense. But this does not imply that the power to actualize these things is found within human nature. A closer look at the Sierpinski pyramid shows that it is an empty structure—much like an atom is mostly empty space.[53] As Charles Taylor characterized premodern views of the person, we are "porous" selves, capable of being filled with God yet vulnerable to other influences.[54]

---

52. When we consider the effect of the ideal self on the other dimensions we are dealing with *evaluated* selves. The evaluated horizontal self, is the conscience directing one's modal functioning: It makes us ask if our modal functioning is what it ought to be. The evaluated vertical self is one's conscience over one's worship: and we ponder whether we worship as we ought. When we consider the influence of the horizontal self on the other two dimensions, we are talking about *embodied* dynamics: the embodied ideal self is the way current modal functioning shapes one's sense of identity or ought. The embodied vertical self is the way current modal functioning shapes the ultimate direction of the heart. Finally, when we consider the influence of the vertical self on the other two dimensions, we are looking at *animated* selves. The animated ideal self is how one's *why* shapes one's ideal or sense of what is desirable. The animated horizontal self refers to the way the direction of the heart shapes our modal functioning.

53. Leanne Payne, in her book on incarnational reality in the thought of C.S. Lewis, alludes to the point I am making here and draws this analogy. See Leanne Payne, *Real Presence: The Christian Worldview of C. S. Lewis as Incarnational Reality* (Grand Rapids: Baker Publishing Group, 1995), 30-31. Also, it should be noted that to create the pyramid, I have students fold a 2-dimensional Sierpinski triangle, hence the middle is actually empty, unlike a full-fledged Sierpinski tetrahedron, in which you have pyramids within pyramids. It very well may be the case in the future that the full tetrahedron is found to be the better model for the human person.

54. Taylor, Charles, *A Secular Age* (Boston, MA: Belknap, 2007), 27, 35-43.

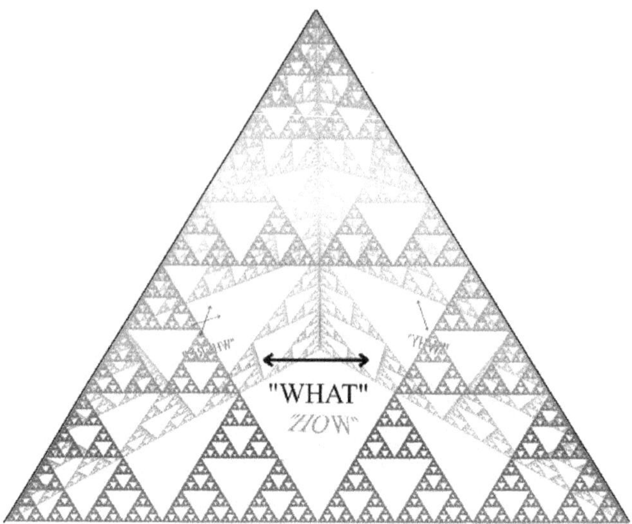

Figure 7: A more accurate view of the pyramidal model, emphasizing the porous self.

A better way of thinking of human beings, then, is to compare them to a lamp, made to be filled with a flame, or to a temple, built to be filled by the Spirit of God. Likewise, the colored pyramid[55] is best thought of as made of stained glass—the brilliance and beauty of the human creation cannot shine forth unless the Light shines forth from within.

The indwelling of God is of course a gift—how could one merit such an infinitely desirable communion? The Roman Catholic notion of *donum superadditum* (or a "superadded gift") seems to imply this, but one of the problems with this Catholic teaching is that it is often taken to suggest that there is an autonomous core to human nature, some part of us that doesn't need God's filling to function properly. In contrast to this, the model posited here states that the human self is made to be filled by God. As Edwards put it, God lived within Adam before the fall as within

55. Colored images are not possible in this volume, but each row of triangles that comprise the Sierpinski pyramid in this theory is shaded with a different color in the visible light spectrum, i.e., the "colors of the rainbow," an allusion to Dooyeweerd's analogy of the modal scale to the colors of the rainbow. In reality, there are millions of shades of color, not seven (as "ROY G BIV" would suggest). Colors such as "red" are actually spectra of colors. This conveys the idea that, while each of the major color categories may be thought to represent a modality, each modality may be further decomposed into submodalities. I hope to further elaborate on this theme (and many others) in a subsequent publication.

a house.[56] We were made to be filled to the measure of all the fullness of God (Ephesians 3:19). God would be before us, and God would be in us. This is the created design.

As this filling of God is—even before the fall—his gift to us, we may call this the "gracious frame of life." We are structurally designed to live by the gift of God's presence and power within us. And the result of this filling is a sense of completion, of happiness, of contentment, of shalom. These things are given gratuitously before we do anything. We are designed to act *from* this happiness and fullness. This is crucial. The "restlessness" of which both Augustine and Dooyeweerd speak is not creational. It is a result of the loss of God's presence in our lives.

The indwelling of God does not imply divinization. A lamp does not achieve its telos without a flame. But this does not make the lamp fire. The temple does not achieve its purpose unless it is filled with God. But that does not make the temple God. The stained-glass pyramid does not shine without the divine Light within. But that does not make the pyramid Light. Pentecost, and the promise of the filling of the Holy Spirit, may thus be understood as the restoration of creational design (grace restores nature), rather than as a new way of existing unavailable to Adam. Grace, as Bavinck said, "does not grant anything beyond what Adam, if he had remained standing, would have acquired in the way of obedience. Grace restores nature and raises it to its highest fulfillment, but it does not add a new, heterogeneous component to it."[57] The presence of God within the human self is creational, i.e., our default design, not a "new, heterogeneous component," or a being "take[n]…up into a supernatural order."[58] As Leanne Payne put it, ours is an *incarnational* reality, where God *comes down* to dwell within us, by design.

The funny thing about Seerveld's tin can is that it seems to be empty. But a tin can is designed to be filled; otherwise it misses its telos. The Sierpinski pyramid implies the same.

---

56. Jonathan Edwards, *Original Sin*, ed. Clyde A. Holbrook, vol. 3, The Works of Jonathan Edwards, (New Haven: Yale University Press, 1758/1970), 382.

57. Jan Veenhof, "Nature and Grace in Bavinck (A. Wolters, Trans.)," *Pro Rege* 34 (2006): 22.

58. Veenhof, "Nature and Grace in Bavinck," 16. Admittedly, this understanding gives grace a larger role than merely to liberate us from sin, which Bavinck seems to have held. Other Reformed thinkers (e.g., Goodwin, Owen, and Witsius) have given an important role for the Holy Spirit in Adam's original righteousness. It is beyond the scope of the present chapter to elaborate on the ways in which these Reformed stalwarts argued that the unfallen Adam was, as a part of his created nature, graciously united to the Spirit of God while still under the covenant of works. For a hint, see Mark Jones, "The (gracious?) covenant of works (again)," 2014. https://reformation21.org/the-gracious-covenant-of-works-1-php/.

The Diachronic Self (The "When")

It's also crucial to acknowledge that human beings were designed to *develop*. Vertically, though we were not to deviate from an upright position, there was also an element of growth in one's devotion to God (we see this in Jesus, who grew in wisdom and stature). Horizontally, each modality of our existence has a developmental trajectory; there is a seemingly infinite potentiality within our various capacities. There is also a sense in which the ideal self develops as well, as our understanding of the universal ideal and of our particular ideal grows. Indeed, our capacities are nearly infinitely developable, another way we manifest the glory of God *ad extra*. While the restlessness of which Augustine wrote is not creational, what Allport called "propriate striving" is, i.e., we long to get better and better at more and more as we actualize the infinite potentiality of our nature. The field of developmental psychology can shed considerable light on some of these realties, though of course the regnant worldview of psychology dims its light.

The Actualized Self (The "Who")

When we ask *who* we are as human beings, then, we would have been considering a work in progress, not from a state of sin and fallenness, but from a state of potentiality to actuality. Who we are at a given point in time could then be called an *actualized* self, denoting that when we function as designed we are forever in progress. Who are we? At any given point in time, we are the totality of our vertical, horizontal, ideal functioning, their interactions with one another, all situated through some foundation or frame of life. This is the ineradicable structure of human nature. Human beings are thus the glory of God *ad extra*, manifesting his beauty as they develop in these multitudinous ways.

Embeddedness

Finally, it must be recognized that human beings do not exist as triangles floating in empty space. Rather, they are embedded in relationships, families, institutions, and cultures. Each person, each family, each institution, and each culture with whom we have to do functions horizontally, vertically, ideally, and in some frame of life. Functioning at an individual level will always be the result of the staggeringly complicated interplay between these factors. To conclude, then, a Christian theory of personality ought to explain the who, what, when, where, why, and how of created human nature, both as individuals and as embedded in the many structures of created reality.

Taking the Fall Seriously in Psychology

According to Kuyper, one of the ways the Christian worldview is to be distinguished from non-Christian worldviews is that ours is an *abnormalist* view of the world. That is a fascinating word choice for psychology, because we psychologists tend to associate abnormality with abnormal psychology, the field interested in the understanding and treatment of mental illness. But there is a crucial sense in which, in this fallen world, all of psychology is abnormal psychology.

Here is why: one of the key concepts in Calvinism is that of "total depravity," an unfortunate name for a good idea. It doesn't mean that people are as bad as they can be. God is gracious, and he typically prevents that from happening, at least in this life. What it does mean is that fallenness affects the entirety of our being, body and soul, or, as we might say, in all dimensions, in all modalities. It affects the who, what, when, where, why and how of functioning. One of the ways modern psychology can distort our understanding is by causing us to forget this. We begin to equate *normality* with *typicality*, i.e., the middle 68 or 95% or so of whatever normal distribution we happen to be considering.[59] But in a Christian sense, *normality* means functioning as God designed, according to his *norms*. It is in this sense that all of psychology is abnormal psychology. But we need to qualify this right away—things are not, after all, as bad as they can be. Far from it. And we need to account for that, too.

Figure 8: *Explsion from the Garden of Eden* by Masaccio.

One benefit of spending considerable time describing our glorious and ennobling created nature is this—it is only when we possess an adequate view of humanity's magnificent design that we can fully appreciate the extent and tragedy of the fall. Masaccio's fresco of the expulsion from Eden powerfully captures the tragedy of this loss. We have, after all, lost just as much as did our first parents; we have just grown accustomed, as Lewis put it, to "making mud pies in a slum because [we] cannot imagine what is meant by the offer of a holiday at the sea."[60]

Part of the tragedy of the fall is the loss of the divine image. Structurally we have not lost

59. That is, one or two standard deviations above and below the mean of a normal distribution.

60. C.S. Lewis, *The Weight of Glory* (New York: Simon & Schuster, 1980), 26.

the image of God. But directionally, we have in many ways.[61]

Due to the limits of space and time, I'll need to be suggestive here. But one of the goals of this volume is to convey something of a Reformational research agenda, both for myself and whoever else might be interesting in picking up some of these pieces.

The Fall and the How: The Descent into the Legal Frame of Life

In their created goodness, humans knew they were empty vessels, meant to be filled with the presence of God. In the presence of God, they knew fullness of joy and were empowered for obedience. We are porous beings meant to be filled with God; our starting point is supposed to be fullness.[62] At the fall, we lost this communion with God, the Westminster Shorter Catechism says, and are under his wrath and curse, and subject to all miseries in this life.

One might argue that the greatest of these miseries is the descent from the gracious frame of life—in which the presence and fullness of God were happily received as the source of our flourishing—to a legal frame of life, in which we no longer see God as life of our life and breath of our breath, but, embracing the satanic "you shall be as God," believe rather that we are to be the source of our success, our self-esteem, of our life. Happiness and joy, rather than gifts to be received from God, are now things that must be earned. This isn't to deny human agency,[63] but rather to say that autonomous agency is the problem. God is no longer the *how* of our choices. In the story of "Jacob's ladder," Jacob isn't climbing up; rather, the angels are descending to him. In the legal frame of life—which is the default setting for fallen humans—we get this precisely wrong. Now, as self-respecting would-be deities, seeking to display our own majesty, we climb upwards in a process of self-glorification and self-justification, building up a life in which we can feel good about ourselves.

But here is the double-bind of living in the legal frame of life. We are, as fallen, by definition, lawbreakers, falling short of the mark in in-

61. This is similar to Edwards who argued that the natural [structural] image of God was not lost, but the moral [directional] image of God was lost. Jonathan Edwards, *The Works of Jonathan Edwards, Volume 2, Religious Affections*, ed. John E. Smith, vol. 2, The Works of Jonathan Edwards, (New Haven: Yale University Press, 1746/1959), 256.

62. This is not far removed from the idea that happiness is the cause rather than the effect of other positive outcomes in life. See Sonya Lyubomirsky, Laura King, and Ed Diener, "The benefits of frequent positive affect: Does happiness lead to success?," *Psychological Bulletin* 131 (2005).

63. I'm grateful to Eric Johnson for helping me formulate this point.

numerable ways. But in the legal frame, we define ourselves by our performance. Lawbreakers who seek to puff themselves up "by the law," as the apostle would put it, are in an inherently unstable position.[64] We instinctively guard ourselves against the knowledge of our faults and shortcomings.

Secular psychologists have noticed this guardedness against seeing our own faults. Bandura talked about mechanisms of self-exoneration, saying that self-reproach is the most intolerable human emotion and we go to great lengths to keep ourselves from a consciousness of falling short of our own performance standards. Daniel Gilbert talked about the psychological immune system, whereby we are unconsciously motivated to maintain a positive view of the self. And Tavris and Aaronson talked about the need to self-justify, a major thrust of the study of cognitive dissonance.[65]

There are two main defense mechanisms we employ to maintain a positive view of ourselves, legalism and antinomianism, which are really opposite sides of the self-justifying coin. In legalism, we persuade ourselves of our goodness by elevating our strengths to the standard by which we ought to be judged. The intelligent judge others by their intelligence; the athletic by their athleticism, the wealthy by their wealth, the artistic by their artistry. And because they tend to be better than most they derive self-worth by being "better than" others. In antinomianism, we devalue or dismiss those aspects of God's law that we transgress. Did God really say that lust is a sin? That lying is a sin? As dissonance theory predicts, one of the best ways to eradicate our discomfort over violating our own principles is to change those principles to line up with our behavior. Psychologists such as Jung and Horney have noted the cycle of pride and shame that humans are prone to; this theory helps account for that. When we live up to our legalisms, and when we dismiss those aspects of God's law we violate, we feel pride. But when we inevitably

64. And this is understandable to some extent in a legal frame of life—the Westminster Confession argues that humans were first put under a "covenant of works," and that future blessings would follow continued obedience. After the fall, with the Spirit of God departed from the temple of the human heart so to speak, we're now determined to carry out this covenant of works on our own. Indeed, we subceive that we remain under such a covenant, i.e., that we owe God our obedience. But since so much is at stake, we are deeply guarded against the knowledge of our own obligations and shortcomings. Freud taught that religion is wish fulfilment, but the actual reality of things is that our deepest fallen wish is that the true and living God not be.

65. Albert Bandura, "Selective Moral Disengagement in the Exercise of Moral Agency," *Journal of Moral Education* 31 (2002); Carol Tavris and Elliot Aronson, *Mistakes were Made (But not by Me) : Why We Justify Foolish Beliefs, Bad Decisions, and Hurtful Acts* (Orlando, FL: Harcourt, 2007); Daniel Gilbert, *Stumbling on Happiness* (Toronto: Vintage Canada, 2006).

meet others better than us, or we fail to attain our own standards, or we subceive the reality of the law we deny, we feel shame.

One significant tragedy of the legal frame of life is that nothing can be fully intrinsic any more. We're designed by God to flourish in all modalities, in all dimensions, to enter into the unique callings and to develop the unique giftedness with which we all are gifted. But in the legal frame of life, they are not ends in themselves but means to self-justification, seen as accomplishments rather than gifts, as identities and sources of pride.

The Fall of the Vertical Self: The Bentness of the "Why"

The vertical self is the *why* of human functioning, the direction of the soul toward or away from the living God and it is the religious core of our nature. Humans are *homo adorans*, man the worshipper: the vertical self is that rock-bottom "god"—the functional deity—that we pursue in all our actions, i.e., that thing we believe (consciously or not) will make us happy[66] which must be distinguished from *how* this happiness is attained.[67]

As empty vessels, without God in the temple of our nature, we are in our fallenness essentially empty, and thus restless and desperate for happiness, reaching out here and there to fill the void. The first thing that we can say about our fallen psychology is that we're no longer properly "vertically aligned," but rather we're bent in toward the creation, as Leanne Payne would say it, and prone to a whole variety of idolatries in which we take some aspect of the good creation and turn them into gods, such as food or sex or you name it. And our development can therefore no longer be multi-modal and balanced but rather prone to lopsided horizontal functioning, much as Karen Horney suggested in her theory of neurotic trends, that neurosis is taking one legitimate aspect or function and absolutizing it.[68]

66. As Edwards taught, self-interest is structural, not an aspect of the fall. We cannot be indifferent to our happiness. When we function as we ought, we make God our happiness.

67. Strangely, it is possible that people may remain in the legal frame of life and still seek to love God with all their hearts—most religious life may very well be like this, featuring man's ascent to God by works. Paul described the Israel of his day this way: "that they have a zeal for God, but not according to knowledge. For being ignorant of the [graciously bestowed] righteousness of God, and seeking to establish their own, they did not submit to God's righteousness" (Romans 10:2-4). This is the reason the *how* and the *why* must be distinguished. We may, in obedience to the commandment of God, seek to make God our *why* but do it on our own, seeking a righteousness "based on the law" or human effort.

68. B.R. Hergenhahn and Matthew H. Olson, *An Introduction to Theories of Personality*, Sixth ed. (Upper Saddle River, NJ: Prentice Hall, 2003), 138-40.

The Fall of the Ideal Self and the Descent into False Identities

There is a kind of logical core to our functioning: from the *how* to the *why*, from the *why* to the *where*, and from the *where* to the *what*. This is the way we ought to function: we ought to begin in fullness (the *how*), and from that fullness, lift our hearts up to God. From him, through him and to him (Romans 11:16). And then with our eyes fixed on God, we can get a correct sense of *where* we ought to go, in our calling both individual and particular.

In the legal frame of life, however, the creational/structural universal ideal self is experienced as a tyrant, a bully a source of condemnation. Much of modern psychology is an attempt to deal with its tyranny. Freud, for example, noted the violence of the "superego" and so silenced its voice by reducing it to "introjected" strictures imposed upon us by a stern father, rather than imperfect articulations of the law of our being. Conversely, Horney dismissed it as an unrealistic "idealistic self," a defense mechanism by which we puff ourselves up with delusions of grandeur. Modern psychologies are legal frame psychologies, and are therefore guarded vis-à-vis the ideal self.

In the legal frame, we're no longer capable of bearing the multi-faceted glory of the divine image; the grandeur of the universal ought (best expressed, as we will see, by Christ himself) is suppressed.[69] In an unconscious attempt to self-justify, we instead define ourselves narrowly, by (what we take to be) attainable standards, by finding our identity in our work, for example, or in our family, or even in one's gender identity. The ideal self is thus incorporated into our self-justificatory compulsions. The tragedy of this narrowing of the ideal self is that it falls far below the actual universal ideal pertaining to our nature. While these truncated identities are enacted in the name of being true to ourselves, they tragically keep us from being true to our deep nature. Our true nature is given to us by God. It is a calling, rather than a construction. Though we are able, via propriate striving, to subceive the existence of the structural ideal self, we tend to repress it and may respond with rage against those who would remind us of this repression.[70]

69. This is not hard to demonstrate. When people are asked to describe their best possible self (a positive psychology intervention), very rarely will they say, "to love the Lord my God with all my heart!"

70. As discussed in the section on creation, there is already within psychological science a literature on concepts such as the true self, and these would be ripe for exploration from a Reformational vantage point. The fact that people experience a disconnect from their true selves is part of this. We understand, on some level, that something is urgently wrong, hence the almost feral protectiveness we may manifest regarding its definition.

The Fall, the Horizontal Self, and the Modal Diversity of Dysfunction

It is when we talk about the horizontal self that our task becomes overwhelming. Martin Seligman, a founder of positive psychology, was famous for claiming that 20th century psychology was focused almost entirely on "the negative." As we consider the various modalities that pertain to our psychological functioning (either by being psychological *per se* or by analogical relation), the breathtaking and tragic scope of the fall becomes readily apparent.

It's helpful to invoke the longstanding distinction between natural and moral evil at this point. The former has to do with dysfunction that is not the result of moral agency or sin. The latter is the realm of sin. Modern psychology deals with both, but tends to treat everything as natural evil, as something that happens to us. The field tends to believe that it's either nature or nurture—choice has nothing to do with the outcomes in our lives (unless we blame the bad choices of parents or other environmental influences). A Reformational research agenda would attempt to tease apart the natural and moral evil in each and every subfield of psychology, to better understand how far the curse is found.[71]

Taking Grace and Redemption Seriously in Psychology

Just as sin affects all aspects of our functioning, so too grace affects all. Once again, we need an adequate understanding of human nature, otherwise we will unduly limit the scope of God's grace; our expectations for transformation will be severely hindered. We're also liable to misunderstand what precisely is *redemptive* in psychology. We therefore immediately need to draw the key Reformed distinction between common and special grace.

Common grace, of course, is the idea that God constrains sin and allows a measure—sometimes a very generous measure—of the richness and joy and complexity and beauty of human life to be experienced, even by those who reject the gospel of Christ. Indeed, created life within this vale of tears is sometimes so captivating that it's hard to imagine that anything greater is possible or desirable. It's the burden of Christian psy-

71. To cut down the length of this chapter I needed to remove a nearly 900-word section which explored themes of natural and moral evil in the psychological modalities, ie., the sensory, fiduciary, ethical, cognitive, lingual, as well as in certain analogical psychologies, i.e., behavioral neuroscience, social psychology, behavioral economics, forensic psychology, and, corresponding to the aesthetic modality, positive psychology. I'd be happy to share these ideas with scholars interested in exploring these themes!

chologists to show that special grace—which has to do with the unique blessings and privileges that come to regenerate persons[72] through faith and union with Christ, such as adoption, justification, and sanctification—does indeed promise something far greater, by restoring us to our glorious original design. Technically speaking, *redemption* in Christ is the domain of special grace, though we may conceive of common grace as in service to special grace (as providing a context in which the gospel may run) and perhaps even a non-salvific outworking of God's victory over sin at the cross. Whatever the relation between the two, we need to take both seriously in psychology.

Taking Common Grace Seriously in Psychology

Let's begin with God's common grace. What would it mean to take common grace seriously in psychology? For one, it would mean appreciating that the creational structure of our human nature (described in the section on creation) is itself a gift, a kind of abiding grace. This is why Eric Johnson calls it "*creation* grace." Breaking the law of our nature is costly. The more we do break it, the more we are harmed and the more prone to deformity we get. So self-interest alone provides some motivation to live carefully according to our nature. As the Reformational tradition says, creation structure "*impinges upon*"[73] us. Of course, the insanity of sin is that we continue to break the law anyway. But the fact that the creation pushes back and says, "Not so fast!" is a grace.

A full-fledged understanding of psychology is therefore going to require that we be keenly aware of the ways in which human suffering can be ameliorated and human flourishing increased without overtly connecting to the gospel. As agents of common grace,[74] there are a whole range of things that Christian psychologists can do to influence and improve human functioning without being overtly Christian. But we need also to be keenly aware that common grace remedies point toward deeper and more abiding remedies in the gospel. Christian psychologists, in oth-

72. As Kuyper called it, "palingenesis," i.e., the status of being truly converted or born again; of being forever united to Christ by faith. This of course presupposes the Reformed and biblical doctrine of the perseverance of the saints, that those who are genuinely converted by the Spirit of God will continue in faith. As John says, sometimes people will leave the church, but this only proves they were never of the church.

73. Albert M. Wolters, Creation Regained: Biblical Basics for a Reformational Worldview (Grand Rapids, MI: Eerdmans, 2005), 62.

74. This winsome phrase (and idea) appears in Richard J. Mouw, *He Shines in All That's Fair : Culture and Common Grace* (Grand Rapids, Mich.: W.B. Eerdmans Pub. Co., 2001), 80.

er words, ought to be able to—and yearn to—lead clients into the special grace "benefits"[75] available in Christ alone.

Common Grace and the How

If our first parents were created in a gracious frame in which the entirety of their lives was received as a gift, humanity has now via the fall descended into a legal frame of life by which we actualize the satanic "You shall be as God," via self-justification and defensiveness. But God by his mercy powerfully restrains sin, and intimations of his grace—which now includes favor toward *sinners*—are shadowed in psychology itself. For example, Carl Rogers famously argued that a client needs to experience "unconditional positive regard" rather than law-like "conditions of worth" if they are to make therapeutic progress. Mindfulness research places a strong emphasis on "nonjudgmental" awareness of our own psychological states. Karen Horney strongly warned against actualizing a false "idealized self." All of these have in common the truth that an unyielding application of the law can cause much harm. All of these things are shadows of the grace that God bestows in Christ, apart from works. Still, much of this "grace" veers into antinomianism ("You're perfect just the way you are!"), in which one's own desires or "organismic valuing" (as Rogers put it) replaces the law of God as the rule of life. The beauty of God's special grace is that he accepts and loves us in spite of our flaws, not because we're perfect just as we are.

Perhaps the purest shadowing of the truth of the gracious frame of life is research in gratitude. The leading figure in the area, Robert Emmons, in light of the extensive benefits of gratitude,[76] says that gratitude is the "queen of the virtues," a sweeping role consistent for what we have called the foundation and frame of life.[77] Habits of gratitude—of seeing life as a gift—certainly point toward the fulness of the gracious frame of life in Christ, even as they often leave unanswered the key question: to whom are we grateful?[78]

---

75. This is the language of the Westminster Standards.

76. Alex M. Wood, Jeffrey J. Froh, and Adam W. A. Geraghty, "Gratitude and Well-Being: A Review and Theoretical Integration," *Clinical Psychology Review* 30 (2010); Lillian Jans-Beken et al., "Gratitude and Health: An Updated Review," *The Journal of Positive Psychology* 15 (2019).

77. Robert A. Emmons, "Is Gratitude the Queen of the Virtues and Ingratitude the King of the Vices?," in *Perspectives on Gratitude: An Interdisciplinary Approach*, ed. David Carr (New York: Routledge, 2016).

78. Russell D. Kosits, "Flatland and the Deep Meaning of Gratitude," *PsycCRITIQUES* 62 (2017). I might also add that there are many normal developmental phenomena that also mitigate and bely the autonomy of the legal frame, such as a sense of dependence upon parents, spouse, communities. All of these things point to the

Common Grace and the Vertical Self

The vertical self is structural—we will worship something. As Scripture, Augustine, Aquinas and others have argued, there will be some ultimate *why* behind our actions. Perhaps the best evidence for the beneficial impact of common grace impact on the vertical self is religion itself. Jesus argued that narrow is the way that leads to salvation (Matt 7:14)—and the Old Testament law was deeply preoccupied with idolatry and false religion. The Scriptures do not give us a blanket endorsement of religion *per se.* Calvin famously said the human heart is "a perpetual factory of idols."[79]

Nevertheless, intrinsically motivated religious people *are* attempting to order their lives around a higher purpose, around some notion of deity. In *Till We Have Faces*, CS Lewis argued that the "primitive" sacrifice-offering pagans are more spiritually advanced than their secular Greek counterparts. So while most religion likely falls short of the true worship of the true God demanded in the Scriptures, we might expect there to be some general overall benefit in religion *per se.*

And of course we do find that. It has been more than two decades since Seybold and Hill published their landmark article cataloguing what was an historic change of opinion about religion.[80] While 20th century psychology had often seen religion as harmful, they showed how "the influence is largely beneficial," for both physical and mental health, while also cataloguing the ways religion can be harmful. These general effects have largely been sustained in subsequent decades.[81]

Yet we need not limit common grace impacts on the vertical self to religion *per se.* Augustine recognized that the human heart is defined by the ordering of its loves. This would imply that even if a human heart has

---

idea that we are not autonomous ladder-climbers but rather rely upon the grace of multitudes. And so, while "the how" is not repaired by God's common grace, the loss of the how is mitigated, and the truth to which it points is shadowed.

79. John Calvin, *The Institutes of the Christian Religion*, ed. John T. McNeill, trans. Ford Lewis Battles, vol. one (Louisville, Kentucky: Westminster John Knox Press, 1559/1960), 108. In its most important sense, the misdirection of the vertical self is absolute. Augustine's two cities differentiate those driven by the love of self from those driven by the love of God, full stop. This is of course a reflection of the dichotomous way the Scriptures conceive of the matter, the saved vs. the lost, the wheat and the tares. Dooyeweerd's approach to the heart was to the same effect.

80. Kevin S Seybold and Peter C. Hill, "The Role of Religion in Mental and Spiritual Health," *Current Directions in Psychological Science* 10 (2001), 21.

81. For example, Samuel R. Weber and Kenneth I. Pargament, "The role of religion and spirituality in mental health," *Current Opinion in Psychiatry* 27 (2014). Sonya Lyubomirsky, *The How of Happiness: A New Approach to Getting the Life You Want* (New York: Penguin, 2007). The benefits for young people in particular may be found in: Timothy A. Sisemore, *The Psychology of Religion and Spirituality* (Hoboken, NJ: Wiley, 2016), 119.

not yet come to love God above all, it may very well value created things more or less in line with their relative merit. Here is how. Aquinas argued that human love includes the incorporation of the happiness of the other into oneself. The self is thus capable of expansion and modern psychology recognizes this.[82] Edwards, in his *Treatise on the Nature of True Virtue* (in which he was in a sense differentiating between common and special grace effects on the vertical self) argued that the human self may be lifted from pure egoism with an ever-widening purview of concern. We may include within the self things like family, or team, or colleagues, or party, or country, etc. This "worship" of things greater than the self may have a positive impact, at least on those within the circle of concern. But in each of these expansions, though better than pure narcissism, the danger of evil and violence lurks. Hence the damage that a "momma bear" mentality can do, for example, when protecting one's own is a pretext for mistreating others. Or how the love of party causes some to de-humanize those in the other party.[83]

But the point is that the proper direction of the vertical self is foreshadowed when the self is expanded to include some notion of divinity or some elevated element of creation within its why. Sometimes these expansions are ennobling, other times they undergird great human evil. But in all cases, the vertical self is ultimately misdirected unless and until the expansion comes to include the true and living God via the virtue of Love.

Common Grace and the Ideal Self

Humanity may very well be the only species that seeks to improve itself. This, like the inevitable quest to direct the heart to some deity (vertical functioning), seems structural. At the beginning of every year, many of us assess how the previous year went, how we need to improve, and set resolutions to get better. And these resolutions often follow the modal scale, desiring to lose weight (biotic), or to learn a new language (lingual) or to learn a new hobby (cultural-formative), to name just a few. Gordon Allport's notion of "propriate striving," is apropos, i.e., that human beings generally do desire to be better than they are, to "intend [our] own perfection." He may very well have been right, that this is "the

82. Arthur Aron et al., "The Self-Expansion Model of Motivation and Cognition in Close Relationships," in *The Oxford Handbook of Close Relationships*, ed. J. A. Simpson and L. Campbell (New York: Oxford University Press., 2013). See also Adler on "social interest" in: Heinz L. Ansbacher and Rowena R. Ansbacher, eds., *The Individual Psychology of Alfred Adler; A Systematic Presentation in Selections from his Writings*, 1st ed. (New York: Basic Books, 1956).

83. Jonathan Edwards, "Two Dissertations," in *Works of Jonathan Edwards, Volume 8, Ethical Writings*, ed. Paul Ramsey (New Haven: Yale University Press, 1989), 555.

only really clean aspect of [fallen] human nature."[84] This yearning to be better is one of the best manifestations of the restraint of sin, even if it is tangled up within the legal frame. In Dante's *Inferno*, the deepest part of hell is frozen, a place where no more becoming is possible. But in this fallen world, the hope for positive change graciously remains and seems universal.

Psychologists also have a large, robust, and useful literature on goal setting, i.e., of determining which standards or ideals we should adopt on our own. Kennon Sheldon, for example, has a multi-step process by which one may evaluate and optimize their own goals, to ensure they are consistent with one's deepest self.[85] This, and work like it, suggests that, via common grace, the internal sense of *ought* remains robustly intact and can motivate positive change.

Common Grace and Horizontal Functioning

Just as the vertical and ideal are structural and remain sources of common or creation grace in this broken world, so too the horizontal self. It turns out that this Reformational ontology is a very powerful framework for engaging the many ways human beings may enjoy a degree of "proximate flourishing"[86] in this life. I have found the theoretical framework developed in this chapter to be a useful way of organizing the entire field of positive psychology, and there is ample empirical evidence to support the role of each of the modalities of the horizontal self in human flourishing. The fact that the modal scale profitably helps organize a field of psychology like positive psychology is strong evidence of its truth. [87]

---

84. Gordon W. Allport, *The Roots of Religion*, Advent Papers, (Boston: Church of the Advent, 1943), 19.

85. Kennon M. Sheldon, *Optimal Human Being: An Integrated Approach* (Mahwah, NJ: Lawrence Erlbaum, 2004).

86. Just as Steven Garber advised that Christians make peace with "proximate justice," which "realizes that something is better than nothing, It allows us to make peace with some justice, some mercy, all the while realizing that it will only be in the new heaven and new earth that we find all our longings finally fulfilled, that we will see all of God's demands finally met. It is only then—there we will see all of the conditions for human flourishing finally in place, socially, economically, and politically." Similarly via common grace, we might argue human beings, regardless of their relationship to God in Christ, are capable of experiencing proximate flourishing. See Steven Garber, "Finding our way to great work, even in politics: Making peace with proximate justice," *Comment*, August 31, 2007.

87. In order to save space, a section of about 2600 words (including 24 mostly scientific references and 22 footnotes) needed to be omitted here. Painful! But again, I am open to conversations with scholars who would like to explore this theme in more depth.

Beyond Common Grace: Taking Special Grace Seriously in Psychology

Explorations of the Christian psychology of the past would often quote Ovid's phrase: "I see and approve the better course; I choose the worse."[88] As a teacher of the science of human flourishing (i.e., positive psychology) for well over a decade, I have lectured for perhaps hundreds of hours of the multitudinous pathways to flourishing, such as those alluded to above. And yet, if I am honest, my own course of action falls far short of what I now know. This drives me back to the grace of God. But it seems an indisputable aspect of biblical revelation that God calls us, even in this life, to a restoration to our created design, that in Christ, we may be restored in our *how*, as well as in our vertical, ideal, and horizontal functioning. Paul chastised the Corinthians thus, "I can only call you merely human" (1 Cor 3:3) by which he meant that the Christians at Corinth lived far below their privileges. We of course are no different. But, today, one of the reasons we live far below our privileges is, frankly, because our psychologies are so impoverished. The Christian psychology of the past was aspirational and ennobling; our efforts in psychology today should aspire to the same.

In the historic Christian psychology of the past, the human soul was understood to be designed for virtue. Aquinas borrowed the four cardinal virtues from the Greeks and argued that these corresponded to different faculties of the soul. Temperance was the virtue that corresponded to the concupiscible power, courage the virtue pertaining to the irascible power. justice the virtue corresponding to the will, and wisdom the virtue corresponding to the intellect. It was an aspirational system well worth careful study. These insights are as pertinent today as they were then, and, in a Reformational framework, would belong to the realm of common grace. These virtues are, by God's gracious restraint of sin, accessible to those outside of Christ, and the world is filled with exemplars of these virtues.

But the tradition recognized that there are virtues that uniquely pertain to the palingenesis.[89] Thomas called these the three theological virtues of faith, hope, and love, and noted that these virtues in turn refashion the cardinal virtues. The theological virtues are among the effects of *special* grace, and pertain to the horizontal, ideal, and vertical selves. That is, faith is the theological virtue pertaining to horizontal functioning (the righteous shall live by faith), hope is the theological virtue pertaining to ideal functioning (our confident expectation or hope is that when he

---

88. Norman Fiering, *Moral Philosophy at Seventeenth-Century Harvard: A Discipline in Transition* (Chapel Hill, NC: University of North Carolina Press, 1981), 115.

89. i.e., to those regenerate in Christ. See footnote 71.

returns we shall become as He is, conforming to the ideal), and love is the theological virtue pertaining to vertical functioning (whereby we love the Lord our God with all our heart, all our mind, and all our strength).

Yes, Christian psychologists are called to be agents of common grace as Mouw said, and we may facilitate proximate flourishing in multitudinous ways. When we are called to give a drink of water, Jesus is not saying, "Save their soul." He is simply saying, "Quench their thirst." People do need water and it is not unspiritual to give people what they need. But if we do not understand the difference between proximate flourishing and the deep flourishing that comes to us through the gospel of Christ, we have failed in our calling, perhaps not as individual Christians in psychology, but certainly as a collective. The cups of water that we bring point to the living water, which is Christ. Christians in psychology need to know what it is to drink the living water, and be ready to pass this along to others. And we need a psychological system that moves us in this direction.

Special grace calls us to a way of functioning that does not cancel out common grace ways of flourishing, but rather complements and completes them. Gospel transformation is not opposed to flourishing in all dimensions—precisely the opposite. As the book of Proverbs attests, the fear of God is the beginning of the wisdom (Prov. 9:10) that leads to shalom in all aspects of life. So what does special grace transformation look like?

"Father": The Restoration of the How Through Christ

The gospel of Christ is at its core about the how. First and foremost—redemption is the righteousness of God (not that of man), received by faith from first to last, by grace and not by works (Rom 1:17; Eph 2:8-9). The gospels repeatedly remind us that the pathway to salvation is "by grace," and "through faith," and "by the Spirit." Any salvation that is not by the grace of Christ, through faith in Christ, and by the Spirit of Christ, is not salvation. Whether we like it or not, this is the clear teaching of Scripture. And we *should* like it—otherwise we're once again putting ourselves and our righteousness on center stage, addicted to works, remaining in the legal frame.

The gospel *how* is in some sense a restoration of our created design, because we were born to live in the gracious frame of life. God was to be the flame in the lantern of our nature. This has not changed. At creation, the presence of the Holy Spirit in the human heart was a grace that we instinctively received as a gift. And he was the light of our light, the light within the lamp. But through the fall something fundamental has changed in that we are now sinners and under his wrath and curse (WSC

Q19), and this light has, apart from his regenerating grace, gone out.

Step number one in moving from common grace to special grace transformation is recognizing, as David did after being confronted with a particularly egregious sin, that "I have sinned against the Lord" (2 Sam 12:13). That *my sins* cry out for retribution. That *my sin* runs deep, and *my disorder* runs deep, even if I've "got my stuff together" when I compare myself to others, because the standard of comparison is not "others," but rather is the law of God in all of its exacting perfection.

We've already discussed how difficult it is to admit wrongdoing in the legal frame of life, even in the most mundane matters. The gospel calls us, then, to the impossible, to recognize our sin, our shortcomings, and indeed even our worthiness of damnation. It seems harsh, but what is the alternative? Thinking we deserve eternal life? The bad news comes before the good.

Every blessing of the gospel comes through Jesus Christ, the spotless Lamb of God who takes away the sins of the world. What is offered to us in the gospel is now mediated to us through him. Special grace transformation begins with a full appreciation of the person of Christ, the God-man. We cannot understand special grace transformation apart from Christ.

Christ entered fully into our humanity. Yet, as sinless, no aspect of his human nature was misdirected. His *how* (frame of life) was God, i.e., he was conceived by the Holy Spirit (Luke 1:35) and filled by the Holy Spirit as he was specially commissioned for his messianic work (Luke 3:22). He knew he could not do anything apart from his Father (John 5:19). His *why* (vertical functioning) was properly directed; he did everything for the glory of God (e.g., John 17:1). He had a clear sense of the *where*, i.e., his particular and general ideal self were properly directed. He knew who he was meant to be as the archetypal human (general ideal self, born under the law of God, Gal 4:4), but he also knew who he was in his particular calling (particular ideal self), as the Messiah, the one who was called to preach the gospel (Luke 4:18) and to bear the sins of the whole world (1 John 2:2), to die, to rise again, and then to share the power of this life and death with others (John 12:24).

John Calvin said in his *Institutes* (3.1.1) that unless this Christ lives in us, he is of no use to us. God's intention is that Christ's human perfection will be graciously given to those who will receive him by faith, through union with him (Col 1:27), by his Spirit. The glory of the gospel is that this fullness is, in one sense, given to us all at once. Every spiritual blessing is ours in union with him (Eph 1:3) and we have been given fulness in Christ (Col 2:10). As we are restored to the redemptive *how*, we no longer attempt to climb the ladder of performance back to God in our own strength, but rather, by the grace of God, receive the fullness of Christ by faith, walk by the Spirit, and are filled with the Spirit.

I have suggested that hints of the redemptive *how* have been hinted at in psychology, especially through research on gratitude, which sees life as a gift. Would it be possible to empirically measure special grace influences on the *how*? Though there is no measure of this construct *per se*, Joshua Knabb's Christian Gratitude Scale—that has items such as "I should thank God daily for his forgiveness" and "I should be thankful to God because I do not deserve all he provides"—may serve as a good proxy.[90]

The Lord's Prayer, as Aquinas taught, is the perfect prayer that tells us not only what to pray, but the order in which we ought to pray these things. It begins with "our Father" (Matt. 6:9) or, as Luke says, "Father" (Luke 11:12). When we, in fellowship with Jesus, look up to heaven and say, "Father," we receive God as gift.

"Hallowed be Thy Name": The Restoration of the Why through Christ

Psychologists in the psychoanalytic tradition will sometimes audaciously talk about "*personality* change," i.e., transformation in the deepest core of who we are. Scripturally, the deepest change imaginable is the very basic promise of the gospel, that our *why* might be changed, i.e., that we may move from egocentric to theocentric beings. That whether we eat or drink or whatever we do we can do it for the glory of God (1 Cor 10:31). That we might no longer live for ourselves, but for Christ (2 Cor 5:5). This is the change that changes everything else. It is to take an idolater, who is bent in toward the creature, and reorient them toward the Father. We see this in the Lord's Prayer. When we pray the Lord's Prayer, we are praying the prayer of Jesus. Part of our "putting on of Christ" (Rom 13:14) comes through praying his prayer. When we pray the first petition[91] of the Lord's Prayer, i.e., "hallowed be thy name" we receive afresh the God-centeredness of Christ into ourselves. But—it bears repeating—this is simply to be restored to our created design, to "normal" functioning. And thus, it ought to be a top priority of Christian psychologists.

When the gospel transforms us and God becomes our why, the theological virtue of love, as Aquinas said, is developed, i.e., we begin to love the Lord our God with all our heart, soul, mind, and strength.

As was the case with the *how*, we shouldn't dismiss this as unmeasurable. Joshua Knabb, once again has a scale that seems to approach this

90. Joshua J. Knabb et al., "The Christian Gratitude Scale: An Emic Approach to Measuring thankfulness in Every Season of Life," *Spirituality in Clinical Practice* (2021). Still, actually *living* in the gracious frame of life is more than a recognition that we "should" be thankful, but rather a deep experience of this gratitude.

91. The Westminster Shorter Catechism divides the Lord's Prayer into a preface, six petitions, and a conclusion. See questions 100-07.

virtue of love to God, the Communion with God Scale. Items like "I feel a deep sense of connection with God," "I pray to fellowship with God," and "having a relationship with God brings me pleasure" approximate the love of God which is the heart of the restored *why*.[92]

"Thy Kingdom Come, Thy Will be Done": Restoration of the Ideal Self through Christ

As our hearts are vertically aligned, our ideal self is also changed. The first change that takes place is the universal ideal. That is, we realize that we were predestined to be transformed the image of the Son (Rom 8:29). Jesus is the one whose *how* was correct, whose *why* was correct, whose *ideal* was correct, whose *horizontal*, while not fully developed was nevertheless non-idolatrous. That's the ideal for us. And so our universal ideal is changed in Christ.

But so too our particular ideal is changed. We can begin to get a sense that our actions in this life are not just for us, but also connect to God's broader redemptive purposes. We can begin to ask, "How does my life uniquely further the kingdom?" Thus, we like Jesus pray, "Thy kingdom come." The particular way that we advance the kingdom is what we typically refer to as *calling* (though of course the universal ideal is the primary calling of all Christians).

As the ideal self is perfected in Christ, we develop the theological virtue of Hope, a confident expectation that we indeed will be conformed to his image (and thus restored to our full humanity).

Though no distinctively Christian scale yet exists to measure this, there are some "secular" analogies. The Moral Self-Image Scale approximates the universal ideal but in a general way, not specifically taking Christ as exemplar, focusing on characteristics like being caring, compassionate, and honest.[93] The Calling and Vocation Questionnaire, approximates the particular ideal, though the scale is oriented toward work—one item on the brief scale is: "I have a good understanding of my calling as it applies to my career."[94] Perhaps versions of these scales specifically designed to access the effects of special grace might be developed, much as Knabb has done in other areas.

92. J. Knabb and K.T. Wang, "The Communion with God Scale: Shifting from an Etic to Emic Perspective to Assess Fellowshipping with the Triune God," *Psychology of Religion and Spirituality* 13 (2021).

93. Jennifer Jordan, Marijke C. Leliveld, and Ann E. Tenbrunsel, "The Moral Self-Image Scale: Measuring and Understanding the Malleability of the Moral Self," *Frontiers in Psychology* 6 (2015).

94. Bryan J. Dik et al., "Development and Validation of the Calling and Vocation Questionnaire and Brief Calling Scale," *Journal of Career Assessment* 20 (2012).

"Give us this Day our Daily Bread, etc.": The Restoration of the Horizontal Self through Christ

I have briefly mentioned that there is ample empirical evidence that human flourishing follows the pattern predicted by the modal scale. In my positive psychology course we talk about the evidence for biotic, sensory, fiduciary, ethical, cognitive, lingual, social, cultural/formative, economic, justicial, and aesthetic aspects of flourishing.[95] I see these forms of flourishing available to all, via common grace. So in a sense, we would not expect the *what* of Christian flourishing to look different from that of non-Christians. Fullness of psychological flourishing would, for example, include normative habits of diet, exercise, sleep, attention, attachment, desire, thinking, self-narration, relating, work, financial management, and giving others their due. But what *would* change is the *how* (from a legal to gracious frame), the *why* (directed to God), and the *where* (actualizing non-idolatrous universal and particular ideals). And these differences, of course, would change everything. This is why in my positive psychology course, the interventions I use (or design) attempt to draw deeply on these Christian motives.

To access the way specifically Christian motivations change horizontal functioning, we would need to consider this aspect by aspect. Here are two examples: in terms of the sensory/attentional functioning, anyone might benefit from mindfulness meditation. But Knabb *et al.* found that specifically Christian forms of meditation were particularly helpful in reliving ruminative thoughts. In our social modality, anyone might benefit from forgiveness (and secular approaches to forgiveness have been developed). But "imbuing forgiveness with sacred meaning" increases the likelihood that forgiveness will actually take place.[96]

To close, one might make the case that when we sanctify all our horizontal functioning to God, we are in a biblical sense, living by faith. That's the spirit behind the fourth, fifth, and sixth petitions of the Lord's Prayer, i.e., to trust that God will give us what we need, protect us from temptation, and deliver us from evil. Thus the perfection of the horizontal self in Christ is the theological virtue of Faith. Here again, Knabb has designed scales that seem relevant. As Aquinas related the theological virtue of Faith to belief in the truth, Knabb's Christian Worldview Scale seems relevant (e.g., "God the Father sent God the Son to atone for my sins"). And since saving faith in the Reformed tradition has been understood to include not

95. But, again, the discussion of these things was removed due to space limitations.

96. Joshua J. Knabb et al., "Christian Meditation for Repetitive Negative Thinking: A Multisite Randomized Trial Examining the Effects of a 4-Week Preventative Program," *Spirituality in Clinical Practice* 7, no. 1 (2020); D.E. Davis et al., "Sanctification of forgiveness," *Psychology of Religion and Spirituality* 4 (2012).

only affirmation of right doctrine (*notitia* and *assensus*—which seem to be measured by the worldview scale), but also trust (*fiducia*), Knabb's Christian Contentment Scale seems to tap into the trust dimension very well (e.g., "I feel at rest within my innermost being because I have confidence in God")."[97]

Initial empirical measurement of this pyramidal theory therefore seems within reach.

Questions for Discussion

1. Would you agree that psychology's major worldview commitments today include empiricism, naturalism, and progressivism? Are there other worldview beliefs that hold sway in the field?
2. When psychologists freely affirm naturalism or progressivism in their publications or conference presentations, how do you respond? If you disagree, do you feel comfortable saying so?
3. The pyramidal personality theory described in this chapter attempts to provide a framework to synthesize the field of psychological science. Is this helpful? Why or why not?
4. I've suggested that this theory may be used to guide research, therapy, and interventions for human flourishing. How might the theory be used to conceive a research agenda, a treatment plan, or a holistic program for wellbeing?
5. The Sociologist C. Smith has argued there are three basic ways in which Christians engage in scholarship: "Baseline compatibility" builds upon the general Christian affirmation of science but without any distinctively Christian content. "Constructive formation" in which the content of one's faith decisively shapes scholarship, although the influence is implicit. Finally, there's "elaboration," in which one attempts to make explicit the connections between faith and scholarship. Where are you most comfortable? Christian universities look for elaboration in teaching and scholarship. What's the biggest hindrance for you to make progress on this front?

Helpful Resources

In my upcoming chapter with Joshua Knabb, we argue that a robustly Christian approach to psychology will have five steps, using the

97. Joshua J. Knabb et al., "The Christian Worldview Scale: An Emic Measure for Assessing a Comprehensive View of Life within the Chrisian Tradition," *Spirituality in Clinical Practice* (2022); Joshua J. Knabb, Veola E. Vazquez, and Kenneth T. Wang, "The Christian Contentment Scale: An Emic Measure for Assessing Inner Satisfaction within the Christian Tradition," *Journal of Psychology and Theology* 49 (2020).

metaphor of a house. The first four of these steps are scholarly, so I'll use this as a framework for this very brief list of helpful resources.

Step One: Laying Foundations and Putting up Framing: Retrieving Christian Psychology

Robert Roberts has argued that our ignorance of the psychological thought of the Scriptures and the Christian past is a great hindrance to our efforts to engage psychology today. Three excellent places to start include:

Johnson, Eric L. *God & Soul Care : The Therapeutic Resources of the Christian Faith.* Downers Grove: InterVarsity Press, 2017.

Lapine, Matthew A. *The Logic of the Body: Retrieving Theological Psychology.* Bellingham, WA: Lexham Press, 2020.

Roberts, Robert C. *Recovering Christian Chaacter: The Psychologial Wisdom of Soren Kierkegaard.* Grand Rapids: Eerdmans, 2023.

Step Two: Making and Gathering Bricks: Empirical Research Within the Christian Tradition

Since psychological science explores God's good creation, there are few areas of psychological science unworthy of Christian attention, and Christians can and do participate in many domains of research. Indeed, to engage psychology as Christians, we need to understand the science as best we can. Of particular interest to exploring the role of special grace in psychology, however, the two big names are PJ Watson and Joshua Knabb, both of whom have done extremely innovative work within mainstream psychological science from a distinctively Christian perspective. I recommend a thorough search of their work.

Step Three: Arranging the Bricks and Finishing the House: Christian Consilience and Synthesis

Psychology today is a cacophony of voices and disconnected findings. How does it all fit together? In the medieval synthesis of Thomas Aquinas and others, Christianity had a way of answering this question, whereas today, in contemporary psychology, evolutionary psychology tends to play the role of unifying theoretical perspective. We need a new Christian synthesis. This chapter describes one such theory. A very important contribution from the Catholic tradition is:

Vitz, Paul C., William J. Nordling, and Craig Steven Titus, eds. *A Catholic*

Christian Meta-Model of the Person : Integration with Psychology & Mental Health Practice. Sterling, VA: Divine Mercy University Press, 2019.

Step Four: Living in the House: Developing Therapies, Interventions, and Trainings

Given common grace insights, a whole range of "secular" therapies and interventions may profitably be employed by Christian therapists and counsellors, and to Christian ends. Indeed, therapies and interventions already exist that address functioning in every dimension, every modality, and the frame of life discussed above. Regarding special grace approaches, Joshua Knabb has developed a range of tools that help clients draw upon the resources of the Christian faith to cope with stress, worry, negative thinking, and trauma-based emotions and rumination. For easy access to these "manualized" approaches see his very helpful website: joshuaknabb.com. He also co-edited a book on distinctively Christian approaches to psychotherapy:

Knabb, Joshua J., Eric L. Johnson, M. Todd Bates, and Timothy A. Sisemore. *Christian Psychotherapy in Context: Theoretical and Empirical Explorations in Faith-Based Mental Health.* New York: Routledge, 2019.

In the Reformed tradition, Eric Johnson and Keith Whitfield have been editing a volume on "Reformational counseling," to be published by Crossway. The concept of "trainings" comes from John Coe, an advocate for a transformational psychology that very much seeks to develop Christian character via spiritual formation. See his work at the Institute for Spiritual Formation and his book:

Coe, John H., and Todd W. Hall. *Psychology in the Spirit : Contours of a Transformational Psychology.* Christian Worldview Integration Series. Downers Grove, IL.: IVP Academic, 2010.

Other Reformed Resources

For big-picture frameworks for understanding psychology in Reformed perspective, I'd recommend these three resources for starters:

Johnson, Eric L. *Foundations of Soul Care: A Christian Psychology Proposal.* Downers Grove, IL: Intervarsity Press, 2007.

Kosits, Russell D. "Whose Psychology? Which Christianity?". *McMaster Journal of Theology and Ministry* 13 (2011-12): 101-95.

Ouweneel, Willem. *Heart and Soul: A Christian View of Psychology.* Grand Rapids: Paideia Press, 2009.

Journals and Societies

Regarding professional societies, The Society for Christian Psychology would be closest to supporting a robustly Christian vision for psychology. The Christian Association for Psychological Studies falls more in the "integration" camp, and publishes the *Journal of Psychology & Christianity*. The other major integration journal is the *Journal of Psychology & Theology*. Both of these journals tend to publish solid empirical work on topics of interest to Christians, though not always from distintively Christian theoretical frameworks, though JPC has under the editorship of Knabb has been moving more in the direction advocated in this chapter. For counselors, the American Association of Christian Counsellors, and the Association of Christian Therapists are available. In the secular sphere, certain divisions of the American Psychological Assocation have been friendly to (implicitly) Christian inquiries such as Division 24 (philosophy) 26 (history) and 36 (spirituality and religion).

Bibliography

Allen, Michael. *Grounded in Heaven: Recentering Christian Hope and Life on God.* Grand Rapids: Eerdmans.

Allport, Gordon W. *The Roots of Religion.* Advent Papers. Boston: Church of the Advent, 1943.

Ames, William. *The Marrow of Theology.* Translated by John Dykstra Eusden. Grand Rapids, MI: Baker Books, 1643/1968. 1624.

Ansbacher, Heinz L. , and Rowena R. Ansbacher, eds. *The Individual Psychology of Alfred Adler; a Systematic Presentation in Selections from His Writings.* 1st ed. New York: Basic Books, 1956.

Aron, Arthur, Gary W. Jr. Lewandowski, Debra Mashek, and Elaine N Aron. "The Self-Expansion Model of Motivation and Cognition in Close Relationships." In *The Oxford Handbook of Close Relationships*, edited by J. A. Simpson and L. Campbell. New York: Oxford University Press, 2013.

Bandura, Albert. "Selective Moral Disengagement in the Exercise of Moral Agency." *Journal of Moral Education* 31 (2002): 101-19.

Basden, Andrew. *Foundations and Practice of Research: Adventures in Dooyeweerd's Philosophy.* United Kingdom: Taylor & Francis, 2019.

"The Pistic Aspect." 1998, https://dooy.info/pistic.html.

Baumeister, Roy F., and Mark R. Leary. "The Need to Belong: Desire for Interpersonal Attachments as a Fundamental Human Motivation." *Psychological Bulletin* 10, no. 3 (1995): 497-529.

Benjamin, Ludy T. *A Brief History of Modern Psychology.* Malden, MA: Blackwell, 2007.

Butterfield, Herbert. *The Whig Interpretation of History.* London: G. Bell & Sons, 1931.

Calvin, John. *The Institutes of the Christian Religion.* Translated by Ford Lewis Battles. Edited by John T. McNeill. Vol. one, Louisville, Kentucky: Westminster John Knox Press, 1559/1960. 1559.

Carver, Charles S., and Michael F. Scheier. "Origins and Functions of Positive and Negative Affect: A Control-Process View." *Psychological Review* 97 (1990): 19-35.

Clouser, Roy A. *The Myth of Religious Neutrality: An Essay on the Hidden Role of Religious Belief in Theories.* Revised ed. Notre Dame, IN: University of Notre Dame Press, 2005.

Davies, Paul. "God and Design: The Teleological Argument and Modern Science." edited by Neil A. Manson, 147-54. London: Routledge, 2003.

Davis, D.E., J.N. Hook, D. R. Van Tongeren, and Everett L. Worthington. "Sanctification of Forgiveness." *Psychology of Religion and Spirituality* 4 (2012): 31-39.

Dik, Bryan J., Brandy M. Eldridge, Micael F. Steger, and Ryan D. Duffy. "Development and Validation of the Calling and Vocation Questionnaire and Brief Calling Scale." *Journal of Career Assessment* 20 (2012): 242-63.

Dooyeweerd, Herman. *A New Critique of Theoretical Thought.* Vol. 2: The General Theory of the Modal Spheres, Philadelphia: Presbyterian & Reformed, 1955.

Dooyeweerd, Herman. *A New Critique of Theoretical Thought. Vol. 1: The Necessary Presuppositions of Philosophy*, Philadelphia: Presbyterian & Reformed, 1953.

Edwards, Jonathan. *Original Sin.* The Works of Jonathan Edwards. Edited by Clyde A. Holbrook. Vol. 3, New Haven: Yale University Press, 1758/1970.

Edwards, Jonathan. "Two Dissertations." In *Works of Jonathan Edwards, Volume 8, Ethical Writings*, edited by Paul Ramsey, 399-627. New Haven: Yale University Press, 1989.

———. *The Works of Jonathan Edwards, Volume 2, Religious Affections.* The Works of Jonathan Edwards. Edited by John E. Smith. Vol. 2, New Haven: Yale University Press, 1746/1959. 1746.

Emmons, Robert A. "Is Gratitude the Queen of the Virtues and Ingratitude the King of the Vices?". In *Perspectives on Gratitude: An Interdisciplinary Approach*, edited by David Carr. New York: Routledge, 2016.

Fiering, Norman. *Moral Philosophy at Seventeenth-Century Harvard: A Discipline in Transition*. Chapel Hill, NC: University of North Carolina Press, 1981.

Friesen, J. Glenn, "Motive." 2010, https://jgfriesen.wordpress.com/glossary/motive/.

Garber, Steven. "Finding Our Way to Great Work, Even in Politics: Making Peace with Proximate Justice." *Comment*, August 31, 2007.

Gilbert, Daniel. *Stumbling on Happiness*. Toronto: Vintage Canada, 2006.

Hergenhahn, B.R., and Matthew H. Olson. *An Introduction to Theories of Personality*. Sixth ed. Upper Saddle River, NJ: Prentice Hall, 2003.

Inazu, John. *Confident Pluralism: Surviving and Thriving through Deep Difference*. Chicago: University of Chicago Press, 2016.

Jans-Beken, Lillian, Nele Jacobs, Mayke Janssens, Sanne Peeters, Jennifer Reijnders, Lillian Lechner, and Johan Lataster. "Gratitude and Health: An Updated Review." *The Journal of Positive Psychology* 15 (2019): 743-82.

Johnson, Eric L. and Russell D. Kosits, "Teaching and Learning in the Social Sciences," in *Christian Higher Education: Faith, Teaching, and Learning in the Evangelical Tradition*, ed. David S. Dockery and Christopher W. Morgan (Wheaton: Crossway, 2018).

Jones, Mark, "The (Gracious?) Covenant of Works (Again)," 2014, https://www.reformation21.org/blogs/the-gracious-covenant-of-works.php.

Jordan, Jennifer, Marijke C. Leliveld, and Ann E. Tenbrunsel. "The Moral Self-Image Scale: Measuring and Understanding the Malleability of the Moral Self." *Frontiers in Psychology* 6 (2015): 1-16.

Keller, Timothy. *Generous Justice: How God's Grace Makes Us Just*. New York: Dutton, 2010.

Knabb, J., and K.T. Wang. "The Communion with God Scale: Shifting from an Etic to Emic Perspective to Assess Fellowshipping with the Triune God." *Psychology of Religion and Spirituality* 13 (2021): 67-80.

Knabb, Joshua J., Veola E. Vazquez, Fernando L. Garzon, Kristy M. Ford, Kenneth T. Wang, Kevin W. Conner, Steve E. Warren, and Donna M. Weston. "Christian Meditation for Repetitive Negative Thinking: A Multisite Randomized Trial Examining the Effects of a 4-Week Preventative Program." *Spirituality in Clinical Practice* 7, no. 1 (2020): 34-50.

Knabb, Joshua J., Veola E. Vazquez, and Kenneth T. Wang. "The Christian Contentment Scale: An Emic Measure for Assessing Inner Satisfaction within the Christian Tradition." *Journal of Psychology and Theology* 49 (2020): 324-41.

Knabb, Joshua J., Veola E. Vazquez, Kenneth T. Wang, and R.A. Pate. "The Christian Gratitude Scale: An Emic Approach to Measuring Thankfulness in Every Season of Life." *Spirituality in Clinical Practice* (2021).

Knabb, Joshua J., K.T. Wang, M.E. Hall, and V.E. Vazquez. "The Christian Worldview Scale: An Emic Measure for Assessing a Comprehensive View of Life within the Chrisian Tradition." *Spirituality in Clinical Practice* (2022).

Kosits, Russell D. "Flatland and the Deep Meaning of Gratitude." *PsycCRITIQUES* 62 (2017).

———. "Sacredness and Heresy in the History of North American Psychology." Presidential Address, Society for the History of Psychology, Division 26 of the American Psychological Association, 2020.

———. "Toward Worldview Pluralism in Psychology." In *The Hidden Worldviews of Psychology's Theory, Research, and Practice*, edited by Brent D. Slife, Kari A. O'Grady and Russell D. Kosits, 68-89. New York: Routledge, 2017.

Kosits, Russell D., and Joshua J. Knabb. "A Christian Psychology View." In *Psychology & Christianity: Four Views*, edited by Eric L. Johnson. Downers Grove: IVP, in preparation.

Lewis, C.S. *The Weight of Glory.* New York: Simon & Schuster, 1980.

Lyubomirsky, Sonya. *The How of Happiness: A New Approach to Getting the Life You Want.* New York: Penguin, 2007.

Lyubomirsky, Sonya, Laura King, and Ed Diener. "The Benefits of Frequent Positive Affect: Does Happiness Lead to Success?". *Psychological Bulletin* 131 (2005): 803-55.

Miller, George A. "The Constitutive Problem of Psychology." In *A Century of Psychology as Science*, edited by Sigmund Koch and David E. Leary. Washington, DC: American Psychological Association, 1992.

Mouw, Richard J. *He Shines in All That's Fair : Culture and Common Grace.* Grand Rapids, Mich.: W.B. Eerdmans Pub. Co., 2001.

Olthuis, James H. "Dooyeweerd on Religion and Faith." In *The Legacy of Herman Dooyeweerd*, edited by C.T. McIntire. New York: University Press of America, 1985.

Ouweneel, Willem. *Heart and Soul: A Christian View of Psychology.* Grand Rapids: Paideia Press, 2009.

Payne, Leanne. *Real Presence: The Christian Worldview of C. S. Lewis as Incarnational Reality.* Grand Rapids: Baker Publishing Group, 1995.

Seerveld, Calvin. "A Christian Tin-Can Theory of Man." *Journal of the American Scientific Affiliation* 33, no. 2 (1981): 74-81.

Seybold, Kevin S, and Peter C. Hill. "The Role of Religion in Mental and Spiritual Health." *Current Directions in Psychological Science* 10 (2001): 21-24.

Sheldon, Kennon M. *Optimal Human Being: An Integrated Approach.* Mahwah, NJ: Lawrence Erlbaum, 2004.

Sisemore, Timothy A. *The Psychology of Religion and Spirituality.* Hoboken, NJ: Wiley, 2016.

Strauss, D.F.M. *The Philosophy of Herman Dooyeweerd.* Jordan Station, ON: Paideia Press, 2021.

Strohminger, Nina, Joshua Knobe, and George Neman. "The True Self: A Psychological Concept Distinct from the Self." *Perspectives on Psychological Science* 12 (2017): 551-60.

Tavris, Carol, and Elliot Aronson. *Mistakes Were Made (but Not by Me) : Why We Justify Foolish Beliefs, Bad Decisions, and Hurtful Acts.* Orlando, FL: Harcourt, 2007.

Taylor, Charles. *A Secular Age.* (Boston, MA: Belknap, 2007), 27, 35-43.

Van Belle, Harry. The Meaning of the Psychical. 1985.

Veenhof, Jan. "Nature and Grace in Bavinck (A. Wolters, Trans.)." *Pro Rege* 34 (2006): 10-31.

Vollenhoven, Dirk H. T. *Introduction to Philosophy.* Sioux Center, IA: Dordt College Press, 1930/2005.

Weber, Samuel R., and Kenneth I. Pargament. "The Role of Religion and Spirituality in Mental Health." *Current Opinion in Psychiatry* 27 (2014): 358-63.

Wolters, Albert M. *Creation Regained: Biblical Basics for a Reformational Worldview.* Grand Rapids, MI: Eerdmans, 2005.

Wood, Alex M., Jeffrey J. Froh, and Adam W. A. Geraghty. "Gratitude and Well-Being: A Review and Theoretical Integration." *Clinical Psychology Review* 30 (2010): 890-905.

Toward A Biblical Grounding for the Profession of Social Work: "No More Death or Mourning or Crying or Pain"

James R. Vanderwoerd

Introduction

The social work profession in the twenty-first century is enormously ambitious. A quick tour through the websites of social work's regulatory, accrediting, and professional organizations reveals a vision for the profession and for society that is unabashedly optimistic and all-encompassing. Social work "...is dedicated to the welfare and self-realization of all people,"[1] and "... promotes social change and development, social cohesion, and the empowerment and liberation of people."[2] "Social workers help people in every stage of life overcome life's most difficult challenges, and the troubles of everyday living."[3] "The purpose of social work is actualized through its quest for social and economic justice, the prevention of conditions that limit human rights, the elimination of poverty, and the enhancement of the quality of life for all persons, locally and globally."[4] Social work education "...envisions an economically, socially, and environmentally just world based on humanitarian and democratic ideals that demonstrate respect for the worth, agency, and dignity of all beings."[5]

This is an alluring agenda. One cannot help but be stirred by the

---

1. Canadian Association of Social Workers, *Code of Ethics,* (Ottawa, ON: Canadian Association of Social Workers, 2005), 3.
2. International Federation of Social Workers. "Global Definition of Social Work," accessed May 18, 2021, https://www.ifsw.org/what-is-social-work/global-definition-of-social-work/.
3 National Association of Social Workers, "About Social Work," accessed May 18, 2021, http://www.helpstartshere.org/?page_id=1999.
4. Council on Social Work Education (CSWE) Commission on Educational Policy and the CSWE Commission on Accreditation, *Educational Policy and Accreditation Standards for Baccalaureate and Master's Social Work Programs* (Washington, DC: Council on Social Work Education, 2015), 5.
5. Canadian Association for Social Work Education [CASWE], *Educational Policies and Accreditation Standards for Canadian Social Work Education*, (Ottawa, ON: Canadian Association for Social Work Education, 2021), 3.

message of hope that social work holds out. At times, that message tilts to an almost religious fervour, for social work promises salvation and healing for a world of hurt and brokenness.

Tapping that inspirational vein, a generation ago the late Harry Specht, a past Dean of the School of Social Work at the University of California Berkeley, and a respected social work educator and author, stirred up a controversy within the profession by boldly claiming, "Social work has been diverted from its original vision, a vision of the perfectibility of society, the building of the 'city beautiful', the 'new society', and the 'new frontier'"[6]. The controversy was that Specht was criticizing social work's abandonment of its commitment to transform society in favor of individual counseling.[7] However, Christians – and perhaps others as well – could hardly miss the eschatological reference to the "city beautiful," which, of course, comes from Revelation 21:

> Then I saw "a new heaven and a new earth," for the first heaven and the first earth had passed away, and there was no longer any sea. I saw the Holy City, the new Jerusalem, coming down out of heaven from God, prepared as a bride beautifully dressed for her husband. And I heard a loud voice from the throne saying, "Look! God's dwelling place is now among the people, and he will dwell with them. They will be his people, and God himself will be with them and be their God. He will wipe every tear from their eyes. There will be no more death or mourning or crying or pain, for the old order of things has passed away." He who was seated on the throne said, "I am making everything new!" (Rev. 21: 1-5).

Is this what the social work profession has in mind when it envisions the "city beautiful" and the "perfectibility of society"? Although most social workers would agree with the vision of a world with no more death, mourning, crying, or pain, it strains belief to imagine that the social work profession today would ever endorse such an explicitly biblical, Christian vision.

The vision articulated by the various social work organizations may indeed be inspiring, but, when put the way Specht does, it's also something else: arrogant. "Fools say in their hearts, 'there is no God'" (Psalm 14:1 and Psalm 53:1), and Christians recognize with the psalmist that social work's ambitious claims tip from inspiration to hubris. Today's so-

6. Harry Specht, "Social Work and the Popular Psychotherapies," *Social Service Review* 64, no. 3 (1990): 354.

7. Harry Specht and Mark Courtney, *Unfaithful Angels: How Social Work Abandoned Its Mission* (New York: Free Press, 1994). Curiously, the first chapter is a revised version of the above 1990 article which includes the same quotation, but without the reference to the "city beautiful."

cial work recognizes the brokenness in the world, but its diagnosis of the roots of this brokenness, and, therefore, its proposed remedies reveal a very different vision than that held by Christians.

Social work's vision for a better world is rooted in fundamental values and assumptions about humans and the nature of the world.[8] In other words, social work has a worldview. To its credit, social work is more open about its progressive, human-centred, and utopian vision, compared to its disciplinary cousin, sociology.[9] Christian Smith, an American sociologist at the University of Notre Dame, has argued persuasively that sociology – despite its claims to be rational, scientific, objective, and ideologically neutral – in fact, has a "sacred project". That sacred project is remarkably similar to social work's vision, and deserves quoting in full:

> American sociology as a collective enterprise is at heart committed to the visionary project of *realizing the emancipation, equality, and moral affirmation of all human beings as autonomous, self-directing, individual agents (who should be) out to live their lives as they personally so desire, by constructing their own favored identities, entering and exiting relationships as they choose, and equally enjoying the gratification of experiential, material, and bodily pleasures.*[10]

As Smith rightly notes, this is a "secular salvation story."[11] And that is what this chapter is about. It seeks to show how the biblical narrative can be marshalled to undergird and inform the profession of social work. Such a biblically informed grounding serves not just as an alternative to other human-centred understandings, but more importantly, as a corrective. This may sound as arrogant as Specht's vision. To say that a biblically grounded approach is a corrective suggests that Christians think that their approach is correct, and that, therefore, others' approaches are incorrect, or at least less correct. Isn't it arrogant to claim that one's own perspective is "true" and that others are not true? Although our twenty-first century sensibilities make anyone hesitant to claim capital-T "truth," the reality is that humans do this all the time. Even someone who says "All truth is relative and therefore you can't impose your truth on others" is imposing

8. Frederic G. Reamer, *The Philosophical Foundations of Social Work* (New York: Columbia University Press, 1993).

9. Terry A. Wolfer and James R. Vanderwoerd, "The Sacred Project of American Sociology: Comparison with Social Work and Implications" (presentation, North American Association of Christians in Social Work Annual Convention, Cincinnati, OH, November 19, 2016).

10. Christian Smith, *The Sacred Project of American Sociology* (New York: Oxford University Press, 2014), 7-8; emphasis original.

11. Smith, *The Sacred Project*, 20.

that truth on others.[12] All truth claims rest on assumptions that are not self-evident, whether one is secular or religious.[13] Christians acknowledge that it is only through the "spectacles of Scripture" that humans are able to understand the world fully, even though we also recognize the imperfect and incomplete human limitations of our knowledge. Social work seeks to address social needs and bring healing to social problems; in this chapter we argue that a Christian understanding of the nature of humans, the reality of sin, and the power of God's redemption provides the best way to do this.

What is Social Work Anyway? A Reformational Perspective

In the early twenty-first century, social work is widely regarded by its practitioners as one among a host of professional occupations within the ever-expanding fields of health, education, and social welfare. Outsiders – those citizens and laypersons not directly involved in the "system" – might be more likely to consider social work as a job where you work with troubled children and poor families. The word "professional" is the lightning rod which attracts ongoing disputes among social work insiders who debate the criteria of professionalization and squabble about what does and does not belong under the label "social work."[14] One hundred years ago, Abraham Flexner gave his (in)famous address to the National Conference of Charities and Corrections (what we today call social workers, a term which was not yet used widely at that time) in which he raised a perennial question: Is social work a profession? No, insisted Flexner, and the repercussions of that address continue to haunt social work to this day, as social work has struggled to define the scope of its practice, particularly the tensions between focusing on social reform and transformation (which falls more on the macro end of the practice continuum) and on individual functioning and well-being (which fits within the micro areas of practice).[15]

The notion of practice is central to understanding social work with-

12. Timothy Keller, *The Reason for God: Belief in an Age of Skepticism* (New York: Dutton, 2008).

13. Nicholas Wolterstorff, *Reason Within the Bounds of Religion* (Grand Rapids, MI: Eerdmans, 1976).

14. Philip Popple and Leslie Leighninger, *The Policy-Based Profession: An Introduction to Social Welfare Policy Analysis for Social Workers,* 7th ed. (New York: Pearson, 2019).

15. See for example Karen Haynes and James Mickelson, *Affecting Change: Social Workers in the Political Arena,* 7th ed. (New York: Pearson, 2010), especially chapter 4, "When Karen Met Harry: *Unfaithful Angels* Disputed"; Therese Jennissen and Colleen Lundy, *One Hundred Years of Social Work: A History of the Profession in English Canada, 1900-2000* (Waterloo: Wilfrid Laurier University Press, 2011).

in the academy, for, despite Flexner's critique, social work has now become understood not only as an academic discipline but also as a professional practice.[16] What is a professional practice? Dutch philosophers Jochemsen and Hegeman draw on Reformational philosophy to extend Alisdair McIntyre's description of a professional practice as a social arrangement in which humans develop specialized expertise to achieve collective ends whose purpose is focused on others' interests, rather than the self-interest of the practitioners.[17] They argue that the central overriding purpose, or *telos*, of helping professions, including social work, is what Dutch philosopher Herman Dooyeweerd called the ethical aspect, which is manifested as love or care for one's neighbour.[18] Of course, social work involves more than just an ethical aspect; one of Dooyeweerd's important contributions was to conceive of created reality in a way that avoids reductionism. Thus, social work, like all other things, reflects many of the fifteen modal aspects.[19] Jochemsen and Hegeman use Wolters' analysis of structure and direction[20] to distinguish between what they call the constitutive and the regulative sides of a professional practice. A practice is constituted – or structured – not simply as a human-invented arrangement, but rather it reflects the order that God has built into creation. However, *how* a practice is carried out – or regulated – involves what humans actually do within the practice that is directed either toward or away from God. Thus, Jochemsen and Hegeman argue that the constitutive side, or structure, of a professional caring practice must be shaped by its ethical *telos*. Further, a professional practice is marked by excellence, that is, competent performance characterized by the appropriate levels of earned knowledge and skills within a specified area. This excellence, however, is not abstract, but shaped by the particularities of social context and time. Excellence in caring for one's neighbour in Canada in the twenty-first century is not necessarily the same as, for example, India in the fourteenth century, or the Netherlands in the nineteenth century. What Jochemsen and Hegeman call the regulative side of a profession involves the way humans understand, respond to, and interpret the con-

16. Steve Hick and Jackie Stokes, *Social Work in Canada: An introduction*, 4th ed. (Toronto, ON: Thomson, 2017), p. 10.

17. Henk Jochemsen and Johan Hegeman, "Equipping Christian Students to Connect Kingdom Citizenship to Issues in Today's Societies," in *Christian Higher Education in the Global Context: Implications for Curriculum, Pedagogy, and Administration*, ed. Nick Lantinga (Iowa: Dordt College Press, 2008), 223-240.

18. Jonathan Chaplin, *Herman Dooyeweerd: Christian Philosopher of State and Civil Society* (Notre Dame, IN: University of Notre Dame Press, 2011), chapter 4.

19. Chaplin, *Herman Dooyeweerd.*

20. Albert M. Wolters, *Creation Regained: Biblical Basics for a Reformational Worldview*, 2nd ed. (Grand Rapids, MI: Eerdmans, 2005), chapter 5.

stitutive elements, as well as other factors in a given social context, and, actually carry out, or practice, the profession. Since this requires judgments and beliefs about the world – that is, one's worldview – Jochemsen and Hegeman argue that "there is no 'neutral' performance of a practice," and thus observe that "relating the performance of practices to one's religious beliefs is fully justified. This always is done, whether implicitly or explicitly."[21] Their use of the phrase "religious beliefs" is intended to refer not just to formal religious doctrine, but rather to underlying worldviews. Thus, even secular social workers base their practice on some set of beliefs, even if they don't think of these as religious.

What is the area of practice that is specific to social work as one type of professional practice distinct from others? As we have already explained, that is a question that has plagued social work throughout its brief history,[22] but here, Jochemsen and Hegeman's use of the Reformational framework of modal aspects of reality[23] unfortunately remains too general and vague to distinguish among different helping professions such as social work, nursing, marriage and family counseling, psychology, or others. However, their identification of the importance of historical contexts does provide a beginning to understanding the differences among related professions. They argue that any professional practice emerges within specific historical circumstances in which humans are called to respond to the particular challenges and demands of their time and place in particular ways. Social work emerged in the nineteenth century as a way to care for – or love – one's neighbour in new ways that took into account the growing demands brought about by industrialization, immigration, and urbanization especially in Great Britain, the USA, and Canada. Loving one's neighbour, of course, was not new; as Chatterjee has pointed out, before the welfare state there were the "welfare church," the "welfare community," and the "welfare family," among others.[24] But doing so through the application of particular techniques by university-trained persons regulated and compensated within the context of the welfare state is what makes the contemporary profession of social work different from approaches to caring for one's neighbour in other contexts and time periods.

21. Jochemsen and Hegeman, "Equipping Christian Students," 230, 231.

22. Specht and Courtney, *Unfaithful Angels;* Haynes and Mickelson, *Affecting Change*; Therese Jennisen and Colleen Lundy, *One Hundred Years of Social Work: A History of the Profession in English Canada 1900-2000* (Waterloo, ON: Wilfrid Laurier Press, 2011).

23. See introductory chapter.

24. Pranab Chatterjee, *Repackaging the Welfare State* (Washington, DC: NASW Press, 1999).

The scope of social work can be described as that area of life related to humans' social wellbeing. The Canadian Association of Social Workers says, "The social work profession is dedicated to the welfare and self-realization of all,"[25] while the National Association of Social Workers in the USA says, "The primary mission of the social work profession is to enhance human well-being and help meet the basic human needs of all people."[26] Focusing only on wellbeing or human welfare suggests that social work's primary attention is to what we could call shalom or flourishing, [27] but this is only one side of social work. The other side – arguably the dominant focus – is not wellbeing alone, but rather the various forces that threaten or undermine wellbeing. Thus, while the above-quoted sections from social work's codes of ethics start with wellbeing, they don't stop there. CASW puts it this way: "The profession has a *particular* interest in the needs and empowerment of people who are vulnerable, oppressed, and/or living in poverty,"[28] and NASW adds "Social workers … strive to end discrimination, oppression, poverty, and other forms of social injustice."[29]

As we have hinted above, Dooyeweerd's scheme of modal aspects is intended in part to show how all of created reality is complex, held together in Christ through God's sustaining power, and thus cannot be reduced to any single aspect. Each social structure is defined by what Dooyeweerd refers to as the "leading" or "qualifying" function that gives that social structure coherence and purpose; for a caring profession such as that of social work, the leading function would be ethical, centred on love or care for one's neighbour. However, that does not mean that other modal aspects are absent. For example, the juridical aspect concerns restoring right relationships which have been broken or betrayed through processes of restitution and retribution, and particularly focuses on systems of injustice, about which the Old Testament prophets said so much.[30] The economic aspect recognizes that the social work relation-

25. Canadian Association of Social Workers, *Code of Ethics*, 5.

26. "Preamble" to *Code of Ethics* by National Association of Social Workers [NASW], (Washington, DC: National Association of Social Workers, 2017), accessed May 19, 2021, https://www.socialworkers.org/About/Ethics/Code-of-Ethics/Code-of-Ethics-English.

27. Lisa Hosack, *Development on Purpose: Faith and Human Behavior in the Social Environment,* (Botsford, CT: North American Association of Christians in Social Work, 2019).

28. Canadian Association of Social Workers, *Code of Ethics*, p. 3; emphasis added.

29. National Association of Social Workers, "Preamble."

30. See for example Gary Haugen and Victor Boutros, *The Locust Effect: Why the End of Poverty Requires the End of Violence.* (New York: Oxford University Press, 2013), which demonstrates that the absence of justice is the central factor contributing to global poverty.

ship is a transaction involving exchanges of scarce resources that must be used wisely. One implication of this aspect is the distinction between a professional relationship and other kinds of human relationships such as kinship or friendship. A social worker is friendly but not your friend; a social worker has a contractual relationship with a client, but that client is not a customer. Other modal aspects particularly relevant to social work include the social, the psychic, and the historical.

Chaplin suggests that the historical aspect is a culture forming one, in which other modal aspects are "opened up" in a particular time and place, and thus draws our attention to the specific historical contexts in which the profession of social work emerged.[31] This aspect alerts us to the importance of particularity and helps us avoid conceiving of a social structure as a generic abstraction. As already noted, social work emerged in the mid to late nineteenth century as a particular organized response to specific types of problems that were emerging in Western societies, especially those associated with industrialization, urbanization, and immigration. Analyzing the historical aspect of social work illuminates two points and raises two questions. First, the responses to social problems in the late modern era are not neutral, but rather are profoundly shaped by the prevailing liberal, modernistic, secularist worldview that prizes progress, science, and human autonomy.[32] Second, a professionalized response to social problems reflects a process of differentiation, in which humans develop increasingly sophisticated and technical social arrangements; where once one relied on family, friends, and church for help, now one turns to professionals.[33] A question then arises: Does this specific historic particularity mean that social work has an enduring normative existence, or is it only a contemporary manifestation of ethical care that could (or should) be done by other means in other historical or cultural contexts? Marvin Olasky argues that the state has become too involved in social welfare, and we should go back to a nineteenth-century model where family, community, and church take back some of that responsibility.[34] A second question, already alluded to above, is whether and how social

31. Chaplin, *Herman Dooyeweerd;* see especially 72-77, 117.

32. Christian Smith, *The Secular Revolution: Power, Interests and Conflict in the Secularization of American Public Life* (Los Angeles, CA: University of California Press, 2003). See also James R. Vanderwoerd, "Reconsidering Secularization and Recovering Christianity in Social Work History," *Social Work & Christianity* 38, no. 3 (2011): 244-266.

33. See as an example John McKnight, "John Deere and the Bereavement Counselor," in *The Careless Society: Community and Its Counterfeits* (New York: Basic Books, 1995), 115-123.

34. Marvin Olasky, *The Tragedy of American Compassion* (Washington, DC: Regnery Publishing, 1992).

work fits within the academy. In Kuyperian terms, this question focuses on the relevant social structures, or spheres, that are involved in contemporary caregiving. Professions are conventionally viewed as autonomous, subject neither to the academy nor the state, but certainly intricately interconnected with both. In fact, one of the contentious issues in the emergence of social work as a profession in the early twentieth century was precisely whether the fledgling profession should hitch its cart to the legitimacy of the academic wagon, or whether it should develop a completely autonomous system of educational institutions outside the realm and grasp of the university. As we now know, it chose the academy, but the tensions remain.[35]

As we have noted above, no human endeavor is neutral. The contemporary social work profession, situated as it is within the secularized Western system of higher education,[36] has become secularized,[37] but that does not mean it is free from underlying values used to evaluate what is wrong and what the solution is. In other words, social work has a narrative about itself and the world that reveals its underlying worldview.[38] Of course, it is too simplistic to say that there is one coherent worldview to which all social workers subscribe; as with any other group, social workers are diverse and reflect a variety of beliefs.[39] Nevertheless, researchers have noted some broad characteristics that describe the mainstream social work profession that give a clue to its underlying belief system.[40] These values include the inherent worth and dignity of all humans, a commitment to pursue social justice and equality, an emphasis on professional competence and integrity, and an obligation to be altruistic rather than

35. Nancy Christie and Michael Gauvreau, *A Full-Orbed Christianity: The Protestant churches and social welfare in Canada: 1900-1940.* (Montreal, PQ and Kingston, ON: McGill-Queen's University Press, 1996); Therese Jennissen and Colleen Lundy, *One Hundred Years of Social Work: A History of the Profession in English Canada, 1900-2000* (Waterloo: Wilfrid Laurier University Press, 2011).

36. Kevin N. Flatt "The Secularization of Western Universities in International Perspective: Toward a Historicist Account" *The Review of Faith & International Affairs* 18, no. 2 (Summer 2020), 30-43.

37. Vanderwoerd and van der Woerd, "Is There More to This Story?" 63-80.

38. See Christian Smith, *Moral Believing Animals* (New York: Oxford University Press, 2003) and *The Sacred Project of American Sociology* (Oxford University Press, 2014).

39. David R. Hodge, "Who We Are, Where We Come From, and Some of Our Perceptions: Comparison of Social Workers and the General Population," *Social Work* 49, no. 2 (April 2004): 261-268.

40. David R. Hodge, "Differences in Worldviews between Social Workers and People of Faith," *Families in Society* 84, no. 2 (2003): 285-295; David R. Hodge, "Value Differences between Social Workers and Members of the Working and Middle Classes," *Social Work* 48, no. 1 (2003): 107-119.

self-serving.[41] As much as social work prides itself on being a value-based profession however,[42] social work's secularization, and the corresponding marginalization of its own religious roots, has resulted in it removing any foundational basis for the source of these values. Social work seeks to value all groups and all perspectives, but its attempt to affirm all systems of belief results logically in a relativistic stance that cannot on its own provide the foundation for its own values. As any philosopher now knows,[43] no system of belief, including a Christian worldview, can be proven beyond a shadow of doubt. Even though we cannot prove it, however, Christians assert both humbly and confidently, that as Keller observes, compared to other belief systems, "...the Christian account of things – creation, fall, redemption, and restoration – makes the most sense of the world."[44]

A Christian worldview rooted in the Reformed tradition provides a worldview that differs from conventional social work and helps reveal key insights that highlight limitations in conventional secular social work. The Reformed Christian worldview framework can be captured in the phrase, "*grace restores nature,*" or in the three-part structure of creation—fall—redemption.[45] To say that grace restores nature is to describe how God in His love relates to the world He made. It points to how God *has* acted, *is* acting, and *will* act intentionally to reclaim and renew all of what He made. God is not distant from His creation, but rather demonstrates His love for all of reality by being actively engaged to restore the world to the flourishing that He intended. A creation – fall - redemption framework highlights three foundational principles that guide how we interpret everything: God created the world as a context for *shalom,* but humans rebelled against God and disrupted not only the intended *shalom* but the very creation itself, and in response, God enters the world and sets about to restore His creation to its original goodness. The following sections will describe how this framework shapes a biblical understanding of the social work profession. But, before we get to each of the sections – creation, fall, and redemption – we need to remember that this framework itself is not by itself an independent source of truth, but rather, is rooted in its Author. In other words,

41. Kip Coggins, *The Practice of Social Work in North America: Culture, Context, and Competency Development* (Chicago, IL: Lyceum, 2016), chapter 2.

42. Frederic G. Reamer, *Social Work Values and Ethics,* 2nd ed. (New York: Columbia University Press); Reamer, *Philosophical Foundations.*

43. Craig G. Bartholomew and Michael W. Goheen, *Christian Philosophy: A Systematic and Narrative Introduction* (Grand Rapids, MI: Baker, 2013).

44. Keller, *Reason for God,* 123.

45. Wolters, *Creation Regained,* 12.

as pointed out in the introductory chapter, we need to begin where the Bible begins, with God.

Taking the Sovereign God Seriously in Social Work

A biblical grounding means taking God at His Word and viewing social work within the grand scriptural meta-narrative in which God acts to carry out His purposes for His creation.[46] A Reformational perspective, rooted in Calvinism, would begin by focusing on the absolute, non- negotiable and incomprehensible sovereignty of the triune God. Jesus declared before issuing the Great Commission that "all authority on heaven and earth has been given to me" (Matthew 28:18 NIV). One insight that flows from recognizing God's sovereignty is captured by Kuyper's arguably most often quoted passage: "There is not a square inch in the whole domain of our human existence over which Christ, who is sovereign over all, does not cry out, 'Mine!'"[47] To get a sense of what this means to a Kuyperian social worker, ask her to give you a tour of her workplace and point out to you which parts of her work are secular and which parts are religious. You will likely see her squirm and frown and stall until eventually she might declare in exasperation (echoing Kuyper), "But that's impossible! It's all religious!" Because God is sovereign over the entire creation, everything is God's and nothing is outside his authority and control.

Recognizing God's sovereignty also means acknowledging oneself as a creature whose first action is to fall on one's face before the living, mighty triune God. As Eugene Peterson puts it, "The Christian life consists mostly of what God – the Father, Son, and Holy Spirit – is and does.... We don't so much lack knowledge, we lack reverence."[48] This entails recognizing the important distinction between God and humans: we are only creatures and only God is the Creator. As Peterson has already hinted, acknowledging God as Creator is more an act of confession than understanding. "Fear-of-the-Lord" is a posture of worship, not simply an intellectual activity.[49] A biblically grounded approach to social work, therefore, must begin with God. As Kuyper unapologetically urged: "The first article of any social program that will bring salvation, therefore, must remain: 'I believe in God the

46. Craig Bartholomew and Michael Goheen, *The Drama of Scripture: Finding Our Place in the Biblical Story*, 2nd ed. (Grand Rapids, MI: Baker, 2014).

47. As quoted in Craig Bartholomew, *Contours of the Kuyperian Tradtion: A Systematic Introduction,* (Downers Grove, IL: InterVarsity Press, 2017), 69.

48. Eugene Peterson, *Christ Plays in Ten Thousand Places: A Conversation in Spiritual Theology*, (Grand Rapids, MI: Eerdmans, 2005), 41, 44.

49. Peterson, *Christ Plays*, 40-44.

Father Almighty, Maker of heaven and earth.'"[50]

Acknowledging God's sovereignty leads to a consideration of two other characteristics of God that are particularly relevant to social work, but which are sometimes considered to be in tension: God is love, and God is just. To say, as we did earlier, that the qualifying function of the social work profession is the ethical modality of love (or care) for one's neighbor begs the question: what is the source and meaning of love? Christians confess that God is the origin of all things, and that such things reflect and emerge out of his very character. *The Belgic Confession* begins with a clear, beautiful, but also mysterious, description of God's attributes:

> We all believe in our hearts and confess with our mouths that there is a single and simple spiritual being, whom we call God—eternal, incomprehensible, invisible, unchangeable, infinite, almighty; completely wise, just, and good, and the overflowing source of all good.[51]

To our twenty-first-century ears the word "love" might appear conspicuously absent from this list, but the concept is undoubtedly embedded within and central to God's character. Indeed, Scripture is clear that "God is love" (I John 4:8, 16), and love appears as a distinct attribute of God in Reformed theology.[52] God's love exists as part of the larger coherent character of God in which love is inseparable from God's holiness and justice. For example, *The Westminster Larger Catechism* lists these together in way that makes clear that they're not meant to be contradictory or in tension: "God is ... most holy, most just, most merciful and gracious."[53] The social work profession identifies social justice as one of its most central values, but is unclear on what the source of that value is. A Christian in social work, however, acknowledges that justice is not a human-centred or derived value, a value centred on or derived from human beings, but arises from the very nature of God. As Timothy Keller puts it, "Biblical justice is … rooted in the very character of God and it is the outworking of that character, which is never less than just."[54]

50. Abraham Kuyper, *The Problem of Poverty: A Translation of the Opening Address at the first Christian Social Congress in the Netherlands, November 9, 1891,* ed. James W. Skillen (Sioux Center, IA: Dordt College Press, 2011), 57-8.

51. *The Belgic Confession,* "Article 1," accessed May 27, 2021, https://www.crcna.org/welcome/beliefs/confessions/belgic-confession.

52. C. Matthew McMahon, "The Attributes of God on A Puritan's Mind," accessed May 27, 2021, https://www.apuritansmind.com/the-attributes-of-god-by-c-matthew-mcmahon/ and "The Attributes of God and Calvin's *Institutes of the Christian Religion,*" accessed May 27, 2021, https://www.apuritansmind.com/the-attributes-of-god-by-c-matthew-mcmahon/the-attributes-of-god-and-calvins-institutes-of-the-christian-religion-by-c-matthew-mcmahon/.

53. "Question 7. What is God?" in *The Westminster Larger Catechism,* accessed May 27, 2021, https://opc.org/lc.html.

54. Timothy Keller, "Justice in the Bible," *Life in the Gospel* (September 2020), ac-

Taking the Wonder of Creation Seriously in Social Work

We are sometimes tempted to think of creation as referring mostly to the natural non-human world. For example, when a Christian says, "I was out enjoying God's creation," we probably imagine he or she went for a walk in the forest, or lingered by a clear lake in the mountains, or perhaps strolled a beach at sunset; what rarely comes to mind is that he or she rode a crowded subway downtown, or took in a game with thousands of other fans, or hung out with friends in a bustling coffee shop. But that's because we sometimes have a stunted sense of what the Bible means when it talks about creation. If, as Wolters affirms, "there is nothing in human life that does not belong to the created order"[55] then we need to train ourselves to see the wonder of God's creation as much in the people and places we encounter in all walks of life as we do when we see the beauty of the natural world.

Social work, as we have seen, deals with people and their difficulties. A Reformational perspective of creation provides insight for how we understand the nature of humans and their roles and characteristics within diverse, pluralistic, and complex societies. The creation story in Genesis 1 makes clear that the fundamental characteristic of humans, according to this view, is that we are created as image-bearers of God.[56] Although there is debate about exactly what that entails,[57] it includes at least that we image God's relational character and his creativity. God said, "Let *us* make man in *our* image, in *our* likeness" (Gen. 1:26, emphasis added). God's plural self-identification alludes to His three-in-one personhood as Father, Son, and Holy Spirit (the relationship of the three persons of the Trinity has been described as *perichoresis*[58]).

God's desire to be in a covenantal relationship with humans means that we, as His image-bearers, are also relational and social. To be human—to image God—is to be in mutual, harmonious, interdependent relationships with others. The reverse is also true. When we are isolated from others or when our relationships are constrained, limited, or broken, then we are in some way less than fully human as God intended. When humans gather together and associate with one another in many types of social arrangements, we get a glimpse of the many ways in which

cessed May 28, 2021, https://quarterly.gospelinlife.com/justice-in-the-bible/.

55. Wolters, *Creation Regained*, 25.

56. Richard Middleton and Brian Walsh, "*Truth is Stranger than It Used to Be: Biblical Faith in a Postmodern Age.* (Downers Grove, IL: InterVarsity Press, 1995), chapter 6.

57. Richard Middleton, *The Liberating Image: The Imago Dei in Genesis 1* (Grand Rapids: Brazos Press, 2005).

58. Keller, *The Reason for God*, 214.

we live out our created relational character.

This biblical conception of the value of human persons rooted in and reflecting God's identity provides the roots and soil out of which springs social work's value in the inherent dignity of every single human being.[59] As David Sherwood has pointed out, "Many in our generation, including many social workers, are trying to hold onto values—such as the irreducible dignity and worth of the individual—while denying the only basis on which such a value can ultimately stand."[60] Being image-bearers of God means that humans have not just rights, but also responsibilities. That is, we are able to respond and act on our own accord. The social work value of the inherent dignity and worth of humans is tightly linked to the value of self-determination and agency.[61] The recognition of human agency does not dismiss the realities of the ways in which social structures and other forces constrain our choices, but points, again, to the relational and loving character of God. As Lisa Hosack poignantly describes it,

> Refusing to control our actions, [God] instead draws us through acts of love that capture our hearts and minds. Even acts of discipline are entirely undergirded by love and a desire to draw us. God does call us to obedience, but not like a tyrannical boss or an oppressive slave master. Instead, he wants willing submission as we trust His goodness.[62]

Rooting the social work value of self-determination in a view of humans as responsible agents made in God's image provides a solid foundation which protects against two extremes. On the one hand, a social worker might use self-determination to give a client the license to do

59. David R. Hodge and Terry Wolfer, "Promoting tolerance: The imago Dei as an imperative for Christian social workers," *Journal of Religion & Spirituality in Social Work: Social Thought* 27, no. 3 (2008): 297-313. Cheryl Brandsen and Paul Vliem, "Justice and Human Rights in Fourth Century Cappadocia," *Social Work & Christianity* 34, no. 4 (Winter 2007): 421-448; Vanderwoerd and van der Woerd, "Is There More to This Story?"

60. David Sherwood, "The Relationship between Beliefs and Values in Social Work Practice: Worldviews Make a Difference," *Christianity and Social Work: Readings on the Integration of Christianity and Social Work Practice,* 6th ed, eds. L. Scales and M. Kelly (Botsford, CT: North American Association of Christians in Social Work, 2020), 89.

61. Terry A. Wolfer, David R. Hodge and Janessa Steele, "Self-Determination in Social Work: A Christian Perspective as a Philosophical Foundation for Client Choice," *Social Work & Christianity,* 45, no. 2 (2018), 3-32.

62. Lisa Hosack, *Development on Purpose: Faith and Human Behavior in the Social Environment,* (Botsford, CT: North American Association of Christians in Social Work, 2019), 23.

whatever he wants in the name of the client's freedom, even if it risks harming himself or others. Another social worker might justify restricting self-determination if she judges that the client's desires are in some way "wrong" or out of step with dominant cultural values. A biblical worldview shows that even inherent human dignity and worth have limits. Of course humans have intrinsic value, but for what? Yes, we have the capacity and freedom to make our own choices, but why? The Christian answer is because we are made in God's image, and as God's image-bearers, we reflect His character and purposes. Since God is a relational being of love who seeks to pour out His love and share it with others for their good, that is a clue to how we are to understand human dignity and freedom. Andy Crouch's discussion of power gives a hint of this:

> There is no explanation for this lavish gift of dignity to creatures formed from the dust.... [T]he gift of glory, like the gift of power and rule, is simply the reflection of true being, the character of the Creator God who always seeks more being, not less, and is glorified by the multiplication and distribution of glory, not by the guarding and hoarding of glory.[63]

Secular social work asserts that we have self-determination because we have inherent dignity, but these are not ends in themselves. Instead, grounding our human dignity in God's image reveals that there are limits to self-determination, and that these limits are not negative, but counterintuitively, these are designed for our good. It is only when we recognize and come to embody the selfless giving nature of God that we begin to truly reflect what it means to be human, and thus come closer to the flourishing that God desires for us and for which we were made.

We humans flourish when we live according to God's design. To say that God created all things, including humans, also means that He orders them. Just as God gives his laws for the operation and regulation of the physical and natural world—laws of gravity, thermodynamics, the changing of the seasons, the ordering and movement of the stars, and so on—so also do God's laws apply to society and culture. Just as there is a structure and proper ordering for the physical world, so there is for the human and social world. Society is God's creation and operates according to God's laws, or at least it should. If you're thinking at this point that there is scant evidence of that, then you are right. The key difference between the laws of gravity, say, and the laws for the social world, is what social scientists call human *agency*, that is, the capacity to act freely and to make choices. The physical world cannot choose to disobey God's

63. Andy Crouch, *Playing God: Redeeming the Gift of Power* (Downers Grove, IL: IVP Books, 2013), 99.

laws, whereas humans can (and do). In other words, there is a *structure* to social arrangements that recognizes that these are not merely human inventions, but rather parts of God's creation. When social arrangements conform to God's laws then we can say that they are operating the way God intended. As noted in the introduction to this volume, the word *norm* can be used in this context to differentiate between God's structures for the non-human world, that is, His laws, and God's structures for the human and social world.[64]

The implication of this insight is that human and social entities—marriages, families, schools, businesses, labour unions, governments, and so on—are part of God's creation and must conform to His norms. There is, in other words, a right way and a wrong way to structure a marriage, or a government, or a school; these social entities do not operate only according to the whims and wishes of humans, but rather must adhere to God's designs. When they do not and things go wrong, it is not because of the way God created them, but rather because of the way humans have misunderstood or misapplied—either wilfully or ignorantly or both—God's norms.

When we say that all of creation is good, therefore, we are saying that there is inherent good in the structures of things that God has made. However, we know full well that that not all marriages or schools or governments (or whatever else) are *actually* good. What we see here are God's good structures that are being distorted or corrupted away from His intentions. They are misdirected away from His norms and instead, pointed in some other direction. This distinction—between the inherent *structures* of things, and their *direction*—either towards or away from God—helps us to avoid the sacred/secular, holy/unholy dualism.[65] That insight leads us to the second part of the biblical framework which faces squarely the ugly reality of sin.

Taking the Ugliness of Sin Seriously in Social Work

Social workers are painfully aware of the many ways in which relationships break down, in which individuals, families, and communities are broken and hurting, and in which vulnerable persons and groups suffer from injustice and oppression. Perhaps nowhere are the awful consequences of sin for human life and relationships more apparent than in the field of social work. Hosack puts it plainly: "…the very existence of social work is a manifestation of the fall…. It might be difficult to find another biblical theme with as much application to social work because

64. Wolters, *Creation Regained*, chapter 2.

65. Wolters, *Creation Regained*, chapter 5.

sin forms the backdrop and the basis for much of our work."[66]

The second act in the drama of Scripture comes quickly on the heels of God declaring that His work of creation is very good. No sooner has God created humans as his stewards over creation and granted them extensive responsibility do Adam and Eve respond by disobeying God and seeking their own way. As the story of Scripture reveals, this has had grave consequences not just for humans but for all of creation itself.

It is sometimes said that social workers work with those who are sinners and those who have been sinned against. Although contemporary social work would not use the language of sin, it readily affirms the latter half of this statement, namely, that its clients are assailed by a host of oppressive forces that unjustly disadvantage them and lead to injustice and inequality. For example, in discussions about how to address poverty, the emphasis is usually on advocating for government programs to correct injustices in the market economy. Rarely does one encounter arguments for interventions that focus on enhancing individuals' capacities for fear that these will be seen as "blaming the victim." Rather, the dominant approaches explicitly identify the cause of poverty as external to the individual, and thus focus on the failings of employers, corporations, laws, institutions, churches, and many other groups in society; in other words, everything but the individual. So for social work, even though they wouldn't use the language of sin, virtually all social problems happen because persons are "sinned against" but rarely if ever because they themselves are "sinners."

In the throbbing rock track "The War Inside," Switchfoot's frontman Jon Foreman wails about a truth that today's social work profession is reluctant to admit:

> Age don't matter like race don't matter like place don't matter like what's inside
> I am the war inside
> I am the battle line
> Ain't no killer like pride, no killer like I, no killer like what's inside."[67]

To really grasp the truth about the depth and reach of sin, the song is best listened to in a car with a great sound system, for there, with the pounding bass and driving guitars, one can feel it reverberate in your body. Sin is not just a superficial veneer, but is much deeper:

66. Hosack, *Development on Purpose,* 13, 14.

67. Switchfoot, "The War Inside," April 9, 2015, YouTube video, 3:38, https://www.youtube.com/watch?v=vaacJQEN3y4&ab_channel=Switchfoot.

I can feel it like a crack in my spine
I can feel it like the back of my mind
I am the war inside."[68]

The pounding insights of a twenty-first century rock band echo the words of Article 15 of *The Belgic Confession*: "We believe that by the disobedience of Adam original sin has been spread through the whole human race. It is a corruption of the whole human nature— an inherited depravity which even infects small infants in their mother's womb, and the root which produces in humanity every sort of sin."[69]

This statement in *The Belgic Confession* would likely be deeply offensive to most social workers today because it is perceived as a denial of the dignity and worth of humans, and because of how such sentiments have too often been used as a justification for all manner of interventions that are judgmental, condescending, and punitive.[70] For most social workers, the war is not inside, but outside; the problem is not that individuals are sinful, but that some external forces have alienated, subjugated, limited, or otherwise perpetrated some form of mistreatment or injustice on them. As the NASW *Code of Ethics* puts it, "Fundamental to social work is attention to the environmental forces that create, contribute to, and address problems in living."[71] And yet here too there are tensions and ambivalence. As noted above, a core value of social work is the inherent dignity and worth of every human being. In contrast to the traditional Christian view that recognizes the paradoxical nature of humans as being both made in God's image *and* tainted by sin, the social work profession has by and large, in keeping with modernist culture,[72] rejected a view of humans as being sinful. Although this is often implicit and assumed, some writers have stated this explicitly. For example, Mullaly and Dupré advocate the value of humanitarianism as central to their progressive and structural vision for social work, and clarify that "humanitarianism de-

68. Switchfoot, "The War Inside."

69. *The Belgic Confession,* "Article 15," accessed May 27, 2021, https://www.crcna.org/welcome/beliefs/confessions/belgic-confession.

70. See for example, Dennis Guest, *The Emergence of Social Security in Canada,* 3rd ed. (Vancouver, BC: UBC Press, 2003); Harry Specht and Mark Courtney, *Unfaithful Angels: How Social Work Abandoned Its Mission,* (New York: Free Press, 1994); Phyllis Day and Jerome Schiele, *A New History of Social Welfare,* 7th ed. (New York: Pearson, 2013).

71. National Association of Social Workers, "Preamble."

72. See for example, Alan Jacobs, *Original Sin: A Cultural History* (New York: Harper Collins, 2008); Rebecca Konyndyk DeYoung, *Glittering Vices: A New Look at the Seven Deadly Sins and Their Remedies* (Grand Rapids, MI: Brazos Press, 2009); Cornelius Plantinga, *Not the Way It's Supposed to Be: A Breviary of Sin* (Grand Rapids, MI: Eerdmans, 1995).

nies this dualism within the individual and claims that people are innately good and reasonable."[73] However, Siporin's frank reflections on the "moral mission of social work" reveal the deep ambivalence of the social work profession and its discomfort with the reality of the idea of sin as a central theme for social work:

> By their very nature, social workers are morally and politically liberal, believing in the inherent goodness and perfectibility of all human beings. This belief is associated with the moral mission of the profession.... But the reality is that social workers seek the good in imperfect people and an imperfect society. The vast majority of social work clients and the major subject of social work ministrations involve sins and evil – conduct which today we politely call dependency, deviant behavior, or even mental illness. These realities of social work practice are hard to reconcile with basic beliefs in the inherent goodness of people when one is at the battlefront of direct social services in urban ghettos.[74]

This is a striking and refreshingly honest admission. It is neither easy nor popular to focus on human sinfulness, especially when one is trying to affirm a person's dignity. Moreover, it feels too judgmental and intolerant to emphasize sin; particularly when the word sin is associated with failure and shortcomings and risks blaming the victim.

But a Reformed understanding of sin helps us to get past this limitation, in part because sin is more – much more – than individual and personal failures. Pulitzer Prize winning author David Shipler inadvertently stumbles upon the reality of the scope of a biblical view of sin with this keen insight from his careful observation of the complex dynamics that lead working people to experience poverty. He astutely notes:

> Each person's life is the mixed product of bad choices and bad fortune, of roads not taken and roads cut off by accident of birth or circumstances. It is difficult to find someone whose poverty is not somehow related to his or her unwise behavior.... And it is difficult to find behavior that is not somehow related to inherited conditions.[75]

His insight, though apparently not biblically informed, reveals the reality of the extensive reach of sin. Yes, people are the victims of sinful structures, but each of us individually is also sinful. We are limited by our poor choices, misguided desires, susceptibility to temptations, lack of self-con-

---

73. Bob Mullaly and Marilyn Dupré, *The New Structural Social Work: Ideology, Theory, and Practice,* 4th ed., (New York: Oxford University Press, 2019), 371.

74. Max Siporin, "Strengthening the Moral Mission of Social Work," in *The Moral Purposes of Social Work: The Character and Intentions of a Profession*, eds. P. Nelson Reid and Philip R. Popple (Chicago, IL: Nelson-Hall, 1992), 93-94.

75. David K. Shipler, *The Working Poor: Invisible in America* (New York: Knopf, 2004), 6-7.

trol, and a host of other personal failures. But that is not the whole story. As Shipler has discovered, individual mistakes cannot account for all of the misery and suffering that humans experience. Whether in spite of or because of our actions, bad things happen that are outside our control. The Bible's concept of sin gives us a language that helps to make sense of this. Wolters describes it this way:

> The effects of sin touch all of creation; no created thing is in principle untouched by the corrosive effects of the fall. Whether we look at societal structures such as the state or the family, or cultural pursuits such as art or technology, or bodily functions such as sexuality or eating, or anything at all within the wide scope of creation, we discover the good handiwork of God has been drawn in the sphere of human mutiny against God.... It is not difficult to find examples of the widespread effects of the fall in our world.[76]

Implicit in Wolters' reference to the "good handiwork of God" is the concept of shalom. Neil Plantinga argues that we cannot understand sin unless we first understand *not*-sin.[77] A rich tradition of authors have described shalom as God's intention for all things in his creation to be rightly ordered and working together harmoniously so that everything is right and good and just and beautiful.[78] As we noted above, God repeatedly declared creation to be good, and then capped it off by creating humans and emphatically describing that as "very good." Shalom is the "very good" that God created. If shalom is the way things are supposed to be, then sin, in Plantinga's words, is "*not* the way it's supposed to be." Sin is a negative thing, and cannot exist on its own; it is a parasite leeching off God's good creation. Sin, therefore, is "the vandalism of shalom," "culpable shalom-breaking"; it is "unoriginal [and] disrupts something that is good and harmonious."[79]

Rather than providing justification for simplistic victim blaming, the biblical concept of sin provides a much broader and more nuanced understanding (which is ultimately more hopeful, as we'll see below when we get to the next section on redemption and restoration) that gives a foundation for a balanced analysis of the complex interplay of personal and systemic/structural sources of human suffering. Since sin is the damaging of shalom, and shalom involves a full picture of all things

76. Al Wolters, *Creation Regained*, 53-4.

77. Plantinga, *Not the Way It's Supposed to Be*, chapter 1.

78. Wolterstorff, *Until Justice and Peace Embrace*; Mark Gornik, *To Live in Peace: Biblical Faith and the Changing Inner City.* (Grand Rapids, MI: Eerdmans, 2002); Steve Corbett and Brian Fikkert, *When Helping Hurts: How to Alleviate Poverty Without Hurting the Poor... and Yourself.* (Chicago, IL: Moody, 2012).

79. Plantinga, *Not the Way It's Supposed to Be*, 14, 16.

being harmonious, it is not surprising that Scripture refers to sin as more than just individual failure, but it also has a corporate and systemic character. In the Old Testament, Moses, Daniel, Nehemiah, Ezra, and others confessed corporate sins for which they were not personally responsible. In addition, the biblical concept of justice reveals God's deep concern for systems, practices, structures, and institutions that are unfair, unequal, or oppressive, [80] and God's heart for those who are most vulnerable, what Wolterstorff has called the "quartet of the downtrodden and excluded."[81]

Taking the Hope of Redemption and Restoration Seriously in Social Work

In the face of the ugly, persistent, unavoidable reality of the way sin has damaged and destroyed human flourishing, where do social workers find hope? How do we face the complex and entrenched systems of injustice, oppression, and marginalization that starkly reveal sin's long reach? Or, as the authors of *Case Critical* ask in their chapter "Challenging Feeling Hopeless": "In the light of the incredible challenges, what on earth would motivate anyone to stay within such a beleaguered environment?"[82] These are questions virtually all social workers face sooner or later in their work. Why go on? What difference am I really making? What good will come of all my work? What can I really accomplish? When and how will things ever be better? One clue is in how the question is asked by the authors of *Case Critical* – "what on earth…?" – because Christians recognize that the source of the answer is ultimately not found on earth, but rather in heaven.

Looking to heaven as the source of our hope highlights a key distinction between a Christian worldview and many others which are either implicitly or explicitly grounded in a human-centric or materialist worldview; or, as Charles Taylor has described it, an "immanent frame" as opposed to an "enchanted" one.[83] That is, Christianity acknowledges God as a Being that is external to creation, and thus Christians submit themselves to an authority that is outside themselves and the world.

80. Timothy Keller, *Generous Justice: How God's Grace Makes Us Just* (New York: Penguin, 2010).

81. Nicholas Wolterstorff, "Justice, Not Charity: Social Work through the Eyes of Faith," *Social Work & Christianity* 33, no. 2 (2006), 126.

82. Banakonda Kennedy-Kish (Bell), Raven Sinclair, Ben Carniol, and Donna Baines, *Case Critical: Social Services and Social Justice in Canada,* 7th ed. (Toronto, ON: Between the Lines Press, 2017), 150.

83. Charles Taylor, *A Secular Age* (Boston, MA: Belknap, 2007); see also James K.A. Smith *How Not to Be Secular: Reading Charles Taylor* (Grand Rapids, MI: Eerdmans, 2014).

These differences are more than just worldviews, since they also reveal differences in stories, or narratives. All humans live by stories of one sort or another, whether explicit or implied.[84] A Reformational approach makes this explicit by describing the Bible as a drama that includes not only an account of things that happened in the past, but also includes ourselves, here and now, in the drama; what is more, it tells the story of the future that God has in store.[85] Christians in social work, therefore, have their hope in the story of a God who promises to "make all things new" (Revelation 21:5).

Many Christians in the Western hemisphere, embedded as we are in modern, liberal individualism, have reduced the entire gospel message to what Jesus has done for *me*.[86] However, the biblical story is not just about our own individual salvation. John 3:16 says, "For God so loved *the world*"—not "For God so loved *the people*," because "world" in this verse is best translated as "cosmos," by which is meant the entirety of created reality, not simply the people in our world. Of course God dearly loves each one of us, but we misunderstand and limit the scope of God's love if we think of salvation as only something that He does for each of us.[87] Paul says in Colossians 1:19-20, "For God was pleased to have all His fullness dwell in Him [that is, Christ], and *through Him to reconcile to Himself all things, whether things on earth or things in heaven*, by making peace through His blood, shed on the cross" (emphasis added).

The Reformational distinction between the structure and direction of creation[88]—that is, in the inherent goodness of all of what God made, intertwined with the sinful human misdirections that have been embedded in everything—alerts us to what God is up to. He is not content just to save our souls; no, He has much grander ambitions than that. God has set out to restore it all! He wants to reclaim and renew *all* of what He created. When Jesus stilled the storm, the disciples said, "Who is this, that even the clouds obey Him?" And, when Christ gave up His life on the cross, the very earth trembled and shook, and the skies went dark. Clearly, this is bigger than we think. In fact, since we see through a glass darkly, we can barely grasp the immensity of God's plans.

---

84. Christian Smith, *Moral, Believing Animals: Human Personhood and Culture* (New York: Oxford University Press, 2003).

85. Bartholomew and Goheen, *The Drama of Scripture.*

86. J. Richard Middleton, *A New Heaven and a New Earth: Reclaiming Biblical Eschatology* (Grand Rapids, MI: Baker, 2014).

87. Eugene Peterson, *Christ Plays*; N.T. Wright, *Surprised by Hope: Rethinking Heaven, the Resurrection, and the Mission of the Church.* (New York, NY: HarperCollins, 2008).

88. Wolters, *Creation Regained,* chapter 5.

A Christian in social work recognizes (and here I echo Kuyper) that the ultimate solution for any and every social problem is Jesus. But, as we've seen, that is not limited to just the salvation of our own souls, but rather it encompasses God's ongoing action plan of redemption to restore His creation and renew it to the glory that He has in mind. Through God's grace, we are restored to relationship with Him through Christ's death on the cross, but Christ's work goes further than just ourselves. God's grace extends to the entire creation. Romans 8:22 describes creation as "groaning as in the pangs of childbirth," and thankfully, God hears those groans. That means that God's redemption restores not just humans, but human and social arrangements and artifacts as well. God wants to renew and restore marriages, families, businesses, choirs, hockey teams, movies, paintings, theatre productions, automobiles, can openers, combines, apps, websites, and on and on and on—all of it. God seeks flourishing and shalom and thriving in His creation, and to do that, He is invested in an immense project of restoration and renewal, the likes of which we can scarcely imagine.

This should give great hope for social workers to invest in the tasks of working within the various settings—agencies, communities, neighbourhoods—in which God has placed us, because these settings are not just earthly things from which God will rescue us. No, these things are part of His creation and He will abandon neither us nor them. (As Wolters pointedly puts it, "God did not make junk, and God does not junk what he made."[89]) In this respect, the Reformed emphasis on the grand scope of God's redemption is what gives social workers the motivation and the theological justification for what is called macro practice.[90] That is, social workers, drawing on the "person-in-environment" theoretical lens[91] seek to bring healing and restoration across the continuum of what they call micro to macro practice, ranging from work with individuals, couples, and families, to work with groups, organizations, communities, and social policies.

Equipped with this vast vision for God's redemptive purposes, then, Christians in social work recognize that the ultimate cause of all social misery is sin, and that the ultimate solution is Jesus. But this is no pietistic and simplistic appeal to some airy-fairy personal salvation. Rather, Wolters puts it this way, "The scope of redemption is as great as that

89. Wolters, *Creation Regained*, 49.

90. Vanderwoerd, "I Am Making All Things New: Biblical Themes for Macro Practice," *Christianity and Social Work: Readings on the Integration of Christianity and Social Work,* 3rd ed., eds. Beryl Hugen and Laine Scales (Botsford, CT: North American Association of Christians in Social Work, 2008), 121-137.

91. Coggins, *The Practice of Social Work in North America.*

of the fall; it embraces creation as a whole.... What distinguishes a reformational worldview is its understanding of the radical and universal import of both sin and salvation."[92] Nor is this an excuse to distance oneself from the world or to seek to escape. Rather, the biblical narrative places us right in the thick of the story through the work of Christ who established His church as His hands and feet to continue the work that He has already begun to reconcile all things to Himself. And further, He has equipped His followers with the power of the Holy Spirit so that we can be Christ's "ambassadors" in His "ministry of reconciliation" (2 Corinthians 5:17-20).

As Kuyper boldly proclaimed, a Christian diagnosis of any social problem reveals the sin at the root of the problem, and bases a solution on the foundation of God's revealed truth. "We as Christians must place the strongest possible emphasis on the majesty of God's authority and on the absolute validity of his ordinances, so that, even as we condemn the rotting social structure of our day, we will never try to erect any structure except one that rests on foundations laid by God."[93] A contemporary example is Corbett and Fikkert's analysis of how a Reformed understanding of poverty leads to a different diagnosis of the problem, and therefore to different solutions. Drawing on the concept of shalom, they argue that poverty is not simply a lack of material resources, but is best seen as a breakdown of four relationships: with God, with oneself, with others, and with the rest of creation.[94] Similarly, Hosack acknowledges that while it is unethical for social workers to coerce clients into accepting Christianity or acknowledging God, social workers can still help clients to make choices that reflect a biblical understanding of flourishing.[95]

Although social work claims a "person-in-environment" perspective, it disproportionately focuses, as we have seen, on external factors and is much more reluctant to assess problems or offer interventions that suggest any failing in an individual. We have described above how a Kuyperian approach certainly gives a clear basis for recognizing the corporate aspects of sin, and thus a solid justification for macro interventions that address systemic injustices. As important as it is to acknowledge and address structural problems, however, a biblical approach also does not allow us to let individuals off the hook. True, God's work of redemption certainly entails more than the salvation of souls, but it also is not less than that. If full shalom involves rightly

92. Wolters, *Creation Regained*, 72.

93. Kuyper, *Problem of Poverty*, 58.

94. Corbett and Fikkert, *When Helping Hurts*, chapter 2.

95. Hosack, *Development on Purpose,* 190.

ordered relationships with God, selves, others, and the rest of creation, then we will never see full shalom in our clients (or ourselves either, for that matter) without *palingenesis.* This is a word that has been described variously as conversion, being born again, renewal, regeneration, and being made anew.[96] In one word it captures the full scope of God's redemptive work; it occurs only twice in the New Testament, once referring to the renewal of creation (Matthew 19:28), and also referring to individual repentance and rebirth (Titus 3:5).[97] Emphasizing only personal salvation is like accepting the King but not seeking His kingdom; emphasizing only structural solutions without acknowledging human sin and failings is like seeking the kingdom without accepting the King.[98] Bartholomew puts it this way, "There is no value in being about 'kingdom business' if one has not been born again! The kingdom is first about coming into a right and living relation to the King."[99] A Christian's hope, then, is in the promise that God is making all things news. No person or system is written off. God can change anyone and anything, and our work as social workers means that we can put our trust in what He is doing and focus on being faithfully obedient to serve where He has placed us, rather than putting our hope in what we can accomplish by our own efforts in our own time.

Toward a Renewed Agenda for Social Work Informed by a Reformed Approach

With this sketch of how a Reformed biblical understanding helps us to view the profession of social work and the social world, we can now begin to imagine how this worldview leads us to ask certain kinds of questions and to investigate and explore particular possibilities that might not be inquired into by others from different approaches. The value of such an exercise, as I have already suggested earlier, is not just in making room for difference, but to push us toward truths that can only begin to be grasped through the illumination of God's word.

96. See Bartholomew, *Contours of the Kuyperian Tradition,* 26-31, 248.

97. John Piper, "Through the Washing of Regeneration," *Desiring God* (February 3, 2008), accessed June 5, 2021, https://www.desiringgod.org/messages/through-the-washing-of-regeneration.

98. This analogy comes from Corbett and Fikkert, *When Helping Hurts,* 37.

99. Bartholomew, *Contours of the Kuyperian Tradition,* 32.

Discovering norms for social structures

How Do We Discern What Is Structural and What Is Directional Variation?

For a profession—and a culture—that believes that individual self-expression is sacred, and that anyone should be free to define his or her own reality, it is anathema to claim that some choices are good and some are bad. A Christian who holds a worldview that affirms the goodness of God's creation, however, does just that.

Think of the example of marriage. Today it is commonly accepted —and legally recognized in many countries—that marriage can consist of any two persons of any sex. Furthermore, marriage is viewed primarily as an optional (but not necessary) arrangement for two (or more) adults who wish to be sexually active. In other words, marriage is seen as nothing more than a consensual (and often temporary) arrangement between adults that is only useful insofar as it allows the participating adults the opportunity to pursue their own desires.

This stands in stark contrast to the historic Christian understanding of marriage in which a man and a woman are joined by God and bound to each other for life. Christian marriage is not just about two adults, but also rooted in larger contexts: an extended family, a supporting community, and the larger body of Christ (i.e., the church).[100] That is why Christian marriage ceremonies are held in community, surrounded by witnesses. Christian marriages connect husband and wife to generations past and future. Children, born as the consequences of a husband's and wife's mutually shared love, are entrusted to their parents, who hold special responsibility to raise such children in the "fear-of-the-Lord."[101]

Accumulating social science evidence now bears witness to the goodness of this God-given norm: marriage is the best arrangement to ensure the long term thriving and flourishing not only of children, but for society.[102] As Novak and Adams show, however, it is widely taught in

---

100. Timothy Keller and Kathy Keller, *The Meaning of Marriage: Facing the Complexities of Commitment with the Wisdom of God* (New York: Penguin, 2013).

101. Peterson, *Christ Plays*, 40-44, 256-257.

102. David C. Ribar, "Why Marriage Matters for Child Wellbeing", *The Future of Children,* 25 no. 2 (Fall 2015): 11 – 28; Wilcox W. Bradford and Wendy B. Wang, "The Marriage Divide: How and Why Working Class Families are More Fragile Today," (Washington, DC: American Enterprise Institute, 2017), accessed March 14, 2019, http://www.aei.org/publication/the-marriage-divide-how-and-why-working-class-families-are-more-fragile-today/ ; Joseph Henrich, Robert Boyd, and Peter J. Richerson, "The Puzzle of Monogamous Marriage," *Philosophical Transactions of the Royal Society B* no. 367 (2012): 657-669.

social work and related disciplines that marriage is "more a problem than a solution. The potential costs of marriage to adults receive exaggerated treatment, while the benefits of marriage, both to individuals and to society, are downplayed."[103] Social work grounded in a Christian worldview, therefore, needs to work harder to discern the goodness of God's given norms for social life and then to show how adherence to these norms leads to shalom.

Diversity and identity

How Can Social Work Affirm Diversity without Idolizing Identity?

Social work, along with other disciplines in the social sciences, has led the way in identifying and uncovering oppression and injustice that are borne disproportionately by those who are identified in various ways as being outside the mainstream, particularly women, ethnic and racialized minorities, persons with disabilities, or persons who fall under the broad acronym LGBTQ (lesbian, gay, bisexual, transgender, queer).[104] Certainly these efforts have done much to expose patterns of unequal and unfair access to resources, and have increased our understanding of the hardships and consequences that these experiences have for persons from these groups, leading to advances in advocacy and improvements in social work interventions.[105]

A key focus in this work draws on the concept of intersectionality and its link to identity.[106] Intersectionality is a term that emerged in the 1990s to convey the complexity of how a person's identity in multiple groups, such as race and gender, leads to additional oppression beyond that associated with either one of the identity categories independently.[107] A central agenda of those using an intersectionality lens is to identify

103. Michael Novak and Paul Adams, *Social Justice Isn't What You Think It Is* (New York: Encounter Books, 2015), 222.

104. Gary C. Dumbrill and June Ying Yee, *Anti-Oppressive Social Work: Ways of Knowing, Talking, and Doing* (New York: Oxford, 2019); Bob Mullaly and Juliana West, *Challenging Oppression and Confronting Privilege,* 3rd ed. (New York: Oxford, 2018).

105. Alean Al-Krenawi, John R. Graham & Nazim Habibov, *Diversity and Social Work in Canada* (New York: Oxford, 2016).

106. Miu Chung Yan, "Multiple Positionality and Intersectionality: Toward a Dialogical Social Work Approach" in *Diversity and Social Work in Canada,* eds. Alean Al-Krenawi, John R. Graham and Nazim Habibov, (New York: Oxford, 2016), 114-138.

107. See for example, Mullaly and West, *Challenging Oppression,* chapter 8; Yan, "Multiple Positionality and Intersectionality," 121.

people according to how much power they have relative to others so that social structures can be radically transformed to correct these power imbalances. Again, while attention to the dynamics of power and injustice has been helpful, this approach rests on categorizing people in a binary way as either oppressed or privileged simply based on their identification with certain groups. Keller, in his critique of intersectionality, puts it plainly: "If you are white, male, straight, cisgender then you have the highest amount of power. If you are none of these at all, you are the most marginalized and oppressed."[108] Keller is not just exaggerating to make a point; proponents of this approach consistently emphasize that the key consideration in whether someone is a victim or a perpetrator of oppression is their membership in certain groups. For example, Mullaly and West argue, "Oppression is determined... not because of individual talent, merit, or failure, but because of their membership in a particular group or category of people." They then later elaborate: "White, bourgeois, Christian, heterosexual males of European origin … enjoy [their] privilege at the expense of other groups in society—people of colour, the working class, non-Christians, gays, lesbians, bisexuals, and transsexuals, women, and so on."[109] Even though proponents of this anti-oppressive intersectionality approach allow in theory for people to hold status as both oppressors and oppressed, most of their analysis divides people into categories that have moral weight: those who are oppressors are morally bad compared to victims of oppression who are morally good. Keller's biblical critique makes this clear: "Most importantly, each category toward the powerless end of the spectrum has a greater moral authority and a greater ability to see the way truly things are. Only powerlessness and oppression brings moral high ground and true knowledge."[110] Dividing people into categories of moral and immoral is ultimately a religious argument, since morality cannot be based on empirical or rational arguments, but rather only on faith claims.[111] In that sense, religious arguments are really worldview arguments that not only identify moral divisions between groups of people, but also provide either explicit or implicit answers to fundamental questions about what is wrong and what the solution is.[112] Intersectionality as an approach to understanding di-

108. Timothy Keller, "A Biblical Critique of Secular Justice and Critical Theory," *Life in the Gospel* (August 2020), accessed May 28, 2021, https://quarterly.gospelinlife.com/a-biblical-critique-of-secular-justice-and-critical-theory/.

109. Mullaly and West, *Challenging Oppression,* 8, 93.

110. Keller, "A Biblical Critique of Secular Justice."

111. Smith, *Moral, Believing Animals.*

112. Brian Walsh and Richard Middleton, *The Transforming Vision: Shaping a Christian World View* (Downers Grove, IL: InterVarsity Press, 1984).

versity and identity reveals a starkly different underlying view compared to a Christian worldview. Andrew Sullivan exposes this reality in his essay "Is Intersectionality a Religion?" with this observation: "Like the Puritanism once familiar in New England, intersectionality controls language and the very terms of discourse.... The saints are the most oppressed who nonetheless resist. The sinners are categorized in various ascending categories of demographic damnation."[113]

Christians in social work, then, need to exercise discernment in sorting through the claims made by those employing an intersectionality lens. This requires, among other things, a greater understanding of the way in which modernist assumptions about the nature of humans and the self have influenced – and distorted – Christian understandings of human identity and selfhood.[114] Although it is important that we be honest about the realities of injustices and oppression, we do a disservice to clients if we suggest that they will find true well-being by rooting their identity in reductionist categories of oppression. Ultimately, such identification becomes a form of idolatry that will not bring satisfaction or solace.[115] Instead, Christians in social work must base their work with clients on a biblical worldview which makes explicit that human identity is oriented toward the ultimate purpose of honoring God, and that true flourishing comes when we put on the new self in Christ and seek others' well-being over our own. Even when we work in settings where we cannot explicitly articulate our Christian convictions, we can still design interventions that are based on a biblical understanding of human identity and diversity.[116] As I have noted in the sections in creation and sin, humans have intrinsic worth yet are prone to sin. The line between moral and immoral persons is not, ultimately, between oppressed and oppressors, but rather within each of us, and thus, we all stand in need of God's grace.

113. Andrew Sullivan, ""Is Intersectionality a Religion?" *New York Magazine* (March 10, 2017), accessed June 6, 2021, http://nymag.com/daily/intelligencer/2017/03/is-intersectionality-a-religion.html. As one might infer from the preceding, Sullivan answers this question in the affirmative.

114. Carl R. Trueman, *The Rise and Triumph of the Modern Self: Cultural Amnesia, Expressive Individualism, and the Road to Sexual Revolution.* (Wheaton, IL: Crossway, 2020).

115. See for example, Crouch, *Playing God,* chapter 3, and Keller, *Reason for God,* chapter 10.

116. Hosack, *Development on Purpose.*

Oppression, freedom, and authority

Can Social Work Imagine Authority as a Positive Force for Flourishing, Rather than as Inherently Oppressive?

If liberation from oppression and emancipation from inequality are central to social work's vision, then wouldn't the best strategy be to confront the powerful, strip away their resources, and redistribute them equally? The only viable response to unequal arrangements of power, according to the social work vision, is to eliminate all hierarchies and distribute power equally.[117] From this vantage point, power is safe only if everyone has equal access to it. Any hierarchy which involves individuals or groups holding disproportionate power, even when it is based on legitimate authority, is seen as inevitably oppressive simply because it is unequal. In response, the liberal impulse is to create a society based on equality, which has come to mean a radical redistribution of many types of resources. The only escape from oppression, it seems, is that the truly free person should have to answer to no one but her- or himself. As Koyzis observes, power and authority are viewed as being a threat to freedom: "Those working from within this perspective tend to view freedom or liberty in a positive light while viewing authority negatively."[118]

But the radical claim of Christianity is that, in Koyzis' words, "we answer to another."[119] In other words, we yield. Our approach to inequality should follow Jesus' example, "who, being in very nature God, did not consider equality with God something to be grasped" (Philippians 2: 6). When faced with the constraining reality of inequality, Jesus did not try to seize power and grasp for equality. Instead, he gave up his power, even as he exercised his rightful authority.

One paradox of a Christian worldview is that properly ordered authority is the means for human flourishing, rather than a threat to freedom. A biblical perspective reveals authority as part of God's design for his creation. Humans, created in God's image, are granted authority over the rest of creation (see Genesis 1:26-28 and Psalm 8) and are expected to use their authority to promote others' flourishing. Furthermore, although all humans have God-given authority by virtue of being God's image-bearers, distinct types of authority are distributed differently. Gov-

117. See, for example, the discussion of anti-oppressive practice in James. R. Vanderwoerd, "The Promise and Perils of Anti-Oppressive Practice for Christians in Social Work Education, *Social Work & Christianity* 43 no. 2 (2016): 153-188.

118. David T. Koyzis, *We Answer to Another: Authority, Office, and the Image of God.* (Eugene, OR: Pickwick Publications, 2014), 62.

119. Koyzis, *We Answer to Another.*

ernments, parents, teachers, social workers, and many others, are each given particular kinds of authority, each of which is limited by specific roles and contexts. Thus, authority is not an open license to dominate others, but rather must be exercised in ways that are appropriate to one's role and setting. As Koyzis argues, "Authority is a lofty office given to all human beings, who exercise it in diverse ways according to their respective callings."[120] Today's social work, rooted in a humanist, liberal worldview, perceives human freedom as being possible only when each individual answers only to her- or himself, and is not subject to any authority. A Christian worldview, by contrast, acknowledges God as the ultimate authority, Who grants humans authority and calls them to use that authority according to His purposes. Paradoxically, true freedom comes only when we recognize God's authority, but we must also recognize various forms of human authority, and be willing to yield to those in authority in appropriate contexts. Of course, that does not eliminate the possibility for exploitive abuse of authority, but such abuse is viewed as a sinful distortion of proper authority, rather than viewing the authority itself as inherently oppressive.

Differentiation and the Limits of the State

What Is the Proper Balance between the State and Other Various Entities Involved in Caring?

In the mid-2000s a marketing campaign entitled "*You'll Need a Social Worker….*" made the rounds. [121] Its purpose was to raise the public profile of social work. The campaign produced a poster that listed dozens of examples of when a person might need a social worker. A quick review of this list revealed that social work was apparently necessary for virtually every event or difficulty at every stage of life, including the following: "When you can't find anyone to play with," "When you can't decide on a career," "When your partner is unfaithful," "When you lose your home in a fire," "When you can't drive any more." Although the point – that social work is a broad field that provides professional help for many kinds of problems – is a valid one, it raises the question of what limits might apply to social work's reach.

As we have seen, social work is a profession that is closely tied to – and dependent upon – the expansion of the welfare state. Thus, extend-

120. Koyzis, *We Answer to Another,* 226.

121. Darlene Lynch and Robert Vernon, "You'll Need A Social Worker…" (2001), accessed June 5, 2021, https://www.wku.edu/socialwork/bsw/bsw_youll_need_a_swer_when.pdf.

ing the reach of social work to all areas of life also brings with it the long arm of the state. Differentiation has resulted in the professionalization of a great many occupations and tasks. However, that does not give license for social work or other related professions, sanctioned by the state, to encroach upon the authority and responsibility of other persons and groups. Thus, a biblically grounded approach to social work needs to explore more carefully the unintended consequences of an ever-expanding state-driven social welfare system over various areas of life.

Conclusion

Earlier we asked a question posed by the authors of a popular introductory social work textbook: "What *on earth* would motivate anyone to stay within such a beleaguered environment?"[122] A Christian in social work would rephrase that question this way, "What *in heaven's name* would motivate me to do this work?" and her answer would be found in the biblical story: God created a world of infinite beauty, crowning it with humans who were gifted with the responsibility to care for and develop God's creation, but He grieved when humans took the gift of freedom, chose against Him, and brought ruin upon themselves and all of creation. But, by God's grace, God did not abandon us or the rest of creation, and instead steadfastly set about to restore the brokenness by entering the world to take on our pain and bear our suffering through His Son, Jesus Christ. Through this loving act of sacrifice, Jesus not only paid the debt for our sins, but also unleashed the full power of the Triune God—Father, Son, and Holy Spirit—in a sweeping reclamation project to restore every aspect of creation.

For social workers working on the frontlines of sin, that project gives us hope because even in the midst of human suffering, we can see evidence of God's redemptive work not just in the stories from the past which are found in the Bible, but all around us, anywhere we see people caring for the poor, the sick, and the oppressed. That hope would be futile if that was all we had, but God has given us a tantalizing glimpse of how the story ends. We need to keep our eyes focused on the end of the story when we bump up against the frustrating reality that our work often seems to make little difference. It is only in the hope of the ending of the story that we can take solace in our tiny accomplishments. Steve Garber's phrase "proximate justice" articulates this hope because

122. Kennedy-Kish (Bell), Sinclair, Carniol and Baines, *Case Critical*, 150 emphasis added.

> It allows us to make peace with some justice, some mercy, all the while realizing that it will only be in the new heaven and new earth that we find all our longings finally fulfilled, that we will see all of God's demands finally met. It is only then – there we will see all of the conditions for human flourishing finally in place, socially, economically, and politically.[123]

We can't do everything, but we can do something. We may not be able to wipe away *every* tear, but we *can* wipe away the tears of the person across from us. Though we do not know the exact details of how or when God will accomplish this, He has given us a hope that is enormously comforting to any social worker: "God himself will be with them and be their God. He will wipe every tear from their eyes. There will be no more death or mourning or crying or pain" (Revelation 21:3-4).

Questions for Reflection and Discussion

1. What kinds of problems should social work be responsible for? What should social work *not* be responsible for? Why? If social work cannot address every human problem, who or what else should be responsible?

2. How do God's laws for social life influence our understanding of the nature of social institutions like the family or marriage?

3. Why is it important for social workers to affirm that every person has inherent worth and dignity? How do Christians and non-Christians differ on the source of human dignity and worth? What difference does that make?

4. Why is it difficult for social workers to accept the Christian belief that humans are sinful? Is that belief incompatible with recognizing inherent human worth and dignity? Why or why not?

5. When you encounter tragic or difficult situations of human suffering, what is your source of hope? When you feel like your efforts are too small to make much of a difference, what motivates you to continue?

---

123. Steven Garber, "Finding Our Way to Great Work, Even in Politics: Making Peace with Proximate Justice," *Comment* (December 1, 2007), https://www.cardus.com/article/finding-our-way-to-great-work-even-in-politics-making-peace-with-proximate-justice/ ; see also Steven Garber, *Visions of Vocation: Common Grace for the Common Good,* (Downers Grove, IL: InterVarsity Press), chapter 8.

6. How does a Christian understanding of human identity differ from one based on intersectionality? Which approach is more useful for addressing conflicts between diverse groups of people? Why?

7. Why are some social workers uncomfortable with the idea of authority? Is authority inherently oppressive? Why or why not?

Helpful Resources on Faith and Social Work

As a relatively recent field, there are fewer resources that apply a specifically Reformed and Kuyperian approach to social work compared to other academic disciplines. In addition, since social work is an interdisciplinary professional practice, it draws from multiple academic areas. That means that readers must mine insights and resources from a range of academic disciplines that can be applied to specific areas of social work practice. Some of these include the following:

Bolt, John. *Economic Shalom: A Reformed Primer on Faith, Work, and Human Flourishing.* Grand Rapids, MI: Christian's Library Press, 2013.

> For a social work profession that typically leans to state-sponsored and more left-wing approaches, Bolt's contribution provides a balanced antidote. He distills insights from key Reformed thinkers including Bavinck, Kuyper, and Wolterstorff to engage critically with economic theories and their contribution to flourishing.

Fikkert, Brian and Kelly M. Kapic. *Becoming Whole: Why the Opposite of Poverty Isn't the American Dream.* Chicago, IL: Moody, 2019.

> Building on his earlier book, *When Helping Hurts*, Fikkert and his co-author work from a Reformed perspective to address the underlying narratives that address poverty alleviation efforts and the pursuit of human flourishing.

Koyzis, David T. *Political Visions & Illusions: A Survey and Christian Critique of Contemporary Ideologies.* 2nd ed. Downers Grove, IL: InterVarsity Press, 2019.

> Since social work is embedded within the institution of the social welfare state, this volume is essential reading to help Christians in social work to develop critical discernment about the political ideologies that influence how social problems are understood and addressed.

MacLarkey, Robert. "Reformational Social Philosophy and Sociological Theory." *Perspectives on Science and Christian Faith* 43 (1991): 96-102.

In this article MacLarkey draws on the philosophy of Herman Dooyeweerd to formulate a Reformational approach to sociology and social structures.

Monsma, Steven V., and Stanley Carlson-Thies. *Free to Serve: Protecting the Religious Freedom of Faith-based Organizations.* Grand Rapids, Brazos Press, 2015.

Monsma and Carlson-Thies present a robust and nuanced defense for faith-based organizations drawing on concepts of pluralism rooted in Reformed thinking. Their analysis provides a solid foundation for understanding the role of religiously-based nonprofit social service organizations.

Mouw, Richard. *Uncommon Decency: Christian Civility in an Uncivil World.* 2nd ed. Grand Rapids, MI: Eerdmans, 2010.

Diversity and inclusion are key themes in social work. Mouw's book discusses what he calls "convicted civility" as a helpful way for Christians to think about how to engage with others across our differences.

Nevertheless, there is a growing literature on the intersection of Christianity and social work practice, most of which has been produced by the North American Association of Christians in Social Work (www.nacsw.org). NACSW publishes a quarterly international peer-reviewed journal, *Social Work & Christianity* (https://www.nacsw.org/publications/journal-swc/), as well as many books, as part of its mission to "to equip its members to integrate Christian faith and professional social work practice." Some notable books include:

Garland, Diana. *Why I Am A Social Worker: 25 Christians Tell Their Life Stories.* Botsford, CT: North American Association of Christians in Social Work, 2015.

Keith-Lucas, Alan, Leslie Gregory, and Sandy Bauer. *So You Want to Be a Social Worker: Reflections for the Christian Student.* 2nd ed. Botsford, CT: North American Association of Christians in Social Work, 2021.

Scales, Laine and Trammel, Regina, eds. *Christianity & Social Work: Readings on the Integration of Christianity and Social Work Practice, 7th Ed.* Palos Heights, IL: North American Association of Christians in Social Work, 2025.

Sherwood, David. *The Challenge of Doing the Right Thing: Real Values, Limited Understanding, and Character-Driven Judgments.* Botsford, CT: North American Association of Christians in Social Work, 2018.

NACSW is an ecumenical organization representing a wide range of Christian traditions, including those from Reformed backgrounds. Some notable resources that are more explicitly rooted in the Reformed tradition include the following:

Hosack, Lisa. *Development on Purpose: Faith and Human Behavior in the Social Environment.* Botsford, CT: North American Association of Christians in Social Work, 2019.

Kuilema, Joseph, "Faith as a Virtue in Social Work Practice: A Reformed Perspective." *Social Work & Christianity* 41, no. 2-3 (2014): 155-174.

Vanderwoerd, James R. "All Things New: Neo-Calvinist Groundings for Social Work." *Social Work & Christianity* 42, no. 2 (2015): 121-148.

Wolterstorff, Nicholas. "Justice, Not Charity: Social Work through the Eyes of Faith." *Social Work & Christianity* 33, no. 2 (2006): 123-140.

In addition to these resources that are primarily addressed to Christians in social work to help them apply a Christian foundation to social work, other authors have published articles and books meant for a broader social work audience and addressing the intersection of Christianity and social work.

Adams, Paul. "Coercing Conscience: Professional Duty or Moral Integrity. *Journal of Social Work Values & Ethics* 8, no. 1 (2011): 50-57.

Bowpitt, Graham. "Evangelical Christianity, secular humanism, and the genesis of British social work." *British Journal of Social Work* 28, no. 5 (1998): 675-693.

Bowpitt, Graham. "Working with Creative Creatures: Towards a Christian Paradigm for Social Work Theory, with Some Practical Implications." *British Journal of Social Work* 30, no. 3 (2000): 349-364.

Braganza, Morgan E. "Introducing a conceptual framework for assessing existing models, frameworks, and approaches for navigating encounters across difficult differences." *Social Work & Christianity* 49 no. 1 (2022): 10-25.

Canda, Edward R., Holly K. Oxhandler, Altaf Husain, Edward C. Polson, Terry A. Wolfer, Michael J. Sheridan, Jeanna Jacobsen, and Kimberly Hardy. "Insights From a CSWE Summit for Critical Conversations on Religion, Faith, and Spirituality in Social Work Education." *Journal of Social Work Education* 59 (3): 635–53. 2023.

Cnaan, Ram. *The Newer Deal: Social Work and Religion in Partnership*. New York, NY: Columbia University Press, 1999.

Coates, John, John R. Graham, Barbara Swartzentruber, and Brian Oulette, eds.

Spirituality and Social Work: Selected Canadian Readings. Toronto, ON: Canadian Scholar's Press, 2007.

Desselman, Adrienne, and Rebecca M. Bolen, eds. *Conservative Christian Beliefs and Sexual Orientation in Social Work: Privilege, Oppression, and the Pursuit of Human Rights*. Washington, DC: Council on Social Work Education, 2014.

Drake, Brett and Hodge, David R. "Social work at the crossroads: The empirical highway or the postmodern/critical offramp? *Research on Social Work Practice* 32, no. 4 (2023): 363-373.

Hodge, David R. "Advocating for the forgotten human right: Article 1.8 of the Universal Declaration of Human Rights – Religious freedom." *International Journal of Social Work* 49, no. 4 (2006): 431-443.

Hodge, David R. "An overlooked human rights crisis: The accelerating persecution of Christians across the globe." *International Journal of Social Work* [published online] (2023). https://doi.org/10.1177/00208728231186521

Hodge, David R. "Does Social Work Oppress Evangelical Christians? A "New Class" Analysis of Society and Social Work." *Social Work* 47, no. 4 (2002): 401-414.

Hodge, David R. "Secular Privilege: Deconstructing the Invisible Rose-Tinted Sunglasses." *Journal of Religion & Spirituality in Social Work* 28, no. 1-2 (2009): 8-34.

Hodge, David R. *Spiritual Assessment in Social Work and Mental Health Practice*. New York: Columbia University Press, 2015.

Marty, Martin. "Social Service: Godly and Godless." *Social Service Review* 54, no. 4 (1980): 463-481.

Novak, Michael, and Paul Adams. *Social Justice Isn't What You Think It Is*. New York: Encounter Books, 2015.

Oxhandler, Holly K; Canda, Edward R; Polson, Edward C; Husain, Altaf; Parrish, Danielle E. "Promoting religious and spiritual competencies in clinical social work: Considerations, potential barriers, and supports." *Spirituality in Clinical Practice* 11, no 4, (Dec 2024): 372-381.

Oxhandler, Holly K., Chamiec-Case, Rick, Wolfer, Terry, and Marraccino, Julianna. "Integrating social workers' Christian faith in social work: A national survey." *Social Work and Christianity*, 48, no.1 (2021) 52-74.

Sherr, Michael, Jon Singletary, and Roger Robins. "Innovative Service or Proselytizing: Exploring When Services Delivery Becomes a Platform for Unwanted Religious Persuasion." *Social Work* 54, no. 2 (2009): 157-167.

Wolfer, Terry. A. "Religion and Spirituality in Health Social Work." In *Handbook of Health Social Work,* 2nd ed., edited by S. Gehlert & T. A. Browne, 263-290. Hoboken, NJ: John Wiley & Sons, 2012.

Finally, there are a number of other organizations, besides NACSW, that explore the relationship between religion and social work or social welfare, including:

Canadian Society for Spirituality & Social Work (https://www.spiritualityandsocialwork.ca/).

Religion and Spirituality Clearinghouse, Council on Social Work Education (https://www.cswe.org/education-resources/religion-and-spirituality-clearinghouse/religion-and-spirituality-educational-resources/).

Society for Spirituality and Social Work (https://spiritualityandsocialwork.org/).

Bibliography

Al-Krenawi, Alean, John R. Graham, and Nazim Habibov. *Diversity and Social Work in Canada.* New York: Oxford, 2016.

Bartholomew, Craig G. *Contours of the Kuyperian Tradition: A Systematic Introduction.* Downers Grove, IL: InterVarsity Press, 2017.

Bartholomew, Craig G., and Michael Goheen. *The Drama of Scripture: Finding Our Place in the Biblical Story.* 2nd ed. Grand Rapids, MI: Baker, 2014.

Bartholomew, Craig G., and Michael Goheen. *Christian Philosophy: A Systematic and Narrative Introduction.* Grand Rapids, MI: Baker, 2013.

Belgic Confession. Accessed May 27, 2021. https://www.crcna.org/welcome/beliefs/confessions/belgic-confession.

Brandsen, Cheryl, and Paul Vliem. "Justice and Human Rights in Fourth Century Cappadocia." *Social Work & Christianity* 34, no. 4 (Winter 2007): 421-448.

Canadian Association for Social Work Education. *Educational Policies and Accreditation Standards for Canadian Social Work Education.* Ottawa, ON: Canadian Association for Social Work Education, 2021.

Canadian Association of Social Workers. *Code of Ethics.* Ottawa, ON: Canadian Association of Social Workers, 2005.

Chaplin, Jonathan. *Herman Dooyeweerd: Christian Philosopher of State and Civil Society.* Notre Dame, IN: University of Notre Dame Press, 2011.

Chatterjee, Pranab. *Repackaging the Welfare State.* Washington, DC: NASW Press, 1999.

Christie, Nancy, and Michael Gauvreau. *A Full-Orbed Christianity: The Protestant Churches and Social Welfare in Canada: 1900-1940.* Montreal, PQ and Kingston, ON: McGill-Queen's University Press, 1996.

Coggins, Kip. *The Practice of Social Work in North America: Culture, Context, and Competency Development.* Chicago, IL: Lyceum, 2016.

Corbett, Steve, and Brian Fikkert. *When Helping Hurts: How to Alleviate Poverty Without Hurting the Poor... and Yourself.* Chicago, IL: Moody, 2012.

Council on Social Work Education, (CSWE) Commission on Educational Policy and the CSWE Commission on Accreditation. *Educational Policy and Accreditation Standards for Baccalaureate and Master's Social Work Programs.* Washington, DC: Council on Social Work Education,, 2015.

Crouch, Andy. *Playing God: Redeeming the Gift of Power.* Downers Grove, IL: IVP Books, 2013.

Day, Phyllis, and Jerome Schiele. *A New History of Social Welfare*, 7th ed. New York: Pearson, 2013.

DeYoung, Rebecca Konyndyk. *Glittering Vices: A New Look at the Seven Deadly Sins and Their Remedies.* Grand Rapids, MI: Brazos Press, 2009.

Dumbrill, Gary C., and June Ying Yee. *Anti-Oppressive Social Work: Ways of Knowing, Talking, and Doing.* New York: Oxford, 2019.

Flatt, Kevin N. "The Secularization of Western Universities in International Perspective: Toward a Historicist Account." *The Review of Faith & International Affairs* 18, no. 2 (Summer 2020): 30-43.

Garber, Steven. "Finding Our Way to Great Work, Even in Politics: Making Peace with Proximate Justice." *Comment* (December 1, 2007). https://www.cardus.com/article/finding-our-way-to-great-work-even-in-politics-making-peace-with-proximate-justice/.

Garber, Steven. *Visions of Vocation: Common Grace for the Common Good.* Downers Grove, IL: InterVarsity Press, 2014.

Gornik, Mark. *To Live in Peace: Biblical Faith and The Changing Inner City.* Grand Rapids, MI: Eerdmans, 2002.

Guest, Dennis. *The Emergence of Social Security in Canada.* 3rd ed. Vancouver, BC: UBC Press, 2003.

Haugen, Gary, and Victor Boutros. *The Locust Effect: Why the End of Poverty Requires the End of Violence.* New York: Oxford University Press, 2013.

Haynes, Karen, and James Mickelson. *Affecting Change: Social Workers in the Political Arena.* 7th ed. New York: Pearson, 2010.

Henrich, Joseph, Robert Boyd, and Peter J. Richerson, "The Puzzle of Monogamous Marriage." *Philosophical Transactions of the Royal Society B* 367, no. 1589 (2012): 657-669.

Hick, Steve, and Jackie Stokes. *Social Work in Canada: An Introduction.* 4th ed. Toronto, ON: Thomson, 2017.

Hodge, David R. "Differences in Worldviews between Social Workers and People of Faith," *Families in Society* 84, no. 2 (2003): 285-295.

Hodge, David R. "Value Differences between Social Workers and Members of the Working and Middle Classes." *Social Work* 48, no. 1 (2003): 107-119.

Hodge, David R. "Who We Are, Where We Come From, and Some of Our Perceptions: Comparison of Social Workers and the General Population" *Social Work* 49, no. 2 (April 2004): 261-268.

Hodge, David R., and Terry Wolfer, "Promoting Tolerance: The Imago Dei as an Imperative for Christian Social Workers," *Journal of Religion & Spirituality in Social Work: Social Thought* 27 no. 3 (2008), 297-313.

Hosack, Lisa. *Development on Purpose: Faith and Human Behavior in the Social Environment.* Botsford, CT: North American Association of Christians in Social Work, 2019.

International Federation of Social Workers. "Global Definition of Social Work." Accessed May 18, 2021. https://www.ifsw.org/what-is-social-work/global-definition-of-social-work/.

Jacobs, Alan. *Original Sin: A Cultural History*. New York, : Harper Collins, 2008.

Jennissen, Therese, and Colleen Lundy. *One Hundred Years of Social Work: A History of the Profession in English Canada, 1900-2000.* Waterloo: Wilfrid Laurier University Press, 2011.

Jochemsen, Henk, and Johan Hegeman, "Equipping Christian students to Connect Kingdom Citizenship to Issues in Today's Societies." In *Christian Higher Education in the Global Context: Implications for Curriculum, Pedagogy, and Administration*, edited by Nick Lantinga, 223-240. Sioux Center, Iowa: Dordt College Press, 2008.

Keller, Timothy. "A Biblical Critique of Secular Justice and Critical Theory," *Life in the Gospel* (August 2020). Accessed May 28, 2021. https://quarterly.gospelinlife.com/a-biblical-critique-of-secular-justice-and-critical-theory/.

Keller, Timothy. *Generous Justice: How God's Grace Makes Us Just.* New York: Penguin, 2010.

Keller, Timothy. "Justice in the Bible." *Life in the Gospel* (September 2020). Accessed May 28, 2021. https://quarterly.gospelinlife.com/justice-in-the-bible/.

Keller, Timothy. *The Reason for God: Belief in an Age of Skepticism*. New York: Dutton, 2008.

Keller, Timothy, and Kathy Keller. *The Meaning of Marriage: Facing the Complexities of Commitment with the Wisdom of God*. New York: Penguin, 2013.

Kennedy-Kish (Bell), Banakonda, Raven Sinclair, Ben Carniol, and Donna Baines. *Case Critical: Social Services and Social Justice in Canada*, 7th ed. Toronto, ON: Between the Lines Press, 2017.

Koyzis, David T. *We Answer to Another: Authority, Office, and the Image of God*. Eugene, OR: Pickwick Publications, 2014.

Kuyper, Abraham. *The Problem of Poverty: A translation of the opening address at the first Christian Social Congress in the Netherlands, November 9, 1891*. Ed. James W. Skillen. Sioux Center, IA: Dordt College Press, 2011.

Lynch, Darlene, and Robert Vernon, (2001). "You'll Need a Social Worker..." Accessed June 5, 2021. https://www.wku.edu/socialwork/bsw/bsw_youll_need_a_swer_when.pdf.

McKnight, John. *The Careless Society: Community and Its Counterfeits*. New York: Basic Books, 1995.

McMahon, C. Matthew. "The Attributes of God on a Puritan's Mind." Accessed May 27, 2021. https://www.apuritansmind.com/the-attributes-of-god-by-c-matthew-mcmahon/.

McMahon, C. Matthew. "The Attributes of God and Calvin's Institutes of the Christian Religion." Accessed May 27, 2021. https://www.apuritansmind.com/the-attributes-of-god-by-c-matthew-mcmahon/the-attributes-of-god-and-calvins-institutes-of-the-christian-religion-by-c-matthew-mcmahon/.

Middleton, Richard. *The Liberating Image: The Imago Dei in Genesis 1*. Grand Rapids: Brazos Press, 2005.

Middleton, Richard. *A New Heaven and a New Earth: Reclaiming Biblical Eschatology*. Grand Rapids, MI: Baker, 2014.

Middleton, Richard, and Brian Walsh. *Truth Is Stranger than It Used To Be: Biblical Faith in a Postmodern Age*. Downers Grove, IL: InterVarsity Press, 1995.

Mullaly, Bob, and Juliana West. *Challenging Oppression and Confronting Privilege*. 3rd ed. New York: Oxford University Press, 2018.

Mullaly, Bob, and Marilyn Dupré, *The New Structural Social Work: Ideology, Theory, and Practice*. 4th ed. New York: Oxford University Press, 2019.

National Association of Social Workers. "About Social Workers." Accessed May 18, 2021. http://www.helpstartshere.org/?page_id=1999.

National Association of Social Workers. *Code of Ethics.* Washington, DC: National Association of Social Workers, 2017.

Novak, Michael, and Paul Adams *Social Justice Isn't What You Think It Is.* New York: Encounter Books, 2015.

Olasky, Marvin. *The Tragedy of American Compassion.* Washington, DC: Regnery Publishing, 1992.

Peterson, Eugene. *Christ Plays in Ten Thousand Places: A Conversation in Spiritual Theology.* Grand Rapids, MI: Eerdmans, 2005.

Piper, John. "Through the Washing of Regeneration." *Desiring God* (February 3, 2008). Accessed June 5, 2021. https://www.desiringgod.org/messages/through-the-washing-of-regeneration.

Plantinga, Neil. *Not the Way It's Supposed to Be: A Breviary of Sin.* Grand Rapids, MI: Eermans, 1995.

Popple, Philip, and Leslie Leighninger. *The Policy-Based Profession: An Introduction to Social Welfare Policy Analysis for Social Workers.* 7th ed. New York: Pearson, 2019.

"Question 7. What is God?" In *The Westminster Larger Catechism.* Accessed May 27, 2021. https://opc.org/lc.html

Reamer, Frederic G. *The Philosophical Foundations of Social Work.* New York: Columbia University Press, 1993.

Reamer, Frederic G. *Social Work Values and Ethics.* 2nd ed. New York: Columbia University Press, 1999.

Ribar, David C. "Why Marriage Matters for Child Wellbeing." *The Future of Children* 25, no. 2 (Fall 2015): 11-28.

Sherwood, David. "The Relationship Between Beliefs and Values in Social Work Practice: Worldviews Make a Difference." In *Christianity and Social Work: Readings on the Integration of Christianity and Social Work Practice*, 6th ed, edited by L. Scales and M. Kelly, 83-102. Botsford, CT: North American Association of Christians in Social Work, 2020.

Shipler, David K. *The Working Poor: Invisible in America.* New York: Knopf, 2004.

Siporin, Max. "Strengthening the Moral Mission of Social Work." In *The Moral Purposes of Social Work: The Character and Intentions of a Profession*, edited **by** P. Nelson Reid and Philip R. Popple, 93-94. Chicago, IL: Nelson-Hall, 1992.

Smith, Christian. *Moral Believing Animals.* New York: Oxford University Press, 2003.

Smith, Christian. *The Sacred Project of American Sociology*. New York: Oxford University Press, 2014.

Smith, Christian. *The Secular Revolution: Power, Interests and Conflict in the Secularization of American Public Life*. Los Angeles, CA: University of California Press, 2003.

Smith, James K.A. *How Not to Be Secular: Reading Charles Taylor*. Grand Rapids, MI: Eerdmans, 2014.

Specht, Harry. "Social Work and the Popular Psychotherapies." *Social Service Review* 64, no. 3 (1990): 354.

Specht, Harry, and Mark Courtney. *Unfaithful Angels: How Social Work Abandoned Its Mission*. New York: Free Press, 1994.

Sullivan, Andrew. "Is Intersectionality a Religion?" *New York Magazine* (March 10, 2017). Accessed June 6, 2021. http://nymag.com/daily/intelligencer/2017/03/is-intersectionality-a-religion.html.

Switchfoot. "The War Inside." April 9, 2015). YouTube video, 3:38. https://www.youtube.com/watch?v=vaacJQEN3y4&ab_channel=Switchfoot.

Taylor, Charles. *A Secular Age*. Boston, MA: Belknap, 2007.

Trueman, Carl R. *The Rise and Triumph of the Modern Self: Cultural Amnesia, Expressive Individualism, and the Road to Sexual Revolution*. Wheaton, IL: Crossway, 2020.

Vanderwoerd, James R. "I Am Making All Things New: Biblical Themes for Macro Practice." In *Christianity and Social Work: Readings on the Integration of Christianity and Social Work*, 3rd ed., edited by Beryl Hugen and Laine Scales, 121-137. Botsford, CT: North American Association of Christians in Social Work, 2008.

Vanderwoerd, James R. "The Promise and Perils of Anti-Oppressive Practice for Christians in Social Work Education." *Social Work & Christianity* 43, no. 2 (2016): 153-188.

Vanderwoerd, James R. "Reconsidering Secularization and Recovering Christianity in Social Work History." *Social Work & Christianity* 38, no. 3 (2011): 244-266.

Vanderwoerd, James R., and Esther R. van der Woerd, "Is There More To This Story? Christianity in Social Work History and Implications for Social Justice." In *Christianity and Social Work: Readings on the Integration of Christianity and Social Work Practice*, 6th ed, edited by L. Scales and M. Kelly, 63-80. Botsford, CT: North American Association of Christians in Social Work, 2020.

Walsh, Brian, and Richard Middleton. *The Transforming Vision: Shaping a Christian World View*. Downers Grove, IL: InterVarsity Press, 1984.

Wilcox, W. Bradford and Wendy B. Wang, "The Marriage Divide: How and Why Working Class Families are More Fragile Today," (Washington, DC: American Enterprise Institute, 2017). Accessed March 14, 2019. http://www.aei.org/publication/the-marriage-divide-how-and-why-working-class-families-are-more-fragile-today.

Wolfer, Terry A., David R. Hodge and Janessa Steele. "Self-Determination in Social Work: A Christian Perspective as a Philosophical Foundation for Client Choice." *Social Work & Christianity* 45, no. 2 (2018): 3-32.

Wolfer, Terry A. and James R. Vanderwoerd, "The Sacred Project of American Sociology: Comparison with Social Work and Implications." Paper presented at the North American Association of Christians in Social Work Annual Convention, Cincinnati, OH, November 19, 2016.

Wolters, Albert M. *Creation Regained: Biblical Basics for a Reformational Worldview*. 2nd ed. Grand Rapids, MI: Eerdmans, 2005.

Wolterstorff, Nicholas. "Justice, Not Charity: Social Work through the Eyes of Faith." *Social Work & Christianity* 33, no. 2 (2006), 123-140.

Wolterstorff, Nicholas. *Reason within the Bounds of Religion*. Grand Rapids, MI: Eerdmans, 1976.

Wolterstorff, Nicholas. *Until Justice and Peace Embrace*. Grand Rapids, MI: Eerdmans, 1983.

Wright, N.T. *Surprised by Hope: Rethinking Heaven, the Resurrection, and the Mission of the Church*. New York: HarperCollins, 2008.

Yan, Miu Chung, "Multiple Positionality and Intersectionality: Toward a Dialogical Social Work Approach" in *Diversity and Social Work in Canada*, edited by Alean Al-Krenawi, John R. Graham, and Nazim Habibov, 114-138. New York: Oxford, 2016.

Our Stories Are Part of God's Story: A Reformed Perspective on the Discipline of History

Kevin Flatt[1]

Prelude: The State of the Discipline

Attempts to make sense of the past are as old as humankind, but the modern discipline of history has its origins in the aftermath of the Enlightenment in the work of historians such as Edward Gibbon and Leopold von Ranke. Despite subsequent historians' shared commitment to the importance of primary sources, careful documentation, and replicable methodology, we have been deeply divided about the way historical scholarship should be carried out.[2]

One division is over the limits of our ability to truly know and rightly interpret the past. Since the birth of the modern discipline, many historians sought to provide historical accounts that would be not only reliable, but scientific and objective: to portray history "as it really was," ("*wie es eigentlich gewesen ist*," in Leopold von Ranke's famous phrase). The job of the historian, according to this way of thinking, was to gather the facts of history and interpret them objectively, such that any fair-minded person would reach similar conclusions from the evidence.

While this "empiricist" view was never universally held, it came under particular attack in the closing decades of the twentieth century. The critics argued that all historical analysis was shaped by the historian's assumptions about which subjects are worthy of study, which evidence is important, and what sorts of interpretations are valid. These assumptions in turn arise, they argued, from the historian's own social and cultural

1. I am grateful to Jacob Ellens, Mark McCarthy, and Harry Van Dyke for their comments on earlier versions of this chapter, and to my colleagues and students at Redeemer University for many good conversations about its subject matter over the years.

2. This chapter assumes the standpoint of the historical profession in the English-speaking world, but many of its observations apply more generally to historians elsewhere with Western-style education.

situation; thus, "objectivity" was an impossible dream.[3] Postmodernist historians, in particular, emphasized the social and contingent aspects of knowledge, the hidden power struggles behind competing claims to historical truth, and the inescapability of language and its limitations.[4] Other historians were unwilling to give up on empiricism, however, and retorted with their own criticisms of the postmodernist approach, which they saw as erasing the line between fact and fiction and endangering the very existence of the discipline.[5] This debate continues today.

Historians also disagree about which aspects of the human experience are most worthy of the historian's attention. One of the oldest approaches to history focuses on politics, especially the lives and deeds of great political leaders and the interactions between states. In an era when advanced education was reserved for elites, such history was seen as especially useful for training the future leaders of society.[6] In modern times, especially in the nineteenth century, political historians were often drawn to the "Whig interpretation" of history, which saw history as a story of steady progress towards greater liberty and enlightenment.[7] The Whig approach fell out of favor in the twentieth century, but there were other ways of doing political history, which continued to be the dominant preoccupation of historians through much of the twentieth century. Although it was elbowed off centre stage in the closing decades of the century, political history continues to be a popular approach, and some historians advocate its return to a central place in the profession.[8]

Over the course of the twentieth century, however, the rise of the social sciences and the growing influence of Marxism led many historians to shift their emphasis away from individual political leaders to large scale social and economic forces that they thought held the key to explaining historical events. For the first time, the advent of accessible computing

---

3. Peter Novick, *That Noble Dream: The "Objectivity Question" and the American Historical Profession* (Cambridge: Cambridge University Press, 1988); for an early example of some of these criticisms, see E.H. Carr, *What is History?* (London, UK: Penguin, 1961).

4. See, for example, Callum Brown, *Postmodernism for Historians* (New York: Routledge, 2004).

5. Examples include Arthur Marwick, *The New Nature of History: Knowledge, Evidence, Language* (Chicago: Lyceum, 2001); Keith Windshuttle, *The Killing of History* (San Francisco: Encounter, 2000), and Gertrude Himmelfarb, *The New History and the Old: Critical Essays and Reappraisals*, rev. ed. (Cambridge, MA: Harvard University Press, 2004).

6. This is a running theme in Machiavelli's *Prince*; see, for example, [XIV chap. 14].

7. Herbert Butterfield, *The Whig Interpretation of History* (London: G. Bell, 1931).

8. For a Canadian example, see J.L. Granatstein, *Who Killed Canadian History?* rev. ed. (San Francisco: Harper Perennial, 2007).

allowed historians to bring large amounts of quantitative data to bear on such questions. Some of these historians focused on what they called "history from below," that is, the history of the experience of the mass of ordinary people rather than social elites. In the words of British historian E.P. Thompson, whose *The Making of the English Working Class* (1963) stands as a milestone in the development of this approach, the historian's work could "rescue" the lives of such people "from the enormous condescension of posterity."[9] Such historians often interpreted history using the broad analytical categories of race, class, and gender, typically in order to expose relationships of oppression or exploitation between groups. This "social history" approach swept the historical profession in the English-speaking world in the 1960s and 1970s, coinciding with a large-scale cultural shift toward skepticism of authority, especially political authority, and toward interest in popular movements for liberation of various kinds. Historians, like many of their colleagues in the humanities and social sciences, have tended to be a left-leaning bunch politically—a bias that has intensified in recent decades—and the social history approach has an obvious affinity with that political orientation.[10] Partly for that reason, it continues to be popular with historians today.

The 1980s witnessed the emergence of yet another approach as the influence of newer intellectual offshoots of Marxism in academia—the Frankfurt School, post-structuralism, second-wave feminism, and post-colonialism—brought about a cultural or linguistic "turn" in historical writing. Like the earlier turn to social history, the cultural turn had primarily Marxist or Marxist-derived ideological roots and consequently reflected a Marxist fixation on oppression as a central category of analysis, an emphasis which resonated with a historical profession that had become almost monolithically left-leaning in its political sympathies. Cultural history shifted the focus, however, onto the relationships between language, power, and identity: for example, how do certain patterns of thinking and speaking perpetuate certain ways of seeing the world, and exclude others? While social historians had often modelled their work after the social sciences, with their confidence in aggregate statistics, patterns, and laws, cultural historians had more affinity with the human-

9. E.P. Thompson, *The Making of the English Working Class* (New York: Pantheon Books, 1963).

10. In 2016, for example, one study of forty leading American universities reported the ratio of registered Democrats to Republicans among history faculty to be more than 33:1—the most heavily left-leaning of the five disciplines included in the study. Sixty percent of history departments had no registered Republicans among their faculty. Michael Langbert, Anthony J. Quain, and Daniel B. Klein, "Faculty Voter Registration in Economics, History, Journalism, Law, and Psychology," *Econ Journal Watch* 13 no. 3 (September 2016): 422-51.

ities and their emphasis on particularity and contingency. Indeed, many cultural historians wrote to subvert and destabilize the categories and concepts taken for granted by social historians by representing those categories as malleable social constructs. Just as social historians imported new modes of analysis from the social sciences, cultural historians have their own preferred analytical styles derived from the literary disciplines, such as the discourse analysis and genealogical method popularized by the French historian Michel Foucault.[11]

Cultural history failed to entirely displace social history, however, just as social history failed to entirely displace political history before it. Rather, each new approach added to the array of methods, ideological perspectives, and topics available to historians. Further complicating the picture, the divisions between topical approaches (political, social, cultural) and philosophies of knowledge (empiricist, postmodernist) overlap, with most (but not all) cultural historians preferring postmodernist views of historical knowledge to the empiricist views assumed by most (but not all) political and social historians.

Many of these developments took place in the context of a rapid expansion in the ranks of professional historians in the second half of the twentieth century along with the advent of mass university education. The result has been a proliferation of subfields and schools of thought within the discipline. Some historians celebrate this proliferation, while others lament what they see as the fragmentation of the discipline and the loss of unifying narratives for the past. Most historians, perhaps, give these debates little direct attention, simply take it for granted that their own approach and subject are worthwhile, and quietly promote their preferred way of doing history through their choices of academic journals and their influence over graduate program reading lists.

What should Christian historians make of this situation? First, we will note that there is now more awareness of the existence of a variety of approaches and points of view in the discipline than there was fifty years ago (more on this later). Second, we should observe that many of the debates that divide the discipline, from questions about objectivity and knowability to questions about focus and methodology, are really foundational questions that cannot be answered from within the discipline itself. No amount of historical study can answer questions such as, "What aspects of history are worth studying?" or "How should we go about studying the past?" Such questions are really prior philosophical questions that can only be answered in terms of underlying presuppositions, which are themselves anchored in one worldview or another. Thus,

11. See, e.g. his *The Archaeology of Knowledge*, trans. A.M. Sheridan Smith (New York: Pantheon Books, 1972).

as Christian historians, we are faced with the challenge of grappling with these questions from a uniquely Christian perspective rooted in a biblical worldview.

A Uniquely Christian Perspective?

But is there such a thing as a uniquely Christian perspective on history? Isn't one's religion irrelevant to studying sources and interpreting the past? Dedicated empiricist historians tend to think so,[12] but as the reader will have noticed, this chapter and this book as a whole take as their starting point the conviction that the work of every discipline is inescapably *religious*, that is, that all academic work depends on and is suffused by presuppositions that have their origin not in the discipline itself, but in the prior convictions of the researcher or writer or teacher about what the world is like at its most fundamental level. The truth of this observation can be seen in the recent history of the historical discipline as summarized above: questions like "What can we know about the past?" and "What historical subjects are important?" can only be answered by stories we tell ourselves, stories that we hold to be the true story of the world. For a long time, the credibility of "objective" scholarship in the Western academy (in history and in other disciplines) depended on keeping these stories out of the limelight to maintain the illusion of neutrality. Nevertheless, as Christian Smith powerfully argues in his short book *Moral, Believing Animals*, all of us inhabit such stories, whether we acknowledge it or not.[13] We are, all of us, believers.

Christian scholars in the Reformed tradition have been making this point for a long time now.[14] At the same time, the role of foundational beliefs in scholarship has been acknowledged more and more widely by all sorts of people in the last several decades. In this respect, the postmodern turn in history and related developments in other disciplines have been a great boon to Christian scholars. Recognition of the "myth of religious neutrality" is now commonplace, though by no means universal.

So far so good: many historians, and most of us who are Christians, know that we are believers whose beliefs shape our scholarship. This continues to be an important insight, and in the aftermath of the Enlighten-

12. For a recent example, see David A. Hollinger, "The Wrong Question! Please Change the Subject!" *Fides et Historia* 43:2 (Summer/Fall 2011): 34-37.

13. Christian Smith, *Moral, Believing Animals: Human Personhood and Culture* (Oxford: Oxford University Press, 2003), chap. 4.

14. Nicholas Wolterstorff, *Reason within the Bounds of Religion*, 2nd ed. (Grand Rapids, MI: William B. Eerdmans, 1988); Roy Clouser, *The Myth of Religious Neutrality: An Essay on the Hidden Role of Religious Belief in Theories*, rev. ed. (Notre Dame, IN: University of Notre Dame Press, 2005).

ment, it will need to be stated and argued again and again by each new generation of scholars.

But once we have acknowledged this situation, then what? If we are all believers, what beliefs should Christians bring with them into their study of history? Or to put it more precisely, if we want to be consistently Christian in our academic work as in other areas of our lives, what implications should our Christian beliefs have for our approach to the study of history? This chapter is an attempt to answer that question from a perspective that is both biblical and Reformed. This chapter's perspective is *biblical* in that it assumes that the Bible, as interpreted by the historic Christian faith, gives us the true and authoritative picture of God and the world. It is *Reformed* in that its interpretation and application of the biblical story draws particularly on themes emphasized by Reformed Christianity, especially the stream that runs from the great North African church father Augustine through to the Dutch scholar and statesman Abraham Kuyper and his heirs. Attentive readers will note that this chapter draws on ideas from other branches of the Christian tradition too.

My central contention is this: the whole human story, and all particular human stories, are really part of a much larger story: God's cosmic story of Creation, Fall, and Redemption. Consequently, God's Big Story is the key that allows us to make sense of the (relatively) small stories of human history. The rest of this chapter works at applying this Big Story to four key questions about the study of history:

1. The *possibility* of studying history: what, if anything, can we know about the past? (The epistemological question.)
2. The *purposes* of studying history: why study history? (The teleological question.)
3. The *purview* of the historical discipline: what history should we study? (The ontological question.)
4. The *practice* of the discipline: how should we go about our study of history? (The methodological question.)

All of these questions are essential for the study of history; every historian operates with answers to each of them, even if these answers are largely implicit. Because the cosmic, biblical story is the key to answering these questions, I address each of them below in turn under the headings of Creation, Fall, and Redemption. First, however, it is necessary to say something about the God whose story this is.

Taking God Seriously in the Study of History

Our God is a God of history. In the beginning he made history possible because he created time and space, and filled them with many creatures, including us, whom he tasked with unfolding the possibilities he built into the creation (Gen. 1:1-28). He continues to make history possible by preserving the world in existence (Col. 1:15-17, Heb. 1:3) and showering his unmerited favor on us (Matt. 5:45). He knows the end of history from the beginning (Isa. 46:10). But God is not only the maker and preserver and knower of history, he is also himself deeply involved in history at every point. Nothing, however mundane, comes to pass apart from him (Matt. 10:29), such that both good and bad events are under his control (Isa. 45:1-7, Acts 2:23). He has always been at work directing human history, from the giving of the cultural mandate to Adam and Eve, through the preservation of Noah and his family, the calling of Abraham, the deliverance of the Hebrews from Egypt, and the sending of the prophets, to entering history himself by becoming a man, Jesus. He continues to direct history in this post-Resurrection era. And he is guiding the history of this age toward its consummation in the New Heaven and the New Earth (Rev. 21:1-5).

Already this gives us some hints about the answers to our four questions about history. It is *possible* to study history because God made it and God made us in such a way that we can know it. The *purposes* of studying history must ultimately relate back to God and his will for us. The *purview* of history will be defined by the way God has made the world and what he is doing with it. And the way we *practice* our discipline as historians and students of history needs to be based on cooperation with God and obedience to his will.

In short, history and the study of history, like the rest of existence, have their final meaning in relation to God. History, therefore, can only be fully and rightly understood if we begin with God and the story he is telling about his cosmos. That story is most simply summarized in biblical terms as Creation, Fall, and Redemption, and so this story acts as a kind of bridge that links our Triune God and the answers to our four questions. The rest of this chapter looks at each major piece of the biblical story in turn to see what it might have to say about the possibility, purposes, purview, and practice of historical study.

Taking Creation Seriously in the Study of History

The study of history, like all academic disciplines, has a creational basis, that is, it is made possible and defined by the character of God's creative work.[15] Much of what we can say here is necessarily modified by the effects of the Fall, but understanding *what* is affected by sin and *why* it is affected requires that we first explore this creational basis.

Possibility

As noted earlier, historians hotly disagree about what we can know about the past, and how we can know it. Is true knowledge of the past even possible? Is Ranke's goal of knowing the past *wie es eigentlich gewesen ist* eminently attainable, or merely a modernist mirage?

First of all, we must recognize that the created world, including its historical or chronological dimension, is real—not a figment of our imaginations, individually or collectively. To dismiss the past as nothing more than the fanciful invention of historians is no more reasonable, and no less disrespectful, than dismissing China as nothing more than the fanciful invention of geographers. To recognize the past as containing the real experiences of real people, on the contrary, is to extend to those people the same recognition we all implicitly extend to ourselves when we think of our own past experiences—whether as recent as what we had for lunch or as distant as our early childhoods—as things that really happened. To argue otherwise is to refuse to give other people the most basic form of respect, which is acknowledgement of their independent existence. In short, admitting the reality of human history is a requirement imposed upon us not only by the doctrine of creation, but also by the second greatest commandment, to love one's neighbour as oneself (Matt. 22:39). Thus solipsism—the denial of reality outside of one's own mind—is not an option for the Christian historian. The past, including the activities and experiences of other people, exists because God made it.

"Fair enough," the skeptical historian might respond, "but the *reality* of the past is not the same thing as the *reliability of our knowledge* of the past. We may agree that things happened in the past, but I do not believe that we can know what they were with any confidence." This is an important distinction that must be acknowledged. Given that the past is real, what if anything can we know about it?

Taking Creation seriously, coupled with taking the Fall seriously (more on this in the next section), allows us as Christian historians to answer this question in a way that avoids some of the opposite extremes that might be championed by empiricist and postmodernist historians respectively.

15. A recent scholarly and wide-ranging survey of the doctrine of creation from a neo-Calvinist perspective can be found in Bruce Riley Ashford and Craig G. Bartholomew, *The Doctrine of Creation: A Constructive Kuyperian Approach* (Downers Grove, IL: IVP Academic, 2020).

On the one hand, the doctrine of creation tells us that our faculties of knowing and communicating, including memory and language, are genuine but limited creational goods. God has made us as creatures that who are capable of remembering and reflecting on the past, and of communicating those memories and reflections to others through speech and writing. Indeed, the Bible itself, as revealed truth in the form of written language, presupposes the possibility of genuine communication between people, including genuine communication about past events. Together with the empiricist, therefore, the Christian historian affirms the possibility of genuine knowledge of the past through the communication of the people who experienced those events—whether in the form of oral accounts and primary documents produced by eyewitnesses, or secondary compilations and interpretations of those reports by historians. There is some sense in which we can reliably know things about the past. Historical knowledge, and the discipline of history, are possible.[16]

At the same time, however, Christian historians must acknowledge that as creatures humans are bound by creaturely limitations. Self-reflection reveals that we remember only a tiny fraction of our own past experiences, and only a tiny fraction of what we remember is ever communicated to others. Only a small fraction of *that* is ever communicated in such a way (e.g. in writing) that it might survive on earth beyond our lifetimes. Only a tiny fraction of what happens to other people, even people we know personally, is ever communicated in a way that could be accessible to us. Furthermore, all of us are more likely to remember and communicate certain kinds of things—such as dramatic events that have a profound emotional impact on us. Likewise, certain kinds of people—people with access to written language or gifted storytellers, for example—are more likely to communicate their experiences in lasting ways than others. All of this means that our possible collective knowledge of the past is necessarily and inescapably *selective*: out of everything that happens, only a miniscule portion is ever recorded in a form that might

16. It is worth mentioning in this connection Alvin Plantinga's argument that the Christian worldview can provide a coherent basis for confidence in the reliability of human powers of knowing, where naturalism fails to do so. See his *Warrant and Proper Function* (Oxford: Oxford University Press, 1993), chap. 12. For most theoretically inclined historians after the cultural turn, however, the operative (though typically unconscious) ontology is more likely to be what Plantinga calls "creative anti-realism," naturalism's main opponent in contemporary Western thought, which he defines as "the view that it is human behaviour – in particular, human thought and language – that is somehow responsible for the fundamental structure of the world and for the fundamental kinds of entities there are." See his essay "Christian Philosophy at the End of the Twentieth Century," in *The Analytic Theist: An Alvin Plantinga Reader*, ed. James F. Sennett (Grand Rapids, MI: Eerdmans, 1998), 313.

be usable by historians.

When records of the past *do* find their way into the hands of historians, moreover, a whole host of creaturely limitations of historians themselves come into play. We can focus on only a limited number of things, we can find and read only a limited number of documents, and (this side of the resurrection) we have only a limited amount of time. When we do set out to write an article or a book, we have only a limited amount of space in which to do it, and what we write will in turn be available to only a limited number of people.

In light of these creational limitations, it is clear that, even before considering the effects of the Fall, any historical account is a massive simplification of the past, just as any map is a massive simplification of the terrain it represents.[17] Thus, the Christian historian must agree with the postmodernist that even our best historical accounts can never *fully* capture the past "as it really was." Our historical knowledge is always partial, selective, and limited. Taking Creation seriously in history, therefore, does yield a "yes" in answer to the question, "Is historical knowledge even possible?" but we need to keep in mind that it is a "yes" with significant qualifications.

Purpose

Granted that it is *possible* to study the past, we next need to address the purpose question: *Why* should we study the past? Fall and Redemption provide their answers to this question as well, which we will consider in the appropriate places, but for now our focus is on the creational basis for studying the past. The Bible affirms that God's creation was originally good (Gen. 1:31) and that before the Fall God gave our first parents the responsibility and privilege of filling the earth and subduing it, including working and keeping the garden (Gen. 1:28, 2:15). In the Reformed tradition this "cultural mandate" is understood as not only referring to *agri*-culture (literally, the cultivation of the field) but also to the whole range of human creative cultural activity whereby we discover, care for, and develop the world.[18] The study of history, like many academic disciplines, involves the discovery of a feature of God's creation (in this case, the past), care for and appreciation of that feature of the creation, and the further development of the potential of the creation through the production of new cultural artifacts (the stories we tell about the past).

Broadly, then, the study of history is a response to the cultural man-

17. For an exploration of this analogy, see John Lewis Gaddis, *The Landscape of History: How Historians Map the Past* (Oxford: Oxford University Press, 2002).

18. Albert M. Wolters, *Creation Regained: Biblical Basics for a Reformational Worldview*, 2nd ed. (Grand Rapids, MI: William B. Eerdmans, 2005), 41-44.

date given to us by God. More specifically, we can identify several reasons for the study of history that are rooted in creation:

1. *To see beyond the horizon.* Without the study of history, our knowledge of the human part of creation would be limited to events within the recollection of our own memory or those of our personal acquaintances. The study of the past—whether it is as simple as an oral account of family history handed down from one generation to another, or as sophisticated as the use of underwater archaeological techniques to investigate an ancient Greek shipwreck—allows us to see beyond this horizon. Historical research is a form of discovery.
2. *To better understand the present by situating it within a historical context.* Not only can historical study uncover features of the past, it can also deepen our understanding of the present. The study of history can help us make better sense of the realities of our own time by uncovering the roots of those realities. One of the best ways to learn about another culture, for example, is to study its history. Similarly, we gain a better understanding of the life of contemporary cities, for instance, by situating them within a historical trajectory of urbanization.
3. *To test our theories about reality.* The theory-making of many disciplines, which is both part of our exploration of the creation and a necessary prelude to much of our own creative activity, relies on a good understanding of the past as a testing ground. This is particularly true of social sciences like economics and political science, which unlike the physical sciences can hardly conduct controlled, replicable experiments in a laboratory to test their theories! Understanding, for example, the effects of an expansionary monetary policy, or the advantages and disadvantages of a bicameral parliament, therefore, requires historical knowledge which can only be gleaned through the study of the past.
4. *To bring delight through well told tales.* We love to tell tales and have tales told to us, and there is something special about a tale "based on a true story." Every historical work is such a tale, and therefore has the potential to delight the teller and the hearers. To tell the true story of the single meeting between the celebrated Baroque composer J.S. Bach and the infamous Prussian despot Frederick the Great, and the clash of musical styles, wits, and political philosophies that ensued, is to create something that has value as a source of delight before whatever other uses it may have.[19] In this respect, at least, the

19. James R. Gaines, *Evening in the Palace of Reason: Bach Meets Frederick the Great in the Age of Enlightenment* (New York: Harper Perennial, 2005).

writing of historical accounts shares a common purpose with the creative arts.

Purview

The doctrine of creation gives us good reasons, then, for studying the past. But which past should we study? Given the proliferation of various forms of social and cultural history alongside political history—not to mention various thematic subfields like religious history, intellectual history, gender history, economic history, and diplomatic history— the historian today is faced with a bewildering variety of subfields to choose from. Are certain subfields more important than others? Does a particular approach such as economic history provide the "key" to understanding the past? Should historians strive to reunite what some see as an increasingly fragmented discipline, perhaps by weaving their investigations into a narrative organized around national political history, or the history of the working class?

The reasons for historical study given above, while crucially important in helping Christian historians direct their investigations, are not much help in answering this particular set of questions. The study of any subfield of history—gender, diplomatic, economic, and so on—could potentially be directed by such purposes. It is possible to answer at least some of these questions, however, using one of the resources of the Reformed tradition: Herman Dooyeweerd's insight that human functioning is irreducibly complex, an insight elaborated in his theory of what he calls the "modal aspects" of reality.[20] The key insight of this theory, for our purposes, is that human beings have many different modes of functioning in creation. For example, we function in the *psychical* mode (because we experience emotions), the *lingual* mode (because we communicate through symbols), the *aesthetic* mode (because we perceive beauty and proportion), and the *juridical* mode (because we make judgments about justice and deservedness).[21] These ways

20. I am grateful to Professor Harry Van Dyke for first making me aware of this connection. For an introduction to Dooyeweerd's understanding of modal aspects, see Jonathan Chaplin, *Herman Dooyeweerd: Christian Philosopher of State and Civil Society* (Notre Dame, IN: University of Notre Dame Press, 2011), 56-61. Readers seeking more detail should consult Herman Dooyeweerd, *A New Critique of Theoretical Thought*, vol. 2, *The General Theory of the Modal Spheres* (Philadelphia: Presbyterian and Reformed Publishing Company, 1969), 1-426, which develops the theory of the modal aspects and some of its implications for the special sciences.

21. Dooyeweerd identifies fifteen modal aspects in total. What is important for our present purposes is not the precise identities or number of modal aspects, but rather the basic idea that creation is modally diverse, that is, it displays a range of different aspects which are not reducible to each other.

of functioning reflect the built-in modal diversity of God's creation. This reality of creational diversity, argued Dooyeweerd, gives rise to the complexity of human societies, including the plurality of social institutions. The essential functional distinctions between the state and the church and the family and the business, for example, are ultimately rooted in the diversity of modal aspects.[22]

Importantly, no modal aspect can be reduced to another modal aspect. Each one is irreducibly unique. The Christian historian working with this insight will resist approaches to history that try to explain it in terms of only one modality (or only one subset of modalities).[23] This would rule out some Marxist approaches, for example, which attempt an economic reductionism by reducing several aspects of human life (religion and politics, for example) to mere by-products of human functioning in the economic mode. This is not to say that the economic mode is irrelevant to the other modes: in explaining any given historical phenomenon, it may even be predominant.[24] But no other aspect of human life besides the economic can legitimately be *reduced to* "nothing but" an expression of the economic mode.[25] All of the modes are important in understanding human functioning, and it follows, the unfolding of history. In short, the theory of modal aspects argues for a broad approach to history, in which various types of thematic historical investigation—social history, political history, economic history, art history, intellectual history, religious history, etc. – all have a place.[26] No one subfield of

22. See Chaplin, *Herman Dooyeweerd*, chap. 6. In this regard the modal aspects are Dooyeweerd's attempt to discern the philosophical basis for Abraham Kuyper's better-known concept of "sphere sovereignty," the idea that each social sphere has a distinct God-given task and realm of authority that should not be confused with or subsumed by other social spheres.

23. Robert K. Burkinshaw, "A Christian Perspective on History," in *Christian Worldview and the Academic Disciplines:* Cross*ing the Academy*, ed. Deane E. D. Downey and Stanley E. Porter (Hamilton, ON and Eugene, OR: McMaster Divinity College Press and Wipf and Stock, 2009), 285, makes a similar point, though not from within an explicitly modal analysis.

24. My thanks to Russ Kosits for bringing to my attention the point that modal diversity need not rule out the possibility that one single type of functioning may be the most important in understanding a given historical phenomenon. This is also recognized in Burkinshaw, "A Christian Perspective on History," 285.

25. Other types of reductionism are possible, of course. It may be that certain forms of postmodernism, where there is "nothing outside the text," involve a lingual reductionism. Sociobiology, not as yet influential in the discipline of history, practices a kind of biotic reductionism in the social sciences. For a brief critique of sociobiology and its cousin, evolutionary psychology, see Smith, *Moral, Believing Animals*, 33-43.

26. Harry Van Dyke, "A Taxonomy of Historical Writing," unpublished document in

history provides a key or central theme for organizing our understanding of the past. There is a place for the social historian as well as the political historian; both of them do valuable work, but neither of them has a monopoly on legitimate historical research.

At the same time, the theory of modal aspects also reminds the historian to be aware of the full spectrum of human experience, even when studying a kind of history that centres on one aspect of human life. For example, the historian of religion cannot solely concern himself with theological matters to the exclusion of all else. In examining the history of the Reformation, for example, which as a religious development is rightly defined by theological concerns, he should remain aware of the economic, political, and artistic dimensions of his subject. Thus, while the theory of modal aspects provides strong justification for various thematic historical approaches, it at the same time warns against the dangers of isolating these approaches from each other. The art historian needs to converse with the historian of ideas; the historian of high politics needs to talk to the historian of popular culture.

Practice

How then should historians carry out their work? The foregoing exploration of the implications of Creation for history suggests five guideposts for practicing historians: *confidence*, *honesty*, *clarity*, *humility*, and *service*.

Confidence

If it is indeed possible to know something about the past, as argued above, then the historian can be confident that her work is not pointless. There is value in the painstaking work of combing through archives, interpreting primary documents, reading and assessing secondary sources, and building carefully argued and clearly written stories on the basis of that research. She can have confidence that such work is never entirely in vain.

There is another sense in which the historian can have confidence as well. She can have confidence that there are worthwhile purposes for the study of history, purposes rooted in God's command to explore and cultivate his creation. If she faithfully strives to fulfill those purposes, her work is an act of obedience to God.

---

possession of author. C.T. McIntire combines this insight with Dooyeweerd's idea of historical development in "The Ongoing Task of Christian Historiography," in *A Christian View of History?* edited by George Marsden and Frank Roberts (Grand Rapids, MI: Eerdmans, 1975), 66-69.

Honesty

Another implication of the possibility of knowing something about the past is that some historical accounts are truer to reality than others. Historical accounts are not simply interchangeable fictions, but attempts to faithfully represent something about the past. The possibility of historical knowledge therefore imposes upon the historian the responsibility to reconstruct the past carefully, with an eye to accuracy, precision, and fairness. There is no place for wilful misrepresentation or selective reading of the evidence to strengthen one's case, no place for unwarranted generalizations, and no place for unfair caricatures of historical figures or the ideas of other historians.

Clarity

Since we can know something about the past, and our purposes in studying it require communicating it to others, we also have a responsibility to be clear in how we communicate. Inescapably, we will sometimes need to deal with complex topics, and specialized language and shorthand references will sometimes be appropriate when writing or speaking for fellow historians. Nevertheless, clarity is to communication what conductivity is to electricity. Without it, we cannot faithfully carry out our tasks as historians. The Christian historian, therefore, should shun unnecessarily obscure jargon, impenetrable prose, and sophistication for sophistication's sake. Instead, he should strive for accessibility, simplicity, and directness.

Humility

Our confidence in our calling and ability to know the past, and our striving for honesty and clarity, however, must always be accompanied by our humility. The past is immense and our knowledge of it is puny, and highly selective at that. The modal diversity of creation ensures that all history is highly complex. Thus, there are many possible alternative accounts of the same historical topic which might be created by selecting different information and focusing on different aspects, each of which may be equally faithful and equally valid, insofar as they do not directly contradict each other. We should resist the temptation to exaggerate the scope or certainty of our knowledge, and keep an awareness of our limitations and the limitations of our enterprise constantly before us.

Service

Finally, it is important to remember that the study of history is not simply an exercise in amusing oneself—though hopefully it is at least that! Instead, the Christian historian puts herself and her work at the disposal of others for their benefit. The purposes of studying history noted above, as well as those which will be mentioned below, are all ultimately about serving other people. The historian who writes to help people to see beyond the horizon, to better understand the present, to test theories, and to bring delight is working for the benefit and flourishing of others. Let us be guided by this calling to service in all of our work, as we obey our Lord's command to love others as ourselves.

Taking the Fall Seriously in the Study of History

Any discussion of the creational basis for the study of history must be followed by an exploration of the effects of sin. In the wake of the Fall, all human activity is distorted in some way by sin; indeed the creation itself groans along with us under the weight of it (Rom. 5:12-14, 8:19-23). Broadly speaking, the impact of the Fall makes itself felt in scholarly pursuits, including the study of history, in two ways. First, historical scholarship is misdirected by sin, marring (though not destroying) its creational contours. Second, faithful historical scholarship must now take the reality of sin into account, introducing new aspects to the practice of the discipline. Let us explore both of these effects of sin in relation to the possibility, purposes, purview and practice of historical study.

Possibility

Earlier we saw that the nature of creation in general and our created nature as human beings make it possible for us to acquire and convey genuine, though limited, knowledge of the past. Just as sin does not destroy our ability to speak, but does twist our speech, so too sin does not erase our ability to know something about the past, but it does distort that knowledge in several ways.

First, the presence of sin can blur or even block our vision of the past. Both the sources used by historians and the historians themselves may engage in deception through lies, half-truths, and wilful omissions. Although cultural diversity is a natural outcome of the God-given cultural mandate in light of the complexity of God's good creation, the curse of Babel (Gen. 11:1-9), which is both a judgment and constraint upon idolatry, impedes our ability to empathize with the people of the past across linguistic and cultural divides.[27] And more generally, our knowl-

27. Augustine (*City of God*, 16.11) takes the position that there was a single human language (Hebrew) before Babel and sees the division of languages as God's punishment for human presumption, a view that has been widely held by Christians and influential in the Reformed tradition. On the other hand, some interpreters, in-

edge of the past exhibits confused thinking rooted in a sin-darkened understanding (Eph. 4:17-18). Sin can even directly destroy our records of the past, as in the wanton destruction of archives and historical buildings during warfare.[28] These fallen distortions compound and complicate the creaturely limitations of historical knowledge we discussed earlier.

Second, the Fall warps the fundamental religious commitments and worldviews that guide all historical interpretation. Erroneous worldviews lead to erroneous interpretations. A materialist who is convinced that all human ideas are a mask for "real" economic interests, for example, or a hard constructivist who denies the existence of any creational norms or constants underlying cultural constructions like gender or law, will both be forced to adopt interpretations of some historical phenomena that are flatly mistaken.

Do the effects of sin obliterate the possibility of historical knowledge? No. God's common grace restrains the effects of sin such that his gifts to us, including the gifts of memory and language, continue to function in this fallen world. Anyone who denies this, to be consistent, would have to give up research and writing about history. Indeed, the fact that someone tries to inquire into the past and ventures to say something about it is evidence enough that he or she does not really believe that such knowledge and communication are impossible. Nevertheless, the effects of sin on the study of history are so profound that our qualified answer of "Yes" to the question, "Can we know anything about the past?" must now be even more heavily qualified. Some of the implications of these new qualifications are discussed below in the *practice* section.

---

cluding leading Reformed thinkers Abraham Kuyper and Herman Bavinck, while agreeing that Babel was the origin of multilingualism and functioned to restrain the sin of the tower-builders, also see the existence of multiple languages as simultaneously a divine blessing. The latter approach seems more consistent with the biblical teachings that God is neither a God of confusion (1 Cor. 14:33) nor the author of sin (James 1:13-17; cf. Westminster Confession 5.4), that the Holy Spirit's response to diversity of languages is not uniformity but gospel translation (Acts 2:1-11), and that linguistic diversity is highlighted along with ethnic diversity in John's vision of the great multitude praising God before his heavenly throne (Rev. 7:9-10). For a thoughtful introduction to the issues, see James Eglinton, "From Babel to Pentecost via Paris and Amsterdam: Multilingualism in Neo-Calvinist and Revolutionary Thought," in *Neo-Calvinism and the French Revolution*, ed. James Eglinton and George Harinck (London: Bloomsbury T&T Clark, 2014), 31-60.

28. Mark McCarthy reports his dismay upon finding that most of the records of the British Foreign Bible Society had not survived the Blitz (personal communication with author).

Purposes

At the same time that the presence of sin in the world distorts our knowledge of the past, it also paradoxically presents the faithful historian with new reasons to study history in the first place. To the four creational purposes for the study of history discussed above, we can now add the following purposes:

To warn. Due to the effects of sin played out in human history, and the temptations of sin in the present, the study of history can now play an important role in displaying the past effects of sin and warning against its consequences in the present. To be clear, the study of history does not furnish us with new moral truths. Instead, it powerfully illustrates and elaborates the moral truths which are already known (or at least, should already be known) to us. Scripture itself often uses history this way, as in Hebrews 3 where the rebellion of the Exodus generation serves as a warning for first-century Christians (and us). Though we cannot claim divine inspiration for our words, contemporary historians can likewise point to arresting historical illustrations of important moral truths as a means of moral formation for our students and readers. For example, the dehumanizing impact of apartheid and the horror of the Holocaust each in their own way warn against the destructive power of racial hatred, just as the terror-famines of Stalin's agricultural collectivization and Mao's Great Leap Forward warn against the dangers of totalitarian economic systems. While historians need to guard against simplistic moralizing and ensure that their judgments are founded in sound moral reasoning, this purpose of historical study is legitimate, and in fact is already a powerful motivation behind much contemporary work.[29]

To correct through perspective. The study of history has some of the same benefits as travel to foreign lands or the study of strange cultures; it frees us from the blinders imposed by our situatedness in only one time and place. In C.S. Lewis's lecture on learning in wartime, he remarks:

> Most of all, perhaps, we need intimate knowledge of the past. Not that the past has any magic about it, but because we cannot study the

29. While it is generally taboo in professional historical circles to explicitly frame one's teaching and writing as a project of moral formation, a cursory survey of journal articles and course descriptions—particularly in cases where the subject is any sort of oppression, imperialism, exploitation, or marginalization—suggests that a large swath of contemporary historical work is in fact driven by such considerations. For a brilliant presentation of similar observations in the field of sociology, see Christian Smith, *The Sacred Project of American Sociology* (Oxford: Oxford University Press, 2014).

> future, and yet need something to set against the present, to remind us that the basic assumptions have been quite different in different periods and that much which seems certain to the uneducated is merely temporary fashion. A man who has lived in many places is not likely to be deceived by the local errors of his native village; the scholar has lived in many times and is therefore in some degree immune from the great cataract of nonsense that pours from the press and the microphone of his own age.[30]

Such advice has special relevance for Western Christians living in an extremely wealthy, democratic, egalitarian, consumerist, structurally differentiated, individualistic, technologically advanced and sexually "liberated" culture that is without historical parallels. We are a historical and global outlier. With such a highly unusual setting as our everyday reference point, our need to be transported beyond our horizon by study of the past is even more pressing.

To combat misleading accounts. Another reason for a historian to take up the task of studying the past is to critique deeply flawed accounts by other historians and advance sound alternative narratives. In some cases the accounts may be flawed because they include factual errors or exhibit outright dishonesty, but more often it will be because they are driven by mistaken agendas, rest on flawed presuppositions, or employ misleading interpretative frameworks. A historian might take the field, for example, to challenge the work of ultranationalist historians who whitewash their country's past by trumpeting its achievements and ignoring its mistakes.[31] A historian might write to vindicate Christian missionaries who have been unfairly portrayed as nothing more than agents of imperialism. Or a historian might devote her life to restoring the place of religion in historical accounts of a period that has been retroactively secularized by short-sighted twenty-first century academics. As these last examples suggest, there is often a desperate need for a Christian point of view in particular to counterbalance the prejudices of the contemporary academy. As long as historians proceed with a humility rooted in the recognition that they have no monopoly on the truth and that their work will have flaws of its own, correcting misleading accounts can be a valid reason for studying the past.

30. C.S. Lewis, "Learning in War-Time," in *The Weight of Glory and Other Essays* (San Francisco: HarperSanFrancisco, 2001), 58-9. My thanks to Heather Laing and Deborah Bowen for reminding me about this quotation.

31. Cf. Burkinshaw, "A Christian Perspective on History," 284.

Purview

The Fall does not obliterate the great variety of aspects of human life and experience. Following Al Wolters, we might call this *structural* variety, that is, a good element of variety built into the structure of creation.[32] Thus, the impact of the Fall does not overturn the creational basis for a wide variety of lines of historical inquiry (political, intellectual, social, and so on). What the Fall does do, however, is to introduce a new kind of variety which we might call *directional* variety. In the wake of sin, human activity in the various areas of life is no longer uniform in its obedience to God. Instead, it is now misdirected by our disobedience to a greater or lesser extent. A line dividing good and evil has been introduced into human history, a line which, as Alexander Solzhenitsyn pointed out, does not cut *between* states, classes or political parties, but rather cuts *through* every area of human endeavour, and indeed, every human heart.[33] In addition to this, the division between good and evil now expresses itself corporately. As Augustine teaches, everyone now belongs to one of two parallel human societies or cities found throughout history: the City of God, made up of those who live according to God's will, and the city of this world, made up of those who live according to human standards.[34] To be sure, the historian needs to remember that at any given time future citizens of the Heavenly City are hidden among the citizens of the earthly city, while in the midst of the City of God are those who will ultimately prove themselves to belong to the city of this world. The two cities "are interwoven and intermixed in this era, and await separation at the last judgment."[35] Likewise, while there is conflict between the two cities, there is also conflict within the city of men, who fight to dominate one another, and even between members of the City of God, because even members of that city have not yet attained perfection in this life.[36] Nevertheless, the differences between the two cities are real, and they can be distinguished by the objects of their loves (God or self) and other signs

32. Wolters, *Creation Regained*, 59-63 proposes the terms "structure" and "direction" for the phenomena discussed in this paragraph.

33. Aleksandr I. Solzhenitsyn, *The Gulag Archipelago, 1918-1956: An Experiment in Literary Investigation, [parts] III-IV* (New York: Harper and Row, 1975), 615-16, quoted in Smith, *What is a Person? Rethinking Humanity, Social Life, and the Moral Good from the Person Up* (Chicago: University of Chicago Press, 2010), 76n74. For an application of the same idea to the different kinds of "creaturely activity," including social institutions, see Wolters, *Creation Regained*, 81-3.

34. Augustine, *City of God*, trans. Henry Bettenson and intro. by G.R. Evans (London: Penguin, 2003), 1.

35. Augustine, *City of God*, 1.35.

36. Augustine, *City of God*, 15.5.

that arise from the difference of their loves.[37]

In contrast to structural variety, this directional variety—this "antithesis" or dividing line between good and evil—is not part of God's good creation. However, it is itself an important, indeed essential, focus of historical study. It is here, rather than in one of the structural areas of human life, that we can legitimately look for a unifying theme or analytical lens through which to understand history. The back-and-forth struggle between good and evil, both within each human heart, and between the Heavenly City and the earthly city, occurs everywhere this side of the Fall. It is a universal theme that exists in the marketplace as much as in councils of state, in the art studio as in the bedroom, on the playing field as much in the workshop. Thus the Fall introduces a theme of historical study that is present across all of the modally defined subject areas. The study of evil, and of the conflict between good and evil, in whatever period and whatever aspect of life, is now part of the historian's job—indeed, it is so much a part of the historian's job that it is hard for us even to conceive of history writing without war and strife and exploitation as a large part of its subject matter. One implication of this responsibility is that Christian historians should not want to whitewash the past or view it through rose-coloured glasses. Instead, we need to realistically face up to and acknowledge the depravity of the human heart.

Before moving on, a note of caution is in order. Christian historians are often drawn to the conflict of good and evil in history, but they are sometimes prone to mistakenly identify the *directional* element of good with a *structural* element of life, the institutional church (that is, Christians gathered and organized under ecclesiastical authority for the purposes of worship, preaching the word, administering the sacraments, and enforcing discipline). This way of thinking tempts Christian historians to see the church institution—its organization, doctrines, leaders, and so on—as the area of God's exclusive concern and therefore the most important or even the only legitimate area of study for the Christian historian. The trouble with this approach is the unbiblical dualism that underlies it, which implicitly consigns aspects of life outside the church institution—craftsmanship, theatre, international relations, and so on—to a "secular" realm regarded as either "neutral," and thus immune to the conflict between good and evil, or as "worldly" and therefore to be shunned.[38] As an antidote to this confusion, Christian historians need to

37. Augustine, *City of God*, 14.28.

38. In *Creation Regained*, Wolters deals with this confusion at various points, diagrammatically illustrating it on pp. 81-82. A related problem is the tendency in some modern theological movements to treat *Heilsgeschichte*, the history of God's saving work, as a completely separate category from "ordinary" history. In extreme cases,

recognize that while God cares how we worship him and what we teach about him, he also cares what we do in the marketplace, how we treat our workers, how we govern, and what we do in every area of our lives. We need Christian church historians, in other words, but we also need Christian economic historians, political historians, and art historians.

Practice

Sin is a part of historical study as it is any human endeavour, so the way we practice it needs to take this reality into account. Sin is not merely an abstract idea that applies to the subjects of our study, or to other historians—though it is those things—but something that applies to each of us in the most personal way.[39] The wise historian needs to respond to the presence of sin in his work in several ways.

We need *proper confidence* in our study of the past, in light of the effects of sin on the possibility of historical knowledge discussed earlier. This means guarding against the temptation to either pride or despair in our attitude toward historical knowledge. The first temptation, the temptation of the modernist, is to ascribe to ourselves godlike powers of knowing, denying for all practical purposes our creaturely limitations and the epistemological effects of sin. The opposite temptation, the temptation of the postmodernist, is to make the limitations on historical knowledge so absolute that we despair of the whole enterprise. The best option for the Christian historian is neither naive realism nor anti-realism, but rather a chastened or critical realism.[40]

We need *discernment* in our study of the past. History contains both good and evil. We need to be able to distinguish between them, while admitting the limitations of our understanding and avoiding rushing to

---

such theologians can be tempted to sever the link between ordinary history and *Heilsgeschichte* entirely, such that they can affirm the reality of Jesus' resurrection as the central event in *Heilsgeschichte* without affirming it as a real historical event that took place in the everyday world of flesh and blood. Needless to say, such an approach runs contrary to the whole thrust of the Bible, most especially the biblical teachings on the incarnation and resurrection of Christ and the final destiny of the world. At the same time, "salvation history" rightly understood ought to include every aspect of human life, since no aspect of it is excluded from the drama of creation, fall, and redemption. For a similar response from Lesslie Newbigin, see George R. Hunsberger, *Bearing the Witness of the Spirit: Lesslie Newbigin's Theology of Cultural Plurality* (Grand Rapids, MI: Eerdmans, 1998), 151-2.

39. "If we say we have no sin, we deceive ourselves, and the truth is not in us." (1 John 1:8, ESV)

40. Christian Smith's proposal for "critical realist personalism" as a way forward for the social sciences also shows promise for historians in this regard. See his *What is a Person?*

judgment. Likewise, powerful but ultimately unbiblical narratives lurk within the work of many historians (including, often, our own); we need to be able to recognize and resist them. For example, Marxist or Marxist-derived assumptions about persons and society, about what is right and wrong and what is important, have exercised a powerful influence on the historical profession in the past fifty years. No doubt this has produced valuable insights, but what serious distortions or blind spots might it have introduced at the same time? How does thinking of every aspect of history as revealing a primary dynamic of oppression, and dividing people into "oppressed" and "oppressor" categories based on some identifying characteristic, impoverish our understanding of the past even while drawing our attention to crucial truths about it? Where does a Christian anthropology and sociology part ways with a Marxist one? And while Marxist or quasi-Marxist narratives may dominate today, they are not the only ones, nor will they reign forever; the task of discernment is multifaceted and must adapt its response to changing circumstances. All of this requires immersion in Scripture to form our judgment, immersion in a Christian community to hold us accountable, and immersion in excellent Christian scholarship to strengthen us for swimming against the stream.

We need *repentance* in our study of the past. We need to be able to acknowledge and turn from our own sins and mistakes as historians in an environment of Christian community, which again means having close relationships with other Christians, including other Christian scholars, who can exhort us to get back up and follow Christ. More generally, it means we need to be open to correction and willing to admit when we are wrong.

Finally, we need *forgiveness* in our study of the past, in two senses. On the one hand, we need forgiveness for our own failures—forgiveness from God, and (especially for perfectionist historians) forgiveness from ourselves. On the other hand, we need a forgiving attitude in our dealings with the people of the past and our fellow historians. We must be willing to see them as fallen people like ourselves, and we must be willing to extend to them the same grace that has been extended to us (Matt. 18:21-25). We are called to be discerning without being judgmental or legalistic.

Taking Redemption Seriously in the Study of History

Sin does not have the last word, thanks be to God! From the beginning, God has purposed to redeem a people for himself, and ultimately to reclaim and restore the rest of creation. By humbling himself even to the point of death on the cross and rising again, Jesus Christ has triumphed over sin, death, and the devil. Reconciliation with God is available to anyone who believes, and sanctification follows through the work of the Holy Spirit in our lives. For our purposes, then, the question is, how does God's work of redemption and restoration change the study of history?

Possibility

As we discussed earlier, some of the limitations to our knowledge of the past are due to the distorting effects of sin, both the deceptions of witnesses and historians, and the faulty interpretative frameworks we apply to the past. Redemption brings the possibility of repentance from deceptions and a straightening of interpretive frameworks through the renewing of our minds (Rom. 12:2). It follows that if we are diligent in making honesty and integrity hallmarks of our lives, and saturate our thinking with biblical truth, we can expect that our vision of the past will grow clearer and more accurate.

This does not mean that Christian historians will necessarily be better at their task than non-Christian historians. To the contrary, because of God's common grace, any given non-Christian historian may be admirably honest and clear-sighted, while any given Christian historian may be mired in self-deception and confusion. Being a disciple of Jesus is no guarantee of perfection this side of glory. Nor does redemption mean that our knowledge of the past becomes boundless; our knowledge of the past is subject to limitations derived from our created nature as well as from sin. What redemption *does* mean, however, is that each of us can be a better historian than we would otherwise be insofar as we open ourselves to the Spirit's work in us.[41] In particular, as we are shaped by the Gospel and develop a thoroughly biblical worldview, we will be less likely to employ interpretive frameworks rooted in flawed worldviews.

Purposes

Redemption in the past and the present also opens up new purposes for historical study:

To inspire. Just as the study of evil in history serves as a warning, so the study of good in history furnishes us with examples to emulate. Provided we keep in mind the necessarily partial character of human goodness before Christ's return, and guard against the temptation to exaggerate or distort the historical record, we can learn much from the people

41. Cf. C.S. Lewis's tooth-whitening analogy in *God in the Dock* (Grand Rapids, MI: William B. Eerdmans, 1970), 59.

of the past who exhibited compassion, heroism, justice, generosity, and the like. Because of God's common grace, such good works can be found among members of the city of man as well as of the city of God, and in either case they should be recognized so that their example can instruct us.[42] But as Christians, we can take particular inspiration from what our brothers and sisters accomplished in past ages as their service to God made possible through his special, saving grace to them, adding to the "great cloud of witnesses" described in Hebrews 11. This is true whether they saw their tasks through to the end or fell as martyrs for their faith. This observation about special grace leads naturally to our next point.

To see God's redemptive work. God's redemptive work—the outpouring of his special grace to those he has chosen as his own possession—takes place in real history; as a result, much of it is visible to us. In addition to the general inspiration that history provides through examples of doing good, therefore, a study of the past provides an opportunity to see, celebrate, and be encouraged by the survival and progress of the Gospel and the effects of the Gospel against great odds. Time and again, God has used the foolish things of the world to shame the wise (1 Cor. 1:27), his people persisting in the face of disdain and prejudice, triumphing in the face of Roman or Soviet or Maoist persecution, shaking off heresies ancient and modern, spreading like wildfire in the most unlikely places through the most unlikely means, overturning infanticide and tyranny and slavery the world over. To be sure, much evil has been carried out in the name of Christ, even by those who could credibly claim to be his followers. But just when the Gospel seems choked beneath the accumulated sins, apathies, and errors of professed Christians, it breaks forth anew with fresh power. The advance of the City of God is a worthy theme for the Christian historian.

Purview

Redemption does not overturn what we discussed earlier about the structural diversity of human society and the directional conflict or antithesis that cuts across it. Nevertheless, it adds a twist to the theme of directional conflict, which is the disruptive power of the Gospel to dramatically roll back the frontiers of evil. As implied by purpose (9) above, this advance of the Gospel should be one of the things the Christian historian

42. See, for example, Augustine's treatment in *City of God* of the wisdom of the Platonists (8.9-10) and of the virtues of pagan Rome (5.12-18). On common grace generally, see Richard Mouw, *He Shines in All That's Fair: Culture and Common Grace* (Grand Rapids, MI: Eerdmans, 2002).

pays attention to across all spheres of life (i.e. across all modal domains). Again, this does not mean that church history *per se* needs to be the focus of every Christian historian, even though every Christian historian should have a good basic grasp of it. No, instead the Christian historian should pay attention to how the Gospel is—or is not—worked out historically in every area of life, in the schoolroom or on the merchant ship as well as in the sanctuary. Awareness of the possibility of redemption and alertness to signs of its presence help the Christian historian steer clear of cynicism or despair.

If part of the Christian historian's task is to note the impact of the Gospel and God's redemptive work in history, does this mean that we can discern and show forth God's purposes in historical events? We know that God directs everything that happens in history; does this mean we can reveal his activities? Although many historians and other Christians ranging from theological giants to televised pseudo-prophets have claimed to see the finger of God in particular events, we have no warrant to proclaim what we do not know. What we do know is God's revealed will: what he wants people to do and how he wants them to live. We can point out, with appropriate caution and humility, historical happenings that are in line with his revealed will (e.g. forgiveness) or contrary to it (e.g. murder). We also know in a general sense that God weaves even great evil into accomplishing his purposes (Acts 2:23), and works all things together for the good of those who love him (Romans 8:28). What we do not, indeed cannot, know with certainty, is God's hidden purpose in specific historical events.[43] We know that the sinking of the Titanic, for example, was somehow part of God's plan for history, but we do not know, and indeed may never know, how that event specifically fit into the larger causal web that ultimately points toward the final victory of Christ.[44] Thus, the Christian historian should be cautious about attributing particular divine purposes to post-biblical historical events, while affirming that God continues to preserve, accompany, and rule his creation throughout history.[45]

---

43. The exception is those historical events clearly explained in Scripture, which is God-breathed and therefore sees "behind the curtain" into God's purposes. A number of ancient Near Eastern events, such as the Babylonian captivity and the rise of Cyrus of Persia, are illuminated this way in Scripture. But Scripture does not tell us God's hidden purposes behind historical events after the closing of the New Testament writings, except in the eschatological writings, which do not appear to be designed to guide us in the interpretation of particular historical events prior to the last days.

44. Cf. Kirk Durston, "The consequential complexity of history and gratuitous evil," *Religious Studies* 36 (March 2000): 65-80.

45. It should be noted that Christian historians have disagreed about whether and how they should recognize God's providential work in history. For an overview of

Practice

Finally, the possibility and presence of redemption should suffuse the way we practice our historical craft. We must never lose sight of the possibility of reconciliation and healing for ourselves and our fellow historians. Thus, when we repent of our sins as historians (which we should do regularly, as argued above) we know that God is ready to forgive us (1 John 1:9). We must be willing to extend the same grace and forgiveness we have received to even our most godless, frustrating, and unkind colleagues, and we should never see them as enemies beyond hope of redemption. Above all, as part of God's redeemed people seeking to do his will, we should bring our work before him in prayer, asking for his guidance and protection over us and it.

Toward a Research Agenda

As the foregoing should make clear, a Christian approach to history is not a matter of studying this or that kind of history, or this or that time period. Rather, it is a matter of pursuing one or more of the legitimate purposes of historical study, with a faithful method and interpretive approach, in any number of modally diverse areas of human experience. The array of topics and eras which can furnish subjects for this kind of faithful scholarship is, for all practical purposes, limitless. What follows, therefore, is not a prescriptive set of marching orders for Christian historians, but a few examples of themes or topics that could be pursued for the purposes and with the tools proposed in this chapter. These examples each lend themselves especially to fulfilling purpose (2)—using the past to make sense of important features of the present—but could serve to fulfill several other purposes as well.

Secularization

The classical secularization paradigm, centred on the notion that the modernization of society causes a decline in the social significance of religion, once reigned supreme, but it has come under sustained attack by creative alternative paradigms and narratives. Some of these alternatives are potentially more attuned to a Christian understanding of the person

---

some of the issues, see Ian H. Clary, "Evangelical Historiography: The Debate over Christian History," *Evangelical Quarterly* 87 no. 3 (2015): 225-51. The threefold conception of God's work of preserving, accompanying, and governing creation stems from the seventeenth-century German theologian Johann Friedrich König; on it, see Ashford and Bartholomew, *The Doctrine of Creation*, 287-96.

than the classical paradigm, which rested on questionable assumptions. Moreover, the debate has so far mostly been carried out by sociologists, often with scant reference to the particularities of history. A Christian historian could explore aspects of secularization in a way that applies, tests, and/or corrects one or more of these paradigms in a concrete historical context.

The Moral Order of Early Modern Economics

The early modern period saw a revolution in Western European economic thinking and practices, a good part of which involved the rise of a new moral order based on individualism, voluntarism, and enlightened self-interest. What was the relationship between the intellectual articulations of this new order and legal, commercial, and social developments? How did the manifestations of this moral order in the economic sphere relate to its manifestations in the political sphere? What were the implications for changes in economic practices for the cosmic order envisioned by early modern Christianity, and vice versa?

Family, Gender, and Sexuality

In the wake of the Sexual Revolution of the later twentieth century, the contemporary West is undoubtedly an extreme historical outlier in its beliefs and customs relating to family, gender, and sexuality. At the time of writing, the headlines almost daily point to further distancing between Western society and the historical mainstream. Much more careful work needs to be done to understand the roots and historical course of this sea change in modern Western society, as well as the attitudes and behaviours of other places and other times. This is particularly important for people in Africa, Asia, and Latin America who are struggling to make sense of the tide of sexual "liberation" reaching their shores from Europe and North America. If such research is exclusively carried out by extreme partisans of the Sexual Revolution, which is a real possibility given the current political and intellectual climate in Western academia, the picture they get is likely to be highly one-sided. Nuanced, rigorous, and irenic but courageous scholarship from a Christian perspective can provide an important counterpoint. Be warned: this option is not for the faint of heart.

Pre-modern China

Due to language barriers, geographical distances, and the limitations of archival records, Western historians who specialize in the history of non-Western countries tend to focus on modern Western imperialism or missionary activity in those countries. While this work is valuable, it illuminates only a very small portion of the history of these places. Given the vast historical expanse of literate civilization in China, and China's contemporary return to central importance on the world stage, there is much room for valuable contributions to the study of pre-modern Chinese history by Christian historians, even Western ones who are able to master one or more Chinese languages and surmount the logistical obstacles. Similar observations, *mutatis mutandis*, apply to the study of many other parts of the world.

Good historical work is already being done on each of these subjects, including good work by Christian historians, and I make no attempt to summarize it here. But there is much opportunity for emerging or established Christian scholars to make a difference in these fields.

Conclusion

To sum up, then, the study of history, like all academic pursuits, is inescapably shaped by fundamental religious commitments. Christian historians, like all historians, need to operate with at least implicit beliefs about the *possibility*, *purposes*, *purview*, and *practice* of historical study. Unless we examine our foundational beliefs and take them captive for Christ (2 Cor. 10:5), we are likely to conform unwittingly to the examples set before us in graduate school, learned societies, and leading journals. These examples are not all bad, of course, but to the extent that they are rooted in non-Christian presuppositions, uncritically imitating them will hinder us from fully following Christ in our work.

In light of these truths, the task for the Christian historian is to develop an integrally Christian approach that addresses the foundational questions in the discipline from the standpoint of a Christian worldview. In this chapter I have drawn on Scripture and the Reformed tradition to argue that God's Big Story of Creation, Fall, and Redemption is the key to rightly forming our understanding of the small stories of human history. This biblical cosmic narrative has much to teach us as we go about our historical task.

No doubt there are many other things that could rightfully be said about a Christian approach to history. I have not said much about things like the modes of God's action in history, the role of spiritual beings such as angels and demons, a Christian assessment of the idea of progress, or many other worthwhile topics. Nevertheless, the principles laid out in this chapter begin to provide the Christian historian with something meaningful to say in conversations with fellow historians, something rooted in the great cosmic story of which we are all a very small part.

Questions for Reflection and Discussion

1. What drew you to the study of history in the first place? Does that interest reflect any themes tied to creation, the fall, or redemption?
2. From the time you first began studying history until now, how has your understanding of the *purposes* of studying history changed? Why do you think that is?
3. Was there anything in this chapter that struck you as completely unexpected?
4. What worldviews or ideological currents have been most influential in your history education/training? (Keep in mind that these may not have been explicit.) Which elements are attractive to you (if any), and which repel you (if any), and why?
5. Why is it, in your view, that many historians are drawn to the oppressor-oppressed dynamic as a central feature of history? A biblical perspective obviously affirms that emphasis to a degree, but how might it also challenge, correct, critique, or broaden it?
6. Do your own instincts lean more towards a modernist/empiricist epistemology or towards a postmodernist one? Why do you think that is? How might a Christian critical realist perspective affirm valid aspects of your preferred approach while challenging others?
7. What modally defined aspect of history (ecclesiastical, political, economic, social, intellectual/theological, artistic, etc.) tends to capture your attention? How might attention to the other aspects enrich your understanding?
8. Think of a friend or colleague (Christian or non-Christian) who would be skeptical about a "Christian approach" to history. How would you explain the attractions of a Christian approach to this person in a way that resonates with some of his or her convictions, but doesn't downplay the antithesis between Christian and non-Christian approaches, or the radically transformative impact of Christ's lordship? What points might you emphasize?
9. Does anything in this chapter challenge your approach to the practice of history in a way that might have a significant impact on your work moving forward? Explain.

10. What aspect of Christian thinking about history do you want to learn more about? Where will you start?

Helpful Resources on Faith and History

The literature relevant to Christian thinking about history is vast, especially if one includes the historical works by Christians of various times and places that implicitly address theoretical questions. A good place to start is the writing of early Christian historians such as Eusebius's *History of the Church*, Augustine's *City of God*, and Bede's *Ecclesiastical History of the English People*, each of which can be read not only as works of theology or history *per se*, but also as containing principles or exemplars for a Christian approach to history worth considering. Such works can profitably be read together with those of Christian historians from subsequent eras, right up to influential twentieth-century writers such as Christopher Dawson, Kenneth Scott Latourette, and Herbert Butterfield.

Much has been written explicitly on the intersection of Christian faith and history in the last fifty years. Some but not all of these recent works follow a "transformationalist" approach to the relationship between the biblical worldview and scholarship, so it would be beneficial to read this "faith and history" literature alongside some of the more general Kuyperian-Reformed resources suggested in this book's introduction. Some of the more important works from recent decades include:

Bebbington, David. *Patterns in History: A Christian Perspective on Historical Thought.* 2nd ed. Vancouver: Regent College, 1990.

Burkinshaw, Robert K. "A Christian Perspective on History." In *Christian Worldview and the Academic Disciplines: Crossing the Academy*, edited by Deane E.D. Downey and Stanley Porter, 278-289. Hamilton, ON and Eugene, OR: McMaster Divinity College Press and Pickwick Publications, 2009.

Dawson, Christopher. *Dynamics of World History.* Edited by John J. Mulloy. La Salle, IL: Sherwood Sugden, 1978.

Fea, John. *Why Study History? Reflecting on the Importance of the Past.* Grand Rapids, MI: Baker Academic, 2013.

Fea, John, Jay Green, and Eric Miller, eds. *Confessing History: Explorations in Christian Faith and the Historian's Vocation.* Notre Dame, IN: Notre Dame University Press, 2010.

Finn, Nathan A. *History: A Student's Guide.* Wheaton, IL: Crossway, 2016.

Green, Jay. *Christian Historiography: Five Rival Versions.* Waco, TX: Baylor University Press, 2015.

Haykin, Michael A.G. *The Empire of the Holy Spirit: Reflections on Biblical and Historical Patterns of Life in the Spirit.* 3rd ed. Peterborough, ON: H&E Academic, 2020.

Irving-Stonebaker, Sarah. *Priests of History: Stewarding the Past in an Ahistoric Age.* Grand Rapids, MI: Zondervan, 2024.

Marsden, George and Frank Roberts, eds. *A Christian View of History?* Grand Rapids, MI: Eerdmans, 1975.

McIntire, C.T. "Dooyeweerd's Philosophy of History." In *The Legacy of Herman Dooyeweerd: Reflections on Critical Philosophy in the Christian Tradition*, edited by C.T. McIntire, 81-117. Lanham, MD: University Press of America, 1985.

McIntire, C.T., ed. *God, History, and Historians: Modern Christian Views of History.* New York: Oxford University Press, 1977.

Seerveld, Calvin. "Dooyeweerd's Idea of 'Historical Development': Christian Respect for Cultural Diversity." *Westminster Theological Journal* 58 no. 1 (Spring 1996): 41-61.

Smit, M.C. *Toward a Christian Conception of History.* Edited and translated by H. Donald Morton and Harry Van Dyke. Lanham, MD: University Press of America, 2002.

Snyder, K. Alan, and Jamin Metcalf. *Many Times and Places: C.S. Lewis and the Value of History.* Hamden, CT: Winged Lion Press, 2023.

Spitz, Lewis W. "The Historian and the Ancient of Days." In *God and Culture: Essays in Honour of Carl F. H. Henry*, edited by D.A. Carson and John D. Woodbridge, 148-161. Grand Rapids, MI: Eerdmans, 1993.

Trueman, Carl R. *Histories and Fallacies: Problems Faced in the Writing of History.* Wheaton, IL: Crossway, 2010.

Wells, Ronald A., ed. *History and the Christian Historian.* Grand Rapids, MI: Eerdmans, 1998.

Wells, Ronald A. *History through the Eyes of Faith.* New York: HarperOne, 1989.

Since history involves the interpretation of human society and culture, Christian thinking in the most relevant neighbouring disciplines such as sociology, political science, theology, philosophy, anthropology, and the creative arts is also indispensable to the Christian historian. For example, even though his approach diverges at some points from the Reformed approach championed in this book, the wide-ranging and theoretically profound works of Catholic sociologist Christian Smith are well worth reading; good places to start include his *Moral, Believing Animals: Human Personhood and Culture* (Oxford University Press, 2003), *What*

Is a Person? Rethinking Humanity, Social Life and the Moral Good from the Person Up (University of Chicago Press, 2010), and *The Sacred Project of American Sociology* (Oxford University Press, 2014).

Christian historians looking for intellectual fellowship beyond their own campus can also consider membership and participation in the Conference on Faith & History (www.faithandhistory.org) an American-based "community of scholars exploring the relationship between Christian faith and history." The CFH publishes the biannual refereed journal *Fides et Historia*. Also of interest is the work of the Davenant Institute (davenantinstitute.org) and its journal *Ad Fontes*, which are dedicated to the retrieval of classical Reformed Protestantism through careful historical and theological study, and which aim to build "networks of friendship and collaboration among evangelical scholars committed to Protestant resourcement."

Bibliography

Ashford, Bruce Riley, and Craig G. Bartholomew. *The Doctrine of Creation: A Constructive Kuyperian Approach*. Downers Grove, IL: IVP Academic, 2020.

Augustine. *Concerning the City of God against the Pagans*. Translated by Henry Bettenson. Introduction by G.R. Evans. London: Penguin, 2003.

Brown, Callum. *Postmodernism for Historians*. New York: Routledge, 2004.

Burkinshaw, Robert K. "A Christian Perspective on History." In *Christian Worldview and the Academic Disciplines:* Cross*ing the Academy*, edited by Deane E. D. Downey and Stanley E. Porter, 278-289. Hamilton, ON and Eugene, OR: McMaster Divinity College Press and Wipf and Stock, 2009.

Butterfield, Herbert. *The Whig Interpretation of History*. London, UK: G. Bell, 1931.

Carr, E. H. *What is History?* London, UK: Penguin, 1961.

Chaplin, Jonathan. *Herman Dooyeweerd: Christian Philosopher of State and Civil Society*. Notre Dame, IN: University of Notre Dame Press, 2011.

Clary, Ian. "Evangelical Historiography: The Debate over Christian History." *Evangelical Quarterly* 87 no. 3 (2015): 225-51.

Clouser, Roy. *The Myth of Religious Neutrality: An Essay on the Hidden Role of Religious Belief in Theories*. Rev. ed. Notre Dame, IN: University of Notre Dame Press, 2005.

Dooyeweerd, Herman. *A New Critique of Theoretical Thought*. Vol. 2, *The General Theory of the Modal Spheres*. Philadelphia: Presbyterian and Reformed Publishing Company, 1969.

Durston, Kirk. "The consequential complexity of history and gratuitous evil." *Religious Studies* 36 (March 2000): 65-80.

Eglinton, James. "From Babel to Pentecost via Paris and Amsterdam: Multilingualism in Neo-Calvinist and Revolutionary Thought." In *Neo-Calvinism and the French Revolution*, edited by James Eglinton and George Harinck, 31-60. London: Bloomsbury T&T Clark, 2014.

Foucault, Michel. *The Archaeology of Knowledge*. Translated by A. M. Sheridan-Smith. New York: Pantheon Books, 1972. {original? L'Archéologie du savoir. Paris: Editions Gallimard, 1969.}

Gaddis, John Lewis. *The Landscape of History: How Historians Map the Past.* Oxford: Oxford University Press, 2002.

Gaines, James R. *Evening in the Palace of Reason: Bach Meets Frederick the Great in the Age of Enlightenment.* New York: Harper Perennial, 2005.

Granatstein, J.L. *Who Killed Canadian History?* Rev. ed. New York: Harper Perennial, 2007.

Hollinger, David A. "The Wrong Question! Please Change the Subject!" *Fides et Historia* 43:2 (Summer/Fall 2011): 34-37.

Hunsberger, George R. *Bearing the Witness of the Spirit: Lesslie Newbigin's Theology of Cultural Plurality*. Grand Rapids, MI: Eerdmans, 1998.

Langbert, Michael, Anthony J. Quain, and Daniel B. Klein. "Faculty Voter Registration in Economics, History, Journalism, Law, and Psychology." *Econ Journal Watch* 13 no. 3 (September 2016): 422-51.

Lewis, C.S. *God in the Dock*. Grand Rapids, MI: William B. Eerdmans, 1970.

Lewis, C.S. *The Weight of Glory and Other Addresses*. San Francisco: HarperSanFrancisco, 2001.

Marwick, Arthur. *The New Nature of History: Knowledge, Evidence, Language.* Chicago: Lyceum, 2001.

McIntire, C.T. "The Ongoing Task of Christian Historiography." In *A Christian View of History?* edited by George Marsden and Frank Roberts, 51-74. Grand Rapids, MI: Eerdmans, 1975.

Mouw, Richard. *He Shines in All That's Fair: Culture and Common Grace.* Grand Rapids, MI: Eerdmans, 2002.

Novick, Peter. *That Noble Dream: The "Objectivity Question" and the American Historical Profession.* Cambridge: Cambridge University Press, 1988.

Plantinga, Alvin. "Christian Philosophy at the End of the Twentieth Century." In *The Analytic Theist: An Alvin Plantinga Reader*, edited by James F. Sennett, 328-52. Grand Rapids, MI: Eerdmans, 1998.

Plantinga, Alvin. *Warrant and Proper Function.* Oxford: Oxford University Press, 1993.

Smith, Christian. *Moral, Believing Animals: Human Personhood and Culture.* Oxford: Oxford University Press, 2003.

Smith, Christian. *The Sacred Project of American Sociology.* Oxford: Oxford University Press, 2014.

Smith, Christian. *What is a Person? Rethinking Humanity, Social Life, and the Moral Good from the Person Up.* Chicago: University of Chicago Press, 2010.

Solzhenitsyn, Aleksandr I. *The Gulag Archipelago, 1918-1956: An Experiment in Literary Investigation, [parts] III-IV*. New York: Harper and Row, 1975.

Thompson, E.P. *The Making of the English Working Class.* New York: Pantheon Books, 1963.

Van Dyke, Harry. "A Taxonomy of Historical Writing." n.d.

Windshuttle, Keith. *The Killing of History.* San Francisco: Encounter, 2000.

Wolters, Albert M. *Creation Regained: Biblical Basics for a Reformational Worldview.* 2nd ed. Grand Rapids, MI: William B. Eerdmans, 2005.

Wolterstorff, Nicholas. *Reason within the Bounds of Religion.* 2nd ed. Grand Rapids, MI: William B. Eerdmans, 1988.

Political Science Regained: The Study of Politics in the Light of Creation, Fall, Redemption and Consummation

David T. Koyzis

What is Political Science? Defining the Discipline

What is political science? If I, as a political scientist, were to apply for a grant to study the role played by turkey vultures in the ecosystem of the Niagara Escarpment, a peer review would quickly inform me that my proposed subject matter falls outside the legitimate range covered by the discipline. But why? Is it not true that ecological issues have been a concern of the political process ever since Rachel Carson published *Silent Spring*[1] more than half a century ago? Yes, it is true, but political debates have also covered a variety of other areas of common concern, such as economic growth, education, road and infrastructure maintenance, and even such contentious issues as the definition of marriage and family. Political scientists do not generally explore ways to stimulate economic growth, how to improve teacher education, which varieties of asphalt will produce durable roads, or how to strengthen communication between spouses. These matters belong to other disciplines with their own legitimate ranges of concern. Political science is not, in short, a "hub science," with the other disciplines extending like spokes from the political centre, the views of Aristotle to the contrary notwithstanding.

What then distinguishes political science from other sciences? To begin with, it is a human or social science insofar as it studies the world of human interactions and interrelationships from a particular vantage point. The habits of the turkey vulture may not fall within this definition, but debates over how best to protect the turkey vulture certainly do. Political scientists themselves may not weigh the factors contributing to a strong economy, but others do so in a variety of settings, and these are of interest to political scientists. Similarly, political scientists do not evaluate the durability of asphalt, but political *leaders* necessarily do so

1 Rachel Carson, *Silent Spring* (Boston and New York: Houghton Mifflin, 1962).

as they address the matter in public forums. It is what these leaders do that political scientists undertake to analyze using the tools of their trade. On the other hand, if my wife and I debate the respective virtues of various brands of asphalt for our front driveway, political scientists will take no notice. If political science is indeed a human science, obviously not everything human beings do socially comes within its purview. Because political science is concerned with political life, this suggests that, before we can properly define the discipline, we must first define politics itself.

What is politics?

Our word *politics* has a Greek root, as cinematic character Gus Portokalos[2] might put it. Polis (πόλις) is sometimes translated as *state* but is more generally rendered as *city*. From this same word come several related words such as *police*, *policy*, *monopoly*, *metropolitan*, and *cosmopolitan*, all of which have to do with human life in community. For the ancient Greeks the polis was the highest of human communities necessary for the attainment of the full measure of the virtues. It was totalistic and multi-functional, ensuring that the local deities were properly placated, that citizens were educated in the ethos of the city, that its borders were defended against external enemies, and that its various social strata were maintained in their respective places. The polis was at once a moral and religious community, commanding the highest allegiance of its citizens. A division between church and state would obviously not be in the cards, because to be a good citizen meant to worship the gods and goddesses of the city as well. Piety and patriotism were a single act aimed at the overall good of the polis. Several points need to be made that are relevant to an adequate definition of politics.

First, there is a persistent tendency to define it with respect to the *scope* of its concerns. Because our driveway is the proper concern of our family alone, most observers would recognize that it is not of political import. On the other hand, the quality of the asphalt on Ontario's 400-series highways is generally acknowledged to be a political matter because it affects so many more people. Yet this may not be enough to bring the matter under the proper purview of political science. If the Vatican clarifies its position on divorced and remarried Catholics receiving the Eucharist, potentially many more people are affected by its ruling than those driving the highways of Canada's Golden Horseshoe. Nevertheless, the guild of political scientists might not approve a grant application for the study of papal teachings on divorce and remarriage, except insofar as

2. Played by Michael Constantine in *My Big Fat Greek Wedding*, directed by Joel Zwick (Golden Circle Films, 2002), 1 hr, 35 min.

they would impact public family law. This tells us that the sheer number of people affected by an action is insufficient *by itself* to place it under the larger rubric of politics.

Second, many observers understand politics to involve some level of *conflict* in the conduct of human affairs. Ely Culbertson defines politics as "the diplomatic name for the law of the jungle."[3] While this is perhaps an overly dark view of politics, it does alert us to the reality that, in a world of natural limits and large egos, human beings tend to make claims on the commons that are mutually incompatible. This raises the distributive element of political life, which is incorporated into the approaches of several political scientists, such as David Easton[4] and Harold Lasswell.[5] Even if the incompatible claims are not of a material nature, participants in the political process still bring to it different expectations, some of which are of a basic ideological character. What is the common good and what does it require? Where do we derive the principles of justice under which we all must live and move and have our being? Socialists and liberals, for example, will give us different answers to these questions, and their efforts to implement them inevitably bring them into conflict. The major wars of the last century were indeed ideological wars, pitting the various political visions and illusions against each other. This underscores the reality that conflict, if left as such, can be deadly—sometimes spectacularly so.

Which brings up the third feature of many standard definitions of politics: if human life is riddled with conflicts, we must have a way to *settle or at least to defuse such conflicts* so that lives are preserved and people can live, if not happily ever after, at least with a reasonable degree of interpersonal harmony. Sir Bernard Crick classically defines politics as the peaceful conciliation of diversity within a particular unit of rule.[6] If we are to live at peace with each other, and if political life is how that happens, then we must focus on those things we have in common, utilizing them to iron out our differences as best we can. If Clausewitz thought of war as the continuation of politics by other means,[7] Crick, Hannah Arendt, Jean Bethke Elshtain, and many others would disagree

3. Mark McCutcheon, *Roget's Superthesaurus* (Cincinnati: Writer's Digest Books, 2004), 443.

4. See, e.g., David Easton, *The Political System: An Inquiry into the State of Political Science*, 2nd ed. (New York: Alfred A. Knopff, 1953, 1971), and *A Framework for Political Analysis* (Englewood Cliffs, NJ: Prentice-Hall, 1965).

5. Harold Lasswell, *Politics: Who Gets What, When, How* (New York: Whittlesey House, 1936).

6. Bernard Crick, *In Defence of Politics*, 5th ed. (London and New York: Continuum, 2000), 21.

7 Carl von Clausewitz, *On War*, Book 1, chapter 1, section 24.

violently—if that adverb is admissible in this context. Instead, war represents nothing less than the breakdown of ordinary politics, which aims at conciliating conflicts before they reach such a fatal impasse.

If such conciliation is to occur, it is scarcely surprising that many observers emphasize human speech as a central component of politics. For Arendt *speech* enables co-operative *action* in the company of one's fellows, preferably in the context of a local body politic where citizens can more easily exemplify the civic friendship extolled by Aristotle.[8] Speech is also central to the advocates of deliberative democracy, which places a premium on the human capacity to talk together and, one hopes, to iron out whatever differences might keep people apart.[9] It is by no means incidental that our word *parliament* stems from the French word *parler*, which means *to speak*. If the two sides to a dispute are still talking, then we take that as a good sign. If they have broken off talks, we get nervous and start to prepare for the worst. Talking seems to be intrinsic to the political process.

But once again, talking for purposes of conciliating conflict is not enough to distinguish politics from the nonpolitical. In ordinary conversations, we are accustomed to hearing people talk about *church* politics, *corporate* politics, *front office* politics, and the like. If we were to accept so expansive an account of politics, it would have to include the deliberations occurring at the Second Vatican Council, the Synod of the Christian Reformed Church, the Board of Trustees of Yale University, and the meeting of the local garden club. Yet once again the guild of academic political scientists would likely see the internal machinations of even a *national* birdwatching society to be beyond the scope of their professional interests. For purposes of defining politics, it seems we shall have to exclude the deliberations of elders in a consistory or session meeting. Deliberation must be about something that is distinctively political. But, as Sheldon S. Wolin asked more than half a century ago,[10] what exactly *is* political?

This brings us to the fourth feature of politics: its *institutional* setting. Strictly speaking, politics takes place within the context of a set of interconnected institutions which together form a systemic whole. Most of us intuitively understand this, but many theoretical efforts to account for politics nevertheless tend to miss it by emphasizing the process that occurs therein. This web of institutions might collectively be called *gov-*

8. Hannah Arendt, *The Human Condition* (Chicago: University of Chicago Press, 1958).

9. See, e.g., Amy Gutmann and Dennis Thompson, *Democracy and Disagreement* (Cambridge, MA: Belknapp/Harvard, 1998).

10. Sheldon S. Wolin, *Politics and Vision* (Boston: Little, Brown & Co., 1960).

ernment, although *state* might be the better term, insofar as it designates a community of citizens bound together by something shared. I am a citizen of the Canadian state, but I am obviously not a member of the Canadian government. As a citizen I have a certain relationship to my fellow citizens characterized by a greater or lesser degree of communal solidarity. This political community of which we are members does not by any means exhaust who we are as persons created in God's image, nor is it our highest loyalty, as the ancient Greeks held. Yet insofar as we are members of this political community, we do have a special relationship with the government, which includes parliaments, executives, courts, bureaucracies, constitutional documents, and legal codes, all of which contribute to human flourishing in a distinctive way.

Although we might be loath to admit it, a fifth feature of politics is its coercive character. The political institutions that govern a community inevitably have at their disposal a variety of means to enforce the decisions they have made for those under their jurisdiction. When a law is enacted or an administrative decision made, it must be obeyed. If it is not, those violating the law must be penalized accordingly. Once more, although Crick, Arendt, and others emphasize the deliberation that goes into political life, this talking cannot go on for ever. At some point, our parliamentary or administrative bodies must come to a decision, and that decision will necessarily be binding on everyone, even on those unhappy with the result. For this reason, our political actors have established domestic police forces, correctional institutions, and military forces to ensure that justice will be done in the real world and not simply remain an ideal to which we earnestly hope everyone will voluntarily conform.

This brings us at last to the sixth feature of politics, which is its *jural* character. Political life is uniquely oriented to the doing of *public justice* within the larger context of a differentiated society. To be sure, all persons and all communities must see that justice be done in all their activities. Marriage requires fidelity between spouses, which is another way of affirming that husbands and wives must treat each other justly by living up to their vows of exclusive sexual faithfulness. If a man cheats on his wife, there is a profound sense in which he can be said to have done her an injustice. Yet the state's justice is different in that it is *public* justice—a justice that is tied to the state's territoriality and impacts all individuals and communities domiciled within its boundaries. This is not to say, of course, that families, marriages, church congregations, labour unions, and businesses are *parts* of the state in the way that arms and legs are parts of the human body. This is a totalitarian understanding of the state's relationship to other communities, each of which instead must be recognized to have its own integrity and distinct status in society. However, it is certainly true that each of these in some fashion functions within the territorial jurisdiction of the state. As such, the state must do justice to each of these, recognizing its distinctive task and its own contribution to the common good. The authority of parents within the family is not a delegated authority enjoyed at the pleasure of king and council. Such authority is conferred directly by the God who has called it into being.

This jural element requires a balancing of legitimate interests. Given the pluriformity of an ordinary human society, these interests are necessarily of a dizzying diversity and are inextricably related to the respective callings we have in the authoritative offices we are granted by God's grace. Human beings are at once kings and commoners, bishops and elders, deacons and lay members, teachers and students, employers and employees, managers and labourers, New Yorkers and Parisians, Italian-Canadians and African-Americans, Christians and Muslims, fathers and mothers, sons and daughters, and so forth.[11] When we think of the need to conciliate *interests* in a polity, our mind tends to gravitate towards the reality of *interest groups* locked in a competitive struggle over the public square or, more crassly, the public purse. To be sure, in the real world, this is what the political process often looks like. In this context political authorities are called to hear the respective claims of these groups and to decide, as Harold Lasswell puts it, who gets what, when, and how.[12]

Crick and Arendt are conspicuously silent on the status of justice as a defining feature of political life, perhaps because they fear that a particular—and contestable—*vision* of justice might short-circuit the deliberative process in the public square, if advanced as undoubted truth. Yet, as Augustine already understood a millennium and a half ago, without justice political rule is indistinguishable from the predations of a band of thieves. How then does political authority wield its coercive power justly? An answer to this question cannot be found simply by an analysis of the mechanics of interest group politics apart from recourse to normative principles. Otherwise, we are left with the bitter reality of a public square being inevitably parcelled out amongst the wealthiest, most powerful, and most articulate such groups. The political process becomes a competitive game, with certain procedural rules to be sure, but also with definite winners and losers. In which case, the most vulnerable and least articulate interests end up with proportionately less of that to which they may have a legitimate claim, namely, justice itself.

11. For an exploration of this pluriformity of authorities, see the present author's own *We Answer to Another: Authority, Office, and the Image of God* (Eugene, OR: Pickwick Publications, 2014).

12. Harold D. Lasswell, *Politics: Who Gets What, When, How* (London and New York: Whittlesey House, McGraw-Hill, 1936).

Crick has the beginnings of an answer to the dilemma raised by ordinary interest group politics in his definition of politics. Yes, it is the peaceful conciliation of diversity, but one in which the various interests are conciliated "by giving them a share in power in proportion to their importance to the welfare and the survival of the whole community."[13] This apparently falls short of the visions he so fears being imposed on the free deliberation characteristic of political life, yet it does constitute a bare-bones principle of justice in all but name. There is still plenty to discuss, but the discussion necessarily occurs within the context of a larger framework of principles. What do these principles look like? The classic definition of justice is *rendering to each his or her due*, that is, giving people what they deserve. The entire history of reflection on the nature of justice revolves around efforts to fill this purely formal definition with substantive content.

But, we might ask, are such debates matters for political science? Although the jural would appear to be a necessary element in comprehending the nature of political life, not all political scientists would regard *justice* as a fit matter for political science *qua* science, except insofar as real flesh-and-blood people have opinions on justice capable of being studied scientifically. Such a study will not, of course, tell us what justice *is*, only what various people *think* it is. We shall return to this issue in a later section.

Creation, Fall and Redemption in Political Life

Now that we have a plausible working definition of politics, we must address this question: Is politics a created good, a necessary evil, a good mandated by the existence of sin, or some combination thereof? What is God's purpose in mandating political rule within the human communities he has brought into being? We know he *has* a purpose, because God has built meaning into all that he has created, and this includes our lives in community. Furthermore, because God is just, he demands that we do justice as well in every one of life's spheres and activities. We noted in the introductory chapter that Christian faith is ineluctably connected to the biblical story, which begins with God. God is a personal God who has brought everything into being and has freely chosen to relate to his creation, and in a special way to human beings whom he has made in his image (Genesis 1:26-27, 5:1, 9:6) and established as rulers over the rest of creation (Psalm 8:4-5). God is God, and we are his divine image. Yet this God, while transcending his creation, is not a distant deistic abstraction. He is a loving God, offering himself to us, not as a specimen

13. Crick, *In Defence of Politics*, 21.

to be examined under glass, but as the living God in whom we live and breathe and have our being (Acts 17:28). The biblical story nowhere tries to persuade the reader of or to offer an apology for God's existence. It does not try to define or conceptualize him. It simply begins with God and quickly moves on to his creative activity in the very first verse.

Thus while the biblical story is undoubtedly complex, stretching over several millennia, it can be comprehended in terms of four central themes: creation (Genesis 1-2), fall into sin (Genesis 3), redemption in Jesus Christ (Genesis 4-Revelation), and ultimate consummation in the kingdom of God (Isaiah, Zechariah, Matthew-John, Revelation). Where does political life fit into this grand redemptive narrative? The answer to this question is complicated by the fact that the Genesis account places our first parents in a garden prior to their fall into sin. Because only two persons are mentioned in this account, and because political life appears to presuppose a more complex and more populous society with a developed culture, it is not immediately clear from the relevant texts whether politics would have developed in the absence of human sin. After all, a garden populated and tended by two naked people would not seem an especially promising setting for political order as we understand it today.

Nevertheless, the authors of Genesis are quite clear that human beings are created to be culture-makers, as we noted in the introduction. Yet even if we admit that politics is part of culture, this in itself cannot answer our question whether it is a pre- or post-lapsarian phenomenon. Is politics needed only to rectify or ameliorate the effects of human sin? Or is it needed because of who we are in our fulness as those created in God's image? Throughout the centuries, Christians have answered these questions differently. On the one hand, we have Augustine, the great fourth- and fifth-century theologian and philosopher whose *City of God* set the tone for a Christian understanding of history for future generations. Augustine saw in political authority a remedial function necessitated by the presence of human sin. On the other hand, Thomas Aquinas, following Aristotle, saw political order as something rooted in our human nature. We are political beings by nature, gravitating to each other in the larger context of community, whose laws are capable of being comprehended by reasonable beings.

John Calvin famously treats political authority in the final chapter of his *Institutes of the Christian Religion* (4.20). Although he is heir more to Augustine than to Thomas, he nevertheless speaks of the calling of the civil magistrate in unusually glowing terms: "Its function among men is no less than that of bread, water, sun, and air; indeed, its place of honour is far more excellent."[14] Similarly, Johannes Althusius (1563-1638), a Calvinist political theorist whose role in the city of Emden paralleled Calvin's in Geneva, could write: "Politics is the art of associating (*consociandi*) men for the purpose of establishing, cultivating, and conserving social life among them. . . . The end of political 'symbiotic' man is holy, just, comfortable, and happy symbiosis, a life lacking nothing either necessary or useful. Truly, in living this life no man is self-sufficient, or adequately endowed by nature."[15] Politics, in other words, is made necessary by the very nature of life in community.

We believe that the historical and perhaps even sociological evidence points to an affirmation of both reasons for political life. Particularly in a society such as ours characterized by a pluriformity of communities, each governed by its own unique structure and purpose, a specialized institution is needed to co-ordinate the interactions and interrelationships amongst them. This need is unrelated to human sin, stemming rather from the intrinsic limits within which we must live and work, not only as individuals but also as communities. Obedience to the word of God entails not claiming more than we have a right to. This is the implication of the proscription against coveting in the Decalogue (Exodus 20:17, Deuteronomy 5:21). As those created in God's image undertaking to fulfil the office that this image entails, we properly desire to see public justice done.

Yet it is easier to will *that* justice be done than to know *what* justice entails in the concrete, simply because our knowledge and other capacities are limited, as is everything in God's creation. Even apart from sin, it is entirely plausible that the claims of diverse interests would conflict, not in the sense of producing overt struggle or violence, but in the sense of being logically mutually incompatible. The jural aspect of reality is a *created* aspect, not the unfortunate by-product of evil. The authors of the Proverbs instruct the reader not to remove the ancient boundary markers (Proverbs 22:28; 23:10), but what if the boundary is not explicitly marked? What is mine and what is thine may not be altogether clear, thus calling for an adjudicating authority to determine what properly belongs to whom. Again this would be the case, even without the presence of sin.

Of course, the fall into sin did take place, as human beings have rebelled against God's intentions for their lives. Because of this, we too often deliberately pervert justice. The relationship between sin and political authority is a complex—and even paradoxical—one. Not only is

14. John Calvin, *Institutes of the Christian Religion*, trans. Ford Lewis Battles, ed. John T. McNeill (Philadelphia: Westminster Press, 1960), 4.20.3, p. 1488.

15. Johannes Althusius, *The Politics of Johannes Althusius*, translated, with an Introduction by Frederick S. Carney (Boston: Beacon Press, 1964), 12.

government needed to remedy the effects of sin, but in so doing governments themselves are affected by sin. Which means that governments, in carrying out their divinely appointed task of doing public justice, are themselves fully capable of committing injustice. The ancient Greeks and Romans recognized that, left on their own with no countervailing institutional checks, monarchy will tend to degenerate into tyranny and aristocracy into self-serving oligarchy. The Bible records that the wisest king on record, namely, Solomon, eventually abandoned his unwavering fidelity to God and became oppressive towards those Israelites not of his own tribe of Judah, thus contributing to the rebellion of the northern tribes against his son and successor Rehoboam (1 Kings 12). Both biblical and extra-biblical histories are replete with episodes of tyrannical rulers preying on their own and neighbouring peoples.

Throughout the centuries political philosophers in a variety of traditions have reflected on the best means of lessening the possibility of such injustices, if not altogether preventing them. In pagan and biblical traditions alike there is remarkable consensus that some form of constitutional checks are needed to ameliorate the effects of sin and to rectify tyranny, often in the form of lower magistrates legally authorized to restrain the power of the chief magistrate. Although the classical mixed constitution is historically associated with the name of the Greek historian Polybius (c. 200-c. 118 BC), we find it already in seminal form in Plato and Aristotle. The mixed constitution combines the best elements of monarchy, aristocracy, and democracy into a composite form which, it was generally thought, would prove more durable than any of the three in their pure forms. Even Samuel's warning against the dangers of monarchy (1 Samuel 8) might be seen as rooted in an entirely realistic appraisal of what happens when a fallible human being is set in a specific office without adequate constraints placed on his powers. The Hebrew prophets' apparent preference for the older power-sharing arrangement of the judges, as established by Moses (Exodus 18), could be viewed as an affirmation of what would come to be labelled the mixed constitution, which is how Thomas Aquinas understands it.[16] We continue to find a preference for the mixed constitution in the writings of Thomas, Calvin, Althusius, Montesquieu, James Madison, and others right up to recent times.

However, we should immediately be aware that the constitutional remedy for tyranny is not itself redemptive. Nor is the role of government in ameliorating the effects of sin. At most government and the laws under which it functions entail what Abraham Kuyper called a "common grace" remedy for sin. Common grace is that divine grace which God bestows on all peoples irrespective of their standing with respect to belief and un-

16. Thomas Aquinas, *Summa Theologiae*, I-II, q. 105, a. 1, resp.

belief. We read in Scripture that "he makes his sun rise on the evil and on the good, and sends rain on the just and on the unjust" (Matthew 5:45, RSV). Government cannot eradicate sin, despite the oft-made claim that we should strive to, say, *end* terrorism, bullying, violence against women, etc. It can be expected to bring about only a proximate justice falling well short of God's ultimate justice.

Does this mean then that government has nothing to do with redemption in Jesus Christ? Not at all. To say that politics cannot redeem is by no means to assert that politics itself is incapable of being redeemed. If redemption in Jesus Christ is cosmic in scope, and if politics is a part of the cosmos, then it too is not exempt in principle from redemption. So what does redeemed politics look like? Or, as some might prefer, what *might* it look like if it were to happen? How do we go about bringing it into being? Quite simply, a redeemed politics is one that is redirected away from sin and towards its created task of doing public justice to individuals and communities alike so that they can more easily fulfil their respective callings. Here is where things become complicated, because many will be tempted to ask: Are we there yet? Or will we see it in our lifetimes?

The first thing to remember, however, is that we are not the ones doing the redeeming, even if, by God's grace, we find ourselves occupying political offices in which even a small measure of this vision of justice might be implemented. God accomplishes his redemption through Jesus Christ in his own time and through his own chosen means. For those of us who are in Christ, this means that we live out his redemption in our whole lives during the time that God in his grace has given us, but we do so as those awaiting the final consummation of God's kingdom, which lies in the unknown future. The kingdom of God is both now and not yet. It has arrived in the person of Jesus Christ, but its ultimate fulfilment awaits his promised return at the end of the present age. It is by no means accidental that the language Scripture uses to describe the present and future age is overtly political language. So much of the language for God used in the Bible makes liberal use of political metaphors. God is a king, that is, a political ruler whose law maintains order within his creation: "The Lord is *king;* let the earth rejoice!" (Psalm 97:1 NLT) "For God is the *king* of all the earth; sing praises with a psalm!" (Psalm 47:7) "Arise, O God, *judge* the earth; for you shall inherit all the nations!" (Psalm 82:8)

Given that we await the final consummation of God's kingdom, even as it in some fashion is already present with us today, we may find ourselves asking what political life will look like in the new heaven and the new earth. Will it be continuous with political life as we know it now? Will there be separate states, governments, parliaments, and bureaucracies? We have reason from the later chapters of Isaiah to believe that nations will not only exist but will bring the riches of their distinctive cultures into God's kingdom (e.g., Isaiah 60:11-13). We can assume there will be no jails or hangmen, which are linked with sin, but beyond that we cannot say with precision what the redeemed world will look like in its mature state and what role political rule will play in it. It is, however, worth noting that the language of city and kingship are applied to this final condition throughout the biblical narrative. Political life will reach its fulfilment in the person of Jesus Christ, whose reign will be unending.

Creation, Fall and Redemption in the Study of Politics

First, politics, and now science. What does it mean to call the study of political life a science? There can be little doubt that, among the disciplines that together comprise the modern academy, political science is by far among the oldest. The term *political science*, or πολιτική επιστήμη, has its origins in Plato and Aristotle, if not earlier. In his dialogue, *The Statesman* (Πολιτικός), Plato discusses the art or craft of politics (πολιτικοὐ τέχνης), which he views as a specialized discipline required for the ruler to discharge his responsibilities well.[17] This art is more important even than the laws, because the laws cannot administer themselves and, more to the point, are incapable of ensuring perfect justice in individual cases. The art of statesmanship is distinguished from other arts by its architectonic focus: it supervises the field of action within which the other arts find their respective places. The statesman has the "task of weaving the web of the state,"[18] which includes, not just the maintenance of institutions, but the pædagogical task of forging the "bond of true conviction" within the young.[19] In *The Republic* (Πολιτεία) Plato more explicitly connects the acquisition of the art of ruling with philosophical knowledge, that is, knowledge of the good, the true, and the beautiful, of which good, true, and beautiful things are but a pale reflection. Such knowledge is gained, not by experience, but by the Socratic method of reasoning. This guarantees the scientific nature of the discipline.

Aristotle differs from his mentor Plato in several ways. Although he agrees that political science possesses a supervisory status within the polis, he is more careful to distinguish amongst the different kinds of human activities, each of which is oriented by nature to its own proper end. Pol-

17. Plato, *The Statesman*, 267a. The Greek term is in the genitive case.

18. Plato, *The Statesman* (308e), trans. J. B. Skemp, in Edith Hamilton and Huntington Cairns, ed., *Plato: The Collected Dialogues* (Princeton: Princeton University Press/Bollingen Series LXXI, 1961), p. 1081.

19. Plato, *The Statesman*, 309d.

itical science he calls the "master art" because "it ordains which of the sciences should be studied in a state [ἐν ταῖς πόλεσι], and which each class of citizens should learn and up to what point they should learn them."[20] Human society is composed of a variety of communities all of which seek the goods which constitute the proper ends of those communities. The polis (πόλις), which translators have sometimes rendered as "the state," is the highest such community and thus "aims at good in a greater degree than any other, and at the highest good."[21] Man by nature is a political animal (πολιτικὸν ζῷον), which means that human beings are constituted by their very being in a way that conduces to the formation of political communities.[22] One can hardly imagine humanity without this form of community, which, as Aristotle believes, is essential to the formation of the virtuous person. Political science (πολιτική επιστήμη) is thus not a superfluous enterprise. It is not a luxury item added on top of the basic needs of human life. Because the virtues constituting the end of human nature cannot be obtained in isolation, only life in the polis can enable us to fulfil our true humanity.

Another difference between Plato and Aristotle is perhaps more subtle but no less significant. While Plato, particularly in *The Republic*, expends considerable energy constructing a city in speech, that is, an ideal polis in which justice will be most easily realized, Aristotle brings a certain empirical orientation to his own political science. His *Constitution of the Athenians*, discovered as recently as 1879, is a description of the Athenian political system as it functioned during his lifetime. Aristotle is said to have authored 170 such accounts of the political systems of various polities of his day, apparently indicative of a turn in the discipline from the ideal to the real. Both the *Nicomachean Ethics* and the *Politics* further demonstrate the turn to the empirical. However, even Aristotle could never consider separating an empirical constitution from the virtue that it facilitated in the person.

The political virtue par excellence is φρόνησις, variously translated as *practical wisdom* or *prudence*. It enables the person, particularly the ruler, to choose wisely in contingent circumstances. Political science as a discipline is ultimately in the service of this practical wisdom, which differs in kind from such other intellectual virtues as τεχνή (art), επιστήμη (scientific knowledge), σοφία (philosophic wisdom), and νούς (intuitive reason). Each of these differs with respect to the degree of certainty at-

20. Aristotle, *Nicomachean Ethics* (1094a-1094b), trans. W. D. Ross, in Richard McKeon, ed., *The Basic Works of Aristotle* (New York: Random House, 1941), p. 936.

21. Aristotle, *Politica* (1252a), trans. Benjamin Jowett, in *Basic Works of Aristotle*, p. 1127.

22. Aristotle, *Politica*, 1253a.

tached to the outcome. One can predict with nearly absolute certainty the phases of the moon or the return of Halley's Comet. By contrast, one cannot be completely sure that Athens' decision to invade Sparta—or Washington's decision to invade Baghdad—is the right one, even if available intelligence is fully taken into account, motives of the relevant actors thoroughly analyzed, and practical considerations exhaustively weighed in the balance. A bad outcome does not necessarily invalidate the rightness of the political decision that led to it, due to what Hannah Arendt has aptly described as the frailty of human affairs.[23]

This implies that, epistemically speaking, the person is more likely to acquire practical wisdom through the experience of making actual decisions rather than by engaging in a method of argumentation such as the Socratic method or even Kant's categorical imperative. This is why Aristotle can make what seems to us a peculiar statement that a young person is not a fit student of political science due precisely to that lack of life experience that makes for virtuous actions. Practice may not make perfect, as the old saying has it, but it does facilitate the acquisition of ordinary virtue. Political science may not approach the status of physics, astronomy, and mathematics, but it has a definite role to play in governing well a community of ordinary citizens.

While Aristotle understood better than Plato that the diversity of fields of study calls for different methods appropriate to each, neither was able to see politics or its study as part of God's creation. For the ancient Greeks matter is eternal, with a divine personage—a *demiurge* (δημιουργός, or "public worker")—imposing form on a chaotic matter.[24] Thus there is no *creatio ex nihilo*, or creation out of nothing, but a pre-existing something that antedates the initial creative act of the *demiurge*. Whatever god might be said to exist is thus less than the God who reveals himself in creation, in Scripture, and, above all, in Jesus Christ. This inability to recognize the cosmos as God's creation is evidence already of the impact of the Fall on both the practice and the study of politics. A major implication of this inability is a failure to see the orderly character of the cosmos and to check one's perceptions against that order. Plato's orientation to an ideal city as the goal of his theoretical reflections, coupled with the form/matter dichotomy, leads him to assume that order must be imposed from without, an assumption that rules out not only widespread participation of ordinary people in political life but an acknowledgement of the ways people order their own lives in community. In short, he detects order only in one facet of creation, seeing it in opposition to another

23. Hannah Arendt, *The Human Condition* (Chicago: University of Chicago Press, 1958), 188-192.

24. See Plato, *Timaeus* 28a.

facet embodying the principle of disorder. The directional opposition between good and evil is now effectively ontologized, with good and evil built into the very structure of the cosmos.

In the thirteenth century the Dominican scholar Thomas Aquinas attempted to synthesize the available knowledge of his day into one systematic whole. For him this entailed borrowing heavily from Aristotle and the Stoics and undertaking to harmonize their insights with biblical revelation and the teachings of the church fathers. While no one can doubt the brilliance of Thomas' philosophical enterprise and the influence it would have on subsequent thinkers over the centuries, Thomas' inattention to the religious worldviews underpinning the ideas he used produced certain tensions in his thought, including that between virtue ethics (Aristotle), which located norms in the actions of virtuous persons, and natural law ethics (Stoics), which viewed norms as conformity to a higher law. These tensions prompted the early modern thinkers largely to abandon the scholastic philosophy of Thomas and his heirs and to reach for something new and ostensibly more rigorous and scientific.

Jumping ahead several centuries, we find two related developments relevant to our understanding of political science. The first is the *establishment of the modern state*, which occurred around five hundred years ago. No single event can be connected with this development, but in general we must credit several royal dynasties with the consolidation of territorial realms within which they could claim undisputed sovereignty or, better, ultimate political authority. Prior to this time western Europe was characterized by a feudal framework in which the distinction between private ownership and public jurisdiction was exceedingly hazy. Did the king *own* his realm outright? Or was he merely the chief magistrate within the realm? This was not altogether clear and would not become so for a number of centuries. Under feudalism a single ruler might have ultimate authority over one piece of land but be vassal to another ruler in a second piece of land and have a completely different title before his name. For example, for not quite two centuries after 1066 the Kings of England were also the Dukes of Normandy and in the latter capacity owed allegiance to the King of France.

The modern state developed under the auspices of these monarchs initially at the far western periphery of Europe. England, Scotland, France, Spain, and Portugal were among the very first of the modern states and were presided over by Tudor, Stuart, Bourbon, Habsburg, and Bragança rulers respectively, all of whom had first to limit, if not destroy, the independent powers of the nobility and of the institutional church hierarchy. These countries, not so coincidentally, were also the first to explore and ultimately settle the New World, primarily because they were the first to establish the political institutional basis for undertaking such huge ventures. When other countries, such as Germany and Italy, finally became unified states in the mid-nineteenth century, they did so following the precedents established three or four centuries earlier by their far western counterparts. The modern notion of the state (*lo stato*) as a community of citizens has been attributed to the sixteenth-century Florentine statesman and publicist Niccolò Machiavelli.[25] It is perhaps one of the ironies of history that our modern democratic states, with their strong emphasis on citizen participation, could not have come about except for the path-breaking efforts of absolute monarchs to consolidate uncontested sovereignty over a specific territorial entity.

The second development relevant to our present discussion is the explosive expansion of knowledge associated with the *scientific revolution* of the seventeenth century in Europe. The pioneering work of Copernicus, Galileo, Newton, and Kepler is familiar enough not to warrant further exploration here. No one can doubt that their efforts radically reshaped our view of the natural world, making possible the great scientific discoveries and technological breakthroughs that would alter the lives initially of westerners and eventually of people around the globe by the beginning of the twenty-first century. What we should note, however, is that this scientific revolution had a paradoxical effect. On the one hand, it represented a huge broadening of our knowledge of God's creation and the ways that it works. Tremendous advances in mathematics, physics, chemistry, and astronomy greatly expanded the horizons of human knowledge as the hold over the popular imagination of astrology, alchemy, and general superstition began to recede. On the other hand, however, along with these undoubted advances in the human project, the scientific revolution represented a pronounced narrowing of the traditional understanding of knowledge.

Up until the dawn of the modern era, it was generally assumed that either all knowledge was of one piece (e.g., Plato), or there were different types of knowledge capable of being grasped by different methods (e.g., Aristotle). But it was generally agreed that the term *knowledge*—in Greek, επιστήμη; in Latin, *scientia*—covered the full range of human faculties for understanding the world. It was possible to have knowledge of the movement of the stars and planets through the heavens. It was possible to know the habits of beasts in the forests and fields, and in the seas and skies. It was likewise possible to know what it means to live the good life and to know what is good and what is evil. We are capable of knowing what is virtuous and what is vicious, what is right and what is wrong. The political side of this had the great philosophers of the past undertaking

25. See Hannah Arendt, *On Revolution* (New York: Viking Press, 1963), p. 32.

to discern what is the best polity and how it might contribute to human betterment. Efforts to define justice and to determine what made for a just constitution were integral components of πολιτική επιστήμη—political science, as understood in its premodern sense.

Beginning with the long-lived English philosopher Thomas Hobbes (1588-1679), however, this began to change. Indeed, Hobbes can with considerable justification be labelled the first modern political scientist, undertaking to anchor the discipline in observable phenomena rather than in metaphysical notions of a normative character. Hobbes is a philosophical materialist and, as such, stakes out his own territory in opposition to those whom he derisively labels "deceived philosophers, and deceived, or deceiving Schoolmen."[26] Thomas Aquinas, following Aristotle, had said that happiness consists in living the life according to virtue. Hobbes, by contrast, defines "felicity" as the continual satisfaction of one's desires, such desires differing according to the subjective preferences of those possessing them. Aristotle had defined virtue as a mean between vicious extremes, such that courage, for example, was a mean between the vices of cowardice and recklessness. Hobbes, however, defines virtue as that quality which others esteem in a person: "And by virtues intellectual, are always understood such abilities of the mind, as men praise, value, and desire should be in themselves. . . ."[27] Similarly, reason, which the scholastic philosophers had understood to prescribe a normative moral framework for human actions, is for Hobbes simply the ability to reckon from consequences within the larger context of the person's aversions and desires.

Hobbes' approach is not only rooted in a radically nominalistic epistemology, but it is predicated on a hard boundary between empirical knowledge and other kinds of purported knowledge. For Hobbes we cannot know what *justice* is as a principle transcending personal preferences. Justice is rooted in the perpetual human quest to avoid a violent death and to advance the power to achieve one's desires. Might and right are coextensive in Hobbes. My complaint of having been done an injustice is invalid if I lack the capacity to back it up. This has significant implications for the political scientist, whose agenda must now undergo a radical shift. No more can the political scientist attempt to build the ideal city along the lines of Plato. Neither can she tell us the meaning of justice. Hobbes begins his brilliant and influential *Leviathan* by treating sensation and appearances, not human nature, which, he asserts, we cannot know scientifically. In the same way, the modern political scientist

26. Hobbes, *Leviathan or The Matter, Forme and Power of a Common Wealth Ecclesiasticall and Civil* (London: Andrew Crooke, 1651), I, 3.1.3.

27. *Leviathan*, chapter 8.

cannot tell us what is just and what is unjust, but she can tell us what people *think* justice is, in other words, she must limit her attentions to what is capable of being observed and measured. We can easily work with survey data tabulating the preferences of so many respondents and in this way make scientific assessments of people's subjective understandings of justice. But we cannot scientifically determine the nature of justice itself, which lies beyond the scope of science, understood in its modern sense.

The upshot of this Hobbesian move is that a principle once understood to stand at the centre of political reflection was now eliminated as a proper object of study. Of course, one could still claim to *know* what justice is and what it demands of political officials, but it would be impossible to anchor this so-called knowledge in anything other than subjective preferences. Science tells us that such a claim to knowledge is not knowledge at all. It lies, rather, within a realm of values which cannot be publicly verified according to the new canons of the scientific method. Within this epistemological framework, the most we can claim to know for certain is what various people value with respect to their notions of justice. If we cannot know what justice truly is, we can nevertheless know what other people *think* justice truly is.

Although this approach to political science would end up carrying the day in subsequent centuries, another form of thinking about politics rooted in the older normative approaches, namely, *political ideology*, would carve out its own space, particularly after the French Revolution of 1789, offering visions proponents would attempt to implement through practical means. Such approaches, grouped under the various partisan labels of liberalism, conservatism, nationalism, democratism, socialism, anarchism, and so forth, would reshape the discipline in ways that did not exactly conform to the canons of the scientific method, and in many cases seemed to run at cross purposes to them, yet managed to captivate and mobilize the efforts of academics and political actors alike.[28] Thus the tradition was spawned of the activist academic, who, while fulfilling the expectations of the larger scholarly community, appears also to be following this well-known Marxian adage: "The philosophers have only interpreted the world, in various ways; the point, however, is to change it."[29] That this approach does not comport very well with the positivism of Hobbes and his heirs has not prevented people from adopting it. Yet

28. See the present author's *Political Visions and Illusions: A Survey and Christian Critique of Contemporary Ideologies*, 2nd ed. (Downers Grove, IL: InterVarsity Press, 2019).

29. Karl Marx, *Theses on Feuerbach* (1845): 11th Thesis, in, *Selected Works in One Volume* by Karl Marx and Frederick Engels (New York: International Publishers, 1968), 30.

its status remains a matter of controversy both within the academy and without.

The tension between theory and practice in the discipline of political science has often been resolved with an appeal to the difference between facts and values, a distinction rooted in the thought of David Hume (1711-1776). Facts are indisputable states of affairs based in empirical observation and capable of being demonstrated via the scientific method. They are publicly verifiable and are thus the common property of all reasonable persons. Values, on the other hand, are idiosyncratic, based on the subjective preferences of committed communities that cannot be easily shared with those lacking these values. Values are divisive, while facts command universal assent. The fact-value dichotomy has had an influence on a variety of academic disciplines, but within political science it has led to a longstanding uneasy relationship between the empirical and normative sides of the discipline. Those working with hard, quantifiable data may even doubt that the normative political theorist belongs within the same discipline. Moreover, given that normative political theory suffers from guilt by association with the purveyors of the ideological visions mentioned above, there seems ample reason to banish what appears to amount to little more than divisive and idiosyncratic preferences from the larger scientific enterprise.

However, the disconnect between facts and values is itself based on a certain "thick" conception of the world incapable of being verified by the standards of modern science. All scientists, even those of a positivist bent, necessarily tailor their research agendas according to what they find of interest, that is, to what they *value.* Furthermore, the empirical political scientist presupposes in his own work a particular normative understanding of the world and the place of politics within it. Practitioners of the discipline generally operate within certain agreed-upon parameters and constraints—that some things are worthy of study under the rubric of political science while others are not. These parameters are definitely of a normative character and are not themselves subject to the canons of the scientific method. The parameters of the discipline are not capable of being either proved or disproved but rest instead upon a worldview that both precedes and transcends it. Here once again is where the Fall has implications for the study of politics. Because of sin, scholars tend to embrace the following errors:

1. a failure to recognize the interconnectedness between so-called facts and values;
2. the implicit substitution of the fact-value dichotomy for the recognition of creational normativity;

3. a failure to recognize the impact of one's own religious presuppositions on the way one engages in the scientific enterprise;
4. insufficient attention to the data one is observing;
5. the ascription of certainty to one's own scientific conclusions in the midst of human frailty and unpredictability; and
6. the imposition of one's own ideological commitments on observed data and the theories growing out of this observation.

While all of these have relevance to the special sciences, the fifth error is especially applicable to the social sciences, whose practitioners often strive to imitate such "hard" sciences as physics and astronomy.

Of course, if worldviews are nonfalsifiable by the scientific method, their validity can still be assessed according to whether they adequately account for reality. This is where we need to return to our discussion above concerning the six components of political life, namely, the scope of its activities, the presence of conflict, the effort to conciliate conflict, the institutional setting, the use of coercive means, and its jural character. If a particular theoretical approach fails to consider one or more of these components, then we can assume its fundamental inadequacy. A positivist political science will tend to insist that, say, *justice* is a value incapable of being verified scientifically and thus ought to be relegated to another less scientific discipline such as philosophy. But if we fail to recognize that all political leaders and institutions in some fashion undertake to adjudicate the various claims of divergent interests, then we are left with the inability to distinguish between a duly-constituted government and Augustine's notorious band of thieves. In other words, if we are adequately to account for the character of political life, we must admit the legitimacy of asking crucial questions about, say, the nature of justice and its relationship to political power.

Towards the Redemption of Political Science: An Agenda for Research

The Christian scholar believes that the grand biblical narrative of creation, fall, redemption, and consummation offers the best account of life in God's world. For him or her the biblical redemptive story is the world's story. All our activities are capable of redemption in Jesus Christ, and this includes political science. While we cannot know what political science will look like in the new heaven and new earth, we can know in part what shape a redeemed discipline—or rather one that is being redeemed—can take. In response to the six points listed in the previous section, we offer the following:

1. A redeemed political science will recognize the integrality of all of life, declining to divide the field of study into facts and values.

2. It will acknowledge that all of God's creation is an orderly creation, and not just some components of it.

3. It will openly acknowledge that all inquiry is rooted in a religious worldview of some sort, declining to claim a neutral stance.

4. It will take into account the data relevant to the field and consider it thoroughly before coming to conclusions.

5. It will manifest a certain humility in stating its conclusions, recognizing that the scholarly enterprise is ongoing and requires many practitioners with varying insights into the cosmos.

6. And finally, while recognizing the impact of the scholar's own worldview on scholarship, it will refrain from imposing overt ideological agendas on it.

Of course, these components of a redeemed approach to the discipline fall well short of the expected glory of the fully consummated creation. Yet in the here and now they will aid us in our continued research into political life in the present world.

What impact might this have on the research agenda of the academic political scientist? Does it or should it make a difference? For many scholars the most obvious candidates for research topics in political science are those related to analysis of empirical data, such as voting behaviour or public opinion. Others, for whom political science is closer to the humanities than to the social sciences, would prefer to interpret the meaning of classic texts or to explore the influence of great political ideas, such as Lockean liberalism or Marxism, on political practice. Above all, we must affirm that the whole of the discipline is worthy of scholarly attentions, and not just those facets that touch on religion.

Helpful Resources

Nevertheless, I believe that the relationship between communal religious faith, that is, the shared redemptive narrative conditioning life together, and political culture is an area that remains under-explored at present. There are, however, two major exceptions to this, Robert Putnam's two-decade-long study of regional political cultures in Italy and

Robert D. Woodberry's work in relating Protestant missionary activity to constitutional democracy.

Putnam's *Making Democracy Work* is a fascinating exploration of the functionality of regional governments throughout the Italian peninsula undertaken between 1970, when most of these governments were established, and 1990.[30] Putnam and his associates discovered that regional governments in the north operated more smoothly and responsively than those in the south. Not so coincidentally, northern Italy is the historic seat of the civic republics, such as Venice, Genoa, and Florence, which were the setting for artistic and intellectual renewal during the Renaissance and the engine for economic growth and innovation in the twentieth and twenty-first centuries. By contrast, the south, which has known only a series of autocratic régimes over the centuries, is much less developed in a variety of areas, including economic and political life. The richer store of social capital in the north has facilitated a variety of endeavours, all of which require a high level of interpersonal trust and co-operation, whereas social capital is much weaker in the south, where a general lack of interpersonal trust outside of extended family networks makes co-operative enterprises more difficult to carry off.

A surprising discovery in Putnam's study is that there appears to be an inverse relationship between conventional religious observance and the vitality of social capital.[31] "Vertical bonds of authority are more characteristic of the Italian Church than horizontal bonds of fellowship." A high level of faithful Catholic practice appears to reinforce vertical ties between patron and client than to facilitate co-operative endeavours among the laity. In other words, church attendance, at least in Italy, seems to suppress the civic virtues needed for democratic governance and economic prosperity. This runs counter to Alexis de Tocqueville's claim that, of all the Christian denominations, Roman Catholicism best embodies the ideal of human equality and is thus conducive to democracy.[32] During his lengthy pontificate, Pope John Paul II promoted democratic forms of government, arguing that their flourishing required a stable moral basis.[33] Clearly the relationship between Roman Catholicism and democracy is a complex one, and this relationship needs further study.

Woodberry's study, "The Missionary Roots of Liberal Democracy," appeared in the premier journal in the discipline in the United States,

30. Robert Putnam, *Making Democracy Work: Civic Traditions in Modern Italy* (Princeton: Princeton University Press, 1993).

31. Putnam, *Making Democracy Work*, 107-109.

32. Alexis de Tocqueville, *Democracy in America*, chapter 9, trans. George Lawrence, ed. J. P. Mayer (Garden City, NY: Anchor Books/Doubleday, 1969), 287-290.

33. See, e.g., Pope John Paul II's encyclical, *Evangelium Vitae*, section 70.

the *American Political Science Review*, in 2012.[34] Woodberry discovered that the global impact of what he calls conversionary Protestant missionaries on the dissemination of democracy has been hugely positive, despite current notions that such missionaries were little more than agents of western imperialism. In fact, they were a "crucial catalyst initiating the development and spread of religious liberty, mass education, mass printing, newspapers, voluntary organizations, and colonial reforms, thereby creating the conditions that made stable democracy more likely."[35] Throughout the world those countries that received conversionary Protestant missionaries, such as Ghana, are more stable and democratic than those, such as neighbouring Togo, which did not. Furthermore, it was the missionaries to the egregiously-misnamed Congo Free State who called the world's attention to the atrocities there under King Leopold II, prompting the Belgian government to intervene in 1908.

Questions for Reflection and Discussion

The results of these two studies suggest the need for further investigation into the relationship between religion, political culture, and the functionality of political institutions. The following questions could provide a basis for further research:

1. Does it matter to political culture and institutions which tradition of Christianity is dominant in a particular national community? Why do some Christian traditions appear to facilitate autocratic and others democratic forms of government?[36]
2. Has the influence of the Second Vatican Council (1962-1965) or recent papal encyclicals decreased the number of autocratic governments in predominantly Catholic countries over the past half century?
3. What does the Muslim redemptive narrative look like and what are its implications for political life? Is Islam intrinsically autocratic, or perhaps even totalitarian, in its political influence? What accounts for the differences between politics in the Arab countries and politics in the largest Muslim country in the world, namely, Indonesia?

---

34. Robert D. Woodberry, "The Missionary Roots of Liberal Democracy," *American Political Science Review*, 106, no. 2 (May 2012), 244-274.
35. Abstract in Woodberry, "The Missionary Roots," 244.
36. See, e.g., the present author's own "Imaging God and his Kingdom: Eastern Orthodoxy's Iconic Political Ethic," *Review of Politics* 55 (Spring 1993), 267-289, for an exploration of this issue relevant to Orthodox Christianity.

4. How has the explosion of Pentecostal and charismatic forms of Christianity in, e.g., Guatemala and Brazil, affected the political life of those countries? Has it encouraged democratic governance or has it simply strengthened autocratic governance?
5. How has the explosion of evangelical Protestantism in Brazil affected politics in the world's fifth largest country?
6. Is biblical religion uniquely conducive to just governance? Is there a necessary connection between Christianity and constitutional governance?

These are a few of the topics that could be explored by future students of political science. Those who understand the place of politics within God's world and within the larger narrative of creation, fall, redemption, and consummation should be uniquely equipped to bring the resources of their faith to bear on these, thereby advancing our understanding of the role religion plays in public life.

As Christians we properly affirm that politics is a legitimate part of the world created and redeemed by God in his grace through Jesus Christ. We thus recognize that the study of political life forms an important part of the university's curriculum. While neither politics nor political science will be wholly redeemed in the present age, by God's grace he has enabled us to catch a glimpse of what this might look like when Christ returns and establishes his kingdom in its fulness. With the psalmist we can thus confess:

> The Lord reigns; he is robed in majesty;
>   the Lord is robed; he has put on strength as his belt.
> Yes, the world is established; it shall never be moved.
> Your throne is established from of old;
>   you are from everlasting (Psalm 93:1-2, ESV).

Bibliography

Adcock, Robert, Mark Bevir, Shannon C. Stimson. *Modern Political Science: Anglo-American Exchanges since 1880.* Princeton: Princeton University Press, 2007.

Adcock, Robert. *Liberalism and the Emergence of American Political Science: A Transatlantic Tale.* Oxford: Oxford University Press, 2014.

Almond, Gabriel A., ed. *A Discipline Divided: Schools and Sects in Political Science.* New York: Sage, 1989.

Almond, Gabriel and Sidney Verba. *The Civic Culture: Political Attitudes and Democracy in Five Nations.* New York: Sage Publications, 1963.

Johannes Althusius, *The Politics of Johannes Althusius.* Translated, with an Introduction by Frederick S. Carney. Boston: Beacon Press, 1964.

Arendt, Hannah. *The Human Condition.* Chicago: University of Chicago Press, 1958.

Arendt, Hannah. *On Revolution.* New York: Viking Press, 1963.

Aristotle. *Nicomachean Ethics.* Translated by W. D. Ross. In The Basic Works of Aristotle, edited by Richard McKeon. New York: Random House, 1941.

Aristotle. *Politica.* Translated by Benjamin Jowett. In The Basic Works of Aristotle, edited by Richard McKeon. New York: Random House, 1941.

Bevir, Mark. *A History of Political Science.* Cambridge: Cambridge University Press, 2022.

Calvin, John. *Institutes of the Christian Religion.* Translated by Ford Lewis Battles. Edited by John T. McNeill. Philadelphia: Westminster Press, 1960.

Carson, Rachel. Silent Spring. Boston and New York: Houghton Mifflin, 1962.

Crick, Sir Bernard. *The American Science of Politics.* Berkeley and Los Angeles: University of California Press, 1959.

Crick, Sir Bernard. *In Defence of Politics.* 5th ed. London and New York: Continuum, 1962, 2000.

Easton, David. *A Framework for Political Analysis.* Englewood Cliffs, New Jersey: Prentice-Hall, 1965.

Easton, David. *The Political System: an inquiry into the state of political science.* 2nd ed. New York: Alfred A. Knopff, 1971.

Easton, David, John G. Gunnell, and Luigi Graziano. *The Development of Political Science: A Comparative Survey.* New York: Routledge, 1991.

Easton, David, John G. Gunnell, and Michael B. Stein, ed. *Regime and Discipline: Democracy and the Development of Political Science.* Ann Arbor, Michigan: University of Michigan Press, 1995.

Eulau, Heinz. *The Behavioral Persuasion in Politics.* New York: Random House, 1963.

Gutmann, Amy and Dennis Thompson, *Democracy and Disagreement.* Cambridge, MA: Belknapp/Harvard, 1998.

Hobbes, Thomas. *Leviathan, or The Matter, Forme and Power of a Common Wealth Ecclesiasticall and Civil.* London: Andrew Crooke, 1651.

John Paul II. *Evangelium Vitae*. https://www.vatican.va/content/john-paul-ii/en/encyclicals/documents/hf_jp-ii_enc_25031995_evangelium-vitae.html

Koyzis, David T. "Imaging God and his Kingdom: Eastern Orthodoxy's Iconic Political Ethic," *Review of Politics* 55 (spring 1993), pp. 267-289.

Koyzis, David T. *Political Visions and Illusions: A Survey and Christian Critique of Contemporary Ideologies*. 2nd ed. Downers Grove, IL: IVP Academic, 2019.

Koyzis, David T. *We Answer to Another: Authority, Office, and the Image of God.* Eugene, Oregon: Pickwick Publications, 2014.

Koyzis, David T. *Citizenship Without Illusions: A Christian Guide to Political Engagemen*t. Downers Grove, IL: IVP Academic, 2024.

Lasswell, Harold. *Politics: Who Gets What, When, How.* New York: Whittlesey House, 1936.

Lipset, Seymour Martin, ed. *Politics and the Social Sciences.* Oxford: Oxford University Press, 1969.

Marx, Karl. *Theses on Feuerbach (1845).* In *Selected Works in One Volume*, by Karl Marx and Frederick Engels, 28-30. New York: International Publishers, 1968.

McCutcheon, Mark. *Roget's Superthesaurus.* Cincinnati: Writer's Digest Books, 2004.

Plato. *The Statesman*. Translated by J. B. Skemp. In *Plato: The Collected Dialogues*, edited by Edith Hamilton and Huntington Cairns, 1018-1085. Princeton: Princeton University Press, 1961.

Putnam, Robert. *Making Democracy Work: Civic Traditions in Modern Italy.* Princeton: Princeton University Press, 1993.

Ricci, David M. *The Tragedy of Political Science.* New Haven: Yale University Press, 1987.

Skillen, James W. "Toward a Comprehensive Science of Politics." *Philosophia Reformata* 53 (1988): 33-58. An abridged version of this was published in *Political Theory and Christian Vision: Essays in Memory of Bernard Zylstra*, edited by Jonathan Chaplin and Paul Marshall, 57-80. Lanham, Maryland: University Press of America 1994.

Strauss, Leo. "What Is Political Philosophy?" *What Is Political Philosophy? and Other Studies*. New York: The Free Press, 1959.

Thomas Aquinas, *Summa Theologiae: Latin text and English translation, introductions, notes, appendices, and glossaries*. New York: McGraw-Hill, 1964-1981.

Tocqueville, Alexis de. *Democracy in America.* Trans., George Lawrence. Ed., J. P. Mayer. Garden City, NY: Anchor Books/Doubleday, 1969.

Voegelin, Eric. *The New Science of Politics: An Introduction.* Chicago: University of Chicago Press, 1951.

Wolin, Sheldon S. *Politics and Vision.* Boston: Little, Brown & Co., 1960.

Woodberry, Robert D. "The Missionary Roots of Liberal Democracy," *American Political Science Review* (May 2012), Vol. 106, No. 2, pp. 244-274.

Zwick, Joel, director. *My Big Fat Greek Wedding.* Golden Circle Films, 2002.

Biomedical Ethics Regained: A Reformed Understanding of the Discipline

James J Rusthoven, MD, MHSc (bioethics), PhD

A Covenant-Making God: Importance of a Reformed Theological Approach to Studying Biomedical Ethics

Ethics is a discipline primarily concerned with doing what is right. At creation, it began with God's command to humankind to be stewards of the created order, tending it and caring for it for God's sake. When the first woman was created, an interpersonal dimension to ethics was also created. That is, human beings were to be in special relationship to God but also to each other. To some Reformed theologians, this relationship with God was covenantal at creation. Human beings would prosper if they were obedient to Him. The first humans failed in keeping that covenant in their disobedience in Eden. And they paid a terrible price, as did all of creation, bearing the burdens of sin, from innate disobedience to God to a final earthly outcome of death. Yet, covenantal relating was given repeated renewal by God's grace in the face of unrelenting covenant-breaking disobedience by his chosen people. Finally, through Christ's sacrifice and resurrection, the Old Testament promise of a new covenant for all who believe and live out their belief in Him is fulfilled.[1]

As I will show later in this chapter, appeals have been made by various healthcare professionals for the development of covenantal relating. While some propose such a relational model of physicians as teachers and friends to their patients, others appeal to a return to a relational grounding of mutual trust between patients and caregivers. Some of these appeals ground their covenantal concept in the pagan Hippocratic tra-

1 Irenaeus (c. AD 130– c. 202) and other late second-century Christian leaders spoke of the apostolic writings as the books of the new or fresh covenant. Through translational missteps, these books have come to us in English as the New Testament, though the term New Covenant more adequately declares the central message of Jesus Christ. See Joseph L. Allen, *Love & Conflict: A Covenantal Model of Christian Ethics* (Nashville, TN: Abingdon Press, 1984), 31–32.

dition while others vaguely acknowledge Judeo-Christian influence. By contrast, I envision "covenantal relating" in medicine and its relationships as founded on, and grounded in, God's faithfulness to humankind. Such an understanding of covenant sees the internal meaning of creation. In medical practice, covenantal relating acknowledges the giving of care by trained healthcare professionals but also an indebtedness to patients for their trust in accepting such care.

In this chapter I present the case for the importance of covenantal relating in medicine, particularly medical practice, with its richest and most meaningful expression as a reflection of the covenantal commitments between God and humankind as taught in Scripture.

Creation: Importance of a Reformational Ontology to Studying Academic Disciplines Including Biomedical Ethics

For Christian scholars, Scripture provides the meaning and direction of reflection for each discipline. The apostle John exhorts Christians to discern the pagan spirits that influence their thinking and daily lives from that of the Holy Spirit.[2] In John's day, one such spirit was Gnosticism which taught that the human body is inherently evil. Under this influence some Christian leaders denied the human nature of Christ, while John declared that Christ was also *God in the flesh*.

For Christians today, such discernment is as crucial to Christian living as it was in John's time. Christian scholars need to identify and understand the worldviews from which theoretical frameworks of the discipline have been developed. Goheen and Bartholomew offer a definition of worldview as "basic beliefs embedded in a shared grand story that are rooted in a faith commitment and that give shape and direction to the whole of our individual and corporate lives."[3] That faith commitment gives ultimate meaning and consequently direction to the thoughts and actions of its adherents.[4] Those spirits described by the apostle John may be expressed by scholars who teach from worldviews that omit, deny, or distort a biblical understanding of creation and the place of their particular discipline in that created order.[5]

2. I Jn 4:1-5 (TNIV) .
3. Michael W. Goheen, and Craig G. Bartholomew, *Living at the Crossroads: An Introduction to Christian Worldview*. (Grand Rapids, MI: Baker Academics, 2008), 23.
4. Sander Griffioen , "The Worldview Approach to Social Theory: Hazards and Benefits," in *Stained Glass: Worldviews and Social Science*, ed. Paul A. Marshall, Sander Griffioen, and Richard J. Mouw (Lanham, MD.: University of America Press, 1989), 87.
5. I Jn 4:5: "They … speak from the viewpoint of the world, and the world listens to them."

To combat the growing spirit and expression of reductionism in the scholarship of his day, Abraham Kuyper recognized distinct relational and institutional spheres of life as irreducible and sovereign structures of created reality.[6] John Calvin, writes Kuyper, spoke of a *Philosophia Christiana* that permeates each special science, uniting the sciences under the Lordship of God as creator.[7] Going hand in hand with theology, a Christian philosophy which Kuyper advocated leads "to unity of interpretation within the circle of regeneration" in fulfilling its task "to arrange concentrically the results of all the other sciences."[8]

Today, we more often refer to special sciences as academic disciplines within which scholars busy themselves with focused reflections on a specific part of created reality. As mentioned in the Introduction to this book, Herman Dooyeweerd heeded Kuyper's call and laboured to develop a Christian philosophy of the created order. It hangs on an empirically based framework of fifteen irreducible aspects of how things and relationships function, an understanding of creation counter to the reductionism prevalent in his and our days.[9] These modal aspects or laws collectively establish a stable, universal order for all "the actual existing individual 'things, events, and relationships' that populate the world."[10] Modal aspects have no meaning apart from the phenomena which they qualify, whether they apply to things like inanimate objects, such as rocks in geology, or to living things or subjects in biology and sociology. This functioning of aspects also extends to relationships among subjects.[11] Each aspect also holds special places in the created order such that academic disciplines may evolve around the functioning of a particular aspect. Thus, the inner structure within disciplines, as well as the relationships between different disciplines, can be studied through the language and understanding of these aspects.[12]

6. Abraham Kuyper, *Lectures on Calvinism* (Grand Rapids, MI: Wm B. Eerdmans1931), 171.
7. Kuyper, *Lectures on Calvinism*, 69, 139, 194.
8. Kuyper, *Principles of Sacred Theology* (Grand Rapids, MI: Eerdmans, 1965), 614–615.
9. Herman Dooyeweerd, *In the Twilight of Western Thought* (Nutley, NJ: Craig Press, 1965), 6-11. Intellectual idolatry is characterized by isolating individual aspects as the "key" to understanding all the rest. See also the Introductory Essay to this book for a listing of these irreducible aspects. Dooyeweerd humbly challenged others to "discover" other irreducible aspects that he might have missed!
10. Jonathan Chaplin, *Herman Dooyeweerd: Christian Philosopher of State and Civil Society* (Notre Dame, IN: University of Notre Dame Press, 2011), 55.
11. Relationships that constitute medicine and its practice can be understood using this framework and will be discussed later in the chapter.
12. J. M. Spier, *An Introduction to Christian Philosophy* (Nutley, NJ: Craig Press, 1966), 34–49.

This author has appreciated the usefulness of this empirical schema to understand the history, foundations, and current dominant theories of biomedical ethics. As a discipline, the primary concern of biomedical ethics is the ethical aspect of medical relationships as expressed in care for others in a medical context. Care for others is the *qualifying* aspect of the practice. That is, it frames and defines its identity and leads in the directing of other various aspects of functioning within the practice. It can also be understood as the *telos*, the core value or reason for the practice to exist.[13] The *founding* aspect, on the other hand, is the historical aspect, best understood as the formative or technical aspect. That is, methods and techniques of diagnosis and treatment are historically developed, imparting formative power and competencies to recommend and supervise appropriate treatments for specific patient circumstances. Clearly, technical proficiency is a requirement of good medical practice. But the care for others leads the relationship and its constitutive aspects and goes hand-in-hand with competence in judgment.

In the next section, I will introduce the reader to a dominant ethical framework in biomedical ethics today, constituted by four principles embedded in a theory of common morality. Using Dooyeweerd's biblically inspired Christian philosophical viewpoint, I will explore the underlying worldview and philosophical underpinnings of this dominant framework, give reasons for its usefulness and its popularity among biomedical ethicists, and uncover its insufficiencies in understanding the relational nature of medicine as manifest in its practice.[14] I will also offer the essentials of a Reformational ethical framework that, in my view, more properly recognizes the relational context of the core ethical aspect of the discipline through the biblical notion of covenant, giving some examples of its practical implications in medicine.

---

13. For a more complete explanation of the qualifying as well as foundational aspects or functions that govern relationships generally and practices more specifically, see Henk Jochemsen, "Normative Practices as an Intermediate between Theoretical Ethics and Morality," *Philosophia Reformata* 71 (2006): 96–112 and Chaplin, *Herman Dooyeweerd:* 66–67.

14. I will use Alasdair MacIntyre's definition of a practice: "By a 'practice' I am going to mean any coherent and complex form of socially established cooperative human activity through which goods internal to that form of activity are realized in the course of trying to achieve those standards of excellence which are appropriate to, and partially definitive of, that form of activity, with the result that human powers to achieve excellence, and human conceptions of the ends and good involved, are systematically extended." See Alasdair MacIntyre, *After Virtue*. 2nd ed. (Notre Dame, IN: University of Notre Dame Press, 1984), 187.

Ethics in a Fallen World: Is There a Common Morality for All?

Principles-based ethics has been a dominant basic ethical framework over 40 years. In developing a Reformational perspective, it is important to understand its history, the worldviews out of which it grew, and its strengths and inadequacies as an ethical framework. Between 1974 and 1978, a single set of principles was distilled from monthly deliberations of a United States federal commission known as The National Commission of the Protection of Human Subjects of Biomedical and Behavioral Research. In its deliberations, Commission members and consultants iteratively navigated multiple ethical theories and methods of moral reasoning that participants brought to the discussion table in order to reach by consensus some basic ethical principles.[15] Three principles were identified in the Commission's final report (the Belmont Report), to be used as aids to exercising ethical propriety when relating to human research subjects. A fourth principle was added and these principles were expanded to medical practice in 1979 in the influential publication *Principles of Biomedical Ethics* by Tom Beauchamp and James Childress.

It is important to distinguish the three basic principles articulated in the Belmont Report from the subsequent promotion of those principles (and the additional principle of nonmaleficence) as a framework for solving biomedical dilemmas. The Belmont Report defined three principles as general judgments "that serve as a basic justification for the many particular ethical prescriptions and evaluations of human actions."[16] Roman Catholic and some Protestant traditions were represented in both the commission membership and in the consultants subsequently called to produce papers to aid in deliberations. However, it remains unclear who selected the commission members and for what particular qualities and expertise. It is also unclear how much discussions were influenced by the various religious traditions represented. In the end, the principles were meant to serve a common good for human research subjects of any faith or secular tradition, reminders that they are human beings and not just research subjects.

What became more problematic was the subsequent development and promotion of a common morality which claims to spring from and embrace these three principles and a fourth principle of nonmaleficence. Developed in their book published a year after the Belmont Report, Tom

15. It is often referred to as the Belmont Commission. More detail concerning its members and their work will be discussed later.

16. Kenneth J. Ryan, et al. *The Belmont Report : Ethical Principles and Guidelines for the Protection of Human Subjects for Research.* (National Institutes of Health, 1979), 4.

Beauchamp and James Childress tried to expand these principles into a method and process of bioethical decision-making, which I believe are insufficient to handle the complexities of ethical decision-making in a contemporary medical context. It is principl*ism* as proposed by Beauchamp and Childress that shall be the focus of my attention and critique in what follows. Principlism is the incorporation of these principles into a common morality framework but without foundational moral grounding that became the focus of much criticism soon after its appearance and continues so to this day. From a Christian perspective, this framework is devoid of moral guidance from the God of Scripture by design; in this effort to be all things ethical to all people, it becomes foundationally deficient in moral meaning. Its moral justification is a sinful reliance in a moral consensus by a process driven by faith in human reason alone, under the influence of both modernist and postmodern worldviews.

While Christian theologians played an important role in the early development of bioethics, by the time of the Belmont Commission their numbers and influence had waned as philosophers and physicians became more prominent in public dialogue and debate. Some theologians remained influential voices, exemplified by Lutheran Gilbert Meilaender's study of human dignity, connecting with Reformed theologian Paul Ramsey's earlier concerns that assisted reproduction technologies were changing procreation as a telos of being human to reproduction as autonomous choice to satisfy parental desires.[17] Yet, such a common recognition of elemental morality might be understood as the ethical component of common goodness still inherent in this fallen world, what Kuyper calls God's common grace as noted in the Introductory Essay. In his Letter to the Romans, the apostle Paul mentions such a common ethical sense in terms of 'law'. He teaches that Gentiles who do not know the law of God can do *by nature* things required by the law and thus show that the requirements of the law are written on their hearts.[18] But they do not acknowledge God as the origin and sustainer of all that is good in creation and in bioethical decision-making. By analogy, the principles-based ethical framework as promoted by Beauchamp and Childress assumes that its adherents have an inherent moral sense, summarized in the four principles.

When reduced to principlism, however, moral communities who consider belief in God as the origin of moral teaching, the influence of sin as a root cause for unethical behaviour, and the subsequent need for redemptive moral correction may be excluded from public moral dis-

17. Gilbert Meilaender, *Neither Beast Nor God: The Dignity of the Human Perso*n (New York: Encounter Books, 2009, 32–36.

18. Romans 2:12ff.

courses. Jesus Christ's death and resurrection have no place in this moral framework, leaving principlism and its common morality without a moral anchor in God and his teachings. Reason alone and iterative rational give-and-take become the empty process by which moral consensus is sought. Consequently, Christians must pay careful attention to how these principles are defined and expressed in various medical contexts and must develop their own response to moral arguments that fail to acknowledge the influence of sin and its disruptive power on biomedical ethics. For Christian bioethicists, moral truth must be pursued by restoring the meaning of the four principles. As will be shown later, when done sensitively, as in the writings of Edmund Pellegrino, William F. May, and others, incorporating these principles into a God-glorifying Christian ethical framework enriches their meaning for non-Christians in the discipline as well.

Such a framework must also give ethical guidance to the relational nature of medicine and its practice. Consequently, the Reformational perspective on biomedical ethics offered in this chapter re-envisions (1) the core ethical aspect of medical relationships as expressed as *relational caring*, the fullest meaning of which can be appreciated through the biblical notion of covenant, and (2) a renewed understanding of the four principles within a covenantal ethical framework. Such a Christian perspective is not the only possible Christian perspective. It also is not novel in its appeal for a biblical understanding of the four principles (developed, for example, by Roman Catholic Pellegrino) or its incorporation of the biblical concept of covenant (explored by Reformed bioethicists Paul Ramsey and William F. May). Rather, its distinctiveness lies in its revaluation of the principles in the context of a covenantal relational model based on Scripture as well as the use of modal analysis to maintain a consistent focus on the ethical core or qualifying aspect of medical relationships.

Development of Principles-based Ethics in Biomedical Ethics

Recognized Need for Moral Guidance in Medical Research Involving Human Subjects

Nineteenth- and early twentieth-century codes of ethics promoted character and personality traits as predictors of desired ethical behaviour befitting a competent and caring physician. However, in 1966 Henry Beecher, an anesthetist at Harvard Medical School, identified studies containing numerous ethical violations involving human subjects.[19]

19. Henry K. Beecher, "Ethics and Clinical Research," *New England Journal of Medicine* 274, no. 24 (1966): 57–63.

Such revelations led to the establishment of the Belmont Commission in 1974. Composed of lawyers, physicians, biomedical researchers, bioethicists, and a civil rights leader, the Commission was asked to identify ethical guidelines to protect the rights and welfare of human research subjects. It is noteworthy that the Commission, in its pursuit of consensual ethical principles, sought and obtained the participation of theologians, although the significance of that input is disputed.[20] After calling in numerous consultants from various disciplines, the Commission's findings were published as the *Belmont Report* in June 1978. Of seven principles initially identified, three were distilled out into the Report: (1) respect for persons as free moral agents, (2) beneficence, and (3) justice.

Three primary applications of these principles were recommended as critical ethical concerns of the day: informed consent, selection of, and weighing of risks and benefits to research subjects. Consequently, the three principles were seen as the conceptual pillars on which the language of ethics discourse regarding ethical concerns could develop. They were also to be used as *reminders of ethical dimensions* to be heeded when relating to human subjects in clinical research.[21] The ethical core of *respect for persons* was applied to informed consent for human research subjects as autonomous agents and protecting disabled persons with diminished capacity. *Beneficence* meant respecting their decisions, protecting them from harm, and securing their well-being. The principle of *justice* was identified out of concern for the fair consideration and treatment of vulnerable subjects in the selection and treatment of research subjects. Discriminating against subjects by mental capacity, race, and gender were identified causes of unfair recruitment strategies into clinical studies in the decades prior to the *Belmont Report.*

In 1979, Commission consultants Tom Beauchamp and James Childress published *Principles of Biomedical Ethics*. In addition to the three principles of the *Belmont Report*, they added the principle of nonmaleficence which was meant to distinguish refraining-from-harm from the more positive and active principle of helping others. The book goes beyond medical research, promoting the application of these principles in medical practice and policy-making as well.[22] The authors call these

20. As noted later by Daniel Callahan ("Religion and the Secularization of Bioethics," *Hastings Center Report* 20, no.4 [1990]: 2–4), a few members of the National Commission were theologians who wrote about bioethical issues. Additional theologians such as Paul Ramsey and Richard McCormick were invited to prepare essays for the commission (see Albert R. Jonsen, *The Birth of Bioethics*. [New York: Oxford University Press, 1998], 99–100).

21. Clinical research is an extension of clinical practice, with much relational ethical behaviour common to both.

22. Tom L. Beauchamp and James F. Childress, *Principles of Biomedical Ethics*, 1st ed.

principles pillars of a common morality. This common morality framework excludes God as the source of moral teaching and sin as the root cause of ethical failing. They become pillars without moral foundation while human intuition and reason become idols when relied on alone as a path to moral certitude.

Beauchamp and Childress's Common Morality Idea and the Emergence of Principlism

In later editions of their book, Beauchamp and Childress give more detail of their concept of a common morality. They insist that those who claim adherence to the common morality idea must adhere to bioethical theories that have the same shared moral beliefs that they label *pre-theoretical* moral values. According to them, the norms of particular moral traditions such as those in Christianity can not be morally justified if they violate norms in the common morality.[23] Elsewhere they refer collectively to their common morality with their principles as a pre-theoretical moral point of view that forms the anchor of moral theory.[24] In still other places they claim these principles are not merely "drawn from the territory of common morality."[25] but also from an entirely sufficient "analytical framework of general norms derived from the common morality that form a *suitable starting point* for biomedical ethics" as well as "general guidelines for the formulation of more specific rules."[26]

Despite these pretensions, Beauchamp and Childress themselves admittedly struggle with the source of their common morality. They have identified no origin other than a history of what they call considered moral judgments, acceptable without argumentative support, and human experience combined into a common language, always subject to revision according to changes in culture and in the persuasiveness of changing moral judgments. But they never justify the normativity of those initial moral judgments.[27]

Beauchamp and Childress claim that their version of common ethics is not grounded in pure reason, rationality, any special moral sense,

(New York: Oxford University Press, 1979); Beauchamp and Childress, *Principles of Biomedical Ethics*, 7th ed. (New York: Oxford University Press 2013).

23. Beauchamp and Childress distinguish particular moralities, with their own moral norms, from their common morality idea.
24. Beauchamp and Childress, *Principles of Biomedical Ethics*, 7th ed., 5, 412.
25. Beauchamp and Childress, *Principles of Biomedical Ethics*, 7th ed., 410..
26. Beauchamp and Childress, *Principles of Biomedical Ethics*, 7th ed., 13. Italics added.
27. This is a concept taken from John Rawls. See Beauchamp and Childress, *Principles of Biomedical Ethics*, 7th ed., 405.

or any idea of natural law.[28] Instead, in the spirit of classical foundationalism, their principles are self-evident and obvious to all who are serious about morality.[29] They claim that their principles are intuitive inductions, implied from previous moral judgments made in particular situations. In putting forward intuition as a source of moral conviction, they appeal to some innate or natural moral understanding.[30] Yet, they claim that even these most basic moral beliefs in their common morality are subject to revision if moral conflict arises. Their morality is held together by a process known as *reflective equilibrium*, the main goal and purpose of which is to continually "match, prune, and adjust considered judgments, their specifications, and other beliefs to render them coherent."[31] These adjust-

28. Beauchamp and Childress, *Principles of Biomedical Ethics*, 5th ed. (New York: Oxford University Press, 2001), 403. I disagree with this premise. Their method of reflective equilibrium is a method requiring iterative rational discourse as the basis of moral decision-making.

29. Alvin Plantinga notes that according to classical foundationalism, humans conform to norms or justify obligations through being and acting rationally. These norms are in turn derived from noetic structures, a set of propositions that are beliefs of the knower regarding these propositions. The most basic of such beliefs, according to classical foundationalists, are self-evident or evident by human sensory perception, a belief that Plantinga exposes as 'false and self-referentially incoherent.' For Reformers such as Karl Barth, John Calvin, and Herman Bavinck, belief in God is properly basic. It is rational to accept such a belief without the need for basing it on any other propositions or beliefs. Calvin, he notes, would think that a Christian should believe in God on the basis of proper Christian noetic structure, with belief in God among its foundations. Thus, in Plantinga's Reformed perspective, being self-evident is not a necessary condition for a properly basic belief. Belief in God is grounded in justifying conditions such as believing through experience God's gracious nature, the wonders and power of his creation, his justice, and his desire to be in covenantal relationship with human beings. See Alvin Plantinga. "Reason and Belief in God,"in *Faith and Rationality: Reason and Belief in God*, ed. A. Plantinga and N. Wolterstorff (Notre Dame: University of Notre Dame Press, 1983); also, Stephen Louthan. "On Religion: A Discussion with Richard Rorty, Alvin Plantinga, and Nicholas Wolterstorff," *Christian Scholar's Review* 26, no. 2 (1996): 177-83 and James Rusthoven. *Covenantal Biomedical Ethics for Contemporary Medicine* (Eugene, OR: Wipf and Stock, 2014).

30. Again, here they seem to allude to common moral awareness.

31. Beauchamp and Childress, *Principles of Biomedical Ethics*, 5th ed., 403. Reflective equilibrium, also called coherence theory, was taken from John Rawls. In this model, justification is a reflective testing of our principles, theoretical postulates, and other moral beliefs in order to make them as coherent as possible. This process begins with considered judgments, judgments in which our moral capacities are most likely to be displayed without distortion. However, even these most generally accepted judgments are liable to revision due to the influence of historical and cultural change over time. For more on this coherence theory, see John Rawls, *A Theory of Justice* (Cambridge, MA: Harvard University Press, 1999) and his later comments on reflective equilibrium in *Political Liberalism* (New York: Columbia

ed judgments are then tested for the consistency of their coherence and must be readjusted if they become incoherent. These judgments are based on consensus, without which such judgments lose their moral meaning since there is no source outside of human iterative reflection for justification of moral normativity.

Yet in acknowledging a lack of moral adhesive that holds their common morality together, Beauchamp and Childress actually ask: "... but can the common morality be made coherent? [....] Is our goal of coherence more *an article of faith* than a demonstrable achievement?" (my emphasis).[32] This remarkable statement gives insight into a major problem with principlism: even the most basic moral beliefs and judgments lack the moral stability and certitude found in moral teaching by divine moral agency outside of human rationality. While moral truth in the Reformational perspective comes from God through his revealed Word, Beauchamp and Childress's common morality lacks morally stable starting points. Even the most basic considered judgments are subject to the winds of cultural and historical change, personal character, and other influences over time. Such moral relativism exposes the fundamental weakness of the common morality idea.

Christian Discernment of the Worldviews Underlying Principlism

An understanding of worldviews that have given direction to principlism is required to see how sin has affected it at its conceptual roots before Christian scholarship can engage in its renewal. Metaphors such as guide, compass, and road map have been used to describe this central and directional role of worldviews.[33] Worldviews often conflict; Sander Griffioen cautions that such conflicts give only incomplete expression to the battle of spirits which we are exhorted to discern in I John 4.[34] In a modernist worldview, faith in Reason is the source of ultimate moral truth, ultimately dominating human activity in the cosmos. By contrast, a postmodern worldview sees moral truth claims among individuals as equally valid or invalid. Consequently, it is important to understand the possible influence of these two conflicting worldviews on principlism.

In discerning these worldviews, and in giving expression to their own worldview, Christian scholars must engage in *double listening*, a no-

University Press, 1996, pp. 8, 381, 384, and 399.

32. Beauchamp and Childress, *Principles of Biomedical Ethics*, 5th ed., 4, 407.

33. Albert M. Wolters, *Creation Regained: Biblical Basics for a Reformational Worldview.* 2nd ed. (Grand Rapids, MI: Eerdmans, 2005), 3–5.

34. Griffioen, *Stained Glass*, 104.

tion credited to John Stott wherein one keeps one ear on Scripture and the other towards the surrounding culture so that Christ's command can be lived out in, but not of, this world.[35] From a biblical vantage point, no aspect of the creation is worthy of such complete trust in rationality alone, including morality. Still, there can be important disagreements among Christian scholars regarding the place of rationality in scholarship. Understanding the basis of such disagreements is critical in developing a Reformational perspective for the disciplines including biomedical ethics. Some Christian scholars such as Carl Henry and Francis Schaeffer see reason as religiously neutral yet supportive of a Christian worldview if operating properly.[36] That is, reason is presupposed and independently gives support to a Christian worldview. For other Christians, such as Kuyper, this claim is too accommodating to a non-Christian epistemology developed from a non-Christian worldview. As Roy Clouser puts it, "reason is not autonomous nor is theorizing religiously neutral."[37] For Roman Catholic scholar Alasdair MacIntyre, rationality is a human capacity that always functions under the influence of a particular set of basic beliefs. Nicholas Wolterstorff and Alvin Plantinga rightly argue that competing secular worldviews at basic and presuppositional levels have distorted a normative understanding of rationality. A fundamental premise of *modernity* is confidence that true and reliable knowledge gained through scientific methods can be objectively understood, is independent of the mind itself, and resists skepticism and doubt.[38] This worldview can subtly influence Christian thinking wherein faith in reason alone can replace faith in God as the creator and maintainer of the cosmos and of the lives of its creatures.[39]

---

35. Goheen and Bartholomew, *Living at the Crossroads*, 108. Wolters (*Creation Regained*, 29) writes about human conscience as intuitive attunement to creational normativity. Through our conscience we witness normative demands of creation law by virtue of our ontic nature as image-bearers of God.

36. This view fundamentally contrasts with that of Abraham Kuyper and later Alvin Plantinga, Nicholas Wolterstorff, and Alasdair MacIntyre, whose position understands reason to be expressed and understood in the context of a worldview. For these Christian thinkers, the starting point of reason is the Word of God. Goheen and Bartholomew, *Living at the Crossroads* , 16, 181n20, 181n21. See also Alasdair MacIntyre, *Whose Justice? Which Rationality?* (Notre Dame, IN: University of Notre Dame Press, 1988); Nicholas Wolterstorff, *Reason within the Bounds of Religion* (Grand Rapids, MI: Eerdmans, 1976).

37. Roy Clouser, *The Myth of Religious Neutrality: An Essay on the Hidden Role of Religious Beliefs in Theories* (Notre Dame, IN: University of Notre Dame Press, 2005), 97–98.

38. Christopher Norris, *Deconstruction and the "Unfinished Project of Modernity"* (New York: Routledge, 2000), 7.

39. Alasdair MacIntyre, *Whose Justice? Which Rationality?* (Notre Dame, IN: Univer-

On the other hand, philosophers with *a postmodern* worldview find the modernist dream of a better life through faith in rationality and science wanting, in light of the horrors of two world wars. They challenge the modernist optimism of objective, verifiable facts with a return to a nominalist view of reality that has no objective ontological standing. Our minds *impose* a framework for reality as we experience the particulars of the universe. Meaning systems become socially and linguistically constructed by way of multiple, open-ended, ever-proliferating narratives and language games, each being no more or less morally valid than any other. Human beings and their societies create their own worlds.[40]

Beauchamp and Childress's common morality idea of their principles-based biomedical ethics has a nominalist view of reality.[41] Such a disconnected understanding of moral reality is also manifest in the attempt to separate, if not to oppose, faith and reason in nominalist thinking.[42] Their principlism distorts the objectively normative character and meaning of biomedical ethics. *Fundamentally then, principlism's source of moral*

---

sity of Notre Dame Press, 1988); Alvin Plantinga, "Reason and Belief in God," in *Faith and Rationality: Reason and Belief in God*, ed. Alvin Plantinga and Nicholas Wolterstorff (Notre Dame, IN: University of Notre Dame Press, 1983); Nicholas Wolterstorff, "Can Belief in God Be Rational If It Has No Foundations?" in *Faith and Rationality: Reason and Belief in God*, ed. Alvin Plantinga and Nicholas Wolterstorff (Notre Dame, IN: University of Notre Dame Press, 1983a),135; Nicholas Wolterstorff, *Until Justice and Peace Embrace* (Grand Rapids, MI: Eerdmans, 1983b), 169–176. Wolterstorff agrees with MacIntyre, arguing that religious beliefs should function as basic control beliefs that help Christian scholars to reject or accept current theories in a discipline and devise alternative theories that are more reflective of a biblically inspired Christian worldview. They reject the foundational contention that belief in God is a falsehood because of lack of evidence.

40. David Naugle, *Worldview: The History of a Concept* (Grand Rapids, MI: Wm B. Eerdmans 2002), 174–179.

41. Nominalistic thinking strips the world of any pre-ordained hierarchical order of being (as proposed in Dooyeweerd's irreducible modal aspects), leaving individuality within reality in an unstructured vacuum, existing as its own truth. This was filled by claiming that the human subject gives order to reality through rational reflection and, with postmodernity, an emphasis on linguistic expression that leaves fundamental ambiguity in understanding moral truth without a creational orderliness of being and, without God as the highest being. For a more detailed history of the effect of nominalism on philosophy, see Danie F. M. Strauss, *Philosophy: Discipline of the Disciplines* (Grand Rapids, MI; Paideia Press, 2009), 370-379.

42. Oliver O'Donovan, *Resurrection and the Moral Order* (Grand Rapids, MI: Wm B. Eerdmans, 1994), 51; Herman Dooyeweerd, *A New Critique of Theoretical Thought* (Philadelphia, PA: The Presbyterian and Reformed Pub. Co., 1969), 1: 558–566; 2: 564–567. O'Donovan acknowledges the insights of Dooyeweerd who describes a form of nominalism whereby disciplines or special sciences see reality too narrowly as a single aspect of reality without properly considering the coherence of that aspect with other aspects that make up the reality of the created order.

truth is expressed through aspects of both modernist and postmodern worldviews. The modernist influence is manifest in the common morality and its foundationalist claim of self-evident moral universality. Postmodern influence is expressed as moral decision-making seeking a consensus of subjective persuasion that *a priori* assumes that moral truth is relative and contingent. It denies privilege to, or primacy of, moral truthfulness from any one set of basic beliefs including belief in the moral authority of God.

This nominalist, postmodern influence can also be seen in the emphasis on procedure and moral language as the means to moral consensus and conditioned truth (This proceduralist distortion will be addressed later in discussing the insights of Charles Taylor). Embedded in the nominalist and postmodern traditions as articulated by Rorty, principlism and its seeking of moral truth by consensus become a historical stream of moral metaphors, with old metaphors constantly dying off, yet serving as a platform and foil for new metaphors,[43]

The distorting influence of these two major non-Christian worldviews accounts for the moral inadequacy of principlism and is a major reason to pursue a Christian perspective in biomedical ethics.[44] With this understanding of influences of these worldviews on principlism and its common morality idea, let's now turn our attention to so-called particular moralities and their relation to the common morality.

The Common Morality and Particular (Customary) Moralities

In addition to this common morality, Beauchamp and Childress acknowledge the existence of *particular,* also called *customary* or *private,* moralities, defined by distinct moral communities with particular moral ideals including those identified by Christian and other particular religious faiths. In the Introduction to this book, it is noted that God's mandate to tend the garden included engaging in cultural activity in com-

43. Strauss, *Philosophy: Discipline of Disciplines*, 374, 375. Further from note 41 above. Richard Rorty's merging of nominalism with his postmodern view of intellectual history as a succession of metaphors led to his adaptation of Nietzsche's definition of truth as a mobile army of metaphors. It is my contention that principlism springs from this, and moral truth consequently becomes ever-changing moral judgments influenced by human history and culture, see Richard Rorty, *Contingency, Irony, and Solidarity*. (New York: Cambridge University Press, 1989).

44. Wolters, *Creation Regained*, 85. Wolters describes this clash of worldviews in terms of a spiritual battle. In this battle, Christian students need "an integral biblical worldview that equips them to fight back with the sword of the Spirit, their alternatives are either to live a life of almost intolerable intellectual schizophrenia (the chapel hermeneutically sealed off from the classroom) or to be swept along in the maelstrom of secular humanism."

munities. Such particular moralities, say Beauchamp and Childress, are distinguishable largely by cultural, religious, and institutional differences. However, they insist that particular moral norms of such communities must be compatible with the fundamental precepts of their common morality. Beauchamp and Childress note "Whereas the common morality … contains moral norms that are abstract, universal, and content-thin (such as 'Tell the truth'), particular moralities present concrete, nonuniversal, and content-rich norms …."[45]

One key distinguishing feature of such particular moralities is their *moral ideals*. For Beauchamp and Childress, moral ideals are universally praiseworthy but are not required of any persons who are members of the common morality. They exemplify such an ideal in the Parable of the Good Samaritan.[46] Common interpretations of the parable, they offer, suggest that the positive charitable beneficence shown by the Samaritan is an ideal rather than a moral obligation. Through the spectacles of their common morality, they cannot expect such *ideal* moral action of any human being. Rather, they minimize the obligations for positive beneficence by listing several rules including preventing harm to others, removing conditions that will harm others, and removing persons from danger. Beneficence *permits* us to help or benefit those with whom we have special relationships, and we often are not required to help or benefit those with whom we have no such relationship.[47] Their common morality has no obligation of beneficence to a stranger and certainly not to one's enemy. Yet calls for covenantal relating in medical practice from the medical literature suggest failings in defining and delivering beneficence as medical care in these settings.

Given the above, one can see a radical difference between the ethical limits imposed by the common morality *ala* Beauchamp and Childress and a biblical view of ethical obligations toward fellow human beings. In the Parable of the Good Samaritan, the priest and Levite passed by the severely beaten man without helping him, presumably either out of fear of violating a Mosaic law against touching a possibly dead body or feeling no obligation to help a stranger. By contrast, the Samaritan acted out of compassion ("… when he saw him, he took pity on him."[48]). It did not seem to matter if the man was a stranger or even a Jew, whom Samaritans generally hated. The Samaritan simply provided help because the man was in need. By the common morality understanding of "moral ideals" noted above, the Samaritan had no obligation to help the man.

45. Beauchamp and Childress, *Principles of Biomedical Ethics*, 7th ed., 5.

46. Luke 10:25–37.

47. Beauchamp and Childress, *Principles of Biomedical Ethics*, 7th ed., 203, 204.

48. Luke 10:33.

Beauchamp and Childress note that "a general obligation of beneficence is controversial" among adherents to the common morality and "the common morality recognizes significant limits to the demands of beneficence."[49] All of this suggests a rationale for Beauchamp and Childress to add nonmaleficence (i.e., do not harm) as a fourth necessary principle, keeping the moral emphasis on not harming that diverts moral attention to beneficence as sacrifice.

As noted earlier, a common morality idea is content-thin, lacking in the content-rich sense of human ethical wisdom found in the teachings of Scripture. As Christian bioethicist Edmund Pellegrino has suggested, incorporation of the four principles into public biomedical discourse can be helpful to get the conversation going.[50] However, as participants with different basic beliefs defend their moral positions in public discourse on particular bioethical issues, they must choose whether to express their faith-based views in the language of the common morality or to give their views their fullest expression in terms that might be perceived as religious in nature. Such is the tension when worldviews collide and their basic beliefs conflict.[51]

For the discerning Christian bioethicist, final ethical decisions sometimes align with those of non-Christian colleagues or fellow caregivers, possibly through recognition of basic norms of ethics that resist the basically sinful nature of human thinking. At other times, basic Christian beliefs may lead to basic disagreement so as to acknowledge the transformative power of God's Word. Examples of such disagreements may be the refusal to engage in *in vitro* fertilization wherein human embryos are killed through discarding them or dissecting them for research purposes. Christians involved in palliative care may refuse to facilitate the death of a patient if requested by the patient in the name of compassion under the medical aid in dying provision in law. Such refusal is grounded in a basic belief that compassion does not include killing on request but involves

49. Beauchamp and Childress, *Principles of Biomedical Ethics*, 7th ed., 204, 205.

50. Edmund D. Pellegrino, "The Four Principles and the Doctor-Patient Relationship: The Need for a Better Linkage," in *Principles of Health Care Ethics*, ed. Raanan Gillon (New York: John Wiley & Sons, 1994), 353.

51. Rawls' restrictive role of religion in political life is even criticized by postmodernist philosopher Jurgen Habermas, who is empathetic to Robert Audi's objection to Rawls' requirements to translate religious belief into secular reasons and language to give them validity in making law or public policy. Alvin Plantinga calls this postmodern mentality "creative anti-realism", where thought and language are somehow held responsible for fundamental structures and entities of the world. See Alvin Plantinga, "Advice to Christian Philosophers." *Faith and Philosophy* 1, no. 3 (1984); Robert Audi and Nicholas Wolterstorff, *Religion in the Public Square* (Lanham, MD: Rowman and Littlefield), 1997); and Jürgen Habermas, *Between Naturalism and Religion: Philosophical Essays* (Cambridge, UK: Polity 2008).

giving care to the naturally dying as skillfully as possible.

Concerns of Formative Christian Bioethicists Regarding Principlism and the Influence of Secular Worldviews

Although the early development of bioethics was heavily influenced by theologians in the decades preceding the Belmont Report, the report was influenced more by other academics and professionals, only some of whom were professing Christians. While the principles articulated in the report were generally not antithetical to Christian moral values, many Christian bioethicists have expressed concerns over the practical outworking of principlism in light of the influence of dominant non-Christian, secular worldviews in our culture.

In judging the worth of a common morality based on four principles, a Reformational perspective takes into consideration both supporting and critical views of principles-based ethics and its common morality idea. Principles-based ethics as promoted by Beauchamp and Childress was dubbed principlism by K. Danner Clouser and Bernard Gert,[52] mainly because it lacks moral content and relational meaning. By the 1990s bioethicist Daniel Callahan was particularly perceptive in his analysis of the fruits of principles-based ethics, suggesting that the roots of principlism were present even in the Belmont Commission itself.[53] Despite his own drift from Roman Catholicism in his personal life, Callahan expressed disillusionment and discontent with the "detached neutrality" (or the "view from nowhere" as characterized by Thomas Nagel[54]) and "culture-free rationalistic universalism"[55] that has materialized in the aftermath of the Belmont Report.[56] This universalism of "the principles movement", as he calls it, was suspicious of the emotions and particularities of actual human communities. Moreover, he observed that many religious believers involved in bioethics also expressed fear of the consequences of revealing their deepest convictions in public moral discourse, a fear that Callahan not only could understand but confessed himself. He bemoans that this disappearing or "denaturing" of Christianity and other

52. K. Danner Clouser and Bernard Gert, "A Critique of Principlism," *Journal of Medicine and Philosophy* 15, no. 2 (1990): 219.

53. Daniel D. Callahan, "Religion and the Secularization of Bioethics." *Hastings Center Report* 20, no.4 (1990): 2–4.

54. Thomas Nagel, *The View From Nowhere.* New York: Oxford University Press, 1989.

55. Callahan, "Religion and the Secularization of Bioethics," 4.

56. For an excellent essay on the myth of religious neutrality in the generation of theories, including moral theories, from a Reformational perspective, see Clouser, *Myth of Religious Neutrality* , particularly pp. 89–109.

religions in public discourse leaves us too heavily *dependent on the law as the working source of morality* and "bereft of the accumulated wisdom and knowledge that are the fruit of long-established religious traditions".[57] Callahan's analysis and critique challenge the tendency of some Christians to mask the Christian beliefs behind their views expressed in public discourse, and to "talk a form of what Jeffery Stout has called moral Esperanto."[58]

Christian philosopher Charles Taylor rightly considers principles-based ethics to be a *proceduralist ethics*, having as its central preoccupation a reflective testing of moral beliefs, moral principles, and judgments with the goal of making them coherent.[59] Taylor attributes the dominance of this approach in contemporary ethics to a belief that special status can be given to universal principles divorced from constitutive goods or standards rooted in authoritative moral sources. Proceduralists come to considerable agreement over the existence of these principles but often disagree over their sources of morality. Taylor sees these sources coming from three major (and diverse) domains (and worldviews): (1) original theistic grounding, (2) naturalism of disengaged reason, usually in a form of scientism, and (3) Romantic expressivism[60].

In the tradition of Enlightenment naturalism, moral proceduralists (like Beauchamp and Childress) distance themselves from "the goods of the spirit" by focusing on so-called universal standards as principles. Taylor systematically documents the deep disagreements within persistent streams of modernity and between the objective order of the modernist and and subjective personal resonance sought by postmodernity. What is lost in this temporal tension is a coherent place for the exploration of

57. Callahan, "Religion and the Secularization of Bioethics," 3–4.

58. Callahan, "Religion and the Secularization of Bioethics," 4.

59. Beauchamp and Childress, *Principles of Biomedical Ethics*, 7th ed., 404-410. As noted earlier in this chapter, Rawls coined the term "reflective equilibrium", whereby iterative reflections on moral judgments are tested repeatedly against other judgments and beliefs held by other moral agents. In theory, this results in considered judgments. The criteria for such judgments and beliefs are consistency, coherence with nonmoral beliefs such as empirical evidence and well-established scientific theories, comprehensiveness in covering the appropriate territory in the moral domain, absence of bias, argumentative support, and restricting starting premises to considered judgments that are worthy of belief independent of any support by reasons. In his critique of Rawls's application of this process to political thought, Wolterstorff disagrees that common reason alone justifies moral judgments coming from such a process. Rather, the use of reason in this process is a function of what we already believe. For Wolterstorff's critique of Rawls's political theory, see Audi and Wolterstorff *Religion in the Public Square*, 90–116.

60. Charles Taylor, *Sources of the Self* (Cambridge, MA: Harvard University Press 1989), 368, 390, 423.

human ethical interaction that draws on extra-human moral sources. In other words, in moral discourse, coherence should not be sought through the exclusion of moral sources outside of human rationality but through their inclusion. According to Taylor, morality becomes the product of individual creative powers alone and the proceduralist is motivated to default to the position of abandoning moral sources altogether.[61] From my Reformational perspective, I believe Taylor's critique of proceduralist ethics masterfully characterizes the dilemma of the common morality wherein God is ignored or moved to the side, the inherent sinful nature of the moral order of creation is not acknowledged, and thus no redemptive need is perceived!

Nigel Biggar has recently claimed that the ideal of secular medicine (including biomedical ethics) as a realm of reason and therefore as untroubled by deep metaphysical and moral disagreements is a fantasy. Secular space should not pretend to be neutral and transcending conflict. Rather, the saeculum should be understood in its original Augustinian meaning of an age of spiritual and moral mix and ambiguity where peace results from negotiation and provisional compromised between rival viewpoints. Such a concept of secularity is more reflective of a "genuinely liberal, plural political ideal than a dogmatically antireligious, secularist version".[62] Principlism was founded on the translational model of Rawls where dialoguing across radical differences ideally starts behind a veil of ignorance, setting aside aspects of their identities and offering compelling reasons irrespective of specific basic beliefs or doctrines people hold. Those engaged in moral dialog are expected to translate their moral concerns into a shared language such as the "broad, abstract, and content-thin" morality of principlism that all should accept, regardless of their particular faith commitments. Against the spirit of this translational model, Jecker et al propose a pluriversal approach to global bioethics whereby persons in bioethical debates are respected in their particularities, including religious beliefs. The latter reflect not only different worldviews, but different ontologies or even very existences.[63]

H. Tristram Engelhardt typifies the struggle of many Christian bioethicists in his time. As a Roman Catholic, he wrote in 1986 that traditional sources of moral authority in Western society had irreversibly fragmented, reiterating Alasdair MacIntyre's insights expressed in *After*

61. Taylor, *Sources of the Self*, 495–518.

62. Nigel Biggar, "Why Religion Deserved a Place in Secular Medicine,' in J *Med Ethics* 2015;41:229–230.

63. Nancy S Jecker, C. A. Atuire, V Ravisky, M. Ghaly, V. Vaswani, and T. C. Voo, "Religion Welcome Here: A Pluriversal Approach to Religion and Global Ethics," Bioethical Enquiry, https://doi.org/10.1007/s11673-024-10410-7.

Virtue.[64] For Engelhardt at that time, moral agreement among moral strangers required commonly accepted procedures for moral reflection. However, he had no Christian critique of, or response to, the proceduralism of principlism. As a consultant, he proposed the principles of respect for persons and beneficence that were largely accepted into the Belmont Report. He later supported principles-based biomedical ethics and argued that moral principles derive their content only through the formation of a web of mutual commitments and understandings that sustain some fabric of moral consensus. Again, he had not formed a Christian response to proceduralist morality. At the time he did not articulate involvement in any particular moral community, considering the principles as necessary for broad moral discourse.

However, following his conversion to Eastern Orthodox Christianity after the first edition of *The Foundations of Bioethics* in 1986, Engelhardt became much more forthright about the influence of his faith on his biomedical ethics. He suggested that if one wishes to engage in what he calls thick morality of moral friends rather than the spare morality of secular reason, one should join a religion and choose the right one![65] As a Roman Catholic, Engelhardt assumed an *accommodating* position with those of secular and other faith traditions at the expense of overtly explicit allusions to the influence of his own faith on his thinking. After his conversion to Eastern Orthodoxy, this changed *transformationally* to an intentional inclusion of the main sources of his moral thinking: Scripture and the writings of the early church fathers of the Eastern Orthodox tradition. Unfortunately, and sometimes to the distraction of even fellow Christian leaders in the field, his critique of fellow non-Orthodox Christians at times could be less than courteous if not offensive.[66]

Roman Catholic bioethicist Edmund Pellegrino is also critical of the lack of moral content and of moral justification in the principles-based framework of Beauchamp and Childress. But he chooses to engage the biomedical ethics community through his faith, setting out to develop a philosophy of medicine rooted in the Thomist tradition and grounded in the good of the patient.[67] He sees common grace features of the

---

64. H. Tristram Engelhardt Jr., *The Foundations of Bioethics* (New York: Oxford University Press, 1986), 39, 75; MacIntyre, *After Virtue.*

65. Engelhardt, *The Foundations of Christian Bioethics* (Lisse, NL: Swets & Zeitlinger, 2000), xvi.

66. Gilbert Meilaender, "Review of *The Foundations of Christian Bioethics,* by H. Tristram Engelhardt, Jr." in *First Things* (November 2000). Engelhardt feels that other Christian views are bound to fall short unless they are restored to the fullness of Orthodox vision. Meilaender quotes from Engelhardt: "The Church may once have had two lungs, but one [i.e., Western Christianity] developed cancer."

67. Pellegrino, "The Four Principles," 360, 362.

principles as a moral *lingua franca* among those with divergent and often incommensurable moral presuppositions. However, for Pellegrino, principlism also fails adequately to account for virtues, particularly the Christian virtues.

True to his Thomist roots, Pellegrino's answer to principlism is its merging with Thomist virtue ethics.[68] In so doing he also seeks to *transform* rather than discard the four principles, redefining and grounding them in the reality of the doctor-patient relationship of medical practice. For Pellegrino, the core of the doctor-patient relationship is beneficence expressed as care and it dominates over autonomy. Pellegrino recognizes the dominance of autonomy and individualism in American society. From his Roman Catholic perspective, he argues that the virtue of love (or charity) binds morality and gives the principles some much needed grounding in a biblical source. Pellegrino considers the principles to be moral structural realities that can be ascertained by reason alone but wants to give them moral substance and authority through his Christian worldview.[69] Pellegrino sees the principles grounded in the moral obligations of humans to each other and in need of a deeper relational context missing in principlism. Beneficence is the guiding principle while love is its informing and illuminating virtue for resolving conflicting principles. For Pellegrino, beneficence unifies biomedical ethics, keeping physicians and patients in relationship through a *beneficence of trust.* In short, the principle of beneficence is given substance through virtue, in capturing care for the needy as an obligation under the overarching principle of love graciously given by God through his covenant.

Put into Reformational terms, beneficence gives expression to the core or qualifying ethical aspect of medicine, practically manifesting as loving care for the needy (discussed later in this chapter in the section on regaining or redeeming biomedical ethics). This obligation of caring is derived from our special status as image-bearers of God. By his grace, God founded a covenantal relationship with humankind and each human being.[70] Pellegrino also maintains that the traditional Hippocratic

68. Beauchamp and Childress do not ignore the importance of virtues but do not give due attention to their importance and, as with their principles, give no moral source for virtue outside of human nature or intuitive induction.

69. This presupposition of reason to worldview was previously suggested in the work of Protestants Carl Henry and Francis Schaeffer (see Goheen and Bartholomew, *Living*, 16). Goheen and Bartholomew contend that Abraham Kuyper's epistemology was fundamentally different, asserting that one's epistemology is a development of one's worldview and hence denies the autonomy and pre-eminence of reason. It further demonstrates the strong influence of rationalism and the dominance of reason on both Roman Catholic and Protestant traditions.

70. Pellegrino 1996, 107, 117.

model has served medicine well as a manifestation of natural law, realized through reason by Aristotle and Hippocratic physicians. In developing a Reformational view of beneficence, however, appeals to Greek views based on reason need to be carefully judged against the biblical concept of morality, including Christian virtues as presented in Scripture.

Anglican theologian N. T. Wright emphasizes the importance of practicing Christian virtues in order to build Christian character, noting that Christians like Pellegrino seek Christian virtues over so-called natural virtues as those more likely to build Christian character. The Christian vision of virtue is about discovering what it means to be truly human and flourishing by putting our humanity in its proper context.[71] Jesus teaches the rich young ruler in Mark 10 that the idea of keeping the old covenant law to earn eternal life needs to be turned inside out. That is, obedience to the law becomes the fruit of our renewed character in Christ and of the virtues expressed through such renewal. Wright notes that the early Christians claimed that in and through Jesus they discovered a totally different way of being human *and* a way which took lessons of ancient wisdom and put them in a framework in which it could now be seen in its fullest meaning. The principles of the common morality and teachings of the Hippocratic tradition might be understood as transformable in this way. The New Testament vision of a genuinely good human life, says Wright, is a life of character formed by God's promised future that is lived within the ongoing story of God's people.[72]

As Reformed theologian Gordon Spykman puts it so well, one *golden thread* that runs through that story is God's gracious creating and keeping of a relational covenant with his people.[73] It is by faith in his promises of life fulfilled in the redemptive power of Christ's death and resurrection and by the work of the Holy Spirit, that virtues and principles can give substance and expression to Christian character. In my view, it is through the relational bond of a biblical idea of covenant for human relationships that Pellegrino's transformation of the principles can be fully realized and expressed in interhuman relationships inherent to medicine. He sees the principles as inherent to a natural created order within a natural ethical mindset, an inner conscience as the apostle Paul put it in Romans 2. However, sin has directed many bioethicists to rely on their own intuition and reason alone, being laws unto themselves, in confronting ethical issues.

71. N.T. Wright, *After You Believe: Why Christian Character Matters* (New York: Harper-Collins), 2010, 25.

72. Wright, *After You Believe*, 25, 26, 48, 57.

73. Gordon Spykman, *Reformational Theology: A New Paradigm for Doing Dogmatics* (Grand Rapids, MI: Eerdmans 1992), 11–12.

Pellegrino and Wright seek to restore God's Word as the true source of ethical wisdom. In acknowledgment of the relational richness offered by a biblical notion of covenant, we can now advance Pellegrino's work beyond the physician-patient relationship to involve *all* care-focused relationships in medicine. Each relationship in medical practice can be expressed through the covenantal responsibilities of all parties to each other, mirroring the covenantal relationship that we need with God through Jesus Christ.

In the next section the case will be made for developing through a Reformational perspective an ethical framework based on the biblical theme of covenant within which the four principles can be re-envisioned through a biblical relational framework. As will be explained later in the section, I will build on such a notion of covenant previously developed and applied in biomedical ethics by William F. May.

Redeeming Biomedical Ethics: Developing a Reformational Framework

In previous sections, I have tried to show how bioethicists have explored structural realities of bioethics in this fallen world, largely working from very basic common morality principles that guide bioethical discourse. Yet, the main elements of redemptive history are not recognized and an ordered creation is not recognized. Sin is not acknowledged as an influence on this common morality, and consensus building through human reason alone is the basis for the moral validity of ethical agreement.

While some Christians have been attracted to the minimalist simplicity of principlism amid the moral uncertainty and confusion caused by sin, formative Christian bioethicists such as Pellegrino and Engelhardt have unabashedly proposed more content-rich ethical deliberations and decision-making informed by Scripture. Their particular Christian moral communities see the normative place of these principles in biomedical ethics as best understood when *faith in moral consensus through reason* is replaced by *faith in the Christ and the Word of God* as the source of moral authority and direction for biomedical discourse and decision-making. From this perspective, beneficence has normative dominance among the principles as the ethical core of relational caring. I am thankful for Pellegrino's work which in many ways comes into close alignment with a Reformational worldview. Importantly, his incorporation of Christian virtue ethics displaces an inherent dominance of autonomy and individualism with beneficence and relational caring, a transforming step toward restoring the principles to their proper normative relationship in light of biblical teaching of moral norms.[74]

Those with a Reformational perspective could be considered members of a particular Christian moral community. In common with some other Christian moral communities is a basic belief in God as the source of moral teaching and truth, in a cosmic order created and overseen by God, in sin as a distorting influence that must be taken into account through biblical teaching, and in the redemptive power of Jesus Christ through the working of the Holy Spirit. A significant insight of this perspective sees reductionism as a major distorting influence of sin that can rob humankind of the richness of creation and of the disciplines that seek to understand it.

This influence of sin on scholarship including in bioethics must be recognized and efforts made to redeem its distortional effects through the covenantal renewing of care relationships in medicine. The importance of this for all scholarly work about the creation order cannot be overly stressed. As Paul told the Corinthians, if anyone is in Christ, he *is* a new creation![75] All of redemptive history comes full circle through the new covenant in Christ. We will next discuss a path forward under that premise of regaining bioethics through the new covenant.

Christian Anthropology and Relationships

As creatures, human beings can be studied and understood in both structural and directional terms. Important to this structure / direction understanding of human functioning is a biblical understanding of human selfhood. Dooyeweerd defines this as "the concentric directedness of the totality of a person's existence toward the Origin of meaning."[76]; that is, being human involves pursuing meaning for one's existence beyond one's self. For many who adhere to the common morality and the reflective equilibrium model, the source of moral meaning comes from within one's humanness and rational capabilities. For Beauchamp and Childress, the common morality with its four principles is "… a product of human experience and history and is a universally shared product…. The common morality comprises moral beliefs (what all morally committed persons believe), not standards prior to moral belief."[77] However,

74. Wolters, *Creation Regained*, 71–72.

75. 2 Corinthians 5:17.

76. Gerrit Glas, "Ego, Self, and the Body: An Assessment of Dooyeweerd's Philosophical Anthropology,"in *Christian Philosophy at the Close of the Twentieth Century: An Assessment and Perspective*, ed. Sander Griffioen and B. M. Balk (Kampen: Kok, 1995), 70.

77. Beauchamp and Childress, *Principles of Biomedical Ethics*, 6th ed. (New York: Oxford University Press, 2009), 3-4.

a source of ethical meaning outside of human beings is either unknown or non-existent.

For Christians, that moral meaning is God and directedness toward God is possible because God first established a covenant with human beings at creation.[78] Within that relationship, human selfhood has its ontological essence in bearing God's image through which a dynamic hearing of and responding to the calling of God is possible. That covenant was re-established specially for a people chosen by God among humankind through Abraham and charged to be God's light to their pagan neighbours. It was renewed through the death and resurrection of Jesus Christ, fulfilling the older covenants established with Adam and Abraham and now made fully accessible to all of humankind. Under this New Covenant in Christ, we gain atonement from his once-and-for-all sacrifice and a vision of how graciously and sacrificially to relate to those around us, whether neighbours, strangers, or enemies.

In a particularly important insight relevant to the contemporary principles of autonomy and beneficence, Roman Catholic theologian Hans Urs von Balthasar warns that the scriptural theme of covenant must be an integral component of the constitutive structure of human nature. Otherwise, *if this covenant component is lost, human nature moves toward an ethic of autonomy, "the very antipode of covenantal ethics."*[79] This insight is applicable to an inadequacy of principlism; that is, the dominant place of autonomy that threatens deep relational and ethical / care aspects of medical practice.[80] The scriptural notion of covenant acknowledges human self as both individual and communal. Just as human beings have a relationship with God and are accountable directly to him, so also human beings have relationships with each other. The African concept of *ubuntu* captures well the importance of the individual and

78. Peter A. Lillback, *The Binding of God: Calvin's Role in the Development of Covenant Theology* (Grand Rapids, MI: Baker Academic, 2001), 1, 27, 51, 135-139; John Calvin, *Institutes of the Christian Religion*, ed. John T. McNeill, trans. Ford L. Battles, (Philadelphia, PA: The Westminster Press, 1960), 241-245, 1294. Some Reformed theologians have made compelling arguments for a creational covenant established by God with Adam and Eve by his gracious willingness to give special status of humankind as his image-bearer. Peter Lillback notes that John Calvin teaches that such a covenant was sealed by the sacrament that was the tree of life.

79. Russell Hittlinger, "Theology and Natural Law." *Communio (International Catholic Review)* 17 (1990): 402-408; Hans Urs von Balthasar, "Nine Propositions on Christian Ethics," in *Principles of Christian Morality*, ed. Joseph Cardinal Ratzinger, Heinz Schürmann, Hans Urs von Balthasar, trans. Graham Harrison (San Francisco, CA: Ignatius Press, 1986), 92–94.

80. Pellegrino and Thomasma, *The Christian Virtues in Medical Practice*, 118-121. Pellegrino calls autonomy "the most problematic of the prima facie principles because it is individualistic rather than communal in focus." (p. 118).

communal nature, conveying a sense of human selfhood wherein one is a person only because of, and through, relationships with other persons. The meaning of the ethic of care in medical relationships depends on what relationship each party has with God or with some other perceived source of moral meaning.

In Dooyeweerd's social philosophy, different relationships across vocations can be distinguished by a particular modal function of reality that qualifies the essence and focus of that relationship.[81] For example, the core or qualifying aspect of a business is economic. In practice, the relationship between a member of the business and a customer or client involves an exchange of products or services for monetary gain sufficient to support the components of the business. There is also an ethical component, a social component, a linguistic component, etc. As noted earlier, differences in qualifying aspects may lead to conflicts in motives within relationships. Conflicts between pharmaceutical companies, patients, and caregivers will be discussed in illustration near the end of this chapter.

A Reformational understanding of the ontological nature of a given relationship helps a Christian medical practitioner to know how best to serve, love and honor whatever party she or he happens to be interacting with at a given moment in time.

Toward a Reformational View of Normative Medical Relationships

In recent decades, Reformed Christians have applied this Christian philosophical understanding of the created order to medical practice. Following MacIntyre, Taylor, and Dooyeweerd, Henk Jochemsen sees inherent value in reality that is independent of its utility for human beings. This contrasts with dominant views of contemporary bioethics, including principlism, whereby meaning is found solely in shared human experience as a construct of human activity. Jochemsen and others see medical relationships between caregiver and patient as historically conditioned, coherent forms of socially established human activity. Seen through his Reformational perspective, medical practice unfolds historically in light of cultural and technical changes that affect how the practice is carried out. Linguistic, psychic, social, and other aspects are *conditioned* by these historical realities and compliance with rules of practice is guided by the qualifying ethical or caring aspect, resulting in a competent implementation of the practice.[82] A covenantal ethic as described previously encom-

81. Chaplin, *Herman Dooyeweerd*, 86–91.

82. Jochemsen, "Normative Practices," 97–105; Chaplin, *Herman Dooyeweerd*, 119.

passes the relational expression of the ethical / caring core aspect of medical relationships and gives depth to the meaning of the four principles.

Some have appealed to a covenantal commitment to medical relationships but have not always grounded them in a biblical notion of covenant. For example, the Patient-Physician Covenant was composed and endorsed by eight prominent physicians out of concern that fundamental values and responsibilities of physicians to the sick through a covenant of trust are being threatened by caregiver self-interest toward monetary and power gains. They cite the ancient Greek medical tradition as the origin of transcendent significance and make no direct appeal to moral authority outside of human common agreement to meet obligations toward such a covenant.[83] Medical educator Jeff Nisker appeals to a covenantal relationship between medical educators and their students to recapture the moral nature of medicine but cites no specific moral tradition or authority to support his appeal. Nurse Sue Coffey calls for a covenantal concept that can improve patient-nurse relationships, alluding to the covenant idea in the Greek medical tradition but also crediting Protestant bioethicist William F. May with leading a resurgence of covenant thought as a prescriptive model for medical relationships without mentioning his biblical source. Through lenses of feminist and care ethics, Coffey presupposes the covenantal nature of patient-nurse relationships which promotes an anthropocentric focus for relationships, caring benevolence, and situational particulars.[84]

Thus, there is a contemporary movement seeking to give deeper meaning to medical relationships through a notion of covenant, though often of pagan Greek origin. This interest has provided an opportunity for Christian caregivers to further develop a biblical notion of covenant through a Reformational perspective in the context of medicine.

The Biblical Notion of Covenant as Applied to Biomedical Ethics

Thankfully, several theologians in biomedical ethics have sought to understand medical relationships through a Reformed interpretation of biblical covenant. As early as the 1950s, Paul Ramsey introduced into biomedical ethics the idea of Christian neighbourly and obedient love as

83. Christine Cassel, "The Patient-Physician Covenant: An Affirmation of Asklepios." *Annals of Internal Medicine* 124, no.6 (1996): 604–605.

84. Susan Coffey, "The Patient-Physician Covenant: An Affirmation of Asklepios," *Annals of Internal Medicine* 124, no.6 (2006): 308–23; Jeffrey Nisker, "A Covenantal Model for the Medical Educator-Student Relationship: Lessons from the Covenant Model of the Physician-Patient Relationship." *Medical Education* 40 (2006): 502–3.

enlightened unselfishness for the sake of others.[85] Later in his writings, he emphasized covenantal love as a means to ensure the protection of vulnerable patients from harm.[86] However, Ramsey's broader application of the covenant idea for both Christians and non-Christians at times drifted into more generic principles of medical ethics. Though remaining a committed Christian, Ramsey appeared to accommodate secular philosophers by using less theological language. Stanley Hauerwas once rebuked Ramsey for leaving his theology behind in the preface of his book *The Patient as Person* rather than making clear the biblical source of his claims in the body of the work.[87] Ramsey sees ethical principles as directions of action, subordinate to *agape* love but emanating from the covenantal relationship of one who loves others and the neighbour in need.[88] Christ's death and resurrection allow for a richer meaning for moral principles and a fresh perspective on what should be done in situations requiring moral discernment.[89]

Hauerwas also imagines medicine in relational terms. It is a commitment of presence for those who suffer in the body and mutually beneficial. As outsiders of the human community, the sick demand a great deal but they also teach the caregiver what it means to be ill and how it is to live with illness. A universal basis for morality is illusory and Christians should speak forthrightly and honestly about the influence of their particularly Christian community beliefs on their moral judgments, particularly the acknowledgment of sin on human moral activity.[90]

Addressing specific key bioethical issues of his day, particularly

---

85 Paul Ramsey, *Basic Christian Ethics* (New York: Charles Scribner's Sons, 1952), 89, 148.

86. As David Smith notes, Ramsey believed the God-human relationship establishes a standard or norm for person-to-person relationships. In Jesus's teaching as the new covenant, Jesus's commandment to love provides us with a norm for each particular relationship that we have with others. See David H. Smith, "On Paul Ramsey: A Covenant-Centered Ethic for Medicine," in *Theological Voices in Medical Ethics*, ed. Allen Verhey and Stephen E. Lammers (Grand Rapids, MI: Wm B. Eerdmans, 1993), 7–9.

87. Paul F. Camenisch, "Paul Ramsey's Task: 'Some Methodological Clarifications and Questions,'" in *Love and Society: Essays in the Ethics of Paul Ramsey*, ed. James Turner Johnson and David H. Smith (Missoula, MT: Scholars Press, 1974), 73, 75, 81. See Stanley Hauerwas, "How Christian Ethics Became Medical Ethics: The Case of Paul Ramsey," *Christian Bioethics* 1, no.1 (1995), 15–16.

88. Smith, "On Paul Ramsey," 11–12.

89. Paul Ramsey, *Deeds and Rules in Christian Ethics* (New York: Charles Scribner's Sons, 1967), 195.

90. Steven Lammers, "On Stanley Hauerwas: Theology, Medical Ethics, and the Church," in Theological Voices in Medical Ethics, ed Allen Verhey and Stephen E. Lammers (Grand Rapids, MI: Wm B. Eerdmans, 1993), 57–76.

informed consent of research subjects and patients,[91] Ramsey laid the groundwork for a more systematic covenantal ethic idea formed by fellow Reformed bioethicist, William F. May. Lutheran bioethicist Gilbert Meilaender believes that Ramsey was an important influence on May and that both were influenced by Karl Barth.[92] Barth sees "creation as the external basis of the covenant", its backdrop, with "covenant as the internal basis of creation" for sharing life with other created persons.[93] May bases his covenantal model for medicine on the new covenant with Christ and on the relationship between Christ and his believers. Its expression in interhuman relationships constitutes a dynamic of giving and receiving, rooted in the created order as the backdrop for human interrelating.[94]

For May, loyalty to God inherent in the covenant requires our loyalty to the care of all God's creatures. Like Pellegrino, he expresses concern that Ramsey's deontological focus on rules and principles undermines the importance of virtuous expression. While May sees value in principles-oriented theories in a pluralistic society, he also believes that a covenantal ethic must be operative in medicine, with more substantive obligations than contractual models, attending to the question of what character we should develop as moral agents when applying those guides and standards.[95] Caregivers are primarily moral agents and their character and virtues brought out in their relationships with others should become the true mark of their practice.

May understands why principles-based ethics, with its problem-solving approach of avoiding "divisive appeals to a particular religious commitment", is attractive to Christians.[96] But like Hauerwas, May expresses regret that some "closet" Christian and Jewish moralists suppress overt references to their religious convictions in their writings, implying that

91. Paul Ramsey, *The Patient as Person* (New York: Yale University Press, 1970), 5, 14. He called informed consent the cardinal canon of loyalty in medical relationships.

92. Gilbert Meilaender, "On William F. May: Corrected Vision for Medical Ethics," in *Theological Voices in Medical Ethics*, ed. Allen Verhey and Stephen E. Lammers (Grand Rapids, MI: Wm B. Eerdmans, 1993), 115.

93. Karl Barth, *Church Dogmatics*, Volume 3, *The Doctrine of Creation, Part 1* (Edinburgh, UK: T. and T. Clark, 1958).

94. William F. May, *Testing the Medical Covenant: Active Euthanasia and Health Care Reform* (Grand Rapids, MI: Eerdmans, 1996), 53.

95. May, *Testing the Medical Covenant*, 54ff. May uses the term "covenant" in its biblical sense, distinguishing its usage in unsavory practices, such as loyalty pledges to professional societies that are intended to take precedent over duties to patients. God's covenant with Israel prefigures the inclusive covenant that is offered up to the whole of humankind in Jesus Christ. See also William F. May, *The Physician's Covenant*. Philadelphia, PA: Westminster Press, 1983), ch. 4.

96. May, *Testing the Medical Covenant*, 55.

society and medicine are confessionally indeterminate.[97]

In spirit, covenants are internal to the parties involved, calling for a *transformation* from expectations of a contractual relationship and going beyond just expediently carrying out obligations and promises. Covenants, says May, have "a gratuitous, growing edge" that comes from fundamental change in a person's being as the relationship grows.[98] A truly covenantal bond with patients leads to discernment, judgments, and actions for the patient's best interests alone.[99] In medicine, a biblical notion of covenant promotes an acceptance of responsibility by the more powerful caregiver partner toward the more vulnerable patient who is a stranger. Jesus Christ has transformed death into the power of donative love through his death and resurrection.[100] For believers, God remains with the dying; he supports them and the caregivers who give aid to their suffering and their dying.[101]

May also sees the ethical struggles in confronting the contemporary notion of medical assistance in dying:

> I favour social policies that would permit allowing to die rather than killing for mercy, policies that would allow caregivers and patients to recognize the moment in illness when it is no longer meaningful to bend every effort to cure or to prolong life, when it is fitting to allow patients to do their own dying with technical assistance in managing pain. This policy seems most consonant with the covenantal obligations of the community to care and of those of us in need of care to rise to the occasion.[102]

This is consonant with a Reformational view of being human and accepting the gift of life that only God can remove. But it also imagines rare instances where actively hastening someone's death might be appropriate. May wishes to retain covenantal responsibility for patients under biblical guidance while resisting law-making that risks bypassing moral concern and turning careful reflection of caregivers into purely autono-

97. May, *The Physician's Covenant,* 24–25, 31.

98. May, *The Physician's Covenant,* 119, 120, 128–130.

99. May, *Testing the Medical Covenant,* 68–72. As a violation of this bond, he gives the example of third-payer payments systems such as health maintenance organizations (HMOs) that may provide profit incentives for physicians in such HMOs to undertreat patients to save costs, thus undermining covenantal fidelity to such patients.

100. May, *The Physician's Covenant,* 124; William F. May, "Code, Covenant, Contract or Philanthropy," *Hastings Center Report* 5, no. 6 (1975): 29–38.

101. Rom 8: 38, 39: "... neither death, nor life, ... nor anything else in all creation, will be able to separate us from the love of God that is in Christ Jesus our Lord."

102. May, *Testing the Medical Covenant,* 48.

mous patient choice. Patients' choices devoid of caregiver counsel deprive the patients of caregiver expertise and wisdom derived from experience of the practice.

Other Reformed bioethicists have contributed to this discussion, but space limits me to mentioning one additional group. Hessel Bouma III and his colleagues show that the covenant relationship with God is at the root of all human relationships and of our relationship with creation as its stewards. Covenantal relationships are more demanding and involve the community more than minimalist moral viewpoints that prioritize the rights of the individual over the caring support of the community. As noted above, minimalist ethics stress negative rights of not inflicting harm but can lead to a one-sided individualism.[103] Covenantal obligation of the caregiver to patients includes the watchfulness to recognize moments when it is helpful to explicitly articulate to patients the truth of Christ as the fulfillment of all human need.

Contemporary Network of Relationships among Strangers in Medical Care

Focusing more on character building applied to covenantal relating than on principles as the core of medicine is a redeeming change toward a more Reformed biblical understanding of medicine. For May, the covenanted unity of character lets the good of the practice become its *telos*. He sees this as the virtue of practice integrity while from a Reformational perspective it is a dimension of the ethic of care core qualifying function of the practice. However, in contemporary society, the ethical emphasis tends to be on rights of patients and duties of caregivers. Such relationships involve a discordance of power between strangers. Campbell and Lustig believe that the caring professions express traditions of duty of care embedded in religiously rooted visions of the good that are intrinsic to such practices.[104] Duty of care for the needs of others draws its deepest meaning from the covenant with God.

Michael Horton argues that overcoming estrangement when meeting the stranger requires an ontology of genuine difference and an episte-

103. Hessel Bouma III et al., *Christian Faith, Health, and Medical Practice* (Grand Rapids, MI: Wm B. Eerdmans, 1989), 88-94. Kenneth Vaux sees a similar role for covenantal relating in medicine, emphasizing the importance of *an ethic of koinonia*, fellowships of believers who are joined together as one body and covenanted community. See Kenneth L. Vaux, *Health and Medicine in the Reformed Tradition* (New York: Crossroad, 1984), 14, 15, 34, 45, 96–98, 105–109, 126–127.

104. Courtney S. Campbell and B. Andrew Lustig, "A Call to Respond: Duties to Others," in *Duties to Others*, ed. Courtney S. Campbell and B. Andrew Lustig (Dordrecht: Kluwer Academic, 1994), ix.

mology of the external word, both grounded in a theology of covenant. Covenant love generates an ethic wherein the biblical new covenant becomes the site where strangers can meet and relational renewal can take place. All human beings exist in a unity of dependence that draws them to each other.[105] In biblical new covenant ethics, human gift-giving has no expectant reciprocation. In medicine, this tempers the power of the caregiver by imparting a greater receptivity to the gift of providing care to the person in need.[106] God repeatedly required that Israel respond to the needs of the aliens among them just as God had provided for Israel's needs when they were aliens in Egypt.[107] This event in redemptive history should be a guide to a Reformational understanding of relationship development in medical practice.

Manifestations of Covenantal Relating: Beyond the Physician-Patient Relationship

Medicine today involves growing *networks of relationships* due in large part to the growing knowledge of health and disease and to the increasing number of therapies that assist in providing care. As a result, a differentiation of care function is resulting in new types of caregivers such as physician assistants and nurse practitioners. In managing a medical illness, there may be a primary caregiver as well as those trained in specialty care. For caregivers, adherence to a covenantal ethic requires professional competence, a disposition toward empathy, conscious character development, and a provision for effective, patient-focused inter-caregiver communication. Attentive caregiver listening is needed to appreciate the degree to which patients understand their illness. Translation of complex medical concepts and jargon is critical to forming a relationship with mutual covenantal trust and understanding. The power difference between the knowledgeable and experienced caregiver and the vulnerable patient must be recognized. Both caregiver and patient should try to understand the source of moral guidance and authority from which each draws moral strength. Even if those sources are very different, sharing their importance can lead to more trusting and honest decision-making

105. Michael S. Horton, "Participation and Covenant," in *Radical Orthodoxy and the Reformed Tradition*, ed. James K. A. Smith and James H. Olthuis (Grand Rapids, MI: Baker Academic, 2005), 115–120.

106. May, *The Physician's Covenant*, 1983, 114; Courtney S. Campbell, "Gifts and Caring Duties in Medicine," in *Duties to Others*, ed. Courtney S. Campbell and B. Andrew Lustig (Dordrecht: Kluwer Academic 1994), 190–194.

107. James B. Tubbs, Jr., "Theology and the Invitation of the Stranger," in *Duties to Others*, ed. Courtney S. Campbell and B. Andrew Lustig (Dordrecht: Kluwer Academic, 1994), 39–41.

regarding prognosis, treatment, and outcome expectations.

Covenantal relating can enrich shared decision-making. The risks and benefits of each treatment option offered must be carefully weighed by caregivers. Expressions of mutual trustworthiness involve patients striving to understand and comply with a mutually agreed upon care plan and communicate fully and honestly with the caregiver throughout implementation of the care plan. Patient charters have arisen in part out of a lack of covenantal trust, stating existing legal rights for patients and empowering them to acquire third-party assistance toward complaint resolution. Such charters have evolved as moral protection against the sin of power abuse by some caregivers who abuse their position of trust.

Covenantal relating should also be fostered between colleagues who provide care to the same patient. Mutual respect for the expertise unique to each party, mutual openness to working out different views regarding optimal treatment, and optimal communication are covenantal elements of such relationships necessary to work toward meeting a mutual patient's needs. For example, a patient with a breast growth may see her primary care physician initially, be referred to an interventional radiologist for a biopsy, and then to a surgeon to remove the growth if malignant. This may be followed post-operatively by visits with a medical oncologist and / or radiation oncologist about preventive therapy, and possibly a physiotherapist or nurse practitioner to help improve post-operative arm swelling. All of these caregivers need to communicate well in order to give expression to practice norms. These include agreeing about realistic therapeutic outcome expectations and delivering coordinated care that addresses a variety of patient needs. When caregivers and patients discover that each are members of faith communities with similar basic beliefs, care can be an even more meaningful experience. As a theme common to Jewish, Islamic, and Christian faith traditions, the concept of covenant can be a powerful focus for sharing how faith traditions can improve relationships and patient care.

Pharmaceutical companies try to be recognized as full participants in medical relationships. However, their core qualifying aspect is economic through which all other aspects of relational functioning are conditioned. They attempt to persuade caregivers that their products are superior to those of competitors, sometimes through incomplete or distorted information. While not primary relational partners in the network of covenantal relationships in medical practice, they could reduce the cost burden through less self-serving profit interests as one way to reform their relationship with caregivers and patients, putting care ethics forward at the benevolent expense of profit motives. Similarly, direct-to-consumer marketing may be done in the name of patient autonomy, taking advantage of patient vulnerability to biased company interpretations of benefits and risks. Caregivers have responsibility to hospital and health care systems regarding the recommendation of cost-effective treatments and stewardly resource usage.

Similarly, experimental therapies may be made available to patients before regulatory approval through so-called compassionate access protocols. While often sanctioned by regulators for patients who have expended all approved therapies and want to try an unproven therapy out of desperation, caregivers should interpret the limited evidence and discourage considering such therapy if significant known or unknown risk outweighs preliminary and often unreliable evidence of meaningful benefit.[108]

Summary and Conclusion

In this chapter, a covenantal ethical framework has been proposed to better conceptualize and give greater meaning to ethical principles articulated by Beauchamp and Childress. A more complete analysis comparing these ethical frameworks can be found elsewhere.[109] The Reformational perspective developed by Kuyper, Dooyeweerd, and others helps to interpret the state and direction of biomedical ethics using major themes in redemptive history. Sin-based structural and directional distortions of the discipline can be recognized and a path toward redemptive renewal can be established through a biblically inspired ethical framework for biomedical ethics in medicine.

I am proposing a more relational ethical working framework recognizing the covenantal thread that permeates redemptive history. While the language of principlism is attractive to many, including some Christians, it fails to characterize the importance of meaningful relationships in medicine. This inadequacy has led to calls for incorporating the concept of covenant by Christian and non-Christian practitioners and educators alike. The most meaningful context of these principles is in interpersonal covenantal relationships modeled after the covenantal relationship between God and human beings. Covenantal relating best gives normative expression to beneficence as the ethical aspect of care which distinguishes care-focused professions from other disciplines and vocations.

A Reformational perspective that envisions this covenantal approach is not the only possible Christian perspective on biomedical ethics. It is an example of a Christian approach that gives guidance in uncovering

108. James J. Rusthoven, "Ethical Issues Raised By Compassionate Access to Experimental Therapies." *Ethics & Medicine* 30, no. 1 (2014a): 17–33.

109. James J. Rusthoven, *Covenantal Biomedical Ethics for Contemporary Medicine* (Eugene, OR: Wipf & Stock 2014b).

the basic belief systems behind a dominant paradigm in the discipline today. It identifies some strengths of that paradigm, and seeks to identify and overcome weaknesses resulting from sin-based distortions that may ignore or minimize biblical norms for ethics.

This author sincerely hopes that readers may see value in this approach, not only specifically for biomedical ethics but perhaps more generally for other disciplines. Whatever follows from this work, may it be done to the glory of God and in a spirit of awe and wonder at his wonderfully created cosmic order. Despite the persistence of sin, care for the stranger in need remains a major responsibility of creational stewardship when mirrored through God's gift of covenantal relationship with him.

Questions for Reflection: Applying Reformational Ideas to Teaching and Research in Biomedical Ethics

1. Do you have a clinical background as a physician or other health care provider or have you previously focused on another discipline such as psychology, philosophy, or theology?
2. How might your academic training help you to enter the study of biomedical ethics?
3. Do you see the value of understanding the basic worldview and beliefs that influence biomedical ethics?
4. Have you thought through how your previous learning has been influenced by non-Christian worldviews such as modernism or post-modernism?
5. Have you found this chapter to be helpful in discerning non-Christian from Christian perspectives?
6. Has the concept of irreducible modal aspects helped you to discern what reductionistic thinking you may have acquired from previous professors or mentors?
7. In engaging in discussion regarding personal perspectives with peers in the discipline:
    - How would you explain a Reformational perspective in biomedical ethics to *non-Christian* graduate students or faculty peers in a way that might be perceived as helpful, relevant, and non-threatening?
    - In order to connect and collaborate with *Christian* colleagues, how could you explain a Reformational perspective in terms that might encourage *Christian* peers to benefit from its insights? How might your approach be different when engaging

Christians of Roman Catholic, Eastern Orthodox, Mennonite, Quaker, or evangelical traditions? In what ways might a Reformational perspective be enriched by their perspectives?

8. Has the approach used in this chapter encouraged you to take further formal studies in biomedical ethics?

Additional Resources on Faith and Biomedical Ethics

A recent book chapter guides the reader through pastoral observations and theological reflections regarding death as seen in the Reformed tradition. While the chapter speaks to the Dutch context and euthanasia, it also addresses end-of-life questions and the medicalization of modern society applicable to other national and cultural settings. The chapter is Van Der Kooi, Margriet and Cornelius Van Der Kooi. "The Dutch and Death," *In Reformed Public Theology: A Global Vision for Life in the World.* Edited by Matthew Kaemingk. (Grand Rapids, MI: Baker Academic, 2021).

An excellent resource on ancient medicine including the Hippocratic Oath and Corpus is Edelstein, Ludwig. *Ancient Medicine: Selected Papers of Ludwig Edelstein.* Edited by O. Temkin and C. L. Temkin. (Baltimore, MD; Johns Hopkins University Press, 1967). *The Birth of Bioethics* (New York: Oxford University Press, 1998) by Albert R. Jonsen is the most comprehensive and authoritative text on the history of this discipline from 1947 to 1987. As a member of the Belmont Commission, he provides a first-hand account of the differences in basic beliefs behind the report. An excellent compilation of articles praising and criticizing principles-based ethics is the work *Principles of Health Care Ethics*, edited by Raanan Gillon (New York: Wiley, 1994). It contains a wide array of perspectives including those from Jewish, Roman Catholic, Anglican, Islamic, humanist, and feminist traditions.

Christian communities continue to struggle over the concept of human personhood and the status of the human embryo. The most comprehensive and insightful book in my reading regarding the status of the embryo is David Albert Jones's *The Soul of the Embryo* (London: Continuum, 2004). Trained in theology at Oxford and in philosophy and natural sciences at Cambridge, Jones goes methodically through Scripture and the history of Christianity for evidence of the status of early human life. He shows how the influence of the pagan Greek philosophers and medical practitioners on early Christian thinking led to contemporary positions on the status of early human life.

Medical assistance in dying (MAID) has recently become legalized in Canada. Also called active euthanasia or physician-assisted suicide, it has been part of accepted practice in the Netherlands, Belgium and Luxembourg for decades. Many Christian caregivers continue to question whether assisting in the acceleration of a patient's death is ethically acceptable and constitutes part of a spectrum of palliative care. In further developing a Reformational perspective for end-of-life medical care, and keeping in mind a covenantal relational framework, specific issues that require reflection and discussion with Christians and non-Christians include:

- Are there circumstances where actively assisting in dying of the terminally ill is ethically acceptable?
- Should MAID be considered simply one extreme of palliative care?
- Can terminal sedation be morally distinguished from MAID?
- Should the practice of MAID be legally required in Christian homes for nursing and other extended care?

Conscientious objection to participating in MAiD occurs at both the individual and institutional levels among those of various faith traditions. Other reasons for objection include violation of the internal morality of medicine itself and attempts to include MAiD as a therapeutic extension of palliative care. Unlike MAiD, notes professional palliative care groups, palliative care does not seek to hasten death nor intentionally end life. Another current concern is an attempt to extend the legal allowance for MAiD to those who wish to die by way of MAiD solely for chronic psychiatric illness. Further current readings on these and other controversies involving MAiD include:

- Daphne Gilbert, "Faith and/in Medicine: Religious and Conscientious Objections to MAiD," *Dalhousie Law Journal*; 43, no.2 (2020):658.
- Philip Shaad and Joshua Shaad, "Institutional Non-participation in Assisted Dying: Changing the Conversation," *Bioethics*; 33, no.1 (2019):207-214.
- Scott Kim and Trudo Lemmens, "Should Assisted Dying for Psychiatric Disorders Be Legalized in Canada?" *Canadian Medical Association Journal*; 188, no.14 (2016): E337-E339.
- Franklin G. Miller and Paul S. Appelbaum, "Physician-Assisted Death for Psychiatric Patients – Misguided Public Policy," New England Journal of Medicine 378, no.10 (2018):883-885.

A recommended source of a Reformational perspective on the distinction between palliative sedation and euthanasia is the excellent analysis "Palliative Sedation Versus Euthanasia: An Ethical Assessment" (*Journal of Pain and Symptom Management* 47(1): 123-136, 2014) by Henk A.M.J. ten Have and Jos V.M. Welie. Two recommended sources that explore a Christian perspective on human dignity are *Neither Beast Nor God: The Dignity of the Human Person* by Lutheran theologian and bioethicist Gilbert Meilaender and *Dignity and Dying: A Christian Appraisal*, edited by John Kilner, Arlene Miller, and Edmund Pellegrino. While Meilaender skillfully lays out an interweaving of philosophical and theological concepts of human dignity through the ages, *Dignity and Dying* speaks to specific issues and experiences of care for the dying in contemporary settings from several Christian denominational perspectives.

On Moral Medicine: Theological Perspectives in Medical Ethics (Grand Rapids, Eerdmans, 2012), 3rd edition, edited by M Therese Lysaught and Joseph J. Kotva, Jr. with Stephen E. Lammers and Allen Verhey is a massive treasury of previously published articles on a wide range of bioethical topics. Such topics include Religion and Medicine, Personhood, Persons with Disabilities, Assisted Reproductive Technologies, Death and its Dignity, and others. Contributors come from many denominational affiliations including those in the Reformed tradition. The tome contains 156 articles and is one of the most comprehensive sources of theological bioethical scholarship available.

Below is a selected list of additional references on links between Christian, Islamic, and Jewish faith traditions and biomedical ethics:

Bartholomew, Craig G. *Contours of the Kuyperian Tradition: A Systematic Introduction*. Downers Grove, IL: IVP Academic, 2017.

Dooyeweerd, Herman. *Roots of Western Culture: Pagan, Secular, and Christian Options*. Edited by D.F.M. Strauss. Lewiston, NY: Mellen, 2003.

Jochemsen, Henk. "Normative Practices as an Intermediate between Theoretical Ethics and Morality." *Philosophia Reformata* 71 (2006): 96-112 (2006).

Glas, Gerrit. "Persons and Their Lives: Reformational Philosophy on Man, Ethics, and Beyond." *Philosophia Reformata* 71 (2006): 31-57.

May William F. *Testing the Medical Covenant: Active Euthanasia and Health Care Reform*. Grand Rapids, MI: Eerdmans, 1996.

Pellegrino, Edmund D. and Alan I. Faden, eds. *Jewish and Catholic Bioethics: An Ecumenical Dialogue*. Washington, D.C.: Georgetown University Press, 1999.

Rusthoven, J.J. "Covenantal Ethics for Health Care." In *Order among Humans: Humanities, Social Science and Normative Practices, Part II Normative Prac-*

tices, edited by Govert J. Buijs and Annette K. Mosher, pp. 195-219. Vol. 2 of *The Future of Creation Order*. Cham: Springer International Publishing AG, 2018. This article gives more detail and additional references regarding how the covenantal framework complements the Reformational Normative Reflective Practices Model for medical practice.

Thomasma, David, David Weisstub, and Christian Hervé, eds. *Personhood and Health Care*. Dordrecht: Kluwer Academic Publishers, 2001.

Finally, I refer the reader to the book *Covenantal Biomedical Ethics for Contemporary Medicine* Eugene, OR: Wipf & Stock, 2014), a companion resource to this chapter. It offers additional breadth to the roots of biomedical ethics today, gives rationale for the broad popularity of principles-based ethics, and provides a more ethically meaningful biblical framework for the various types of medical relationships.

Bibliography

Allen, Joseph L. *Love & Conflict: A Covenantal Model of Christian Ethics*. Nashville, TN: Abingdon Press, 1984.

Audi, Robert and Nicholas Wolterstorff. *Religion in the Public Square*. Lanham, MD: Rowman and Littlefield, 1997.

Balthasar, Hans Urs von. "Nine Propositions on Christian Ethics." In *Principles of Christian Morality*, edited by Joseph Cardinal Ratzinger, Heinz Schürmann, Hans Urs von Balthasar, and translated by Graham Harrison. San Francisco, CA: Ignatius Press, 1986.

Barth, Karl. *Church Dogmatics*, Volume 3, *The Doctrine of Creation, Part 1*. Edinburgh, UK: T. and T. Clark, 1958.

Beecher, Henry K. "Ethics and Clinical Research." *New England Journal of Medicine* 274, no. 24 (1966): 57–63.

Beauchamp, Tom L. and James F. Childress. *Principles of Biomedical Ethics*, 1st ed. New York: Oxford University Press, 1979.

Beauchamp, Tom L. and James F. Childress. *Principles of Biomedical Ethics*. 5th ed. New York: Oxford University Press, 2001.

Beauchamp, Tom L. and James F. Childress. *Principles of Biomedical Ethics*, 6th ed. New York: Oxford University Press, 2009.

Beauchamp, Tom L. and James F. Childress. *Principles of Biomedical Ethics*, 7th ed. New York: Oxford University Press, 2013.

Biggar, Nigel. "Why Religion Deserved a Place in Secular Medicine." *Journal of Medical Ethics* 41 (2015): 229-233.

Bouma, Hessel, III, Douglas Diekema, Edward Langerak, Theodore Rottman, and Allen Verhey. *Christian Faith, Health, and Medical Practice*. Grand Rapids, MI: Wm B. Eerdmans, 1989.

Callahan, Daniel D. "Religion and the Secularization of Bioethics." *Hastings Center Report* 20, no.4 (1990): 2–4.

Calvin, John. *Institutes of the Christian Religion*. Edited by John T. McNeill. Translated by Ford L. Battles. Philadelphia, PA: The Westminster Press, 1960.

Camenisch, Paul F. "Paul Ramsey's Task: 'Some Methodological Clarifications and Questions.'" In *Love and Society: Essays in the Ethics of Paul Ramsey*, edited by James Turner Johnson and David H. Smith. Missoula, MT: Scholars Press, 1974.

Campbell, Courtney S. "Gifts and Caring Duties in Medicine," In *Duties to Others*, edited by Courtney S. Campbell and B. Andrew Lustig. Dordrecht: Kluwer Academic, 1994.

Campbell, Courtney S., and B. Andrew Lustig. "A Call to Respond: Duties to Others," In *Duties to Others*, edited by Courtney S. Campbell and B. Andrew Lustig. Dordrecht: Kluwer Academic , 1994.

Cassel, Christine. "The Patient-Physician Covenant: An Affirmation of Asklepios." *Annals of Internal Medicine* 124, no.6 (1996): 604–606.

Chaplin, Jonathan. *Herman Dooyeweerd: Christian Philosopher of State and Civil Society*. Notre Dame, IN: University of Notre Dame Press, 2011.

Clouser, K. Danner and Bernard Gert. "A Critique of Principlism." *Journal of Medicine and Philosophy* 15, no. 2 (1990): 219–236.

Clouser, Roy. *The Myth of Religious Neutrality: An Essay on the Hidden Role of Religious Beliefs in Theories*. Notre Dame, IN: University of Notre Dame Press, 2005.

Coffey, Susan. "The Nurse-Patient Relationship in Cancer Care as a Shared Covenant: A Concept Analysis." *Advances in Nursing Science* 29 (2006): 308–23.

Dooyeweerd, Herman. *In the Twilight of Western Thought*. Nutley, NJ: Craig Press, 1965.

Dooyeweerd, Herman. *A New Critique of Theoretical Thought*. Vols 1 and 2. Philadelphia, PA: The Presbyterian and Reformed Publishing Company, 1969.

Engelhardt, H. Tristram, Jr. *The Foundations of Bioethics*. New York: Oxford University Press, 1986.

Engelhardt, H. Tristram, Jr. *The Foundations of Christian Bioethics*. Lisse, NL: Swets & Zeitlinger , 2000.

Glas, Gerrit. "Ego, Self, and the Body: An Assessment of Dooyeweerd's Philosophical Anthropology." In *Christian Philosophy at the Close of the Twentieth Century: An Assessment and Perspective*, edited by Sander Griffioen and B. M. Balk. Kampen: Kok, 1995.

Goheen, Michael W. and Craig G. Bartholomew. *Living at the Crossroads: An Introduction to Christian Worldview*. Grand Rapids, MI: Baker Academics, 2008.

Griffioen, Sander. "The Worldview Approach to Social Theory: Hazards and Benefits." In *Stained Glass: Worldviews and Social Science*, edited by Paul A. Marshall, Sander Griffioen, and Richard J. Mouw. Lanham, MD.: University of America Press, 1989.

Habermas, Jürgen. *Between Naturalism and Religion: Philosophical Essays*. Cambridge, UK: Polity, 2008.

Hauerwas, Stanley. "How Christian Ethics Became Medical Ethics: The Case of Paul Ramsey." *Christian Bioethics* 1, no.1 (1995): 11–28.

Hittinger, Russell. "Theology and Natural Law." *Communio (International Catholic Review)* 17 (1990): 402–408.

Horton, Michael S. "Participation and Covenant." In *Radical Orthodoxy and the Reformed Tradition*, edited by James K. A. Smith and James H. Olthuis. Grand Rapids, MI: Baker Academic, 2005.

Jecker, Nancy S., Caesar A. Atuire, Vardit Ravitsky, Mohammed Ghaly, Ashish Vaswani, and Teck Chuan Voo. *Journal of Bioethical Inquiry* (2024). Published on-line at https://doi.org/10.1007/s11673-024-10410-7.

Jochemsen, Henk. "Normative Practices as an Intermediate between Theoretical Ethics and Morality." *Philosophia Reformata* 71 (2006): 96–112.

Jonsen, Albert R. *The Birth of Bioethics*. New York: Oxford University Press, 1998.

Kuyper, Abraham. *Lectures on Calvinism*. Grand Rapids, MI: Wm B. Eerdmans, 1931.

Kuyper, Abraham. *Principles of Sacred Theology*. Grand Rapids, MI: Eerdmans, 1965.

Lammers, Steven. "On Stanley Hauerwas: Theology, Medical Ethics, and the Church," in *Theological Voices in Medical Ethics*, ed. Allen Verhey and Stephen E. Lammers (Grand Rapids, MI: Wm B. Eerdmans, 1993).

Lillback, Peter A. *The Binding of God: Calvin's Role in the Development of Covenant Theology*. Grand Rapids, MI: Baker Academic, 2001.

Louthan, Stephen. "On Religion: a Discussion with Richard Rorty, Alvin Plantinga, and Nicholas Wolterstorff." *Christian Scholar's Review* 26, no. 2 (1996): 177-83

MacIntyre, Alasdair. *After Virtue.* 2nd ed. Notre Dame, IN: University of Notre Dame Press, 1984.

MacIntyre, Alasdair. *Whose Justice? Which Rationality?* Notre Dame, IN: University of Notre Dame Press, 1988.

May, William F. "Code, Covenant, Contract or Philanthropy," *Hastings Center Report* 5, no. 6 (1975): 29–38.

May, William F. *The Physician's Covenant.* Philadelphia, PA: Westminster Press, 1983.

May, William F. *Testing the Medical Covenant: Active Euthanasia and Health Care Reform.* Grand Rapids, MI: Eerdmans, 1996.

Meilaender, Gilbert. *Neither Beast nor God: The Dignity of the Human Person* (New York: Encounter Books, 2009.

Meilaender, Gilbert. "On William F. May: Corrected Vision for Medical Ethics." In *Theological Voices in Medical Ethics*, edited by Allen Verhey and Stephen E. Lammers. Grand Rapids, MI: Wm B. Eerdmans, 1993.

Meilaender, Gilbert. "Review of *The Foundations of Christian Bioethics*, by H. Tristram Engelhardt, Jr." *First Things* (November 2000).

Nagel, Thomas. *The View From Nowhere.* New York: Oxford University Press, 1989.

Naugle, David. *Worldview: The History of a Concept.* Grand Rapids, MI: Wm B. Eerdmans, 2002.

Nisker, Jeffrey. "A Covenantal Model for the Medical Educator-Student Relationship: Lessons from the Covenant Model of the Physician-Patient Relationship." *Medical Education* 40 (2006): 502–503.

Norris, Christopher. *Deconstruction and the "Unfinished Project of Modernity."* New York: Routledge, 2000.

O'Donovan, Oliver. *Resurrection and the Moral Order.* Grand Rapids, MI: Wm B. Eerdmans, 1994.

Pellegrino, Edmund D. "The Four Principles and the Doctor-Patient Relationship: The need for a Better Linkage." In *Principles of Health Care Ethics*, edited by Raanan Gillon. New York: John Wiley & Sons, 1994.

Pellegrino, Edmund D., and David C. Thomasma. *The Christian Virtues in Medical Practice.* Washington, D. C.: Georgetown University Press, 1996.

Plantinga, Alvin. "Advice to Christian Philosophers." *Faith and Philosophy* 1, no. 3 (1984): 253-271.

Plantinga, Alvin. "Reason and Belief in God." In *Faith and Rationality: Reason and Belief in God*, edited by Alvin Plantinga and Nicholas Wolterstorff. Notre Dame, IN: University of Notre Dame Press, 1983.

Ramsey, Paul. *Basic Christian Ethics*. New York: Charles Scribner's Sons, 1952.

Ramsey, Paul. *Deeds and Rules in Christian Ethics*. New York: Charles Scribner's Sons, 1967.

Ramsey, Paul. *The Patient as Person*. New York: Yale University Press, 1970.

Rawls, John. *Political Liberalism*. New York: Columbia University Press, 1996.

Rawls, John. *A Theory of Justice*. Cambridge, MA: Harvard University Press, 1999.

Rorty, Richard, *Contingency, Irony, and Solidarity*. New York: Cambridge University Press, 1989.

Rusthoven, James J. *Covenantal Biomedical Ethics for Contemporary Medicine*. Eugene, OR: Wipf & Stock, 2014b.

Rusthoven, James J. "Ethical Issues Raised By Compassionate Access to Experimental Therapies." *Ethics & Medicine* 30, no. 1 (2014a):17-33.

Ryan, Kenneth J. The Belmont Report: Ethical Principles and Guidelines for the Protection of Human Subjects for Research. DHEW Publication No. (OS) 78-0012 (National Institutes of Health, 1978) 4.

Smith, David H. "On Paul Ramsey: A Covenant-Centered Ethic for Medicine." In *Theological Voices in Medical Ethics*, edited by Allen Verhey and Stephen E. Lammers. Grand Rapids, MI: Wm B. Eerdmans Publishing Company, 1993.

Spier, J. M. *An Introduction to Christian Philosophy*. Nutley, NJ: The Craig Press, 1966.

Spykman, Gordon. *Reformational Theology: A New Paradigm for Doing Dogmatics*. Grand Rapids, MI: Eerdmans, 1992.

Strauss, Danie F. M. *Philosophy: Discipline of the Disciplines*. Grand Rapids, MI; Paideia Press, 2009.

Taylor, Charles. *Sources of the Self*. Cambridge, MA: Harvard University Press, 1989.

Tubbs, James, B., Jr. "Theology and the Invitation of the Stranger." In *Duties to Others*, edited by Courtney S. Campbell and B. Andrew Lustig. Dordrecht: Kluwer Academic Publishers, 1994.

Vaux, Kenneth L. *Health and Medicine in the Reformed Tradition*. New York: Crossroad, 1984.

Wolters, Albert M. *Creation Regained: Biblical Basics for a Reformational Worldview*. 2nd ed. Grand Rapids, MI: Eerdmans Publishing Company, 2005.

Wolterstorff, Nicholas. "Can Belief in God Be Rational If It Has No Foundations?" In *Faith and Rationality: Reason and Belief in God*, edited by Alvin Plantinga and Nicholas Wolterstorff. Notre Dame, IN: University of Notre Dame Press, 1983a.

Wolterstorff, Nicholas. *Reason within the Bounds of Religion* (Grand Rapids, MI: Eerdmans, 1976).

Wolterstorff, Nicholas. *Until Justice and Peace Embrace*. Grand Rapids, MI: Eerdmans, 1983b.

Wright, N. T. *After You Believe: Why Christian Character Matters*. New York: Harper-Collins, 2010.

Language and Literature in Reformed Perspective

Ben Faber

> For nothing is more preposterous than to enjoy the very remarkable gifts that attest the divine nature within us, yet to overlook the Author who gives them to us at our asking.
>
> Calvin, *Institutes of the Christian Religion*, 1.5.6[1]

Introduction

The thesis of this essay is that language and literature are two gifts that attest the divine nature within human beings. The metaphor that John Calvin favors when referring to creation and that readers of his *Institutes* cite most frequently is that of the theatre: "such a dazzling theatre" (1.5.8), "this most glorious theatre" (1.6.2), "this most beautiful theatre" (1.14.20), and "this magnificent theatre of heaven and earth" (2.6.1). Whereas Calvin's theatrical metaphor attests the divine nature of the Creator, this essay will focus on authorship as metaphoric of the divine nature within us. Among the divine attributes that distinguish human beings from other creatures, I will argue, is *the ability to create, by means of language, worlds that invite our responsible participation*. My thesis is not particularly original as it follows a tradition of Christian theories of literary creativity begun by Sir Philip Sidney, a Protestant Renaissance man in the court of Queen Elizabeth I, in *An Apology for Poetry* (1595):

> Neither let it be deemed too saucy a comparison to balance the highest point of man's wit with the efficacy of nature; but rather give right honor to the heavenly Maker of that maker, who, having made man to His own likeness, set him beyond and over all the works of that second nature: which in nothing he showeth so much as in poetry, when with the force of a divine breath he bringeth things forth far surpassing her [nature's] doings [...].[2]

1. John Calvin, *Institutes of the Christian Religion:* vol. 1, trans. Ford Lewis Battles, ed. John T. McNeill (Philadelphia, PA: Westminster John Knox, 1960), 58-59.
2. Sir Philip Sidney, *An Apology for Poetry*, in *The Critical Tradition: Classic Texts and Contemporary Trends*, 3rd ed., ed. David H. Richter (New York: Bedford/St. Mar-

In elaborating upon Sidney's thesis in this chapter, I also want to echo his caveat that any claim for the divine nature within us should not deny the uniqueness of God's creation of the universe nor dim his glory as the almighty Creator of heaven and earth. Furthermore, whatever reflected glory human beings enjoy when they create, by means of language, worlds that invite our responsible participation is derivative of God's glory and is diminished by our finitude and by our sin. Nevertheless, the Reformed apology for literature and literary studies that will follow unabashedly grounds the activities we perform as writers, readers, critics, scholars, teachers, and students in the goodness of God in whose image we are made.

We begin with a reflection on the state of the discipline in 2020, and then proceed in the way of the preceding chapters to describe a distinctly Reformed approach to language and literature in reference to creation, fall, and redemption. The concluding section brings together into nine propositions what I believe are hallmarks of a Reformed way of thinking about literature for writers and readers alike, and it suggests possible research topics for a literary scholar to undertake.

The State of the Discipline

To borrow a distinction that Abraham Kuyper makes regarding the church, an academic discipline has both an institutional and an organic aspect. Thus, when we speak of English as a discipline in its institutional sense, we are referring to an *administrative unit or department*. The panoply of connotations of the institutional dimension of "English" as a discipline includes:

- *Physical.* The discipline occupies a suite of offices, with a bulletin board, a display case with new publications, and a rack with current journals and brochures about career opportunities and graduate schools. This is the literal address to which mail, packages, and promotional materials are sent.
- *Personnel.* The discipline consists of full-time faculty in varying degrees of precarious-to-secure standing, sessional and part-time instructors, an administrative assistant or two, and graduate and undergraduate students. It includes everyone, in fact, who identifies with the tribe and wears the "English" hoodie.

tin's, 2007), 139. Some prefer to denote the literary creation as "sub-creation", following J.R.R. Tolkien's essay "On Fairy-Stories" (1938) in C.S. Lewis, ed., *Essays Presented to Charles Williams* (London: Oxford University Press, 1947); see, among others, David Bratman, "Tolkien's Subcreation," *Tolkien Studies* 13 (2016): 293-295.

- *Program.* The discipline is also the academic programs with their requirements and electives, course offerings, all identified in the academic calendar under "English". At graduation, students are announced as having fulfilled the degree requirements for "English". They have a piece of paper to prove it.

For the organic aspect of the discipline, we might turn to Alasdair MacIntyre's idea of the social practices that describe the relationships, practices, and habits—in short, the virtues—of those who participate with others in these activities.[3] In this sense, when we speak of the discipline of "English", we are also referring to the *materials, methods, manners, and media of literary study*:

- *Materials.* In a word, "texts". Historically, as the object of study, "text" referred to poems, prose, and plays deemed by the academy to be of quality and importance. Currently, "text" refers to any artifact that signifies meaning beyond itself, whether it is a performed or a printed work, culturally dominant or marginal, literally verbal or loosely discursive. It therefore includes William Shakespeare, Marvel comics, and body writing.
- *Methods.* The practice of those in the discipline calls for the close reading of the text, with the technical analysis of the formal attributes of the text within its historical context. More recently, the methods involve theory-inflected interdisciplinary explorations of the construction of gender, the negotiation of power, the machinations of empire, the inscription of ecological attitudes, and the erasure (and subsequent re-inscription) of racialized peoples from the discipline. From reading the text as an aesthetic object to deconstructing "text" as a performance of intersecting social practices, the focus may have shifted, but the method remains that of the analysis of texts.
- *Manners.* Although Stanley Fish may claim that "there is no such thing as critical self-consciousness",[4] the discipline today asks practitioners to self-identify with theoretical perspectives as they read texts. While acknowledging such bias, the reader at the same time stands prepared to revise theoretical assumptions and readerly predispositions. To borrow from Paul Ricoeur's notion of the hermeneutic arc, the critical reader holds in abeyance any openness to the text and undertakes a deliberate application of

3. Alasdair MacIntyre, *After Virtue: A Study in Moral Theory* (Notre Dame, IN: University of Notre Dame Press, 1981).
4. Stanley Fish, *Doing What Comes Naturally: Change, Rhetoric, and the Practice of Theory in Literary and Legal Studies* (Oxford: Oxford University Press, 1989), 465.

formal modes of analysis. Despite Rita Felski's critique of skepticism as the critical *mood*, the contemporary reader's orientation toward the text is a hermeneutic of suspicion, approaching a text warily with a view to revealing the text's constructedness and its complicity in hegemonic structures.[5] Conference panels have become sites for advocacy and agency.

- *Media*. The social practice of "English", similar to other disciplines, becomes public through academic presses, peer-reviewed journals, and generalist and specialist conferences organized by associations and organizations. Increasingly, social media have become platforms for disseminating scholarship in the discipline via Podcasts, Twitter, Facebook, Academia.edu, Wordpress, and the Humanities Commons. English as a discipline has gradually accepted the potential for the Digital Humanities to reimagine how texts can be read, from the digitization of medieval manuscripts to stylometric evidence of Shakespeare's additions to Thomas Kyd's *The Spanish Tragedy*.

The institutional and organic aspects of a discipline are inseparable and interdependent: members are habituated to the social practices of the discipline through the formal, institutional means of an English degree, postgraduate studies, learned societies, and appointment as faculty. Presumably, the state of the one informs the other. As goes one, so goes the other.

From its formation as an academic discipline in the 1920s to its current state at the end of the twentieth century, "English" has undergone a radical transformation. Terry Eagleton describes the rise of English as discipline as the confluence of three streams: the gentlemanly pursuit of *belles lettres*, the Victorian concern for culture, and the classical philology of the research university.[6] The person who embodied the values of English as a discipline was Matthew Arnold (1822-1888) whose "The Function of Criticism at the Present Time" (1865, 1888), together with *Culture and Anarchy* (1869), identified literary criticism as the "disinterested endeavour to learn and propagate the best that is known and thought in the world."[7] From the outset, then, English as a discipline was

5. Rita Felski, "The Stakes of Suspicion," in *The Limits of Critique* (Chicago, IL: University of Chicago Press, 2015) 14-51.

6. Terry Eagleton, "The Rise of English," in *Literary Theory: An Introduction* (Oxford: Blackwell, 2008), 15-46. See also Gerald Graff, *Professing Literature: An Institutional History* (Chicago, 1987).

7. Matthew Arnold, "The Function of Criticism at the Present Time" (1864) in *The Critical Tradition: Classic Texts and Contemporary Trends*, 3rd ed., ed. David H. Richter (New York: Bedford/St. Martin's, 2007), 427.

driven by secular humanist impulse, seconded from time to time for a Christian recovery of the cultural tradition, such as T.S. Eliot's *The Idea of a Christian Society* (1939). In early modern literary studies, for instance, A.C. Bradley's emphasis on the nobility of personhood in *Shakespearean Tragedy* (1904) and E.M.W. Tillyard's focus on worldview in *The Elizabethan World Picture* (1957) can serve as examples of the humanist criticism that continued the line of approach from Arnold. The New Critics of the 1940s and '50s, likewise, though more business-like and technical in their close reading of texts than their psychological and historicist forebears, were rooted in the conviction that literary analysis reveals something timeless and transcendent. Cleanth Brooks, in the preface to his collection of New Critical essays, *The Well Wrought Urn* (1947), implies affirmative answers to both "the question as to whether the critic can make normative judgments" and "the related question as to whether a poem represents anything more universal than the expression of the particular values of the time."[8] Paul de Man summarized the attraction of English for a humanist agenda: "as a depositor of human experience of considerable variety and scope, it gains access to questions of moral philosophy—questions of value and normative judgment. Its technical and descriptive aspects as a science of language dovetail with its historical, theological and ethical function."[9]

But with the post-war era, especially in the Paris of the 1960s, came the Postmodernist challenge to the various strains of humanism in the discipline. Loosely aligned with what can be called "spectral Marxism", Jacques Derrida, Roland Barthes, and Michel Foucault undertook a deep critique of the metaphysical commitments of literary studies in the first half of the twentieth century. The ensuing Poststructuralism "rejects structuralist claims to objectivity and comprehensiveness, typically emphasizing instead the instability and plurality of meaning, and frequently using the techniques of deconstruction to reveal unquestioned assumptions and inconsistencies in literary and philosophical discourse" (*OED Online*, "post-structuralism").[10] The keyword of this turn to theory is *deconstruction*, the term that captures the attitude of incredulity toward the transcendentals of beauty, truth, and goodness. In place of the Victorian and Modernist trust in literary art, Poststructuralist theory and criticism became masterfully suspicious of literature as political hegemony (James-

8. Cleanth Brooks, *The Well Wrought Urn: Studies in the Structure of Poetry* (New York: Harcourt, Brace & World, 1947), xi.

9. Paul de Man, "Return to Philology," in *The Resistance to Theory* (Minneapolis, MN: University of Minnesota Press, 1986), 22.

10. *Oxford English Dictionary*, s.v. "post-structuralism, n.," accessed June ? 2021, www.oed.com/view/Entry/240113.

on), of language as illusory of reality (de Man), and of the culture industry as Ideological State Apparatus (Althusser). While some readers may rue the dominance of the phrase, most will agree that "critical theory" has come to describe theories and practices of interpretation that are critical of the Western literary and philosophical traditions.

For now we simply note that, as a consequence of the persuasive and pervasive presence of critical theory, the institutional or administrative identity of the discipline has become unstable. In colleges and universities around the world, English departments are being rebranded as "cultural studies", are redeployed as "composition and rhetoric" for Gen. Ed. purposes, or they are being combined with other units, such as "modern languages" or "film studies", still within the area traditionally known as the Humanities. However, because the very notion of "Humanities" is predicated on an essentialist view of being human, the Poststructuralism currently dominant in literary studies rejects this home for the discipline of English. With the loss of its exceptional status, literature no longer has an exceptional place in the academy. In short, the discipline formerly known as "English" has changed significantly from the historical and philological reading of the canon of Western civilization to the social and political critique of the cultural hegemony of literature. The current crisis in the Humanities is thus most acutely experienced in the discipline of English because its rise as an institution rests on the belief in literature as a supremely humanizing agent.

But the organic aspect of the discipline has also become unstable. Formerly, the social practice of the discipline was centred in the analysis of canonical literature—the materials, methods, and manners were exemplified by the textual scholarship published in academic presses, journals, and lecture halls. Student apprentices in the critical guild learned their trade at the feet of masters in the arts of the close reading, textual analysis, and editorial practice. Now, however, as discourse analysis from complex interdisciplinary perspectives replaces the close reading of texts in the canon of literature, "English" has lost its purposeful identity as a discipline. As literary studies lose their distinct disciplinary character, they run the risk of no longer having a place—either literal or figurative—from which to contribute to the interdisciplinary enterprise. Just as one may lose one's cultural identity in the great melting pot of American society, so "English" may no longer have its separate, special identity. The irony, of course, is that the rebranded new edition of the non-discipline of English loves to deconstruct ways by which identities are constructed. Furthermore, scholars of colour working with critical race theory have called for "undisciplining" the discipline to expose the inherent and problematic white-ness of the materials, methods, and manners of English as a discipline.[11] We may have deconstructed ourselves out of a discipline.

What are we to make of the current state of the discipline? First, we note the paradox of defining a discipline that has embraced indecipherability, indefinability, incommensurability, and supplementarity. Given the current post-Saussurean linguistic framework in the discipline (the paradigm-shifting equivalent in English of post-Euclidean geometry), it is hardly surprising that attempts at defining the discipline are futile. At the same time, Poststructuralism is to be thanked for providing the tools to reveal the secular humanist, colonialist, and patriarchal biases of the discipline. From my perspective, as the disassembling of cultural artifacts, Deconstruction has exposed the *hubris* of the implicit or explicit claims that have been made in both the institutional and organic expressions of the discipline. Further, the deconstructing of the very concept of "discipline" suggests that the identity crisis in English has an ideological origin in the worldview of the social practices that are associated with the discipline. Consequently, the resources in the Reformational philosophical tradition, with its strengths in worldview analysis, allow us to envision literary studies as a discipline which has a distinct identity in the linguistic and aesthetic aspects while participating fruitfully in dialogue with other disciplines (or with other modal aspects) relevant to the understanding of literature.

A Reformed Approach to Language and Literature

The response to the current state of the discipline can be hope or despair, and I choose hope. In God's providence, we are neither orphans of Descartes nor children of Derrida. In the Kuyperian tradition in which I write, one holds in dynamic tension the blessing of common grace and the curse of the antithesis. In fact, as a heuristic for identifying spiritual struggle in the human heart, the doctrine of the antithesis is itself a blessing.

In other words, we receive with one hand the gift from contemporary critical theory of insight into the foundational assumptions of the discipline that require correction, and we point with the other to the radical incompatibility between the control beliefs that underwrite our competing theories and practices. Or, in yet other words, in God's providence we have the resources of Poststructuralist critiques of the ideological commitments of twentieth-century literary theory to form an alternative account of the discipline's contribution to the coming of God's kingdom. Or, in explicitly Reformational philosophical terms, while we can

11. Christina Sharpe, *In the Wake: On Blackness and Being* (Durham, NC: Duke University Press, 2016), 13.

accept the dismantling of the pseudo-*religious* nature of the discipline of English, we reject the complete removal of the *pistic* or *faith aspect* from the conversation about literary and other texts. The idols of the English academy may have been smashed, but the iconoclasts are reluctant to talk about faith. A state of crisis is an opportunity for renewal; the discipline needs faithful Christian witnesses—perhaps it was for such a time as this.

Creation

As with other chapters in this volume, the starting point for a biblical approach to literature begins with creation. At the conclusion of each of the six days, God declared the moral, aesthetic, and functional goodness of what He had made. Each aspect of each day of creation reveals something of God's wisdom, making the universe for Calvin "a sort of mirror in which we can contemplate God, who is otherwise invisible" (*Institutes*, 1.5.1, p. 52-53). Consequently, according to Calvin, there are "not only those more recondite matters for the closer observation of which astronomy, medicine, and all natural science are intended, but also those which thrust themselves upon the sight of even the most untutored and ignorant persons.... Indeed, men who have either quaffed or even tasted the liberal arts penetrate with their aid far more deeply into the secrets of the divine wisdom" (1.5.2, 53). But we must move from the biblical truism about the goodness of creation to its discipline-specific relevance by asking an important question: how do the act of creating and the fact of creation relate to literature and its study?

First, *language*. The Dutch theologian Herman Bavinck alludes to Augustine when he locates the originating moment of creation in the conversation among the three Persons of the Trinity: "the self-communication that takes place within the divine being is archetypal for God's work in creation."[12] Reformed theology draws attention to the deeply covenantal nature of God's relationship with creation in general and with human creatures in particular. All covenants enact through language the reciprocal obligation among parties. In the divine counsel of Elohim before creation and then in the *fiats* of the six days of creation, language is the mode, means, and manner of God's primary attribute, love. For the student of literature, Genesis 1 reveals that the most basic function of language is to perform or enact relationships, first, among the Father, Son, and Holy Spirit, and, second, between God and his creation. An explicitly Reformed approach to creation rests on the covenantal nature of language itself. Later in this chapter we will return to the implied cov-

12. Herman Bavinck, *Reformed Dogmatics*, vol 2, *God and Creation*, ed. John Bolt, trans. John Vriend (Grand Rapids, MI: Baker Academic, 2004), 333.

enant of author and reader that is at the heart of English as a discipline.

Second, *word-wrought worlds*. It is stating the obvious to say that fiction is the making of worlds out of mere words: worlds come into existence in fiction through the same medium—language—as the creation itself. The writer takes formless materials and by means of language shapes them into the forms of fictional worlds. A playwright begins with an empty stage, calls for light and calls forth persons who did not exist. Sir Philip Sidney, quoted in the introduction to this essay, claimed that the poet-creator is "lifted up with the vigor of his own invention [and] doth grow in effect another nature, in making things either better than nature bringeth forth, or, quite anew, forms such as never were in nature."[13] All the arts derive their creative impetus from God's acts of creation, but the medium of language *per se* makes the writer uniquely and closely imitative of God the Creator. The sequential act of writing—word by word, phrase by phrase, sentence by sentence, chapter by chapter—is the day-by-day speaking into existence of the fictional universe: "Writing cannot reveal itself all at once but must write a world slowly into life," as Joe Moran eloquently puts it.[14]

Third, *imago creatoris*. Not only are the creations of writers closely analogous with the creation of the universe through the instrument of language, the person of the writer is a clear reflection of God the Creator. The various disciplines are busy with aspects of the universe that manifest different attributes of God as they are successively revealed in time: the mathematician reflects God's logical, orderly nature; the historian reflects God's providential care in the unfolding of his plan for creation; the doctor (as well as the artist) reflects God's fearful and wonderful fashioning of the human body; and the musician reflects the harmonies and resolutions that are intrinsic to God. But it is the writer who reflects the first revealed aspect of God: his creativity through the word. In creating, the writer performs in the function "sub-creator" (to borrow Tolkien's term from "On Fairy-Stories") in that they derive their craft, materials, and purpose from God the Creator.[15] The capacity to project possible worlds through the word is distinctly human and inherently a function of being God's image.

Of these three reasons for rooting an apology for literature in creation, it is the reality-constituting power of the word that is of special relevance. The biblical account of creation is profoundly invested in

13. Sidney, *An Apology for Poetry*, 138.

14. Joe Moran, *First You Write a Sentence: The Elements of Reading, Writing ... and Life* (London: Penguin, 2018), 162.

15. J.R.R. Tolkien, "On Fairy-Stories" (1938), in *Essays Presented to Charles Williams*, edited by C.S. Lewis (Oxford: Oxford University Press, 1947), 60, 67.

language. Speech is the figure by which the author of Genesis describes the intra-trinitarian counsel of the Father, Son, and Holy Spirit: "God said, 'Let us make mankind in our image, in our likeness'" (Gen. 1:26). Speech is the figure by which God brought matter into existence: "And God said, 'Let there be light!' (Gen. 1:3). Speech is the image which describes the communication between God and Adam in the garden. The naming of the animals is the primary task of Adam after his creation and before the formation of Eve, whom Adam later names 'mother of all living'. Speech is the mode by which relationships are established, maintained, and fulfilled: God with Adam in the cool of the garden; Adam with Eve in their Edenic state; and Adam and Eve over the creatures who accompany them. We can conclude that naming is the means by which symmetrical and asymmetrical relationships are performed: symmetrical in the *ad intra* dialogue of the Godhead, asymmetrical in the *ad extra* conversation of God with Adam and Adam with creation. These symmetrical or horizontal relationships are ones of *mutuality*, whereas the asymmetrical or vertical relationships are ones of *dominion*. In the prelapsarian world, such divine and human exercise of dominion through language is the norm, whereas at the Fall language is perverted into a tool for abusive power, as we will see in the following section.

It logically follows, then, that human beings, bearing God's image, enact these attributes of God naturally. From birth, humans are designed to express God's image through speech (Ps. 8:2). Evolutionary neuroscientists cannot explain the development of letter-recognition hardware in the human brain after only 4000 years of literacy.[16] The theological answer to this neurological puzzle is that human beings are specially-endowed creatures who uniquely echo the creative and covenanting function of divine discourse: human beings have the capacity for speech and literacy *in order that* they may read and respond to God's self-revelation in the two books of creation and Scripture (*Belgic Confession*, Article 2). This theo-anthropological explanation for the neuroscientific evidence of literacy in humans gives literary study a special place among the disciplines, a place where the divine image imprinted on humankind is particularly in play. The discipline of English is where this divine attribute is most directly evident and, potentially, most authentically human in expression.

Next to the creative function of language is the capacity for mean-

16. See, for example, Stanislas Dehaene, *Reading in the Brain: The New Science of How We Read* (New York: Penguin Books, 2009): "If the brain did not evolve for reading, the opposite must be true: writing systems must have evolved within our brain's constraints. [....] In brief, our cortex did not specifically evolve for writing—there was neither the time nor sufficient evolutionary pressure for this to occur. On the contrary, writing evolved to fit the cortex" (8, 150).

ing-making, also known as *interpretation*. Some theorists of interpretation would argue that human interpretation is not different in kind from the signifying processes (semiotics) of animals more generally. In this view, the classic fight-or-flight response to threats in the environment joins primates with protozoa in one continuum of "reading" or decoding the signs available to the senses. The capacity to interpret complex linguistic structures, according to this view, is simply a higher degree of interpretation that humans possess over other animals. Again, this way of understanding "interpretation" derives from evolutionistic presuppositions about what it means to be human. But when we understand "interpretation" to be a conscious act by which we construe (or construct, conjecture) the significance of individual signs within their local (semantic, generic) and global (discursive, cultural) systems and contexts, we begin to see the special nature of the human being as a "language animal", to use Charles Taylor's phrase. Johann Michel, writing from within an evolutionary framework, nevertheless recognizes these "lines of demarcation" as a "radical discontinuity" between humans and animals: animals respond to signs, whereas humans interpret symbols.[17] James K.A. Smith has argued persuasively for a *creational hermeneutic* that "understands interpretation and hermeneutical mediation as constitutive aspects of human being-in-the-world": "Hermeneutics, then, is not an evil to be overcome (or in the case of Derrida, an inescapable, violent state of affairs) but rather an aspect of creation and human life that ought to be affirmed as 'good'."[18] Such affirmation of interpretation as a characteristic of being human means, furthermore, that this aspect of humanity is redeemable in Christ from this present darkness and for the new creation. For the Reformed Christian literary scholar, philosophical hermeneutics provides an ontological--as well as epistemological and ethical--argument that places the writing and reading of texts at the heart of being human, made in God's image, called to responsible participation in his word and in his world.

With good reason, then, Calvin uses analogies from the arts to emphasize the whole duty of the human creature to take up and read the evidences of God's glory and wisdom in the universe around and within us: "For nothing is more preposterous than to enjoy the very remarkable gifts that attest the divine nature within us, yet to overlook the Author who gives them to us at our asking" (*Institutes*, 1.5.6). Despite being deeply suspicious of *artistic representations* of the divine, Calvin highlights the potential

17. Johann Michel, *Homo Interpretans: Towards a Transformation of Hermeneutics*, trans. David Pellauer (London: Rowman & Littlefield International, 2019), 19-20.

18. James K.A. Smith, *The Fall of Interpretation: Philosophical Foundations for a Creational Hermeneutic* (Downers Grove, IL: InterVarsity Press, 2000), 22.

of *natural manifestations* of God to be seen in creation: "We must therefore admit in God's individual works—but especially in them as a whole—that God's powers are actually represented as in a painting" (1.5.10, p. 63). If we were to extrapolate from Calvin's view of creation an Aristotelean-inflected literary theory, it would be this: whereas a textual object exists in its material, formal, and efficient causes as an expression of the author/artist, its purpose is to elicit from the reader/viewer a faithful response. The Reformed theology of creation thus aligns with the hermeneutical approach to literature that I have been implying throughout this section, one that foregrounds the subjectivity of both the author and the reader as human beings against the text as object. This aligns literary creativity with God's act of creation: not only does an author reflect God's image when they create a literary world, the reader owes a duty to respond to that world rightly. Nicholas Wolterstorff calls this way of understanding the relationship of author and reader as "authorial-discourse interpretation": "what all of us do most of the time when interpreting is try to discover and understand the illocutionary act that the person who authorized the words before us performed by authorizing them. Having succeeded in this, we often go on to do other things that can also be called interpretation."[19] The creature to the Creator, the reader to the author.

Fall

Although language is constitutive of creation at the beginning and is distinctive of human activity from the outset, language also carries the main burden of the Fall. The words of the serpent to Eve are a revision of the truth that God speaks, whereby the trustworthy correspondence between word and thing is destabilized. The power of language to constitute reality can also be used to destroy. What was at the beginning the benign exercise of power through naming, with the entry of sin into creation has become a tool for the abuse of power. What was at the beginning the means of covenantal communion between God and creation, human beings and animals, and man and woman, at the Fall became an instrument of separation, blame, recrimination, and discord. We could say, using the distinction between structure and direction from Albert Wolters in *Creation Regained*, that, while the human capacity for language to create, order, and communicate remained intact, the ability to use language aright was deeply marred by sin. Because language is covenant, the disruption of language is covenant-breaking: just as the constitutive nature of creation is language, so is language the mode and

19. Nicholas Wolterstorff, "Resurrecting the Author," *Midwest Studies in Philosophy* 27, no. 1 (2003): 24.

means of the Fall. This will point in a way that is more than symbolic to the recreation of the fallen world through the Word (John 1).

We must highlight three characteristics of language between Fall and Redemption, characteristics that also pertain to the writing and reading of literature today. First, language continues as an instrument of grace after the Fall. God speaks words of judgment on Adam, Eve, and the serpent, but He also declares the promise of victory through the Seed of the Woman. Adam's immediate response to God's words of justice and mercy is to name the woman "Eve" ("mother of all the living", Gen 3:20). This act of naming involves much more than the accuracy of a scientific, taxonomic classification: it is an act of faith by which Adam accepts as true God's promise in the *protoevangelium*. The fact that God speaks the words of promise and Adam answers with faith again shows that language is the mode of covenantal relationship: the medium of verbal communication is the message of covenantal relationship. In faith, the creative and covenantal functions of the language of paradise remain after the Fall.

However, before we get too excited, language is also the medium of humankind's rejection of God and his proffered grace. Students of literature should always remember that the first recorded poem in human history is Lamech's vaunting declaration of independence from God in a vicious celebration of violence (Genesis 4:23-24). The account in Genesis 11 of the confusion of tongues at the Tower of Babel further reminds us that language is central to the development or unfurling of the potentials of creation. Earlier, in the narrative about the growth of civilization with Jubal and Tubal-Cain in Genesis 4, human beings create culture through technology and music. The impulse to develop human society in Genesis 11 extends to technological innovations, such as the invention of brick and mortar, as well as political organization into a single community. But essentially, it is the common language that unites the descendants of Cain on the plain of Shinar:

> The Lord said, "If as one people speaking the same language they have begun to do this, then nothing they plan to do will be impossible for them. Come, let us go down and confuse their language so they will not understand each other." (Gen 11:6-7 NIV)

Read along Reformational lines, this passage demonstrates the directional distortion of the structurally good gift of language. The *protoevangelium* and the naming of Eve, on the one hand, and Lamech's song and the Tower of Babel, on the other, reveal language as more than merely a functional or instrumental tool: the crucial factor is not the accuracy with which language corresponds with reality, but the way words speak with or against God's intended goodness for creation.

Third, through Moses and the prophets, God speaks his grace

through literary means. One could rightly say—in a rephrasing of Romans 5:8—that God demonstrates his love for us in that, while we were sinners, He gave us his Word. In a Reformed apology for literature, we must grant a significant place to the literary nature of God's special revelation in Scripture. Thanks to the cultural sophistication of that remarkable prince of Egypt, Moses, the Bible opens with a poetic account of creation, followed by thematically-structured narrative accounts of the calling of Abram, the exodus out of Egypt, and the receiving of God's law. The shaping of the micronarratives of the Book of Judges to reflect the arc of the redemptive metanarrative is another illustration of the rules of composition serving the redemptive purpose of language. Many literary aspects of the Old Testament are adopted and adapted from Ancient Near Eastern poetic and narrative practices. From the vivid imagery of the prophets to the affective force of the Psalms of David, the Old Testament exhibits the traits of literature: genres and their conventions, narrative and poetic structures, and poetic devices for affective impact. Recognizing the literariness of the Bible need not be a rejection of its authority, as *The Westminster Confession of Faith* states:

> [T]he heavenliness of the matter, the efficacy of the doctrine, the majesty of the style, the consent of all the parts, the scope of the whole (which is, to give all glory to God), the full discovery it makes of the only way of man's salvation, the many other incomparable excellencies, and the entire perfection thereof, are arguments whereby it doth abundantly evidence itself to be the Word of God: yet notwithstanding, our full persuasion and assurance of the infallible truth and divine authority thereof, is from the inward work of the Holy Spirit bearing witness by and with the Word in our hearts. (I.5)

The literary qualities of the Old Testament testify to the value of literature as a means of grace, as rainbows in the fallen world, to borrow Calvin Seerveld's marvelous phrase.[20]

Again, however, before we get too optimistic about the potential for the structurally-good but directionally-ambivalent nature of language and its literary uses, we need to consider the Poststructuralist insight about the slippery, indeterminate, and supplemental nature of language. In short, Poststructuralism emphasizes the lacunae in linguistic and literary communication, the fissures through which meaning threatens to drop out of sight, and the ultimate undecidability of signification. Think here of Jacques Derrida's famous play on the word *difference* as *deference*: meaning is not a stable system of referentiality but is always already deferred, replaced, or supplemented by other words in a theoretically infinite regress

20. Calvin Seerveld, *Rainbows for the Fallen World: Aesthetic Life and Artistic Task* (Toronto, ON: Tuppence Press, 2005).

that never can definitely define meaning. But the Poststructuralist problem of *supplementarity* is a problem only if one wants to make absolute claims for language, which is not what the Reformed view of language does. The correspondence view of language correlates the sign (word) and the signified (thing), what in the classical tradition is heard in the phrase *res et verba*. The Reformed view of language—and, consequently, of literature—holds that the relationship between word and thing is proximate, not absolute, even when speaking about Scripture. When Scripture is viewed from the Reformed theological perspective of the covenant, the Word of the LORD has primarily a testamentary authority as God's self-revelation. With divine discourse, the question of fidelity revolves around the trustworthiness of the Author, which Kevin Vanhoozer associates with the fiduciary framework in epistemology.[21] The limited reliability of the medium, however, does not necessarily preclude the trustworthiness of the speaker, nor should the Poststructuralist suspicion of language lead to radical relativism or nihilism. We need not be afraid, as James K.A. Smith has argued, to admit the contingency of knowledge: "To recognize contingency is not the equivalent of saying 'anything goes'."[22] In fact, the humility that we learn from the doctrine of the Fall makes us wary of totalizing claims about anything, including claims about language's reliability. We may be so fearful of reducing the authority of Scripture when we admit the insight of the Poststructuralist deconstruction of language and its attendant relativism that perhaps we may overcompensate in the other direction and unduly exaggerate the reliability and efficacy of language. As Elaine Botha argues in *Metaphor and Its Moorings*, recognizing the metaphorical nature of language is not a denial of Scripture's claim upon the reader.[23] From the Reformed theological perspective, Scripture is infallible because he who gives it to us is faithful (Heb 6:16-18), not because the medium of language is inerrant. Likewise, what is redeemed by the Incarnate Word through the Spirit of Pentecost, as we will see in what follows, is not the medium but the messenger.

Redemption

For an apology for literature to be Christian, it must be Christocentric. When we consider the *who* and the *what* of the Son's ministry, we will see that the person and the ministry of Jesus offer three valu-

21. Kevin Vanhoozer, *Biblical Authority after Babel: Retrieving the Solas in the Spirit of Mere Protestant Christianity* (Grand Rapids, MI: Brazos Press, 2016), 100-103.

22. James K.A. Smith, *Who's Afraid of Relativism? Community, Contingency, and Creaturehood* (Grand Rapids, MI: Baker Academic, 2014), 100.

23. M. Elaine Botha, *Metaphor and Its Moorings: Studies in the Grounding of Metaphorical Meaning* (Bern: Peter Lang, 2007), 209–233.

able insights for an understanding the role of language and literature post-Pentecost: the person of the Word; the ministry of the parable; and the person and ministry of the Spirit.

First, the Gospel of John begins with the affirmation of language and creation in a reprise of the motif of the life-giving *fiat* of Genesis 1:

> In the beginning was the Word, and the Word was with God, and the Word was God. The same was in the beginning with God. All things were made by him; and without him was not any thing made that was made. In him was life; and the life was the light of men. And the light shineth in darkness; and the darkness comprehended it not. (John 1:1-5, KJV)

The central claim of the Gospel of John is the divinity of Jesus the Christ, and the rhetorically powerful opening statement of the theme declares the mystery and miracle of the Incarnation by means of the metaphor of language. The Old Testament is rich in similes, metaphors, and analogies to reveal God's character, but nothing prepares us for the startling metaphor of the Word to reveal the two natures of the Incarnate Son. This metaphor affirms what has been implied throughout the Old Testament, namely, that God's light- and life-giving Speech Acts, from the first naming of "the greater light" (Genesis 1:16) to the last prophecy of "the Sun of Righteousness with healing in its rays" (Malachi 4:2), entwine the creative and redemptive dimensions of God's eternal counsel. If we earlier highlighted the significance of the creative word in Genesis 1 for the student of literature, we can now extend the significance to include the redemptive Word in John 1.

Augustine uses Christ's incarnation in *De Doctrina Christiana* (*On Christian Teaching*) to illustrate how language works. The union of human and divine natures in Christ's person expresses well the collocation of idea and sign in Augustine's theory of language:

> In what way did He come but this, "The Word was made flesh, and dwelt among us"? Just as when we speak, in order that what we leave in our minds may enter through the ear into the mind of the hearer, the word which we have in our hearts becomes an outward sound and is called speech and yet our thought does not lose itself in the sound, but remains complete in itself, and takes the form of speech without being modified in its own nature by the change: so the Divine Word, though suffering no change in nature, yet became flesh, that He might dwell among us. (1.13)[24]

Just as the Son of God did not lose his divine nature when He took

24. Augustine, *On Christian Doctrine*, 1.13. Christian Classics Ethereal Library, https://ccel.org/ccel/augustine/doctrine/doctrine.xiii.html.

on flesh, so the word which we have in our heart retains its nature when it has been uttered as spoken word. The utterance is not a *reduction* of the ideal thought as it assumes physical form and as it is expressed in material sound; it is the fulfilment of the potentiality for human communication. The word is spoken [*dictio*] precisely in order to bring the inner word [*dicibile*] into a dimension that admits relationship between and among human beings, for this is the purpose of speech.

> Conventional signs are those which living beings mutually exchange for the purpose of showing, as well as they can, the feelings of their minds, or their perceptions, or their thoughts. Nor is there any reason for giving a sign except the desire of drawing forth and conveying into another's mind what the giver of the sign has in his own mind. (2.2.3)[25]

What is remarkable here, of course, is that the incarnation/language metaphor of John 1 is transposed so that the incarnation is the metaphor for the word rather than the other way around.

It is worth noting at this point that Christian approaches to literature often invoke the theological term "incarnation" in a general rather than a specifically Christological sense. When a character is said to embody an idea or a plot makes a theme or motif physical, this is referred to as the incarnational quality of the artistic imagination. This loose use of incarnation as a metaphor for how literature translates an idea into a (fictional) reality runs the risk of diminishing the unique event of the Incarnation. Terry Eagleton argues that the idea of language-as-incarnation is merely metaphorical: "all language is conceptual, and making it seem otherwise is just a kind of poetic sleight of hand. It may feel as though the words of the Heaney poem ["Digging"] somehow embody the very stuff they speak of, but what looks like incarnational is really associational."[26] For Augustine, however, Christ's incarnation not only serves as an illustration or analogy, but is the very basis of meaningful speech and of relationships made possible through language. Augustine reflects on this reality in *Confessions* (11.5-9), too. Since Christ as the Word-made-flesh is the instrument of creation (John 1), he is the very ground of language as the means of communion between God and humanity and amongst human beings. Unlike Plato's disdain for the word-as-material-idea in *Phaedrus* and elsewhere, Augustine's incarnational view of language values the word precisely at its intersection of thought and utterance. For Plato, a word is a sensible thing that contains an idea—as soul is to body,

25. Augustine, *On Christian Doctrine*, 2.2.3. Christian Classics Ethereal Library, https://ccel.org/ccel/augustine/doctrine/doctrine.iv.iii.iii.html.

26. Terry Eagleton, "The Incarnational Fallacy," in *How to Read a Poem* (Oxford: Blackwell, 2007), 61.

so idea is to word; for Augustine, a word is the hypostatic union of the thought to be uttered (*dicibile*) and the word that is spoken (*dictio*).

Second, the ministry of the Incarnate Word validates the use of fiction. Throughout the Old Testament Scriptures, God reveals aspects of his infinite Being by means of metaphors, similes, and analogies. The prophet Hosea is unique in that he literally embodies the analogy of God's betrothal to his people, Israel. Israel is already metaphorically God's firstborn son (see Hosea 11:1-2), but by virtue of the covenant, Israel is also God's wife and, furthermore, mother to his offspring. In Hosea, then, we have not only verbal metaphors of God's commitment to Israel but also the living embodiment in Hosea's marriage with Gomer, a prostitute. The prophecy of Hosea is unique in that he does not speak to Israel—there are no "Thus saith the LORD" passages—but his body speaks figuratively on God's behalf. Ezekiel, likewise, pictures forth the LORD's prophecy against Jerusalem by creating a model of the city and its besiegement: "This will be a sign to the people of Israel" (Ezek. 4:3). Jonah is miraculously revived after three days in the belly of the fish, thereby physically prefiguring Christ's resurrection, as Jesus explains to the Pharisees (Matt. 12:39-41). Leaving aside the visual figures embedded in the ceremonies of the tabernacle and temple, the Old Testament Scriptures are replete with verbal images by which God reveals himself metaphorically. As Thomas Aquinas puts it in *Summa Theologica*:

> It is befitting Holy Writ to put forward divine and spiritual truths by means of comparisons with material things. For God provides for everything according to the capacity of its nature. Now it is natural to man to attain to intellectual truths through sensible objects, because all our knowledge originates from sense. Hence in Holy Writ, spiritual truths are fittingly taught under the likeness of material things.[27]

By its extensive use of imagery to reveal aspects of God and his relationship with Israel, Scripture already demonstrates the legitimacy of using fiction to speak truth.

But it is especially in the ministry of Jesus, in whom the prophetic images of the Old Testament find their meaning, that we encounter the full force of verbal pictures and fictional narratives. Many of the "I am" statements that Jesus makes are metaphors: the door, gate, vine, way, light, shepherd, and bread. These metaphors are exemplary in their effectiveness. They are fresh and innovative, universally relatable, and evocative of much more than the immediate point of comparison. In a way, each metaphor is a micro-parable that suggests a narrative behind it for

27. Thomas Aquinas, *Summa Theologica*, Part 1, Article 9. Christian Classics Ethereal Library, https://www.ccel.org/ccel/aquinas/summa.FP_Q1_A9.html.

the listener and reader to realize in their imagination. Occasionally, the figures that Jesus employs are substitutionary, such as the metonym of the cup and the bread at the Last Supper. When he says, "This is my body, which is for you; do this in remembrance of me" and "This cup is the new covenant in my blood; do this, whenever you drink it, in remembrance of me," Jesus is doubling the substitutionary figure as he describes the sacrament of his substitutionary atonement: "cup" *stands in* for what it contains ("wine"), as wine *stands in* for the blood Jesus will shed for his people, and "bread" *stands in* for body, as "body" *stands in* for Christ's sacrifice. Whether it is a metaphor or a metonym, Jesus appropriates for his divine purposes these ordinary poetic devices, thereby redeeming the figures that are central to the way literary texts work.

The same can be said for the parables. If the central theme of the Old Testament is *covenant*, then the central theme of Christ's ministry is *kingdom* and the primary means by which he describes the kingdom is by parable. Indeed, Christ's ministry is unique in the extent to which he uses parables to reveal to those who accept him and to conceal from those who reject him as the Son of God (Luke 8:9-10). Unlike metaphor and metonym, which are primarily visual images, parable is a narrative mode that invites the listener/reader to situate him- or herself in the world of the story, to identify with its characters, and to realize the truth about the kingdom of heaven that the parable narrates. Because the kingdom of heaven is a reality to be experienced more than it is an idea to be conceptualized, the realistic form of the parable perfectly matches its content. As stories that function on the affective plane, the parables of Jesus require the listener/reader to respond to the voice of the narrator, to feel the truth concerning the kingdom of heaven, and to make the story their own. In this regard, it is crucial to see parable not as allegory, which has meaning only when the features of the story are abstracted through symbolism, but as realism. To say that Jesus's telling of parables validates fiction as a means of speaking truth is also to affirm realism as a mode.

Third, the person and ministry of the Spirit in the New Testament make accessible to fallen human beings the goodness of language as it was intended at creation. This aspect of a Reformed theological perspective on language and literature extends the doctrine of the Word-made-flesh of Christology into pneumatology, the doctrine of the Holy Spirit. The application of the redeeming work of Christ in the linguistic aspect comes powerfully after Pentecost as the Holy Spirit opens the eyes of the Old Testament reader to the ultimate signification of its signs and figures.[28] Central among the sanctifying functions of the Spirit is illumi-

28. See Craig Bartholomew, Colin J.D. Green, and Karl Möller, eds. *After Pentecost: Language and Biblical Interpretation* (Carlisle: Paternoster Press, 2001).

nation, the understanding of the coherence of all things in Christ: "we have received is not the spirit of the world, but the Spirit who is from God, so that we may understand what God has freely given us" (1 Cor 2:12 NIV). Having "the mind of Christ" means seeing the fullness of things from his perspective, the scales taken from our eyes. The focus on the Spirit's work at Pentecost is often on the speaking in tongues, rather than on the understanding by the hearers of what was being said; they not only understood the words, they understood and responded to the claim that these words had. Pentecost was an event that demonstrated what Spirit-filled understanding consisted of: it was the ministry of the Spirit that enlightened the minds and hearts of the hearers to grasp the full meaning of what was being said.

The best exemplar of the new pneuma-hermeneutics is the Apostle Paul. In his Epistles, particularly when he addresses Jewish Christians, Paul configures the meaning of the Old Testament in terms of the lived experience of the redeemed-but-persecuted followers of Christ. In his letter to the Galatians, Paul reads the narrative of Hagar and Sarah in Genesis in a way that gives significance to the trials that the Galatian believers experience. After Paul explains that the Galatians are children of the promise, descendants of Abraham by Sarah rather than by Hagar ("his son by the free woman was born as the result of a promise," 4:23), he adds: "These things may be taken figuratively" (4:24). The Apostle Peter, when he refers to the days of Noah's persecution, reads the event of the flood in terms of a new understanding of baptism (1 Pet. 3:21). The Letter to the Hebrews is an extended exercise in the post-Pentecost reading of the Old Testament, from the mysterious origins of Christ's priesthood in Melchizedek to the design of the temple, in which the lived experience of the Hebrews is read into the narrative of God's covenant and kingdom. It is important to recognize in the pneuma-hermeneutic of the New Testament the practice of apostolic reading in which the text is understood to convey a meaning with propositional truth *and* to impact the reader through its affective force. Paul, Peter, and the writer to the Hebrews are not just making impressive analytical moves on Old Testament allegories, they are practising a form of reading that releases the power of the Spirit through the letter. As David Lyle Jeffrey and Alan Jacobs have amply proven, the New Testament teaches us how to read.[29]

29. David Lyle Jeffrey, *People of the Book: Christian Identity and Literary Culture* (Grand Rapids, MI: Eerdmans, 1996) and *Houses of the Interpreter: Reading Scripture, Reading Culture* (Waco, TX: Baylor University Press, 2003); Alan Jacobs, *A Theology of Reading: The Hermeneutics of Love* (Boulder, CO: Westview Press, 2001).

Conclusion

Among the divine attributes that human beings possess, as I noted in the introduction, is *the ability to create, by means of language, worlds that invite our responsible participation.* We temporarily inhabit the world created by the words of the text, whether that is as members of the audience who react in sympathy with what we see on stage or as listeners at a poetry reading in which the poet's voice conjures up new ways of seeing the world or as readers absorbed by the people, places, and plot of a novel. Building on the theological tradition of Calvin and Calvinism, we can name the central tenets of a Reformed theory of literature and literary criticism that, though not a method or a practice, can animate our scholarship and teaching today:

1. Every human being reflects that most glorious of God's attributes—creativity. Writers and readers share the capacity to generate, through an imagination that conceives and perceives, new worlds and alternate realities.
2. Language, as the enactment of covenant relationships, is a special gift of God's grace entrusted uniquely to human beings. As a means of grace, language is never neutral but is ever oriented either toward or away from the good purposes ordained by its Giver to reveal truth, beauty, and goodness.
3. Literature, as language given meaningful shape in form by an author to produce an effect, elicits from the reader a response. Understanding a literary text is more than the mere apprehension of an idea as the meaning of the text; it is the engagement of the reader's cognitive and affective faculties. A literary text—whether poem, play or prose work—is not simply an inert object, a historical artifact, or a puzzle in code; it is a fictional universe in which the reader participates while reading. The reader meets historical and contemporary texts in the present moment, in the act of reading, and responds to the converging of historical horizons, as Hans-Georg Gadamer describes the phenomenon in *Truth and Method,*[30] in terms that include an array of aesthetic, moral, ethical, and spiritual aspects of the reading activity. While these aspects of reading can be distinguished for the purpose of analysis, they cannot be totally separated

30. Hans-Georg Gadamer, *Truth and Method*, in *The Critical Tradition: Classic Texts and Contemporary Trends*, 3rd ed., ed. David H. Richter (New York: Bedford/St. Martin's, 2007), 735-737.

or removed while reading.[31]

4. Despite the fallen condition in which all humans partake, authors often have insight into the human condition that rings true. Even in literary texts in which God seems absent, the worlds created by literature reveal a yearning for coherence, order, wholeness, and closure that is native to being human. We can ascribe this recognition of humanity's congenital condition of loss to common grace, even though the literary text does not account for the brokenness specifically in terms of humanity's original and actual moral lapse. In his commentary on Jabal, the descendent of Cain who is credited with inventing the harp, John Calvin sounds positively surprised "that this race, which had most deeply fallen from integrity, should have excelled the rest of posterity of Adam in rare endowments."[32]

5. Fiction is a means by which the truth about reality can be revealed. As in the metaphors and parables of Jesus, make-believe opens the complexity of reality to the reader by activating cognitive and affective faculties. The reader's response to fiction involves an affirmation of its truthfulness as analogy. As fiction relates to reality indirectly, reading is the translating of the imagined world in terms of the real world; as Rita Felski puts it, "texts draw us into imagined yet referentially salient worlds."[33] Because the fictive world may bend or distort the truth of the world in its reflection, the reader actively evaluates the fidelity of the analogy in relation to his or her understanding of reality.

6. The two branches of axiology in philosophy—aesthetics and ethics—are simultaneously in play in both the writing and in the reading of literary texts. The aesthetic sphere is never neutral because decisions regarding form, both in the creating and critiquing of literature, are inflected by worldview. Because language and literature are speech acts among human agents (see points 2 and 3 above),

31. See Rita Felski, *The Limits of Critique*, for a positive description of the affective domain in the practice of literary criticism. Citing Michel Chaouli, Felski concludes: "the literary work discloses itself to the reader's experience of it—such that an effacement of that experience, in the name of analytical rigor and detachment, also fails to do justice to the work" (191). See further Cristina Vischer Bruns, "The Varied Effects of Literary Experience and Why They Matter" in *Why Literature?: The Value of Literary Reading and What It Means for Teaching* (New York: Continuum, 2011), 18-26.

32. John Calvin, *Commentary on Genesis*, vol. 1, trans. John King, (Grand Rapids, MI: Christian Classics Ethereal Library, 1847), https://www.ccel.org/ccel/calvin/calcom01.x.i.html.

33. Rita Felski, *Uses of Literature* (Oxford: Blackwell Publishing, 2008), 104.

writing and reading necessarily involve ethical categories. If justice is defined as the performance of obligation that can legitimately be claimed by another, as Nicholas Wolterstorff does, then writers and readers are required to fulfil their respective duties to each other in the contract, the tacit exchange of trust that is implicit in writing and reading.[34] When encountering a character in a literary text, such as the speaker of a lyrical poem or a protagonist in a play, the reader's feelings toward that character are of an ethical nature.[35] Consequently, many view the development of empathy in the reader as being the primary function of literature.[36] Revulsion, disgust, pity, fear, guilt, remorse, self-congratulation, envy, and admiration are some of our responses to the characters we encounter in literature, responses that have complicated origins in our personal experiences, our value systems, and our control beliefs. Furthermore, ethics also pertains in the practice of criticism in the academy, the classroom, and the media in the way that we treat others justly and humbly in all contexts of literary studies.

7. Appreciation, delight, and enjoyment are valid responses to literary texts, whether or not such a response is accompanied by instruction. Every element of literature—diction, imagery, form, characterization, plot—has the capacity to delight the reader. Rather than mere delight for delight's sake, enjoyment is made complete when experienced as grace. "All things that are connected with the enjoyment of the present life are sacred gifts of God," Calvin notes in his commentary on 1 Corinthians 7:29.[37] Just as our delight in the aesthetic goodness of creation is made meaningful against the backdrop of faith in the goodness of the Creator, so the pleasure derived from literary texts is sanctified by receiving language as a gracious gift of God and by recognizing the author as *imago Dei* (see "A" and "B" above). To quote again from Calvin's commentary on Genesis 4:20,

34. Nicholas Wolterstorff, introduction to *Justice: Rights and Wrongs* (Princeton: Princeton University Press, 2008), 4-5.

35. Ben Faber, "Ethical Hermeneutics in the Theater: Shakespeare's *The Merchant of Venice*." In *Hermeneutics at the Crossroads: Interpretation in Christian Perspective*, eds. Kevin Vanhoozer, James K.A. Smith, and Bruce Ellis Benson (Bloomington, IL: Indiana University Press, 2006), 211-224.

36. See, for instance, Suzanne Keen, *Empathy and the Novel* (New York: Oxford University Press, 2007). See also Martha C. Nussbaum, "Perceptive Equilibrium: Literary Theory and Ethical Theory," in *Love's Knowledge: Essays on Philosophy and Literature* (New York: Oxford University Press, 1992), 168-194.

37. John Calvin, *Commentary on the Epistles of Paul the Apostle to the Corinthians*, vol. 1, trans. by John Pringle (Edinburgh: Calvin Translation Society, 1848), https://ccel.org/ccel/calvin/calcom39/calcom39.xiv.vii.html.

"Pleasure is indeed to be condemned, unless it be combined with the fear of God, and with the common benefit of human society."[38]

8. "Emplotment", a term used by Hayden White to describe the way historians shape events into a certain type of story, in narratology refers to the way a narrative in poem, play, or prose embodies assumptions about agency and time in its plot.[39] The Christian metanarrative of creation, fall, restoration, and consummation, also known simply as the Story of Scripture, can often be discerned in the beginning, middle, and end of narratives in literature.[40] The Bible consists of discrete books in a wide range of genres, but it is itself a complete story in the comic mode. As Paul Fiddes has argued, the narrative momentum toward resolution in literature—what Frank Kermode called "the sense of an ending"—mirrors the historical momentum toward the eschaton.[41]

9. "Poetic faith" is an act of the imagination whereby the reader accepts as true the givens of the fictive world that he or she encounters in the text. Michael Tomko, in his study of Samuel Taylor Coleridge's phrase "the willing suspension of disbelief", describes "poetic faith" as analogous to "a religious faith that awakens all the human faculties, prompts reason to ascend to its greatest capacity, and educes meaningful experience not otherwise available."[42] Rather than denigrating the imagination, we can recognize this image-forming faculty as crucial to memory, hope, and faith. Not only does Jesus powerfully draw on his hearers' imagination in the parable, the biblical definition of faith itself relies on the imagination to picture-forth "the substance of things hoped for, the evidence of things not seen" (Heb. 11:1).

---

38. Calvin, *Commentary on Genesis.*

39. Hayden White, *Metahistory: The Historical Imagination in Nineteenth-Century Europe* (Johns Hopkins, 1973), 7-11. See also Hayden White, "The Historical Text as Literary Artifact" in *The Critical Tradition: Classic Texts and Contemporary Trends*, 3rd ed., ed. David H. Richter (New York: Bedford/St. Martin's, 2007), 1384-1397.

40. See Albert M. Wolters, *Creation Regained: Biblical Basics for a Reformational Worldview*, 2nd ed. (Grand Rapids, MI: William B. Eerdmans, 2005); Craig G. Bartholomew and Michael W. Goheen, *The Drama of Scripture: Finding our Place in the Biblical Story* (Grand Rapids, MI: Baker Academic, 2004).

41. Paul Fiddes, *The Promised End: Eschatology in Theology and Literature* (Oxford: Blackwell, 2000). See also Frank Kermode, *The Sense of an Ending: Studies in the Theory of Fiction* (Oxford: Oxford University Press, 2000).

42. Michael Tomko, *Beyond the Willing Suspension of Disbelief: Poetic Faith from Coleridge to Tolkien* (London: Bloomsbury Academic, 2016), 145.

Research Agenda

With the turn to political ways of reading in the Humanities generally and in literary studies in particular, the Christian scholar has an opportunity to speak into contemporary social justice concerns legitimately within the discipline. It is here that scholars interested in the Neo-Calvinist philosophy of Herman Dooyeweerd can push the boundaries of literary studies beyond the linguistic and aesthetic aspects (see Koyzis and Kosits, "Introduction"). The concept of sphere sovereignty, while praiseworthy in distinguishing the roles of discrete institutions in society generally, can inhibit interdisciplinarity in the academy. While some would argue that the disciplines of political science, psychology, sociology, and even theology have no business in the close reading of literary texts, such insularity is difficult to maintain in literary studies today. Since the decline of New Criticism and the rise of Critical Theory in the 1960s, the discourse of literary studies has become increasingly interdisciplinary. Class, race, and gender have come to dominate literary studies in the twenty-first century, thereby weakening the sacred sovereignty of the disciplinary spheres. The worldview analysis with which Neo-Calvinist scholars have distinguished themselves in the arts sets an example for literary scholars to imitate in the current critical environment. Perhaps the best way to apply Dooyeweerd is by following the example of his critique of Enlightenment philosophy in identifying the *ground motive* of the critical practices that pertain in the academy today. It is a platitude in our discipline that there is no practice without theory. To which someone applying Dooyeweerd's critique would add: there is no theory without a prior faith commitment or basic orientation. This is what Nicholas Wolterstorff nicely demonstrates in Part II of *Reason within the Bounds of Religion*.[43]

It should be noted, however, that Herman Dooyeweerd's *A New Critique of Theoretical Thought* does not offer specific direction for the literary scholar. Even though Dooyeweerd wrote poems under the influence of Romanticism in his younger years, he clearly rejects the Romantic worldview as being antithetical to the theme of Christ's supremacy over all things. Together with Groen Van Prinsterer, Willem Bilderdijk, and Abraham Kuyper, Dooyeweerd associates Romanticism in the arts with the humanistic spirit of the French Revolution. Thus, when it comes to his description of the *aesthetic modal aspect*, Dooyeweerd is firmly Neo-Classical, as though the order, control, restraint, structure, and balance that the Neo-Classical writers, such as Alexander Pope, discerned in

43. Nicholas Wolterstorff, *Reason within the Bounds of Religion*, 2nd ed. (Grand Rapids, MI: William B. Eerdmans, 1984), 109-146.

Nature aligns with his own cosmonomic idea:

> First follow NATURE, and your judgment frame
> By her just standard, which is still the same:
> Unerring Nature, still divinely bright,
> One clear, unchang'd, and universal light,
> Life, force, and beauty, must to all impart,
> At once the source, and end, and test of art.
>
> (*An Essay on Criticism*, Part 1, lines 68-73)[44]

Perhaps it is telling that the modal aspect that is contiguous with the *aesthetic* aspect in Dooyeweerd is the *economic*, whose kernel characteristic is frugality. It follows, then, that the principle of frugality carries over to the ideal of moderation in Dooyeweerd's aesthetic. Is this a function of Dooyeweerd being influenced by Modernism in the arts? Or is his allergic reaction to exuberance and excess in the arts typical of Dutch Protestant attitudes toward the baroque excesses?

Here follows a series of suggested topics for further research by literary scholars, particular those engaged in British, American, Canadian, and world literature. The final set of research ideas is for those who are interested in applying Neo-Calvinist or Reformational philosophy to the theory and practice of literary studies.

Literary Theory

(1) Poststructuralism:

Christian literary scholars are generally nervous about the claims of Poststructuralist literary theory. Many of us feel unequipped or underequipped to speak into issues in contemporary critical theory. Because some aspects of Poststructuralist theory seem incompatible with or inimical to Christian faith, we may shy away from debating these theories with our peers in the academy. Christian scholars with expertise and interest in contemporary theory should lead the way in demonstrating how we may benefit from the insights of Poststructuralist theories of literature, even while we register our disagreement with their faith assumptions, philosophical presuppositions, and critical practices.

(2) Ecocriticism:

One of the current critical approaches that most naturally aligns with a Reformed biblical perspective is ecocriticism. The doctrines of creation, fall, and re-creation (Rom 8: 20-25) that impel the stewardship for

44. Alexander Pope, *An Essay on Criticism* (1711), Representative Poetry Online, University of Toronto, https://rpo.library.utoronto.ca/content/essay-criticism-part-1.

creation also provide the framework for Christian ecocriticism. This is a field in literary studies that can fruitfully be worked by Christian scholars who want to shift the discourse about the environment from material or natural determinism to include the transcendent.

(3) Metafiction:

Gallagher and Lundin's *Literature through the Eyes of Faith*, a text that remains popular in undergraduate literature courses at American Christian colleges, damns metafiction with faint praise and ultimately rejects it as a mode of representation because of its skeptical epistemology and "denial of absolute truth."[45] An explicitly Christian engagement with metafiction can align this mode of writing with a biblical appreciation that human knowledge is relative, constructed, and limited.

(4) Magic Realism

Christian scholars who want to explore the relationship between the mundane and the miraculous, the real and the fantastic, can speak to contemporary concerns by delving into the history and practice of magic realism.

Language, Rhetoric, and Composition

(1) Fake News and the Post-Truth Era:

Marilyn Chandler McEntyre's *Caring for Words in a Culture of Lies* sets a good example of the calling of Christian scholars to articulate how language relates to truth.[46] We need more analysis of public discourse and political speech acts. This can be theoretical (discourse analysis), historical (close reading of cultural artifacts), and contemporary (linguistic algorithms on social media), with a view to demonstrating the nexus of language and truth.

(2) Race and Rhetoric:

Critical Race Theory opens the door Christian scholars to identify how language constructs both social distinctiveness and racial discrimination. It would be helpful to have an evaluation of the way Critical Race Theory has changed the discipline. With the biblical revelation of Babel and Pentecost on the one hand and the lived experience of writers of color on the other, we need to bring theological insight to bear on the

45. Susan V. Gallagher and Roger Lundin, *Literature through the Eyes of Faith* (San Francisco: Harper Collins, 1989), 164.

46. Marilyn Chandler McEntyre, *Caring for Words in a Culture of Lies* (Grand Rapids, MI: Eerdmans, 2009).

way language expresses difference.

(3) Fiduciary Commitment:

How has language eroded trust? With the covenantal model for language, the Christian scholar can develop a framework that (re)inserts trust into communication in its various modes.

Race

(1) Canon Formation:

The process of truth and reconciliation involves the recovery of lost or suppressed voices. We need scholars who are Black, indigenous, or persons of color to curate collections of texts—oral and written—that reflect these communities, their histories, and their present.

(2) Postcolonial Criticism:

Postcolonial theory is a space that currently lacks a clear Christian presence. Whether out of fear or guilt, or both, Christian scholars are wary of openly addressing literary works that implicate Christianity in the history of colonization. Honest, direct, and courageous work needs to be done from a Christian perspective to complement the growing body of Postcolonial scholarship.

(3) Critical Re-vision of the Western Canon:

Critical Race Theory and Postcolonial criticism can help Christian scholars reread "classics" in order to place the literary monuments of the past in their proper context. Instead of a radical de-colonization of the Western canon, Christian scholars have an opportunity to situate new readings of literary texts within a historical context that includes our present moment. Christian scholars have an opportunity to rise above the political partisanship of the culture wars by participating in the critical discourse about race and colonialism with truth and trust.

Pedagogy

(1) Teaching Digital Orphans:

As anyone teaching literature at the post-secondary level knows, students are finding it increasingly difficult to maintain the attention, focus, and discipline to read their assigned texts well. Maryanne Wolf, in *Reader, Come Home*, maintains that democracy itself is in peril unless the so-called "digital natives" in college classrooms re-learn the art of deep reading: "If we in the twenty-first century are to preserve a vital collective conscience, we must ensure that all members of our society are able to read and think both deeply and well."[47] The threat is real for the Christian church, too, as the faithful increasingly become the Bad Readers that C.S. Lewis decries in *An Experiment in Criticism*.[48] We need a critical pedagogy for literature classes for students to develop habits of deep reading for the cause of democracy and the Gospel.

(2) Spiritual Formation:

Literature classes are frequently places of reflection on a variety of religious experiences, whether it is reading a medieval mystic or a Southern Gothic Catholic writer. For those teaching in Christian colleges, sometimes the text becomes a pretext for students' self-reflection (even self-absorption) rather than an entity in its own right (and rite). A pedagogy that respects the text and encourages centripetal reading, and that also dovetails with the spiritual formation of students outside the classroom, would form the foundation for teaching and learning that is faithful to the specific literary text and to the broader mission of the Christian college.

Three Themes

(1) Christian-Islamic Worlds:

As a subfield of Postcolonial criticism, the long history of engagement between the Christian West and the Islamic world holds promise especially for scholars in Medieval and Early Modern literatures. What distinguishes the literature of these two cultures? What influences and confluences are perceptible? How do Christian readers receive the literatures of their Abrahamic relatives?

(2) Global English:

The global economy, dominated by a predominantly American tech industry, has ensured that English is the *lingua franca* in social media, entertainment, and commerce. How has English altered the realities of non-English speaking communities in culturally inflected ways? How has English adapted to the new media?

(3) Residual Calvinism in Contemporary American Fiction:

Perry Miller famously outlined the contours of Puritan thought in early American literature. A similar project on the enduring legacy of Protestantism in literature today, not only in Christian authors such as

47. Maryanne Wolf, *Reader, Come Home: The Reading Brain in a Digital World* (New York: HarperCollinsPublishers, 2018), 201..

48. C.S. Lewis, *An Experiment in Criticism* (Cambridge: Cambridge University Press, 1961).

Marilynne Robinson and Wendell Berry, but also in fiction that explores the American psyche from an agnostic or atheistic position.

Neo-Calvinist and Reformational Topics

(1) Dooyeweerd and Structuralism:

One could argue that Dooyeweerd is very much a product of his time. The systems theory that forms the basis of much Structuralist thought between 1900 and 1950 may also be the animating force behind Dooyeweerd's cosmonomic idea. One could fruitfully compare Saussurian Structuralism with the structuralism of Dooyeweerd's philosophy. Is a Poststructuralist Reformational philosophy possible?

(2) Modal Aspects and Literature:

One of the strengths of Dooyeweerd's approach is that it resists reductionism. Even though each modal aspect is discrete, independent, and governed by its own law, Dooyeweerd clearly intends for artificial entities (i.e., human constructions, cultural products, social practices) to be analyzed through the constellation of aspects that comprise these entities. When it comes to literary texts, one could situate the close reading of a text in relation to the material, economic, aesthetic, and social dimensions of the text.

(3) Genre:

Contemporary theories of genre have moved away from the transcendent, universal forms that have dominated the critical description of genre from Aristotle (form and matter) to Frye (myth and genre). Dooyeweerd's notion of "historical time" allows for the dynamic interaction between the human, subjective experience and the object reality in "cosmic time". Does Dooyeweerd's philosophy of time allow enough space for the social construction of literary form? Would New Formalism offer a potential détente between the cosmonomic and the historical timezones in the "disclosure" (*ontsluiting*) of aesthetic conventions?

(4) Worldview and Literature:

With the boundaries between disciplines becoming increasingly blurred in the academy, the literary scholar has the opportunity to unpack the philosophical grounding of the theories that drive literary criticism. A Neo-Calvinist critique of the discipline would expose the religious foundation of contemporary critical practices, such as Post-Humanism, Queer Theory, and Ecocriticism.

Questions for Reflection and Discussion

1. How does the Reformed understanding of the Lord's Supper differ from that of the Lutheran and Roman Catholic understanding of the sacrament? Consider the difference between George Herbert (Protestant) and Gerard Manley Hopkins (Roman Catholic) in their use of figurative language. What implications might this have for using the word "sacramental" to describe how the imagination gives real presence to an abstract idea in fiction?
2. Given the uniqueness of the coming of the Son of God in the flesh, should readers use the word "incarnational" for the process by which literature realizes imagined people, places, and things?
3. What role does the imagination play in the exercise of faith? Is imagination a function of belief, or vice-versa?
4. To what extent can the relationship between an author and their reader be described as a "covenant"? How does this way of construing the writer-reader contract imply *obligation* and *responsibility*?
5. To what extent is the reading of Scripture similar to the reading of non-biblical texts?
6. Is the doctrine of common grace sufficient to account for the goodness of literature in a fallen world?
7. In what respects is literary criticism *political*?
8. Discuss the relative importance of the following aspects of literature's function in a Reformed Christian literary theory. How would you rank them?:
   a. correspondence to reality;
   b. moral formation of the reader;
   c. appreciation of beauty;
   d. advocacy for social justice; and
   e. worldview critique.
9. How does the *creation-fall-redemption-restoration* framework help scholars in Christian colleges teach contemporary literature?
10. Which Poststructuralist literary theory aligns most closely with Christian faith? What can be gained by a Christian literary scholar identifying with a Poststructuralist school or theorist?
11. What are some possibilities for the Christian literary scholar to engage prophetically in the secular academy?

Helpful Resources

Anonby, John A. "A Christian perspective on English literature." In Dean E. D. Downey and Stanley E Porter, eds. *Christian Worldview and the Academic Disciplines: Crossing the Academy*, 233-247. Eugene, OR: Pickwick Publications, 2009.

Barratt, David, et al. *The Discerning Reader: Christian Perspectives on Literature and Theory*. Downers Grove: InterVarsity Press, 1995.

Berry, Wendell. *Standing by Words*. San Francisco, CA: North Point Press, 1983.

Edgar, William. *Created & Creating: A Biblical Theology of Culture*. Downers Grove, IL.: InterVarsity Press, 2017.

Gallagher, Susan V., and Roger Lundin. *Literature through the Eyes of Faith*. San Francisco: Harper Collins, 1989.

Jacobs, Alan. *A Theology of Reading: The Hermeneutics of Love*. Boulder, CO: Westview Press, 2001.

Jeffrey, David Lyle, and Greg Maillet. *Christianity and Literature: Philosophical Foundations and Critical Practice*. Downers Grove, IL: InterVarsity Press, 2011.

Lewis, C.S. *An Experiment in Criticism*. Cambridge: Cambridge University Press, 1961.

Lundin, Roger. *The Culture of Interpretation : Christian Faith and the Postmodern World*. Grand Rapids, MI: W.B. Eerdmans, 1993.

Ryken, Leland. *The Christian Imagination: The Practice of Faith in Literature and Writing*. Colorado Springs, CO: Shaw Books, 2002.

Ryken, Leland. *The Liberated Imagination: Thinking Christianly About the Arts*. Colorado Springs, CO: Shaw Books, 1989.

Van Til, Henry R. *The Calvinistic Concept of Culture*. Grand Rapids, MI: Baker, 1972.

Zylstra, Henry. *Testament of Vision*. Grand Rapids, MI: Eerdmans, 1958.

Bibliography

Arnold, Matthew. "The Function of Criticism in the Present Time." In *The Critical Tradition: Classic Texts and Contemporary Trends*, 3rd ed., edited by David H. Richter, 415-429. New York: Bedford/St. Martin's, 2007.

Aquinas, Thomas. *Summa Theologica*. Christian Classics Ethereal Library, https://www.ccel.org/ccel/aquinas/summa.

Augustine. *On Christian Doctrine in Four Books*. Christian Classics Ethereal Library, https://www.ccel.org/ccel/augustine/doctrine.html.

Bartholomew, Craig, Colin J.D. Green, and Karl Möller, eds. *After Pentecost: Language and Biblical Interpretation*. Carlisle: Paternoster Press, 2001.

Bartholomew, Craig G., and Michael W. Goheen. *The Drama of Scripture: Finding our Place in the Biblical Story*. Grand Rapids, MI: Baker Academic, 2004.

Bavinck, Herman. *Reformed Dogmatics*. Vol. 2, *God and Creation*. Edited by John Bolt. Translated by John Vriend. Grand Rapids, MI: Baker Academic, 2004.

Belgic Confession. In *Our Faith: Ecumenical Creeds, Reformed Confessions, and Other Resources: Including the Doctrinal Standards of the Christian Reformed Church in North America and the Reformed Church in America*. Grand Rapids, MI: Faith Alive Christian Resources, 2013.

Botha, M. Elaine. *Metaphor and Its Moorings: Studies in the Grounding of Metaphorical Meaning*. Bern: Peter Lang, 2007.

Bratman, David. "Tolkien's Subcreation." *Tolkien Studies*, vol. 13, 2016, pp. 293-295.

Brooks, Cleanth. *The Well Wrought Urn: Studies in the Structure of Poetry*. New York: Harcourt, Brace & World, 1947.

Bruns, Cristina Vischer. *Why Literature?: The Value of Literary Reading and What It Means for Teaching*. New York: Continuum, 2011.

Calvin, John. *Commentary on Genesis*. Vol. 1. Translated by John King. Grand Rapids, MI: Christian Classics Ethereal Library, 1847. https://www.ccel.org/ccel/calvin/calcom01.

Calvin, John. *Commentary on the Epistles of Paul the Apostle to the Corinthians*. Vol. 1. Translated by John Pringle. Edinburgh: Calvin Translation Society, 1848. https://ccel.org/ccel/calvin/calcom39/calcom39.

Calvin, John. *Institutes of the Christian Religion*. 2 vols. Translated by Ford Lewis Battles. Edited by John T. McNeill. Philadelphia, PA: Westminster John Knox, 1960.

Dehaene, Stanislas. *Reading in the Brain: The New Science of How We Read.* New York: Penguin Books, 2009.

De Man, Paul. *The Resistance to Theory.* Minneapolis, MN: University of Minnesota Press, 1986.

Eagleton, Terry. *How to Read a Poem.* Oxford: Blackwell, 2007.

Eagleton, Terry. *Literary Theory: An Introduction.* Oxford: Blackwell, 2008.

Faber, Ben. "Ethical Hermeneutics in the Theater: Shakespeare's *The Merchant of Venice.*" In *Hermeneutics at the Crossroads: Interpretation in Christian Perspective*, edited by Kevin Vanhoozer, James K.A. Smith, and Bruce Ellis Benson, 211-224. Bloomington, IL: Indiana University Press, 2006.

Felski, Rita. *The Limits of Critique.* Chicago, IL: University of Chicago Press, 2015.

Felski, Rita. *Uses of Literature. Oxford: Blackwell Publishing, 2008.*

Fiddes, Paul. *The Promised End: Eschatology in Theology and Literature.* Oxford: Blackwell, 2000.

Fish, Stanley. *Doing What Comes Naturally: Change, Rhetoric, and the Practice of Theory in Literary and Legal Studies.* Oxford: Oxford University Press, 1989.

Gadamer, Hans-Georg. *Truth and Method.* In *The Critical Tradition: Classic Texts and Contemporary Trends*, 3rd ed., edited by David H. Richter, 718-737. New York: Bedford/St. Martin's, 2007.

Gallagher, Susan V., and Roger Lundin. *Literature through the Eyes of Faith.* San Francisco: Harper Collins, 1989.

Graff, Gerald. *Professing Literature: An Institutional History.* Chicago, IL: University of Chicago Press, 1987.

Jacobs, Alan. *A Theology of Reading: The Hermeneutics of Love.* Boulder, CO: Westview Press, 2001.

Jeffrey, David Lyle. *Houses of the Interpreter: Reading Scripture, Reading Culture.* Waco, TX: Baylor University Press, 2003.

Jeffrey, David Lyle. *People of the Book: Christian Identity and Literary Culture.* Grand Rapids, MI: Eerdmans, 1996.

Keen, Suzanne. *Empathy and the Novel.* New York: Oxford University Press, 2007.

Kermode, Frank. *The Sense of an Ending: Studies in the Theory of Fiction: With a New Epilogue.* Oxford: Oxford University Press, 2000.

Lewis, C.S. *An Experiment in Criticism*. Cambridge: Cambridge University Press, 1961.

MacIntyre, Alasdair C. *After Virtue: A Study in Moral Theory*. Notre Dame, IN: University of Notre Dame Press, 1981.

McEntyre, Marilyn Chandler. *Caring for Words in a Culture of Lies*. Grand Rapids, MI: Eerdmans, 2009.

Michel, Johann, and Hans Joas. *Homo Interpretans: Towards a Transformation of Hermeneutics*. Translated by David Pellauer. London: Rowman & Littlefield International, 2019.

Moran, Joe. *First You Write a Sentence: The Elements of Reading, Writing... and Life*. London: Penguin, 2018.

Nussbaum, Martha C. *Love's Knowledge: Essays on Philosophy and Literature*. New York: Oxford University Press, 1992.

Pope, Alexander. *An Essay on Criticism* (1711). Representative Poetry Online, University of Toronto, https://rpo.library.utoronto.ca/content/essay-criticism-part-1.

Oxford English Dictionary, s.v. "post-structuralism, n." Accessed May 31, 2021. www.oed.com/view/Entry/240113

Richter, David H., ed. *The Critical Tradition: Classic Texts and Contemporary Trends*. 3rd ed. New York: Bedford / St. Martin's, 2007.

Seerveld, Calvin. *Rainbows for the Fallen World: Aesthetic Life and Artistic Task*. Toronto, ON: Tuppence Press, 2005.

Sharpe, Christina. *In the Wake: On Blackness and Being*. Durham, NC: Duke University Press, 2016.

Sidney, Philip. *An Apology for Poetry*. In *The Critical Tradition: Classic Texts and Contemporary Trends*, 3rd ed., edited by David H. Richter, 132-159. New York: Bedford/St. Martin's, 2007.

Smith, James K.A. *The Fall of Interpretation: Philosophical Foundations for a Creational Hermeneutic*. Downers Grove, IL: InterVarsity Press, 2000.

Smith, James K.A. *Who's Afraid of Relativism? Community, Contingency, and Creaturehood*. Grand Rapids, MI: Baker Academic, 2014.

Tolkien, J.R.R. "On Fairy-Stories" (1938). In *Essays Presented to Charles Williams*, edited by C.S. Lewis, 38-89. London: Oxford University Press, 1947.

Tomko, Michael. *Beyond the Willing Suspension of Disbelief: Poetic Faith from Coleridge to Tolkien*. London: Bloomsbury Academic, 2016.

Vanhoozer, Kevin. *Biblical Authority after Babel: Retrieving the Solas in the Spirit of Mere Protestant Christianity*. Grand Rapids, MI: Brazos Press, 2016.

Westminster Confession of Faith. The Committee on Christian Education of the Orthodox Presbyterian Church, 2005. https://www.opc.org/wcf.html.

White, Hayden. "The Historical Text as Literary Artifact." In *The Critical Tradition: Classic Texts and Contemporary Trends*, 3rd ed., edited by Daniel H. Richter, 1384-1397. New York: Bedford/St. Martin's, 2007, pp. 1384-1397.

White, Hayden. *Metahistory: The Historical Imagination in Nineteenth-Century Europe*. Johns Hopkins, 1973.

Wolf, Maryanne. *Reader, Come Home: The Reading Brain in a Digital World.* New York: HarperCollinsPublishers, 2018.

Wolters, Albert. *Creation Regained: Biblical Basics for a Reformational Worldview*. 2nd ed. Grand Rapids, MI: William B. Eerdmans, 2005.

Wolterstorff, Nicholas. *Justice: Rights and Wrongs*. Princeton: Princeton University Press, 2008.

Wolterstorff, Nicholas. *Reason within the Bounds of Religion*. 2nd ed. Grand Rapids, MI: William B. Eerdmans, 1984.

Wolterstorff, Nicholas. "Resurrecting the Author." *Midwest Studies in Philosophy* 27, no. 1 (2003): 4-24.

Music as a Science and an Art

Janet R. Danielson

Music as an Academic Subject

Oh, sing to the Lord a new song,
Sing to the Lord, all the earth!

—Psalm 96:1

I don't mean to complain, but serious musicians
seem to be getting more expendable by the hour.

—Richard Taruskin, 1989

Music presents unique challenges to academic study. Intangible, ephemeral, and multifarious, its mysteries defy our ontologies and epistemologies, resist our analyses, and sidestep our semantics. Yet amongst humankind, music-making is as widespread and ancient as language. From precisely tuned 9,000-year-old Jiahu bone flutes to present-day laptop orchestras, music's interplay of melody and rhythm has been a continual source of fascination and delight. And music seems to be in no danger of extinction: Longplayer, a British work for Tibetan bowls, is slated to ring on for another thousand years.

Ancient writings and archeological findings also show that, whether as a performing art or as the subject of cosmic speculation, music has displayed surprising consistency over time. For example, the scale was carved in bone in the later Jiahu flutes (ca. 6000 BC),[1] demonstrated in geometry in Mesopotamia (ca. 1500 BC),[2] cast in bronze in the bells of Marquis Yi (433 BC),[3] and calculated algebraically in the writings of Bharata Muni (ca. 200 BC).[4] Recent research confirms music's power to modulate emotion,

1. Juzhong Zhang et al., "The Early Development of Music. Analysis of the Jiahu Bone Flutes," *Antiquity* 78, no. 302 (December 2004): 769-778.

2. Leon Crickmore, "A Musical and Mathematical Context for CBS 1766," *Music Theory Spectrum* 30, no. 2 (2008): 333-4.

3. Robert Bagley, "The Prehistory of Chinese Music Theory," *Proceedings of the British Academy* 131, 58.

4. Wolfgang von Steinitz et al, Bharata Muni's Experimental Tuning Procedure with Two Identical Vinas; P. Sambamurthy, Experimental Vinas; Bharata-Muni, The

transcending culture and language. Neuroscientist Walter J. Freeman sees music as essential for the development of cooperative societies, a "human technology for crossing the solipsistic gulf."[5] For it is the music of human speech—its rhythm, tempo, pitch, and amplitude—that communicates intentions, enabling us to distinguish sarcasm from sincerity and desperation from delight.[6] Freeman argues that music thereby creates channels of trust that are essential for the transfer of meaningful information: musical communication, in his view, was a precondition for the earliest human inventions such as fire and tools.[7] There have been contesting views on whether music is a "universal language," or a cultural convention. But music's significance over broad spans of human geography and history, together with its key role in human social behaviour, suggest that it is indeed integral to human life. As a non-verbal, non-visual, quintessentially human communicative activity, music presents a unique challenge to the higher educational system of the European tradition, whose disciplines favor empirical research, analysis, and documentation.

The Conundrum of Music in the European Academy

Music was one of the earliest subjects of academic study, yet its place in the Western academy has been curiously inconsistent. Originally a quantitative science along with arithmetic, geometry, and astronomy in the medieval Quadrivium, music hovered around the humanities in the Renaissance, migrated into the fine and performing arts in the eighteenth century, returned to academe in the nineteenth century restyled as musicology, and more recently has been problematized by critical theory as a means either of constituting identity or reinforcing cultural hegemony. It is tempting to wonder whether music, given such a checkered history, is less an academic discipline than an academic vagrant, finding accommodation where it can but never earning its keep, scrounging bits of regalia from the castoffs of more respectable disciplines. Music's academic unsettledness is due at least in part to the philosophical frameworks within which mu-

---

Natyasastra: A Treatise on Hindu Dramaturgy and Histrionics, Vol. II: 5-8, translated by Manomohan Ghosh (Calcutta: The Asiatic Society, 1961. https://www.plainsound.org/pdfs/bharata.pdf. See also Figure 1 in this chapter.

5. Walter J. Freeman, Societies of Brains: A Study in the Neuroscience of Love and Hate (Hillsdale, NJ: L. Erlbaum, 1995), 131.

6. B. Dichter, J. Breshears, M. Leonard, and E. Chang, "The Control of Pitch in the Human Laryngeal Motor Cortex," *Cell* 174: 1 (June 2018). https://doi.org/10.1016/j.cell.2018.05.016

7. Walter J. Freeman, "A Neurobiological Role of Music in Social Bonding," in *The Origins of Music,* ed. Nils. L. Wallin, Björn Merker, and Steven Brown (Cambridge, MA: MIT Press, 2000), 419.

sic-making occurs. Can a Christian worldview enhance music scholarship?

Recent Trends in the Academic Study of Music

A 2016 report on college undergraduate music curricula for the College Music Society calls for a shift away from what its authors describe as a "creativity-deficient, hegemonic, and ethnocentric college curriculum" towards greater diversity, creativity, and integration. The goal of this shift would be to harness the "transformative power of the musical river that connects all the world's cultures"[8] by training music majors to become composer-performer-improvisers fluent in a rich array of jazz, global, popular, and European classical practices. Implicit in this report is a construct of culture as a humanly-generated and humanly-transmitted totality of knowledge, behaviours, ideas and artifacts of a particular human group. This modernist construct has profoundly shaped the academic study of music, trickling down to undergraduates through texts such as Bonnie Wade's *Thinking Musically: Experiencing Music, Expressing Culture.*[9] Yet it presents significant challenges: composer-performer-improvisers-in-training find themselves between the Charybdis of engaging in cultural appropriation of other cultures, and the Scylla of advancing the cause of cultural hegemony should they draw on the lexicon of musical conventions that they and their audiences hold in common. And beyond Scylla and Charybidis, Mammon awaits. While the College Music Society Report assures students that "few, if any, cultures are not enriched by the creative syncretism that increasingly defines the planetary musical landscape,"[10] students find themselves confronting a US$30 billion-dollar music industry[11] which underwrites the proliferation of popular "genres" by minimalizing stylistic diversity in order to maximize airplay. A startling 2012 study of a million-song dataset of popular music from 1955 onwards found not the hoped-for greater diversity and creativity, but rather growing conventionalism:

8. Patricia Shehan Campbell, David E. Myers, Juan Chattah, Victoria Lindsay Levine, David Rudge, Ed Sarath, Lee Higgins, and Timothy Rice, *Transforming Music Study from its Foundations: A Manifesto for Progressive Change in the Undergraduate Preparation of Music Majors* (Task Force on the Undergraduate Music Major, 2016). https://www.music.org/pdf/pubs/tfumm/TFUMM.pdf, 21.

9. Bonnie Wade, *Thinking Musically: Experiencing Music, Expressing Culture,* 2nd ed. (New York: Oxford University Press, 2009).

10. Campbell et al., *Transforming Music Study* (2016), 7.

11. IFPI Global Music Report 2025." https://ifpi-website-cms.s3.eu-west-2.amazonaws.com/GMR_2025_State_of_the_Industry_Final_83665b84be.pdf

> We find three important trends in the evolution of musical discourse: the restriction of pitch sequences (with metrics showing less variety in pitch progressions), the homogenization of the timbral palette (with frequent timbres becoming more frequent) and growing average loudness levels (threatening a dynamic richness that has been conserved until today).[12]

The music industry has pushed traditional virtuosic practices around the globe to the margins, reducing them to artifacts, though some virtuosic streams such as free jazz at the fringes and metal at the edges maintain a stance of creative resistance. Commercials use music powerfully to influence social identity and cultural expression. College music programmes face the challenge of equipping students to stem this tide of homogenizing commodification, yet confining music within the compass of cultural expression may vitiate rather than promote musical creativity. Artists in "diverse cultures" may have quite different views of music, and be offended when their music is torn from its ritual or devotional context. Students trying to make their way in a culture shaped by their wearisome elders may prefer to reject or transcend, rather than to express culture: they refer to their own experience of music, music that engages them and moves them deeply, even to awe. There is therefore an urgent need for a fuller and more coherent understanding of music, one that takes into account the intense, even sublime experiences music affords.

Music and Ground-Motives

Reformational philosophy has proven remarkably effective in detecting distortions of otherwise compelling systems of thought and in opening fruitful ways of understanding the reality we have been given. Reformational philosopher Herman Dooyeweerd developed the concept of *ground-motive* to capture the sense of a pervasive theme that is both foundational and driving.[13] Ground-motives are spiritually formative in that they pertain to ultimate issues such as good and evil, life and death; they help establish what is really meaningful, and show how things connect in a totality of meaning. The driving power of ground-motives is ev-

---

12. See Joan Serrà, Álvero Corral, Marián Boguña, Martin Haro, and Josep Ll. Arcos, "Measuring the Evolution of Contemporary Western Popular Music," in *Nature.com Scientific Reports 2,* Article 521, (July 2012). http://www.nature.com/srep/2012/120726/srep00521/full/srep00521.html.

13. Compare Max Weber: "Magical and religious forces, and the ethical ideas of duty based upon them, have in the past always been among the most important formative influences on conduct." *The Protestant Ethic and the Spirit of Capitalism,* trans. Talcott Parsons, introduction Anthony Giddens (London and New York: Routledge, 1992), *xxxix.*

ident in the history of music; we will look at three dualistic or polarizing ground-motives, *form-matter, nature-grace*, and *nature-freedom.*

In the *form-matter* motive elaborated in the Platonic tradition, reality is bifurcated into flawless and eternal forms which impose order upon the ceaseless flux of base matter. The perishable human body becomes inferior to the eternal human soul, and action inferior to contemplation. Thus music, being immaterial, is particularly well regarded. But fear of anarchic formlessness, as we shall see, privileged a tuning system that was not conducive to harmony.

When Charlemagne established academies at the end of the eighth century, the authoritative music text was *De Institutione Musica* by Boethius (d. 524 AD),[14] which summarized the Pythagorean/Platonic tradition. For Boethius, music encompassed a vast array of topics, ordered hierarchically from the silent circuits of the stars and the march of the seasons *(musica mundana)*; to harmonious human relationships and the attunement of soul and body *(musica humana)*; and finally, at the lowest level, to the audible music we experience as performers and listeners (*musica instrumentalis). Musica instrumentalis* makes the inaudible music of cosmic and human relationships accessible to the senses and thus potentiates in its hearers the order and virtue of the higher levels of harmony. The word *instrumentalis* denotes music's role as agent, leading the capricious senses to certain knowledge.[15]

Boethius and his contemporaries enriched and transformed the Platonic model of a cosmos ordered by concord. The redemptive work of Christ revealed concord not as an impersonal ideal, but rather as a symbol of the divine covenant, of God's loving intention to sustain and order a cosmos charged with yearning. Boethius wrote:

> The world, always changing, persists in harmony;
> A covenant secure unites the warring atoms
> [...]
> The universe itself is ruled by Love.[16]

14. Boethius, *Five Books on Music,* trans. J. Garceau, K. Long, S. Burnham, M. Waldstein, T. McGovern. Privately published, 1985. http://static1.squarespace.com/static/5a6b9486e9bfdfc602d49f99/5a6bb5a2edce67763886f611d/5a6bb5b9edce67763886f7691/1517008313635/Five-Books-of-Music-1.pdf?format=original Accessed July 2019.

15. David S. Chamberlain, "Philosophy of Music in the *Consolatio* of Boethius," *Speculum* 45, no.1 (Jan. 1970): 81, footnote 7.

16. Dennis Danielson, "Their Peculiar Behavior Confounds Mortals' Minds: Boethius and Martianus Capella," in *The Book of the Cosmos: Imagining the Universe from Heraclitus to Hawking,* ed. Dennis Danielson (Cambridge, MA: Perseus Publishing 2000), 81.

Boethius's contemporary Dionysius portrayed God's sustaining, gracious provision for the entire universe in terms that set the tone for a truly Christian philosophy:

> The gifts of the unfailing Power pass on, both to men and living creatures, and plants, and the entire nature of the universe; and It empowers things united for their mutual friendship and communion, and things divided for their being each within their own sphere and limit, without confusion, and without mingling; and preserves the order and good relations of the whole, for their own proper good.[17]

The Platonic cosmos, in which eternal perfect forms impose order on a chaotic, evil material world, was thus replaced by a transcendent and compelling dynamic of reconciliation. Once the works of Boethius and Dionysius became available to scholars in the mid-800s, a new practice of music composition arose, a brilliant sonic interpretation of the Dionysian vision. It featured simultaneous yet independent melodies, "each within their own sphere and limit," sung simultaneously yet "without confusion" as the onward drive of dissonance was resolved and stabilized by recurring harmonies. This early *counterpoint* reflected the yearning cosmos Dionysius had described, and in so doing, it changed the course of Western music. As medieval scholar Nancy van Deusen notes:

> Music uniquely exemplified an absolutely pivotal concept. [...] Motions—of discourse, of physical bodies, of thoughts, and, especially, of musical melodic lines—which appeared to oppose one another by their contrary impulses, their sources of directions, their movements toward goals—could be made to be reconciled with one another. No other concept in the history of Western music has had such power.[18]

Counterpoint dynamically reconciled the form-matter opposition.

Nature-grace, a second ground-motive identified by Dooyeweerd, stemmed from Scholasticism, a profound interaction between Aristotelian and Christian thought in the thirteenth century. For Aristotle, divine activity did not penetrate the material (sublunary) sphere, yet material things tended towards their own perfect or complete form. In the heavenly realm, perfection was exemplified by the perfect cyclic motion of heavenly bodies. Aristotle's categories re-shaped Christian concepts: grace was immaterial, eternal, and perfect, while nature, being material, was corrupt and subject to mortality. Boethius's hierarchical vision of

---

17. See Dionysius the Areopagite, "Divine Names," in *The Works of Dionysius the Areopagite*, trans. Rev. John Parker (London: James Parker and Co., 1897): 8.5, https://ccel.org/ccel/dionysius/works/works.i.ii.viii.html, accessed June 24, 2019.

18. Nancy van Deusen, *Theology and Music at the Early Universities: The Case of Robert Grosseteste and Anonymous IV* (Leiden, New York: Brill, 1995), 18.

cosmic, human/moral, and instrumental music—all integrated by harmony—was replaced by a dualistic division between *musica speculativa* (harmonics and theory) and *musica practica* (performance). The Greek doctrine of opposites—perfection vs imperfection, eternal vs perishable—replaced the earlier chain-of-being model in which the microcosm participated and reflected the macrocosm.

Traces of scholastic dualism persist to this day in music notation. *Tempus perfectum* (triple metre, now ¾ time), was originally indicated by a perfect circle. Though numbers are now used to indicate metre in music notation, we have retained the broken circle for *tempus imperfectum* (duple or quadruple metre). We still use *perfect* and *imperfect* cadences, to refer to the chords marking phrase boundaries. The *perfect* cadence returns to the harmony established at the beginning of a composition, completing a harmonic circle. Likewise, the pairs of tones that blend most smoothly—the octave, fifth, and fourth—are designated *perfect* consonances.

Three Scholastic concepts were particularly important for music: first, a natural goal-orientation—i.e., the tendency for everything to seek its perfection; second, the idea of the composite; and third, the durability of individual identity. Zarlino's influential *Le Istitutione Harmoniche* (1558) acknowledged perfection as the ultimate goal of a nature characterized by variety and change:

> Thus [the ancients] held that when a perfect consonance was reached, it was an end, a perfection toward which music strives. They did not want to repeat perfection many times so as not to satiate the ear. Their fine and useful observation confirms how true and good are the workings of wondrous nature, which does not produce identical individuals in a species [...]. Every composer ought to follow the beautiful order of nature [...] we should seek to vary constantly the sounds, consonances, movements, and intervals; and thus through diversity we will attain a good and perfect harmony.[19]

While Reformational philosophers have cautioned against synthesis with "Greek thought," the magnificence of Renaissance contrapuntal music shows that careful engagement can be fruitful, too.

A more recent ground-motive, *nature-freedom*, holds that for humanity to reach its true potential, the forces of nature, including disease and possibly death itself, must be brought into subjugation through the exercise of human reason. The effect of this ground-motive on music has been far-reaching—extensive enough to justify the following lengthy and fairly technical account.

---

19. Gioseffo Zarlino, *The Art of Counterpoint*: Part Three of *Le Istitutioni harmoniche* (1558), trans. Guy A. Marco and Claude V. Palisca (New York: Norton, 1976), 60-61.

In 1585 Simon Stevin, a Dutch engineer, published *The Art of Tens,* a brief paper demonstrating the usefulness of decimals. Stevin believed that decimals would replace cumbersome fractions, eliminating the ancient Greek distinctions between numbers (discrete integers) and magnitudes (continuous quantities), and between rational and irrational numbers. Decimals had obvious implications for musical tuning systems previously based on simple rational proportions.

On the authority of Boethius, Pythagorean tuning was retained in early counterpoint. As mentioned earlier, Pythagoreans feared irrationality. Believing that everything was generated from the *tetractys,* [20] that is, the numbers 1, 2, 3, and 4, they constructed their 7-note scale using only multiples of 2:3. In order to make the major third (e.g. *do-mi*) conform to the *tetractys*, they rejected the smooth 4:5 ratio in favor of the harsh-sounding 64:81. So in early counterpoint, sustained thirds were avoided, and when they did occur, performers could spontaneously adjust their tuning to sweeten the harmony. But the rise of fixed-tuning keyboard instruments, especially the organ, drove the search for a more satisfactory tuning system. There were no obvious solutions: the scale with the simplest ratios, *just intonation* shown below, produces a twangy 27:40 between *re* and *la*.

The Diatonic Scale in Geometric Form

Dimensions represent vibrating bodies of equal mass per unit length under equal tension. Solfège syllables indicate the tones produced by the vibrations of each line.

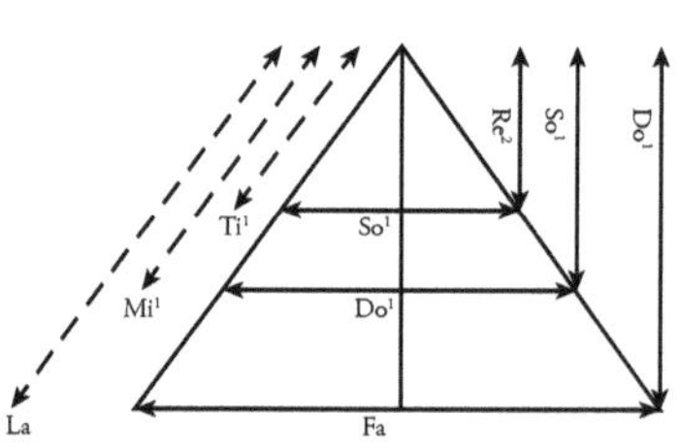

5-limit just intonation as an archetype:

- Bharata Muni (India, ca. 2nd century BC)
- Ptolemy (Greece, 1st century AD)

Tone	Frequency	Length
Do	1	1
Re	1.125	.88
Mi	1.25	.8
Fa	1.333	.75
So	1.5	.667
La	1.667	.6
Ti	1.875	.533
Do¹	2	.5
Re¹	2.25	.44
Mi¹	2.5	.4
Fa¹	2.667	.35
So¹	3	.333
La¹	3.333	.3
Ti¹	3.75	.2666
Do²	4	.25
Re²	4.5	.22

Figure 1: The Diatonic Scale in Geometric Form © 2021 Janet R. Danielson, all rights reserved.

20. Greek music theorists used an instrument called a *helikon* with a diagonally-swinging bridge dividing the 1:2 ratio into its harmonic and arithmetic mean: low *do* - *fa, so* - high *do*. The step between *fa* and *so* is the ratio 8:9. The helikon provides a geometrical justification for the bass line of twelve-bar blues.

In just intonation, all tones are derived from a single keynote. If, for example, an organ is justly tuned relative to C, the scale of Ab will not be in tune. The price of purity, then, is a restricted palette of key changes.

Tuning exemplifies the problems inherent in the nature-freedom ground-motive. Stevin's sixteenth-century "equal temperament"[21] made all tonal relations except octaves irrational, dividing the octave by factors of twelfth root of two into twelve equal half-steps. To the incredulity of his musical contemporaries, Stevin asserted the "articulateness, rationality, appropriateness, and natural, wonderful perfection of these [irrational] numbers."[22] In other words, in the whole infinite array of numbers, none was more rational, pure, perfect, originary, primary, or unitary than any other. The proportions of the tones—1:2, 2:3 and so on—were irrelevant. Even the famously skeptical Descartes was appalled: in a 1634 letter to his friend Marin Mersenne, he wrote, "As for the reasons given by your musicians who deny the proportions of the concords, I find them so absurd that I hardly know any more how to reply."[23]

Mersenne, a Minim priest and major figure in the development of modern science, feared that Stevin's proposed tuning corroborated philosophical skepticism's claim that "music is nothing but appearance, since that which I find pleasant someone else will find discordant according to his whimsy."[24] With no distinction between irrational and rational numbers, music would lose its basis in a shared experience of reality. Mersenne's own proposal was a keyboard in just intonation augmented by six extra black notes. His rationale had a decidedly Aristotelian flavour:

> Augmented keyboards should not be deemed extraordinary, for they do nothing other than that which voices do; they simply place harmony [in that state of] perfection which the mind and the ear desire.[25]

It was not until the late nineteenth century that Stevin's system, so abhorrent to the musicians of his time, finally took hold. Like the slogan of the French Revolution, it promised *liberty* to modulate into any key

21. "Temperament" means a fine adjustment of a purely tuned interval. Composer Lou Harrison calls it "tampering."

22. Mark Lindley, "Mersenne on Keyboard Tuning," *Journal of Music Theory*, 24.2 (Autumn 1980): 173.

23. "Pour les raisons que disent vos musiciens, qui nient les proportions des consonances, je les trouve si absurdes que je ne saurais quasi plus y répondre." http://ckcc.huygens.knaw.nl/epistolarium/letter.html?id=desc004/1062

24. Marin Mersenne, *La Verite dessciences contre les Sceptiques ou Pyrrhoniens* (Paris: Toussainct du Bray, 1625; facs. edition, Stuttgart-Bad Cannstatt: Friedrich Frommann / Gunther Holzboog, 1969), 32.

25. Lindley, "Mersenne on Keyboard Tuning," 173.

without increasing the number of out-of-tune intervals; *equality*, in that all major scales had the same proportions due to the division of the octave into 12 equal half-steps; and *fraternity*, in that scales were related by the cycle of fifths. But purity of tuning was thoroughly compromised, and the expressive potential of a distinct tuning for each key centre was entirely lost.

By the nineteenth century, the concordant cosmos of *musica speculativa* had been eclipsed by the mechanomorphic cosmology embraced by modern science. However, *musica practica* came back into academic purview on the coattails of culture. "Culture," in the sense of an overarching and determining force subsuming everything except nature, was actually a new coinage, contrived by Jacob Burckhardt in the 1860s and then promulgated by his protegé Friedrich Nietzsche.[26] The definition of "culture" was crystallized by Edward Burnett Tylor in his 1871 work *Primitive Culture: Researches into the Development of Mythology, Philosophy, Religion, Art and Custom.* His first chapter, "The Science of Culture," opened with the following magisterial pronouncement:

> Culture or civilization, taken in its wide ethnographic sense, is that complex whole which includes knowledge, belief, art, morals, law, custom, and any other capabilities and habits acquired by man as a member of society.[27]

Cultural progress is advanced by artists, scientists, and composers, the best of whom—such as Beethoven—were deemed to possess the superhuman power of genius:

> After [Beethoven's] death, of course, his music entered into the lives not of thousands but millions, and with the passing of generations his name stood not only for music in its sublimest form, but for a Being, strange, passionate, and unapproachable, more God than man.[28]

Wrested from alleged servitude to court and church, and pressed into the forward march of culture, music was once again a legitimate academic discipline.

Music's re-entry into the academy was catalyzed by Guido Adler's seminal publication *The Scope, Method and Aim of Musicology* (1885). He modelled musicology on the science of paleontology, which had captured public imagination after the 1859 publication of Darwin's *Origin of the*

---

26. See Nicholas Boyle, "Redeeming Culture" in, *Sacred Imagination,* Garaventa Center for Catholic Intellectual Life and American Culture, ed. Charles B. Gordon, and Margaret Monahan Hogan (Portland: University of Portland, 2009), 123.
27. Edward Burnett Tylor, Primitive Culture: Researches into the Development of Mythology, Philosophy, Religion, Art and Custom, (London: John Murray, 1871), 1.
28. Alexander Brent-Smith, "Ludwig Van Beethoven" in *Proceedings of the Musical Association* 53 (1926): 86. http://www.jstor.org.proxy.lib.sfu.ca/stable/765532.

Species. Adler's method was to identify the *species* of a musical score in order to classify it historically. "Just as the earth's crust was fashioned out of formations belonging to different epochs, so also the total picture of an age reveals a distinctive artistic character."[29] This historical character could be determined from analysis of the musical laws of masterworks in notated score format. As Bruno Latour has argued, inscripted objects such as scores transform ephemeral, non-replicable, local practices into immutable, easily reproducible, portable objects, [30] abstracted from real time and accessible to visual examination. Notated scores are essential for coordinating the large orchestras, choirs, and bands that made Western music such an impressive adjunct to the imposition of colonial power. However, they are unique to the West and cannot adequately capture the nuances of their own, let alone other musical traditions. Though musicology as a science promised to chart the musico-cultural progress of humankind in general, by limiting the scope of his new science to notated music, Adler covertly promulgated a Eurocentric worldview.

The sudden attribution of sweeping powers to Culture transformed the academic treatment of music. A Culture to which belief, art, morals, law, and customs were all relativized was harnessed to a History of inexorable human development from a primitive childlike state to the "full manhood" of European genius. Historicist explanations of the practice of singing Gregorian chant in unison, for example, might cite a primitive inability to sing parts or clerical oppression or both, overlooking the church's scrupulous adherence to the injunction to glorify God with one voice.[31] Similarly, the development of counterpoint was explained—despite evidence to the contrary—as an evolutionary progression from unison to harmony to dissonance, with allegations of the church permitting some intervals and prohibiting others, thus impeding musical "development."[32]

29. Erica Mugglestone, "Guido Adler's The Scope, Method, and Aim of Musicology (1885): An English Translation with an Historico-Analytical Commentary," *Yearbook for Traditional Music*, 13 (1981): 5-6.

30. See Bruno Latour, "Visualization and Cognition: Drawing Things Together," in *Knowledge and Society Studies in the Sociology of Culture Past and Present* 6, no. 1 (1986): 1-40. Latour argues that the role of inscription in European expansion has not been fully appreciated; it was not so much superior munitions that secured new territories for Europe, but the cheap and accurate reproduction of Mercator projection maps and treaties that defined and established boundaries.

31. Rom. 15:6; see also Bennett Zon, "Science, Theology, and the Simplicity of Chant: Victorian Musicology at War," *Journal of the History of Ideas* 75, no. 3 (2014): 453.

32. See H. C. Colles, *The Growth of Music: A Study in Musical History*, 3rd ed., ed. Eric Blom, (London: Oxford University Press, 1956) 6-7; and Donald Jay Grout, *A History of Western Music* (New York: W. W. Norton, 1960), 31. Groen van Prinsterer and Abraham Kuyper countered the absolutist claims of cultural historicism with the concept of "sphere sovereignty": "But behold now the glorious Freedom

The horrors of World War I and genocides of World War II unmasked the dark side of historicism and shook confidence in the agenda of musicology. The idea of culture, however, retained its power. Music was re-framed as an emblem of technological progress and human creative freedom, an emblem whose salient characteristic was not its display of genius, but its *style.* In his 1957 essay *The Place of Musicology in American Institutions of Higher Learning,* Manfred Bukofzer articulated the shift from the study of historical *musical laws* in the nineteenth century to cultural *style* in the twentieth. "Style criticism must be recognized as the core of modern musicology," he wrote. "Only the stylistic method will permit a correlation of music history with the history of ideas and the general cultural history of mankind."[33] Style classifies historical eras and cultures and thus assigns *meaning.* Music during an era of advanced technology, for example, would have an "advanced technology" style. Accordingly, post-World War II French composer Pierre Boulez organized his music using complex number series which eliminated harmony, coherence, and predictability, thus situating himself at the avant-garde's cutting edge. Composers in the Cold War era had total freedom of style as long as their music sounded as if it came from the cockpit of the Starship Enterprise. The cool hyper-rationalism of Mr. Spock became the ideal: "Debussy said: penetrate to the naked flesh of emotion; I say: penetrate to the naked flesh of evidence."[34] But even Boulez the arch-iconoclast deferred to culture: "I may be wrong, but I equate music with culture. I don't think music is an entertainment product. It's a product of culture—not for marketing, but to enrich lives. All these years, I've been trying to convince people that music is not there to please them; it's there to disturb them."[35] As Mersenne feared, the "emancipation of the dissonance,"[36] the logical conclusion of Stevin's irrational tuning, was

idea! That perfect and absolute Sovereignty of the sinless Messiah at the same time contains the direct denial and challenge of all absolute Sovereignty on earth in sinful man because of the division of life into spheres, each with its own Sovereignty." Abraham Kuyper, *Sphere Sovereignty: A Public Address Delivered at the Inauguration of the Free University,* Oct. 20, 1880, trans. George Kamps. www.reformational-publishingproject.com.

33. Manfred Bukofzer, *The Place of Musicology in Institutions of Higher Learning* (New York: The Liberal Arts Press, 1957), 16, 30-31.

34. Pierre Boulez, *Boulez on Music Today,* trans. Susan Bradshaw and Richard Rodney Bennett (Cambridge MA: Harvard University Press, 1972), 34.

35. Philip Clark, "Face to Face with Pierre Boulez", *Gramophone* (March 20, 2015). https://www.gramophone.co.uk/feature/face-to-face-with-pierre-boulez-'acquire-and-destroy-acquire-and-destroy-then-go-further'. Visited July 12, 2019.

36. See Arnold Schoenberg's essay "Opinion or Insight?" in *Style and Idea: Selected Writings of Arnold Schoenberg, ed. Leonard Stein* (New York: St. Martin's Press; London: Faber & Faber, 1975), 258-64.

pronounced by Schoenberg and broadened by John Cage to encompass all sounds. But it was a pyrrhic victory: emancipated dissonances failed to captivate audiences.

Post-structuralism profoundly impacted academia from the 1980s onward. Denouncing the power dynamics behind traditional musicology's canon of masterworks, the new musicology proposed instead a multiplicity of "musics" so as to include previously marginalized practices. Ethnomusicology provided a badly needed corrective to the progressivist view that had ranked cultures from primitive to advanced, redefining music as "sound that is organized into socially accepted patterns" and asserting that "musical styles are based on what people have selected from nature as part of their cultural expression."[37] Historicism had undermined the spiritual, cosmological, and numeric meanings of music, assigning music's meaning as an emblem of progress. But the deconstruction of "progress" threatened to devolve music into a mere compilation of arbitrary conventions.

Post-structuralism also legitimized research into power structures outside the imperatives of history and culture: context, patronage, and the requirements of social groups shaped music, too. In her stunning study of arts patronage, *Who Paid the Piper: The CIA and the Cultural Cold War,* Frances Stonor Saunders documents how the meteoric rise of the artistic avant-garde in the USA and in Europe was covertly promoted and lavishly funded by the CIA and US Army using agencies such as the Ford Foundation as fronts. Works of art and music that had been trotted out as displays of genius, nurtured by American artistic freedom and undergirded by advanced technology, were unmasked as instruments of propaganda. Boulez's postwar music was "for marketing" after all.

Another contribution of post-structuralism was its linguistic turn. The idea that social groups construct reality through language led to research into musical semiotics and narrative structures. Semiotics was most applicable to Western music of the eighteenth and nineteenth centuries which had a notated literature; a narrative structure; the ability to convey suspense, climax, and resolution; and analytical accessibility. But the music of Southeast Asia, based on external narratives such as rituals or shadow plays, was not as amenable to semiotic analysis. Musical semiotics thus ran the danger of privileging Western music once again.[38]

The distorting, polarizing effects of dualistic ground-motives can be

37. John Blacking, *Music, Culture, and Experience: Selected Papers of John Blacking,* ed. Reginald Byron, foreword Bruno Nettl (Chicago: University of Chicago Press, 1995), 23.

38. See Ray Jackendoff, "Parallels and Nonparallels between Music and Language," in *Music Perception: An Interdisciplinary Journal* 26, no. 3 (February 2009): 195-204.

clearly seen through the lens of music studies. But the biblical ground-motive of *creation, fall, and redemption,* which extends beyond the realms of culture and even personal belief, offers an integrating framework for reality from which the value and meaning of everything, including music, is derived: a reality whose origin, existence, and ultimate destiny is in God.

Music in Reformational Philosophy

Reformational philosophy, with its emphasis on a spiritually-rooted diversity and its commitment to a biblical worldview, has much to contribute to our understanding of music. Calvin demonstrated a deep understanding of music, commissioning and overseeing the Geneva Psalter, one of the most influential and widely-disseminated musical projects of the early modern period. Calvin first introduced rhythmic phrasing to liturgical music and insisted that the Psalter tunes be simple enough to be sung well by untrained men and women together—a radical change from the gender-segregated skilled monastic choirs. Calvin's rigorous re-thinking of the Christian faith had major implications that reached beyond the ecclesiastical and theological to the political, moral, and artistic life of his time.

Calvin set the stage for a distinctively Reformational philosophy by emphasizing five Biblical teachings: first, that the sovereignty of God extends over all creation, including inanimate objects "into which God constantly infuses what energy he sees meet";[39] second, that true wisdom consists of knowledge of God and knowledge of ourselves; third, that humans have a proclivity to construct and worship false gods: "The human mind is, so to speak, a perpetual forge of idols";[40] fourth, that those redeemed in Christ—clergy and laity alike—make up a new royal priesthood extending the Levitical line;[41] and fifth, that the world is a theatre of divine glory. All creation, not only humanity, participates in the glory of God: "the faithful, to whom he has given eyes, see sparks of his glory, as it were, glittering in every created thing."[42] These five principles, which can be summarized as Sovereignty, Wisdom, Idol-

39. John Calvin, *Institutes of the Christian Religion*, translated by Henry Beveridge (Grand Rapids, MI: Eerdmans, 1989), vol 1, 1.14.2.

40. Calvin, *Institutes,* vol. 1 1.11.8.

41. Actually, the renewal of the priestly order of Melchizedek: see Calvin's *Commentaries on Hebrews.*

42. John Calvin, *Commentaries on the Epistle of Paul the Apostle to the Hebrews 11: 2-4,* trans. and ed. John Owen (Edinburgh: The Calvin Translation Society, 1853), 266. https://hdl.handle.net/2027/uva.x000427932. See also Calvin's *Catechism of the Church of Geneva, Being a Form of Instruction for Children.* https://reformed.org/documents/calvin/geneva_catachism/geneva_catachism.html, Questions 1-3.

averse, New priesthood, and Glory[43] was given vigorous re-articulation by Abraham Kuyper in the late nineteenth century. Kuyper saw in them an antidote to modernist constructivism, which "build[s] a world of its own from the data of the natural man, and construct[s] man himself from the data of nature."[44] Kuyper realized that Calvinism's dominating principle, "the sovereignty of the Triune God over the whole Cosmos, in all its spheres and kingdoms, visible and invisible,"[45] implied an expansion of the priestly calling into all kingdoms and spheres, including philosophy.

The biblical ground-motive of creation, fall, and redemption encapsulates the five principles mentioned above: God is sovereign over all; he established the world by wisdom; humankind yielded to the temptation to become as gods, and has since been prone to idolatry, which includes enslavement to some aspect of the temporal creation; yet through redemption and sanctification, humans can participate in Christ's priestly service of interceding for the world and glorifying God.[46]

God

Reformational philosophy assumes the sovereign presence of God in every area of life. God, who transcends space and time, is beyond human comprehension; but God's invisible attributes can be clearly perceived in the things that have been made.[47] Eighteenth-century American theologian Jonathan Edwards emphasizes the complete dependence of the cosmos on God, whose excellence and beauty are pre-eminent:

> God is not only infinitely greater and more excellent than all other Being; but he is the head of the universal system of existence; the foundation and fountain of all Being and all beauty; from whom all is perfectly derived, and on whom all is most absolutely and perfectly dependent; *of whom*, and *through whom*, and *to whom* is all being and all perfection; and whose Being and beauty is as it were the sum and comprehension of all existence and excellence: much more than the

43. *It don't mean a thing (if it ain't got that SWING)*, attributed to jazz trumpeter James "Bubber" Miley and immortalized by Duke Ellington's composition of the same name.

44. Abraham Kuyper, *Lectures on Calvinism* (Grand Rapids, MI: Eerdmans 1931), 11.

45. Kuyper, Lectures on Calvinism, 79.

46. Karl Barth's discussion of Calvin's *Geneva Catechism* is particularly instructive here: "The Doctrine of Creation," vol. 3 part 2 of Church Dogmatics (Edinburgh: T & T Clark, 1960), 183.

47. Rom. 1:20.

> sun is the fountain and summary comprehension of all the light and brightness of the day.[48]

The *Shema* (Deuteronomy 6:4-5) declares that God is one, or perhaps more accurately, unity; and that the proper response to God is love. On the basis of the *Shema* and Edwards' description, we can appreciate how God's power and divine nature are exemplified in harmony. First, harmony is the product of unity and power; second, harmony is both cosmic and local; third, harmony links beauty and goodness.

When any unity, such as a string fixed at both ends, or an enclosed column of air, is set into motion by a force, it vibrates not only over its entire length, sounding a *fundamental* tone, but also in halves, in thirds, in fourths and so on *ad infinitum*. What to the naked eye appears to be random jiggling when a string is plucked is actually an orderly, precise division into partials. The largest partials—the divisions into 2, 3, 4, and 5—have the greatest amplitude or loudness, and blend smoothly together into a harmonious chord. The sound of smaller partials played together—say, the divisions into 21, 22, 23, 24, and 25—produce interference, perceived as noise. Harmonious chords, then, are maximally clear when they consist of a fundamental tone and its first four divisions.

This harmonic pattern was evident in creation, when primordial formless white noise inflated from quantum to cosmic dimensions. This white noise formed sound waves with harmonics generated by gas bouncing in and out of valleys of dark matter, which then densified into stars. Mark Whittle describes the instant after inflation:

> Evidence supporting the theory of inflation has now been found in the detailed pattern of sound waves in the CMB [Cosmic Background Radiation]. Because inflation produced the density disturbances all at once in essentially the first moment of creation, the phases of all the sound waves were synchronized. The result was a sound spectrum with overtones much like a musical instrument's.[49]

Cosmic background radiation confirms that the ancient postulate of *musica humana* (cosmic harmony) was no mere fantasy. Harmony was foundational for the discoveries of both Kepler and Newton. Harmony is not only cosmic, but also local and embodied: with a little practice, most people can create harmonics in their own vocal tracts by shaping different vowels over a steady sung pitch.[50]

48. Jonathan Edwards, *An Essay on the Nature of True Virtue* (London: W. Oliver, 1778), 40-41.

49. Wayne Hu and Martin White, "The Cosmic Symphony, *Scientific American* 290 no. 2 (February 2004): 46. http://background.uchicago.edu/~whu/Papers/HuWhi04.pdf

50. For example, Tuvan Overtone Singing. Some singers are able to create polyphony

Finally, harmony is beautiful, and the fittingness of musical consonance maps onto goodness. Roger Bacon observed, "Whatever also is said concerning the commensurability of quantities can be fittingly applied to acts of love."[51] And Calvin said of music, "There is hardly anything in the world with more power to turn or bend, this way and that, the morals of men, as Plato has prudently considered. And in fact we find by experience that it has a secret and almost incredible power to move our hearts in one way and another."[52] Abraham Kuyper sees creation as an invitation to experience God's presence:

> God is invisible. He hides Himself behind the veil of nature. But the folds of that veil move themselves in undulations and vibrations whereby we perceive that God Himself behind that veil is close to us [. . .] [E]ven in nature everything is for the sake of religion, to reveal to you the glorious presence of God.[53]

Harmony is a vibrant witness to God's glory.

Creation

1. *Music and Creation in Ancient Cosmologies*

The idea that music is a manifestation of the order and beauty of a divinely-governed cosmos is ancient and widespread. Hsün Tzu, one of the founders of Confucian philosophy, wrote that "The purity of [the gentleman's] music is modeled after Heaven, its breadth is modeled after the earth, and its positions and turnings imitate the four seasons."[54] In India, Matanga Muni (6th-8th centuries) described sound, *nada*, as the form in which the highest deity, Brahma, exists; the entire world, then, is the embodiment of this causal sound, the source of all song and even the scale-degrees from which music is made.[55] In Navajo cosmology,

between their normal voice and the overtones. See Anna-Maria Hefele, "O Antiqui Sancti - Polyphonic Overtone Singing," YouTube video, 2:34, November, 2014, https://www.youtube.com/watch?v=letfkSJ92Js

51. Roger Bacon, *Opus Majus,* trans. Roger Belle Burke (Philadelphia: Pennsylvania Press; London: H. Milford, Oxford University Press, 1928), vol. 1, part 4: 238-40.

52. John Calvin, "Epistle to the Reader," *Geneva Psalter* (1542), in *Source Readings in Music History* edited by Oliver Strunk, revised and ed. Leo Treitler, (New York: Norton, 1998), 366.

53. Abraham Kuyper, *To Be Near unto God,* trans. John Hendrik de Vries (Vancouver: Regent College Publishing, 2005), 268-9.

54. Mo, Di, Xunzi, and Fei Han, *Basic Writings of Mo Tzu, Hsün Tzu, and Han Fei Tzu,* trans. Burton Watson, (New York: Columbia University, 1967), 116.

55. "Without *nāda,* song cannot exist; without *nāda,* the scale-degrees cannot exist; Without *nāda,* the dance cannot come into being; for this reason the entire world

sung rituals are vital for maintaining, restoring, and celebrating *Hózhó*, a term encompassing order, health, beauty, harmony, happiness, and moral good.[56]

Pythagoreans such as Theon of Smyrna (ca. 70 AD) also understood harmony as the principle of cosmic order.

> Since people also call some numbers 'concordant', and without the science of number the proper account of concordance could not be discovered, and since this concordance possesses the greatest power, in speech being truth, in life happiness, and in nature *harmonia,* one could also not discover what this *harmonia* was in the cosmos if one had not first discovered fully what it is in numbers.[57]

Nearly two hundred years later, Plotinus, whose re-interpretation of Platonism influenced Augustine, wrote that "The Ideal-Form [...] has grouped and coordinated what from a diversity of parts was to become a unity: it has rallied confusion into co-operation: it has made the sum one harmonious coherence."[58]

2. *Music and Creation in Ancient Israel and Early Christianity*

The Pentateuch establishes the proportions of harmony with precision and significance. The proportions for Noah's Ark[59] and the tabernacle[60]—centuries before Pythagoras—included not only the numbers 1, 2, 3, and 4, but significantly, the number 5. The 3:5 ratio is found both in Noah's ark and in the mercy seat within the Holy of Holies. The harmonic proportions of the Hebrew tabernacle and temple set them apart from the concentric circles or squares of the temples of India and Southeast Asia and the ziggurats of Mesopotamia and Central America. Recent biblical scholarship suggests that the temple was a re-creation of

---

becomes the embodiment of *nāda*. In the form of *nāda*, Brahma is said to exist." Quoted in Lewis Eugene Rowell, *Music and Musical Thought in Ancient India* (Chicago: University of Chicago, 1992), 43.

56. Gary Witherspoon, and Glen Peterson, *Dynamic Symmetry and Holistic Asymmetry in Navajo and Western Art and Cosmology* (New York: Peter Lang, 1995), 15.

57. Andrew Barker, "Minor Authors Quoted by Theon and Porphyry," in *Greek Musical Writings II: Harmonic and Acoustic Theory,* ed. Andrew Barker (Cambridge: Cambridge University Press, 1989), 211-212.

58. Plotinus, *The Six Enneads* I.6.2, trans.Stephen MacKenna and B. S. Page (South Bend, IN: Infomotions, Inc., 2000), 1.6.2. , https://ebookcentral-proquest-com.proxy.lib.sfu.ca/lib/sfu-ebooks/detail.action?docID=3314722, .

59. Gen. 6:15.

60. Exod. 25.

the garden of Eden,[61] and the books of Hebrews and Revelation affirm that the proportions of the eternal city of God are harmonic.[62]

In the Temple of ancient Israel, the reading of the Law was always chanted or sung, not spoken. The early church maintained the Temple practice of singing the Scriptures. Athanasius (AD 295-373) commended this practice, pointing out that singing requires unity of intent, strength, power, and integrity:

> For to sing the Psalms demands such concentration of a man's whole being on them that, in doing it, his usual disharmony of mind and corresponding bodily confusion is resolved, just as the notes of several flutes are brought by harmony to one effect; and he is thus no longer to be found thinking good and doing evil.[63]

Athanasius acknowledged harmony's agency in bringing several notes "to one effect," and John Scotus Eriugena (810-877 AD), scholar in the Carolingian Palatine Academy, saw harmonic agency as a direct manifestation of Divine agency:

> For [God] gathers and puts all these things together by a beautiful and ineffable harmony into a single concord; for those things which in the parts of the universe seem to be opposed and contrary to one another and to be discordant with one another are in accord and in tune [when] they are viewed in the most general harmony of the universe itself.[64]

"Beautiful and ineffable" are not just vague superlatives here; on the contrary, Eriugena defines harmony in precise quantitative integer ratios 1:2 and 2:3,[65] situating musical harmony within a God-gathered harmo-

---

61. See G. K. Beale, *The Temple and the Church's Mission: A Biblical Theology of the Dwelling Place of God* (Downers Grove, IL: Apollos/IVP, 2004).

62. Heb. 8:5: They [priests] serve a copy and shadow of the heavenly things. For when Moses was about to erect the tent, he was instructed by God, saying, "See that you make everything according to the pattern that was shown you on the mountain."

    Heb. 9:23: Thus it was necessary for the copies of the heavenly things to be purified with these rites, but the heavenly things themselves with better sacrifices than these. For Christ has entered, not into holy places made with hands, which are copies of the true things, but into heaven itself.

    Rev. 11:1 Then I was given a measuring rod like a staff, and I was told, "Rise and measure the temple of God and the altar and those who worship there."

63. Athanasius, *The Life of Antony and the Letter To Marcellinus*, trans. Robert C. Gregg (New York: Paulist Press, 1980), 127.

64. John Scotus Eriugena, *Periphyseon: de divisione naturae*, ed. I. P. Sheldon-Williams, with Ludwig Bieler (Dublin: Dublin Institute for Advanced Studies, 1968), 207.

65. "For opposites by relation are always so opposed to one another that they both begin to be at the same time and cease to be at the same time, whether they are of

ny of the universe in which apparent opposites are ultimately reconciled. Around 1200 years after Eriugena's time, Abraham Kuyper continued the theme:

> It may not be inferred that this broken life which has burst into all sorts of differences and contrasts is our real life. Life in holy harmony and unbroken unity stands infinitely higher and shall one day show itself to be our real, truly human existence, as it now is for God's angels.[66]

3. *Music and Creation: Reformational Philosophy*

Are we to conclude that music is numeric and not cultural or historic? Is it a physical or an aesthetic phenomenon? Reformational philosophy invites us to expect evidence of God's beneficent sovereignty and wisdom over the full range of aspects or modalities of creation. Dooyeweerd proposed fifteen modalities, of which historical/formative is only one. The first five—numerical, spatial, kinetic, physical, and biotic—pertain to the structure of creation. The next five modalities—the psychic (feeling), analytical, historical/formative, lingual, and social modalities—are concerned with sentient beings, particularly humans. The last five—economic, aesthetic, juridical, ethical, and faith—pertain to worth: what we have, what we value, and what we love. We can look at music from the modality of number, of kinetic motion, of the senses and psyche, of social groups, of history, and so on, taking care that none of these modes be arbiter over the others, and that each maintains an unbroken coherence of meaning while retaining its own central nucleus of meaning.

This comprehensive understanding reveals music's *structure*—i.e., how it functions in all the diverse modes of our experience—and its *direction*, its referring character. As Dooyeweerd asserted, "*Meaning* is the *being* of all that has been *created*."[67] In this pithy formulation Dooyeweerd set aside durable *substance*—which according to Aristotelians made things real—in favor of *meaning*, reflecting the contingent, temporal, and referential character of the created order. Thus music, reverberant

---

the same nature, like single to double [the octave] or 2:3 or 3:2 [the fifth], or of different natures, like light and darkness, or in respect of privation, like death and life, sound and silence [...] For those things which are in discord with one another cannot be eternal" (Eriugena, *Periphyseon*, 77).

66. Abraham Kuyper, *On Scholarship: Two Convocation Addresses on University Life*, ed. Harry van Dyke (Grand Rapids, MI: Christian's Library Press, 2014), 453; italics added.

67. Herman Dooyeweerd, *A New Critique of Theoretical Thought* vol. 1 (Philadelphia: Presbyterian and Reformed Press, 1969), 4.

both with the unbroken unity of the Godhead and with the harmonious diversity of the cosmos, becomes much more than an invention of human whimsy—the skeptic's "mere appearance" that Mersenne feared. Music refers us to that which is of ultimate importance, to the source and meaning of our existence.

In order to illustrate the explanatory power of the structure-direction approach, let us see how harmony, the nucleus of the aesthetic aspect, reveals music's *numerical* and *spatial* modalities. In music, tones and rhythms are organized through three simple number series, the arithmetic (1, 2, 3…), the geometric (1, 2, 4, 8…), and the harmonic. The arithmetic and geometric series are repetitive: the arithmetic series has equal differences between each value (imagine a series of steady beats, or a sustained tone); and the geometric simply doubles each value, producing octaves. But the harmonic series (1, ½, 2/3, 3/4 …) has a *different difference* between each value, which is why it is a beautiful symbol for the concord of diverse elements. Harmony functions as an ordering principle in music, science, and nature. Exploring music's numeric aspect reveals harmony as a key player in the development of science because harmonic proportions create linear perspective.

Linear perspective allows us to perceive three-dimensional objects on a two-dimensional surface. Samuel Y. Edgerton's book *The Heritage of Giotto's Geometry: Art and Science on the Eve of the Scientific Revolution* presents compelling evidence that linear perspective, discovered in 1420 by Brunelleschi,[68] was in effect the midwife of modern science. Artists such as Leonardo da Vinci[69] and Alberti[70] acknowledged that the proportions for *perspectiva* were borrowed from those of musical harmony.

Indeed, centuries before painters and architects discovered linear perspective, monastic and cathedral choirs had conclusively demonstrated the projective property of the harmonic mean, as they sought sonically

68. This discovery predated Desargue's formulation of projective geometry by more than 200 years.

69. "From these shapes is born the proportionality called harmony, which delights the sense of sight with sweet concord just as the proportions of diverse voices delight the sense of hearing." "The painter measures the distance of things as they recede from the eye by degrees just as the musician measures the intervals of the voices heard by the ear." Jean Paul Richter, *The Literary Works of Leonardo da Vinci.* 3rd ed. (New York: Phaidon Press, 1970), 1: 61, 77.

70. "We shall therefore borrow all our Rules for the Finishing our Proportions, from the Musicians, who are the greatest Masters of this Sort of Numbers, and from those Things wherein Nature shows herself most excellent and compleat." Leon Battista Alberti, *The architecture of Leon Battista Alberti. In ten books. Of painting. In three books. And of Statuary. In one book,* trans. James Leoni (London: Edward Owen, 1755), 9.5.[?]

to model the grace of Christ the mediator.[71]

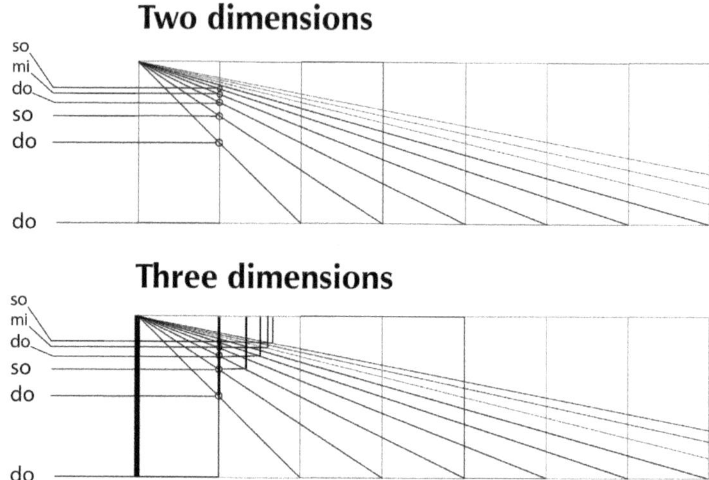

Figure 1: Perspective is Harmonic © 2021 Janet R. Danielson, all rights reserved.

Boethius discerned the breadth and power of harmony as a natural, human, and spiritual organizing principle. Its musical manifestation refers us to a glorious reality. Johann Walther, friend of J. S. Bach, made this inspiring observation: "Through music man rejoices not only because he sees his own image [...], but music also confronts God with His own Divine Wisdom."[72]

Music also functions *kinetically*: audible tones are produced by vibrations. Though sound is temporal rather than spatial, we experience music as virtual motion: melodies seem to move up or down, phrases move towards culmination, themes move from one key to another, "catchy" rhythms seem to invite us to move, and we ourselves may feel deeply moved by solemnly beautiful music. Within the *physical* modality, sound waves dissipate over distance according to the inverse square law, and at the right frequency and intensity, tones can shatter glass. The *biotic* modality invites us to observe the precise control of muscle and breath needed for virtuosic live music performance, as well as the unsurpassed

71. For example, *Anonymous IV*, trans., ed. Luther Dittmer in *Music Theorists in Translation*, vol. 1 (New York: Institute of Mediaeval Music 1939), 72. https://archive.org/stream/anonymousivconce00ditt/anonymousivconce00ditt_djvu.txt

72. Johann Walther, *Praecepta*, vol. I, pp. 5-6, quoted in Ruth Tatlow, "Theoretical Hope: A Vision for the Application of Historically Formed Theory," *Understanding Bach* 8 (2013): 56.

properties of biotic materials for the production of beautiful musical tones. As Kuyper wrote:

> A piece of brass, a tightly-stretched hide, [...] a horn from an animal's head, even down to a reed cut by the riverside, such are the seemingly futile, and yet, in their effect, the glorious means, which God himself has ordained for man as supports for the human voice, to unite human voices in grand chorus, and to bring the human heart into co-operation and into harmony with the world of sounds that surrounds it.[73]

The next group of modalities demonstrates how Reformational philosophy exposes reductionism and provides the basis for a richer understanding of all musical traditions. The *psychic* or sensitive aspect reveals the power of music to activate the brainstem and limbic system, evoking powerful emotions that trigger muscular and hormonal responses. Overturning the assumption of the primacy of human rationality over perception and emotion, Jaap Panksepp and Colwyn Trevarthen, pioneers of affective neuroscience, argue instead for the passionate nature of the mind, positing a quasi Dooyeweerdian "core SELF with central SEEKING urges transported through Intrinsic Motive Formations."[74] Panksepp and Trevarthen see musicality as the basis for both intersubjective and multisubjective communication because of music's unparalleled capacity to communicate and modulate emotions, warning that "without the intrinsic ancestral dynamics of emotional systems, learned musical facility remains affectively flat, its intricacies becoming only an intellectual exercise or a muscular tour de force."[75] Communicative musicality opens up exciting avenues of research that we can explore through the *analytic* modality.

Undergraduate courses in musical analysis include chord analysis, formal analysis, musical set theory, tone-row theory, and sometimes semiotics. But analysis is reductionist when in the grip of a single absolutized modality. Dualisms arise: *both-ands* such as nature/culture are often mistaken for *either-ors*. The late nineteenth-century commitment to the absoluteness of *historical* or *formative* modality is still in evidence in twenty-first century musical semiotics:

> For semioticians to model a phenomenon in "hard-science" is a kind of mystification, since we deal primarily with human, cultural, and

73. Kuyper, *To Be Near unto God*, 377-378.

74. Jaap Panksepp and Colwyn Trevarthen, "The Neuroscience of Emotion in Music" in *Communicative Musicality: Exploring the Basis of Human Companionship*, ed. Stephen Malloch and Colwyn Trevarthen (Oxford: Oxford University Press, 2009), 133.

75. Panksepp and Trevarthen, "The Neuroscience of Emotion in Music," 133.

> social behaviours—not physical laws. Music is not based on natural or physical law, although it has been argued many times (e.g. music as an elaboration of the overtone series). Rather, various *cultures choose*—from the continuum of tones, noises, and sounds *offered by nature*—those which they consider to be music.[76]

Where and when did nature "offer" the major chord, the diatonic scale, or common-time metre, let alone the complex interlocking rhythms of Ewe drumming or the intricate handling of srutis in the music of North India? Such *either/or* thinking appears in serious musical scholarship all too often, inhibiting the free exploration of musical meaning through the full range of modalities.

Discussion of the remaining aspects lies beyond the scope of this single chapter; but having glimpsed how richly music is embedded in the created order, let us consider how music is affected by the fall of humankind.

Fall

> [D]isproportioned sin
> Jarred against nature's chime, and with harsh din
> Broke the fair music that all creatures made
> To their great Lord.
> —John Milton, *At a Solemn Music*, 19

Music operates within a fallen world, a world that in 2019 had a 20 billion-dollar music industry that provided professional performing artists with a paltry annual income averaging $21,000.[77]

Economic injustice arouses our indignation, but Reformational philosophy takes a deeper view, showing how the fall into sin permeates all modalities of reality including the analytic mode of human reason. Dooyeweerd emphasizes that the absolutization of any modality is a form of idolatry which distorts and conceals the Divine order. "If there were no sin, the harmony among the law-spheres [modalities] would be fully realized, just as in a perfect work of art." But he adds, "If the Divine order in the temporal cosmos were not kept intact and elevated above any kind of human *hubris*, the manifestation of sin in time would not even be possible. For the whole of temporal reality would then burst like a

76. Eero Tarasti, *Signs of Music: A Guide to Musical Semiotics*," Approaches to Applied Semiotics, vol. 3 (Berlin: Mouton de Gruyter, 2002), 24; italics added.

77. Hogan, "The Record Industry Expects a Windfall," *Pitchfork* (May 30, 2019). https://pitchfork.com/features/article/the-record-industry-expects-a-windfall-where-will-the-money-go/

soap-bubble."[78] An escapist view of reality finds no justification in Reformational philosophy.

However, music can facilitate an escapist response to reality. Philosopher and musician Roger Scruton attributes such escapism to "fake emotion," something that distinguishes kitsch from authentic art:

> The kitsch work of art is not a response to the real world, but a fabrication designed to replace it. Yet both producer and consumer conspire to persuade each other that what they feel in and through the kitsch work of art is something deep, important and real [....] Fake emotion seeks to discard the cost of feeling while receiving the benefit.[79]

In other words, music can be fabricated for the purpose of manipulating the listener's mood rather than stimulating the kind of reflection that leads to personal integrity and ethical relationships. For Scruton, kitsch music is self-gratifying ear candy that fails to nourish.

Scruton is among many who affirm 'authentic' art music's ennobling effects. But Joseph J. Moreno's chapter "Orpheus in Hell"[80] documents the opposite: the use of classical music to soothe and inspire perpetrators of callous brutality in the death camps of the Holocaust. Even if extreme cases make bad law, and the Holocaust is an extreme case, the question remains how a culture claiming to be the centre of the classical music tradition could descend to mass cruelty. Researcher Helmut Loos has traced how the arts, especially music, became an ersatz religion in Leipzig during the rise of the Third Reich.[81] Musicology redefined its mandate to reflect Darwin's theory of natural selection and Herbert Spencer's social Darwinism: a 1902 treatise on Bach claims that "the music of a people is on a higher level than its language, and is thus a truer expression of its cultural ranking."[82] A lower "cultural ranking" implied an expendable life.

Neither Scruton's kitsch nor the highbrow music of Leipzig impli-

---

78. Dooyeweerd, *New Critique* 2: 335.

79. Roger Scruton, "The Great Swindle," *Aeon* (December 2012), https://aeon.co/essays/a-cult-of-fakery-has-taken-over-what-s-left-of-high-culture

80. Joseph J. Moreno, "Orpheus in Hell: Music in the Holocaust," in *Music and Manipulation: On the Social Uses and Social Control of Music*, ed. Steven Brown and Ulrik Volgsten (New York and Oxford: Berghahn Books, 2006), 264.

81. Helmut Loos, "Die Kunstreligiöse Botschaft der Leipziger Musikwissenschaft im späten 19. und frühen 20. Jahrhundert," in *Musicological Annual* 50, no. 2 (2014): 43-51.

82. Arthur Prüfer, *Sebastian Bach und die Tonkunst des neunzehnten Jahrhunderts* (Leipzig: Poeschel & Trepte 1902), 7-8; translation mine. http://hdl.handle.net/1802/14405

cates music itself; rather, they warn us that music, as a powerful modulator of human emotions and drives, has serious potential for abuse. Music can activate the same reward centres in the brain as hard drugs such as cocaine and heroin.[83] Loud, highly rhythmic music can bring on oceanic experiences of oneness or facilitate self-destructive behaviour. Music over 90 decibels stimulates the vestibular (balance) system with "pleasurable sensations of self-motion,"[84] but at a cost: exposure to music at 90 Db for two hours permanently damages hearing ,[85] and the time required for damage halves for each three-decibel increase over 90 Db. Music can be an emblem of allegiance for a certain group or way of life, and as such can be a means of social exclusion; it can incite mob behaviour; and it has been used in torture, notoriously in Guantanamo Bay.

Biblical Hebrew differentiates sin, iniquity, and transgression. Sin (*hatta'at*) is "missing the mark." and iniquity (*avon*), "distortion." Transgression (*pesha*) means "stepping across," with connotations of intentional rebellion and infringement. These words describe three types of motion with which we disconnect ourselves from God, the source of all life, goodness, and love. As Isaiah says:

> Behold, the Lord's hand is not shortened, that it cannot save, or his ear dull, that it cannot hear; but your iniquities have made a separation between you and your God, and your sins have hidden his face from you so that he does not hear.[86]

Reformed theology emphasizes that the fall corrupts every aspect of life. But in order to treat of this topic with comprehensive rigor, Reformed writers have been known to deploy highly abstract concepts and to favor analytical and juridical modes of thinking. By contrast, sonic analogies or models have an immediacy which enables us to apprehend the concrete reality implied by *hatta'at*, *avon*, and *pesha*. Sin or shortcoming finds its sonic analogy in being out of tune: if a singer fails to reach a high note, for example, audience and singer alike instinctively avert their gaze. Iniquity is analogous to musical dissonance or distortion; dissonant sustained tones literally interfere with each other, obscured by electrical

83. Ann J. Blood and Robert Zatorre, "Intensely Pleasurable Responses to Music Correlate with Activity in Brain regions Implicated in Reward and Emotion," *Proceedings of the National Academy of Sciences of the United States of America* 98, no. 20 (Sept. 25, 2001): 11818-11823.

84. Neil P. McAngus Todd and Frederick W. Cody, "Vestibular Responses to Loud Dance Music: A Physiological Basis of the 'Rock and Roll Threshold'?" *The Journal of the Acoustical Society of America* 107, no. 1 (2000): 496. doi: 10.1121/1.428317

85. Barry Blesser, "The Seductive (Yet Destructive) Appeal of Loud Music," http://www.blesser.net/downloads/eContact%20Loud%20Music.pdf

86. Isa. 59:1-2.

interference or static as they are carried by the auditory nerves into the brain. Iniquity scrambles the signals between God and humanity.

Transgression finds a sonic analogy in the interval of the tritone (three whole steps), the square root of two in sound. Dubbed *diabolus in musica* in the early eighteenth century[87] (*dia* means through and *bolus* means thrown), the square root of two irreconcilably divides the pure 1:2 octave ratio. An unresolved tritone maps fittingly onto the experiences of separation and alienation, for example in the opening notes of "Maria" in Leonard Bernstein's musical *West Side Story*; or in *YYZ* (referencing Toronto Airport) by the Canadian band Rush; or in the ancient Dhaivati mode of India, associated with disgust and terror.[88]

Futility, another effect of the fall, has its sonic counterpart in *Shepard tones,* tones sounding in all their audible octaves. Shepard tones create a perpetual ascent (or descent) that actually goes nowhere, the sonic equivalent of the Penrose staircases famously portrayed in the lithographs of M. C. Escher. When a culminating direction or dimension is removed, what remains is the sort of endless hellish tedium described in Ecclesiastes, or the subjugation to futility of Romans 8:20.

Music, then, can hide shame or justify idolatry; musical tones themselves can instantiate shortcoming, interference, alienation, and futility in a direct and emotionally salient way. But dissonance can be resolved: thus we turn to the third component of our Biblical ground-motive, redemption.

Redemption

> Men had been lost, and angels were not beyond the reach of danger. By gathering both into his own body, Christ hath united them to God the Father, and established actual harmony between heaven and earth.
> —John Calvin, *Commentary* on Ephesians 1:10

The Reformational tradition emphasizes the restoration and renewal of the whole of creation including care for the earth, relief for the destitute, social justice, and the transformation of culture. As Albert Wolters succinctly writes, "Redemption [...] is the recovery of creational goodness through the annulment of sin and the effort toward the progressive

87. Margo Schulter, "Tritones in Early Music: Were They Always Prohibited?" http://www.medieval.org/emfaq/harmony/tritone.html. Schulter provides evidence that in the medieval period, the tritone, far from being viewed as "diabolic," is treated as an interval which can be pleasing and even "consonant" in the right context. .

88 Nazir Ali Jairazbhoy, "What Happened to Indian Music Theory? Indo-Occidentalism?" *Ethnomusicology*, 52, no. 3 (Fall 2008): 358-359.

removal of its effects everywhere."[89]

Redeeming culture, a popular theme in recent Reformational philosophy, can be explored in light of the priestly calling of all believers and specifically, in the role of the high priest who enters the presence of God. Recent biblical scholarship suggests that we view Eden not primarily as a paradise for humans, but as a temple or dwelling-place for God, a place of beauty, abundance, and delight[90] that humans were invited to share. This view of Eden enriches our understanding of the cultural mandate, God's appointment of Adam to cultivate and keep the garden.[91] G. K. Beale points out that the words translated "cultivate" and "keep" are, in every other Old Testament instance, translated "serve" and "guard,"[92] which are also the two main priestly duties: service[93] to God, and protection of the Temple from defilement.

Whereas in Eden God walked openly, in the tabernacle and the temple a thick curtain representing the cosmos hid the Divine presence. Continual sung praise, blessings, sacrificial and feast cycles, incense, prayers, and rites of purification[94] all served to attract and maintain God's presence in the Holy of Holies.[95] As King David emphasized, the Temple was "not for man, but for the Lord God";[96] the vast scope of Temple operations indicates no less than the symbolic consecration of the whole cosmos to the service of God. Kuyper describes this as the "universal character of religion":

> If everything that is, exists for the sake of God, then it follows that the whole creation must give glory to God. [...] [T]he whole of Nature around us, but above all, man himself, who, priestlike, must consecrate to God the whole of creation, and all life thriving in it.[97]

89. Albert M. Wolters, *Creation Regained: Biblical Basics for a Reformational Worldview*, 2nd ed. (Grand Rapids, MI: Eerdmans, 2005), 83.

90. Isa. 51:3, Ezek. 28:13, Ps. 36:8.

91. Gen. 2:15.

92. Gregory K. Beale, "Eden, the Temple, and the Church's Mission in the New Creation," *Journal of the Evangelical Theology Society* 48, no. 1 (March 2005): 7-8.

93. Theophilus of Antioch writes that "And by the command, 'till it' no other kind of labour is implied than the observance of God's command." Theophilus, "Letters to Autolycus" 2.24, in *Fathers of the Second Century: Hermas, Tatian, Athenagoras, Theophilus, and Clement of Alexandria*, vol. 2 of *The Ante-Nicene Fathers*, ed. Alexander Roberts and James Donaldson (Buffalo: The Christian Literature Publishing Company, 1885) 104.

94. 1 Chron. 9:33.

95. Jonathan Klawans, *Purity, Sacrifice, and the Temple* (New York: Oxford, 2005), 71, 119.

96. 1 Chron. 29:1.

97. Kuyper, *Lectures on Calvinism*, https://archive.org/details/calvinismsixst00kuyp/

Priestly service involves presenting and representing the world to God, a service most perfectly fulfilled by Jesus Christ in his earthly life, death, resurrection, ascension, ongoing reign, and intercession. "You yourselves," wrote the apostle Peter to the churches in Greece, "like living stones are being built up as a spiritual house, to be a holy priesthood, to offer spiritual sacrifices acceptable to God through Jesus Christ."[98] Kuyper warns,

> Do not misunderstand me. I do not say: The Church consists of pious persons united in groups for religious purposes. [...] The real, heavenly, invisible Church must manifest itself in the earthly Church. If not, you will have a society, but no church.[99]

Echoes of the call to priestly service can be heard in the 2016 Report of the College Music Society:

> The proposed transformation of music study offers potential to shape a new generation of artists-visionaries who may then transmit their broad and transformative wisdom to society and positively impact many of the most pressing issues of our times: ecological crises, poverty, famine, disease, violence against women, child abuse, ideological and extremist tensions, the threat and manifestation of war and violence. The time has come for a world that is also brimming with beauty, ingenuity, connection, and peaceful interchanges through the transformative power of the musical river that connects all the world's cultures.[100]

But Gramsci-esque[101] overtones are also evident: the Report's authors "view the culturally narrow horizons of music study as nothing short of a social justice crisis."[102] They propose a shift away from pedagogy based on the "European classical tradition" which is now "out of step" (p. 7-8) with the "broader reality" (p. 16) of the twenty-first century. They specifically single out four-part harmony and counterpoint for

---

page/n107/mode/2up?view=theater 108. Many thanks to Hendrika who pointed out the mistranslation in the 1931 edition.

98. 1 Pet. 2:3.

99. Kuyper, *Lectures on Calvinism*, 108.

100. Campbell et al., *Transforming Music Study*, 21.

101. Antonio Gramsci was an Italian Marxist who defined hegemony as "the 'spontaneous' consent given by the great masses of the population to the general direction imposed on social life by the dominant fundamental group; this consent is 'historically' caused by the prestige (and consequent confidence) which the dominant group enjoys because of its position and function in the world of production." Antonio Gramsci, *Selections from the Prison Notebooks*, ed. and trans. Quentin Hoare and Geoffrey Nowell Smith (New York: International, 1971), 12.

102. Campbell et al., *Transforming Music Study*, 5.

"streamlining," acknowledging that the viability of large ensemble programmes that rely on sheet music—bands, choirs, and orchestras—may well be compromised under their new regime.

In their attempt to redress an ethnocentric past, the Report's authors swap Tylor's progressive/primitive polarity for a global/ethnocentric polarity. However, the absolutized cultural modality remains fully intact, inhibiting exploration of music's full diversity of modal meanings. Are diatonic and pentatonic scales sonic "geometry"; or does harmony enhancing music's emotional salience by expanding melody into three dimensions? Even Gramsci might have appreciated how counterpoint sonically models the coherent independent identity of an individual voice within an ever-changing environment of other voices, resolving conflict (dissonance), preventing trespass (voice crossing), repairing breaks (steps after leaps), resisting dominance by another voice (parallel fifths or octaves), and culminating in concord. Denying students adequate time to acquire fluency in such foundational skills on the grounds that harmony and counterpoint originated in Europe makes no more sense than "streamlining" geometry requirements for civil engineering students because Euclid was a member of the privileged Greek class in colonial Egypt. The Reformational understanding of modal diversity and coherence provides a robust alternative to academia's confusion between culturally specific surfaces and deep musical infrastructures proper to humanity as a whole. This fuller understanding would advance the Report's laudable goal of "an authentic transcultural understanding"[103] of music. A redemptive academic study of music would inspire students to seek out the glory of God in the *structure* of music as it functions in all modalities.

A redemptive study of music will also acknowledge music's *direction*, which might best be exemplified in musical virtuosity. Music in virtuosic performance allows us to experience the highest aspirations of a community because it is charismatic—compelling, inspiring, and magnificent. It draws audiences and challenges apprentices. Virtuosity is celebrated across cultures and genres, from the rap of Kendrick Lamar to the Jaipur style of North Indian *dhrupad*:

> The psychological impact of this kind of musical presentation [i.e., Jaipur] on the audience is such that the listener reacts to this music with awe. He feels that he is listening to something which is unfathomable and beyond reach [....] The structure emerging out of such a presentation has an undeniable quality of grandeur.[104]

---

103. Campbell et al., *Transforming Music Study*, 6.

104. Shrikrishna Haldankar, *Aesthetics of Agra and Jaipur Traditions* (Mumbai: Popular Prakashan, 2001), 23-24.

Virtuosity attests to the devotion of the performer who has acquired total command of his or her voice or instrument, resulting in an awe-inspiring freedom of performance; technical hurdles are overcome with ease, intricate forms with unerring memory, and vast ranges of expression with exquisite sensitivity. Charismatic virtuosity celebrates the promise of a culmination in which devotion and freedom are reconciled in glory.

Culmination

As royal priests with an eternal inheritance, Christians serve God in view of the culmination of time when the New Jerusalem in its indescribable splendour appears at the proclamation, "Behold, the dwelling place of God is with man. He will dwell with them, and they will be his people, and God himself will be with them as their God."[105] What the Revelation reveals is not mere restoration, but cosmic celebration. The new priesthood's exalted task is one of preparation and rehearsal for the wedding feast of the Lamb. Music features prominently in John's vision: the redeemed sing the praises of the slain Lamb,[106] and play "harps of God."[107] Biblically speaking, the direction of music—its ultimate reference-point—is the new song of the *eschaton*,[108] a song of glorification. Glory is so beautifully experienced through music that any discussion of music, particularly a truly biblical and philosophical discussion, must take glory into account.

There has been little philosophical or artistic attention to glory in the past century. Against the backdrop of such aesthetic concerns as irony, play, embodiment, and antinarrative, glory seems a fusty throwback indeed. However, Giorgio Agamben's *The Kingdom and the Glory* reopens the discussion of glory, situated within the context of political theology. Agamben traces conceptions of glory from Greek, biblical, and patristic sources through to the writings of twentieth-century theologians. Rejecting the idea that glory is merely aesthetic, Agamben argues that glory establishes, dignifies, and perpetuates power. Kingdoms—including secular contemporary regimes—are made effectual by glory just as a signature makes effectual a cheque, treaty, or decree. Similarly, public bodies, whether citizenry or *ecclesia*, are constituted and established by [their] common voice of acclamation and praise. The reciprocal function of glory uniting a populace as subjects of a sovereign, while in the same action establishing the sovereignty of the ruler, is found in the Hebrew word *kabod*, which means both glory and glorification. Glory is given its

105. Rev. 21:3.

106. Rev. 5:12-13.

107. Rev. 15:2-3.

108. Rev. 5:9.

fullest expression in the mysterious dynamic circularity of glorification of the Trinity. As Cyril of Jerusalem explains:

> When the Father is glorified, the Son also shares the glory with Him, because the glory of the Son flows from His Father's honour: and again, when the Son is glorified, the Father of so great a blessing is highly honoured.[109]

Having probed the crucial connection between glory and power in theology, Agamben proceeds to analyse our present situation. Our widespread uneasiness with the trappings of glory—best safely confined to museum-cases—masks a pervasive secularized dynamic of glorification in the form of media-manipulated public opinion: "The doxological function [i.e. public acclamation], freeing itself of liturgy and ceremonials, absolutizes itself to an unheard of extent and penetrates every area of social life."[110] This secularized glorification endlessly solicits acclamations in the form of "likes," ratings, stars, and feedback for virtually any object or service that can be bought and sold, yet leaves us more vulnerable and exposed than ever before. Our "likes" are turned into data to be mined and manipulated by unknown powerful interests, which in turn define our "needs." As Shepard tones remind us, acclamation becomes illusory and futile when diverted from its proper end.

Glory is not optional for Christians: consider its importance in Jesus' high priestly prayer. His first words, "Father, the hour has come; glorify your Son that the Son may glorify you,"[111] show the mysterious mutuality of glory, stranger still in light of Christ's impending humiliation, torture, and crucifixion. He continues, "The glory that you have given me I have given to them, that they may be one even as we are one."[112]

Calvin's *Geneva Catechism* brilliantly encapsulates the High Priestly prayer:

> Qu. 1. What is the chief end of human life?
> — To know God by whom men were created.
>
> Qu. 2. What reason have you for saying so?

109. Cyril of Jerusalem, "Catechetical Lecture 6: Concerning the Unity of God. On the Article, I Believe in One God. Also Concerning Heresies," in *Cyril of Jerusalem, Gregory Nazianzen,* Series 2, vol. 7 of Nicene and Post-Nicene Fathers, trans. Edwin Hamilton Gifford (Grand Rapids, MI: Eerdmans, 1893), http://www.ccel.org/ccel/schaff/npnf207.ii.x.html.

110. Giorgio Agamben, *The Kingdom and the Glory: for a Theological Genealogy of Economy and the Government,* trans. Lorenzo Chiesa (Stanford: Stanford University Press, 2011), 259.

111. John 17:1.

112. John 17:22.

—Because he created us and placed us in this world to be glorified in us. And it is indeed right that our life, of which himself is the beginning, should be devoted to his glory.

Qu. 3. What is the highest good of man?
—The *very same thing* (italics added).

Devotion to God's glory has inspired extraordinary musical achievements, even within the European classical tradition. J. S. Bach famously concluded his compositions with the ascription *Soli Deo Gloria* (to God alone be the glory). His brilliant canonic unfolding of brief themes in a unified but exuberant plenitude expressly represented God's activity in creating and sustaining the universe.[113] Bach's music is a consummate expression of faith, of art, and, in his own words, of science: "a small work of that science which I have achieved in music" was how he described his *Mass in B Minor.*[114]

Arvo Pärt is amongst the composers currently living whose music intentionally echoes God's glory. It took Pärt nearly a decade to develop what he calls his *tintinnabulation* technique, a highly rigorous and frugal interpenetration of octaves, pure triads, and stepwise segments of a single mode. Pärt saw the tintinnabulation of the simplest musical elements as a symbol for the relationships of body and spirit, of earth and heaven. *Fratres* and *Spiegel im Spiegel,* Pärt's early explorations of this new technique, were internationally acclaimed for their extraordinary beauty and emotional depth. "Art," in Pärt's understanding, "has to deal with eternal questions, not just sorting out the issues of today."[115] Neither Pärt's disdain for modernism nor his use of Christian liturgical texts have curbed public enthusiasm for his music: according to bachtrack.com, Pärt held the distinction of being the world's most performed living classical composer for eight years in a row ending in 2019 and has remained in first or second place until 2024.[116]

Musical examples from around the globe attest that the highest good of music, to paraphrase Calvin's catechism, is to manifest the glory of God. This should come as no surprise: as one precocious student concluded in 1915,

113. David Yearsley, "Alchemy and Counterpoint in an Age of Reason," *Journal of the American Musicological Society* 52, no. 2 (Summer 1998): 238.

114. Christoph Wolff, "Bach's Music and Newtonian Science: A Composer in Search of the Foundations of His Art," *Understanding Bach* 2 (2007): 96.

115. Paul Hillier, *Arvo Pärt* (Oxford: Oxford University Press, 1997), 65.

116. "All in the Balance: Bachtrack's Classical Music Statistics of 2025." https://bachtrack.com/classical-music-statistics-january-2025.

> After all, everything moves in one direction, everything develops from one single thought, namely, the glory of Him who was from the beginning and who created heaven and earth and all creatures that dwell in it.[117]

Proposals for A Reformational Study of Music

Abraham Kuyper challenges scholars to make the glory of God the ultimate aim of their research:

> There are three wonderful things about science: it brings to light the hidden glory of God; it gives you joy in the act of digging up the gold that lies hidden in creation; and it grants you the honour of raising the level and well-being of human life. [118]

What would music research and composition look like in view of Kuyper's challenge? If we expand music's role beyond that of a mere emblem of human progress or showcase of cultural identity, what areas need to be brought to light, or better, to be given audible expression?

1. It would explore music as a precise speculative art—speculation being a mirroring of God's wisdom in creation—thus re-establishing the link between music, mathematics, and world structure.
2. It would explore how music unites intentions and builds trust, looking across cultures and through history for examples, and exploring the properties that enable music to perform this function.
3. It would explore harmony as a principle of distribution, design, and planning.
4. It would develop a theory of melody; Kepler's 1619 *Harmonice Mundi,* book 3, chapters 13-16 presents the most coherent theory of melody I have found.
5. It would work closely with neurology, aiding in research on emotions and the language of the brain.
6. It would explore the intimate connection between music and speech and endeavour to develop ways of "giving words wings" more effectively.

---

117. Herman Dooyeweerd, "De Troosteloosheid van het Wagnerianisme" [The Comfortlessness of Wagnerianism], *Opbouw* 2 (1915): 110-112. I am indebted to Glenn Friesen for this reference.

118. Abraham Kuyper, *On Scholarship*, 9, 13.

7. It would explore new ways for music to display God's glory in the confidence that God's glory is a fount of inspiration that can never be exhausted.

> We have in this visible world, a conspicuous image of God; and thus the same truth is taught here, as in Romans 1:20, where it is said, that the invisible things of God are made known to us by the creation of the world, they being seen in his works. God has given us, throughout the whole framework of this world, clear evidences of his eternal wisdom, goodness, and power; and though he is in himself invisible, he in a manner becomes visible to us in his works.[119]

Topics for Reflection and Discussion

1. Questioning the Categories

Current musical scholarship is hampered by an inherited set of vague categories such as "Western," "Classical," "Pop," "World," or "Folk," which serve to stereotype music, justifying insensitivity to the deep significance that a particular musical practice or heritage might have for its performers. How would it look to categorize music according to structure and direction—that is, based on the characteristics of the music itself and the typical purpose of the music in the setting where it developed?

2. Is Glory a Given?

Christian musical scholarship should be marked by enthusiastic curiosity and humility: curiosity motivated by the expectation of encountering the glory of God, a glory that knows no cultural boundaries (Rev. 21:24); and humility in acknowledging that the European system of harmony, keyboard, and notation is not a gold standard by which other music can be judged. Humility admits that those of us trained in the European tradition struggle to hear, let alone to comprehend, the nuances of melody and rhythm of virtuosic non-notated musical traditions. Should we then maintain a respectful and appreciative distance; or undertake a deeper study of such traditions?

3. Centrality of the Heart?

There are several reasons why Reformational philosophy, like philos-

119. John Calvin, *Commentaries on Hebrews,* www.ccel.org/ccel/calvin/comment3/comm_vol44/htm/xvii.ii.htm.

ophy in general, has been more comfortable with the visual and discursive rather than with the aural and emotional. The aural and emotional are always fleeting and therefore difficult to objectify. Scholarship aspiring to credibility in the academic world must of course be objective and indifferent. And in an intellectual framework dominated by rationalism, modernism, and secularism, emotions (along with faith commitments) become both trivial and dangerous. Kuyper's contemporary Max Weber blamed Calvinism for the worldly asceticism from which this framework arose, but Kuyper's devotional writings and Dooyeweerd's emphasis on the centrality of the heart attest to a consistent Reformed resistance against rationalism, and to a wholistic, emotionally engaged faith. And in the last couple of decades, neuroscience, using video technology and fMRI brain imaging, has pinned emotion down and thus opened up an entirely new view of what it means to be human, with emotions taking centre stage. Can we, however, benefit from studies that presuppose a mechanistic model of the brain, or that incorporate an imprecise or culturally-defined category of music? Are emotions in some sense supra-temporal?

4. Music and Presence

Studies of musical ontology have run aground over questions such as whether music's "being" is to be found in live performance; or in an ideal version of the live performance in a composer's head; or in music's reception in the auditory processing channels of the listener's brain. However, another way to tackle this rocky problem is to study music and presence. A great deal of ingenuity, from music notation to talking drums to microphones to recordings, has been devoted to making music performable without aural instruction and audible to remote listeners. The Reformed emphasis on *Coram Deo* provides a deep foundation for a discussion of music and presence. What are the strengths and weaknesses of music notation? How does the presence of the performer impact the musical experience of the listener? How do amplification and digital streaming change the nature of musical experience?

5. Musical Multisubjectivity

Daniel Stern and Colwyn Trevarthen's research on mother-infant intersubjectivity—the sharing of attention, feelings, and intentions—has impacted not only infant development studies, but also linguistics, the arts, and the social sciences. Interpersonal communion through the attunement of affect and matching behaviours enables two unique, embodied selves to reach beyond their hidden interior worlds into a coherent flow of shared meaning. There is much in Stern and Trevarthen's proposal that resonates with Dooyeweerd's concern for meaning, naïve experience, temporal coherence, the selfhood, and especially the ground-motive of creation, fall, and redemption: we are conceived *in utero*, ejected from the nurturing womb in a helpless state, and receive our true selfhood through loving communion with God. Stern and Trevarthen's findings help us see the *Shema* not as the edict of a remote despot, but rather as the imperative for our life and our growth, our engagement with God our creator, who like a loving parent rejoices over us with singing (Zeph. 3:17, NIV). *Multisubjectivity* through shared musical participation may also be important, as the synchronized heart rates of choral singers suggest; African drumming rituals and Southeast Asian gamelan music may also afford the experience of multisubjectivity.

But many questions remain: *how* does music facilitate sharing of intentions and physical states, and for whom? Can *multisubjectivity*, rather than cultural dominance, explain the international popularity of such made-in-America traditions as shape-note singing and gospel choirs? What are musically-facilitated multisubjectivity's implications for the standard model of cultural silos?

6. *Composing a Renewed Creation*

While Stern and Trevarthen's research has underscored the importance of musical forms of vitality in intersubjective dialogue, Bruno Latour's *Compositionalist Manifesto* invites us to shoulder the task of the composition—the act of putting things together while retaining their heterogeneity—to build a beautiful, harmonious, common world, released from the Cartesian view of "nature" as mere mechanistic *res extensa.* He also argues that the academic preoccupation with critique has, in the end, so undermined epistemology that the findings of science, which purports to speak for nature, are met with skepticism and political disarray. "Universities no longer offer a preview of what will become future common sense, but rather isolated archipelagos in a sea of discontents."[120] Compositionalists, by contrast, bring immanence and truth together with regard not only to matters of fact, but also to matters of concern. Latour sees the need for mobilization on an unprecedented scale. Without mutual bonds of trust between individuals, nations, and powers, we will never mobilize the concerted forces needed to heal our feverish planet. The need for music sensitive to the song of creation and attuned to the song of God has never been more urgent: how can musicians help fill this need?

120. Latour, "Is Geo-logy the New Umbrella for All the Sciences? Hints for a Neo-Humboldtian University,"(lecture, Cornell University, Ithaca, NY, October 2016), 9.

Helpful Resources

Music and Culture

The website of the *Centre for the Interdisciplinary Study of Music*, University of California, Santa Barbara, has an excellent media section.

Music and Neuroscience

The *Zatorre Lab*, McGill University, Montreal, QC, Canada, has a fascinating programme of research and good website.

Juslin, Patrik and John A. Sloboda, eds. *Handbook of Music and Emotion: Theory, Research, Applications* (Series in Affective Science). Oxford: Oxford University Press, 2010.

Music, Theology, Worship

The *Calvin Institute of Christian Worship* (*CICW*), Grand Rapids, Michigan, promotes the interdisciplinary study of the theology, history, and practice of Christian worship and the renewal of worship in worshiping communities across North America and beyond.

Yale Divinity School Institute of Sacred Music, New Haven, CT, is an interdisciplinary graduate center for the fostering, exploration, and study of engagement with the sacred through music, worship, and the arts in Christian communities, diverse religious traditions, and public life.

Christian Congregational Music: Local and Global Perspectives is an annual conference held during August at Ripon College, Cuddesdon, Oxfordshire, UK.

Music Theology Durham holds study days and conferences.

Reformation Musical History and Theology, a project of the Theological University Kampen and Melanchthon-Academy Bretten, has annual conferences.

General Music Scholarship

The *Society for Christian Scholarship in Music* has annual meetings and also maintains a blog at medium.com.

Networking and Support

Crescendo: A Worldwide Network and Community of Musicians and Dancers https://www.crescendo.org.

Bibliography

Agamben, Giorgio. *The Kingdom and the Glory: For a Theological Genealogy of Economy and Government.* Stanford, CA: Stanford University Press, 2011.

Alberti, Leon Battista. *The Architecture of Leon Battista Alberti. In ten books. Of Painting. In three books. And of Statuary. In one book.* Translated by.James Leoni. London: Edward Owen, 1755.

Athanasius. *The Life of Antony and the Letter to Marcellinus.* Translated by Robert C. Gregg. New York: Paulist Press, 1980.

Bacon, Roger. *Opus Majus.* Translated by Roger Belle Burke. Philadelphia: Pennsylvania Press; London: H. Milford, Oxford University Press, 1928.

Bagley, Robert. "The Prehistory of Chinese Music Theory." In *Proceedings of the British Academy* 131(London, 2005) 41-90. Accessed June 2021.

Barker, Andrew. "Minor Authors Quoted by Theon and Porphyry." In *Greek Musical Writings*, vol 2: *Harmonic and Acoustic Theory,* edited by Andrew Barker, 209-244. Cambridge: Cambridge University Press, 1989.

Barth, Karl. *The Doctrine of Creation.* Vol. 3, part 2 of *Church Dogmatics.* Edinburgh: T & T Clark, 1960.

Beale, Gregory K. "Eden, the Temple, and the Church's Mission in the New Creation." *Journal of the Evangelical Theology Society* 48, no. 1 (March 2005): 5-31.

Beale, Gregory K. *The Temple and the Church's Mission: A Biblical Theology of the Dwelling Place of God.* Downers Grove, IL: Apollos/IVP, 2004.

Bell, Clive. *Art.* London: Chatto & Windus, 1914.

Blood, Ann J., and Robert Zatorre. "Intensely Pleasurable Responses to Music Correlate with Activity in Brain Regions Implicated in Reward and Emotion." *Proceedings of the National Academy of Sciences of the United States of America* 98, no. 20 (Sept. 25, 2001): 11818-11823.

Boethius. *Five Books on Music.* Translated by J. Garceau, K. Long, S. Burnham, M. Waldstein, and T. McGovern. Privately published, 1985. http://static1.squarespace.com/static/5a6b9486e9bfdfc602d49f99/58a6bb5a2edce67638866f611d/5a6bb5b9edce67638866f7691/1517008313635/Five-Books-of-Music-1.pdf?format=original Visited July 2, 2019.

Blacking, John. *Music, Culture, and Experience: Selected Papers of John Blacking,* edited by Reginald Byron. Foreword by Bruno Nettl. Chicago: University of Chicago Press, 1995.

Blesser, Barry. "The Seductive (Yet Destructive) Appeal of Loud Music." http://www.blesser.net/downloads/eContact%20Loud%20Music.pdf

Boulez, Pierre. *Boulez on Music Today.* Translated by Susan Bradshaw and Richard Rodney Bennett. Cambridge MA: Harvard University Press, 1972.

Boyle, Nicholas. "Redeeming Culture." In *Sacred Imagination,* edited by Charles B. Bordon, C. S. C, and Margaret Monahan Hogan, 121-131. Portland, OR: University of Portland, Garaventa Center for Catholic Intellectual Life and American Culture, 2009.

Brent-Smith, Alexander. "Ludwig van Beethoven." *Proceedings of the Musical Association,* Oxford University Press—Royal Musical Association 53 (1926 - 1927), 85-94. http://www.jstor.org.proxy.lib.sfu.ca/stable/765532

Braun, Martin. "Bell Tuning in Ancient China: A Six-Tone Scale in a 12-Tone System Based on Fifths and Thirds." *Neuroscience of Music.* Klässbol, Sweden, 2003. http://web.telia.com/~u57011259/Zengbells.htm.

Bukofzer, Manfred. *The Place of Musicology in Institutions of Higher Learning.* New York: The Liberal Arts Press, 1957.

Burckhardt, Jacob. *The Civilization of the Renaissance in Italy.* Translated by Samuel George Chetwynd Middlemore. Project Gutenberg Ebook, 2014.

Calvin, John.*Catechism of the Church of Geneva, being a form of instruction for children.* https://reformed.org/documents/calvin/geneva_catachism/geneva_catachism.html

Calvin, John. *Commentaries on the Epistle of Paul the Apostle to the Hebrews.* Edited and translated by John Owen. Edinburgh: The Calvin Translation Society, 1853. 266. https://hdl.handle.net/2027/uva.x000427932

Calvin, John. "Epistle to the Reader," *Geneva Psalter* 1542. In *Source Readings in Music History,* edited by William Oliver Strunk, and revised and edited by Leo Treitler, New York: Norton, 1998, 364-367.

Calvin, John. *Institutes of the Christian Religion.* 2 vols. Translated by Henry Beveridge. Grand Rapids, MI: Eerdmans, 1989.

Campbell, Patricia Shehan. *Music, Education, and Diversity: Bridging Cultures and Communities.* New York: Teachers College Press, 2017.

Campbell, Patricia Shehan, Davie Myers, Juan Chattah, Victoria Lindsay Levine, David Rudge, Ed Sarath, Lee Higgins, and Timothy Rice, *Transforming Music Study from its Foundations: A Manifesto for Progressive Change in the Undergraduate Preparation of Music Majors.* Task Force on the Undergraduate Music Major, 2016. https://www.music.org/pdf/pubs/tfumm/TFUMM.pdf

Carey, John. *What Good Are the Arts?* London: Faber and Faber, 2005.

Chamberlain, David S. "Philosophy of Music in the *Consolatio* of Boethius." *Speculum* 45, no.1 (Jan. 1970): 80-97.

Chua, Daniel KL. *Absolute Music and the Construction of Meaning.* Cambridge: Cambridge University Press, 1999.

Colles, H. C. *The Growth of Music: A Study in Musical History.* 3rd ed. Edited by Eric Blom. London: Oxford University Press, 1956.

Clark, Philip. "Face to Face with Pierre Boulez." *Gramophone* (March 20, 2015). https://www.gramophone.co.uk/feature/face-to-face-with-pierre-boulez-'acquire-and-destroy-acquire-and-destroy-then-go-further'. Visited July 12, 2019.

Crickmore, Leon. "A Musical and Mathematical Context for CBS 1766." *Music Theory Spectrum* 30, no. 2 (2008): 327-38. Accessed June 10, 2021. doi:10.1525/mts.2008.30.2.327.

Cyril of Jerusalem. "Catechetical Lecture 6: Concerning the Unity of God. On the Article, I Believe in One God. Also Concerning Heresies." In *Cyril of Jerusalem, Gregory Nazianzen.* Series 2, vol. 7 of Nicene and Post-Nicene Fathers. Translated Edwin Hamilton Gifford. Grand Rapids, MI: Eerdmans, 1893. http://www.ccel.org/ccel/schaff/npnf207.ii.x.html

Danielson, Dennis, Richard. "Their Peculiar Behavior Confounds Mortals' Minds: Martianus Capella and Boethius." In *The Book of the Cosmos: Imagining the Universe from Heraclitus to Hawking,* edited by Dennis Danielson, 78-81. Cambridge, MA: Perseus Publishing 2000.

Danielson, Janet. *Basic Organization of Music.* Sidney, BC: Vibrant Air Music, 2014.

Deusen, Nancy van. *Theology and Music at the Early University: The Case of Robert Grosseteste and Anonymous IV.* Vol. 57 of Brill's Studies in Intellectual History. Leiden: Brill, 1997-98.

Dichter, B., J. Breshears, M. Leonard, and E. Chang. "The Control of Pitch in the Human Laryngeal Motor Cortex," *Cell* 174, no. 1 (June 2018): 21-31.

Dionysius the Areopagite. "Divine Names." In *The Works of Dionysius the Areopagite,* 8.5. Translated by the Rev. John Parker. London: James Parker and Co., 1897. http://www.ccel.org/ccel/rolt/dionysius.html. Viewed June 24, 2019.

Dittmer, Luther, ed., trans. *Anonymous IV.* Vol. 1 of Music Theorists in Translation. New York: Institute of Mediaeval Music 1939. https://archive.org/stream/anonymousivconce00ditt/anonymousivconce00ditt_djvu.txt

Dooyeweerd, Herman. *A New Critique of Theoretical Thought.* Philadelphia: Presbyterian and Reformed Publishing Company, 1969.

Dooyeweerd, Herman. "De Troosteloosheid van het Wagnerianisme" [The Comfortlessness of Wagnerianism]. *Opbouw* 2 (1915): 97-112.

Edwards, Jonathan. *An Essay on the Nature of True Virtue.* London: W. Oliver, 1778/

Edwards, Jonathan. "On the Nature of True Virtue" (1765)." In *Ethical Writings.* Vol. 8 of Works of Jonathan Edwards, edited by Paul Ramsey, 403-536. Haven, CT: Yale University Press, 1989.

Eriugena, John Scotus. *Periphyseon: De divisione naturae.* Edited by I. P. Sheldon-Williams, with Ludwig Bieler. Dublin: Dublin Institute for Advanced Studies, 1968.

Freeman, Walter J. "A Neurobiological Role of Music in Social Bonding." In *The Origins of Music,* edited by Nils. L. Wallin, Björn Merker, and Steven Brown, 411-424. Cambridge, MA: MIT Press, 2000.

Freeman, Walter J. *Societies of Brains: A Study in the Neuroscience of Love and Hate.* Hillsdale, NJ: L. Erlbaum, 1995.

Gramsci, Antonio. *Selections from the Prison Notebook.* Edited by Quintin Hoare and Geoffrey Nowell Smith. New York: International Publishers, 1971.

Grout, Donald Jay. *A History of Western Music.* New York: W. W. Norton, 1960.

Haldankar, Shrikrishna. *Aesthetics of Agra and Jaipur Traditions.* Mumbai: Popular Prakashan, 2001.

Hefele, Anna Maria. "O Antiqui Sancti - Polyphonic Overtone Singing." YouTube video. 2:34. Nov.27, 2014. https://www.youtube.com/watch?v=letfkSJ92Js

Hicks, Andrew James. *Composing the World: Harmony in the Medieval Platonic Cosmos.* New York: Oxford University Press, 2017.

Hillier, Paul. *Arvo Pärt.* Oxford: Oxford University Press, 1997.

Hogan, Marc. "The Record Industry Expects a Windfall: Where Will the Money Go?" *Pitchfork* (May 30, 2019). https://pitchfork.com/features/article/the-record-industry-expects-a-windfall-where-will-the-money-go/

Hu, Wayne and Martin White. "The Cosmic Symphony." *Scientific American* 290 no. 2 (February 2004): 44-53.

Huron, David. *Sweet Anticipation: Music and the Psychology of Expectation.* Cambridge, MA: MIT Press, 2007.

Jackendoff, Ray. "Parallels and Nonparallels between Music and Language." *Music Perception: An Interdisciplinary Journal* 26, no. 3 (February 2009): 195-204.

Jairazbhoy, Nazir Ali. "What Happened to Indian Music Theory? Indo-Occidentalism?" *Ethnomusicology*, 52, no. 3 (Fall 2008): 349-377.

Kepler, Johannes. *The Harmony of the World*. Translated by E. J. Aiton, A. M. Duncan, and J. V. Field. Philadelphia: The American Philosophical Society, 1997.

Klawans, Jonathan. *Purity, Sacrifice, and the Temple*. New York: Oxford, 2005.

Kuyper, Abraham. *Lectures on Calvinism*. Grand Rapids, MI: Eerdmans 1931.

Kuyper, Abraham. *On Scholarship: Two Convocation Addresses on University Life*. Edited by Harry van Dyke. Grand Rapids, MI: Christian's Library Press, 2014.

Kuyper, Abraham."Sphere Sovereignty: A Public Address Delivered at the Inauguration of the Free University, Oct. 20, 1880." Translated by George Kamps. www.reformationalpublishingproject.com

Kuyper, Abraham. *To Be Near unto God*. Translated by John Hendrik de Vries. Vancouver: Regent College Publishing, 2005.

Latour, Bruno. "An Attempt at a Compositionalist Manifesto." *New Literary History* 41, no. 3 (2010): 471-490.

Latour, Bruno. *An Inquiry into Modes of Existence: An Anthropology of the Moderns*. Translated by Catherine Porter. Cambridge, MA: Harvard University Press, 2013.

Latour, Bruno. "Is Geo-logy the New Umbrella for All the Sciences? Hints for a Neo-Humboldtian University." Lecture, Cornell University, Ithaca, NY, October 2016.

Latour, Bruno. "Visualization and Cognition: Drawing Things Together." *Knowledge and Society: Studies in the Sociology of Culture Past and Present* 6, no. 1 (1986): 1-40.

Latour, Bruno. *We Have Never Been Modern*. Translated by Catherine Porter. Cambridge MA: Harvard University Press, 1993.

Lindley, Mark. "Mersenne on Keyboard Tuning." *Journal of Music Theory* 24, no. 2 (Autumn 1980): 166-203.

Loos, Helmut. "Die Kunstreligiöse Botschaft der Leipziger Musikwissenschaft im späten 19. und frühen 20. Jahrhundert." *Musicological Annual* 50, no. 2 (2014): 43-51.

Malloch, Stephen, and Colwyn Trevarthen, editors. *Communicative Musicality: Exploring the Basis of Human Companionship.* Oxford: Oxford University Press, 2009.

McKinnon, James. *Music in Early Christian Literature.* New York: Cambridge University Press, 1987.

Mersenne, Marin. *La Verite dessciences contre les Sceptiques ou Pyrrhoniens.* Paris: Toussainct du Bray, 1625; facsimile edition, Stuttgart-Bad Cannstatt: Friedrich Frommann / Gunther Holzboog, 1969.

Mo, Di, Xunzi, Fei Han. *Basic Writings of Mo Tzu, Hsün Tzu, and Han Fei Tzu.* Translated by Burton Watson. New York: Columbia University Press, 1967.

Moreno, Joseph J. "Orpheus in Hell: Music in the Holocaust." In *Music and Manipulation: On the Social Uses and Social Control of Music,* edited by Steven Brown and Ulrik Volgsten, 264-286. New York and Oxford: Berghahn Books, 2006.

Mugglestone, Erica. "Guido Adler's *The Scope, Method, and Aim of Musicology* (1885): An English Translation with an Historico-Analytical Commentary," *Yearbook for Traditional Music,* 13 (1981):1-21.

Orsini, Francesca. 2014. "“Krishna Is the Truth of Man”." In *Culture and Circulation,* 46:222–46. https://doi.org/10.1163/9789004264489_010. Accessed June 2021.

Panksepp, Jaap, and Colwyn Trevarthen. "The Neuroscience of Emotion in Music." In *Cummunicative Musicality: Exploring the Basis of Human Companionship,* edited by Stephen Malloch and Colwyn Trevarthen, 105-146. Oxford: Oxford University Press, 2009.

Papastathopoulos, Stathis. "Thinking Intersubjectivity in Daniel N. Stern's Work." *Eleutherna: Journal of Psychology and Behavioral Sciences* 7 (2015): 62-91.

Plotinus, *The Six Enneads.* Translated by Stephen MacKenna and B. S. Page. South Bend, IN: Infomotions, Inc., 2000. https://ebookcentral-proquest-com.proxy.lib.sfu.ca/lib/sfu-ebooks/detail.action?docID=3314722

Prüfer, Arthur. *Sebastian Bach und die Tonkunst des neunzehnten Jahrhunderts.* Leipzig: Poeschel & Trepte, 1902. http://hdl.handle.net/1802/14405

Richter, Jean Paul. *The Literary Works of Leonardo da Vinci.* 3rd ed. New York: Phaidon Press, 1970.

Rowell, Lewis Eugene. *Music and Musical Thought in Ancient India.* Chicago: University of Chicago, 1992.

Schulter, Margo. "Tritones in Early Music: Were They Always Prohibited?" http://www.medieval.org/emfaq/harmony/tritone.html.

Schweinitz, Wolfgang von. *Bharata Muni's Experimental Tuning Procedure with Two Identical Vinas;* P. Sambamurthy, *Experimental Vinas;* Bharata-Muni, *The Natyasastra: A Treatise on Hindu Dramaturgy and Histrionics,* Vol. II: 5-8. Translated by Manomohan Ghosh. Calcutta: The Asiatic Society, 1961. https://www.plainsound.org/pdfs/bharata.pdf. Accessed July 2019.

Scruton, Roger. "The Great Swindle," *Aeon* (December 2012). https://aeon.co/essays/a-cult-of-fakery-has-taken-over-what-s-left-of-high-culture.

Serrà, Joan, Álvero Corral, Marián Boguña, Martin Haro, and Josep Ll. Arcos. "Measuring the Evolution of Contemporary Western Popular Music." *Nature.com Scientific Reports 2,* Article 521, July 2012. http://www.nature.com/srep/2012/120726/srep00521/full/srep00521.html

Stern, Daniel. *Forms of Vitality.* New York: Oxford University Press, 2010.

Tarasti, Eero. *Signs of Music: A Guide to Musical Semiotics.* Vol. 3 of Approaches to Applied Semiotics. Berlin and New York: Mouton de Gruyter, 2002.

Tatlow, Ruth. "Theoretical Hope: A Vision of for the Application of Historically Formed Theory." *Understanding Bach* 8 (2013): 33-60.

Thakar, Markand. *Counterpoint: Fundamentals of Music Making.* New Haven, CT: Yale University Press, 1990.

Theophilus of Antioch. "Letters to Autolycus" in *Fathers of the Second Century: Hermas, Tatian, Athenagoras, Theophilus, and Clement of Alexandria.* Vol. 2 of *The Ante-Nicene Fathers: Translations of the Writings of the Fathers Down to A.D. 325,* ed. Alexander Roberts and James Donaldson. 10 vols. 1885–1887. (Buffalo: The Christian Literature Publishing Company, 1885), 87-121.

Todd, Neil P. McAngus, and Frederick W. Cody. "Vestibular Responses to Loud Dance Music: A Physiological Basis of the 'Rock and Roll Threshold'?" *The Journal of the Acoustical Society of America* 107, no. 1 (2000): 496-500. doi: 10.1121/1.428317

Treitler, Leo, ed. *Strunk's Source Readings in Music History,* Rev. ed. New York: Norton, 1998.

Tylor, Edward Burnett. *Primitive Culture: Researches into the Development of Mythology, Philosophy, Religion, Art and Custom.* London: John Murray, 1871.

Wade, Bonnie. *Thinking Musically: Experiencing Music, Expressing Culture,* 2nd ed. New York: Oxford University Press, 2009.

Weber, Max. *The Protestant Ethic and the Spirit of Capitalism.* Translated by Talcott Parsons. Introduction by Anthony Giddens. London and New York: Routledge, 1992.

Whittle, Mark. "Quantum Hiss." Big Bang Acoustics: Sounds from the Newborn Universe. http://people.virginia.edu/~dmw8f/BBA_web/bba_home.html. Accessed July 2019.

Witherspoon, Gary, and Glen Peterson. *Dynamic Symmetry and Holistic Asymmetry in Navajo and Western Art and Cosmology.* New York: Peter Lang, 1995.

Wolff, Christoph. "Bach's Music and Newtonian Science: A Composer in Search of the Foundations of His Art." *Understanding Bach* 2 (2007): 95-106.

Wolters, Albert M. *Creation Regained: Biblical Basics for a Reformational Worldview.* 2nd ed. Grand Rapids, MI: William B. Eerdmans, 2005.

Wolters, Albert M. "The Intellectual Milieu of Herman Dooyeweerd." In *The Legacy of Herman Dooyeweerd: Reflections on Christian Philosophy in the Christian Tradition*, edited by C. T. McIntyre, 4-10. Lanham, MD: University Press of America, 1985.

Wolterstorff, Nicholas. *Art in Action: Toward a Christian Aesthetic*. Grand Rapids, MI: Eerdmans, 1980.

Yearsley, David. "Alchemy and Counterpoint in an Age of Reason." *Journal of the American Musicological Society* 52, no.2 (Summer 1998): 201-243.

Gioseffo Zarlino, *The Art of Counterpoint:* Part Three of *Le Istitutioni harmoniche* (1558). Translated by Guy A. Marco and Claude V. Palisca. New York: Norton, 1976.

Zhang, Juzhong, Xinghua Xiao, and Yun Kuen Lee. "The Early Development of Music. Analysis of the Jiahu Bone Flutes." *Antiquity* 78, no. 302 (December 2004): 769-778. DOI: https://doi.org/10.1017/S0003598X00113432. Accessed June 2021.

Zon, Bennett. "Science, Theology, and the Simplicity of Chant: Victorian Musicology at War." *Journal of the History of Ideas* 75, no. 3 (2014): 439-69. http://www.jstor.org/stable/43289676. Accessed June 2021.

Marketing Redeemed:
Toward a Reformational Perspective

Vahagn Asatryan

Introduction

The purpose of this chapter is to:

1. briefly discuss the modern definitions of marketing, which generally suggest that marketing is an activity for creating and exchanging value between a provider and a consumer as well as to provide a brief overview of the discipline from a Christian Reformed perspective;
2. discuss why such limited definitions of the discipline conceal the purpose or *telos* of marketing and introduce a revised view of the discipline based on the biblical concept of *shalom* to fill the gaps in the existing Christian scholarship on this subject;
3. introduce the philosophical framework of Modal Aspects proposed by Herman Dooyeweerd and discuss possible applications of that framework in marketing;
4. discuss an extension and application of Dooyeweerd's framework to marketing practices; and
5. propose research methods to examine marketing practices in the proposed context as well as to advise Christian marketing professionals on how to conduct marketing activities to the glory of God.

Modern Marketing and Its Limitations

The most recent definition of marketing according to the American Marketing Association conceptualizes the discipline as "the activity, set of institutions, and processes for creating, communicating, delivering, and exchanging offerings that have value for customers, clients, partners, and society at large."[1] Marketing guru Phillip Kotler broadly defines market-

1. American Marketing Association, "Definition of Marketing," accessed July 24, 2024, https://www.ama.org/AboutAMA/Pages/Definition-of-Marketing.aspx

ing as a "social and managerial process by which individuals and groups obtain what they need and want through creating and exchanging value with others."[2] These and similar definitions suggest that marketing ultimately involves actions of stakeholders (such as consumers, managers, and government agents, among others) that benefit more than one party. Thus, the task of marketing as a science is to research, explain, predict, and influence behaviour of the exchange participants, especially those of consumers, for a monetary or otherwise societally beneficial gain. In short, the goal of marketing is to assist creators and consumers of value to find the right product, in the right place, at the right time, and at the right price (also known as the 4 Ps of the marketing mix[3]): to facilitate an exchange of value.

This traditional 4P model of marketing examines activities related to product and service design, including research on product features and benefits favored by specific consumer or business groups, product life-cycle analysis, packaging and labeling tactics, as well as brand development and brand management, whereby an organization applies a name, symbols, phrases, and other visual and auditory elements to identify its economic offerings and to distinguish them from those of competitors. Marketers also spend significant effort on identifying the most effective and efficient ways of delivering products and services to consumers. These functions include identifying appropriate channel structures (direct vs. indirect), building strategic alliances (such as distribution of Starbucks coffee through a series of global retail chains; for example, in Denmark's largest retailer, Dansk Supermarked), as well as nurturing relations with various and often numerous distributors (merchant wholesalers, agents, and brokers.) Pricing strategies play a crucial role in business profitability and in the rewarding of stakeholders and owners. They even affect the not-for-profit organizations' ability to fulfil their mission and to serve its customers. Marketers must identify pricing objectives, determine the effects of operational (internal) and market (external) constraints, evaluate customer preferences and estimate market demand, as well as determine cost, volume, and profit relations to exercise their responsibilities in a stewardly fashion. In the traditional 4P model, marketers need to communicate or promote the value of their product's selling proposition in a convincing and truthful manner to the target audiences of consumers. These activities typically include choice of promotional elements or alternatives among the following: advertising, personal selling, sales

2. Philip Kotler and Gary Armstrong, *Principles of Marketing,* 15th Global ed. (Harlow, UK: Pearson, 2013), 6.

3. E. Jerome McCarthy, *Basic Marketing: a Managerial Approach* (Homewood, IL, Richard D. Irwin, 1960).

promotion, public relations, and direct marketing. Furthermore, each of these activities require careful planning, identification of specific target audiences, specifying objectives, setting budgets, and designing of the promotional messages, as well as selecting of the appropriate promotional tools and scheduling. Finally, marketers need to keep track of dynamic external environment factors such as changes in regulatory compliance, environmental sustainability and ethical considerations, to name a few.

Although many Christian writers have often been critical of traditional views of modern marketing theory and practice, some authors have recognized the important role marketing plays in modern society and have attempted to reconcile the practice with business principles found in the Scriptures.[4] Writers from the Reformed Christian perspective explore the discipline and the role of its practitioners in the context of the biblical metanarrative: Creation, Fall, Redemption, and Consummation. We learn that we are God's image-bearers with a purpose: to "be fruitful and multiply," to fulfill the *cultural mandate* – to "rule over the fish of the sea... The Lord God took the man and put him in the Garden of Eden to work it..." (Gen. 1:26; 2:15). Thus, Christian marketing thinkers frequently reflect on the Biblical themes of God's provision (Gen. 9:3; Exod. 16:1-30; 1 Tim. 6:17; Mt. 6:30) and God's sovereignty (Gen. 1:1; Deut. 5:7) as well as the participatory nature of human beings, created in his image, with gifts of creativity (Gen. 1:1), freedom and autonomy (Gen. 2:16; Rom. 8:21; 1 Cor. 10:23-31; Gal. 5:1), stewardship (Gen. 1:28; 2:5,15), and personhood (Gen. 1:26-27) when describing the discipline-related activities. Chewning suggests that being made in the image of God includes such characteristics as "holiness, righteousness, and true knowledge," in addition to attributes of truth (John 1:14), justice and faithfulness (Deut. 32:4), love (1 John 4:7-8), mercy (Psalm 145:8), goodness (Psalm 34:8), and grace (Eph. 2:8, Exod. 33:19).[5] *The Westminster Shorter Catechism* describes God as "a Spirit, infinite, eternal, and unchangeable, in his being, wisdom, power, holiness, justice, goodness, and truth."[6] Karns suggests that "exchange and marketing are the avenues for participating creatively with God in work that provides for each other's needs, whether recognized as such by those engaged in it or not."[7] We were created to emulate these Christ-like qualities in the

4. Richard C. Chewning, *Biblical Principles and Business: The Practice,* Christians in the Marketplace, vol. 3. (Colorado Springs, CO: NavPress, 1990).

5. Richard C. Chewning, *Biblical Principles and Economics: The Foundations,* Christians in the Marketplace, vol. 2 (Colorado Springs, CO: NavPress, 1989), 315.

6. G. I. Williamson, *The Westminster Shorter Catechism: For Study Classes,* 2nd ed. (Phillipsburg, NJ: P & R, 2003).

7. Gary L. Karns, "A Theological Reflection on Exchange and Marketing: An Exten-

process of cultivating the earth and in our relationships in all spheres of life, including those of business and marketing in particular.

However, although humans are made in the image of God, they are fallible and prone to wander away from their Creator. The Fall refers to the failure of Adam to comply with God's good and pleasing will by his disobedience to God's law. The introduction of sin has direly affected not only man's relationship with the holy God but also the entire creation which now "groan[s] as in the pains of childbirth right up to the present time" (Rom. 8:22). Hence, man's relationships with God, with self, and with fellow human beings, as well as the created order has been corrupted by sin.[8] This distortion of relationships as a result of the Fall has introduced deceptive practices into the work of business and marketing as well, such as dishonesty, falsehoods, coercion, manipulation, denigration, neglect, to mention only a few of the corrupted practices.[9] It is as if some modern marketers compete to denigrate goodness, kindness, loyalty (see for example many Axe deodorant advertisements) and delight in evil. Furthermore, branding activities designed to elevate the brand to achieve a cult-like status (e.g., Apple, Lululemon or Harley-Davidson)[10] with its own worshipers and disciples is another illustration of the idolatry which dominates some marketing approaches. We should mention, of course, that even the most innocent and ethical marketing activities may evoke

sion of the Proposition that the Purpose of Business is to Serve," *Christian Scholar's Review* 38, no. 1 (Fall 2008): 97-114.

8. Craig G. Bartholomew and Michael W. Goheen, *The Drama of Scripture: Finding our Place in the Biblical Story*, 2nd ed. (Grand Rapids, MI: Baker Academic, 2014).

9. David Hagenbuch, *Honorable Influence: A Christian's Guide to Faithful Marketing* (Spring Valley, CA: Aldersgate Press, 2016).

10. The image shows a motorcyclist riding a Harley-Davidson motorcycle straight toward the viewer. The rider is positioned in the center of a long, empty road that stretches toward the horizon. The road is wet or glossy, reflecting the light from the motorcycle's headlamp. The rider's arms are extended outward, away from the handlebars, giving a crucifix-like pose. The rider has long hair and a beard, visually reminiscent of traditional Western artistic representations of Jesus. The background features a dramatic sunset or sunrise, with deep orange, gold, and purple tones. Clouds are dark and heavy, adding intensity and drama to the sky. Silhouetted, leafless trees appear on either side of the road, contributing to a stark, almost biblical landscape. The lighting is high-contrast, with the motorcycle headlight glowing brightly in the foreground while the horizon glows softly behind the figure. At the bottom right, the Harley-Davidson Motorcycles logo is clearly displayed. Across the bottom of the image, in bold capitalized letters, is the tagline: "THOU SHALT HAVE NO OTHER GODS BEFORE ME." The rider's pose combined with the religious language invokes a deliberate comparison between Motorcycling / Harley-Davidson ownership and religious devotion, worship, or ultimate allegiance. Ads Spot, "Harley-Davidson: Jesus," accessed July 20, 2022. https://adsspot.me/media/prints/harley-davidson-jesus-e240df3bab58.

undesired or unintended reactions from consumers who (choose to) misinterpret intentions and worship the brand or its creators.[11]

This rebellion against God's normative laws usually translates into hiding the truth (e.g., in advertising and product design) or, in cases of consumers' dissatisfaction with product features, blaming the unscrupulous marketers for evoking misguided desires and causing temptation of at times catastrophic proportions (e.g., the failure of corrupt management practices at Ashley Madison, the dating website which promotes adultery).[12] The encouragement and even at times promotion of lust, greed, covetousness, sexual immorality, and similar vices appears to have a strong grip on marketing.[13] Karns labels deviations from Christian worldview themes (such as stewardship, love and holiness, among others) as "misalignments."[14] Indeed, the practice and the outcomes of the discipline have become distorted and misguided by sin. Materialism (the importance an individual attaches to worldly possessions), hedonism (the idea that pleasure is the only good in life, including avoidance of pain),[15] and consumerism have become the predominant elements of the modern marketing paradigm[16] and its idols. Consumerism is a particularly self-centered social phenomenon as it "points to a culture in which the core values of the culture derive from consumption rather than the other way round."[17]

This discussion leaves us with the question of the *telos* or purpose of marketing: why do we need such a creative activity and what role does it play in our civilization, in the context of the Creation, Fall, Redemption, Consummation framework? And more importantly, what role *should* it play in the Kingdom of God? How do we, as Christian marketers and researchers redirect our discipline away from this corrupting misalignment?

---

11. David J. Burns, and Jeffrey K. Fawcett, "The Role of Brands in a Consumer Culture: Can Strong Brands Serve as a Substitute for a Relationship with God?" *Journal of Biblical Integration in Business* 15, no. 2 (2012): 28-42.

12. I. Szmigin, "Sex, Lies and Exposure: Is Ashley Madison To Blame, or Its Customers?" CNN.com, August 21, 2015. https://www.cnn.com/2015/08/21/opinions/ashley-madison-blame/index.html

13. Laurie R. Busuttil, "Toward a Practical Theology of Marketing: A Five Ps Approach to the Business of Persuasion," *Journal of Biblical Integration in Business* 20, no. 2 (2017): 30-41.

14. Karns, "A Theological Reflection," 97-114.

15. John O'Shaughnessy and Nicholas Jackson O'Shaughnessy, "Marketing, the Consumer Society and Hedonism," *European Journal of Marketing* 36, no. 5-6 (2002): 524-547.

16. Russell W. Belk, "Materialism: Trait Aspects of Living in the Material World," *Journal of Consumer Research* 12, no. 3 (1985): 265-280.

17. Thorsten Moritz and Craig G. Bartholomew, *Christ and Consumerism: Critical Reflections on the Spirit of Our Age* (Carlisle: Paternoster, 2000).

The Purpose of Marketing

I agree with Rae's[18] general proposition that business has two main purposes: (1) to serve the common good of the society with valuable offerings (i.e., goods, services, experiences, etc.) that contribute to human flourishing and (2) to provide meaningful work that creates an environment for the growth and development of the organization's employees. The purpose of marketing as a business sub-discipline *is* flourishing. Flourishing is *shalom* and is defined here as "the human being dwelling at peace in all his or her relationships: with God, with self, with fellow, with nature. ...[;] at its highest, shalom is enjoyment of one's relationships. [....] Shalom [...] incorporates right, harmonious relationships to God and delight in his service, ... delight in human community, ... and delight in our physical surroundings."[19] Hence, the purpose of marketing is to enhance shalom in our interactions or relationships with the aforementioned "valuable offerings," including activities that brought forth those offerings, such as the creativity and work of product designers, advertising message creators, production managers, among many others – all for the common good and to the glory of God. Karns argues that a Christian worldview envisions business activities and marketing in particular "as a means to serve one another and not as a means to exploit"; they give preference to "distributive justice and self-sacrificial love over greed" and they contribute to the aforementioned "enjoyment."[20] For example, he suggests that shalom is being enhanced where marketing activities develop "cooperation among people and the rule of law."[21] Marketing, therefore, was not intended only to effectively and efficiently solve humanity's problems of exchange and service, facilitating the creation and transfer of value from producers to consumers, but also to enhance the relationships among the stakeholders as well as other elements of creation involved in this process. Shalom is God's vision of what "ought to be." It is a vision of peace, justice, and salvation. It is a vision of spiritual, physical, and social wholeness and well-being. (I will adapt this working definition and expand on its implications and applications in marketing activities in later sections). We might ask then: what kind of practice could bring about such a vision? What kind of marketing activities can contribute to the ushering in of shalom?

---

18. Scott B. Rae, *Doing the Right Thing: Making Moral Choices in a World Full of Options* (Grand Rapids, MI: Zondervan, 2013).
19. Nicholas Wolterstorff, *Until Justice and Peace Embrace* (Grand Rapids, MI: W.B. Eerdmans, 1983), 69-70.
20. Karns, "A Theological Reflection," 97.
21. Karns, "A Theological Reflection," 107.

Redemptive Marketing and Its Practitioners: Toward a Restorative Practice

God imposes his law over creation in two distinct ways: (1) by direct governance through the laws of nature (*creatio secunda*)[22], and (2) through human beings, through norms, or *creatio tertia*. He maintains created order through the laws of nature and norms. Spykman states: "This good order for creation holds for all our life relationships. It defines our manifold callings. . . . This cultural mandate [Genesis 1:26-31] lays its claim on us both as a benediction and a command. . . . It delineates in a typically biblical way the potentials for every human enterprise as well as the limitations on it. ... Viewed in this light, every calling is a religious calling. . . . Our calling is to bring the order *of* our life in God's world, whether in the pulpit or in politics, in our halls of learning or in our marketplaces, into conformity with God's good order *for* our life in this world."[23] Our role as the culture makers, as marketers and consumers, is to reveal and apply these creational, *structural* norms in carrying out respective duties in our lives, including our economic relations; to discern and to do God's will to his glory and human well-being. Karns claims that "the exchange and marketing processes would be at play even if the Fall had not occurred"[24] and they are designed to promote "Genuine relationships between persons [which] model the relationships between God and persons." Sometimes the extraordinary happens, as Andy Crouch says, "And from time to time human culture is so carefully tended and developed that the artifacts that emerge are something even more than very good. They approach something we could call glory. Glory is the magnificence of true being, the captivating beauty of something that is so rich in realization that it leaves us in awe and close to worship."[25] Thus, the goals of marketing are ambitious indeed: at its best, marketing should lead to awe and worship of God.

Thus, one of the first tasks of a faithful marketing practitioner is to recognize, define, and organize those structural norms – the order of creation – in specific contexts of marketing exchanges, as well as to reform or redirect them when they appear to deviate from God's instituted intentions. The performance of these tasks is possible because of humans' "intu-

22. Albert M. Wolters, *Creation Regained: Biblical Basics for a Reformational Worldview*, 2nd ed. (Grand Rapids, MI: William B. Eerdmans, 2005): 42.
23. Gordon J. Spykman, *Reformational Theology: A New Paradigm for Doing Dogmatics* (Grand Rapids, MI: W.B. Eerdmans, 1992): 179-180.
24. Karns, "A Theological Reflection," 104, 105.
25. Andy Crouch, *Playing God: Redeeming the Gift of Power* (Downers Grove, IL: IVP Books, 2013): 105.

itive attunements to creational normativity"[26] or conscience. For example, because market exchanges need norms of trust and efficiency to perform their basic functions, the cultivation of this kind of confidence and reliance in the other party is necessary for the proper functioning of marketing.

First, we need to recognize the roots of normative marketing practice. I agree with Steen and VanderVeen[27] who cite Spykman and boldly proclaim that the norm of marketing is found in "the mediating Word of God given with creation ..., reaffirmed in the redeeming work of Christ, and illumined by the witness of the Scriptures."[28] Thus, to recognize and apply such redemptive practices we need to turn to Scripture as well as theological tradition as the source of wisdom and inspiration. Furthermore, redemptive marketing practice is discerned with the presence and influence of the Holy Spirit (Gal. 5:18; Rom. 8:9) and is aimed at the reorientation or reordering of love toward God, the self, others, and creation. Beyond Scripture, we learn about God's norms in marketing practices through intuition, experience or interactions with each other and creation, and the empirical study of various phenomena. We also need to acknowledge the effects of sin as a result of the Fall, which produces tension and acts as a counterweight to our own efforts. This varying nature of good and evil provides a helpful guide for developing a theoretical and practical framework within which to research the extent to which a practice or a process conforms to God's ordained norms and how it deviates from them.

The current discussion rests on the fundamental assumption that the direction of activities allows for two end-points: toward God and away from God. Wolters brands it as "direction, ..., [which] designates the order of sin and redemption, the distortion and perversion of creation through the fall on the one hand and the redemption and restoration of creation in Christ on the other" and "either in obedience or disobedience to his law."[29] Thus, identification of practices directed toward God and their incorporation into various marketing activities, outcomes, and institutions is the first serious and laborious task that Christians must undertake to reform the discipline. However, not only is it important to discern what the Bible and one's theological tradition reveal about the full spectrum of God's good norms or cursed "glittering vices,"[30] it is

26. Wolters, *Creation Regained*, 29.

27. Todd Steen and Steve VanderVeen, "Will there be Marketing in Heaven?" *Perspectives* (November 2003): 6-11.

28. Spykman, *Reformational Theology*, 62.

29. Wolters, *Creation Regained*, 59.

30. Rebecca Konyndyk DeYoung, *Glittering Vices: A New Look at the Seven Deadly Sins and their Remedies* (Grand Rapids, MI: Brazos Press, 2009).

also important to identify the nature of application of the various ways in which these encouragements and prohibitions can be implemented. Spykman argues that we come to know God "by studying how his various creatures respond to the holding power of his Word,"[31] which is encapsulated in his commandments and laws.

Furthermore, as we examine "the drama of Scripture"[32] in the context of Creation, Fall, Redemption, and Consummation, we focus on the biblical story of the restoration of created order through the death and resurrection of Jesus Christ. Wolters argues that in followers of Christ this "process of progressive inner renewal in every phase of human life (not just in the context of worship activities) is a unique feature of biblical religion" and that "everything in principle can be sanctified and internally renewed – our personal life, our societal relationships, our cultural activities."[33] Hence, redemptive marketing includes strategies with the intent, means, and end to contribute to this process and to the edification of the members of Christ's church. I agree here with Busuttil who suggests that marketing actions can "draw on edifying motives through techniques that are restorative and that strengthen godly values."[34] These practices are inspired by the redemptive and restorative work of Jesus Christ and are responsive to the call of the Holy Spirit and God's law (Col. 3:12-13). Redemptive marketing activities are focused on the restoration of God's good creation order and contribute to the process of divine reconciliation. For example, marketing practices that are driven by "the ministry of reconciliation" (2 Cor. 5:18) as applied in product design and development, attempt to incorporate features and benefits in such a way that "they [can] be made answerable to their creational structure."[35] A Christian marketer may even use strategies to design products and services that contribute to the renewal of the mind (Rom. 12:2), usher in justice and peace (Zech. 7:9), and enhance shalom through genuinely flourishing relationships among users or designers of the product. Furthermore, Wrenn, Hoover, and Warwick, for example, argue that "Scripture calls for Christian marketers to market the value of a product in ways that make the need for that product transparent" and that "marketers should not suggest that the consumption of material or physical goods or services can add meaning to life."[36] Hence, we need to

31. Spykman, *Reformational Theology*, 80.

32. Bartholomew and Goheen, *The Drama of Scripture.*

33. Wolters, *Creation Regained*, 91.

34. Busuttil, "Toward a Practical Theology," 33.

35. Wolters, *Creation Regained*, 78.

36. Bruce Wrenn, Harwood Hoover Jr. and Jacquelyn Warwick, *Scriptural Foundations for Marketing* (Berrien Springs, MI: Andrews University Press, 2013), 13.

identify the normative goodness or God's "law that is in force for it"[37] to properly market goods or services and capably participate in this ministry of reconciliation.

Meaning-Makers:
A Dooyeweerdian Approach to Reforming Marketing

We now turn our attention to the examination of this normative goodness through the Dooyeweerdian philosophical approach. The marketing practice framework presented below allows us to devise proactive and reactive transformative strategies as well as to determine their potential implications. Van Duzen and his co-authors argue that as a result of the Fall "managers now need to understand that their redemption work has two components: it needs to be both corrective and restorative – in going back to heal, and fill in – as well as additive."[38] Unfortunately, the available Christian business literature still lacks a comprehensive approach and provides few specific guidelines for practitioners in the various realms of marketing practice, with few exceptions.[39] The following sections represent my attempt to provide such an approach and to discuss its implications for marketing practice in order to add to the growing body of research and to enrich Christian practitioners' portfolio of methods. First, I present the philosophical framework developed by Herman Dooyeweerd as a useful tool for a comprehensive analysis of marketing activities. Second, I examine how normative perspectives rooted in biblical principles of justice and love, among others, may assist in enhancing the Dooyeweerdian framework's application in marketing. Third, I discuss how this proposed approach helps marketing practitioners discern redemptive marketing activities. Finally, I discuss opportunities for future research to enhance the framework's application to the glory of God.

Herman Dooyeweerd's Philosophy: A Brief Introduction

Image-bearing is a lofty yet joyful responsibility. The rich intellectual tradition of Dooyeweerd equips us with useful frameworks for reforming research and practice in the discipline of marketing. First, it identifies and classifies the plethora of ways in which humans relate to the Creator, to others, and to his creation; this includes a multi-as-

37. Wolters, *Creation Regained*, 62.

38. Jeff Van Duzer et al., "It's Not Your Business: A Christian Reflection on Stewardship and Business," *Journal of Management, Spirituality & Religion* 4, no. 1 (2007): 99-122.

39. Karns, "A Theological Reflection, 104.

pectual analysis (which we will discuss in the following sections) or "ways in which things can be meaningful."[40] Second, Dooyeweerd's framework describes and characterizes the nature of laws and norms designed to govern these relationships. Finally, the framework allows practitioners to develop marketing techniques and researchers to study the discipline of marketing as it relates to the enhancement of the common good and to flourishing.

We begin with a critical reflection on the nature and the direction of the relationships among the participants and objects involved in a marketing activity (e.g., the sale of an item or a television commercial). Imagine a consumer, an item (e.g., a car, toy, vacation package, or college education), a manufacturer or marketer of that item, other stakeholders, as well as the rest of the created order (e.g., environment), and the Creator. The process of developing redemptive or reconciliatory marketing strategies must include a comprehensive analysis of such relationships. My proposition here is consistent with the Model of Reconciliation as Vocation proposed by Hagenbuch, who argues for reconciliation and support of strong relationships "between oneself and God, oneself and others, others and God, and others and others."[41] The proposed framework allows us to shape responses to questions related to marketing activities such as the following: What characteristics of a vehicle would constitute a healthy and flourishing relationship between the driver and her car? How would the promotion of a particular cooking utensil enhance God's shalom at the dinner table of a family? What kinds of relationships is a board-game designed to promote (e.g., competitive vs. collaborative) among the participants during and after the game? What vision of the Kingdom is encapsulated in the practices or, as Smith calls them, liturgies,[42] of shopping, consuming, and disposing?

Dooyeweerd's theory of modal aspects attempts to examine the diversity and coherence of Creation. He argues that all of created reality does not *have* meaning, but *is* meaning, which points beyond itself to the Creator. The "structure of individuality" refers to the ways a thing (an entity such as a car, a movie, a human being) is meaningful in the various aspects or modes of being: it is what enables the entity to

40. Andrew Basden, *Philosophical Frameworks for Understanding Information Systems* (Hershey, PA: IGI Global, 2007), 127.

41. David J. Hagenbuch, "Marketing as a Christian Vocation: Called to Reconciliation," *Christian Scholar's Review* 38, no. 1 (2008): 83.

42. James K.A. Smith, *Desiring the Kingdom: Worship, Worldview, and Cultural Formation* (Grand Rapids, MI: Baker Academic, 2009).

be that particular individual despite changes.[43] An *aspect* is a mode, a fundamental way of being. According to Dooyeweerd there are fifteen irreducibly distinct aspects (spheres of meaning) of life: quantitative, spatial, kinematic, physical, biotic, sensitive, analytical, formative, lingual, social, economic, aesthetic, juridical, ethical, and pistic. The model suggests, for example, that an advertising billboard can be counted (numerical aspect), can be distinguishable (logical aspect), can evoke emotion (psychic aspect), and can be the advertiser's property (juridical aspect). Moreover, according to the Dooyeweerdian view, marketing itself as a discipline is a social entity governed by laws and norms. Marketing is a set of individual things, practices, events, and social relationships (e.g., advertising billboards, new product launches, and interactive sales presentations, respectively) that function in all modal aspects. Each of these aspects has a distinct set of laws that enables things to exist and interact.[44] Dooyeweerd proposes that each aspect has a meaning-nucleus, a kernel which can only be grasped intuitively, and which "always indicates a *how*, never a *concrete something*."[45] Table 1 further explains the differences among the different aspects or modalities (as they are at times called) including their corresponding meaning-nuclei. The table lists all fifteen aspects and descriptions of how an entity, a print ad from Federici, a gelato marketer (included in the table), functions within that modality as presented by Kalsbeek[46] (with some expansions). This advertisement shows an attractive, young, and pregnant woman dressed as a nun in a traditional black-and-white habit, sitting in what appears to be a dimly lit church or chapel. She is holding a container of Antonio Federici Gelato labeled "Pistachio" and delicately eating it with a spoon. The woman is looking contemplative and sensuous, with eyes half closed as she tastes the gelato.

"Immaculately Conceived" is written in ornate gold font, referencing religious language. The ad is prominently featuring the brand—"Antonio Federici Gelato Italiano"—and the message: "Ice Cream is our religion."[47]

43. Herman Dooyeweerd, *A New Critique of Theoretical Thought*, trans. David H. Freeman and H. De Jongste (Jordan Station, ON: Paideia, 1984), 7-8.

44. For a more comprehensive review of Dooyeweerd's philosophy, see Leendert Kalsbeek, Bernard Zylstra and Josina Van Nuis Zylstra, *Contours of a Christian Philosophy: An Introduction to Herman Dooyeweerd's Thought* (Toronto, ON: Wedge, 1975).

45. Kalsbeek, Zylstra and Van Nuis Zylstra, *Contours of a Christian Philosophy*.

46. Ibid., p. 100.

47 Contrast Creative Ltd., "Antonio Federici Campaign," accessed July 20, 2024, https://www.contrastcreative.co.uk/portfolio/antonio-federici-2/.

Table 1. Aspects and their meanings.

Aspect	**Its meaning-nuclei**	**Examples**[48]
Numeric	Discrete quantity (numerable, calculable)	This 1 page contains about 4 product attributes, and has a certain number of words.
Spatial	Continuous extension or expansion	This advertising (ad) page is laid out in rectangular areas.
Kinematic	Motion (extensive movement)	The ad invites your gaze to move across it.
Physical	Energy and matter (physico-chemical)	This ad emits light.
Biotic	Life and vitality	Certain areas of your nerve cells are activated by interacting with this ad.
Sensitive	Feeling, sensation	This ad can be seen, and the reader may have an emotional reaction to its content.
Analytical	Distinction, logic, cognition	The reader can distinguish things in this ad and think about them.
Formative	Formative power	The reader can construct an impression of this ad.
Lingual	Symbolic representation	The reader can understand some of what this ad describes.
Social	Social intercourse	The reader has a role as reader or "encounter." This page is not conventional.
Economic	Frugality	The writer attempts to get all that is needed into this page.
Aesthetic	Harmony, beautiful proportion	Is this ad interesting? Does it "work" as a whole?
Juridical	Retribution (what is due)	Does this page do justice to the topic and to the reader?

48. Examples of aspectual functioning of the text of an advertising page in a magazine (adapted from Andrew Basden, "Aspects of Reality as We Experience It," updated March 2017, http://kgsvr.net/dooy/aspects.html.)

Ethical	Love in temporal relationships (self-giving)	Information contained on this page is truthful and the writer is "generous" with the reader.
Pistic	Faith, firm assurance, and vision	The writer believes in the truth and importance of what he or she is writing on this page.

There are also intricate and complex relations between *subjects* and *objects* in creation. *Subjects* are the "active" participants, originators of an action (for example, a person on an exercise bike). *Objects* play a passive role as recipients of the subject's actions (the aforementioned bike), all operating under God's laws within a specific aspect. Thus, under all modalities or aspects, there exist both laws and phenomena or entities (i.e., subjects and objects) that operate under these laws. Hence, a person functions in each aspect either as a subject (i.e., an initiator of action) or an object ("things" can be done to him or her). Chaplin suggests that object-subject functioning is straightforward: for example, he suggests that an entity operates as a subject (i.e., "it extends in space, grows, feels, thinks, claims legal rights").[49] Alternatively, that entity can "function objectively" so that when other subjects act upon it "they can perceive it, use it, develop affection for it, own it, and so on."[50] In our earlier example of the Federici advertising, a person (i.e., subject) viewing the ad (i.e., object) may discern the written message, feel excitement toward the content, consider the legal limitations of its usage in the context of advertisement law, or imagine some spiritual implications of the ad's content in light of his or her own beliefs. Dooyeweerd argued that all of nature has been created to be in a coherent relationship with each other. Human functioning in *sensitive* and post-*sensitive* aspects (i.e., analytical through pistic, see Table 1, according to Kalsbeek)[51] is subject to "normative laws" as opposed to the laws of physics, mathematics, and other laws in the modalities ranging from the numeric to sensitive aspects (although there is some debate among the scholars as to where that line of demarcation between laws of nature and normative laws should be drawn, which is beyond the scope of this chapter). Our functioning or interactions, including those in the context of marketing activities, are governed by normative law-spheres, which are "distinctive and irreducible logical, linguistic,

49. Jonathan Chaplin, *Herman Dooyeweerd: Christian Philosopher of State and Civil Society* (Notre Dame, IN: University of Notre Dame Press, 2011), 90.
50. Chaplin, *Herman Dooyeweerd*, 90.
51. Kalsbeek, Zylstra, and Van Nuis Zylstra, *Contours of a Christian Philosophy*.

social, economic, legal, aesthetic, ethical, and pistical norms."[52] Chaplin also concludes that Dooyeweerd's "normative principles" or "rules of conduct," which appear in all post-sensitive modalities, "are thus much wider in scope than the field designated by the term ethics in contemporary philosophy and theology; it includes, unusually, norms of language, aesthetics, and even faith. What he [Dooyeweerd] terms 'ethical norms' are merely one variety of normative rules of conduct."[53]

The general conceptual model that I propose here based on Dooyeweerd's philosophy for identification and analysis of the normative dimensions suggests that a practice or an activity may be examined and judged in terms of its functioning "well" within each aspect or modality. However, proper functioning in one aspect may be combined with distortions in others. For example, a magazine advertisement for a car may appear to "do justice" and treat properly all parties involved in the production of the promotional material. Alternatively, it may apparently conform to aesthetic norms, but may nonetheless lack integrity in the pistic modality by appealing to idolatry and utilizing sacrilegious language. (Appendix 1 contains an example of such a sacrilegious advertisement from a well-known brand.)

The Dooyeweerdian theory of created order further helps us refine the concept of human flourishing as proper, good, and obedient to God's norms in its functioning in all aspects and in all subject-object relations. Dooyeweerd also argued that our harmonious functioning in all aspects (particularly as it relates to the normative laws of aspects, above the *sensitive*) leads to a full, healthy, godly life, whereas violations of such laws result in harmful and unholy living, which is unsustainable. Furthermore, this flourishing motive is never self-centered or self-serving. Shalom-enhancing activities attempt to bring peace and balance into relationships among members of society and elements of creation even in the absence of the agent of reconciliation – human beings, and especially Christians, guided by the power of the Holy Spirit. Dooyeweerd called the implementation of normative principles through human activities "positivization."[54] For example, the positivized relationship between a believer and her client improves and enhances relations between that client and his or her own customers, or positively influences the client's environmental stewardship practices (i.e., relations with the elements of creation in the context of value-creation). I am convinced, through my own research[55]

52. Chaplin, *Herman Dooyeweerd*, 62.

53. Chaplin, *Herman Dooyeweerd* , 62.

54. Chaplin, *Herman Dooyeweerd*, , 63.

55. Vahagn Asatryan, "Promoting Gifts of Common Grace in Marketing" (paper presented at the Symposium on Common Grace in Business at Calvin College, Grand

and class-room experiences,[56] that not only can Christian educators, researchers, and practitioners share such shalom-enhancing marketing activities but that they can also educate and convince their co-workers and other organizational stakeholders to implement the normative practices.

Applications in Marketing

Although aspectual and normative laws can never be fully known, we can attempt to find reasonable approximations and apply them in marketing. New product development and design of advertisement campaigns or branding exercises are among the most important, accessible, and potentially productive areas in marketing practice and research that may benefit from the analysis and application presented here. Hence, this multi-aspectual approach allows for simultaneous and comprehensive analysis of functioning in all aspects of all forms of being.

Let us now consider an application of such analysis for a new product design: a luxury SUV (Sport Utility Vehicle). This task includes research and discernment of proper structures and practices that are best suited to meet the demands of the non-normative (i.e., quantitative, spatial, kinematic, physical and biotic) aspects as well as identification and application of the normative proper functioning of the vehicle and its user. Analysis of the non-normative (pre-*sensitive*) elements of a motor vehicle is quite complex and technical, and more suitable for the field of engineering, but, in short, it includes considerations for quantitative (number of seats), spatial (layout and configuration of the interior or the engine compartment), kinematic (the movement of headlights as the vehicle turns), and similar considerations.[57] These characteristics, of course, are predetermined by the purpose of the vehicle and its intended audience or users. Hence, marketers should always recognize that such analysis and product design are context- or purpose-specific. For example, some SUVs are designed to excel in truly harsh terrains and weather conditions with high ground clearance and shock absorbers, while others are created as family recreational vehicles with enhanced driving and handling capabilities suited for a comfortable ride.

The normative aspects require our attention to discern God's laws

Rapids, MI. October 31, 2014).

56. Vahagn Asatryan, "Taught or Caught? The Learning and Teaching of Virtues for Future Entrepreneurs" (paper presented at the Kuyers Institute for Christian Teaching and Learning Conference on Virtues, Vices, and Teaching at Calvin College, Grand Rapids, MI, October 3-5, 2013).

57. We will focus on the normative aspectual analysis here due to the lack of space in this volume.

and norms for the well-functioning of the car and the relationship of the consumer with the car (as well as the relationships of all others who are involved in activities related to the conceptualization, design, sale, and even disposal of the car).[58] The effects of our fallenness and, hence, our tendency to misinterpret the intended structure for things, may result in unintentional or even intentional deviations and distortions. Basden, for example, provides an excellent discussion of dysfunction or evil in each aspect, such as the curse of disease in the biotic, confusion in the analytic, waste or squandering in the economic, and idolatry or disloyalty in the pistic.[59] Basden's proposed framework may be applied in our example of SUV design (see Table 2).

Table 2. Multi-Aspectual Analysis of Car Design.

Aspect	Benefits to users	Detriments to users
Biotic	Ergonomic design with adjustable seat parts enhances health and vitality.	Poor seat design features and limited adjustment options threaten and diminish users' health.
Sensitive	Individualized environment control features enhance users' happiness and psychological well-being.	Lack of adjustable vent controls or seat configurations frustrate and aggravate passengers.
Analytical	Dashboard design and layout improve clarity and readability of performance indicators.	Poor visibility of dashboard instruments or cumbersome navigation interface increase confusion and endanger performance.
Formative	Voice activated features or foldable seats for storage availability allow for efficient planning and effective goal achievement.	Navigation software glitches or faulty brake mechanisms increase potential destruction and harm.

58. Notice here that we stress "relationship" rather than *usage* or *consumption* of the product or service in general to include the multitude of possible interactions with a consumer, including idolatrous attachments and conspicuous consumption.

59. Andrew Basden, *Philosophical Frameworks*.

Lingual	External noise reduction features and easy person-to-vehicle communication system improves quality of communication and user information satisfaction.	Deficient or distracting car-to-user communication system reduces access to information and poor symbols or icons on dashboard diminishes understandability.
Social	Swivel seats which allow for passengers in the second row of a minivan to turn seats to face third-row passengers may enhance respect and friendliness.	Closely and confusingly placed seatbelt buckles promote hostility and disrespect among passengers attempting to use them.
Economic	Hybrid engine and LED lamps lead to fuel economy and lower maintenance costs.	Disproportionately large engine and difficult-to-reach storage compartments increase waste and mismanagement of space.
Aesthetic	Harmoniously integrating variety of textures (e.g., wood, chrome, fabrics) are pleasing to the eye and evoke interest.	Misaligned and unfitting design elements suggest ugliness and evoke boredom.
Juridical	Safety features alert the driver to the right of way of other vehicles at the intersection or when the driver inappropriately occupies two lanes on the road.	Emissions control software reports corrupted data.
Ethical	Car access features (e.g., pin-code entry pads) and tracking capabilities allow the owner to share the vehicle selflessly with others.	Exclusive and rare design materials (e.g., ivory, one-of-a-kind fossilized dinosaur bone trims, or panels made from remnants of a meteorite) promote elitism and self-centeredness.
Pistic	The car's brand and reputational features (e.g., Volvo's renown for safety) help define consumer identity and reflect personal belief system.	The car's features (e.g., exclusivity, elitism) help develop a cult-like following among its users, promoting misguided loyalty and idolatry.

Source: Table by author based on information in Basden, *Philosophical Frameworks.*

In this quest for discernment, a Christian researcher and practitioner may turn to many disciplines besides theology to find answers to the following questions: What kind of car design and features may facilitate formative and positive social interactions?[60] What design characteristics allow for an efficient and effective entry into and operation of the vehicle? What kind of features may prompt the driver of the vehicle to "worship" it and become susceptible to idolatry (i.e., a distortion in the pistic modality)? I agree with Schuurman who argued that "the designers of technical objects embed their personal or corporate values into their devices" and that "technological objects are biased toward certain uses, which in turn bias the user in particular ways."[61] I have also discussed these dangerous implications and an application of the proposed framework in my earlier publications.[62] For example, I conducted normative analysis of a product design and provided recommendations for improving the modern methods of new product development. And more generally, what are the appropriate levels of interactions and extent of relationship between the marketing organization and its stakeholders? Notice, however, that most of these "normative" features contain some potential for abuse and misdirection in the hands of the consumer or user beyond the marketer's control (i.e., a car may serve as a weapon or a get-away vehicle for bank robbers). At the very least we may use aspectual analysis to identify issues from multiple perspectives and share such awareness with others in our workplaces or in academic research. We as Christians can be creative in our approaches in raising issues of our professional functioning in, for example, juridical or ethical aspects, including appeals to professional codes of ethics (common grace language) such as the American Marketing Association's Code of Conduct.[63] The Code's ethical norms clearly state that marketers should do no harm, foster trust in the marketing system, and embrace ethical values. The Code further identifies and defines these ethical values as: honesty, responsibility, fairness, respect, transparency, and citizenship. Christians can find comfort and encouragement in these statements of professional conduct which contain reflections of the biblical principles of justice, integrity, stewardship, and respect for

60. For example, a recent Toyota Sienna mini-van design includes a "Driver Easy Speak" feature to amplify the parent-driver's voice for the children in the back row to facilitate a peaceful and stress-reducing means of communications.

61. Derek C. Schuurman, *Shaping a Digital World: Faith, Culture and Computer Technology* (Downers Grove, IL: InterVarsity Press, 2013), 15.

62. Vahagn Asatryan, "Product Development in HD: A Christian Philosophy in Action" (paper presented at the Christian Business Faculty Association Conference, Mount Vernon, OH, June 28, 2011).

63. American Marketing Association, "Code of Conduct,", accessed April 17, 2017, https://www.ama.org/codes-of-conduct/.

the human dignity of creatures made in the Image of the Most High. Furthermore, we ought to distinguish between liberating, restorative, or transformational movements (toward God) and enslaving or destructive directions (away from God). We need to distinguish between wholesome or shalom-seeking states and harmful deviations.

New Horizons in Marketing Practice and Research

The proposed Dooyeweerdian framework's emphasis on normativity advances a new agenda for marketing research and practice. Christian marketing researchers, in collaboration with experts in other fields (including people of other faiths and secular researchers), may contribute to conceptualization and measurement of normativity in each of the post-sensitive modalities proposed by Dooyeweerd. We may explore the normative and the anti-normative spectrum for analysis of product features, advertising elements, and even consumer experiences. We do need to keep in mind the role of the Holy Spirit in the lives of Christians in this journey of discernment of God's "good and perfect will" (Rom. 12:2) – guided by special or saving grace and by Scripture itself. The ultimate goal is the human flourishing of all stakeholders and their relationships with the creation through conceptualizing, creating, communicating, delivering, and exchanging value offerings in ways which give honour to God.

The concept of normativity is certainly not new in marketing literature. Hunt and Vitell[64] argue, for example, that marketers have *prima facie* duties which constitute moral obligations, especially as they are reflected in the juridical and ethical modalities. These normative obligations include fidelity, justice, beneficence and non-injury, and much research has been completed on these moral imperatives. In my own practice I have successfully used virtue-based methods to advise marketing professionals on such normative practices.[65] However, the proposed Dooyeweerdian framework provides a much richer and more comprehensive view of normativity with its multi-dimensional focus. Because normativity is so central to the Dooyeweerdian framework, the exploration of possible measurement scales and their application in empirical studies may prove to be a fruitful area for an innovative research agenda.

What are the possible sources which can be used to help develop

64. Shelby D. Hunt and Scott Vitell, "A General Theory of Marketing Ethics," *Journal of Macromarketing* 6, no. 1 (1986): 5-16.

65. Vahagn Asatryan, "Ethical Marketing" (workshop presented at the Partners Worldwide Business SEVA Christian Business Conference, Bangalore, India, January 29, 2015).

such normative measurements? Normative characteristics in some modalities are often associated with virtuousness (justice, love, honesty) and often find their roots in virtue ethics. Discussion of their application in marketing is often found in normative marketing literature. Normative marketing is a prescriptive practice which is rooted in normative ethics and is "anchored in moral philosophy, business ethics research, corporate social responsibility frameworks, public policy thinking, religious values, legal guidelines, and a modicum of utopian idealism." [66] This view of the discipline may serve as a useful conceptual and methodological foundation for further exploration. Furthermore, a growing body of research on human flourishing and holistic development has been emerging in the field of positive psychology.[67] Despite its numerous shortcomings (e.g., its focus on the self-centeredness of an individual's "happiness") this field of psychology may provide a lucrative harvest for developing psychometric tools for a possible assessment of normativity. For example, one can modify and apply the various developed scales to measure the extent to which justice is manifest in a car's design or how frugality (e.g., efficient fuel consumption) can do justice to the user's relationship with creation. Furthermore, we may research the normativity of marketing-related activities, such as purchasing behaviour and its effects on others. I have attempted to construct such scales for the ethical and pistic modalities in my research on ethical marketing and business practices, which I tested in developing countries.[68] Preliminary results indicate that managers can intuitively gauge the normative aspects of various marketing practices. For example, consider the normative analysis of the aforementioned Federici advertisement (Table 1). For the "ethical" aspect of "generosity, giving, sacrifice, hospitality vs. selfish, taking advantage of others, competition"[69] or moral aspect as "humanitarian love for one's neighbor,"[70] one may explore the Sexual Embeds in Advertising: VASE Scales,[71] which offers four scales that measure attitudinal aspects of sub-

66. Gene R. Laczniak and Patrick E. Murphy, "Normative Perspectives for Ethical and Socially Responsible Marketing," *Journal of Macromarketing* 26, no. 2 (2006): 154-177.

67. Martin E. P. Seligman and Mihaly Csikszentmihalyi, "Positive Psychology: An Introduction," *American Psychological Association* 55, no. 1 (2000): 5-14.

68. Vahagn Asatryan, "Marketing and Ethical Business" (paper presented at Partners Worldwide Business SEVA Christian Business Conference, Bangalore, India. January 30-31, 2015).

69. Andrew Basden, *Philosophical Frameworks*, 78.

70. Kalsbeek, Zylstra, and Van Nuis Zylstra, *Contours of a Christian Philosophy*, 102.

71. Robert Widing, et al., "The VASE Scales: Measures of Viewpoints about Sexual Embeds in Advertising." *Journal of Business Research* 22, no. 1 (January 1991): 3-10.

jects finding the use of sexual embeds in advertisements to be objectionable, manipulative, morally harmful, and insufficiently controlled. The respondents were asked to respond to or finish the following statements:

I feel the use of sex in advertising that the viewer is not intended to be consciously aware of is ...

On the moral dimension:
Morally harmful – not at all morally harmful
A cause of lower moral values – not at all a cause of lower moral values

On the objectionable dimension:
Very objectionable – not at all objectionable
Very offensive – not at all offensive
Very unethical – not at all unethical

These statements may perhaps serve as guides for developing scales for measuring normativity redefined in accordance with the Dooyeweerdian framework. Furthermore, moral foundations theory[72] may provide insight into how Christian and non-Christian viewers of the advertisement differ in evaluating its normativity (e.g., examining statements such as "sacrilegious – not sacrilegious at all").

A number of scales have been also developed to measure viewers' responses to commercials that encompass a few of the aforementioned aspects or dimensions in one instrument (e.g., Leavitt's now classic Reaction Profile[73], which originally produced 525 words that could be used for scaling ads or Reaction Profile for TV commercials[74] which may further enhance our understanding of the multi-aspectual analysis. Indeed, much of the reviewed literature lacks cohesive, useful scales to measure the more nuanced, if not elusive, aspects: i.e. the pistic and the juridical. (For example, how does the "Immaculately conceived" tag-line affect the viewer's perception of the Federici ad's appropriateness or normativity from the pistic perspective?)

Furthermore, other elements of the marketing mix may also undergo a similar analysis. Consider the difference between the two following statements measuring price perception: "Buying a high price brand that causes jealousy in others makes me feel good about myself," and "I enjoy

72. Jonathan Haidt and Craig Joseph, "Intuitive Ethics: How Innately Prepared Intuitions Generate Culturally Variable Virtues." *Daedalus* 133, no. 4 (2004): 55-66.

73. Clark Leavitt, "A Multidimensional Set of Rating Scales for Television Commercials." *Journal of Applied Psychology* 54, no. 5 (1970): 427-429.

74. William Wells, Clark Leavitt, and Maureen McConville, "A Reaction Profile for TV Commercials." *Journal of Advertising Research* 11, no. 6 (1971): 11-17.

telling people how much they might expect to pay for different kinds of products,"[75] or "I am usually delighted to see my friends enjoy their new purchases." A researcher may hypothesize that the first statement, with its focus on the self and its desire to evoke negative emotions in another fellow human being is likely anti-normative. The other two statements appear to be subdued with their focus on personal humility and intent to serve others, as well as contentment and delight in the neighbour's flourishing. We may use similar scales in marketing research when evaluating consumer behaviours or attitudes. This example suggests that in addition to the normativity of aspects, we should also acknowledge and measure the powers of the "dark side" in order to curtail their presence and influence on marketing exchanges. For example, Edell and Burke[76] created a "feelings toward ads" survey which measures consumers' feelings while watching a commercial. The items and scales, which ranged from "very strongly" (5) to "not at all" (1), incorporated such descriptors as "angry," "disgusted," and "irritated" balanced with "cheerful," "inspired," and "good." We may create semantic differential scales to measure consumer attitudes toward ads or products with items ranging from "deceptive" to "truthful", from "dull" to "interesting", or from "promotes greed" to "encourages generosity." Once again, one ought not to appeal to envy, jealousy, anger, hopelessness, or other vices to promote a product or service. Thus, the proposed framework allows for a systematic development of scales, and we may apply *exploratory* and *confirmatory factor analysis*[77] in refining the various measurements.

Multi-aspectual analysis can significantly contribute to the development of positioning strategies and to the creation of positioning statements. *Conjoint analysis* assists researchers in gauging consumers' preferences or in evaluating trade-offs for various predetermined combinations of product attributes or other marketing stimuli (e.g., advertisement text or imagery). Using this methodology, researchers could show consumers different versions of print advertisements and then ask them to rank order or rate particular attributes or indicate preferences for specific features. For example, following the various methodologies

75. The scale items are adapted from Donald R. Lichtenstein, Nancy M. Ridgway and Richard G. Netemeyer, "Price Perceptions and Consumer Shopping Behavior: A Field Study," *Journal of Marketing Research* 30, no. 2 (May 1993): 234-245.

76. Julie A. Edell and Marian Chapman Burke, "The Power of Feelings in Understanding Advertising Effects," *Journal of Consumer Research* 14, no. 3 (1987): 421-433.

77. Factor analysis is a statistical method used to describe variability among correlated, observed variables in order to identify potentially lower number of unobserved variables (i.e., factors).

described by Green, Krieger, and Wind[78] as well as studies conducted by Tscheulin and Helmig,[79] researchers may prepare "prop cards" which describe numerous attributes of an advertising poster (e.g., one including pictures appealing to sex, temptation, envy, or jealousy contrasted with another one containing images appealing to normative aspects of generosity, loyalty, and kindness) and invite the respondents to rate the normativity of the various aspects and perhaps even indicate preferences on a 0 to 100 likelihood-of-purchase scale or likelihood-of-referral scale. Potentially these methodologies may guide researchers to explore and measure the respondent's perceived normativity in various aspects. A positive relation between normative characteristics of an advertising poster or product features and likelihood-of-purchase may prompt the practitioner to craft "normative" positioning statements or choose effective advertising text. *Perceptual mapping*, using attribute-based approaches, which rely on feature-by-feature assessment of various product or brand characteristics and Likert-type scales (ranging from "strongly agree" to "strongly disagree") or semantic differential scales, will assist marketers in meaningful comparisons of product offerings vis-à-vis their competition (e.g., using a combination of typically two select modalities or dimensions, such as social and juridical or aesthetic and ethical).

Qualitative research methods may also provide a fruitful soil for elaboration on the nature of normativity in marketing activities and artifacts. *Photo sorts*, for example, encourage study participants to express their attitudes towards brands by sorting through a stack of pictures of brand-sponsored advertisements with different imagery and text, which are designed to appear as either normative (e.g., context-appropriate imagery and norm-promoting accompanying text, such as "Good to the last drop" by Maxwell Coffee or "Grace. Space. Pace." by Jaguar) or anti-normative (e.g., explicitly seductive bodies of human models which denigrate human dignity, and "Cheat on your girl-friend, not your work-out" accompanying text for a gym). Consumers then connect those ads with the brands they are likely to purchase or use. Furthermore, individual *in-depth interviews, focus groups and Delphi panels*, as well as hermeneutic research techniques, which focus on the interpretation of consumers' motivations for purchase of a product in an open conversation with the researchers and usually without a predetermined list of questions, will also shed light on how consumers perceive normativity and deviations in

78. Paul E. Green, Abba M. Krieger and Yoram Wind, "Thirty Years of Conjoint Analysis: Reflections and Prospects," *Interfaces* 31, no. 3_supplement (2001), S56-S73.

79. Dieter K. Tscheulin and Bernd Helmig, "The Optimal Design of Hospital Advertising by Means of Conjoint Measurement," *Journal of Advertising Research* 38, no. 3 (1998): 35-46.

different modalities. Probing customers' deep motives for a decision may reveal normative elements in the desire to purchase or use an item.

However, we do have to proceed with caution. We must recognize the limiting effects of our fallen nature on the process, methods, and interpretation of our knowledge. "The total depravity of all humankind implies that this problem is not simply one of imperfect management of carnal impulses; it is also a problem of biased perceptions, fallacious reasoning, and an unfaithful will. The failure to think, feel, speak, and act in ways that are consistent with our new identities in Christ is a thoroughgoing problem."[80] Hence, we need to consider that our own theorizing, conceptualization of the normative laws, methods, and instruments of measurement, as well as the research subjects' or interviewees' perceptions, interpretations, and judgements may all be tainted by that sinful nature. Furthermore, we should consider the devious, perhaps even subliminal, effect of the (consumerist) culture, which often attempt to "normalize" attitudes and behaviours that are antithetical to godly living. We must also recognize that the various definitions, measurements, and instruments we conceive and apply to examine normativity in various aspects will themselves undergo revisions in light of new discoveries and theological or anthropological revelations, including developments in the Reformed tradition: *Ecclesia reformata, semper reformanda!* ("The church reformed, always reforming.") And this formative process should always be directed by submission to the Scriptures and the guidance of the Holy Spirit.

Restoration

Our earlier discussion on redemptive marketing may lead us to consider the following question: what would marketing look like in the new heavens and the new earth? Here we are firstly and strongly encouraged to practice humility in exploration of this matter, because our knowledge of this new, restored state of our presence with God, one in which, "He will wipe every tear from [our] eyes [and in which] [t]here will be no more death or mourning or crying or pain, for the old order of things has passed away." (Rev. 21:4) is limited. In this new home of righteousness (2 Peter 3:13), one that is ushered in by Christ's return, we may imagine a role for marketing. Steen and VanderVeen[81] articulate such a possibility and make three cautions assumptions about the reality in the new heavens and the new earth. First, they assume that despite God's abundant provisions in the New Jerusalem, some types of scarcity will exist:

80. Jason Stansbury, "Moral Imagination as a Reformational Influence in the Workplace," *Journal of Markets & Morality* 18, no. 1 (2015): 21-22.

81. Steen and VanderVeen, "Will there Be Marketing?", 6-11.

> "[T]here presumably will be choices to make about the temporal ordering of activities that we choose to engage in. Will we choose to read a novel or till a garden, sing songs of worship or hike a mountain, prepare a meal or build a treehouse? We may need goods (or products) in all of these cases to participate in these activities. Temporal issues may sound unusual in a place where there is no more night and the Lord will reign for eternity. However, if we exist in time as we experience it now, some things will have to come before others."[82]

Hence the role of a marketer will be modified to that of an advisory mentor or a guide to help neighbours navigate through the sequence of experiences (e.g., taking kayaking lessons or building a house). However, these choices will be free from the effects of sin and interference from the forces of evil.

Second, Steen and VanderVeen assume that "although all of God's people will be in full communion with the Holy Spirit, there will still be a distribution of gifts among his people, and that we will still function as a body."[83] Our diversity of gifts (1 Cor. 12) and our exercise of the fruit of the Spirit (Gal. 5:22) will continue in the new heaven and new earth. We will likely share our gifts with the other inhabitants of our new dwelling, in the presence of God himself. The structure of the exchange will not likely change, but its nature and motivation will: no longer will we pursue it with any ulterior motive agenda.

Finally, we are unlikely to become omniscient; however, "all information available in heaven will be completely true and useful to God's people. In addition, we will know things to a greater depth than ever before and appreciate God's goodness and sustaining love throughout all of his redeemed creation."[84] This lack of complete knowledge, which is somewhat similar to the their first assumption about scarcity, suggests, that "we will be able to process only limited amounts of information at one time, and will need to make decisions about which information is useful in completing a particular task at any one time."[85] Hence, we can assume that marketers will specialize in acquiring and sharing such knowledge in the context of exchanges, much as farming individuals in our community will share theirs.

The discussion above leaves room for creative imagination about what marketing envisioned with such an end in sight might look like in the present times. We may re-imagine, for example, advertising approach-

82. Steen and VanderVeen, "Will there Be Marketing?", 9.

83. Steen and VanderVeen, "Will there Be Marketing?", 9.

84. Steen and VanderVeen, "Will there Be Marketing?",10.

85. Steen and VanderVeen, "Will there Be Marketing?", 10.

es that incorporate or evoke biblical principles of justice, compassion, grace, and forgiveness. We can design inclusive distribution channels and innovative ways of delivering our selling propositions to the marginalized or underserved target markets. We can design biodegradable packaging solutions that contain built-in features for easy product disposal or recycling (e.g., mail-back envelopes for small electronics). Product design may incorporate removable components for easy upgrades and reduction of waste (e.g., a removable smartphone camera or battery which allow for easy upgrades and replacements). Scripture tells us that in the new heaven and the new earth we will worship God for eternity, that we were made to worship the Author of Creation and of our Salvation; hence, we need to design and apply marketing activities that bring glory to God and are acts of worship.

We may also need to distinguish among the different ways in which the laws and norms we have described relate God's will to two distinct groups: (1) those who recognize Yahweh's sovereignty and the Lordship of Jesus Christ; and (2) those who are ignorant of or refuse to submit to His authority. Here we have to make a distinction between the "language" of *special* grace and that of *common* grace. The Scriptures are clear: "Therefore, if anyone is in Christ, he is a new creation; the old has gone, the new has come!" (2 Cor. 5:17) and that a New Covenant is in place (2 Cor. 3:6). The mediation of the Holy Spirit allows ministers of the New Covenant to abide in and benefit from the Word (special revelation). Thus, it appears that the task of a Christian marketer in restoring and reconciling the current practice of marketing in conformity with God's law needs to be adjusted to meet specific participating stakeholders, particular circumstances, and specific marketing activities.[86] These activities may take on the nature of what Kosits (citing Heie[87]) refers to as "strongly perspectival" practices that "lean[s] upon Christian sources (scripture, Spirit, tradition) and draw[s] explicitly Christian conclusions" and are contrasted with "weakly perspectival" activities.[88] Furthermore, in terms of "strongly perspectival" practices one should recognize the variety of Christian traditions and diversity in the levels of faith commitment and daily practice[89] in this generical-

86. Richard J. Mouw, *He Shines in All That's Fair: Culture and Common Grace* (Grand Rapids, MI: Wm. B. Eerdmans, 2002), 44, 50.

87. Harold Heie, *Learning to Listen, Ready to Talk.* (Lincoln, NE: iUniverse, 2007), 158.

88. Russell D. Kosits, "Deeply Engaged and Strongly Perspectival? The Impasse in the Psychology-Christianity Dialogue and its Missional Resolution," *Perspectives on Science and Christian Faith* 65, no. 3 (2013b): 163-179.

89. Helen Lee, "5 Kinds of Christians: Understanding the Disparity of Those Who

ly labeled group, and, hence, the aforementioned activities (i.e., marketing practices) can be adjusted to the preferences of the particular tradition and circumstances. Indeed, Spykman suggests that "God accommodates his Word to our changing situations. He meets us where we are in order to bring us back and onward to where we ought to be. Therein lies the redirecting power of the good news proclaimed in both law and gospel. ... God by his Word also repeatedly creates radically new situations."[90] Thus, we need to examine marketing activities in various contexts of production and consumption of value as well as in relations among various stakeholders (i.e., suppliers, consumers, government agencies, etc.). However, we need to keep in mind that the normative laws revealed in the Bible are not completely hidden from non-believers; they are graciously given the capacity to recognize goodness, kindness, gentleness, and other normative attributes, through common grace.

Conclusion

In this chapter I have attempted to (re)define marketing and its purpose from a Christian perspective and to discuss a shalom-based view of the discipline. I have introduced a framework to distinguish between normative and anti-normative marketing practices and their effects on target audiences. I have also discussed the applications of Herman Dooyeweerd's philosophical framework to distinguish among the marketing practices as well as various methods to research and examine marketing practices as a guide for Christian marketing professionals. The journey ahead, in terms of research, teaching and practice, is long and challenging, but exciting. Flourishing in these areas will require the Christian marketing professional and researcher to show courage in theorizing, strength in methodology, zeal in application, and experience the joys of collaboration. We are reminded that we ought to conduct this mission prayerfully, faithfully, diligently, sacrificially, and all for the glory of God (1 Cor. 10). Promoting shalom through marketing activities requires a renewed attitude (2 Cor. 5:17). We are instructed that we should be guided by the theory and practice of marketing in a way that reflects God's character – we glorify God by becoming like Him (3 John 1:11; Eph. 5:1) and by pursuing normative practices. We are called not only to enhance our relations with God, our own selves, our neighbours, and the rest of the creation but also to contribute to flourishing in the relations of

---

Call Themselves Christians Today", *Christianity Today* (October 1, 2007), last accessed July 5, 2015, www.christianity today.com/le/2007/fall/1.19.html.

90. Spykman, *Reformational Theology*, 85.

others with the Creator and His domain. Stuart Fowler reminds us that we must "see eating and drinking as a way of expressing our love for God, not by means of accompanying words of grace, but by an act of eating and drinking itself."[91] We are also called to collaborate with others (e.g., secular scholars and marketing professionals, even those of other faiths) to unveil the normative mysteries of the created order. The classification of the practices as normative is intended to serve as a helpful guide to marketing activities that are pleasing to God and, hopefully, by using this means we will invite all people to unite under the banner of the Lamb. The God of the Bible wants to be known, glorified, and worshipped. For this reason, our motives, goals, and methods should be driven by this meta-narrative in the context of the Creation-Fall-Redemption-Consummation discourse. Be holy, for He is holy!

Questions for Reflection and Discussion

1. What kind of marketing activities can contribute to the ushering in of shalom?
2. What implications does the vision of the new heaven and the new earth have for present marketing practices? What vision of the Kingdom of God is encapsulated in the practices of designing, distributing, consuming, and disposing of products?
3. What features of products and services would constitute a healthy and flourishing relationship between that product or service and its user?
4. How would a promotion of a product or service enhance God's shalom? What kinds of relationships is a product advertisement promoting among its viewers and its creators or the actors who were used in it?
5. What kind of pricing strategies promote justice, frugality, and even moral behaviour in the purchasers and users?
6. How does the understanding or perception of "normativity" differ for various audiences (e.g., Christians compared to non-Christians)?

Helpful Resources and Further Readings in Marketing and Christian Worldview

The literature on Christian business practice and marketing in particular has been growing in the last three decades. Christian authors often

91. Stuart Fowler, *On Being Human: Toward a Biblical Understanding* (Blackburn, Vic.: Foundation for Christian Scholarship, 1980), 7.

focus on the identification and examination of biblical principles applied to various sub-disciplines: accounting, management, leadership, and others. Marketing literature and research have been gaining momentum in recent years; however, exploration of comprehensive approaches, especially in such challenging areas as branding, advertising, and sales, has been slow. The resources cited below constitute an important collection of works in the discipline that stretch over a number of decades and focus on various areas of business and marketing.

Busuttil, Laurie R. "Toward a Theology of Marketing: A Five Ps Approach to the Business of Persuasion." *Journal of Biblical Integration in Business.* 20, no. 2 (2017): 30–41.

Burns, David J., and Jeffrey K. Fawcett. "The Role of Brands in a Consumer Culture: Can Strong Brands Serve as a Substitute for a Relationship with God?" *Journal of Biblical Integration in Business* 15, no. 2 (2012): 28-42.

Chewning, Richard C. *Biblical principles and business: The practice*. Christians in the Marketplace, vol. 3. Colorado Springs, CO: NavPress, 1990.

Engelland, Chad, and Brian Engelland. "Consumerism, Marketing, and the Cardinal Virtues." *Journal of Markets & Morality* 19, no. 2 (2016).

Hagenbuch, David J. "Marketing as a Christian Vocation: Called to Reconciliation." *Christian Scholar's Review* 38, no. 1 (2008): 83-96.

Hagenbuch, David. *Honorable Influence: A Christian's Guide to Faithful Marketing*. Spring Valley, CA: Aldersgate Press, 2016.

Hagenbuch, David. *Mindful Marketing: Business Ethics That Stick*. Dubuque, IA: Kendall Hunt Publishing, 2024.

Hutchins, Bob, and Greg Stielstra. *Faith-Based Marketing: The Guide to Reaching 140 Million Christian Customers.* [Hoboken, NJ]: John Wiley and Sons, 2009.

Karns, Gary L. "A Theological Reflection on Exchange and Marketing: An Extension of the Proposition that the Purpose of Business is to Serve." *Christian Scholar's Review* 38, no. 1 (2008): 97-114.

Schneider, John R. *The Good of Affluence: Seeking God in a Culture of Wealth.* Grand Rapids, MI: Wm. B. Eerdmans, 2002.

Steen, Todd, and Steve VanderVeen. "Will there Be Marketing in Heaven?" *Perspectives* (November 2003): 6-11.

Van Duzer, Jeff, Randal S. Franz, Gary L. Karns, Kenman L. Wong, and Denise Daniels. "It's Not Your Business: A Christian Reflection on Stewardship and Business." *Journal of Management, Spirituality & Religion* 4, no. 1 (2007): 99-122.

Van Eman, Sam. *On Earth as It Is in Advertising?: Moving from Commercial Hype to Gospel Hope*. Eugene, OR: Wipf and Stock, 2010.

In addition, Christian Business Faculty Association (CBFA, https://www.cbfa.org/), with a mission to "empower Christian business faculty to transform the world for the glory of God," publishes *Journal of Biblical Integration in Business* (JBIB) and *Christian Business Academy Review* (CBAR), and hosts annual conferences devoted to Christian perspectives in business, with some sessions devoted to marketing. The Association of Christian Economists (ACE, http://christianeconomists.org/) exists to "encourage Christian scholars to explore and communicate the relationship between their faith and the discipline of economics"; it also publishes *Faith & Economics*, a peer-reviewed journal, and holds annual sessions at the Allied Social Science Associations meetings. Finally, *Philosophia Reformata* (https://brill.com/view/journals/phir/phir-overview.xml), a biannual peer-reviewed academic journal of the Association for Reformational Philosophy, is another source of insight into the Reformed philosophical worldview and occasionally contains useful content on economics and business.

Bibliography

Ads Spot. "Harley-Davidson: Jesus." Accessed July 20, 2022. https://adsspot.me/media/prints/harley-davidson-jesus-e240df3bab58.

American Marketing Association. "Definition of Marketing." Accessed July 24, 2024, https://www.ama.org/AboutAMA/Pages/Definition-of-Marketing.aspx

Asatryan, Vahagn. "Ethical Marketing." Workshop presented at the Partners Worldwide Business SEVA Christian Business Conference, Bangalore, India, January 29, 2015.

Asatryan, Vahagn. "Marketing and Ethical Business." Paper presented at Partners Worldwide Business SEVA Christian Business Conference, Bangalore, India. January 30-31, 2015.

Asatryan, Vahagn. "Product Development in HD: A Christian Philosophy in Action." Paper presented at the Christian Business Faculty Association Conference, Mount Vernon, OH, June 28, 2011.

Asatryan, Vahagn. "Promoting Gifts of Common Grace in Marketing." Paper presented at the Symposium on Common Grace in Business at Calvin College, Grand Rapids, MI. October 31, 2014.

Asatryan, Vahagn. "Taught or Caught? The Learning and Teaching of Virtues for Future Entrepreneurs." Paper presented at the Kuyers Institute for Christian Teaching and Learning Conference on Virtues, Vices, and Teaching at

Calvin College, Grand Rapids, MI, October 3-5, 2013.

Bartholomew, Craig G., and Michael W. Goheen. *The Drama of Scripture: Finding our Place in the Biblical Story*. 2nd ed. Grand Rapids, MI: Baker Academic, 2014.

Basden, Andrew. "Aspects of Reality as We Experience It." Updated March 2017. http://kgsvr.net/dooy/aspects.html.)

Basden, Andrew. *Philosophical Frameworks for Understanding Information Systems*. Hershey, PA: IGI Global, 2007.

Basden, Andrew. Foundations and Practice of Research: Adventures with Dooyeweerd's Philosophy. Routledge, 2021.

Belk, Russell W. "Materialism: Trait Aspects of Living in the Material World." *Journal of Consumer Research* 12, no. 3 (1985): 265-280.

Burns, David J., and Jeffrey K. Fawcett. "The Role of Brands in a Consumer Culture: Can Strong Brands Serve as a Substitute for a Relationship with God?" *Journal of Biblical Integration in Business* 15, no. 2 (2012): 28-42.

Busuttil, Laurie R. "Toward a Theology of Marketing: A Five Ps Approach to the Business of Persuasion." *Journal of Biblical Integration in Business*. 20, no. 2: 30–41.

Chaplin, Jonathan. *Herman Dooyeweerd: Christian Philosopher of State and Civil Society*. Notre Dame, IN: University of Notre Dame Press, 2010.

Chewning, Richard C. *Biblical Principles and Business: The Practice*. Christians in the Marketplace, vol. 3. Colorado Springs, CO: NavPress, 1990.

Chewning, Richard C. *Biblical Principles and Economics: The Foundations*. Christians in the Marketplace, vol. 2. Colorado Springs, CO: NavPress, 1989.

Contrast Creative Ltd. "Antonio Federici Campaign." Accessed July 20, 2024. https://www.contrastcreative.co.uk/portfolio/antonio-federici-2/

Crouch, Andy. *Playing God : Redeeming the Gift of Power*. Downers Grove, IL: IVP Books, 2013.

DeYoung, Rebecca Konyndyk. *Glittering Vices: A New Look at the Seven Deadly Sins and their Remedies*. Grand Rapids, MI: Brazos Press, 2009.

Dooyeweerd, Herman. *A New Critique of Theoretical Thought*. Trans. David H. Freeman and H. De Jongste. Jordan Station, ON: Paideia, 1984.

Edell, Julie A. and Marian Chapman Burke. "The Power of Feelings in Understanding Advertising Effects." *Journal of Consumer Research* 14, no. 3 (1987): 421-433.

Fowler, Stuart. *On Being Human : Toward a Biblical Understanding*. Blackburn, Vic.: Foundation for Christian Scholarship, 1980.

Green, Paul E., Abba M. Krieger, and Yoram Wind. "Thirty Years of Conjoint Analysis: Reflections and Prospects." *Interfaces* 31, 3_supplement (2001): S56-S73.

Haidt, Jonathan, and Craig Joseph. "Intuitive Ethics: How Innately Prepared Intuitions Generate Culturally Variable Virtues." *Daedalus* 133, no. 4 (2004): 55-66.

Hagenbuch, David. *Honorable Influence: A Christian's Guide to Faithful Marketing*. Spring Valley, CA: Aldersgate Press, 2016.

Hagenbuch, David J. "Marketing as a Christian Vocation: Called to Reconciliation." *Christian Scholar's Review* 38, no. 1 (2008): 83-96.

Heie, Harold. *Learning to Listen, Ready to Talk.* Lincoln, NE: iUniverse, 2007.

Hunt, Shelby D., and Scott Vitell. "A General Theory of Marketing Ethics." *Journal of Macromarketing* 6, no.1 (1986): 5-16.

Kalsbeek, Leendert, Bernard Zylstra, and Josina Van Nuis Zylstra. *Contours of a Christian Philosophy: An Introduction to Herman Dooyeweerd's Thought.* Toronto, ON: Wedge, 1975.

Karns, Gary L. "A Theological Reflection on Exchange and Marketing: An Extension of the Proposition that the Purpose of Business is to Serve." *Christian Scholar's Review* 38, no. 1 (2008): 97-114. http://search.ebscohost.com/login.aspx?direct=true&db=aph&AN=34969290&site=ehost-live.

Kosits, Russell D. "Deeply Engaged and Strongly Perspectival? the Impasse in the Psychology-Christianity Dialogue and its Missional Resolution.". *Perspectives on Science and Christian Faith* 65, no. 3 (2013): 163-179.

Kotler, Philip, and Gary Armstrong. *Principles of Marketing,* 15th Global ed. Harlow, UK: Pearson, 2013.

Laczniak, Gene R., and Patrick E. Murphy. "Normative Perspectives for Ethical and Socially Responsible Marketing." *Journal of Macromarketing* 26, no. 2 (2006): 154-177.

Leavitt, Clark. "A Multidimensional Set of Rating Scales for Television Commercials." *Journal of Applied Psychology* 54, no. 5 (1970): 427-429.

Lee, Helen. "5 Kinds of Christians: Understanding the Disparity of Those Who Call Themselves Christians Today." *Christianity Today* (October 1, 2007). Last accessed July 5, 2015. www.christianity today.com/le/2007/fall/1.19.html.

Lichtenstein, Donald R., Nancy M. Ridgway, and Richard G. Netemeyer. "Price Perceptions and Consumer Shopping Behavior: A Field Study." *Journal of Marketing Research* 30, no. 2 (May 1993): 234-245.

McCarthy, E. Jerome. *Basic Marketing: A Managerial Approach*, Homewood, IL, Richard D. Irwin,1960.

Moritz, Thorsten, Craig G. Bartholomew. *Christ and Consumerism : Critical Reflections on the Spirit of Our Age.* Carlisle: Paternoster, 2000.

Mouw, Richard J.*He Shines in All That's Fair: Culture and Common Grace.* Wm. B. Eerdmans, 2002.

O'Shaughnessy, John, and Nicholas Jackson O'Shaughnessy. "Marketing, the Consumer Society and Hedonism." *European Journal of Marketing* 36, no. 5-6 (2002): 524-547.

Rae, Scott B. *Doing the Right Thing: Making Moral Choices in a World Full of Options.* Grand Rapids, MI: Zondervan, 2013.

Schuurman, Derek C. *Shaping a Digital World: Faith, Culture and Computer Technology.* Downers Grove, IL;InterVarsity Press, 2013.

Seligman, Martin E. P., Mihaly Csikszentmihalyi. "Positive Psychology: An Introduction." *American Psychological Association* 55, no. 1 (2000): 5-14.

Smith, James K.A. *Desiring the Kingdom: Worship, Worldview, and Cultural Formation.* Grand Rapids, MI: Baker Academic, 2009.

Spykman, Gordon J. *Reformational Theology : A New Paradigm for Doing Dogmatics.* Grand Rapids, MI: W.B. Eerdmans, 1992.

Stansbury, Jason. "Moral Imagination as a Reformational Influence in the Workplace." *Journal of Markets & Morality* 18, no. 1 (2015): 21-41.

Steen, Todd, and Steve VanderVeen. "Will there Be Marketing in Heaven?" *Perspectives* (November 2003): 6-11.

Strauss, D. F. M. Discovering Dooyeweerd. Lightning Source Inc, 2023.

Strauss, D. F. M. *The Philosophy of Herman Dooyeweerd.* Jordan Station, Ontario, Canada: Paideia Press, 2021.

Szmigin, I. "Sex, Lies and Exposure: Is Ashley Madison to Blame, or Its Customers?" CNN.com. August 21, 2015. https://www.cnn.com/2015/08/21/opinions/ashley-madison-blame/index.html

Tscheulin, Dieter K. and Bernd Helmig. 1997. "The Optimal Design of Hospital Advertising by Means of Conjoint Measurement." *Journal of Advertising Research* 38, no. 3 (1998): 35-46.

Troost, Andree. *What is Reformational Philosophy?: An Introduction to the Cosmonomic Philosophy of Herman Dooyeweerd.* Paideia Press, 2012.

Van Duzer, Jeff, Randal S. Franz, Gary L. Karns, Kenman L. Wong, and Denise Daniels. "It's Not Your Business: A Christian Reflection on Stewardship and Business." *Journal of Management, Spirituality & Religion* 4, no. 1 (2007): 99-122.

Wells, William D., Clark Leavitt, and Maureen McConville. "A Reaction Profile for TV Commercials." *Journal of Advertising Research* 11, no. 6 (1971): 11-17.

Widing, Robert E., Ronald Hoverstad, Ronald Coulter, and Gene Brown. "The VASE Scales: Measures of Viewpoints about Sexual Embeds in Advertising." *Journal of Business Research* 22, no. 1 (January 1991): 3-10.

Williamson, G. I. *The Westminster Shorter Catechism: For Study Classes.* 2nd ed. Phillipsburg, NJ: P & R, 2003.

Wolters, Albert M. 2005. *Creation Regained: Biblical Basics for a Reformational Worldview*. 2nd ed. Grand Rapids, MI: William B. Eerdmans, 2005.

Wolterstorff, Nicholas. *Until Justice and Peace Embrace*. Grand Rapids, MI: W.B. Eerdmans, 1983.

Wrenn, Bruce, Harwood Hoover Jr., and Jacquelyn Warwick. *Scriptural Foundations for Marketing.* Berrien Springs, MI: Andrews University Press, 2013.

Index

In addition to listing names, this index focuses on concepts and terms used across the book, with the intention of highlighting the unity of the volume. However, the diversity of the volume must be sought in the individual chapters, each of which has its own unique subject matter and conceptual scheme which is not to be found in this index.

C

I

J

T

W

Y

Z

www.ingramcontent.com/pod-product-compliance
Lightning Source LLC
LaVergne TN
LVHW052339100826
845147LV00021B/1114

* 9 7 8 0 9 3 2 9 1 4 3 9 2 *